The Economics of European Integration

The Economics of European Integration

Theory, Practice, Policy

WILLEM MOLLE
Erasmus University Rotterdam, The Netherlands

ASHGATE

Published by
Ashgate Publishing Limited
Gower House
Croft Road
Aldershot
Hants GU11 3HR
England

Ashgate Publishing Company
Suite 420
101 Cherry Street
Burlington, VT 05401-4405
USA

Ashgate website: http://www.ashgate.com

British Library Cataloguing in Publication Data
Molle, Willem
    The economics of European integration : theory, practice
    policy. - 5th ed.
    1.European Union 2.Europe - Economic integration 3.European
    Union countries - Economic policy
    I.Title
    337.1'42

Library of Congress Cataloging-in-Publication Data
Molle, Willem.
    The economics of European integration : theory, practice, policy / by Willem
Molle.--5th ed.
        p. cm.
    Includes bibliographical references and index.
    ISBN 0-7546-4805-2 (hardback) -- ISBN 0-7546-4812-5 (pbk.)
1. European Economic community. 2. Europe--Economic integration--History. 3.
Monetary policy--European Economic Community countries. I. Title.

    HC241.2.M58 2006
    337.1'42--dc22

    2005035222

ISBN-13 978 0 7546 4805 5 (Hbk)
ISBN-13 978 0 7546 4812 5 (Pbk)

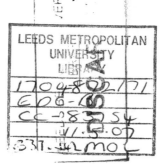
Printed and bound in Great Britain by TJ International Ltd, Padstow, Cornwall.

Contents

Part 5 Conclusions and Lessons

List of Figures

List of Tables

Acknowledgements

In writing this book I have been supported by many, in particular students and colleagues. The book's present form owes much to students at the various universities where I have lectured, particularly in Maastricht and Rotterdam, but also at universities where I have been a guest lecturer. My students' critical comments on the text have resulted in this adapted fifth version, which should be better suited to students' needs than the previous. Many colleagues, too numerous to list here, have helped me by correcting errors in the text and by making suggestions for including new material or presenting the existing material in a different way. Their expertise in their own fields has made it possible for me to cover areas far beyond the territory I could possibly have hoped to become an expert in myself. Very valuable has been the research assistance of Walter Lutz, who updated the various tables and has been very helpful in tracking down new material for this fifth edition. I have also highly appreciated the secretarial support of Ineke van der Stap.

I thank them all for their help and encouragement. Needless to say, all remaining errors and shortcomings are my responsibility.

List of Abbreviations

ACP	African, Caribbean and Pacific Countries
BEUC	Bureau Europeen des Unions de Consommateurs
BIS	Bank for International Settlements
CAP	Common Agricultural Policy
CCP	Common Commercial Policy
CEC	Commission of the European Communities
CEEC	Central and Eastern European Countries
CEN	Comite Europeen de Normalisation
CENELEC	Comite Europeen de Normalisation Electronique
CEP	Common Energy Policy
CEPT	Conference Europeenne des Postes et Telecommunications
CET	Common External Tariff
CI	Community Initiative
CM	Common Market
CMEA	Council of Mutual Economic Assistance (Comecon)
CMU	Capital Market Union
CNIR	Covered Nominal Interest Rate
CU	Customs Union
COREPER	Committee of Permanent Representatives
DI	Direct Investment
EAEC	European Atomic Energy Community (Euratom)
EAGGF	European Agricultural Guidance and Guarantee Fund
EC	European Commission/Community
EBRD	European Bank of Reconstruction and Development
ECA	European Court of Auditors
ECB	European Central Bank
ECE	Economic Commission for Europe
ECJ	European Court of Justice
ECSC	European Coal and Steel Community
ECU	European Currency Unit
EDC	European Defence Community
EDF	European Development Fund
EDIE	European Direct Investment in Europe
EDIUS	European Direct Investment in the US
EEA	European Economic Area
EEC	European Economic Community
EFTA	European Free Trade Association
EIB	European Investment Bank
EMCF	European Monetary Cooperation Fund

EMI	European Monetary Institute
EMS	European Monetary System
EMU	Economic and Monetary Union
EP	European Parliament
EPC	European Political Community/Cooperation
ERDF	European Regional Development Fund
ERM	Exchange Rate Mechanism
ESC	Economic and Social Committee
ESF	European Social Fund
EU	European Union/Economic Union
FCMA	Free Capital Movement Area
FDIE	Foreign Direct Investment in Europe
FED	Federation
FLMA	Free Labour Movement Area
FPC	Foreign Profit Creation
FPD	Foreign Profit Diversion
FRG	Federal Republic of Germany
FTA	Free Trade Area
FTL	Full Truck-loads
FU	Full Union
GATS	General Agreement on Trade in Services
GATT	General Agreement on Tariffs and Trade
GDP	Gross Domestic Product
GDP/P	Gross Domestic Product per Head of Population
GFCF	Gross Fixed Capital Formation
GJ	Gigajoule
GNP	Gross National Product
GSP	Generalised System of Preference
HFL	Dutch Florin
IBRD	International Bank for Reconstruction and Development (World Bank)
ICM	Incomplete Common Market
ICU	Incomplete Customs Union
IIT	Intra-Industry Trade
ILO	International Labour Organisation
IMF	International Monetary Fund
ISIC	International Standard Industrial Classification
LDC	Less Developed Country
LEC	Labour-Exporting Country
LFTL	Less Than Full Truck-loads
LIC	Labour Importing Country
LMU	Labour Market Union
LPG	Liquefied Petroleum Gas
MCA	Monetary Compensatory Amounts
Mecu	Million ECU
MFA	Multi-Fibre Arrangement
MFN	Most Favoured Nation
MNC	Multinational Company

MNF	Multi National Firm
MU	Monetary Union
Mt/y	Million (1 000 000) tons per year
Mtoe	Million (1 000 000) tons of oil equivalent
NATO	North Atlantic Treaty Organisation
NG	Natural Gas
NIC	Newly Industrialising Countries
NORDEL	Nordic Electricity
NTB	Non-Tariff Barriers
OCA	Optimum Currency Area
OECD	Organisation for Economic Cooperation and Development
OIA	Optimum Integration Area
OMA	Orderly Marketing Arrangements
OPEC	Organisation of Petroleum Exporting Countries
PTA	Preferential Trade Agreement
PTT	Post Telegraph Telephone
PU	Political Union
QR	Quantitative Restrictions
R & D	Research and Development
RIR	Real Interest Rates
SDR	Special Drawing Right
SEA	Single European Act
SSR	Self Sufficiency Ratio
TEU	Treaty on European Union
TRIMS	Trade-related Investment Measures
TRIPS	Trade-related Intellectual Property Rights
UCPTE	Union for the Coordination of the Production and Trans-mission of Electric Power
UK	United Kingdom
UNCTAD	United Nations Conference on Trade and Development
UNIDO	United Nations Industrial Development Organisation
UNIR	Uncovered Nominal Interest Rate
UNO	United Nations Organisation
USA	United States of America
USDIE	US Direct Investment in the US
VAT	Value-Added Tax
VER	Voluntary Export Restraint
WEU	Western European Union
WTO	World Trade Organisation

PART 1

General Issues

1 *Introduction*

Objectives

Progressive integration has been one of the most characteristic aspects of economic development in the last decades, worldwide and in Europe, where it has found expression notably in the European Union (EU). The EU has had a direct and profound influence on the economy of member states and third countries.

Much has been written about European economic integration. In the 1950s and 1960s, the discussion on economic integration was concentrated on international economic relations, as witness the specialised books on the subject from that period. In the 1970s and 1980s, the idea of economic integration quickly spread to the economics of the sectors of economic activity (agriculture, energy, manufacturing, services, transport) and to such aspects as market regulation, macro-economic equilibrium, monetary control, regional equilibrium or social welfare. At the end of the 1980s and during the 1990s, the issues of the completion of the internal market and the realisation of monetary integration were central to the discussion on European economic integration. In all fields mentioned, the body of specialised literature has grown very rapidly to become a real avalanche in recent years.

To *students of the economic integration process per se* this abundant specialist literature is inconvenient. Indeed, as economic integration touches ever more areas of society, more and more people are confronted by the bewildering complexity of the functioning of the EU. The past decades have witnessed the publication of a large number of books that aim to help readers find their way. The present book differentiates itself from these titles in that it aims to:

- place the wide variety of issues in a robust conceptual structure;
- integrate theoretical developments with the results of empirical research and of policy analysis;
- explain the logic of the dynamic processes;
- describe the structural features of the European economy;
- highlight the response of private companies to changes in the regulatory environment;
- depict the 'historical' developments so as to give a sound basis for the understanding of the present situation and the likely future development;
- set the European developments in the light of global developments;
- draw lessons from the EU experience for other regional integration schemes and for global institutional developments.

Three fundamental concepts

INTEGRATION

The expression 'economic integration' covers a variety of notions.[1] It may refer to the absorption of a company in a larger concern. It may also have a spatial aspect, for instance if it refers to the integration of regional economies in a national one. In this book, the expression is always used with respect to international economic relations. The *definition* of integration that is used here is the gradual elimination of economic frontiers between independent states. As a result the economies of these states end up functioning as one entity.

Economic integration is not an *objective* in itself, its *rationale* is to serve higher objectives, both of an economic and of a political nature.[2]

- Economic welfare. The prosperity of all participating countries is enhanced by overcoming the inefficiencies of nationally segmented economies through specialisation of production and through cooperation in policy making, the two basic elements of economic integration.
- Peace and security. When countries become dependent upon each other as a result of economic integration this reduces the chance of armed conflicts between them.[3]
- Democracy. If participation in a group that brings benefits through integration is made conditional on the existence of a parliamentary form of democracy, it is less likely that attempts to overthrow this system of government in a member country will stand much chance of success.
- Human rights. In much the same way, the respect for human rights may be safeguarded if this is set as a precondition for participation in a scheme for economic integration.

In this book we will not go further into the last three objectives, which are of a political nature; we will henceforth concentrate on the economic objective.

The term 'economic integration' can be interpreted in two senses. In a dynamic sense, it is the process whereby economic frontiers between member states are gradually eliminated (that is to say, whereby national discrimination between integration partners is abolished), with the formerly separate national economic entities gradually merging into a larger whole. In a static sense, it is the situation in which national components of a larger economic zone function together as one entity. The dynamic interpretation is the more usual, and the one to be used in this book. Of course, the static meaning of the expression will apply in full once the integration process has passed through its stages and reached its object.

The attention we give to the dynamics of integration is reflected in each of the following chapters. Indeed, for each of the aspects of integration we will describe how things have evolved over time while the EU passed though different stages of integration.[4]

---

1   The expression 'economic integration' has become so current that it gives the impression of a fundamental notion with a long historical background. Actually the term does not occur until after the Second World War.

2   The first of these objectives has been central to all stages of the deepening and widening of European integration. The three others have had different weights in each round of extension (see Chapter 18).

3   Empirical support for this statement in matters of trade is given by Polachek (1980), Hirsch (1981), Buzan (1984). In matters of institutions (arbitrage) we refer to the WTO and in matters of trade and monetary relations to for example, Gartzke et al. (2001). Note that on the other hand, security (for example, NATO) stimulates economic integration (for example, EU, OECD).

4   In this respect the present book distinguishes itself from many others that tend to describe only what is (present policies); whereas we describe also how things have evolved and why they did evolve in that way.

ECONOMICS

As to economics[5], three elements will recur throughout the book. We will analyse and describe:

- Theoretical principles. We will present a selection of theory most relevant to explaining the dynamics of economic processes associated with the integration of (segments of) the economy.
- Empirical facts. We will describe how the various segments of the European economy have evolved over the past fifty years under conditions of integration, using selected long-term statistical series on the one hand[6], and using case studies of the behaviour of the business sector on the other.
- Public policy. We will discuss why and how the EU and national governments influence the economic process with policy measures; and what effect these interventions have.

We will not deal with these elements separately. On the contrary, while dealing with different aspects of integration we will combine a brief theoretical treatment with an analytical description and with the relevant elements of policy of the subject at hand.

In all parts of the book we will finally evaluate the results of the integration processes in economic terms. To measure advantages and disadvantages of integration, use will be made of the well-known concepts of welfare economics.

EUROPE

The word 'European' refers in principle to the whole geographical entity of Europe. In practice the European Union will be the focus of major parts of this book. The EU, extended since its foundation from six to nine, then to 10, 12, 15 and 25 member states, and open for further enlargement, forms the core of the European integration process. For reasons of simplicity we will henceforth use the term 'European Union (EU)' to indicate for the whole period of analysis and irrespective of the prevailing precise legal situation both the group of member states and the policy system drawn up on the basis of the various treaties.

While describing developments we will as much as possible refer to the whole area of the present EU. However, in many cases it is not feasible to include data for the period that countries were not yet members. The problem pertains mostly for the new member states (NMS). During the 1990s the NMS have gone through a transition from a centrally planned economy to a market economy. So, as for the period up to 1990, comparable data for the NMS are mostly lacking; therefore we have to limit ourselves to the former EU15.

European integration is not an isolated process: it takes place in a world in which national systems become more and more interwoven. Therefore we must keep an eye on external aspects. Speaking of labour market integration, for instance, we will discuss not only

---

5   The accent in this book is on economics in the narrow sense of the word. Students of business will, however, find it very useful too, as the book depicts, on the one hand, the changing environment of corporations due to the integration process and, on the other hand, the reactions of firms to this new environment (notably in Chapters 9–13).
6   Note that the statistics used in this book up to the year 1990 do not cover the regions that joined as a result of the reunification of Germany. Note also that figures are given in euros for the whole period; the values of other currencies and the predecessors of the euro (such as the ECU) have all been recalculated to form a comparable statistical base. Note finally that the 25 present EU member countries have been ordered in the various tables on the basis of two criteria: 1 by round of accession; 2 within each of these group by size (GDP).

internal migration within the EU, but also migration from and to third countries, distinguishing between different groups of countries[7].

Organisation of the material

Part 1 lays the *foundations* for the rest of the analysis. First it gives the fundamental concepts that will be used in this book, such as the definition of integration. Next it gives a theoretical treatment of the dynamics of the integration process. Third, it presents an historical overview of the process of integration, which makes it easier to understand the present dynamics. Fourth, it exposes the objective, the institutional set-up and the regulating capacity of the European Union.

Part 2 is devoted entirely to *market integration*. It starts with separate chapters on goods and services. The next two chapters deal with the liberalisation of the markets for production factors. In each of the chapters on labour and capital, the results of empirical studies are set on a solid theoretical basis and in the framework of the dynamic development of the European policy regimes for both production factors.

Part 3 is devoted to *business*. The integration of markets of products and of production factors permits entrepreneurs to make their operations more efficient. The way enterprise responds to the opportunities created by integration is analysed for five sectors of economic activity[8]. For each of them we will follow the same process. We describe first the EU regulatory framework. Next we depict the sectors' development under conditions of integration, referring, wherever useful, to theoretical notions specific to the sector concerned. For each sector we will single out two branches for which detailed case studies will be presented. In these case studies we follow the same logic: description of the evolution of the regulatory framework; sketch of the development of the industry in terms of production, trade, etc; and, finally, the response of companies to their changing environment.

Part 4 deals with *policy integration*; the objective is to create the conditions for a balanced growth of the EU economy. For the discussion of these policies a division into chapters has been made into the following four objectives:[9]

---

7   We will give an overview of these aspects in Chapter 17 on external relations.

8   The breakdown into sectors is based, on the one hand, on the famous Clark (1957)/Chenery (1960)/Kuznets (1966) triad and, on the other hand, on the differences in EU policy regime. This leads to a division into five main sectors: agriculture, manufacturing, energy, services and transport.

9   The categories chosen are not the only ones possible. The first three have been inspired by ideas of fiscal federalism (see Musgrave and Musgrave 1989). In the EU policy documents, quite similar breakdowns are used that tend to get other labels through time. Recent policy documents speak for instance about the objectives of competitiveness and (real) convergence with respect to the first and third objective (EC 2004a) or of prosperity, solidarity and external projection with respect to the first, third and fourth objectives (EC 2005a). Note that the non-economic objective of security is now often mentioned too.

         The distinction between allocational efficiency, macro-economic stability, redistributive equity and external identity, relatively neat in theory, is often blurred in practice in the process of political bargaining. Indeed, instruments devised to serve policies in one area are often adapted under political pressure to serve other objectives as well. A good example is allocational efficiency. The instrument of guaranteed prices, introduced to make agricultural markets function properly (see Chapter 9), has also been used for redistribution purposes. Another example is state aids for the restructuring of industries that in practice may become an instrument for permanent subsidisation of certain sectors (for example, shipbuilding), in order to enhance their competitiveness on external markets. Indeed, original objectives are often lost sight of as policies, including common policies, develop.

- efficiency in allocation of resources, requiring mainly micro-economic policy instruments aiming at the efficient use of resources; this function comprises the policies aiming at the competitiveness of European business and the proper functioning of the internal market;
- stability of development, requiring mainly macro-economic and monetary policy instruments to attain such objectives as high growth rates, price stability and full employment;
- cohesion of constituent parts, requiring (redistribution) policies that aim to ensure that different social and regional groups will get a fair share in the benefits of integration should the market mechanisms fail to achieve an equitable outcome;
- external projection: at each stage of integration the union has to define itself vis-à-vis the outside world; its external relations develop from commercial policies in a customs union up to defence in a full union. The EU strives towards a situation in which the values it respects internally are also fostered globally.

The policies designed to realise the first two objectives are essential to gather the full benefit of integration, those for the third are indispensable to gaining and keeping the necessary political support from all participants in an integration scheme and for the fourth to contribute to a better world in which the EU has a stable and secure place.

Part 5 contains an *evaluation* of the results presented in Parts II to IV. In a first chapter we give the lessons from the EU development for the EU itself. In the following two chapters we draw lessons from the EU experience for the other regional integration schemes and for the design of global integration.

Specification of the readership

The book addresses primarily two groups of readers. First it addresses *students* – in particular students who are following courses on European integration. In this book they will find a general introduction to the dynamics of economic integration, covering in a systematic and coherent way the areas that are most relevant, ranging from agriculture to trade, monetary matters and cohesion. However, experience has shown that the book is also useful for two more categories of students. The first of these is students of economics specialising in specific fields, such as industrial economics, international economic relations, and monetary and financial economics, who are all increasingly confronted by the European dimension of their specialisation. In this book they will find a general framework for the study of their own special area. The second category is students of business, who will find in this book much information about the changing regulatory environment of the firm, and about the response of companies to these changes.

Second, this book is written *for all those professionally interested in the economic aspects of European integration* in the widest sense, including the increasing number of people who in their professional activities are faced with questions as to the organisation and functioning of the European economy (researchers, consultants, journalists). To these professionals can be added all those who are interested in the lessons that can be drawn from the European experience for the set-up and development of regional integration frameworks in other parts of the world (Mercosur, and so on) and those who are interested in the improvement of worldwide integration and global governance.

The material in the book has been organised and presented to allow both groups of readers to fruitfully study individual subjects without having to go through the complete text. To facilitate deeper and more complete study starting from this text, ample references to more specific literature are given. To facilitate access to the material presented, the book has been written in such a way that only a basic knowledge of economics is needed; the use of mathematics has been reduced to a minimum[10].

Constant update

A difficulty encountered in writing about the EU is that the text needs continuous adjustment and updating. Indeed in the past the EU policy environment and the response of firms and individuals have shown a remarkable dynamism. In the past decades some really dramatic changes have occurred. The first is the move into higher stages of integration with the completion of the internal market, the introduction of the euro as a common currency and the elaboration of an external policy. The second is the stepwise extension with new members. The latest one concerns the integration of the Central and Eastern European countries. This fifth revised edition comes, therefore, only a few years after the publication of the fourth edition.

The present edition differs from the previous one in that it:

- addresses the integration of the new member states (NMS) and the association of the remaining Central and Eastern European countries;
- integrates new insights from theoretical and empirical analyses in many policy fields (for instance the introduction of the euro); updates with figures for recent years and complements for the NMS the series of data that highlight the long-term structural changes that are entailed by the integration process;
- draws lessons from the EU experience for the development of other integration areas in the world and for world governance.

Summary and conclusions

- Economic integration is the gradual elimination of economic frontiers between partner countries. It is a dynamic process in which the economies of partner states become more and more interwoven.
- The main objectives of economic integration are of an economic nature: for example, higher growth, hence more prosperity. Other objectives are of a political nature: for example, the reduction of the chance of armed conflicts among partners, the safeguard of democracy and the respect for human rights.

---

10   Only basic knowledge of linear equations and their graphical representation and the essentials of regression analysis is required to understand the whole text.

2 Dynamics of the Integration Process

Introduction

For a proper understanding of the details of the process of economic integration as described in the subsequent chapters, it is essential to know a few fundamental elements about the dynamics of the integration process.

To start we will make a basic distinction between the integration of markets and of policy. The former relates to the taking away of barriers to movement of products and production factors between member states, the latter to the setting up of common policies for the Union. The integration of markets (products and production factors) and the integration of different areas of economic policy follow, in practice, a sequence of forms. We will describe these stages of integration in some detail, specifying markets and policies.

The rest of this chapter will be devoted to the dynamics of the integration process. We will describe the essentials of the different approaches that try to respond to the questions of why and how further integration develops. We make a distinction here between deepening and widening. We define deepening as the involvement of Union institutions in an increased number of policy matters. We define widening as the geographical enlargement of the Union – in other words, the increase in its membership. A short summary will complete this chapter.

Two dimensions: markets and policies

MARKET INTEGRATION

The *economic logic* of market integration is mainly based on welfare economics. Indeed, the free exchange of goods promises a positive effect on the prosperity of all concerned. It permits consumers to choose the cheapest good, generally widens the choice, and creates the conditions for further gain through economies of scale. Free movement of production factors permits optimum allocation of labour and capital. Sometimes certain production factors are missing from a place where otherwise production would be most economical. To overcome this problem, entrepreneurs are apt to shift their capital from places of low return to those which give more promising results. The same is true of labour: employees will migrate to regions where their labour is more needed and therefore better rewarded. An enlarged market of production factors favours new production possibilities which in turn permit new, more modern or more efficient uses of production factors (new forms of credit, new occupations and so on).

Institutional economics provides the reason why most integration schemes start with market integration. Market integration can proceed without much demand on institutions and policy making. The taking away of barriers can in general be easily and clearly defined, and once laid down in treaties is binding on governments, companies and private persons. There is little need for a permanent regulatory and decision-making machinery. The respecting of these measures is a matter of law; any firm, person or institution may appeal to the courts if infringements damage his interest.

POLICY INTEGRATION

In an economy which leaves production and distribution entirely to the market, the elimination of obstacles to the movement of goods and production factors among countries would suffice to achieve full economic integration. This is not the case in modern economies where the government frequently intervenes in the economy. In all European countries there is substantial government intervention with the aims of enhancing economic welfare (by correcting imperfections of markets) and of realising a number of political objectives (such as an equitable income distribution).

The *economic arguments* for policy integration are based on the welfare increasing effects of integrated policy making. This comes about in the following way. The objectives and forms of regulations diverge among countries owing to differences in preferences (traditions, institutions and so on). As a result of the considerable international interwovenness, the policy of one country has effects in another. If the objectives of two governments are inconsistent, the policy of one country will frustrate that of the other. Policy integration may bring economic benefits as it leads to the recovery of effectiveness in policy making. It will also take away the extra cost of compliance for companies that operate internationally under a multitude of different national regulations. Therefore, as the economic integration progresses, strong impulses are given towards the integration of various segments of the national regulatory systems.

Institutional economics provides another argument for policy integration. The aim of policy integration is the creation of a common policy framework that creates equal conditions for the functioning of the integrated parts of the economy. Common policies require common institutions. These need to be stronger, the larger the competences of the Union and the higher the complications of the various packages of common policies.

Stages[1]

MARKETS

There are three stages:

* Freetrade area (FTA). All trade impediments such as import duties and quantitative restrictions are abolished among partners. Internal goods traffic is then free, but each country can apply its own customs tariff with respect to third countries.

---

1   Many authors have used different definitions (for example, Tinbergen (1954); Scitovsky (1958). The definitions given here largely follow the classical work of Balassa (1961); other sources are the major reports preceding the various jumps that mark the European integration process, such as Spaak et al. (1956), Werner et al. (1970), MacDougall et al. (1977), Padoa-Schioppa et al. (1987) and Delors et al. (1989). See also Pelkmans (1991). Note that the definitions given here are conceptual ones that do not always correspond to the setting up of concrete integration schemes (Balassa, 1976; Pelkmans, 1980). Note also that the various stages distinguished here can be split up further: see, for example, for the CM, Pelkmans (1986) and, for the MU, Gros (1989).

- Customs union (CU). All obstacles to internal free movement are abolished without exception as to category of product or type of barrier. A common external tariff is implemented.
- Common market (CM). This consists of (1) an internal market: that is, fully free internal movement of products (goods and services) and of production factors (labour and capital); and (2) common external regulation for both products and production factors (so this definition encompasses a CU).

ECONOMIC POLICY

There are three forms of integration of economic policy:

- Economic union (EU). The common market is complemented with a high degree of coordination or even unification of the most important areas of economic policy. As a minimum these comprise those that are associated with the CM, such as market regulation, competition and industrial structure. Next come those that are related to the MU, such as macro-economic and monetary policies. Finally there are those that refer to the more social aspects, like redistribution policies and social and environmental policies. Towards third countries common policies are pursued on trade, production factors, economic sectors, monetary stability and so on.
- Monetary union (MU). One common currency circulates in all member states. Capital movements within the union are free.
- Economic and monetary union (EMU) combines the characteristics of the economic and the monetary union. The latter implies quite a high degree of coordination of macro-economic and budget policies. In view of the close interweaving of monetary and macro policies, integration evolves mostly simultaneously for both policy fields.

Other policies Two further aspects of integration policy should be considered:

- Political union (PU). Integration is extended beyond the realm of economics to encompass such fields as anti-crime policy (police) and foreign policy, eventually including security policy.
- Full union (FU). This implies the complete unification of the economies involved, and a common policy on many important matters. For example, social security and income tax are likely to come within the competence of the union. The same holds true for macro-economic and stabilisation policy; this implies a budget of sufficient size to be effective as an instrument of these policies. The situation is then virtually the same as that within one country. Hence some form of a confederation or federation will then be chosen.

INTERMEDIATE STAGES

The stages that are given here are theoretical constructs. The first stages, FTA, CU and CM, seem to refer to market integration in a classical *laissez-faire* setting, the higher stages (EU, MU, FU) to policy integration. In practice, however, the former three stages are unlikely to stabilise without some form of policy integration as well (for instance, safety regulations for an FTA, commercial policy for a CU, or social and monetary policies for a CM). On the other hand they may not be fully comprehensive; for instance an FTA and a CU may be incomplete in the sense that some categories of goods are excluded. In the same way an incomplete common market may develop; internal free movement may be limited to certain segments of labour and capital, while external relations may be comparable to the FTA or to a CU (common regulation).[2]

THE SUBSIDIARITY PRINCIPLE

In the course of the movement through the stages of integration, competences are handed over from the member states to the union. So the presumption is that powers are best executed by the nation and only in specific circumstances handed over to the higher level. Theory[3] gives us a number of reasons why policy is best executed at the lowest level of government.

- differences in needs and in preferences will be better taken into account; implementation cost will be lower and the accountability of the institutions for their actions will be higher;
- innovation and experiment will be given more latitude; competition between jurisdictions will bring forward the best solutions.

In the EU these considerations have found their translation into the so-called subsidiarity principle.[4] It says that a matter has to be assigned to the Union only in case the member states cannot effectively deal with it and the EU is better qualified. Cases in point are corrections of market failures, compensation for externalities and economies of scale.

Forms

REGIMES

All forms of policy integration require permanent agreements among participating states with respect to procedures to arrive at resolutions and to the implementation of rules. In other words, they call for partners to agree on the rules of the game. For an efficient policy integration, common institutions (international organisations) are created. Organisations such as the European Union encompass different regimes.

Regimes are defined as special sets of understandings, rules, organisations and compliance mechanisms that govern the relations between private and public actors in a given area of public interest. They are organised on a functional basis as an answer to a sectoral problem. Initially regimes tend to give answers only to the most pressing needs. The development of a new regime or the change in an existing regime tends to be influenced by the following factors (Molle, 2003):

- Awareness. The awareness that there is a real problem comes often after events that have a high bearing on the mass public (for example, ecological disasters).

---

2   One may also distinguish an incomplete monetary union, where the exchange rates of the currencies of the member countries are (irrevocably) pegged to a reference currency.
3   See, for example, Begg et al. (1993) and Tabellini (2003).
4   In the works of classical thinkers the most commonly used term was 'principle of federalism'. It lies at the basis of the constitutions of many federations such as Germany, Switzerland and the USA. The term subsidiarity was first used in the papal encyclical Quadragesimo Anno (1931). It was introduced into EU jargon in the 1980s and subsequently it has been developed in theoretical terms (for example, CEPR 1993) and enshrined in the constitutional treaties. For the economic inspiration of the same principle, see Oates (1999).

- Knowledge. The clearer and more unequivocally the problem can be defined and the more there is a common understanding of the best way to solve it, the easier it will be to find a cooperative solution. In this respect scientific evidence is of great importance.
- Attitudes. Change in ideas about major issues (for example, the role of the state in the economy), change in political fundamentals (such as the demise of communism) lead to changes in positions of political actors and may lead to convergence about needs and means.
- Interdependence. The decreased ability of states to realise their goals autonomously enhances their willingness to cooperate.
- Interest. Regime formation is more likely the higher the interest of the parties involved. Interest increases with benefits and benefits increase with the intensity of transactions between participants (benefits are the mirror image of the transaction cost a regime takes away).
- Pre-existing structures. Setting up a whole new set of rules and their associated organisations is a difficult exercise. It is much more easy to hook on new functions to an existing structure, with clear rules about the legal effects, the compliance mechanisms and so on.

Once in place, regimes matter. They create conditions and set the rules and thereby influence the behaviour of actors in such a way that they become conducive to the reaching of objectives.

INSTRUMENTS

All forms of integration diminish the freedom of action of the member states' policy makers. The following *hierarchy of policy cooperation* is usually adopted:

- *Information*: partners agree to inform one another about the aims and instruments of the policies they (intend to) pursue. This often induces partners to change their own policies in order to achieve a more coherent set of policies for the group. However, partners reserve full freedom to act as they think fit, and the national competence is virtually unaltered.
- *Consultation*: partners agree that they are obliged not only to inform but also to seek the opinion and advice of others about the policies they intend to execute. In mutual analysis and discussion of proposals the coherence is actively promoted. Moreover they learn from each others' experiences (best practices) and can exert some peer pressure in case of undesirable developments. Although formally the sovereignty of national governments remains intact, in practice their competences are affected.
- *Coordination* goes beyond this, because it commits partners to agreement on the (sets of) actions needed to accomplish a coherent policy for the group. If common goals are fixed, some authors prefer the term 'cooperation'. Coordination often means the adaptation of regulations to make sure that they are consistent internationally (for example, the social security rights of migrant labour). It may involve the *harmonisation* (that is, the limitation of the diversity) of national laws and administrative rules. It may lead to convergence of the target variables of policy (such as the reduction of the differences in national inflation rates). Although agreements reached by coordination may not always be enforceable (no sanctions), they nevertheless limit the scope and type of policy actions nations may undertake, and hence imply limitation of national competences.
- *Unification*: either the abolition of national instruments (and their replacement with union instruments for the whole area) or the adoption of identical instruments for all partners. Here the national competence to choose instruments is abolished.

THE PROPORTIONALITY PRINCIPLE

The higher the form of integration, the greater the restrictions on and loss of national competences and the more power will be transferred from national to union institutions. The question comes then; what justifies the use of the more constraining instruments? In line with the considerations that lie at the basis of the principle of subsidiarity, the answer to this question is that unnecessary constraints lead to welfare losses as they preclude the optimal use of instruments. So, for putting union policies into effect the least constraining instruments should be used. The EU has translated this understanding into the *principle of proportionality*.

For the application of this proportionality principle, effectiveness and efficiency to realise the objectives of the EU policies is the norm. In case the matter can be dealt with by less constraining instruments (such as coordination) these have to be chosen; in case these are not effective, more constraining instruments (such as harmonisation or even unification) have to be chosen.

RELATION BETWEEN STAGES AND INSTRUMENTS

There is a certain relation between the stages of integration and the instruments of policy integration mentioned above, in the sense that, in the early stages, the less binding instruments of integration will be applied. On the way to a common allocation policy, member states may begin by consulting one another with respect to certain elements (systems of value-added tax, the structure of tariffs, for example), to end up with the full unification of value-added tax rates and so on. Between the two stages, harmonisation may be practised. Parallels can be found in external policy. A freetrade area may start with consultations on the level of the external tariff, may next review the advantages of harmonisation of the structure of tariffs and may end up with unification by the adoption of a common external tariff (which turns the freetrade area into a customs union).

Another option is the distinction within one policy area between cases calling for integration and others for which partner-state competencies are maintained. Examples are the fixing of a common external tariff while maintaining partner competence with respect to quotas *vis-à-vis* third countries.

Each step towards further integration depends on an evaluation of advantages and disadvantages by a set of actors under specific institutional circumstances. Therefore policy integration will vary in extent and nature according to the prevailing political circumstances; *there is no theoretical optimum blueprint for the intermediate stages between the FTA and the FU.* As a consequence the transitions between stages are fluent.

As one moves through the various stages of integration, more and more competences of the member states will be handed over to the union (implying a loss of national autonomy). We can schematise the dynamics of integration as follows (see Figure 2.1). First the number of economic matters that are integrated increases (such as fair competition and monetary stability). Next integration also covers non-economic areas (such as culture, social areas, defence). Moreover the intensity with which the union is involved will increase (from consultation to unification).

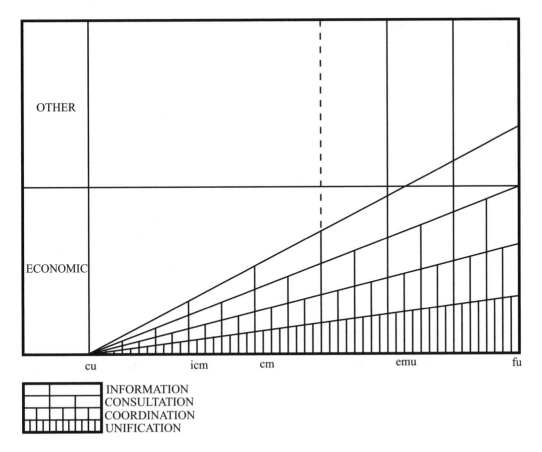

Figure 2.1   Distribution of competences between nation and union in several stages of integration

COMPLIANCE

There are different means for stimulating compliance of member states with Union rules. We detail their use by the EU as follows:

- Coercion. This is mostly done in a hierarchical situation, where orders are given. The EU does not have such powers; it has no police or military force to discipline member states.
- Reputation. States want to behave in a correct way so as to benefit from the advantages that this brings. They want to be part of a respectable set. Most of the compliance in the EU (including the observance of European Court decisions) is based on this form.
- Sanctions. The instrument is used in a number of cases, for example in the Stability and Growth Pact (see Chapter 15). Most organisations have as their ultimate sanction only the expulsion of the violating member from the club. This withdraws the benefits of the club good. The EU has not yet used this.
- Incentives. This instrument is the opposite of sanctions or fines. It exists in many forms; for instance in the Structural Funds that support cohesion (see Chapter 16).

Dynamics of deepening

COST-BENEFIT APPROACHES

Progress towards further integration depends on the proof that the gains from each individual step towards integration will outweigh the cost. The basic notion of the approach of the cost-benefit analysis is that major decisions are based on the well-understood interest of the parties involved. In this view decisions to integrate the economies of member states are based on the net advantages that the members of the group can draw from this integration. So the potential members of an integration area all make their calculations and, on the basis of the outcome, make a 'rational' choice.

Over the years, economists have developed a toolbox to identify first and to quantify next the cost and benefits of each step of integration.[5] They have combined insights from welfare economics and trade theory and later welfare economics and aspects of monetary theory. The types of cost and benefit change as one moves to higher stages. In the first instance:

- Gains come from better allocation of resources (market integration). They come moreover from enhanced competition and innovation that stimulates economic growth. In other words, firms can operate in a larger market and under more favourable conditions, permitting them to produce at lower cost and obtain better starting positions to compete on global markets. The basis for a systematic analysis of this phenomenon has been laid by customs union theory (notably Viner, 1950), that tries to determine the welfare implications of the merging of markets (for a further elaboration, see Chapter 5).
- Costs of integration will come first from the adaptation to new circumstances (short-term) – for instance, from the reinsertion of the labour made redundant by international competition.

In the higher stages of integration the situation changes:

- Gains come from the increased effectiveness of common allocation, stabilisation and redistribution policies (see Chapters 14–17). This positive effect of policy integration stems from the decrease in the cost of policy delivery (economies of scale), the increase in its effects (credibility) and, finally, in the decrease in the transaction cost for business (see also Box 2.1).
- Costs come from the impossibility of meeting national preferences owing to a loss of autonomy, in terms of taxes, consumer protection, health and other matters (long-term). Moreover centralised solutions to policy problems bring a reduction in the variety of solutions and hence imply increased costs in terms of loss of innovation and experimentation.

The *size of countries* plays a determinant role in the decision to participate in an integration scheme. Indeed factors such as economies of scale and externalities are more relevant for a small than for a big country.

---

5   The earlier approaches could only account for the static effects of trade changes. Later methods were devised to quantify the cost and benefits of the higher stages of integration. We will come back to the problems and their solutions in the relevant later chapters of this book.

The *distribution of cost and benefits* over members depends on the level of development and the competitive position of members with respect to union partners and the rest of the world. Theory tends to predict that integration among low-income countries tends to lead to divergence of incomes, while agreements between high-income countries tend to lead to convergence (Venables, 2003).

BOX 2.1
REASONS FOR CENTRALISATION

Competencies should be handed over to the next highest level of government (for example, from a nation to the union) for five main reasons:

- Transaction costs. The diversity of rules in a decentralised system may make it costly for private actors such as firms and owners of production factors to know what the best options are. Assigning this competence to a higher level of government may bring more uniformity, hence more transparency and lower cost.

- Economies of scale. For the production of public goods and policies there exists an optimal scale much in the same way as for private goods and services. Policy competencies should be given to the layer that can provide the lowest cost, given the level of output. An example is monetary policy, which is better organised by a union central bank than by a loosely coordinated group of independently operating local central banks.

- Spill-overs (externalities). There are cases where outsiders – that is, non-residents – may benefit from, or have to bear the cost of, actions of the insiders of a specific jurisdiction. For example, if the pollution of a firm in country A is carried by the wind to country B, country B incurs a high environmental cost, while country A has the economic benefits. In such cases the matter needs to be dealt with by a higher authority. If not, the spill-over of important cost or benefit elements to other areas will lead to inefficiencies – that is, to, respectively, an over- or undersupply of public goods (such as clean air). As integration advances, spill-over effects are likely to increase in importance, and hence more competencies need to be transferred to the union level.

- Credibility. In many cases countries have a stimulus to enter into cooperative solutions for common policies (common advantage) but may also have a stimulus to break them (free-rider). Although the choice of the latter is diminished by the fear of retaliation, many may be seduced into selecting this option for short-term policy reasons. The market will put little faith in the effectiveness of cooperative policies. So the better solution in these cases is to hand over the competence to the union level.

- Insurance. If parts of an integrated area are subject to macro-economic shocks that have a particularly high impact in one or a few of them, there is scope for the pooling of risks. Transfers within a centralised system may be most efficient, as there is no market for macro-economic insurance.

OPTIMAL DECISION MAKING

Progressive integration implies the gradual transfer of policy competencies from national to union institutions. Hence the explanation of progress lies in the reasons why a matter could better be entrusted to the union instead of to the national state (see Box 2.1). These reasons are not specific to integration schemes; any state, be it unitary or federal, has to decide on the best way to distribute competencies over the various layers of government. Important in this respect is the notion of governments providing *public goods*. The different regimes all deal with a specific public good; for example, safeguarding fair competition, macro-economic stability or social justice. Each of these is in turn associated with a particular stage of integration. The question becomes then: which government layer is best suited to provide each of these public goods?

The economic theories of optimal distribution of powers over different layers of government take efficiency as the main criterion.[6] There is an economic rationale to choose the lowest form of integration needed to achieve the goals set. The growth of integration – that is, the increase over time of the number of matters that are assigned to EU level – is then determined by a bigger weight of the set of factors that determine centralisation. One such factor is market integration that engenders the need for policy integration for the same geographical area (for instance, competition policy). Another factor is technical progress that increases the areas where economies of scale in government prevail and externalities occur (for instance, monetary stability). A final factor is the shift in societal preferences towards equity issues and hence centralised redistribution policies.

In practice the application of the notions of 'optimal level of decision making' will not always come to clear-cut conclusions.[7] It may then lead to a situation whereby the Union is responsible for certain matters and the member states for other matters. Defining criteria to come to a clear cut allocation of functions to the two levels and hence the setting up of so-called *competence catalogues* is not very easy; moreover a catalogue once adopted is difficult to change to new environments (Kirchner, 1997).

A specific argument about the assignment of functions is the *quality of the administration* at different levels. Some refer to the fact that high layers tend to be rather ineffective and powers should not be entrusted to this layer.[8] On the other hand much concern also exists about devolution of powers to lower layers of government. The argument here is that the possibilities for corruption are enhanced as local elites tend to rely more on personalism and favouritism than elites on the higher level.

In practice there are large numbers of policy matters for which the two levels have to come together to exercise authority jointly. One might call this 'cooperative federalism' (Casella and Frey, 1992). An example of a policy measure that brings economic advantages of integration, but jeopardises certain national social objectives may illustrate this. The harmonisation of taxes is considered necessary to the undisturbed movement of capital in the integration area. However, that may bring about a shift from direct to indirect taxes in some countries, so that

---

6   The theory of transfer of power from nations to the union has gradually been worked out. The impetus to the exploration of this line of thought has been given by Tinbergen (1959, 1965) who elaborated the basics of the theory of optimal level of decision making. The first applications of this sort of reasoning to the reality of the EU relied heavily on the theory of fiscal federalism (see Oates, 1972; and the pioneering work by MacDougall et al., 1977; Emerson, 1977; Forte, 1977; and Pelkmans, 1982). A consistent presentation of the theory of regulation at various levels of government in integrating areas has been given by Pelkmans (2001), particularly chapter 4.
7   See Breuss and Eller (2004) for a very good review of the economic perspective in the theoretical and empirical literature on optimal assignment of functions.
8   This argument has often been voiced to plead against further involvement in global public good provision by the United Nations.

the tax system can no longer be used to reduce income inequality. Whether the positive effects outweigh the drawbacks is uncertain. As a result, the Union and the member states may come to the essentially political decision not to centralise fully the competence in matters of taxes, but to share the responsibility, limiting integration to the coordination of those aspects of the tax system that impinge most on allocational efficiency. Similar political trade-offs, but with different outcomes in terms of integration, exist over a wide range of matters of public concern, leading to a large variety of practical solutions to integration problems.[9]

INSTITUTIONAL ECONOMICS

Integration starts with private commercial transactions, governed by local or national rules. International transactions take place after an agreement is reached among traders on the basic rules that will govern these transactions. A more efficient solution is reached where the respective governments agree on these rules and on the way to enforce them (for example, mutual recognition of property law and rules for the applicable legal system). Governments incur costs in solving problems they have in common with others and in implementing collective action to arrive at common goals. These costs can be reduced by creating international institutions that permit concluding stable contracts between partners (see, for example, Molle, 2003).

Institutional economics has two objectives. The first is to explain why international institutions are created; the central argument has been borrowed from transaction cost economics and says that dealings among governments and collective actions by governments are more efficient within the framework of an institution. The second objective is to explain why institutions, once created, develop as they do; in our case why integration proceeds and takes the form of the sequenced transfer of national competencies to the Union.[10]

The minimum requirement for a decision on joining an institution (framework for integration) to be taken is that the partners need to have a positive balance of cost and benefit. However, many more aspects enter into the decision process. This process can be modelled along the lines of *becoming members of a club*.[11] Clubs are voluntary agreements created to let the members (consumers) share in the benefits of an excludable public good. The application of the club goods idea to the EU is fraught with difficulties. However, under certain assumptions, one can see the provision of free access to the internal market as a club good of EU members. Another example is the EMU: the European Central Bank provides price stability for the members of the EMU only; non-EMU members and non-EU countries are excluded.

When founding a club (in our case, an integration scheme) the partners generally concentrate on one issue. In the case of the EU that was internal free trade. In the course of the existence of a club it becomes apparent that the organisation can efficiently be used for other purposes as well (Casella, 1994). Consequently, many clubs diversify the club goods they deliver in the course of their existence. Compare, for example, the services delivered by automobile clubs: initially only information about roads and petrol stations, later all sorts of tourist information and, finally, financial services such as credit cards and insurance. In

---

9   An example is regional policy, which is carried out in 'partnership' between European, national and regional authorities (see Chapter 16).

10   For an excellent overview of this body of literature (set in a coherent theoretical framework) see Vromen (1995); see further, for example, Pejovich (1998) for the basics of the comparative approach in institutional economics. The absence of the EU in these and other studies shows that the application of the institutionalist theory to the EU is still in its embryonic stage.

11   See, for the basics: Buchanan (1965) and Olson (1965), and for problems of application: Streit and Voigt (1997).

the case of the EU this has been done by using the EU framework for new subjects such as industrial policy, innovation policy and so on.

The *constitutional economics*[12] school (Buchanan, 1987, 1998) examines the rationale for accepting constraints and for the choice of specific constraints. There are mainly two reasons for policy makers to tie their hands by international conventions or by economic integration. Firstly, because by tying their own hands they also tie the hands of their partners. Secondly, external constraints limit the room for manoeuvre of domestic interest groups. This happens for instance when a country adheres to a customs union type integration scheme that is based on open borders, thereby 'locking in' internal reforms towards liberalisation. The same is true for adhering to an EMU that obliges members to stick to strict budget rules (Quaglia, 2003).

In the approaches described up until now, national states are neutral agents that make rational choices based on cost and benefit considerations in the common interest. Authors from the *public choice* school reject this hypothesis. They consider that the polity (politicians and bureaucrats) working in symbiosis with other actors (like special interest groups and voters) are not only able, but even inclined, to pursue personal goals which do not conform to the public interest. An example is the choice between an FTA and a CU that is made on the basis of elements of rent seeking and lobbying (Panagariya and Findlay, 1996).

The development of the degree of centralisation will differ by public good (Dur and Roelfsema, 2005). For public goods for which all costs are shared through a common budget, policy makers tend to delegate to 'public good lovers'. The polity (national administrations) may permit (or even promote) such 'excessive' transfer of regulatory powers (beyond rational choices) from the nations to the EU.[13] However, the opposite 'under-integration' may occur. For public goods for which cost cannot be shared, under-provision of public goods on the central level will occur. This comes about in the following way. If it is the constituent units that decide on the centralisation of functions and about the sharing of the cost (as is the case in the EU) then the degree of centralisation will be sub-optimally low. Voters will strategically delegate to representatives who are averse to public spending and hence prefer decentralised decisions (Lorz and Willmann, 2005).

BUSINESS ECONOMICS

In using concepts from business economics countries can be regarded as producers, trying to create conditions for profitable operation in the medium and long term (continuity). The theoretical starting point is that firms, and in particular multinational firms, are a rational institutional solution to an economic problem (Coase, 1937/1988). The question is why a firm would produce certain intermediate products instead of buying them on the market. The answer is that the coordination costs within the firm are less than the transaction costs on the market (Williamson, 1985). In markets, where transaction costs are particularly high, integration of activities in one firm will be profitable. This business economics idea of introducing hierarchy within a multi-layer firm as opposed to contractual relations between independent firms is similar to the notion of institutional economics of the unification of regulation in an integration area as opposed to incidental negotiation between independent nations.

---

12   Unfortunately, progress in explaining why institutions develop their rules as they do has been slow. This seems particularly true for the EU (Hodgson, 1988; Hodgson et al., 1994; Schmidtchen and Cooter, 1997).
13   See notably Vaubel (1986, 1994) and, for constitutional safeguards against such developments, Vaubel (1996).

BOX 2.2
COMPARISON OF FIRM MERGERS AND EUROPEAN INTEGRATION

The *progress of integration* seen from a firm perspective is determined by the factors that determine success of cooperation and of mergers. The following factors identified for firms can be transposed to the integration of countries:

- External circumstances. The chances are better if the economies grow and can adapt easily to new circumstances: this was the case for the EU in the period up to 1973 and again in the period since 1985, when the single market initiative was stimulated by the economic recovery.

- Cultural differences and identity. The larger the differences, the larger the potential for conflicts, misunderstandings and so on. The cultural differences within the EU are very large. The success of the EU has been based on the fact that it has not gone immediately towards a full merger but to less stringent forms of integration. Indeed, the EU has integrated first the domains where cultural conflicts were likely to be small (the economic domain – in particular, manufacturing activities) leaving free the other domains where strong feelings existed about national preferences.

- Leadership. The clearer the direction of the new group, the more successful the integration. The importance of leadership in the creation and growth of the EU is often underestimated.* In the EU the success factor has been divided between three entities: the Commission for its independent role; the European Council for general orientation, and the Franco-German tandem.

- Organisation. A form of cooperation between firms, where partners remain in principle independent, sets high demands on the structure of organisation. The EU has been endowed with strong institutions even for limited forms of cooperation.

---

*   On the occasion of the commemoration of the 40th anniversary of the Treaties of Rome I made a short survey among persons who had played key roles during different stages of the EU integration process. It revealed the critical role of these political entrepreneurs. Under conditions of considerable uncertainty in economic, social and political terms, they were convinced they were making the right choices, they were leading the way of a group of hesitant followers and finally had their views accepted by a majority of the voters.

Extending the comparison, it could be said that the integration of countries in the EU is akin to a process of merging of firms into a larger, multinational and or multi-product group.[14] The comparison between firms and states can be made for each stage of integration (see Box 2.2). The early stages of integration of countries can be compared to loose forms of cooperation among firms. The stage of the common market (in which only part of the sovereignty of countries is transferred) can be compared to a joint venture of firms, as the essential freedom to make independent strategic choices for the participants is not hampered. On the other end of the scale, a political union (federation) can be compared to a complete merger of firms.

---

14   Kool and Olie (1997) based on Olie (1996).

Related to these theoretical approaches is the theory of the Multi-national Firm and Foreign Direct Investment. They create a series of dynamic effects due to enhanced competition, transfer of knowledge that increases efficiency and access to new technologies which tends to stimulate innovation.[15]

POLITICAL ECONOMY (SCIENCE)

Decisions on economic integration are not taken only on the basis of economic considerations, but are part of a much larger political process in which other considerations weigh very heavily too. Indeed, the final decision is taken by politicians on political grounds. Thus it is useful to look briefly at the contributions that political economy and political science have made to the explanation of the dynamics of integration. This is all the more relevant because a number of strands of thought in modern economics, discussed in the previous sections, have become close neighbours of political science and international relations.[16]

The approach that has had the strongest resonance in academic and political circles is known as the *neo-functionalism theory* of integration or neo-federal point of view.[17] According to this theory the process of integration is driven by spill-overs from one policy area to another (see Box 2.3). The transfer of powers to the EU in the first field (for instance, goods markets) is based on the considerations of costs and benefits. Such integration generates adjustment needs in other fields that change the costs and benefits and leads to centralised solutions in that field too. This process is reinforced by such factors as:

- issue linkage and the need for package deals;
- the increased power of the EU institutions to influence public opinion as resources increase;
- shared understanding of the advantages of adopting certain common regimes; and
- causal connections between issues documented by expert committees.

Another line of thought that has received much attention recently is the so-called *liberal intergovernmentalism* (Moravcsick, 1993). It explains integration by the interest which national governments have in handing matters over to a higher level authority in order to solve, in an efficient way, some of their domestic problems. One such problem may be standing up to strong rival powers in the world. The views of this school can be related to the views of the institutional economics school. In so far as progressive integration is felt to have gone beyond the level which an economic cost-benefit analysis would predict, this can also be related to the insights of the public choice school.

Finally, we mention a third view, based on *multi-level governance*. Some explain progressive integration by the fact that, beyond a certain stage, national states are aware that they have lost so much power to the centre that they no longer have control over the integration process (Marks, 1996). Others (Chryssochoou, 1997) stress the interest of national governments confronted with high interdependency to create a 'confederal consociation', a regime of

---

15   For the theoretical basis, see Dunning (1979, 1980, 1988, 1993). See Chapters 8, 10 and 14 for further details.

16   For early attempts at integration of various strands of thought, see Hirschmann (1981) and for a practical guide to the various forms of political science theorising, see Rosamond (2000).

17   In the simple view of neo-functionalism the integration proceeds more or less linearly from the initial stage of free trade area to the final stage of the political union (Haas, 1958; Mitrany, 1966). However, the theory has been developed to accommodate other development paths too (Keohane and Hoffmann, 1991; Kahler, 1995). Wessels (1997) has tried to integrate several of these views in a fusion thesis of structural growth in cycles whereby the end outcome is open.

BOX 2.3
A FUNCTIONAL VIEW OF THE DYNAMICS OF EUROPEAN INTEGRATION

Customs union Impulses to policy integration come from both the external and internal dimension of the free movement of products. Externally, the setting of a common external tariff and its regular adjustment to changed circumstances call for a common trade policy. Indeed, negotiations with third countries can be conducted to greater advantage by the customs union acting as an entity than by each member state on its own. Internally, the abolishing of many non-tariff barriers (NTBs) implies the harmonisation of many regulations in such widely divergent fields as taxation and safety. For the internal market to function properly, measures are also needed to prevent competition distortion. Hence the need for a common competition policy, with rules for private and public sectors.

Common market The establishment of free movement of productive factors also gives strong impulses towards the coordination of policy. Free movement of workers requires in practice the mutual recognition of diplomas or certificates of professional proficiency and some harmonisation of measures of social security. Free movement of capital necessitates the elimination of some administrative obstacles, such as exchange control, and some harmonisation of fiscal rules to prevent capital flowing to states with a favourable tax regime. Finally the mobility of capital demands the adjustment of monetary policies (rates of exchange, interest and so on) to diminish economic disturbances caused by speculation. The creation of a common market may lead to concentrated investments in certain regions, and growing unemployment in others. Such situations call for measures of common social and regional policy. The proper functioning of the integrated market can be severely impeded by monetary disturbances. Moreover, countries with a stable currency will want to prevent countries with a depreciating currency from using their monetary policy as a means to enhance their international competitiveness. So the single market pushes towards monetary union.*

Economic and monetary union The pursuit of the objectives of an EMU means that integration extends into a large number of different policy areas. A major policy is to foster favourable and stable conditions. As the free movement of goods and factors renders the economies of member states more mutually dependent, economic or fiscal measures taken by one member state become more likely to affect all others, perhaps conflicting with their policy. Because member states no longer have authority to counteract such disturbances by measures of trade or monetary policy, coordination of the macro-economic and other economic policies of member states becomes imperative.

---

*   The thesis that market integration pushes towards monetary integration was well formulated in the EU report, One Market, One Money (EC, 1990a).

power sharing that strikes a balance between the concurrent demands for territorial segmental autonomy and central Union authority. The fundamentals of these views are similar to those of constitutional economics; their operationalisation refers back to the arguments of the school of optimal decision making.

   The size of a country does influence the decision as it influences its capacity to use power in international relations.

- Small countries (see Molle, 2002b) are pushed towards regionalism as they think that if they are left out in the cold their relative position can be impaired. To them Regional Integration Agreements (RIAs) are in a sense insurances against the risks of trade disputes with major partners (Perroni and Whalley, 2000). However, they also fear regionalism with a major partner, as the forces of the economy may lead to concentration in the largest market freezing out the smaller ones.
- Large country participation means an increase in both its power inside the RIA where it can extend its influence, and its power outside the RIA as it can enter into trade negotiations as a bigger block.

Widening

COST BENEFIT

The decision of any country to join an integration scheme is based to a large extent on the balance of the economic costs and benefits involved for that country. In the same way, the decision by the EU to adopt a new member should equally be based on an evaluation of the costs and benefits to the EU.[18]

The evaluation of costs and benefits suggests different sizes of the integration area at different stages of integration. To start with the Free Trade Area, international trade theory suggests that the best option for the integration of markets is the global one. And if this option is not feasible, customs union theory suggests the option of regional integration. Refinements of the original contributions to customs union theory and common market theory suggest that the net gains increase with the size of the union.[19] However, policy integration theory comes to the opposite conclusion. The transaction cost between governments increases with the increase in the numbers of negotiators and the diversity of the paradigms in which they work. So the best option from an economic point of view is to start with a limited number of members and, once the required institutional effectiveness is secured, to enlarge the number of participants.

The costs and benefits are influenced in a number of ways of which we note two important ones:

- Geographical. The very fact that a number of countries agree to form an integration area changes the game for non-participants. The costs of staying out are different and so are the advantages of getting in (this point is elaborated in the section on institutional economics).
- Temporal. The pace at which the EU has been enlarged can be considered as very rapid, in the light of the historical experience of other integration areas. The causes of this high speed are, however, not well known (Tinbergen, 1991).

The specification and quantification of the advantages and the disadvantages of integration can be set in a time scheme, showing for each of the (potential) participants in the scheme

---

18   In trying to calculate the cost and benefits of enlargement of the EU, economists have coped with the same set of problems as they had while assessing the cost and benefits of deepening. However, some new approaches have given interesting results. See, for example, Kohler (2004).

19   See, for example, Viner (1950); Meade (1955); Tinbergen (1959); see also Chapters 6–10.

when each occurs. This approach to integration (Martin, 1996) allows the optimal sequencing of integration measures to be determined.

OPTIMAL DECISION MAKING

The basic idea of optimality has also been applied to the geographical aspect of integration schemes. The theoretical foundation of the *optimum integration area* approach was laid down quite some time ago. Rather astonishingly, this has not been done for the lower stages of integration (for example, free trade) but for one of the higher stages, *viz.* the monetary union. It has become known under the name of the Optimum Currency Area (OCA) approach.[20] In this approach one defines first the conditions necessary for the good functioning of the integration scheme. Next, one translates these in terms of criteria for membership. The approach has been applied to the EU by many authors, but the results were rather inconclusive. The approach has also been applied to the extension of the EMU to include the NMS, giving indications about the countries that are likely to participate in the foreseeable future and those which still have a long way to go (see Chapter 15).

    Applied to the case of the monetary union, OCA theory predicts that an EMU can the better be sustained when: the lower the chances of asymmetric shocks to occur; the higher the flexibility of the system to adapt; and the higher the credibility of the institutions.

    Generalising the concepts developed in the framework of OCA theory to all stages of integration one can speak of an optimum integration area (OIA) (see, for example, Tichy, 1992). On the basis of this idea we have identified the criteria for determining which countries would belong to such an OIA at each stage of economic integration (see Table 2.1).

Table 2.1   Criteria for participation at different stages of integration

Stage	Criteria
Free Trade Zone	High exchange of goods and services
	Equality of production structure
	Equality of economic order
Common Market	Equality of markets for labour and capital (prices and availability)
	Freedom of movement (migration and investment)
	Convergence of policy (e.g. taxes)
Economic Union	Effective coordination
	Comparability of institutions
	Transfer payments
Monetary Union	Production factor markets: a high degree of capital and labour mobility
	Institutional development: a high degree of political integration

    The establishment of a currency union tends to push the number of members beyond the optimum size. As they admit more members, currency unions face a rising marginal cost curve, which cuts the marginal benefit curve from below. Costs and benefits will both be

---

20   See, notably, Mundell (1961) Chapter 15.

highest when joining with those partners that are the most suitable. Any additional partner will bring extra costs (coming from different industrial structures) but these may not be that high because the largest cost, coming from the loss of independence, has been accepted anyway. The additional partner may also bring proportional benefits. If members are myopic, the currency union may be enlarged beyond the point where the marginal cost and marginal benefit curve intersect for the group (Maloney and Macmillen, 1999).

The OIA approach, so neat in theory, is far from simple to put into practice. At all stages of integration one is confronted with two problems. The first concerns the lack of empirical foundation for a quantification of the criteria. Indeed, little basis exists to specify what the threshold level is for such criteria as a high degree of intra-union trade or of labour mobility. If one sets the threshold low, it will mean that many countries can participate. If one sets it high only a very limited number of countries can be accepted as members. The second problem stems from the parallel use of several criteria: it then depends on the weight one attaches to each of them what the end result will be.[21] Confronted with these problems, policy makers have adopted a simple solution – namely, to define rule-of-thumb criteria based on averages (see Chapter 15 for the EMU criteria).

To these criticisms of a practical nature one can add a more fundamental one – namely, the lack of empirical support when seen in the light of the dynamics of integration. Indeed, in the past, countries that did not fulfil the criteria for an OIA at the outset and were accepted as participants nevertheless proved to be able to come up to standards quickly under the influence of integration. Examples for the EU are the customs union in the 1960s, the EMS in the 1980s and the EMU in the late 1990s.

INSTITUTIONAL ECONOMICS

Recently, a new perspective on the widening of institutions has been given. It takes its starting point in the *rationale for the formation and break-up of nations*. The central element in this line of thought is efficiency in the provision of public goods. Any model with economies of scale in the provision or financing of such goods will lead to a small number of big countries rather than to a single country because it is assumed that, beyond a certain point, decreasing returns and increasing coordination costs occur due to larger heterogeneity of the constituencies. The push towards larger countries is stronger the lower the degree of integration with third countries. The widening of an integration area can be explained by the reaping of the benefits of the larger area without being obliged to come to one state (see Alesina and Spolaore, 1997).

One of the first questions the potential members of a club need to tackle is with whom they will form the club – in other words, how they define its optimum size and composition. The first suggestion comes, of course, from the advantages a group can have in integrating markets; the next derives from the advantages this group can draw from further integration (Casella, 1994). The optimal club size depends on the specific public good. Take the example of an Optimum Currency Area seen as a club. 'If money is viewed mainly as a means of transactions, then it is a fully non-rivalries collective good: more people using the same currency increase the benefits to the original users. In this case the optimal club size is as large as possible. However, if money is viewed as a sort of budget finance, or as a tool for stabilisation, then the optimal size of the monetary club is given by the requirement that preferences over the use of money be somewhat homogeneous within the club' (Casella and Frey, 1992, p. 644).

---

21   See Chapter 15 for substantiation in the case of the EU.

If the optimal club size depends on the specific public good, then all users should be divided into a complex system of overlapping clubs. Applied to integration this means that countries can join different functional integration areas. In this respect, one can see the notions of variable geometry, two-speed Europe and so on that often come up to account for flexibility in the integration process; that means that member governments choose whether or not to join certain elements of integration (Frey and Eichenberger, 1997). The higher functional jurisdictions have to compete for members and may overlap with other functional jurisdictions. The obvious advantage of this set-up is flexibility and adaptation to needs; the obvious disadvantage is high transaction costs for both private and public actors. As the rationale of institutions is to lower transaction costs this is not a minor objection. Sometimes functional clubs are merged to exploit economies of scale. In integration matters this would mean that only one organisation (for example, the EU) would exist; this would take care of the interests of its club members for a whole range of subjects, with members using, to different degrees, the various club goods offered (for example, EMU).

There are *political economy* forces at work that may accelerate the widening beyond the degree that would be indicated by mere costs and benefits to club members. This effect is based on the external impact of the creation of a club by changing the policy options of non-members. If the non-members are small with respect to the club, they can suffer from the effects of the arrangement on their economy. So joining is a sort of insurance against possible adverse effects (Ghosh, 2002). This is the more so because setting up an alternative to the existing club may be very costly and risky (Baldwin, 1994, 1997). This will then unleash forces within the non-member country that push towards the joining of the club. For example, firms in non-member countries that are in a disadvantaged position with respect to EU firms will lobby for their country to become a member too. Their incentive to invest considerable sums of money in lobbying is greater the more they have to deal with sunk cost. This phenomenon has led to the *domino theory* of integration: each time the weight of the core causes a non-member country to fall into the group, it increases the incentive for the remaining non-member to join. The EU has increasingly become the dominant power on the European subcontinent. In the process it has changed the relative attractiveness of the various options of the non-EU members. Both membership of alternative clubs and staying alone outside quickly became unattractive options to many non-members. In the past this has been the case for most EFTA countries (which have almost all switched from the EFTA to the EU club). At present the same is the case for CEFTA (Central European Free Trade Association). The EU club exerts such power that it is very difficult for the smaller countries of Central Europe to organise themselves into a club that can hope to provide the advantages of the EU (even without redistribution).

BUSINESS ECONOMICS

The theory of the firm applied to the widening issue also gives an interesting perspective. This may be seen as a parallel to the rationale for multinationalisation of firms by merger or acquisition.[22] The central element here is the industrial complex, defined as a bargaining configuration organised around a core firm in which the major actors are suppliers, workers, dealers, financiers and governments. Relations between the industries in the complex are characterised by their degree of dependency. The question as to which companies can create

---

22   For example, Hymer (1966); MacNamus (1972); Dunning (1979). From this extensive literature we have selected the view of international restructuring (Ruigrok and van Tulder, 1995; see also van Tulder and Ruigrok, 1997), as it relates, in an interesting way, international business to international political economy considerations (see the next section).

synergy by joining forces while keeping the problems of management under control is comparable to notions about the OIA and of effective club size.

At one end of the spectrum partners are independent and may decide to cooperate or compete; at the other end, the core firm has structural control over the dependent firm. National situations have given rise to five different concepts of control, each favouring a certain degree of dependency relation. At the low end of the spectrum we see the idea of flexible specialisation – independent firms working together in a network. At the high end we see Toyotism where the core firm controls its environment. Core firms with a relatively cohesive complex have generally invested heavily in well-functioning bargaining practices. Governments have favoured such more cohesive complexes, as they facilitate coherent trade, industrial and other policies on the national level. This has led to the development of specific national bargaining arenas.

Several factors have created a need for openness and have induced firms to go international. The nature of a firm's domestic bargaining area determines its internationalisation strategy. Firms that tend to favour control will opt for subsidiaries abroad that depend on coordination by international headquarters. On the other hand, firms that favour networks would do so internationally as well. Firms that go international penetrate countries that may have another regime (or bargaining arena), thereby triggering changes that may erode the cohesion of these arenas. The EU has tried to develop a new regime of its own in order to replace the weakened national arenas of its members.

Several of these notions have parallels to our problem of the widening of an integration scheme. We can develop these as follows:

- Firms that internationalise by dependency can be compared to the enlargement of a union by the integration of a new member, whereas firms that opt for networks would be comparable to countries that develop their international relations.
- Firms that have grown strong by merging limit the strategic choices of their weakened competitors and force them into a dependency relation (possibly a take-over). This is a parallel to the domino theory. The more difficulties encountered by weak firms in competing, and the less their likelihood of creating a credible alternative option by teaming up with other weak partners, the more these firms will be inclined to accept a take-over bid by a larger competitor or be forced to accept any other relation of dependency.
- The creation of a dependency relation between firms will entail the harmonisation of the rules for the management of the new company. This is not easy in the medium stages. It can be likened to the situation of the EU in its efforts to define a new regime starting from a number of rival national regimes, which has resulted, over the decades, in the development of its own elaborate regime, thereby altering the game for new entrants. In much the same way as a large firm which is taking over a small one (or a series of small ones) will impose its existing organisation on the new subsidiaries, the EU imposes the obligation to adopt the '*acquis communautaire*' on all its new members.

Firms from modern economic sectors tend to bring to the mergers process a dimension that can be compared to the accelerator of other approaches. Indeed, these activities are often characterised by network economics. The quicker one can attain the status of the provider of the dominant technology for a set of activities, the better are the chances of reaching a position of almost complete dominance of that sector. This means that firms do have a much increased incentive to merge, and this is enhanced by the so-called positive feedback that stems from the fact that the product becomes more interesting the more people are using it (see Shapiro and Varian, 1999).

POLITICAL ECONOMY (SCIENCE)

The neo-functionalist view (that is, spill-overs from one integrated policy area lead to the integration of another policy area) can also be set up for widening. Both the potential member and the union have interest in joining. The potential member's interest is to regain credibility, as their national capacity for dealing with a number of issues is no longer sufficient to provide a good answer to the problems (see also the discussion on the domino theory). The interest of the union to respond to the application of the potential member by integrating the fringe is more of a political than an economic nature. We need but refer to the decision on the integration of East Germany into the Federal Republic. History shows that great powers have extended their influence over neighbouring areas first and integrated them next because of the need to deal with insecurity at borders (Kennedy, 1988). Similar factors play a role in the EU: in the 1960s France blocked the first enlargement on essentially political considerations. Security issues have been and still are prominent in the motivations of many EU member countries to stimulate the Eastern enlargement of the EU.

The multi-level governance view can also be extended to cope with the widening issue. Indeed, in a number of cases, incidental decisions by individual members on enlargement with another specific potential member based on political considerations are replaced by explicit rules to which all present members adhere and that are communicated to new members. Sometimes such rules are even put into the form of constitutional requirements. In practice this means that the potential member knows the criteria that must be met in order to join the club. Should it not yet meet them all, a catch-up programme can be put in place in time.[23]

Overview of the various theoretical economic approaches

ESSENTIAL FEATURES

The approaches that have been discussed in the previous sections draw, from different sources, elements that can be helpful in understanding the dynamics of integration. In order to facilitate the *construction of a complete picture* we have regrouped in Table 2.2 the basic elements organised by the dimensions: theoretical foundation; deepening; widening; and accelerator.

---

23   The EU has clearly stated the requirements that applicant countries have to meet in order to qualify for membership (for example, stable institutions, a well-functioning market economy and so on; see Chapter 18 for further details). This need not only apply to membership of the club as such, but also to the membership of sub-clubs. A case in point is membership of the EMU for which specific criteria have been formulated.

Table 2.2   Key features of the various theoretical economic approaches distinguished

Approach/ Aspect	Cost-benefit	Optimal decision making	Institutional economics	Business economics
Theoretical foundation	Welfare economics; Cost-benefit analysis	Optimal regime; Fiscal federalism; Theory of regulation	Institutional economics; Constitutional economics	Theory of the firm; Transaction cost theory
Deepening	Customs union theory (based on trade theory); Common market theory	Optimal level of regulation (subsidiarity)	Clubs; Public choice	Merger; Theory of multi-nationalisation
Widening	Trade (from second-best to first-best solution)	Optimum Currency Area	Optimal club size	
Accelerator		Small extra cost coupled with proportional benefits	Existing institution used for additional purpose; Domino effects; Specific interest group (polity)	Dependency on hegemon; Network economics

COMPLEMENTARITY AND SIMILARITY OF APPROACHES

The analysis of the economic approaches to the dynamics of integration has shown that the various 'schools' do not give rival explanations. On the contrary they are rather *complementary* and there are many *similarities* between them. However, they do not yet form a consistent well-structured grand design.

We can detail this remark as follows:

- *Complementarity.* The approach of optimal decision making makes use of the notions of the cost-benefit approach. Together they do not give the whole picture; institutional economics shows how decisions are influenced by the interests of the actors involved (public choice) and by institutional design.
- *Similarity.* Concepts and arguments used by the business economics approach reveal a high degree of similarity with those used in institutional economics. Yet there is a very limited degree of cross-referencing between authors of the approaches reviewed.

MAJOR CAUSES OF THE PROGRESS OF INTEGRATION

The review leads to identification of the major *causes of the progress* in integration.

First, the progress in terms of *deepening* (extension of scope) is determined in all stages by the interest of the various actors, in other words by the economic advantage that can be derived from integration. For instance, integration of markets permits the reaping of economies of scale. To facilitate integration, union institutions are created because they are more effective and more efficient than national ones (lower transaction costs and cheaper delivery of public goods). Integration is further enhanced by the complex interplay of economic and political actors – trying to use their power to secure as large a share as possible of the advantages of integration and avoiding the problematic aspects of national decision making. Another important factor is the sense of fairness of the distribution of the benefits of the integration; as the distribution that develops spontaneously is often not equal, progress depends then on the capacity to use redistribution policies to arrive at a better balance. Finally the quality of the mechanisms for compliance is important as it enhances the confidence of all participants in the system and reduces the risks of cheating and opportunism.

Second, the progress in terms of *widening* (extension of the geographical area) is determined to a large extent by the net advantages cited under deepening. However, here the very dynamics of the union deteriorates the relative position of the non-members. This increases their incentive to join.

Finally, there is as yet *no coherent framework to explain the development of integration systems* in general, nor to explain the path European integration has taken in particular. For answers to the latter type of question one has to look beyond the economic approaches reviewed here. Political economy and political science will then help out.[24]

Summary and conclusions

- Market integration is needed because it improves efficiency and hence welfare. Policy integration is needed because the intervention of national governments in modern mixed open economies has lost its effectiveness.
- The main stages in the process of economic integration are the customs union, the common market and the economic and monetary union, representing the integration of, progressively, the markets of goods and services, of production factors and, finally, of economic and other policies. The assignment of functions to the EU needs to meet the subsidiarity principle.
- The main instruments for policy integration are consultation and the coordination (harmonisation) or unification of government regulations; the higher forms of integration require more binding instruments. The use of the more constraining instruments has to be justified (application of the proportionality principle).
- The dynamics of integration are determined by a complex interplay of forces. The assignment of new functions to the EU (deepening) is a function of the net advantages that market and policy integration produce. It is enhanced by efficient institutions. Economic factors are only one set among others. In the last instance major decisions on further integration are taken on political considerations.
- The process of widening (that is the enlargement of the integration area or the integration of new members) is largely dependent on the cost-benefit calculations of both present and

---

24   For an assessment of the situation, see, for example, Bhagwati and Panagariya (1996). For the political economy line of thought, see, for instance, Scharpf (1999); Marks et al. (1996); Majone (1996).

new members. The benefits can also be seen in terms of the advantages of belonging to a club. The stronger the existing club the higher the attraction for potential new members.

3 *Short History*

Introduction

Economic integration, defined as a process of economic unification of national economies, has been going on all through modern European history.[1] Two factors have always stimulated integration:

- *Technical progress.* Mechanisation and automation of the production process have completely changed production methods. Advances in energy technology, for instance, led to the replacement of human and animal power with steam and, later, with electricity. With respect to transport, horse-drawn vehicles gave way to railways and lorries. As a result, goods can be produced and distributed cheaply in large numbers.
- *Political idealism.* Since the Middle Ages there has been virtually no period in which statesmen or philosophers did not point to the common European heritage and the necessity for more 'political' unity in Europe.[2]

In the following sections we will describe the progress of economic integration for five periods. We will thereby concentrate on the structural adaptations of the economy and the institutional arrangements that accompanied integration. The chapter will be concluded by a brief summary.

Until 1815: a traditional world with little integration

THE MIDDLE AGES TO THE FRENCH REVOLUTION

In the early Middle Ages, the European economy was marked by a great fragmentation of markets. The feudal system had made all regions almost perfectly self-supporting. Under the influence of urban development in the 12th century, interregional trade was re-established for an increasing number of goods. In the following centuries this tendency continued, bringing about an increased integration of markets of products and production factors.

---

1   The organisation of the subject matter of this chapter has been largely borrowed from Pollard (1981a; see also Pollard, 1981b); the setting of the European process in the framework of a worldwide development towards internationalisation leans on Kenwood and Lougheed (1999). For the history of the 'ideology' of European unification, see Brugmans (1970).

2   For a description of the changes in the perceptions of Europe in history, see A. Rijksbaron et al. (eds) (1987) and Wilson and van der Dussen (1995). We will not go further into this aspect here.

The *movement of goods* – that is, trade among regions and countries – developed only slowly; yet up to the 18th century trade remained of limited scope, being mostly concerned with luxury goods. There were three reasons for this:

- Countless obstacles. Tolls, different weights and measures and coins, staple rights and the privileges of merchant groups hindered trade between regions and cities of the European countries.[3]
- Primitive means of transport. On land, everything had to be hauled by waggon and pack animal. Most tradesmen preferred the cheaper transport by water: sea or river. The fleets of river barges and sea-going vessels increased steadily, but the tonnages of the vessels remained small.
- Economic policy. The aim of mercantilist policy was, first, to be as much as possible self-sufficient and, next, to achieve the highest possible export surplus. To that end, rudimentary trade and industrial policies were pursued with often very crude instruments.

The *movement of production factors* was also very gradually improved. The reasons differed for labour and capital:

- Labour movements used to be hampered because under the feudal system virtually the entire population, with the exception of the nobility and the clergy, was bound by law to a certain place (serfdom). Over the centuries, citizens fought for, and gained, the right to move and trade freely everywhere. Europeans were adept at long-distance searches for employment and opportunity (Canny, 1994). Later some monarchs pursued active migration policies to increase the productive and military capacity of their country.
- Capital movements were in principle free. In practice, however, the transfer of money was much hindered by the defective monetary system and the limited means to convey money from one place to another. Money traffic consisted not only of payments for commercial transactions, but also of loans to princes to cover their military expenditure. Investments in trade, craft and infrastructure were mostly made and financed locally.

THE INNOVATIONS OF THE FRENCH REVOLUTION

The French Revolution, a political event, was soon developed by the citizens, who became all-powerful, into an economic revolution, totally upsetting the 'feudal' economy. The following measures show clearly the essence of this revolution, *the integration of the regional and local economies into a national economy*:

- abolition of all rules impeding the free traffic of goods;
- shift of customs duties to the outer frontiers;
- creation of quota systems and tariffs to protect national production;
- abolition of all privileges of guilds, and of rules about the manner of production;
- introduction of a uniform system of weights and measures;
- introduction of new legal rules for trade;

---

3   These intra-national barriers were comparable to those that prevailed until recently between European states, for national frontiers then did not have the economic function they have now: tolls were levied at bridges, town gates, locks and so on, rather than at the national frontier. In the late Middle Ages, the citizens of towns tried to obtain privileges so as to get around tolls and other trade obstacles. The resulting patchwork of privileges for various groups heralded in a way the complex systems of trade discrimination by country groups that developed in the 19th and 20th centuries.

•   construction of new infrastructure.

Owing to the national character of these measures, at first economic integration increased internally but decreased externally. During the Napoleonic regime the above novelties were introduced all over the European sub-continent. Moreover the so-called 'continental system' was created, intended to make the continent independent of Britain. The ensuing selective international integration was the fruit of a politico-military concept rather than economic logic.

With the collapse of Napoleon's empire, the continental system broke down as well. Once more British goods could be sold on the continent and, given Britain's technological leadership, a whole range of industries on the continent had to be closed down owing to British competition. That put free trade, and international integration, in a bad light. On the other hand, measures like the removal of tolls, which had fostered economic integration at the national level, were found useful and were maintained practically everywhere in Europe.

1815–1870: progressive integration following the industrial revolution

THEORY AND POLICY

'Protection or free trade' had become the central theme of discussions between politicians and economists in many countries, and until the middle of the 19th century the free-traders were in the ascendency. The successful coalition of economists and politicians opened a new era of closer integration of European economic life, in which governments took conscious decisions to open out the opportunities to international trade and competition. Total external trade increased rapidly (see Table 3.1). Intra-European trade in this period relied strongly on sectoral specialisation, itself the result of different technologies practised in different countries. At the end of the period international trade, migration and capital movement were practically free all over Europe.

Table 3.1   Some indicators of European[a] economic development, 1810–70

Indicator	1810	1830	1850	1870
Gross National Product per head (index 1900 = 100)	47	53	62	79
Industrial production (index 1900 = 100)	n.a.	20	33	51
Production of pig iron (MT/y)	1	2	4	10
Production of coal (MT/y)	20	29	67	180
Share of exports in GNP (%)	3	4	7	11
Share of foreign investment in GNP (%)	—	1	2	3
Railway track (x 1000 km)	—	—	24	105

Notes: [a] All of Europe (West, Central and East). n.a. = not available.

Source: Bairoch (1976).

In the period from 1815 to 1870, the progress of economic integration differed according to the initial situation of the European countries.

Unity Far-reaching integration was realised by the UK. In this country the ideas of free trade were given a theoretical foundation and a political shape.[4] Obstacles to the free movement of goods, people and capital were increasingly felt as suffocating and were gradually removed. The UK, as the leader in innovation of industrial technology, initially prohibited the exportation of machinery and the emigration of skilled workers. Nevertheless many British craftsmen went to work in other countries of Europe, often using smuggled machinery. Because the prohibition could not be enforced, the UK abolished all legal barriers to the emigration of skilled workers in 1825 and of capital goods in 1842. It moved further towards free trade with the abolition of the Navigation Acts and the repeal of the Corn Laws.

Homogeneity In areas such as Germany, Austria and Italy, where economic frontiers were dividing a space felt to be culturally united, economic integration spelled a way to political unity. For example, Germany tackled the problem of trade obstacles by means of the *Zollverein*.[5] Under Prussian leadership a customs union was created in 1834 and gradually expanded. It involved the abolition of all duties at inner borders, and a duty levied on the outer frontier which was low for 'European' and high for colonial goods. Gradually more and more states in central and southern Germany joined this union. The rapid industrialisation of Germany during this period contributed much to the success of this type of integration, and was itself stimulated again by progressive integration.

Diversity It is interesting to see that integration was progressing even among countries that were clearly independent from one another. Most European countries adopted more liberal external policies.

TECHNOLOGY AND DIPLOMACY

While integration was clearly stimulated by industrialisation, founded on technological innovation[6] and by the ensuing fast economic growth, the rapid industrialisation marking most West European countries in this period was in turn fostered by progressive integration. Indeed the application of modern technology made further specialisation not only possible but also desirable (see Table 3.1).

A second important component of the 'natural techno-economic process' is the means of transport and communication and in particular the railways. The tremendous accumulation of capital required for the construction of railways was often warranted only if transport nodes and feeding points were also internationally connected; moreover, to be feasible, railway transport had to be liberalised to a high degree. River transport, too, was liberalised: the new, larger steamships called for flexible exploitation. Successive international agreements ensured free navigation on the Rhine,[7] the Danube, the Scheldt and so on.

---

4   Great classical economists such as Smith, Ricardo and Mill emphasised in their work that free national and international trade would lead to the greatest possible prosperity. They paved the way for political aspirations towards free trade (Gomes, 1987).
5   Theoretically underpinned by the German economist, List.
6   See, for example, Mathias and Davis (1991).
7   Central Committee for Rhine Navigation, 1815, and Mannheim Treaty, 1868.

Monetary integration was also attempted in this period.[8] Many of the large states of Western Europe had already reached a considerable degree of internal monetary integration.[9] After the Napoleonic wars, practically every country had developed its own national currency system. International monetary cooperation was set up by the German and Italian states before unification. International monetary integration without political integration was attempted by the Latin Monetary Union, which was based on the French franc and to which the Belgian, Swiss, Italian and later the Greek and Spanish currencies were joined. All these systems suffered from the lack of mechanisms obliging the participants to practise consultation and cooperation. These experiences show that a monetary union seems to have to go hand-in-hand with some degree of political union.

The form in which integration was expressed varied over the years. International integration had always been a more or less factual process partly consolidated in bilateral agreements. This continued in the period under discussion, for instance with the famous Cobden–Chevalier freetrade Treaty of 1860, which gave French industry access to cheaper and better coal and iron from Britain. It was copied by many other countries for similar matters. Its importance lies in its unconditional most-favoured-nation clause, which had considerable implications for Europe-wide tariff reductions. These treaties were drawn up and implemented through the usual diplomatic channels, no permanent international institutions being created for the purpose.

1870–1914: stagnating integration

DEPRESSION AND PROTECTIONISM

Around 1870 the long period of growth came to a sudden end, in a depression which has been compared to the Great Depression of the 1930s. Many governments responded to it in a protectionist fashion. The French–German war and the Italian struggle for unity had completely upset the situation. The powers demanding more protection for economic reasons were reinforced by a desire for autarky of mostly political and military inspiration. As a result, in many places attempts were made to curtail the existing freedoms of trade and traffic of production factors; straight tariff and subsidy wars were fought between some countries. Having become far better organised than before, national states found themselves in a better position to impose taxes and customs duties, regulate their social affairs and pursue a protectionist, nationalist policy.

Trade in goods developed slowly, but it increased at the same rate as production, which indicates that protectionist inclinations did slow down, but not reverse, economic integration (see Table 3.2, row 5). Indeed some countries soon found out that complete autarky was an illusion, given the international specialisation which had developed. Far-reaching sectoral specialisation, not different natural endowment, had become the main reason for goods trade, a specialisation based on economies of scale and technological leadership. Improved transport techniques (leading, among other things, to lower freight rates) also made for continued economic integration in Europe; the railway and canal networks proliferated during this

---

8   See Bartel (1974) for overview, Holtfrerich (1989) for the FRG, Sannucci (1989) for Italy; see also Hamada (1985).
9   As early as the 13th century, Saint Louis, King of France, introduced one single coin, the ECU, for his entire kingdom!

period (see Table 3.2). However, in the construction of infrastructure, nationalist tendencies were becoming more and more manifest.

Table 3.2   Some indicators of European[a] economic development, 1870–1910

Indicator	1870	1880	1890	1900	1910
Gross National Product per head (index 1900 = 100)	79	80	85	100	110
Industrial production (index 1900 = 100)	51	61	77	100	136
Production of pig iron (MT/y)	10	14	17	25	37
Coal production (MT/y)	180	217	328	438	574
Share of exports in GNP (%)	11	13	13	11	13
Share of foreign investment in GNP (%)	3	4	4	4	5
Ocean freight rates (index 1900 = 100)	212	180	127	100	83
Railway track[b] (x 1000 km)	105	169	225	292	351

Notes: [a] All of Europe (West, Central and East). [b] Including Asian parts of Russia.

Source: Bairoch (1976).

Movement of production factors, that is, of workers and capital, also remained free to a large extent during this period.

Labour International migration mainly involved seasonal workers. Several thousands of Italians were employed in France, Germany and Austria. Some hundreds of thousands of Poles went to Germany every year, as did quite a number of other East Europeans. Many of them were employed in manufacturing industry, the mining industry or the construction trade, but many also filled the jobs in agriculture left open by the urbanising rural population. Many specialised labourers tended to move from country to country to operate special machines in regions and countries starting up new industrial projects.

Capital During this period the financial sector developed quickly (Cassis, 1991). Europe became the banker of the world. Its total stock of foreign investment rose significantly to reach, in 1913, a level that exceeded its GDP. Annual flows amounted to more than 5 per cent of GDP in 1913. About a quarter of outgoing capital was oriented towards other European countries, one-quarter to the USA and half to the rest of the world. Banking organised itself internationally to engage in large investment projects: railways in Russia, textile factories in Silesia. As a consequence, the total foreign investment of European countries increased faster than their Gross Domestic Product .

The *monetary relations* of all major countries were governed by the automatic rules of the gold standard. The combination of free movement of goods, labour and capital with fixed exchange rates was achieved by abstaining from an independent monetary policy. The increased integration was reflected by the coincidence of economic cycles across European countries.[10]

---

10   See Craigh and Fisher (1996).

INTERNATIONAL ORGANISATION AND COORDINATION

At the turn of the century, forms of integrated policy were practised for the first time, international institutions being founded for the purpose. This was the logical outcome of increased government intervention in the economy, combined with intensified international exchange. Not surprisingly, this policy integration concerned areas directly connected with the conditions for international trade and competition.

- *Transport.* The technical standardisation of railway equipment was mainly due to the British system of measures being adopted by most states. The coordination of other elements, such as the exchange of rolling stock, the treatment of goods, time schedules and so on, was accomplished in international committees.
- *Post and telecommunication.* Among the first international organisations were the International Telecommunication Union (1865) and the Universal Postal Union (1874). Both were established to harmonise internationally all national regulations with respect to rates, procedures, infrastructure (cables) and so on. The harmonisation has contributed much to the rapid growth of PTT traffic.
- *Agriculture and fishery.* Several attempts were made at international coordination and regulation; a first, limited success was the abolition of sugar premiums. An effort was made to achieve one European tariff for foodstuffs, to protect European producers against competition, on their home market, from new producer countries.
- *Social policies.* Efforts towards integration were inspired largely by the fear that the improvement of social services and work conditions in one country would put that country at a competitive disadvantage. The abolition of slavery was among the first steps towards social policy integration: in 1890, a General Act against Slavery was signed.

Some hesitant steps were taken to bring about some coordination in other areas. However, the pressure of the techno-economic circumstances was not strong enough to make them successful.

1914–1945: disintegration

THE FIRST WORLD WAR AND THE PEACE TREATY

With the outbreak of the First World War, every country started to practise autarky: they reasoned that to depend economically on foreign countries makes a country vulnerable in military terms. The result was a process of disintegration. This had its effects both on markets and on policy.

- *Markets.* The first victim was international trade, which showed a steep drop, owing to government intervention. The next was production factors, their movement being more and more curtailed. Under the pressure of conscription, among other things, the free movement of individuals collapsed completely. Capital was more and more contained within national borders by a multitude of national rules. The international loans concluded during this period concerned exclusively the assistance of one government by another.

- *Policy.* The state began to interfere intensively with trade and industry, organising them for purposes of war. Because the control was strictly national, a coordinated international policy was practically impossible. Even within a political bloc, integration was shunned for fear of disloyalty of allied states. Agreements concluded between the members of each bloc covered only restricted areas. For instance, during the First World War the Allies only coordinated the use of shipping tonnage, and made some attempt at specialising production.

The Peace Treaty of Versailles consolidated the disintegration brought about by war. The central theme of this treaty was the nations' right to self-determination. On that basis, many new states were formed in Europe, which instantly began to quarrel about frontiers, debts, minorities and so on. The result was a great length of new frontiers (some 11 000 km) with corresponding customs barriers. To support the autonomy of the national economies, most barriers were made sky-high. Thus the industry and transport structures were forced to adapt themselves to a multitude of small territories. Factories were built at uneconomic locations, railways rerouted, and so on.

THE PERIOD UP TO THE END OF THE SECOND WORLD WAR

After the First World War some countries (notably Germany) were left with enormous debts, leading to serious balance-of-payment difficulties. These were aggravated by low prices and diminishing sales prospects on export markets. Under such circumstances, non-competitive companies, traditionally in favour of protection, grasped their chance, and the enormous unemployment consolidated the protectionist tendencies. This movement spread quickly through Europe and, as a consequence, imports were reduced to almost half the pre-war level; this in turn led to a decrease in exports as well (as illustrated by Table 3.3). An even greater decrease befell international capital movements, which fell back to about one-fifth of their pre-war level.

Table 3.3   Some indicators of European[a] economic development, 1913–38

Indicator	1913	1920	1930	1938
Gross National Product per head (index 1938 = 100)	n.a.	73	89	100
Industrial production (index 1938 = 100)	n.a.	59	84	100
Production of pig iron (MT/y)	42	22	37	39
Coal production (MT/y)	515	395	483	485
Share of exports in GNP (%)	16	9	9	6
Share of foreign investment in GNP	5	n.a.	1	1
Railway track (x 1000 km)	217	215	226	229

Notes: [a] *Only former EU15 countries. n.a. = not available.*

Source: *Calculated on the basis of figures given in OECD (1964), Bairoch (1976), Mitchell (1981).*

The disadvantages of the economic disintegration were increasingly recognised and attempts were undertaken to reintegrate the economies of certain groups of states.

- *Markets*. The plan to unite in a customs union the old Habsburg states failed, as did a freetrade scheme in which 29 states agreed to abolish all trade restrictions within six months and never impose them again (Conference of Geneva, 1927).
- *Policy*. The League of Nations, founded by the Allies, came into operation in 1920; its object was to maintain peace in Europe. The League developed some activity in economic and social affairs (among others it created the ILO, the International Labour Organization). However, all those initiatives hardly made an impact. In this period of general disintegration one example of effective international integration by institution building can be mentioned. The Bank for International Payments, a joint venture of the central banks in Europe, was founded in 1930 to facilitate payments, quite a feat in a period of great monetary disorder.

In the 1920s the average dependency on external trade remained virtually stable. Even that comparatively modest integration was curtailed by the depression of the 1930s. Again there was a sharp effect on both markets and policy integration.

- *Markets*. The United States' introduction of the very high Smoot–Hawley tariff in 1930 sparked off a further wave of protectionist measures in Europe, leading to tariffs of unprecedented height and the multiplication of the number of quotas.
- *Policy*. The most important area of disintegration was monetary policy. The gold standard, which had not worked very well during this period, collapsed. A period of currency competition ensued, one devaluation following upon the other. All attempts to solve the crisis by international agreements failed. In other fields, too, policy integration decreased. To overcome the depression, states began to intervene even more than before in the economy, and Keynes (1936) furnished the theoretical foundation. Solutions (armament, infrastructure works) to the unemployment problem were governed by national circumstances, and the economy was often made subservient to military objectives.

The Second World War brought about some integration among members of the same political blocs. On the side of the Axis powers it was achieved by enlisting the economies of territories occupied by Germany in the German war efforts. The integration concerned not only products (agricultural as well as industrial): production factors were forcefully integrated as well (*Arbeitzeinsatz*, war loans). On the side of the Allies some integration could also be perceived: once more, production and means of transport were to some extent normalised for the sake of the war effort. The integration efforts hardly touched the other sectors of the economy, however.

1945 to the present: a new upsurge of integration

EUROPE AND WORLD POLICY

Integration, which had come to a halt during the war, was gradually re-established during the 1945–1955 period. It has been accompanied by the development of major international economic institutions (Molle, 2003). First, there was a move towards free trade. The task of fostering worldwide free trade liberalisation has been entrusted to the General Agreement on Tariffs and Trade (GATT) transformed in the 1990s into the World Trade Organization

(WTO). One important instrument against the occurrence of trade disputes is the so-called 'most-favoured-nation' clause, according to which any favourable tariff which two countries accord to each other is essentially valid for all other participants in the General Agreement. The GATT/WTO has accomplished a considerable worldwide tariff decrease; many non-tariff impediments have been eliminated as well.

Next there was a move towards convertibility of currencies and free capital movements, with exchange rates pegged to the dollar. This task has been entrusted to the World Bank (IBRD) and International Monetary Fund (IMF). The combined task of these organisations was to ensure well-regulated international monetary relations (Conference of Bretton Woods). That meant fixed exchange rates between currencies. Countries that, through temporary balance-of-payment problems, found it hard to maintain these fixed exchange rates could obtain hard-currency loans. The monetary and macro-economic coordination schemes of the IMF and the Organisation for Economic Cooperation and Development (OECD: see below) had worked well for several decades. However, in the 1970s they could no longer cope with the emerging inconsistencies, and the Bretton Woods system collapsed. The experiences of the period led to the conclusion that free movement of goods and capital cannot be combined with pegged exchange rates and independent macro-economic policy making of member countries.

After the Allied victory, Europe was cut in two. If at first the spheres of influence of the western Allies and the Soviet Union were not precisely delimited, soon afterwards the outbreak of the Cold War led to the very sharp dividing line which went by the name of the Iron Curtain. Economic integration of European countries from the western bloc with those from the eastern bloc was thus excluded for a long time.[11] Any further integration has proceeded within each separate bloc. Some integration of the economies of Central and Eastern Europe has taken place in the framework of the Council of Mutual Economic Assistance (CMEA or Comecon).[12]

THE PURSUIT OF EUROPEAN UNITY

The ravages of war made it clear that Europe's only chance of survival lay in progressive (economic) integration. To that end some important multinational agreements were concluded and some international bodies, widely different in structure and authority, were created.[13] Examples are the Council of Europe, concerned in particular with cultural affairs and human rights, and the West European Union, mainly occupied with defence. The generally felt need for economic integration soon generated a favourable climate to create, with American support, an international organisation covering all Western Europe, an intergovernmental set-up and a wide range of policy objectives: the Organisation for European Economic Cooperation.[14]

---

11   The only platform where 'integration' of East and West was still a point of discussion was the Economic Commission for Europe (ECE), a regional organisation of the United Nations. Its role has been very modest.

12   See Kozma (1982); Pinder (1986); van Brabant (1989).

13   See, for instance, Palmer, Lambert et al. (1968); van Meerhaeghe (1998). A forerunner of the European Union is the Benelux Economic Union (1944), which joins together the Netherlands, Belgium and Luxembourg. The importance of the Benelux lies in particular in the opportunity it has given to gain experience in certain forms of integration, an experience which has often proved very useful for the European Union.

14   The Organisation for European Economic Cooperation (OEEC) (1948) was created to administer the Marshall Aid which the US provided to Europe. The OEEC aimed for trade liberalisation and provided for some coordination of national policies, for instance at the macro-economic level and with respect to manufacturing industry and energy. The OEEC was extended and relaunched in 1961 under the new name of Organisation for Economic Cooperation and Development (OECD); at present it comprises the entire industrialised world: that is, Western Europe, North America (United States, Canada, Mexico), the Antipodes (Australia, New Zealand) and Asia (Japan, Korea).

A limited set of countries pushed towards further integration. The UK appeared to set greater store by an empire than a European orientation, and the British gradually withdrew from initiatives towards greater European integration. However, continental nations continued to strive for closer cooperation. This is not surprising, as most initiatives were inspired by the hope of eliminating forever the potential war threat posed by French and German differences. That political aim was to be achieved, not through unrealistic plans for complete political union, but through a strategy of gradual integration of certain functions. These could then later be followed by other functions. The first function chosen was of an economic nature, which seemed the most practical as very good economic reasons were pushing in that direction.[15]

TWO VIEWS ON INTEGRATION

To safeguard the durability of an integration scheme international institutions need to be set up. There has been considerable debate about the degree to which national governments needed to transfer powers to such organisations. One can distinguish essentially two rival concepts:

- a *supranational* organisation, with an organ that independently executes policies and prepares decisions, and where the representatives of national governments may take decisions by majority rule; and
- an *intergovernmental* organisation, characterised by a small secretariat, and where the representatives of the national governments take decisions by unanimity.

The *supranational road* has been indicated by Jean Monnet, 'generally considered the father of United Europe', in the following words: '*Europe will not be made in one go; nor in a comprehensive construction; she will be made through concrete realisations that create first a factual solidarity*' (Monnet, 1976, p.335). On 9 May 1950 the French foreign minister Schuman (inspired by Monnet) presented a plan to join together the French and German basic industries under a European High Authority. After negotiation the plan was accepted not only by France and Germany but also by the Benelux countries and Italy. The UK, having serious reservations about its supranational character, kept aloof. In 1952 the Treaty of Paris created the European Coal and Steel Community (ECSC). The ECSC was based on a functional/supranational approach. The functional character appears in the choice of the strategic sectors of coal (the major form of energy) and steel (the basic material). The supranational character appears in the attribution of considerable powers in matters of regulation of markets.

After the successful creation of the ECSC, new initiatives were taken to extend the functions to be integrated beyond economics into fields such as defence and foreign policy. However, the ratification of the treaties of the European Defence Community (EDC) and of the European Political Community (EPC) eventually miscarried in the French parliament. The pressure of those striving for further integration was then once more brought to bear on the economic function. The choice of this avenue of functional integration seemed the more appropriate as the sectoral limitation of the ECSC had proven to be a serious handicap. First because the interrelations between different sectors of the economy (some of which were integrated and

---

15   See Chapter 2 for the basics of functionalism. See Machlup (1977) for a review of the contributions to the thinking on integration of historians (ch. 5), political economists (ch. 6), statesmen, men of affairs and men of letters (ch. 7), committee members and organisation staff (ch. 8) and economic theorists (ch. 9).

others not) caused a series of practical problems. Second, and more importantly, the integration of the markets of these other products could significantly contribute to economic growth.

Studies were made (Spaak report) and negotiations started (Messina conference) that resulted in 1958 in the Treaty of Rome. This treaty created, on a supranational basis, the European Economic Community. The member states were the same six mentioned above, the UK again keeping apart. With the EEC, European integration reached a decisive stage in its development, for the Treaty of Rome set ambitious goals. In that same year, 1958, the same countries also founded the European Atomic Energy Community (EAEC or Euratom). Since then the Communities have extended both their membership and their competences, which led to the merger into the *European Community*, which later became the *European Union* (see next section).

The *intergovernmental road* has been taken by the other countries of Western Europe. Under the leadership of the UK they created in 1959 the *European Free Trade Association* (EFTA). While recognising the advantages of further integration, these countries could not, for different reasons, accept the objectives and the organisation of the Community. The objectives of EFTA were far less than those of the EC, only a freetrade zone being established. The institutional organisation of EFTA was no different than the usual intergovernmental structure of most international organisations. Over the decades it became clear to an increasing number of EFTA members that their interest would be better served by joining the EC. Almost all have successively left EFTA to become members of the EC. Their accession to the EC has been facilitated by the *European Economic Area* (EEA), a pact signed and ratified in 1992. It merged the EC and the EFTA into a single market with one set of regulations.[16]

FROM EUROPEAN COMMUNITY TO EUROPEAN UNION

The legal foundation of the European Community has evolved over time. Initially it consisted of the three treaties of the ECSC, the EEC and the EAEC. Right from the start of the latter two organisations, two of its institutions (Parliament and the Court of Justice) assumed responsibilities for the three organisations. In the 1960s, the executive bodies (Commission and Council) of the ECSC, the EEC and the EAEC were merged as well. From that moment one institutional structure was in operation for the three separate legal entities. Of these three, the EEC has come to occupy a paramount place. Its treaty has been constantly adapted to cope with the new constitutional needs of the dynamics of the European integration process. For example, the Single Act of 1987 provided among other things for further market and policy integration. The Maastricht and Amsterdam Treaties formalised the colloquial name 'European Community' and created the European Union. The latter encompasses cooperation of member states in matters of foreign and security policy and justice and home affairs. The Treaty of the ECSC had been concluded for 50 years. So in 2002 it expired. It has not been renewed and the functions of the ECSC have been taken over by the EC.

Deepening The EU has gradually extended its field of activity and intensified its involvement in already existing common policy areas. The first objective of the EEC was to create a customs union and an incomplete common market. The next was to create an economic union by setting up common policies and to coordinate many national policies. Market integration made rapid progress in the 1960s and the beginning of the 1970s; a customs union was indeed

---

16   The EEA now encompasses, apart from the EU, Liechtenstein, Norway and Iceland; Switzerland has decided not to participate. These countries have agreed to harmonise their legislation with the 'acquis communautaire'.

quickly realised for most of the sectors of the economy. Similar results were obtained for major parts of the labour and capital markets. Policy integration made headway, for example with the setting up of a common agricultural and a common trade policy. The economic crisis of the middle of the 1970s and early 1980s brought the integration process practically to a halt. When the negative effects of this situation became evident, new impulses were given. Over the years a gradual extension of policy integration took place, based on agreements on new objectives. At some points an acceleration of this process took place. The Single Act (1987) codified the objectives of the completion of the single market, of the protection of the environment and of the improvement of social and economic cohesion. In the 1980s attempts were made to reduce exchange rate volatility (the European Monetary System). The Maastricht Treaty (1992) provided for an Economic and Monetary Union and for more social protection. Moreover the Treaty extends the integration process into a number of non-economic fields, such as justice and home affairs, defence and foreign policy and European citizenship. The Treaty of Amsterdam (1997) has further reinforced the role of the EU in these areas. Recently the EU has set itself new objectives; central is the aim to become the most competitive knowledge-based economy in the world.

The patchwork of treaties and protocols that had accompanied and structured the growing integration in the EU became very ill adapted to the new needs of the enlarged Union. So a new Constitution has been drafted that streamlines and systematises the different 'constitutional' rules that govern the functioning of the European Union.

All during its development the EU has used a French term to designate the integration it had achieved both in market terms and in policy terms. The so-called *'acquis communautaire'* consists of the total body of EU legislation and practices and its common policies. It is sometimes also called 'patrimony'.

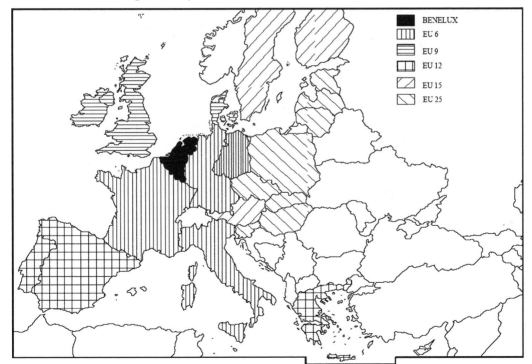

Figure 3.1   Gradual extension of the membership of the European Union

Widening The number of member countries of the EU has gradually increased (see Figure 3.1). This was the result of the success of the EU in the realisation of its objectives. When other European countries realised that they had no part in these advantages, they decided to apply for EU membership. In 1972, the UK, Denmark and Ireland left the EFTA to join the EU. In 1981, Greece was admitted, followed in 1986 by Spain and Portugal. Sweden, Finland and Austria joined in the early 1990s. Recently the geographical coverage of the EU has been further widened. The collapse of the system of central planning in the countries of Central and Eastern Europe (CEEC) opened a new perspective for both the EU and the CEEC. The latter have created the CEFTA, the Central European Free Trade Agreement, that has served as a pre-accession instrument to the EU (Dangerfield, 2000). The German Democratic Republic was taken into the EU when it was united with the Federal Republic of Germany in 1990. Eight of the CEECs that had applied for membership in the 1990s have become members in 2004, together with Malta and Cyprus. EU membership is imminent for Bulgaria and Romania. The other countries on the Balkan peninsula are also striving for membership.

At each enlargement the EU has asked the new members to accept the '*acquis communautaire*' in order to avoid legal and political uncertainties.

Summary and conclusions

- Economic integration of Europe has been not so much an objective as a by-product of technological progress, on the one hand, and aspirations to political unity, on the other.
- The two most important technical-economic factors were large-scale production (attended by mechanisation and automation) and the development of new means of transport (such as trains and lorries).
- Not only can integration cease to make progress, it can also, once achieved, be reversed. Especially in times of economic depression and decline, the forces arguing against integration tend to become harder to resist. War tends to have a very negative influence.
- Integration of goods and factor markets and of macro-economic and monetary policy making is most effective in a strong institutional setting.
- From a multitude of institutions dealing with economic integration the European Union has emerged as the most dynamic. It has extended both its fields of activity and its geographical coverage. The success of the deepening integration in the EU engendered discriminatory effects on European non-member countries that incited them to join the EU.
- The velocity of integration of the EU exceeds the speed with which other integration schemes have proceeded (for example, France, Switzerland, the USA).

4 *Institutions*

Introduction

Economic integration is dependent on the institutional framework that is set for it. The EU is a special specimen of international organisation. International organisations can be defined as purposive entities, with structures for decision making, dispute settlement and policy implementation permitting them to employ their resources to deliver public goods and to respond to events. The EU has from the start been endowed with a strong and original institutional framework that has provided the necessary stability in difficult times and the desirable dynamics when faced with new challenges.

In this chapter we will give the essential aspects of the EU system. This book is on economics; therefore we will not go into the many formal details of the institutions such as size, composition, mode of the election, and so on[1] We will limit ourselves here to those elements that are necessary for the understanding of many of the issues dealt with in later chapters.[2] In the next section we will present the various institutions and the original way in which they relate to each other. We will thereby refer in broad terms to their present competences.[3] Four of these institutions that form the backbone of the system merit fuller treatment, and we will describe in some detail the composition, procedures, tasks and competences of each.

The realisation of the objectives of any organisation and also the EU is giving effect in two different ways: setting rules and providing financial means. In the following sections we will detail the specifics of the EU way in both areas. We will first indicate the different legal forms in use, the diversity of the decision-making processes to initiate new or adapt existing EU regulation. We will next turn our attention to the financial resources, describing briefly the structure of expenditure and receipts and the way budgetary powers are executed. A summary section with some conclusions will round off the chapter.

---

1   We recognise that constitutional aspects such as electoral rules and vote attribution are also important from an economic point of view. They determine the type of cooperation and choices with respect to centralisation of policies (see, in this respect, Chapter 2). For an economic analysis of voting rules, see Mueller (1989), especially page 105 and studies such as Persson and Tabellini (2003).

2   The EU has a very complicated institutional structure. The structure is often defined as resting on three pillars. The central pillar consists of economic matters. The second pillar consists of justice and home affairs and the third of foreign and security aspects. The workings of this system differ according to field of competence. As we confine ourselves in this book to economics we will only mention the institutional aspects of that part.

3   These competences have developed gradually; we will not refer to that evolution here, but only deal with the essentials of the present situation.

Institutional framework

MAJOR AND OTHER INSTITUTIONS

The institutional set-up of the EU is rather original. On the one hand, it has traits of an international organisation, as the member states have kept their sovereignty and competence in essential areas. The member states are represented in the Council of Ministers; as in all traditional intergovernmental international organisations, this is the dominant institution where final decisions are made. On the other hand, the European Union also has some obvious traits of a federal union. Its institutions exercise a clearly defined authority in an increasing number of areas.

The formal institutional framework[4] of the EU consists of some ten different bodies (see Table 4.1 for a schematic representation). The five most important institutions of the EU are the Council, the Commission, the Parliament, the Court of Justice and the European Council. We will deal with these institutions in detail in the following sections. The five other institutions will be discussed briefly in a separate section. Finally there are a number of institutions that do not have a high constitutional status but that nevertheless are very important for the smooth functioning of the EU. These concern notably committees and lobby groups; we will deal with these briefly as well.

Table 4.1   The main institutions of the EU

Council	Commission	Parliament	Court of Justice	European Council
Court of Auditors	European Central Bank	European Investment Bank	Economic and Social Committee	Committee of the Regions

THE COMMISSION

The European Commission (EC) occupies a special position in the system of the Union. Its role is much stronger than that of the secretariat of other intergovernmental institutions, which can only prepare decisions and implement them by delegation of authority of the representatives of member states. On the other hand it falls short of that of the government of a sovereign member state, which has full executive power, whereas the Commission shares these powers with the Council of Ministers.

The major tasks of the Commission are:

---

4   Until 1967, the three Communities (ECSC, EEC and Euratom) had separate executive bodies (Commissions and Councils); the two other institutions (Parliament and Court) had decided to act for all three Communities. In 1967, a treaty merged the executive bodies of the three Communities as well. Although institutions were merged, treaties were not. Indeed the merged bodies have continued to act according to the legal rules and procedures valid for the individual Communities, as the matter in hand required. For a long time plans have been made to merge the treaties into one, with a single set of legal rules. The Treaty on European Union went a long way to integrating the various legal set-ups. The Treaty of Amsterdam has finally resulted in a consolidation of the various set-ups. The daft treaty on the European Constitution sought to finalise this work.

- Initiation of actions. The Commission has the right of initiative; it develops new policies, proposes new legislation. To fulfil its role effectively, the Commission is represented in the meetings of the Council and COREPER (see next section). The role of initiator enables the Commission to safeguard the Union interests against the national interests dominating the Council. The Commission is not the sole initiator; the European Council (of heads of government) has reserved for itself the initiating of major new developments of a strategic nature.
- Execution of policies. EU legislation on the whole scope of its policies calls for implementation by the Commission. In many cases the Council has tied up the Commission in its executive task with some form of consultation, for instance with the so-called 'management committees' (see the following section).
- Implementation of the budget. This includes the operations of the various funds (Agricultural, Regional, Social, Cohesion and Development Funds). The Commission is also authorised to raise loans to finance investments in energy, industry and infrastructure projects envisaged to help realise certain policy objectives.
- Enforcement of the laws. The Commission supervises the correct implementation of treaties and decisions. When the Commission finds, through an inquiry, that a company, individual or member state has violated the EU rules, it invites the offender first to explain its behaviour and next to stop it. Should that prove ineffective, the Commission will institute legal proceedings before the Court.

To perform its task, the Commission has at its disposal an international staff. Each member of the Commission is responsible for one policy sector or, in more concrete terms, for the work of one or more Directorates General (comparable to national ministerial departments).

Members of the Commission are nominated and appointed (after scrutiny by the European Parliament) by the governments of the member states. Once appointed, the members of the Commission have a European responsibility; a member state cannot call 'its' Commissioner to account. The Commission is accountable to the European Parliament. It can be forced to resign by a motion of censure of the Parliament. In that event a new Commission must be appointed.

THE COUNCIL

The Council of Ministers is the principal decision-making body of the EU. It consists of one representative minister of the government of each of the member states. The composition of the Council varies with the matter in hand. In general, the Council consists of the ministers of foreign affairs of the member states, but it may also consist of the ministers responsible for a specific policy field, for instance Agriculture, Transport or Finance. The Council of Ministers meets as often as it considers necessary.

The member states take the presidency in turns, for six months each. The president of the Council takes responsibility for the progress of the work of the Council. The ministers on the Council are accountable to their national parliament and not to the European Parliament (EP). There is, however, a dialogue between the two bodies. The Council has a small separate staff of European officials who prepare the meetings. It is a small staff compared to that of the Commission. Important in the preparatory work is the Committee of Permanent Representatives, often indicated by the French abbreviation of COREPER. This Committee meets every week in task-oriented workgroups, in which civil servants of national departments also take part. COREPER deals with the Commission's proposals. If COREPER is agreeable to the proposal, the Council's final decision is no more than a formality. If not, the proposal is further negotiated in the complete Council of Ministers.

THE EUROPEAN COUNCIL

The European Council is composed of heads of government (and head of state for France) and the president of the Commission. The foreign ministers of the member states and of the EU may also participate in the meetings, usually called 'summits', that take place some four times a year.

The European Council's role is to give direction to provide the Union with the necessary impetus for its development and define the general political guidelines and priorities thereof. In practice this means that the European Council decides (by consensus) on the passing into new stages of integration (for example, single market, EMU). Moreover, it takes decisions on current policy issues that have proved too involved for the Council of Ministers. In the past the role of the European Council has been greatly enhanced as an increasing number of thorny issues are transferred to it by the Council of Ministers.

THE EUROPEAN PARLIAMENT

The members of the European Parliament (EP) are elected directly for a term of five years. From the start, EP members have grouped themselves, not by national delegations, but along party-political lines. The preliminary work of the Parliament is carried on in the parliamentary committees. From their members, the committees choose rapporteurs, who report on subjects to be treated in the full Parliament. Most reports contain a draft resolution, to be voted on by the full EP.

The *competences* of the EP differ according to area:

- Legislation.[5] Parliament has to approve all legislation that applies to matters related to the internal market, framework programmes for the environment, technology and transport and the conclusion of treaties with third countries, notably those for extension of the Union.
- Budget. The competence of the EP is quite extensive. It can accept the complete budget or reject it. It has different powers regarding the various parts of the budget. With regard to expenditure necessarily resulting from the Treaty ('obligatory' expenditure) it can only propose modifications within the total expenditure set. With regard to other expenditure, however, it can amend the draft budget.
- Policy. The EP can influence the scope of EU activities; it is entitled to ask for existing policies to be extended or amended and for new ones to be initiated.
- Control. The major aspect of control is that the Commission has to account to the EP for its actions. It does so in answer to spoken or written questions and in the discussion of its annual General Report.

---

5   Four different procedures exist: consultation, cooperation, co-decision and assent. The last two are most important for the matters dealt with in the present book. In the procedure of consultation (in the past the main one) the role of the EP is limited to advice. In the cooperation procedure the position of the EP is strengthened, as the Council can reject amendments of the EP only unanimously.

COURT OF JUSTICE

One of the essential roles of any efficient international organisation is to provide a system that is able to settle disputes when they arise. The EU has been endowed with a particularly efficient system[6] that is in line with the original legal order established by the treaties. They confer rights and impose obligations directly on citizens and authorities of member states by European law. Moreover, citizens can appeal to European rules in national courts. The proper and consistent interpretation and application of European law in all member states evidently called for a supreme body to settle conflicts; this task was entrusted to the European Court of Justice (ECJ). In its interpretation of the EU legislation the Court has on many occasions taken an 'integrationist' view, which has broken political stalemates on important dossiers.[7]

Who has access to the European Court? Member states and EU institutions (Council, Commission and Parliament) have unlimited access. Natural and legal persons (companies, for instance) have only limited access; they may initiate proceedings in disputes relating to such acts, or the failure to act or give compensation, of the Commission and the Council as affect their interests directly. In a national lawsuit, too, judgement may depend on relevant European law. Individuals can request a national judge who is not sure about the interpretation of European law to demand, before pronouncing judgement, a preliminary ruling from the European Court of Justice. The subject matters brought before the Court were concentrated in the main areas of European policy making. The action of the Court has been very important in maintaining dynamism in the process of European integration. For example, the Court has repudiated, in many judgements, any form of protectionism and in this way the realisation of the internal market has been safeguarded.

OTHER FORMAL INSTITUTIONS

Five other 'institutions' exist that need some brief introduction.

- The Court of Auditors (ECA). This body examines the accounts of the EU to determine not only whether all revenue has been received and all expenditure incurred in a lawful manner, but also whether the financial management has been sound.
- The Economic and Social Committee. The ESC, composed of representatives of employees and employers, professionals and consumers, advises the Commission and the Council on their policy plans.
- The Committee of the Regions. The CR also acts in an advisory capacity to the Commission and the Council on matters regarding local authorities and regional interests.[8]
- The European System of Central Banks (ESCB) and the European Central Bank (ECB). These have the task of maintaining price stability. To that end the ESCB/ECB define and implement the monetary policy of the EU. Moreover, they support the general economic policies of the EU.[9]
- The European Investment Bank. The EIB grants credits to business companies and governments, notably for projects of common interest to several member states that are of

---

6   Most international organisations have to function with dispute settlement procedures that are simply extensions of the negotiation processes between members. The World Trade Organization stands out as it has expert panels. However, even the latter type is much less effective then the EU set up (see Molle, 2003).
7   See for instance the case in insurance (Chapter 12) or transport (Chapter 13).
8   The strong institutional set-up of the regional representation is a consequence of the growing importance of sub-national government through decentralisation in many member states. See, further, Chapter 16.
9   See, further, Chapter 15.

such a nature or size that they cannot be entirely financed by one state. Moreover, the EIB can finance projects in less developed regions.

COMMITTEES

In order to optimise the effectiveness of the preparation and execution of EU policies it is necessary to involve major stakeholders. The major actors in this respect are the member states that wish to keep as much control as possible. The form that has been chosen to accommodate these interests is the committee.[10] In some committees only experts of the Commission and of the member states are represented, in others experts from special interest groups or from the academic world are called upon too.

After their function in the policy process one distinguishes several *types of committee*, the most important[11] of which are:

- Advisory (for example, internal market policy). The Commission determines the agenda and the Commission has only to take the opinion of the committee into account; it is not binding.
- Management (notably used in the field of agricultural markets, see Chapter 9). The Commission proposes; the conclusions of the committee are not binding on the Commission.
- Regulatory (harmonisation of national rules – for example, technical standards, see Chapter 14). The Commission can only take action on the basis of the positive advice that the committee has formulated with a qualified majority.

LOBBY GROUPS

European decision making involves not only EU institutions, but many others.[12] These range from national ministries via regional authorities to industry and professional associations and individual firms. They generally act as lobby groups. Lobbying is best defined as the informal exchange of information in order to try to influence the decisions of public authorities. EU lobbying has increased considerably, for two reasons:

- *Growing regulatory authority*: the areas in which the EU has acquired authority have gradually increased (including the internal market, economic and monetary union). Moreover, the areas in which the Council decides with qualified majority have been stepped up considerably, which implies that national interest groups could no longer count on their national representations to block decisions that would harm their interests. To safeguard these interests it became necessary to try and influence all the stages of the European decision-making process.
- *Discretion over spending considerable funds*: the increased attention that the EU gives to aspects of economic and social cohesion has given rise to a sizable European redistribution. Being eligible for EU structural funds can make a big financial difference for a local authority infrastructure development. The same is true for a firm that may be eligible for funding of part of its research and development under an EU programme.

---

10   Committees have become very important elements in the EU policy-making process (Pedler and Schaefer, 1996; van Schendelen, 1998).
11   The number of committees is increasing fast; a 2005 report listed some 1700 advisory and some 1000 management committees.
12   See, for example, Keohane and Hoffmann (1991); van Schendelen (1993); Pedler and van Schendelen (1994).

These developments have led to the increase in both the number and size of lobby groups that evolve around the EU institutions, notably Commission and Parliament.

Regulation

LEGAL INSTRUMENTS

In order to put its policies into effect the EU, like other organisations, uses regulation. Rules form a whole hierarchy; they range from constitutions to by-laws and contracts. The basic rules of the EU have indeed been given in the treaties. On the other hierarchical levels the EU makes regulations, issues directives, takes decisions.[13]

- A *regulation* is general in its application; it is binding in its entirety and directly applicable in all member states. This means that national legislation, if existent, is overruled by regulations; indeed European law takes precedence over national law. The national governments have no right or need to take action once a matter has been settled by a European regulation, for it is automatically valid in all member states.
- A *directive* is binding, as to the result to be achieved, upon each member state to which it is addressed, but leaves the national authorities the choice of form and methods. So, to implement directives, action of member states is needed in the form of national laws and decrees.
- A *decision* is binding in its entirety upon those to whom it is addressed.

THE PROCESS OF LEGISLATION

Decisions about legislation have in the past been made according to a multitude of procedures, depending on the character of the matter at hand. We present here only the main common features of the legislative process (Figure 4.1).

1 Preparation

The Commission elaborates a planned proposal with the help of its staff; to that end work discussions are often held with committees of national experts.
- The Commission presents its opinions and outlines its planned strategy in communications to the Council and the Parliament.
- The Council and the Parliament communicate their reactions to the Commission; the Commission revises its plans and establishes its proposal.

2 First reading (consultation)

- The proposal is discussed in the Economic and Social Committee, in the Committee of Regions and in the Parliament.

---

13   These are the terms used by the EEC and Euratom; we disregard the slightly different terms used in the past by the ECSC for practically the same notions. The proposal for the Constitutional treaty introduces new forms. We will not go into these legal intricacies here. The EU has the obligation to indicate in each proposal for legislative action whether the subsidiarity and proportionality criteria (see Chapter 2) are met.

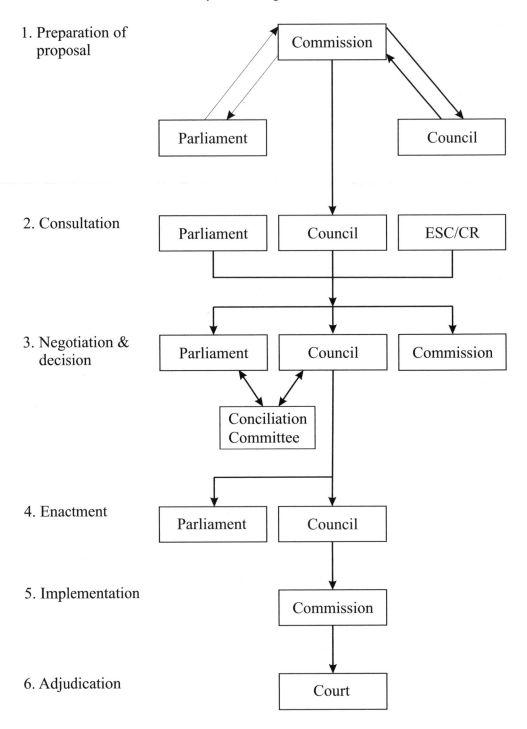

1. Preparation of
   proposal

2. Consultation

3. Negotiation &
   decision

4. Enactment

5. Implementation

6. Adjudication

Figure 4.1   A schematic view of the legislation-making process

- The ESC, CR, EP and Commission form their opinions and communicate these to the Council.

3 Second reading (negotiation)

- The Council's decision on the proposal is prepared by the Committee of Permanent Representatives (COREPER). Any amendments proposed will be submitted by the COREPER to the Council, together with the ESC and EP positions and recommendations.
- The European Parliament discusses the Commission proposals, the Council's position and, in case it has competence in the matter in hand, negotiates with the Council in the framework of a Conciliation Committee.
- The Commission participates in this stage by adapting proposals, intermediating and so on.

4 Enactment

- Depending on the procedure followed, the Council (or in other cases the Council and Parliament) decides about enactment.
- The regulation, directive and so on is enacted by publication in the Official Journal.

THE PRACTICE

The process as described in the previous section passes through the critical stage of the decision making in the Council where specific voting rules apply. These differ according to the matter at hand. In matters of economic policies we can distinguish two cases:[14]

- Qualified majority. Decisions are taken in case the threshold is passed.[15] Its field of application started with internal market issues and has been increased gradually to cover most areas where the EU has shared responsibilities with the member states (in practice this now concerns almost 80 per cent of Council decisions).
- Unanimity. This is the classical method of inter-governmental cooperation. It applies notably to sensitive areas such as cohesion, taxation, and so on that are thought to be critical to national sovereignty.

In many cases decisions are taken on the objectives of the policy and about the system to be set up for implementing them. The member states are then left with the responsibility (in line with the subsidiarity principle) to find ways and means to put the policy into practice. Often the so-called Open Method of Coordination (OMC) is then used which implies an exchange of best practices between member states. This method, which may lead to policy convergence, applies notably to social policy issues. A more constraining method of coordination is used in macro-economic policy making (see Chapter 15) where rigid quantitative objectives are set and where sanctions exist about non-compliance.

---

14   In the past, unanimity was very often the rule. The Single European Act established that many decisions about the internal market, regional policy, and research and technology could be taken by qualified majority. The Treaties of Maastricht (1992) and Amsterdam (1997) have enlarged these areas.

15   Each member state has been attributed a certain number of votes in line with its size. We give here neither the specific numbers per member state, nor the threshold in numbers of votes as they depend on the size of the EU and the specific treaty in force. For our purpose it should suffice that a qualified majority is obtained in case a proposal gets about 70 per cent of the weighted votes cast by a majority of member states.

The EU institutional set-up in general and the qualified majority voting in the Council in particular do represent very efficient forms for reaching international cooperative agreements. Moreover, by simultaneously playing both the EU and the national political game, the governments of member states can use the legitimacy of the EU to overrule domestic lobbies, or to mobilise domestic coalitions in favour of agreements reached at the European level.[16]

Two factors complicate EU decision making:

* Size. The increase in the number of actors that followed from the widening of the EU (from six to 25) and the increased diversity of interests of its members.
* Detail. There has been a tendency to lay down in the European law not only the general principles but also most technical details.[17]

In some cases progress can only be made by abandoning the idea of equal forms and full participation for all member states. The EU permits groups of member states to advance on specific subjects using the legal framework of the EU. This option has been adopted for the European Monetary System, for the European Monetary Union and for social policy. Its application gives rise to expressions such as 'two-speed Europe', 'variable geometry', 'Europe à la carte' or 'flexibility'. The composition of the groups that participate in specific integration projects can be determined on the basis of the interests of each country and the efficiency of the integration process in the context of clubs.

The EU decision-making process is *segmented by sector*. The expert Council (of agriculture, for example) cooperates with the expert member of the Commission, seconded by his expert Directorate General, the expert Committee of the EP and with expert committees of national civil servants, after hearing experts from lobby groups. This practice has led to widely divergent forms of integration models for different areas (as we shall see in the next chapters), notwithstanding the efforts of the Commission and the European Council to maintain as much consistency and unity as possible.[18]

EVALUATION

The present institutional set-up has been devised for a small group of countries (originally six) and a limited task (a Common Market). In the past it has been regularly adapted to cope with an increase in the number of members and with an increase in the EU competences. In general these changes have been adequate to permit the EU to cope with its tasks. However, the limits of the set-up have become visible (EC, 2001d). Most observers do agree that the present institutional set-up is inadequate for coping with the circumstances that prevail after the latest enlargement, let alone any future enlargement. The simple question then is how the Union can maintain its decision-making capacity and its cohesion under these circumstances?

---

16   See the discussion in Chapter 2 on institutional economics and political science; see in particular Moravcsik (1993).

17   National officials have been insistent on this point (hence many delays in COREPER), because their main concern was national acceptance and the consistency of national policy.

18   How serious the damage to consistency could be is illustrated by the outcomes of past negotiations concerning agriculture. In the 1970s and early 1980s, decisions repeatedly went against the principles of the EU, violating the unity of the market, exploding the financial frameworks and jeopardising the integration reached in other areas (monetary, for example). Even a kind of legal restraint imposed by the ministers of finance on the agricultural ministers met with no success.

In this respect the draft constitutional treaty is of importance. Its aims are broad[19] but for us two elements are important:

- The streamlining of the decision-making processes. It generalises in economic matters the system of qualified majority voting in the Council followed by a co-decision procedure for legislative decisions.
- The strengthening of the principles of subsidiarity and proportionality. The EU should limit itself to its main tasks; thereby limiting the burden on decision making and policy implementation.

Budget

GENERAL

The second major instrument to put policies into effect is through the provision of financial resources. In this matter the EU has an intermediate position between a traditional international organisation and a federal state. The cost of international institutions is almost invariably paid from member states' contributions, each country paying a fixed percentage of total expenses. Most international organisations only incur staff and household expenses, larger outlays for special programmes being taken care of by those member states wanting to participate. With the European Union, things are different, on two essential counts. On the expenditure side, the EU has the cost of the large programmes it executes. On the receipts side, the EU has an embryonic form of its own resources. These are pre-federal traits.

The budget of a national state is generally of a considerable size, owing to the important financial consequences of many of its socio-economic policies. The EU budget is small: its total weight is a little over 1 per cent of EU Gross Domestic Product, against some 40 per cent of GDP in some member states (so the total EU budget is about 2 per cent of national budgets). As a consequence the functions of the EU budget differ from those of a national state in the following respects:

- Allocation. With the relatively limited EU budget divided among a long list of programmes in different fields, only limited influence can be directly exerted in most policy fields, like transport, banking and so on. Agriculture, which devours huge sums, is traditionally the only field in which EU policy influences in detail developments in markets of a whole range of products.
- Stabilisation. The EU budget is not an instrument of macro-economic policy; the treaty stipulates that each year the revenues and expenditure shown in the budget shall be in balance. Anyway the total size of the budget is too low for an effective macro policy.
- Redistribution. Although the expenses on EU regional and social policies have increased considerably over the past years, both in absolute and in relative terms, the redistributive

---

19   The changes that the draft Constitution proposes are mostly in areas that fall outside the scope of the present book. A first set of articles concerns deepening: for example, EU powers in matters of asylum and security. A second set concerns changes in the number of members of each of the institutions. A third set concerns consistency and unity of policy making: for example, a president of the Council appointed for five years and a European foreign minister. Finally a Charter of Fundamental Human Rights is included.

power of the EU budget is still very limited if compared to national budgets (which include income tax and social security payments).[20]

EXPENDITURES

In order to put its policies into effect the EU has developed a large number of programmes to which it devotes considerable resources. In order to cope with the expansion of policy areas (for example, agriculture) and the introduction of new ones (cohesion, for instance) the total EU expenditure has shown a substantial real increase over the past decades. The major categories are:[21]

- *Agriculture and fishery* (44 per cent). This category used to absorb a very large portion (two-thirds) of the total budget, mainly through the European Agricultural Fund's outlays for guaranteed prices. A series of decisions have been taken to control agricultural outlays with the effect that their relative share has considerably decreased (see Chapter 9).
- *Structural adaptation* (35 per cent). Expenditures to reinforce social and economic cohesion have assumed increasing weight over the years. Much of the outlay is financed from the so-called 'structural funds', like the European Regional Development Fund and the Social Fund (see Chapter 16).
- *Internal* (6 per cent). The programmes of major policy fields like energy, manufacturing industry, transport and research fall into this category. No large funds have been created; the amounts are spent directly on programmes (see Chapters 10 to 13).
- *External* (5 per cent). Under this heading falls development aid. In addition the European Development Fund (EDF) grants credits to developing countries (see Chapter 17).
- *Running costs* (5 per cent). This consists of cost of staff, offices, travel, and so on.

The categories just mentioned are no longer thought adequate in the light of the growth of EU policy competences and the adoption of new policy objectives. For the period up to 2013 the two major objectives are competitiveness (Lisbon agenda) and cohesion (consequence of accession of NMS). The category 'internal' is recast to accommodate competitiveness. The category 'structural adaptation' is to be recast to accommodate cohesion; its share is supposed to remain in the near future at about 33 per cent (EC 2004a).

RECEIPTS

In order to pay for its expenditure the EU needs income. For some time the EU has had its own funds, but, unlike most federal and confederal structures, the EU cannot itself levy taxes, as it has no fiscal sovereignty. Its revenues consist essentially of EU claims on fiscal and para-fiscal levies and other receipts of the member states.[22] The EU's own resources consist mainly of the following:

---

20   Aid to developing countries (Lomé), to the CEEC (Tacis and Phare programmes) and to the Mediterranean countries (MEDA programme) constitute the reflection in the budget of redistribution through external policy of the EU (see Chapter 17).

21   In brackets averages of 2000/2003 budget figures. The remaining 5 per cent of costs fall under the category of miscellaneous expenses.

22   Several proposals have been made to give the EU a 'fifth resource; one that is not tied to member states' contributions'. This would give the EU its own tax base. The Commission has analysed the pros and cons of several options, such as carbon tax, corporate tax and seigniorage of the European Central Bank (EC, 1998a). None has as yet been adopted.

- *Customs duties* (14 per cent) are levied from products imported from outside the EU. The member state levying these duties will often be the one most favourably situated for importation into Europe, which is not necessarily the one for which the goods are destined (think, for instance, of German imports through the Dutch port of Rotterdam). In such a case, to allocate the duties to one member state seems unjust, so, from 1971, they have flowed into the EU treasury. Their share in the total has decreased over time as external tariffs of the EU have been lowered continuously (see Chapters 5 and 17).
- *Agricultural levies and contributions* (1 per cent). Special types of import levies are the variable agricultural duties levied at the outer frontiers of the EU to adjust the price level of imported produce to EU prices. Duties and contributions are levied from internal EU produce as well, to control production and thus limit the need for financing from the Agricultural Fund. Once more, logically these levies accumulate to the EU. The levies have tended to decrease over time as the EU has changed its agricultural support policies and its external regime for agricultural products (see Chapter 9).
- *Value-added tax* (36 per cent). A uniform basis has been established for value-added tax in all member states. A fixed percentage (at present 1) has to be transferred to the EU. Value-added tax was introduced in 1960 to replace fixed national contributions.
- *GDP-related income* (48 per cent). Since 1988 each member state pays a certain percentage of its GDP to the EU budget; this percentage is fixed every year. The relative importance of this revenue source has increased constantly. With GDP as indicator, the contributions to the EU budget tend to take relative wealth levels of each member into account, thereby limiting the need for redistributive measures on the expenditure side.

THE PROCEDURE

The budget is established by an involved procedure (EC, 1993a, 2000a), the main steps of which are as follows:

1 Preparation. The Commission establishes a preliminary draft budget and submits this to the European Parliament and the Council of Ministers. The Council goes into consultation and turns it into a draft budget (acting by qualified majority). This draft is then sent to the EP.

2 First reading. The Parliament discusses the draft budget. If no amendments are proposed, the budget is adopted. If the EP votes proposals for change, the procedure moves into its next stage.

3 Second reading. The Council of Ministers receives the draft budget with proposals and amendments. To resolve conflicts a Conciliation Committee will be convened (involving Parliament, Council and Commission).

4 Adoption. After a final round of negotiations between Council and Parliament, the president of the European Parliament signs the budget, thus formalising its adoption.

EVALUATION: SOME MAJOR ISSUES

The budget procedure is subject to continuous criticism. There are five major points on which improvements are sought:

Annuality   The fact that the budget needs to be balanced every year conflicts with the need of the EU to engage in multi-annual programmes. Multi-annuality is often necessary to give sufficient predictability to the beneficiaries of such programmes. In order to avoid such problems the EU also adopts Financial Frameworks for a period of at least five years. The upcoming one covers the period 2007-2013 (EC 2004a).

Responsibility   The budget authority of the EU is vested in the Council of Ministers and in the European Parliament. The Commission is involved only in the proposition of a draft budget. Conflicts that result from this situation are now largely resolved in the so-called 'consultation procedure'. The Parliament tries to have the final responsibility in all budget matters.

Discipline   Many decisions bearing on expenses are made in a fragmented way, by specialised Councils of Ministers (for instance, of agriculture). Moreover, some decisions of the Commission entail expenses. Many expense categories (such as the Agricultural Guarantee Fund) depend on market and monetary developments. The Council of Ministers draws up the framework for the budget. The Commission is responsible for making sure that policy measures that entail expenses are financed within the limits set by the Council.

Equity   The contribution to and the receipts from the budget are not in equilibrium for each member state. Some are net contributors, others net beneficiaries. The distribution of income and outlays over member states is a bone of contention and is the subject of very fierce negotiations that often can only be concluded in the framework of package deals.[23]

Controls   The execution of many European policies demands the participation of member states, which makes the control function of the budget difficult to accomplish. The European Court of Auditors, charged with the control of expenditure and revenues and endowed with powers of investigation with regard to EU institutions as well as national administrative bodies, reports every year on the most important deficiencies, amongst them fraud. To remove their causes has proved extremely difficult, but should be improved in future by specific measures.

Summary and conclusions

- A strong institutional set-up has stimulated the continuous development of the integration process.
- The usual division of powers in a state is partly to be found in the EU in the sense that legislation is with Parliament, execution with the Commission and adjudication with the Court. The Council does not fit very well in this scheme as it has both important legislative and executive powers.
- Decision-making procedures in the EU are rather involved and differ according to subject area. The gradual generalisation of the qualified majority voting rule has been critical in the balanced development of the integration process.
- The budget of the EU is relatively small. Notwithstanding that, the EU expenditure serves important allocation (competitiveness), redistribution (cohesion) and external (for example, aid) purposes. It has no role in matters of stabilisation. To pay for the outlays, the EU has its own financial means.

---

23   A correction mechanism decreases the total contribution of the UK; the financing of these forgone receipts is made proportionally by the other member states.

- The EU has to adapt its institutions and streamline its decision-making processes in order to continue to function effectively after further enlargement.

2 *Common Market*

5 *Goods*

Introduction

autricula

The centrepiece of most integration schemes is the integration of goods markets. In this chapter we describe first in a theoretical way how markets evolve when barriers to movement are torn down. Next, we will describe the way in which the EU has realised the integration of the markets for manufactured goods of its member countries.

In the first section we treat some basic theoretical concepts and we will define and specify the advantages of integration, the barriers to trade and the reasons for protection. Next we will turn our attention to the way the EU has regulated the free movement of goods between its member states. We will also pay some attention to the external trade relations of the EU, although the main discussion of this point will be presented in Chapter 17.

The main body of the chapter will be devoted to a close analysis of the changes in the geographical as well as the product structure of the internal and external trade of the EU under the influence of integration. Having thus dealt with the quantity aspect of trade, we will next turn to the price aspect, finding out whether or not prices have converged under the pressure of integration.

Finally, we will indicate how liberalised goods movements in Europe have affected welfare and economic growth. As usual, the chapter will be rounded off with some conclusions and a summary.

Some basic theoretical concepts

MOTIVES FOR OBSTACLES

Many countries have protected their domestic producers from foreign competition by introducing obstacles to free trade (see Chapter 3). Protection against third countries is mostly achieved by *import restrictions*. From the extensive literature we have distilled the following arguments for such measures:

- Strategic independence. In times of war and supply shortages, a country should not depend on unreliable sources in other countries as far as strategic goods are concerned.
- Nurturing so-called 'infant industries'. The idea is that young companies and sectors which are not yet competitive should be sheltered in infancy in order for them to develop into adult companies holding their own in international competition.
- Defence against dumping. The health of an industry may be spoiled when foreign goods are dumped on the market (sale prices below the cost in the country of origin). Even if the action is temporary, the industry may be weakened beyond its capacity to recover.

- Defence against social dumping. If wages in the exporting country do not match productivity, the labour factor is said to be exploited; importation from such a country is held by some to uphold such practices and is therefore not permissible.
- Boosting employment. If the production factors in the union are not fully occupied, protection can turn local demand towards domestic goods, so that more labour is put to work and social costs are avoided.
- Diversification of the economic structure. Countries specialising in one or a few products tend to be very vulnerable; problems of marketing such products lead to instant loss of virtually all income from abroad.
- Easing balance-of-payment problems. Import restrictions reduce the amount to be paid abroad, which helps to avoid adjustments of the industrial structure and accompanying social costs and societal friction (caused by wage reduction, restrictive policies, and so on).

Pleas for *export restriction* have also been heard. The underlying ideas vary considerably. The arguments most frequently heard are the following:

- Strategically important goods must not fall into the hands of other nations; this is true for military goods (weapons) but also for incorporated knowledge (computers) or systems.
- Export of raw materials means the consolidation of a colonial situation; it is hoped that a levy on exports will increase the domestic entrepreneurs' inclination to process the materials themselves. If not, then at any rate the revenues can be used to stimulate other productions.
- If exported goods disrupt foreign markets, the importing country may be induced to take protective measures against the product and a series of other products; rather than risk that, a nation may accept a 'voluntary' restriction of the exports of that one product.

CATEGORIES OF OBSTACLES TO FREE TRADE

Obstacles or trade-impeding factors fall into two categories, tariffs and so called 'non-tariff barriers', or NTBs.[1] They can be described as follows:

- Tariffs, or customs duties or import duties are sums levied on imports of goods, making the goods more expensive on the internal market. Such levies may be based on value or quantity. They may be in fixed percentages or variable amounts.
- Levies of similar effect are import levies disguised as administrative costs, storage costs or test costs imposed by the customs, and so on.
- Quantitative restrictions (QR) are ceilings put on the volume of imports of a certain good allowed into a country in a certain period (quota), sometimes expressed in money values.
- Currency restrictions mean that no foreign currency is made available to enable importers to pay for goods bought abroad.
- Other non-tariff impediments are all those measures or situations (such as fiscal treatment, legal regulations, safety norms, state monopolies or public tenders) which ensure a

---

1   Non-tariff barriers are very common, because international agreements forbid countries to have recourse to tariffs. The negative effects are similar to those of tariffs; see, for instance, Krauss (1979); Greenaway (1983). For a more thorough treatment of voluntary export restraints (VERs), see Jones (1984).

country's own products' preferential treatment over foreign products on the domestic market.

WHY DO AWAY WITH PROTECTION?

Classical international trade theory teaches us that protection has important negative effects on prosperity[2] and that the best way to avoid these negative effects is for all the countries of the world to adopt perfect free trade. The advantages of free trade are:

- more production and more prosperity through better allocation of production factors, each country specialising in the products for which it has a comparative advantage;
- more efficient production thanks to scale economies and keener competition;
- improved 'terms of trade' (price level of imported goods with respect to exported goods) for the whole group in respect of the rest of the world.

WHY A CUSTOMS UNION?

Countries, finding progress on the score of worldwide trade liberalisation too slow, try to adopt as a second-best strategy a geographically limited form of free trade, as represented by a customs union. Recall that a CU implies free trade among partners, but protection of the entire union against the rest of the world. So we move from a situation in which country A operates tariffs against all other countries to a situation in which it applies tariffs to third countries only.

The *theory of customs unions*[3] relates to the gains and losses incurred by the establishment of such unions. In economic terms, the creation of the CU is warranted only if the former outweigh the latter. In political terms, it is feasible only if the advantages and disadvantages are fairly distributed among partners.

The effects of a customs union between countries A and B are best studied by making a distinction between trade creation, trade diversion (Viner, 1950) and trade expansion (Meade, 1955). We can explain these effects as follows:

- *Trade creation* will occur when trade between partners A and B increases. In country A, demand will shift from the expensive protected domestic product to the cheaper product from the partner country, implying a shift from a less efficient to a more efficient producer.
- *Trade diversion* will occur when imports from the efficient or cheap producer 'world market' are replaced by imports from a higher-cost (or less efficient) producer, namely, the 'partner country'. That country's products can be sold more cheaply in country A than world market production, because the CU imposes a protective tariff on imports from W, while leaving imports from the partner country free.

---

2   The arguments for protection and the (lack of) economic basis for them have been extensively studied in the literature. We refer here only to the authoritative work of Corden (1971, 1974), the handbook by Caves and Jones (1984), the case studies by Meyer (1973), the political economy approach of Frey (1985), the inventory of the OECD (1985c) and the European study of new protectionism by Page (1981).

3   See, for the origins of this theory, Machlup, (1977). Classical economists occupied themselves quite frequently with the problems of preferential trade agreements (some sparked off by the creation of the German Zollverein in the 19th century). International economic integration actually only became a separate object of economic thinking after the Second World War (Viner, 1950). The post-war integration processes have greatly stimulated profound theoretical studies (Tovias, 1991).

- *Trade expansion* will occur because the lower market price in A stimulates total domestic demand, which will be satisfied by foreign trade (either from the partner or from the world market).

For a better understanding of the nature and volume of these three effects, let us take a close look at Figure 5.1, which gives the situation for country A on the left-hand side and for country B on the right. We assume that the supply from producers in the rest of the world is fully elastic at a price level p_w. The corresponding supply is represented in the diagrams by the horizontal line S_w. Assume that, as a high-cost producer, country A enables its industry to capture part of the home market by introducing a fairly high tariff. Country B, on the contrary, produces at rather low costs, and needs only a low tariff to make sure that its producers can cover the entire internal demand. Assume now that countries A and B form a customs union which establishes a common outer tariff t^*, the average of the tariffs of countries A and B. Once the customs union is established, supply and demand in the area will settle at a price p_{cu}. Now, country A will buy all its imports (BE) from the partner country, p_{cu} being lower than p_{w+t^*}. Production in country A will be O_aB. Country B, for its part, produces the quantity O_bE', of which $B'E'$ (equal to BE) is in excess of its home demand (O_bB'); B exports this quantity to the partner country.

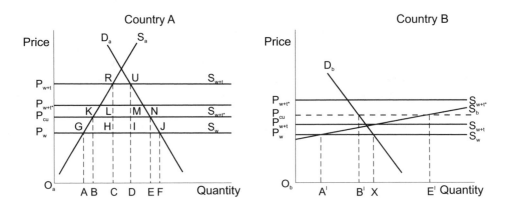

Figure 5.1   Trade and production effects of a customs union, countries A and B

What, then, are the trade effects of the creation of this customs union? The effects differ according to the initial situation (see Table 5.1). Let us take the two cases of protection and free trade of the previous section as examples.

Table 5.1   Trade effects of a customs union, countries A and B

| Effect | Starting situation | | | |
| | Free trade | | Protection | |
	A	B	A	B
Creation	−AB	−A′B′	BC	*
Expansion	−EF	−B′X	DE	B′E′
Diversion	BE	*	CD	*

*Note: * Not applicable.*

- *Country A.* If protection marks the initial situation of country A, a positive development occurs. A new trade flow (*BE*) occurs between partners, of which *CD* is trade diversion; it replaces the imports that used to come from other countries in the world. Trade creation is *BC* and trade expansion *DE*. On balance, trade has increased in our example (*BC* + *DE* being larger than *CD*) and international specialisation has intensified accordingly. Starting from free trade for country A, a negative development occurs. Trade actually diminishes by *AB* on the producer side and by *EF* on the consumer side. Moreover *BE* is diverted from the lower-cost world producer to the high-cost partner country.
- *Country B.* Starting from free trade, the introduction of a common tariff stops the trade that existed between B and W, which implies negative trade creation (−*A′B′*) and expansion (−*B′X*) as less efficient home producers take over from more efficient world producers. Starting from a situation of protection in B, a customs union does not give rise to trade effects (but for the exports *B′E′*), as there were no imports from the world anyway.

WELFARE EFFECTS OF A CUSTOMS UNION

What are the advantages and disadvantages ensuing from the customs union and the tariff? On the one hand, trade diversion tends to make production less rational, which is a disadvantage. On the other hand, trade creation and trade expansion make production more efficient, which is advantageous. To get an idea of the magnitude of the effects, consider Figure 5.2, starting from protectionism. We assume that the price for the customs union is p_{cu}.

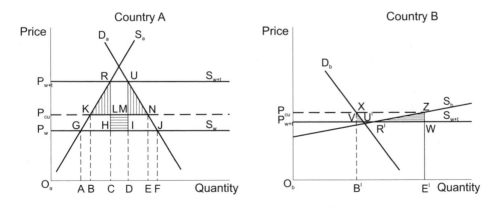

Figure 5.2   Welfare effects of a (trade-diverting) customs union

- *Country A.* The advantages on the production side (trade creation *BC*) are represented by the triangle *KRL*. This indicates that the saving on production cost equals, on average, half the difference in costs between home production and that in country B ($p_{w+t} - p_{cu}$), leaving economic resources available for other purposes. On the consumption side (trade expansion equal to *DE*) the advantages are represented by the triangle *MUN*. The disadvantages for country A are represented by the square *HLMI*. For the amount of trade equal to *CD*, which has been diverted, production inputs have been higher than necessary. In our example the establishment of a customs union produces a net advantage for country A.
- *Country B.* The disadvantages are on the consumer as well as the producer side. The consumer gets less quantity for more money; his loss is indicated by the horizontally shaded little triangle *VXU'*. On the producer side, there is a production loss indicated by the horizontally shaded triangle *R'ZW*. The producers in B will of course enjoy a net gain.

Alternative cases can be imagined in which the profits or the losses are heavier. If, for instance, the only effect is trade expansion, there will be larger net advantages, as can be shown by a slight variation of the former example. Assume the supply curve of country B is equal to that of the world. The net effect of a customs union between countries A and B will be positive, in fact the reverse of the negative one found for country A passing from free trade to protectionism (Figure 5.1). We can vary the differences between p_{cu} and p_w and the gradient of the supply and demand curves in such a way that the trade diversion exceeds trade expansion, so that the establishment of a customs union produces a net disadvantage to the world as a whole.

The present examples have a number of limitations. First, they refer to only one product. To judge the economic desirability of a customs union by its static effects, the profits and losses for all products involved need to be calculated, under consideration of the specific circumstances obtaining for each. Next, they treat only tariffs. The production and welfare effects of non-tariff barriers differ from those of tariffs, but are quantitatively at least as important.[4]

Modern analysis based on mathematical models shows that regional integration unambiguously benefits the member countries and hurts the outside country (Olofsdotter and Torstensson, 1998).

THE INCIDENCE OF POSITIVE AND NEGATIVE EFFECTS

Various factors influence the occurrence of positive and negative effects of a CU:[5]

- *The production structure.* Two countries can be complementary or competitive. If one country is a potential competitor of the other, specialisation along the lines of inter-industry trade is probable and the advantages of a CU are likely to be important. With complementary production structures the advantages of a CU cannot be very important.
- *The size of the union.* The more numerous and the larger the countries participating in the CU, the larger its share in total world trade, the better the prospects for division of labour and the smaller the risk of trade diversion.
- *The level of the tariffs.* As the initial tariffs of the trade partners are higher, the attendant inefficiencies will be worse and the welfare effects of the abolition of tariffs greater. On the

---

4   For a detailed treatment of these effects, see previous editions of this book.
5   Contributions by Viner (1950); Meade (1955); Tinbergen (1959); Balassa (1961); Petith (1977); Krugman (1980).

other hand, the introduction of high common external tariffs against third countries will reduce the positive effect.

- *Transport and transaction costs.* The increased trade has to be realised physically, for which efficient transport is required. Failing that, the transport costs will replace the tariffs as an obstacle to further specialisation. For that reason, customs unions tend to be concluded between contiguous countries.
- *Flexibility.* The advantages are smaller if production bottlenecks prevent the full accomplishment of advanced specialisation and the corresponding reallocation of production.
- *Terms of trade.* Importing countries united in a customs union can enforce (by their stronger bargaining power) lower supply prices on the world market, thus improving their terms of trade (export price divided by import price). The increase in the members' welfare would then be accompanied by a loss in non-members' welfare).
- *Improved technical efficiency.* An economy that is subject to new competitive pressures will try to improve its production methods. This will lead to a lowering of the supply curve of domestic producers, in turn leading to welfare increases exceeding the static welfare increases described in the previous section.
- *Economies of scale.* For many production processes average cost decreases with the increased scale of production. Integrated markets permit the taking advantage of such low-cost production (see Chapter 10). Countries with domestic production of industries subject to economies of scale are likely to benefit from integration.

EU regime

RATIONALE AND PRINCIPLES

The advantages from free trade predicted by theory have incited the founders of the EU to adopt very clearly *the principle of the free internal movement of goods*. The freedom of movement within the EU extends to goods from third countries for which, in the importing member state, the administrative conditions have been met, and the (common) customs tariffs, or measures of equal effect, have been settled by the importing member state.

GRADUAL ELABORATION OF A COMMON POLICY

In the 1960s the most important targets as to the liberalisation of goods trade among the original six member countries could be realised.

- *Import duties and levies* of equal effect in force between member states could be abolished a year and a half earlier than foreseen in the Treaty (July 1968).
- *Quantitative restrictions and measures of equal effect* among member states were also eliminated, most already in the early 1960s.
- A number of NTBs were abolished, partly under the impulse of the Commission's action programmes, partly as the result of verdicts of the Court of Justice.

In the 1970s and 1980s the new member states – both those which joined in 1972 (the UK, Ireland and Denmark) and those which joined in the 1980s (Spain, Portugal and Greece)

– abolished all quotas and tariffs in intra-EU trade during a transition period of several years. However, the removal of many NTBs proved very difficult as they were closely related to national regulations set up to pursue important objectives of public policy. Examples include the differences between member states in:

- levels and structure of indirect taxation (as on tobacco and liquor);
- technical standards set for the protection of the worker, the consumer and the general public (for example, for pharmaceuticals);
- the consequence of the external policy (national quotas for textile products);
- national industry-oriented government procurement policies (such as those on telecommunications, computers and defence equipment); and
- administrative stipulations for such diverse matters as statistics and crime.

During the 1985–2000 period the Commission took a bold approach to end the fragmentation of important segments of the European market for goods (and services). Its White Paper on the completion of the internal market (EC, 1985a) proposed doing away with all these remaining barriers by 1992 by abolishing the controls at the internal frontiers. The so-called 'Single Act' (EC, 1986a) laid down these objectives in a treaty and gave increased powers to the institutions of the EU to pass all necessary legislation to reach them. This programme has since been executed and a huge number of regulations and directives have been adopted, with the result that the single market for goods is now practically completed (see also Chapters 10 and 14). Note that the accession of Austria, Sweden and Finland in the middle of the 1990s could be realised without special rules as their trade with the EU had already been liberalised in the framework of the European Economic Area (see Chapter 3).

EXTERNAL SITUATION

In line with the definition of the customs union (Chapter 2) the EU has adopted a common customs tariff in their relations with third countries. At the end of the transition period, the *common external tariff* (CET) came into force. For the CET the arithmetical average of the duties applied in the various countries was to be taken as the basis. The national tariffs have been gradually adjusted to that CET as the mutual tariffs were broken down.

The level and structure of the CET have been adapted several times under the influence of a drive for *worldwide liberalisation of trade* relations. The EU has supported this drive in view of the advantages it entails both in economic (more welfare) and political terms (more stability). This has taken place in the framework of negotiations on tariffs and quotas of the General Agreement on Tariffs and Trade (GATT) (the so-called 'Dillon round' of 1960–62, the Kennedy round of 1964–7, the 'Tokyo round' of 1973–9 and the 'Uruguay round' that was completed in 1993) This has led to a considerable decrease in protection levels.[6] The EU has negotiated trade privileges with certain groups of countries with which it wants to keep up *special relations*. The most advanced agreement is the Free Trade Treaty with the countries in Western Europe that are not EU members (see Chapter 17).

The CET system applies in general to all manufactured products. Until recently it did not apply to agricultural products: the agricultural market of the EU was protected by a separate system of variable levies on imports and subsidies on exports (see Chapter 9).

---

6   See Kock (1969); Hoekman and Kostecki (1996). Empirical analyses of the welfare effects of these liberalisation measures (see, for the Tokyo round, for example, Deardorff and Stern, 1981; Whalley, 1985) have shown that these are mostly positive for all partners (EU, USA, LDCs, NICs and so on).

Trade patterns

RELATIVE IMPORTANCE OF TOTAL FOREIGN TRADE

International goods trade is essential to the economies of EU member states, as is illustrated by the figures of Table 5.2, representing the relative importance of goods trade in gross domestic product.[7] First, the table shows that the trade–GNP ratio, indicating the degree to which a country participates in international goods trade, seems dependent on two factors:

- *Size of economy.* For large countries, the value of goods trade (average of imports and exports, including intra-EU trade) amounts to about one-quarter of their GDP, while for smaller countries with an open economy (the Netherlands, Belgium and Ireland) the percentage rises to some two-thirds.
- *Structure of the economy.* Countries in the Mediterranean basin (for example, Spain), having specialised in services such as tourism, show relatively low figures; countries with major ports, such as the Netherlands, show high figures and the NMS that are concentrating on manufacturing (for example, the Czech Republic) also show high figures.

The figures show further very clearly that, over the years, the international integration of the economies of the EU member states by the exchange of goods has considerably increased (EU15 average from 16 to 28).[8]

Finally the table shows that the high increase in the trade–GDP ratios is notably due to the increase in *intra-EU trade*, itself the result of the progressive integration of the goods markets of the EU. The involvement of the EU as a whole in trade with the rest of the world has not suffered from this intra-EU dynamism; indeed the ratio for extra-EU trade stayed more or less on the same level over the whole period. The orientation of trade changed over the period under discussion. In 1960, trade was relatively more oriented towards third countries than to the countries that are now part of the EU15. By 1970, this situation was reversed; in line with theoretical expectations, integration has led to intra-EU trade increasingly outweighing extra-EU trade.

INTERNAL TRADE AMONG MEMBER STATES OF THE EU

In the period 1960–2000 intra-EU trade has grown by almost 7 per cent per annum, which is significantly in excess of GDP growth. The major determinants of this growth were EU integration and the gradual liberalisation of world trade.[9] The member states of the EU trade more among themselves than with third countries. We know from a previous section that the creation of a customs union may divert, or create, trade flows. Despite measures taken to prevent large-scale shifts (EFTA/EU custom tariff agreements), trade-creating and trade-diverting effects were experienced at the moments of the formation and enlargement of the

---

7   Naturally one should keep in mind that the goods trade is given at production value and GDP value added. On the other hand, GDP also comprises some activities which do not enter into the international commercial circuit. For lack of basic data, the ratio has not been corrected for these influences.

8   This increase has followed a consistent and gradual development over the years: for the values in intermediate years, see earlier editions of this book.

9   For the earlier period, see Cherif and Ginsburgh (1976) and for the whole period see Badinger and Breuss (2004).

Table 5.2   Percentage share of goods imports and exports[a] in total GDP of member states (current prices), 1960–2004

	1960		1970		1980		1990		2000		2004	
	imp	exp	imp	exp	imp	exp	imp	exp	imp	exp	imp	exp
Germany	14	16	16	19	23	24	23	26	27	30	25	31
France	10	11	13	12	20	17	19	18	26	25	22	22
Italy[b]	12	9	14	12	22	17	16	15	22	22	20	20
Netherlands	38	34	39	35	45	43	44	46	59	63	51	57
Belgium/Lux	34	32	43	44	57	51	58	57	76	79	75	81
UK	18	15	18	16	22	22	23	19	24	20	22	17
Ireland	34	23	38	24	55	42	46	52	54	81	35	61
Denmark	30	24	27	20	29	24	24	26	29	32	27	32
Spain	6	6	13	6	16	10	18	11	28	21	25	18
Portugal	19	12	22	13	32	16	37	24	38	23	31	21
Greece	17	5	16	5	22	11	24	10	29	10	25	8
Austria	n.a.	n.a.	24	19	31	22	31	26	37	35	39	38
Sweden	n.a.	n.a.	21	20	27	24	24	25	30	36	28	34
Finland	n.a.	n.a.	24	21	30	27	34	20	29	38	26	33
EU15 (average)	16	15	18	17	24	22	24	23	36	37	32	34
Intra	6	6	10	10	13	13	15	15	n.a.	n.a.	19	19
Extra	10	9	8	7	11	9	9	8	n.a.	n.a.	9	9
Czech Rep									57	52	57	54
Estonia									78	58	71	50
Cyprus									35	5	32	4
Latvia									41	24	47	26
Lithuania									46	31	52	38
Hungary									69	60	58	52
Malta									89	64	66	46
Poland									29	19	33	26
Slovenia									53	46	50	46
Slovakia									63	58	69	67
EU25 (average)									45	39	41	37

Notes: [a] *The exports of goods comprise all (national or nationalised) goods carried permanently, free or against payment, from a country's economic territory abroad; for imports, a similar definition applies.* [b] *Upward correction of GDP in the mid-1980s.*

Source: *European Commission, Statistical Annex of European Economy, several years, Tables 38, 39, 42, 43.*

EU. Figure 5.3 gives an illustration of these effects. It shows the development over time of trade between the successive old and new members of the EU.[10]

Since 1960, for the six original member states, the EU share in trade has risen considerably faster than trade with other countries. Trade among the six original EU member states between 1958 and 1972 (the year of the extension with the UK, Ireland and Denmark) had increased ninefold, while goods trade with the rest of the world grew by a factor of three. In the same period the importance of the EU as a trade partner increased with respect to two of the three new member states (trade with Denmark declined).

---

10   More detailed statistics specifying exports and imports and individual members show that the tendencies that have been given in the graph for groups of countries do apply in general also to all its members. More detailed material specifying manufacturing imports by product (Jacquemin and Sapir, 1988) corroborate the findings as to the integration effects.

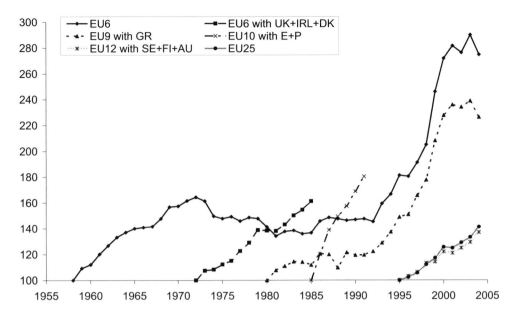

Figure 5.3   Impact of accession on trade

After 1972, the year of *the first enlargement*, the picture changed somewhat. The trade of the six original member states with the three new ones increased very fast between 1972 and 1978, showing an effect of integration. Trade between the original six between 1972 and 1985 was less dynamic, owing partly to the effect of the oil crisis and partly to some relative trade diversion to the three new member countries. For the candidate members, Greece, Spain and Portugal, however, the relative importance of the EU to their foreign trade remained fairly constant during the 1960s and 1970s.

The *post-1985* period is marked by three major events:

- *Second enlargement.* The integration of the Iberian countries has entailed a very dynamic expansion of intra-Union trade. However, this was not immediately so for Greece; it took this country some time to seize the new oppportunities.
- *Completion of the internal market.* In the 1985–95 period, the growth of intra-EU trade has been particularly dynamic.
- *EFTA-EU agreements.* The growth of trade with Austria, Sweden and Finland is spread over a long period. Its dynamics resembled that of the internal growth of the EU12.

The *post-1995 period* is dominated by the fast liberalisation of trade between the EU15 and the NMS in Central and Eastern Europe. Figure 5.3 shows that this resulted in a very dynamic growth of trade between these two groups of countries.

GEOGRAPHICAL PATTERN OF INTERNAL TRADE

The geographical structure of internal trade in the EU is marked by large flows between some pairs of countries and much smaller flows among others. By far the largest trade partner (accounting for almost one-quarter of the total) is Germany. This country is the largest exporter to and importer from all other EU member states, with the exception of Spain (France), Ireland (UK) and Portugal (Spain).

Has the integration process changed the trade orientation of the member states? A linkage model clustering countries by their trade orientation in different reference years shows that the answer is yes. The 1955 pre-EU situation predicted neither the formation of the EU6 (Italy, Germany, France and the Benelux belonging to different blocs) nor that of EFTA (whose member countries also belonged to different clusters). Actual integration did not change that picture very fast: by 1975, the nucleus of the EU (though without Germany) shows up but EFTA had not yet emerged. Only in 1981 did trade figures begin to reflect the institutional arrangements: a central cluster is clearly visible, made up of the member states of EU9, to which Greece and Spain were already associated but from which Denmark was still keeping apart.[11] By 1997 the process seemed completed as the whole of the EU shows up as a distinct cluster, although with several sub-clusters based on geographical proximity (for example, the British Isles and the Nordic countries).

The dissolution of the Comecon group and the opening up to world trade of the CEEC has profoundly changed the situation of these countries. The 1997 data show that all CEECs had dissociated themselves from the former USSR. Their trade integration with the EU had progressed but not sufficiently far so as to let them join the EU15 cluster.

We have shown the trade orientation of such sub-clusters within the EU25 in Table 5.3. It confirms the dominant position of Germany as a trade partner but also the importance of geographical proximity, even between sub-clusters (for example, low for the link Iberia-Nordic countries, and Iberia-Central European countries; high for Iberia-France and for Germany/Austria with the Central European countries.

EXTERNAL TRADE OF THE EU, BY PARTNER

The EU is the world's largest trade partner. Over the past decades, exports and imports of the EU (without intra-EU trade) amounted to some 20 per cent of total world exports and imports, so trade of the EU has increased at about the same pace as total world trade.

Table 5.4 shows the relative importance of *EU trade with groups of third countries* (without intra-EU trade). Owing to data limitations it is split up in three parts. For the period 1960–80, the data refer to the EU12, so give the situation as if that grouping had existed all over the period. For the 1980–2004 period, the data refer to the EU15. For 2004 we have data for the whole EU 25. Taking the change in statistical basis into account, one observes that, for the whole period 1960–2004, trade relations were much closer with one group than with others. This is due to a number of factors, such as attraction (highly developed economies), friction (distance, see also the next section) and policy (see Chapter 17). Let us look briefly at each of the different *categories of countries*.

Paramount among trade partners of the EU are the countries in the western industrialised world. Within that group, the small group of countries that formed EFTA held a large share in the EU12 trade and, even after the joining of the EU of three of their members, in EU 15 trade. This feature can be explained by their high income-level, their small distance from the EU and the absence of trade barriers (the EU has concluded a freetrade arrangement with these countries). The high figures for the USA and the medium ones for Japan reflect not only the

---

11   See Peschel (1985, 1999). In 1990, only two small sub-clusters subsisted (France–Spain and UK–Ireland–Norway) (Poon and Pandit, 1996). This analysis was carried out with a somewhat different methodology focusing on developments at the world level. The clustering of countries on the basis of these world trade data suggests the emergence of a large block centred on the EU to which also belong Central and Eastern Europe and Africa.

Table 5.3   Intra-EU trade (billion euro) by country, 2004

	AUS & GER	FRANCE	UK & IRE	IT, GR, CY & MA	BENE- LUX	ESP & POR	DEN, SWE & FIN	CEEC	EU25
AUS & GER	63	73	64	21	84	41	34	67	490
FRANCE	56	0	35	131	41	40	9	11	228
UK & IRE	38	32	33	46	50	17	13	7	209
IT, GR, CY & MA	45	34	21	8	15	23	6	16	168
BENELUX	119	68	53	21	66	23	18	13	393
ESP & POR	22	30	17	46	11	20	4	4	125
DEN, SWE & FIN	28	9	17	21	16	7	26	9	121
CEEC	63	9	9	3	11	4	10	23	140
EU25	435	255	249	311	294	176	119	151	1874

Note: *Totals may differ due to rounding.*
Source: *Eurostat, External and Intra-European Union Trade, Monthly Statistics, 2004.*

economic power of the two countries, but also the high level of intra-industry trade among highly developed economies.

The developing countries have a more modest, and since 1980 a decreasing, share. Within that group the associated African (ACP) countries and Latin America lose ground, the ACP notwithstanding their privileged access to the EU market. The Asian countries gain considerable market share, which is due to their competitive advantage in many labour-intensive industries. The position of OPEC increased dramatically as a result of the increases in oil prices of the 1970s, to decrease as dramatically since 1980 with the fall in oil prices.

The centrally planned economies accounted for only a small portion of the EU12 trade (just under 10 per cent), reflecting to a large extent a deliberate choice by their governments to keep trade with the West to a minimum. About ten years ago that strategy was drastically changed for the CEEC/NMS, who have improved their position since as the result of their rapid transition to a market economy, their proximity to the EU15, and their free trade with the EU in view of their accession. For Russia the situation changed more hesitantly; however, in recent years trade has picked up significantly due to the gradual opening up of the Russian economy and the surge in their energy exports.

EXTERNAL EU TRADE, BY COMMODITY GROUPS

The type of commodity[12] internationally traded by the EU[13] has changed quite significantly in the period of the past decades (Table 5.5). The change in the structure of *EU import trade* reflects the shift away from the heavy dependence on other parts of the world for food and raw materials towards imports from low cost countries and inter-industry trade with developed countries of various manufactured goods.[14] On the *export side*, manufactured products, with

---

12   A major shift in the pattern that is not revealed by the table concerns agricultural produce. Although agricultural imports increased considerably in the period analysed, their relative share dropped steeply, and by 1990 was on a level with exports. That development is closely tied up with the common agricultural policy, to be described in Chapter 9.

13   The figures given here for the EU12 are not available in a comparable form for the EU15. Fragmentary information permits us to say, however, that the figures presented are likely to be representative for both the structure and the development of the commodity trade of the EU15 too.

14   Not visible in the table is the steep increase in the money value of energy imports that occurred in the 1970s and 1980s (see Chapter 11), an effect that had been expunged by 1990, but has been lost again by the recent increase in energy prices (for figures see earlier editions of this book).

Table 5.4   Geographical distribution (in percentages) by groups of countries, of extra-EU trade in goods, 1960–2004

Country (group)	Imports							Exports						
	EU12		EU15				EU25	EU12			EU15			EU25
	1960	1970	1980	1990	2000	2004	2004	1960	1970	1980	1990	2000	2004	2004
Industrialised	49	51	39	52	43	36	40	46	53	38	51	46	42	52
EFTA	15	17	10	13	10	11	12	22	25	16	15	10	10	12
United States	20	22	18	21	19	14	15	14	18	14	21	24	21	27
Japan	1	3	6	12	8	6	7	1	3	3	6	5	4	5
Rest of OECD	12	8	5	6	6	5	6	10	7	6	8	7	7	8
Third World	47	43	52	38	42	43	47	48	40	50	39	38	37	41
Mediterranean	7	9	9	10	6	7	7	13	10	15	12	8	8	9
ACP	10	9	8	5	4	4	4	9	8	9	5	4	4	4
OPEC	9	8	20	5	6	6	6	3	6	10	6	5	6	5
Latin America	9	8	6	6	3	4	4	8	7	5	3	4	3	4
Asia	8	5	7	12	19	21	24	10	7	7	11	13	13	14
Other Third World	12	9	3	1	4	2	2	15	10	4	2	4	3	5
Former centrally planned	5	6	10	10	15	21	13	5	7	12	10	16	21	13
CEEC	3	4	4	5	9	13	3	3	5	7	6	13	16	3
USSR/CIS	2	3	5	5	5	7	10	2	3	5	4	3	5	4

Source: *Eurostat, External trade, Statistical Yearbook; External and intra-European Union trade, Statistical Yearbook, various years.*

machinery and transport equipment in the lead, are observed to account for about three-quarters of total exports. The accession of the NMS has not changed the export structure of the EU very much. However, on the import side the EU15–NMS trade in machinery and other manufactured products has caused a switch between these two categories in the external trade figures of the EU15 and the EU25.

Table 5.5   Distribution of the EU's[a] foreign trade by commodity group, in percentages, 1960–2000

Commodity group	Imports			Exports		
	1960	2000		1960	2000	
	EU-12	EU-15	EU-25	EU-12	EU-15	EU-25
Food, drink, tobacco	25	5	6	9	5	6
Energy products	16	15	16	4	3	3
Raw materials	26	5	5	4	2	2
Chemicals	4	7	7	10	14	14
Machinery, transport equipment	10	38	27	37	47	46
Other manufactured products	17	27	36	33	27	27
Miscellaneous	2	3	3	3	2	2
Total	100	100	100	100	100	100

Note: [a] 1960: EU12, 2000: EU15: estimates based on figures for 1999.

Source: Eurostat; various statistics; External and Intra-European Trade 1958-2003, Statistical Yearbook, External and intra-European Union trade, various months, Luxembourg.

Is the pattern of specialisation reproduced in Table 5.5 also indicative of the sectors for which the EU is most competitive on international markets? Indeed the EU is generally considered strongest in capital-intensive industries (where wage costs are less relevant) and in knowledge-intensive products (for which other countries do not always have the qualified labour).

In the 1970–90 period, the EU used to specialise rather in medium technology products and to hold a neutral position in low technology products. For the products of the former categories (motor vehicles, wireless and television sets, office machinery, other machinery) the competitive position of the EU on its own market has been gradually eroded.[15] This deterioration of the EU's position was thought to be caused by a segmented home market. To remedy that situation, two types of action were taken: an industrial policy specifically aimed at stimulating innovation (see Chapter 10) and a policy focusing on the improvement of market conditions (see Chapter 14). In the 1990-2005 period these policies seem to have had a positive effect. The performance of the EU needs to be seen in the framework of its ambition to become the most competitive area in the world in knowledge-based activities.

Explanation of spatial trade patterns

SOME 'TRADITIONAL' APPROACHES

Trade theory puts a heavy accent on comparative advantage. In practice, the concept is rather difficult to work with, however. Prices and availability of factors are not easy to integrate in our

---

15   See Jacquemin and Sapir (1988); EC (1993b).

framework with export and import structures. The suggestion has been made (Balassa, 1977) first to analyse the so-called 'revealed comparative advantage' (RCA) and then relate that RCA to relative cost. However, systematically relating these RCA indices for the EU to explanatory factors proves too difficult.

Trade patterns may also be influenced by trade impediments. Among these we find structural factors as well as government and private distortions. Tariffs occupy a preponderant place in integration theory. Distance has also been cited in that respect. Distance-bridging transport has a clear effect on aggregate trade flows. This is also the case in the EU on the disaggregate level of manufacturing industries.[16] We will come back to the integration effects of tariff cuts in the last part of this chapter. In recent times the study of goods trade has tended to focus on other aspects, highlighting the role of industrial organisation (see Chapter 10), technology and so on.

INTRA-INDUSTRY SPECIALISATION

Contrary to what some had expected, the further opening up of the national markets for manufactured goods by the integration schemes of the EU and EFTA and the liberalisation in GATT has not produced specialisation among countries along the lines of traditional trade theory. According to this theory one country will specialise in one good, for instance steel, and the other in other goods, for instance port wines, on the basis of comparative advantages. On the contrary, at the beginning of the 1960s it became clear that the specialisation occurred *within sectors*, with, for example, both countries producing cars, but of different types: 'The more similar the demand structures of two countries, the more intensive potentially the trade between these two countries' (Linder, 1961).

Trade liberalisation in Europe has been accompanied by considerable increases in the extent of intra-industry trade (IIT). This was the case for all member countries of the EU6 in the 1958–77 period,[17] of the EU9 in the 1970–87 period[18] and of the EU15 during the period up to 1997 (EC, 1996a). The increase in IIT is particularly striking for the traditionally less developed member states (Portugal, Spain and Ireland) which reflects the reorientation of their production towards higher value-added activities.

Several factors can explain intra-industry trade. The first is scale economies; if there is much product differentiation and a wide range of products, each country will produce only a limited sub-set (such as the trade in cars produced in different European countries). Technology is another factor; if R&D produces a rapid turnover of products protected by patents, each country will specialise in different segments of the market (pharmaceutical products are a case in point). Moreover, the strategies of multinational companies lead to flows of intermediary goods among plants (for example, parts and components of cars) and the delivery of final goods in their distribution systems (Caves, 1982).

Now *is the observed growth of IIT also due to integration?* A set of studies would suggest so. In the 1959–80 period, intra-EU, intra-industry trade grew more rapidly than total EU intra-

---

16   See Linnemann (1966); Aitken (1973); Bröcker (1984).

17   See Balassa (1966, 1975). The question of how to measure and explain IIT has received much attention in the literature (see among others, Balassa, 1986; Grubel and Lloyd, 1975; Tharakan, 1983; Greenaway and Milner, 1986; Kol, 1988).

18   Results for the EU in Greenaway (1987). Information for EFTA countries shows the same tendency, but at a lower level; for CMEA the indices are lower (Drabeck and Greenaway, 1984). The EU results are also corroborated by Bergstrand (1983), who calculated IIT indexes for the years from 1965 to 1976 for the four large EU countries; he found that, on average, in three-quarters of the sectors he analysed IIT had increased, sometimes considerably (30–50 per cent). See also Sapir (2000).

industry trade (Greenaway, 1987). In addition, the level of IIT in Western Europe was positively influenced by the factors just cited and negatively by increasing distance and differences in culture (Balassa and Bauwens, 1988). There is clear econometric evidence that the cancellation of border formalities in the framework of the single market programme has contributed importantly to the growth of intra-industry trade. Some other factors such as returns to scale and foreign direct investment did also have a significant influence on IIT growth in the 1985–93 period (CEPII, 1996). Finally, the convergence of national industrial structures is an important factor which is itself dependent on integration (see Chapters 9–16).

TECHNOLOGY

Modern theory of trade tends to look towards technological and industrial factors for the explanation of trade patterns. The idea is that the level of innovation determines the quality of the product, which in turn determines its competitive position on external markets. This leads to specialisation: some countries specialise in high-tech goods, others in low-tech goods; the latter are generally believed to create less value added.

Within the EU, countries show a wide variation in innovation efforts, the pattern being that R&D per head is highest in the relatively rich countries and very low in the relatively poor ones. Differences in a country's innovative capacity have been found to influence significantly their trade performance in high-tech products (Soete, 1987).

High innovation leads to a strong competitive position in high-quality products for which higher prices are paid on international markets. For a given product one can distinguish between low, medium and high unit values. In the 1980s and early 1990s the dispersion of unit values in intra-EU trade grew, which meant a stronger specialisation of member countries over the quality spectrum. The picture is in line with theory: the most developed countries in the North West of the EU tended to specialise in high value products; those in the Mediterranean basin in low value-added products (CEPII, 1996).

Price differences

EVOLUTION OF DIFFERENCES FOR SEPARATE PRODUCTS

The degree of integration can be measured by the degree of convergence of the prices for various products in the member countries of the EU.[19] Under the law of one price, undistorted markets would result in completely equal prices, and trade would reflect the location of demand and the location of the lowest-cost producers. However, the opening of markets alone is unlikely to lead to complete price equalisation: numerous factors cause price differences between countries to persist. We mention differences in transport costs, in collusion practices, in tariffs and taxes (in particular value-added taxes and excises), in distribution networks, in quality on account of regional and cultural differences in taste, in monetary policy on account of exchange rate changes and in margins on account of differences in competitive pressures.

---

19   To compare price levels in different countries is a hazardous undertaking. To be meaningful, such a comparison should be made between products which are not only available in all the countries surveyed but also representative of all the national (and regional!) consumption patterns. This is not easy as the size of the EU and the many differences in historical origins within its borders give rise to a great variety of consumption patterns.

These factors work out differently for different products due to their tradability, company structure, and so on (Chen, 2004).

A number of interesting studies have shed some light on the price effects of the different stages of the European integration process.

For the initial *period of integration 1958–72* a comparison of the prices before (1958) and after (1970) the creation of the EU did not give very conclusive results; out of 36 products, 15 showed a tendency towards greater disparity and 21 a tendency towards convergence (Glejser, 1972).

The evolution of prices for the *period 1975–85*, broadly speaking the period between the first enlargement and the second, has been characterised by considerable monetary unrest (with exchange rate changes) and was prior to the Single Market programme, so conditions for convergence were not very good. The figures reveal two major features:

- Price levels differed appreciably from one member state to another, more so for consumer goods than for investment goods. Indirect taxes, which in the period of study varied considerably among countries, were responsible for a significant share of the total price differences. However, even net of indirect taxes, prices differed considerably.
- The evolution of the dispersion of prices is different for different sub-groups. In those sectors where there were non-tariff barriers, price dispersion tended to increase, whereas it narrowed appreciably in the sectors more open to competition. There remained a large potential for price convergence, as price dispersion in the EU was still double that within Germany (Emerson et al., 1988).

In the *1985–2001 period* we see (EC, 1996a, 2000f, 2001a) the effect of two major aspects of integration:

- Widening: the price structures of Spain, Portugal and Greece did show a very clear convergence with those in the rest of the EU (Hoeller and Louppe, 1994). There are indications that this effect has also occurred after the integration of the NMS.
- Deepening: the completion of the internal market brought increasing competition for a large range of products, which in the 1990s brought convergence of prices. This was notably the case for tradable goods; little convergence could be seen for non-tradable goods and goods that are subject to special taxes and regulation.[20] The convergence was most significant for countries that had participated in the EMS; the introduction of the euro has had a significant further positive effect on convergence (Allington et al., 2004).

EVOLUTION OF THE PRICE DIFFERENCES BETWEEN A BASKET OF PRODUCTS

We can also study the evolution of price dispersion with the help of figures for a basket of consumer goods. Figure 5.4 shows the long-term evolution of the standard deviation of the Harmonised Index of Consumer Prices (HICP). This indicator takes the value 0 for full price convergence and 1 for full price dispersion.

The figure shows that price differences have almost halved in the 43-year period. At the moment the differences are comparable with those between the DM zone (Germany, Benelux and Austria) in the 1960s. In the latter zone price differences have practically disappeared. The

---

20   See, for example, Rogers et al. (2001); Engel and Rogers (2004); and Sosvilla-Rivero and Gil-Pareja (2004). Convergence was strongest the higher the initial dispersion (EC, 2004b). See Chapters 10–13 for specific cases such as cars.

convergence for the EMU and the DM zone has been stimulated by the convergence of cost and of indirect taxes, by the increase in international trade and by exchange rate stability. The main factor for the stagnation of convergence is the increased volatility of exchange rates that occurred in certain periods (Faber and Stokman, 2004, 2005).

Welfare effects

EFFECTS ON MEMBER COUNTRIES[21]

At the time of the creation and successive enlargements of the EU, various attempts were made at quantification of the effects as given in the theoretical framework depicted earlier in this chapter.[22]

Let us first look at the *trade effects*. For the first period of the EU6, from 1955 to 1969, the period of eliminating high tariffs, some estimates amounted to a doubling of trade in comparison to a situation without EU. The first enlargement that created the EU9 has been estimated to have produced a 50 per cent rise in trade between the UK and the EU. A survey of the results of computations of the trade effects of the creation of the EU in the 1960s and 1970s

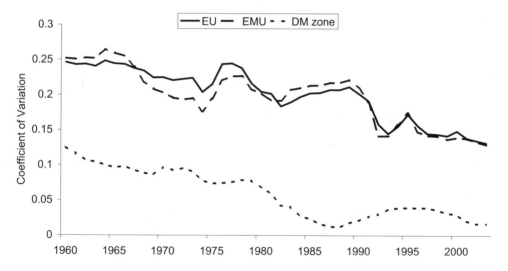

Figure 5.4   Price convergence in the EU by country group, 1960–2003

showed that trade creation has amounted to between 10 and 30 per cent of total EU imports of manufactured goods. Trade diversion is on the whole estimated much lower, at between 2 and 15 per cent. Agriculture is an exception to the general picture; considerable trade diversion occurred for this sector. The second enlargement creating the EU12 was thought (in an *ex*

---

21   To calculate the trade and welfare effects of integration, methods varying in sophistication have been applied. For a brief review of methods and outcomes, we will borrow from the surveys made by, in particular, Verdoorn and Schwartz (1972); Balassa (1975); Mayes (1978); and El-Agraa and Jones (1981).
22   See, for example, Krauss (1968); Williamson and Bottrill (1971); Resnick and Truman (1975); Balassa (1975); Waelbroeck (1976); Miller and Spencer (1977); Petith (1977); Viaene (1982); Grinols (1984); Winters (1985); and Jacquemin and Sapir (1988). Note that many of the methods and definitions used by these authors are not directly compatible with the theoretical conception of the CU.

ante study) to be of limited importance, given the low initial tariffs. As it coincided with the completion of the internal market, we should rather look for the combined effect of the two. Substantial trade creation has been found; over the 1985–93 period intra-EU import market shares increased by at least 3 per cent in average sectors and by 8 per cent in sectors sensitive to competition.[23]

The next step is the calculation of *welfare effects*. The income effects of the dismantling of tariffs measured with static models were in the order of magnitude of 1 per cent of GNP.[24] There was quite some dissatisfaction with static models, notably because they fail to take the dynamic effects of goods market integration into account (ensuing from economies of scale, efficiency or learning by doing). This has stimulated work along new lines.

In some, a macro model is used to calculate the effects of changes in trade and in terms of trade. The percentage growth of GDP actually observed can be split into a part due to the EU and a residual part. The effects of the EU6 appear to be quite substantial, particularly for the smaller countries,[25] much larger anyway than the effects calculated by the Vinerian type of study discussed earlier. The effects of the EU9 present quite a different picture. Of course the period differs from the preceding one in many respects. At the start of the EU9 most tariffs were lower than at the time of creation of the EU6; besides, a profound need for economic restructuring was recognised, energy prices were on a steep increase, trade balances were adversely affected and new protectionism was becoming generally accepted.[26] Macro models applied to the single market programme find an initial effect of some 1 per cent of GDP. The same is true for a growth factors approach (Henrekson et al., 1997) and for a computed general equilibrium approach (Gasiorek et al., 2002). Unfortunately the dynamic effects could not be heeded in the approaches described (see Chapter 14).

In others, micro-economic studies were made, better suited to deal with the dynamic effects. One (Owen, 1983) estimated that the effects of the opening of the European markets in the 1960s on increased competition, economies of scale and restructuring of firms have increased prosperity with some 40 to 100 per cent of the additional trade involved, or some 5 per cent of GDP.

The *accession of the Central and Eastern European countries to the EU* has been estimated to be marginally beneficial for the EU (some 0.2 per cent of GDP) and very beneficial for the CEECs (some 1.2 per cent increase in GDP) (Baldwin, François and Portes, 1997). In a less conservative scenario that takes into account the decrease in the risk for investors to the Portuguese level, the accumulated benefits for the East will go up to 20 per cent of the income.

EFFECT OF THE EU CUSTOMS UNION ON TRADE WITH THIRD COUNTRIES

The formation of a customs union also affects the patterns of trade with third countries. The taking away of the internal barriers in the EU has been a catalyst for the reduction of external barriers as well (Hufbauer, 1990; Messerlin, 1992).

---

23   See, for quantitative studies, Mayes (1978); Winters (1987); and Allen et al. (1996).

24   See the pioneering study by Verdoorn (1952) for a European Free Trade Area, and the studies by Johnson (1958); Miller and Spencer (1977); and Balassa (1975) for the EU. The studies cited have a number of drawbacks. Many use simplified methods to avoid data problems. Most studies, moreover, confine themselves to manufactured goods, leaving agriculture largely out of account.

25   Marques-Mendes (1986a, 1986b); the result is in line with the suggestions made by Petith (1977).

26   In later chapters we will take up the other effects of integration, such as mobile production factors and/or common policies. For instance, the effect of stable exchange rates on the volume of trade will be taken up in Chapter 15, on monetary policy.

The effects of the *formation of the EU6* on trade with third countries differ by good category (Sellekaerts, 1973; Balassa, 1975). Particularly large positive trade-creation effects occurred for machinery, transport equipment and fuels, and negative ones for food, chemicals and other manufactures. The EU formation caused a significant trade gain for associated less developed countries and somewhat lesser positive trade effects for the UK and the USA. By contrast, net trade-diversion effects occurred for the other developed countries and the centrally planned economies; very small negative effects could be observed for the other EFTA and other LDC groups.

The effects of the *first enlargement* on trade partners (Kreinin, 1973) were found to be largely trade-diverting; they were heaviest for the group of other developed countries (approximately 20 per cent) and somewhat less heavy for the LDCs (approximately 15 per cent). The effects of the *completion of the internal market* for goods on the trade partners of the EU were very diverse. For the group of EFTA countries the analyses (Haaland, 1990; Norman, 1991; Lundberg, 1992) all indicate significant increases of EU/EFTA trade, notably of the inter-industry type, going hand-in-hand with substantial welfare gains. For the group of LDCs the conclusion of an overview of studies (Koekkoek *et al.*, 1990) is that the trade effects of 1992 *vis-à-vis* developing countries are more likely to be positive than negative. Overall there has not been any trade diversion. On the contrary, trade with third countries has actually increased, which is in a sense plausible as it is easier to penetrate a market with one regime instead of a patchwork of 15 regimes (EC, 1996a).

The effects of the *third enlargement* of the EU with three former EFTA countries (in other words of the European Economic Area) on third countries were found to be very positive for all trade areas of the world (Haaland, 1990; Haaland and Norman, 1992; CEPR, 1992). The magnitude of the effects is different for different countries: highest for EFTA, average for the EU and small for third countries.

Summary and conclusions

- The integration of the economies of EU countries through the mutual exchange of goods has greatly increased over the past decades; more than the exchange with third countries.
- Specialisation took the form, not so much of each country concentrating on a specific sector, but of specialisation within sectors (intra-industry trade).
- The prices of most goods tended to converge, in line with theoretical expectations.
- Trade creation has on the whole been considerably greater than trade diversion; so, on balance, the EU has contributed to the efficient allocation of production factors in the world.
- Where the EU was externally open (manufacturing), the welfare effects were positive; where it was externally protected (for example, agriculture) the effects were negative.
- Integration has entailed only limited static welfare effects; the great advantages came from its dynamic effects (increased competitiveness on internal and global markets).

6 *Services*

Introduction

Over the last decades the importance of services in the economy of the EU has increased dramatically (see Chapter 12). Trade in services has increased also; both intra-EU trade and trade of the EU with the rest of the world. So the discussion that follows is well warranted.

Like the previous chapter the present one will go first into a few basic concepts; although in many aspects services can be thought of as comparable to goods, they nevertheless reveal some specific characteristics that call for preliminary elucidation. Next we will consider the EU regime. This is of particular relevance because the EU has played a crucial role in the process of both internal (internal market programme) and external (GATT/WTO round) liberalisation of trade in services.

The specific patterns of trade in services will be described in the next section with the help of statistical series, detailing the structure by area and by branch of activity. As trade in services is much less well documented than trade in goods, the description will be much less complete with regard to the length of the time series, the detail of products and the coverage of geographical areas. This is even more so with respect to the prices and the welfare effects of service trade, so we can only devote very short sections to each of these problems. The chapter will be concluded by a short summary of the main findings.

Basic (theoretical) concepts

FORMS OF INTEGRATION

The integration of service markets can be considered complete in cases where there are no obstacles to cross-border trade. We distinguish three types of international transaction.[1] For each type of transaction we will consider service markets to be integrated if the following obtain:

- Cross-border supply. No spatial move of either producer or consumer is needed because the service is rendered through trans-border flows of information. Integration is considered to exist if a consumer in country A is free to contract a service (for instance, an insurance policy) with a company in country B.
- Consumption abroad. Consumers of one country move to producers in another country to receive the service offered. Personal services (such as staying at a seaside resort), education

---

1   Following Bhagwati (1987a) and the WTO/GATS typology. The four modes are of different importance; it has been estimated that the first takes about 40 per cent, the second mode about 20 per cent, the third only 2 per cent and the fourth the remaining 38 per cent of total world trade in services (Karsenty, 1999).

(such as a student studying abroad) and retail services (such as British people shopping in Paris) are cases in point. Integration exists when consumers can move freely abroad to obtain a service.

• Production abroad from home base. Producers of one country move to a foreign country to provide their services there. Managing a construction site, a plumber fixing a problem in a house across the border, or a teacher giving guest lectures, are cases in point. Integration exists if the provider can render the service freely to a client abroad.

A fourth type named 'commercial presence' is often distinguished. It is 'establishment-based trade', which occurs when service providers create a permanent subsidiary in the importing country in order to produce and sell the service, parts of which will have to be imported (compare direct investment (DI)-induced trade in goods!) There is quite a difference between the liberalisation of the setting up of an establishment and of cross-border provision of services. The former maintains the coexistence of different national regulations, whereas the latter implies a direct competition between the various services produced under divergent rules.

MOTIVES FOR OBSTACLES

Traditionally the markets for services are not integrated but segmented. Many reasons are given to justify such obstacles to free trade in services. Most of the obstacles are allegedly drawn up to *protect consumers*. A few examples from different sectors may illustrate this.

• In banking and insurance, regulation serves to limit the risk of insolvency through surveillance of private operators by (semi-) public organisations (central banks, among others). Since foreign suppliers are hard to control, access to the national market is barred to them.
• In air transport, the safety of the passenger is the main concern. Standards are accompanied by mutual import controls in the form of landing rights.
• In communication and energy (electricity), services are regulated to protect consumers from unfair pricing by a natural monopolist.
• In medical services, the interests of the patient are protected by the enforcement of standards for the qualifications of personnel (medical doctors and so on).

Although the arguments for consumer protection are valid, they do not necessarily have to lead to trade protection; indeed other policy measures can be devised with the same effect for the safety and health of consumers while leaving international competition free.

Many other obstacles overtly aim at *protecting national companies*. There are several reasons to do so:

• strategic importance: an example is maritime transport, where international trade is restricted by a complex system of cargo reservation; a national merchant navy is thought to be necessary in times of war to provide the country with essential goods;
• economic policy: the control of macro-economic policy (through the banking system);
• enhancing national prestige (civil aviation);
• control of key technologies (telecommunication);
• safeguarding cultural values (movies, television).

However, even if consumer protection is the official reason for this protectionist regulation, in practice the real reason is often that domestic firms want to be sheltered from international competition.

TYPES OF OBSTACLES

The forms in which the free trade in services is impeded cover a wide spectrum. Many of them are fairly comparable to those that hinder goods trade.[2] However, as the value of a border-crossing service is harder to control than that of a good, tariffs are seldom practised, and restrictions on the trade in services are mostly of the non-tariff type. Moreover, because the provision of some types of service across the border involves direct investments, a set of restrictions to entry of markets is relevant too.

Trade in services can be hampered by the following instruments:

- quantitative restriction, notably on domestic consumption[3] (for instance, advertising, air transport);
- shares of markets reserved for home producers (for example, for movies);
- subsidies (for instance, in construction);
- government procurement (for instance, construction, data processing);
- currency controls on transfers to foreign countries for services provided;
- restrictions on the qualifications of manpower required to perform certain services (legal, medical);
- technical requirements for capital goods (transport, for example);
- customs valuation problems for goods required to perform services (for instance, plumbers' tools).

Entry restrictions on a profession or restrictions on setting up in business are the second category of barriers. These can take the following forms:

- restrictions on the right of foreign firms to set up or take over subsidiary companies;
- exclusion of foreign firms from certain types of activity;
- discriminatory performance requirements;
- selective taxation;
- restrictions on the transfer of profits.

The effects of these obstacles on the cost of a service provider who wants to export are illustrated in Figure 6.1. As many of the measures lack transparency they are difficult to quantify.

---

2   A detailed description of these trade barriers is given in OECD (1981b, 1983a, 1984a, 1985b, 1986a). See, further, Tucker and Sundberg (1988).
3   These measures are favoured by many policy makers, for several reasons. First, they are particularly well suited to being applied in times of economic downturn, to increase the effectiveness of stabilisation policies. Next, their protectionist impact is independent of substitution between foreign and domestic producers. Finally, their enforcement is often done through the involvement of agencies in which domestic producers are represented.

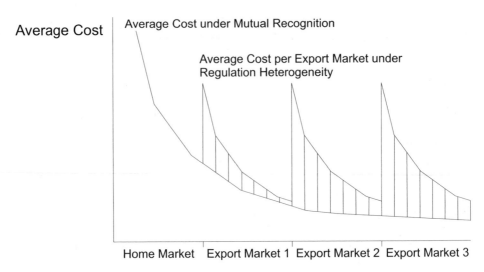

Figure 6.1   Effect of heterogeneity of regulation of service markets on cost of the provider

ADVANTAGES OF INTEGRATION

Markets that are segmented tend to be inefficient. Hence there is a drive towards doing away with obstacles and liberalising trade. The theoretical foundations of the integration of service markets are largely akin to those of the trade in goods. In practice there is much difference. Indeed, the analysis based on differences in factor endowments of different countries has not given very rich results for services.[4] Alternative approaches, involving aspects of industrial organisation theory, are giving more promising results. These refer to notions such as economies of scale and scope and transaction cost. High transaction cost means that sourcing from abroad is expensive for the user or alternatively that the provision of a service by a provider from abroad is in practice prohibited because the latter is confronted with extra cost each time he wants to export to another member state. The development of multinational firms using economies of scale and the beneficial effects of increased competition are therefore largely forgone.

The arguments for the integration of service markets are similar to the ones for goods markets.[5]

- Higher international specialisation raises the efficiency of resource allocation and hence income. In other words, consumers will have more choice and the products produced and consumed will be better matched.
- Economies of scale and scope will be better exploited (for instance, in banking through spreading risks; in consulting by using international databases). So cost will go down.

---

4   See, for a review, Landesmann and Petit (1995).
5   See the survey in Messerlin (1993) and Chapter 5.

As with goods, the liberalisation of international trade in services alone does not suffice to integrate markets. Most of these markets have been regulated for several reasons (to protect consumers, for example) and a certain degree of harmonisation of the rules is necessary to avoid distortions. In much the same way, competition rules must be enforced and the relations to third countries defined.

The proximity of the supplier to the customer being of crucial importance for many services, the creation of a foreign establishment by a direct investment is a solution that is more often chosen for services than for goods. However, as technological progress in telecommunications lowers the transaction costs, integration according to one of the three models described may be expected to intensify, particularly for the third category of transactions.

EU regime

RATIONALE AND PRINCIPLES

The advantages of liberalisation that apply for goods also apply to services (see the previous section). So there is a case for the integration of service markets. The EU has recognised these advantages and has enshrined free trade in services in the Treaty of Rome. The Treaty reflects awareness of the wide variety in products of the service branches. They include in particular activities of an industrial or commercial nature and those of craftsmen and professions. For all these activities the Treaty stipulates two freedoms:

- to provide services; that is a company of member country A can provide services in member country B without having an office there;
- to set up an establishment: that is, companies (or persons) of country A wishing to set up an establishment (that is, a legal entity with, in general, premises, staff and so on) in member country B are free to do so under the same conditions as are laid down for the nationals of the country of establishment.

There are a few exceptions to this general freedom:

- activities which are connected with the exercise of official authority are excluded completely;
- medical and pharmaceutical professions: here liberalisation depends on coordination of the conditions for their exercise in various member states;
- transport services are governed by another title of the Treaty;
- banking and insurance services: as they are closely connected with movements of capital, their liberalisation will be effected in step with the progressive liberalisation of capital.

So one can say that the Treaty considers that services and goods can be subjected to the same type of general rules for liberalisation of markets, irrespective of whether the service is provided by cross-border trade or by establishment.

GRADUAL ELABORATION OF A POLICY

In the lengthy negotiations carried on to substantiate the freedom to provide services, the equivalence of qualifications proved one difficult point, another being the way in which governments had organised certain markets (or sanctioned private groups to organise and protect them). The general result was that some foreign penetration through subsidiaries had occurred in several service markets, but that very little progress towards liberalisation via cross-border trade had been made. Conflicts occurred between countries and cross-border operators. The country where the service was delivered claimed the right to supervise that service or subject it to licensing. The cross-border operator maintained that compliance with the rules of his home country was sufficient.

In a set of famous rulings in such conflicts the Court of Justice has clarified the meaning of freedom of services. The Court has ruled that a service lawfully provided in one member country can in principle also be freely provided in another member state. The common element in the rulings was the consideration that governments have to demonstrate clear reasons of public interest before imposing requirements on a foreign trader over and above those fulfilled to receive a permit from his home authorities, or duplicating qualification checks already performed at home. When applying these principles to insurance, for example, governments may regulate to make sure that individual private consumers do not get confused by the (lack of) coverage from an insurance policy imported from abroad. On the other hand, corporate clients of insurance companies need less regulation of this type because they are often very competent buyers.

The rulings of the Court have in principle liberalised all services connected with agriculture, manufacturing, craft and trade (commerce).[6] However in actual practice this is not the case and many obstacles to the freedom to provide services subsist even today. As the service sector is now dominant in the economy (see next sections) this means that a very substantial segment of the EU economy is not as competitive as it might be, so growth and employment are impeded.

The Commission has worked for some time on liberalisation/harmonisation programmes for several service sectors.[7] Special attention has been given to the sectors of transport, telecommunication and finance. The example of two sectors may illustrate this specific sector approach.

Financial services (banking and insurance) are regulated on a national basis to permit prudential control of the soundness of the undertakings to make sure that they will be able, for instance, to pay the client at the moment a life insurance comes to term. The harmonisation of these rules has been extremely involved. A number of directives have in the meantime been adopted. However, the market is still very segmented and the Commission has announced its intention to attack the remaining obstacles in its new Financial Services Action Plan (FSAP).[8] The FSAP is very dependent on the implementation of the various measures by the member states.

---

6   The Court has also clarified the role of competition on service markets by ruling that the EU competition rules apply fully to the service sector. This is in respect of both firms that set prices (such as airlines) and governments that influence quantities (for example, public procurement).

7   In other sectors similar attempts were made. For instance in professional services (lawyers and auditors, engineers and so on), strong national corporations had either regulated the profession themselves (allegedly in the interest of the consumer) or were subject to detailed government regulation concerning both access to the profession and the type of products supplied. The instrument used to regulate access is the specification of qualification requirements (diplomas, for instance). The EU has been working on the mutual recognition of diplomas, but for a long time progress has been extremely slow (Pertek, 1992).

8   See www.europa.eu.int/comm/internal_market/finances/actionplan

Internet-related services, notably e-commerce, made a new directive of the EU necessary in order to develop the potential of the internal market to the full. In line with the new approach sketched above, the directive states that any firm engaging in e-commerce has to comply with the rules of the country where it is established. This has to be a real establishment; a mere server would not be sufficient. The directive stipulates next that, in all member states, electronic contracts must be recognised. The directive finally gives rules for the accountability of intermediaries, the so-called Internet service providers. The most important aspect of this latter rule is that providers cannot be held responsible as long as they have no information about illegal activities or information on their net or server. With the further development of e-commerce it is likely that more rules will be needed to cope with problems of privacy, safeguards of rights (industrial property) and so on.

However the Commission has found that this process was too slow[9] and, when successful, ran the risk of leading towards too detailed and sectoral-specific European regulation. So, while proposing the liberalisation necessary for the completion of the internal market in services, a new more fundamental and encompassing approach was to be adopted (EC, 2000b, 2004b). This proposed directive would cover all market services other than those mentioned earlier for which sector-specific regulation is already in place. It foresees three groups of measures:

*   Take away obstacles to the freedom of establishment, such as a ban on legislation with discriminatory stipulations for foreign providers; the creation of a single office for licences where operations can be made electronically and the adoption of fundamental principles governing the licensing systems of member states.
*   Promote the free movement of services. Adoption of the country of origin principle implies that service providers, having obtained a licence in due form of their own country, are entitled to deliver services in the whole EU.
*   Promote trust among the member states. Monitoring of the quality of the national systems so as to improve mutual trust. Harmonisation of national regulation so as to come to common levels of consumer protection, and of other matters of public interest.

The proposed directive has run into many political difficulties, due to vested interests in specific aspects of national service regulation; consequently decisions about the course to take were still pending in mid 2005.

EXTERNAL SITUATION

Contrary to the situation for goods, the Treaty is silent as to the organisation of an external policy in matters of services. As a consequence the external regime for a large number of services was in fact not a common one, but a set of national ones. Indeed, each country had regulated the industry on a national basis and maintained an external regime *vis-à-vis* both EU partners and other countries to protect its industries from foreign competition.

Three factors have changed this situation in the last two decades. First, the pursuit of an internal market in services has considerably changed the outlook for the external regime. Second, in the framework of the GATT/WTO the EU has worked on the GATS, the General Agreement on Trade in Services. This agreement sets rules and creates a framework for basic fair trading principles such as non-discrimination. Individual signatories, among them the

---

9   A specific example of such regulation was the proposal to facilitate the cross-border trade in services (EC, 2000b) involving non-EU nationals who are lawfully established in one of the member states but do not have the right to work in other EU member states.

EU, pledge market opening in a wide range of service branches. For some branches special provisions have been made, as for financial services, telecommunications and sea and air transport.

GATS is not of the same inspiration as the single market. The latter tries to do away with all remaining barriers in one go, and to create a new competitive situation. The former has listed the present barriers, evaluated the problems they create, has drawn up an inventory of the potential for liberalisation by each of the negotiating partners, and finally has worked out an agreement on a reduction of protection. The more partial and segmented approach of GATS is the result of the great diversity of preferences of the national governments that take part in the GATT/WTO negotiations.

BOX 6.1
THE INTERNET

Throughout modern history the growing integration of the world economy and technological development have created the need for governments to set up international organisations to regulate the international aspects of the use of the new technology. This has been the case, for instance, for the railways and for telecommunications (see Chapter 3). The typical form of such organisations was an intergovernmental agreement on technical standards, cost and revenue sharing, and so on. Compliance was guaranteed by the national governments that had become members of the organisation.

The Internet has not developed in the same way. Its regulation has emerged largely bottom-up, meaning that its rules are the result of consensus building among its users. The process of policy formation on the Internet is largely carried out by the *Internet Engineering Task Force (IETF)* which functions as an on-line community of interested parties and is in charge of developing technical standards such as communication protocols.

So far, this original decision-making process has proved to be remarkably robust, notwithstanding its inherent flaws. However, there are signs that this may not be sufficient in the future. The problems that arise are multi-faceted. On the one hand there is the increasing risk of commercial or special interest groups taking over control of certain parts of the net. On the other hand there is the growing concern about the inability of governments to safeguard certain public goods (such as a reliable legal system for dispute settlement) or their capacity to tax international and national transactions on an equal basis.

The problem is particularly acute with the property of Internet names and numbers. Indeed, there is a very high commercial interest involved in the possibility of using company and brand names on the net. In order to cope with these problems the *Internet Corporation for Assigned Names and Numbers (ICANN)* has been created. It is a hybrid form of an on-line community (such as IETF) and a real-world government structure. It comprises accredited organisations such as the World Intellectual Property Organisation, and national governments have a voice via a governmental advisory committee. This structure has yet to prove its effectiveness.

The European Union, just like national governments, is aware of these problems. However, it has not yet established a clear position with respect to the future development of the Internet.

The third new factor is the emergence, in recent years, of the Internet which facilitates the global exchange of information and the creation of many new services, generally called e-business or e-commerce. The development of the Internet has taken place almost without any international intergovernmental regulation (see Box 6.1).

It will be some time before the EU manages to set up a consistent external regime for services from these rather dispersed elements. It takes the standpoint that most new Internet-related services have to fall under the GATS as well.

Trade patterns[10]

RELATIVE IMPORTANCE OF TRADE IN SERVICES

Services are to an increasing extent traded internationally. The transaction costs involved in international service trade are often considerable, and not all services are susceptible to economies of scale. Hence services tend to be traded less than goods. To analyse the development of service market integration we are hampered by deficiencies in the data. Those for the period before 1980 concern 'invisibles' that encompass, besides services, such items as income from investment. For the period 1960–80 they show that service trade has increased its share in GDP for all EU member countries.

For the 1980–2000 period (where data are adequate) there has been a somewhat slower growth of integration (see Table 6.1). Some countries appear to specialise in services. If we compare the intra-EU cross-border trade of services with that of goods (Table 5.2) in the same period, we see two features. First, the transactions in services appear to be relatively small (less than one-third of those in goods). Second, the increase of the service trade, notably in the recent period, has been much faster. One explanation for the low level is that in services the internationalisation process has proceeded much more by establishment-based competition, rather than in terms of cross-border trade-based competition.[11] The explanation for the strong increase in recent years is to be found in the institutional and technological changes that have had a big impact on many services (see Chapters 12 and 14). We refer here in particular to the influence of the internal and external liberalisation programmes. The *internal market programme* started in 1985, but the actual liberalisation of the various markets of branches of the service sector has taken quite some time. However, the effects are becoming visible: indeed the intra-EU trade share in total trade in services did go up for all member countries. Moreover, the intra-EU trade did go up for most service branches in the course of the second half of the 1980s (Messerlin, 1993) and after some stagnation in the first part of the 1990s picked up recently.

---

10   To measure trade in services is quite a complicated proposition. For a service incorporated in an information carrier, for instance a consultancy report, the international transaction can in principle be recorded the moment the report passes the frontier. In cases where either the consumer (a student who studies abroad) or the producer (a professor who teaches abroad) travels from one country to another, the transaction is difficult to register. To overcome such difficulties, most international service transactions are registered only at the moment the payment is made (through the records of the central banks). The criterion for the international export of a service is then that it be paid for by a person resident or a company established in a country other than the home country of the producer. As a consequence of these recording problems, most statistics on trade in services are very deficient. Consistent series over a long time period are not available. For this reason we have to limit ourselves here to relatively short series.

11   See Messerlin (1993); see also the sections on direct investment in Chapter 8.

Table 6.1   Percentage share of service imports and exports in total GDP of member states (current prices), 1980–2003

	1980 Import	1980 Export	1990 Import	1990 Export	2000 Import	2000 Export	2003 Import	2003 Export
Germany	4	3	3	6	7	5	7	5
France	3	5	4	5	5	6	5	6
Italy	2	4	4	5	5	5	5	5
Netherlands	7	8	6	8	14	14	12	12
Belgium/Lux.	8	11	13	16	17	20	18	21
UK	3	6	4	5	7	8	7	8
Denmark	4	8	6	9	14	15	14	15
Ireland	6	5	7	6	30	18	33	24
Spain	3	6	2	7	5	9	5	9
Portugal	4	8	3	9	6	8	5	8
Greece	—	5	4	7	10	17	6	14
Austria	7	14	7	14	15	16	16	17
Finland	4	8	5	3	7	5	6	5
Sweden	4	6	6	5	10	9	10	10
EU15	4	5	4	6	8	8	8	8
Intra	3	3	3	3	4	4	4	4
Extra	1	2	1	3	4	4	3	4
Poland					5	6	5	5
Czech Rep					10	12	8	9
Hungary					11	13	11	10
Slovakia					9	11	9	10
Slovenia					8	10	8	10
Lithuania					6	9	7	10
Cyprus					13	35	17	39
Latvia					9	15	8	14
Estonia					17	27	15	24
Malta					19	29	18	27
EU25					8	8	8	8
Intra-EU25					n.a.	n.a.	5	5
Extra-EU25					n.a.	n.a.	3	3

Note: *Due to rounding, figures do not add up.*

Source: *Statistical Annex of European Economy, June 1996, EC; Table 6.1; Eurostat, Eurostatistics, January 2000; Eurostat, Geographical Breakdown of the current account, various years.*

The *worldwide drive for liberalisation* of trade in services got off the ground only in 1993 with the GATS agreement. However, the progress in liberalisation has been rather cumbersome and little effect on extra-EU trade can yet be reported.

MAIN TRADING PARTNERS

The exports and imports of total services by the EU are not only fairly balanced for the total extra-EU trade (Table 6.1) but they are also very balanced for the various (groups of) trading partners (see Table 6.2, taking account of the statistical error margin). The large surplus the EU had in 1980 with the Third World (notably ACP countries) has disappeared since and the same is true for its deficit with EFTA. The similarity in the patterns of exports and imports is typical for services; it does not appear for other types of current account transactions.

Table 6.2   Geographical distribution (percentages) by groups of countries, of extra-EU trade in services, 1980–2003

Country group	1980 Imp	1980 Exp	1990 Imp	1990 Exp	2000 Imp	2000 Exp	2003 Imp	2003 Exp	2003[a] Imp	2003[a] Exp
Industrialised	66	57	69	68	64	65	60	61	61	61
EFTA[b]	25	19	24	24	13	14	14	16	15	17
USA	30	28	33	31	42	39	37	34	38	35
Japan	2	3	4	6	4	6	3	5	2	5
Other[c]	8	7	8	7	5	6	5	6	6	5
Third World	31	39	27	29	34	33	38	37	37	36
ACP	10	16	5	8	4	4	4	4	4	5
OPEC	6	9	5	6	4	6	3	4	3	4
Other	15	14	17	15	27	23	31	29	30	28
Other (ex state trading)	4	4	4	3	2	2	2	2	2	2
Total	100	100	100	100	100	100	100	100	100	100

Notes: [a] *1980-2003: EU15, 2003[a]: EU25.* [b] *From 1998 onward only Norway, Switzerland, Iceland and Liechtenstein.* [c] *Australia, Canada, New Zealand and Turkey.*

Source: Eurostat, Geographical Breakdown of Current Account, various years.

The table also shows that the EU trade in services has always been geared very much more to the industrialised countries than to developing countries (the same structure that obtains for goods: see Table 5.4). The main trading partner for the EU in services over the past 20 years has been the USA (much larger than for goods). The paramount place of the USA in EU services trade can be explained by the weight of its economy and the importance services have in its branch structure (notably services such as software and audiovisual productions). Exchanges with the EU have, moreover, been enhanced in the past decades by the considerable drop in the cost of transport, of telecommunications and of information processing. EFTA was second for services, which can be explained by the geographical proximity and EU/EFTA market arrangements.

TRADE IN SERVICES BY BRANCH

The structure of the external trade in services by sector of activity (see Table 6.3) has remained fairly stable over the past 25 years. Transport and tourism were by far the most important items in terms of exports as well as imports. Over the whole period the EU has had a net surplus on its balance of trade in services. The main contributors to that surplus have changed over time. Around 1980, exports of almost all branches were slightly in excess of imports. Around 1990, tourism stood out somewhat more. By then the EU was attracting more foreign tourists than it sent (a difference, more or less, of 15 million a year). But in recent years the position of the EU in tourism has been reversed; the EU has become a net importer of tourist services. This is due to the strong demand among EU citizens for non-EU destinations (for example, Turkey and the Far East). Moreover, banking and business services showed good performances. The specialisation on the latter branches has been accentuated in recent years. The surpluses of financial services (banking) would appear to reflect their strong competitiveness on world markets.

Table 6.3   Extra-EU trade in services, by branch (billion euro), 1980–2003

	1980		1990		1998		2000		2003		2003[a]	
Category	Exp	Imp	Exp	Imp	Exp	Imp	Exp	Imp	Exp	Imp	Exp	Imp
Transport	27	25	46	44	60	57	81	73	77	72	79	70
Sea freight	11	11	15	17	22	25	31	23	32	19	32	18
Air freight	1	1	3	1	4	3	5	3	4	3	4	3
Air passenger	5	4	10	9	17	12	23	14	17	13	17	13
Other	10	9	18	17	17	17	23	33	24	37	25	36
Travel and tourism	14	13	34	29	61	62	75	83	62	82	64	76
Other	30	22	55	43	116	104	154	147	189	145	186	146
Construction	6	3	6	3	12	7	10	6	11	6	11	6
Merchanting	4	5	7	9	12	12	4	0	11	0	10	0
Banking and nsurance	3	2	11	6	18	9	31	15	37	15	37	16
Communication	1	1	2	3	4	5	6	7	6	7	6	7
Business	8	4	12	8	43	39	58	57	71	57	70	58
Computer and information	–	–	–	–	6	4	2	1	1	1	2	1
Films, TV	0	0	1	1	1	4	2	6	3	4	3	4
Other	8	7	16	13	20	24	41	56	50	54	48	54
Total	71	60	135	116	237	223	311	303	327	300	328	292

Note: 1980-2003: EU15, 2003a: EU25. Due to rounding, figures do not add up.

Source: Joint Publication OECD & Eurostat, *International Trade in Services*, various years, 1980–90 EU12, 2000 EU15. Eurostat, *Geographical Breakdown of the Current Account*, 2005.

The relative importance of external trade in the total of the branches is still limited. For most sectors the share of trade in total turnover is around 5 per cent; somewhat higher figures (10 per cent) can be found for specialist services such as computer and information, while only very specialist services such as R&D consulting come up to shares of around 80 per cent. Of course, sea and air transport are by nature very much oriented to external trade as well.

In recent years there has been an explosive growth of electronic commerce, or the trade in services on the Internet. This explosive growth is expected to continue for some years in the future. As yet only rough estimates are available on the magnitude and geographical pattern of this type of trade. These estimates show that US-based companies had some 50 per cent share in this trade around the turn of the century. Most of this commerce is e-business (inter-company trade).[12]

Price differences

The comparison over time and space of prices for typical services is a rather complicated operation. In the past a few attempts have been made for specific products; the scanty evidence produced showed that the lack of integration that has characterised service markets until recently tended to maintain considerable price differences.

In the 1990s some better information became available, showing that in the 1985–93 period prices converged somewhat as a result of the 1992 liberalisation programme (EC, 1996a). Similar information about the 1993–6 period shows a continuation of the cautious trend towards convergence for services in general and most service branches. This convergence has been much less general and much less pronounced than in manufacturing (see Chapter 12 for more details).

For some specific branches there is evidence of the remaining price differences. For instance differences in the prices of the many services of the financial sector varied from almost nil for money markets to almost full for retail bank services (Baele *et al.*, 2004).

Welfare effects

There are no comprehensive empirical studies that permit us to evaluate the trade, let alone the welfare effects of decreased protection, in services, due to the integration of different national economies. The reason for this is that the conceptual and statistical basis for such studies is very weak. For example, the estimation of '*ad valorem*' equivalents of restrictions to trade in services is very difficult, and hence the economic cost of these restrictions cannot be established. This is contrary to the case of goods, where welfare cost of protection and welfare benefits of liberalisation have been estimated on several occasions.

There are numerous examples of firms that have increased their exports or imports of services to or from other EU member states following the internal market programme. However, the increase is moderate if compared to manufacturing (EC, 1996a). There is also substantial evidence of increases in efficiency due to liberalisation. The completion of the internal market for services (conform the draft directive EC, 2004d) would lead to an increase of total intra-EU trade of 1 to 3 per cent and a growth impulse of some 1 per cent for GDP and 0.3 per cent for total employment (Kox *et al.*, 2004; Copenhagen Economics, 2005).

There remains much room for further welfare increases as the internationalisation of the sector is still in its infant stage (for example, banking). Yet the evidence from the manufacturing sector shows that penetration via FDI of protected markets by multinational firms (MNF) entails in general an increase in productivity.[13] Some information exists about the potential welfare effects of individual service branches. For instance the integration of the European financial markets will increase the productivity of the manufacturing sector by about 1 per cent a year (CEPR, 2002); the integration of the stock and equity markets alone may result in an increase of some 1 per cent of GDP (LE/PWC, 2002).

---

12   Its composition in terms of the traditional sectors cannot be given for lack of a statistical basis.
13   As evidence from the manufacturing sector shows; see Faini et al. (2004).

In large part the argument that trade liberalisation leads to positive welfare effects rests on the assumption of increased (potential) competition. It is here that some caution is needed. Indeed, in many cases where liberalisation went hand-in-hand with deregulation, an initial period of enhanced competition was followed by a period of concentration of firms, leading to a situation of limited oligopolistic competition. So a prudent policy of regulation and of enforcement of competition rules is needed (see Chapter 14).

Summary and conclusions

- Until recently many service markets have been protected from foreign competition by a variety of instruments; often the official reason was the protection of the consumer, but in practice the consumer has often borne a high cost while the producer has mostly profited.
- International trade of services is relatively limited. This is partly due to protection. It is also partly due to the need for proximity of producers and consumers that induces firms which undertake internationalisation to prefer the setting up of an establishment in the country to cross-border trade.
- The EU has liberalised the internal trade in services; this has been accompanied by a mutual recognition of home country supervision and a minimal set of EU regulations.
- The effects of liberalisation have started to become visible in terms of increases in cross-border trade and direct investment; however, the deficient data situation precludes as yet any conclusion as to price convergence and positive welfare effects.

7 *Labour*

Introduction

Under certain conditions, the creation of a common market entails movements of labour which in turn have a levelling effect on the price of labour (the wages). In this chapter we will describe in some detail how these two phenomena have taken shape in practice with the integration of the labour markets of the EU member countries.

We will start the discussion with the presentation of a few *basic concepts*, such as the definition and specification of barriers to movement and the forms and advantages of integration.

Next we will devote a section to *regulation*. Each country has tried to regulate the labour market with a complex set of legislation and administrative rules and practices and multinational or bilateral agreements. The EU has first of all ensured unrestricted migration for work reasons within its border to nationals of member states. Next it has gradually increased its regulating of aspects of social policy that influence the functioning of labour markets.

The *exchange of labour* among member states through international migration is the subject of the following section.[1] Although labour is much less mobile than goods and capital, labour migration is an important phenomenon.[2] In this section we will give the results of studies that have tried to explain movements of labour to and in the EU.

Next we will turn to the development of the *price of labour* under the influence of integration. After a theoretical treatment of the question we will examine with empirical data how far wages in the member states of the EU have actually adjusted to the new conditions. Finally, we indicate both in a theoretical and an empirical way the *welfare effects* of migration. A brief summary of the main findings concludes the chapter.

Some basic concepts

FORMS OF INTEGRATION

There is labour market integration if (1) nationals of one member state may unrestrictedly look for and accept a job in another, and (2) self-employed people from one member state are free to settle in another member state to exert their profession or activity.

---

1   The definition of movement of labour refers to persons residing and working outside their home country; frontier zone workers are therefore generally excluded. Although they also reflect the integration of labour markets, their motives are different from those of actual migrants.

2   In Western Europe, labour has always been on the move (see, for instance, Winsemius, 1939; Lannes, 1956); the movements were often inspired by political motives. The migration wave just after the Second World War comes immediately to mind; examples from the 1960s and 1970s are the repatriation of French people from North Africa and of Portuguese citizens from Angola and Mozambique, while very recently emigration from the war-ridden former Yugoslavia is a case in point.

There are as yet no generally accepted notions to capture the various *forms* in which the labour market may be integrated, but here, too, a distinction can be made along the lines of free trade area and customs union made in Chapter 2. In both a free labour movement area (FLMA) and a labour market union (LMU), employed persons are free to accept a job in any of the partner countries. However, in the FLMA, participant countries are free to establish their own conditions with respect to third countries, while in the LMU that competence is transferred to the union. In the former case, therefore, employed persons from third countries admitted to one member state would not automatically have the right to move freely into other member states. With the fully integrated labour markets in a union, this last limitation does not exist. Full labour market integration means, indeed, that among partner countries (all) restrictions are abolished. But to achieve real integration, measures of positive integration are needed as well. Such positive integration will mostly be realised by coordinating labour market and employment policies, as well as social policies and taxes.

MOTIVES FOR IMPEDIMENTS

Integration means the taking away of obstacles to movement. This triggers the question why these obstacles do exist. The proponents of obstacles to the free movement of production factor labour justify such measures by arguments, which are mostly directed against immigration. The following arguments against immigration are frequently heard:

- pressure on wages due to increased supply with stable demand;
- increase in unemployment: demand remaining the same, additional supply expels existing supply;
- rise in government expenditure: foreigners are supposed to need costlier social provisions (education and housing, for instance) and to make more demands on social security than nationals;
- societal disruption: cultural differences tend to disturb the social equilibrium;
- increase in regional disparities: labour tends to move to concentrations of economic activities;
- balance of payments deterioration: via increased remittances;
- high cost of recruitment, travel, management, personnel services and so on.

On the other hand, arguments are also raised against emigration, such as:

- loss of human capital essential to the development of the economy;
- depopulation of certain regions, causing waste of societal capital;
- opportunity cost of forgone output.

RESTRICTIONS

What instruments are used to control the international exchange of labour? Most governments use permits as a tool (comparable to quantitative restrictions in the exchange of goods), forbidding all immigration without a permit. The permit may be accompanied by all kinds of restriction, sometimes defined so sharply that in practice no immigration is feasible. The mere abolition of such permits does not mean that factor markets are integrated. There are, indeed, several ways to impede migration of workers; they can be divided into the following categories.

- Access to functions and professions. This can be limited by direct conditions stipulating, for instance, that foreign nationals cannot be lawyers. It can also be done in a subtler way, as with the setting of professional demands which foreigners cannot satisfy (for instance because foreign certificates are not recognised); or by making public labour exchange services accessible to a country's own nationals only.
- Accommodation conditions. To accept a job, a person must have accommodation. A residence permit for foreigners can be refused or made hard to get. Restrictions can also be imposed on obtaining residential accommodation or schooling for children, and so on.
- Financial disadvantages. These can be created, for instance, by imposing higher taxes, or charging premiums for social security without granting rights to benefits. Finally the transfer of earnings can be restricted (foreign currency).

ADVANTAGES OF INTEGRATION

The advantages from the integration of labour markets (the taking away of obstacles to free movement) depend on the type of exchange chosen. In general terms, the following advantages are expected from permanent migration:

- for supply of labour (employed persons) a better chance to capitalise on their specific qualities;
- for those demanding labour, better possibilities of choosing a technology with an optimum capital/labour ratio from the management point of view;
- levelling of differences in production cost as far as they were due to the compartmentalisation of the labour market.

In the case of temporary migration, a distinction must be made between advantages to the emigration country and those to the immigration country.

- Emigration countries expect three major advantages: (1) to ease their unemployment situation (and lower the budgetary cost of unemployment benefits); (2) to ease their budget and balance-of-payments problems through remittances; and (3) to improve the quality of the labour force (return migrants having acquired skills abroad).
- Immigration countries hope to gain a direct production effect: by adding foreign workers with skills that are scarce to their own manpower in places where investments require it, they are able to make the most of their own capital stock and indigenous manpower. These advantages are most manifest in times of cyclical highs, as they enhance production without increasing the pressure on inflation. Some countries hope that the inflow of young migrants will improve the capacity of the country to offset the negative effects on the labour force and on public finances of an ageing population.

The profitable effects of international migration may well be distributed unevenly between sending and receiving countries. In politics, the voices pleading restriction are often louder than those pleading full freedom. The outcome is often free movement of labour within a common market, but a policy of restriction towards third countries. This is the more likely in cases where the common market is supplemented by some form of redistribution mechanism which could offset the potential negative effects of emigration for the less developed member countries (see Chapter 16).

EU regime

RATIONALE AND PRINCIPLES

The EU has adopted the principle of free movement of workers within the area of the EU. The treaties work out the principle of non-discrimination differently for employed persons and persons practising an activity on their own account and responsibility.

- Workers are persons performing work in an employment situation against payment. They have the right to move freely within the EU. All discrimination based on nationality between workers of the member states as regards employment, remuneration[3] and other conditions of work and employment is forbidden.
- Self-employed or independent persons are those who exercise an economic activity in their own interest and on their own responsibility. Member state nationals have the right to set up businesses abroad (agencies, branches, subsidiaries, self-employed) on the same conditions as those laid down for its own nationals by the law of the country where the establishment is effected.

These rules apply to all sectors of the economy. There is one exception: the public sector. Given the prominent place which the government now occupies in the economy of many member states, large portions of the labour market could thus be excluded from free migration. However, the Court of Justice has pronounced clearly in several verdicts that this exception does concern only those jobs that are related to the exercise of official authority.

GRADUAL ELABORATION OF A COMMON POLICY

The free market for labour had been realised for most activities by 1970. This was the result of two actions. One was the application of the fundamental principles of the free movement of salaried workers and of the free establishment of independents by the Court of Justice. The second was the efforts made by the Commission to harmonise related issues. However, for a large number of professions, problems continued to exist (see Chapters 12 and 14) that stemmed from deeply rooted differences in culture and in legal or administrative practices.

The Commission has tried to reduce the remaining obstacles as much as possible by further harmonisation of matters such as social security, residence permits, diploma recognition, work conditions, health and safety conditions (EC, 1992a). Another initiative has been to set up a European network of consultants (often housed in the labour exchanges) who electronically exchange data about job opportunities and working conditions in other EU countries (EC, 1992b). The *objective* of all these measures is to create the conditions for facilitating the efficient functioning of the EU labour market (see EC, 1997a).

---

3   Non-discrimination does not mean that wages in the different member countries have to be equal, but that there shall be no difference in the remuneration of workers of different nationalities working in the same establishment and country.

WAGES

Neither the (original and amended) Treaties nor the relevant regulations and directives contain rules about the harmonisation of wages.[4] This implies that the remuneration discrepancies that exist among countries are accepted; indeed wages remain a matter of concern for national contractual parties. Wage differences are due to several types of differences between EU countries, such as industrial structure, productivity and supply factors. Moreover, institutions are different, and so are the attitudes of trade unions and of employers' organisations, the legal frameworks in which they operate and their respective bargaining strengths.[5]

In the future the EU may have some influence on wage formation. The legal base for this has been developed in the framework of the building up of a 'Social Europe'. Now, if management and labour so desire, their dialogue (in other words, negotiations) may lead to contractual relations. Until now this framework has not been used for wage negotiation. The argument against Europe-wide wage formation is that it will lead to inflexibilities and regional unemployment. Indeed, in many European countries, the drive of labour unions towards nationwide bargaining has made regional differences in wages disappear and thus widened the regional differences in unemployment. As the same tendency would manifest itself on the European scale, most parties involved (trade unions, employers' organisations and governments) in high- and low-wage countries alike agree that wage formation should for some time remain a national issue.

EXTERNAL RELATIONS

The notions of free trade area and customs union can be transferred from goods trade to the movements of production factors. While the EEC Treaty clearly laid down the external regime for goods trade, it was silent on the movement of persons. Neither did the regulations and directives implementing the Treaty give common rules about the treatment of nationals of third countries (EC, 1979a). The EU regime has not changed much since.

Apparently, as far as the movements of active persons are concerned, the EU resembled a free trade area rather than a customs union. Obviously such a situation was difficult to maintain as physical frontiers were abolished (see Chapter 14). For that reason attempts have been made to work out a common admission policy for workers and independents (and other non-active immigrants) from third countries. This policy is rather restrictive and is actually only promoting the immigration of high-skilled knowledge workers in order to help the EU attain the objective to become more competitive on world markets (see Chapter 18).

OTHER MIGRATION THAN LABOUR

Much migration no longer concerns only labour but other categories of the population as well. Of course the motives for such migration are different than for labour migration. The EU has had to cope with this phenomenon both internally and externally. One major aspect of this has been the elaboration of the new area of competence of the EU: justice and home affairs. Its objective is to ensure that the EU is an area of freedom, safety and justice.

---

4   Before the Treaty of Rome was drafted, there had been a discussion about the need to harmonise wages and the other elements of manpower cost firms have to pay (such as social security contributions, holidays and fringe benefits) prior to the internal liberalisation of labour movements. Most of those participating in the debate did not recognise such a need, however. The basic idea of the founding fathers was that wages were to be determined in the process of national bargaining between trade unions and employers.

The EEC Treaty did, however, prescribe equal pay for men and woman.

5   See, for example, EC (1967); Seidel (1983); Ferner and Hyman (1992).

Internally In the course of its development the EU has passed through the stages that have a purely economic rationale into a Union with a political rationale. In step therewith the EU has developed the concept of EU citizenship. One of the aspects is of course that citizens are free to move from one member country to another and take up residence there. This freedom has in practice given rise to fairly limited flows; most of it concerns more or less permanent changes of (secondary) residence for leisure reasons.

Now the right to move and live in other member countries does not by definition imply absence of controls. These are costly and against the spirit of belonging to the same Union. In the framework of the completion of the internal market border controls were abolished (see Chapter 14). For reasons of safety, the combat of crime and terrorism, some countries have thought that they also needed to maintain border controls for personal movements within the EU. However, most member countries have adhered to the so-called Schengen agreement that does away with such controls and they mutually rely on each others' services for the control of the outer borders.

Externally[6] The EU economy has changed over time and is now characterised by persistent high unemployment. Under the influence of increased globalisation many low-skilled jobs are now transferred to low-wage countries. Moreover, the integration of the previous immigrants into society reveals itself as much more problematic than was initially thought; unemployment hits more than proportionally second and third generation immigrants. Claims on welfare benefits are mounting. So the general feeling is that the EU does not need any more immigration apart from some selected for their capacity to fill skill shortages of strategic importance (for example, knowledge workers).

The pressure on the EU from the non-EU countries is, however, mounting. Political and social unrest in many areas of the world increases the number of asylum seekers. Bad employment opportunities at home push many to try to enter the EU. Some try to enter under the title of asylum seeker. Others try to enter illegally. As an area of justice the EU accepts people that have left their homeland because they feared prosecution for political or religious reasons. However, it wants to keep out the others. In order to cope with these problems the EU is in the process of elaborating a common asylum and immigration policy. It involves harmonisation of rules, close cooperation between national immigration authorities and the setting up of a Union Agency for Border issues. The Commission (EC, 2003d) is in favour of a unification (which in matters of migration would make the EU comparable to the customs union in trade. However, many observers consider that the arguments for this option are not very strong (see discussion on subsidiarity in Chapter 2) and plead rather in favour of an open form of coordination (Bruecker, 2002).

International exchange of labour (migration)

THE SIX ORIGINAL MEMBER STATES (1958–73)

In the first decade after the Second World War, international migration of labour in Western Europe had been on a small scale. In the 1950s, Italy provided about half the supply of migrant

---

6   International organisations, such as the International Labour Organization (ILO), the OECD and the Council of Europe, have each assumed a coordinating role; however, this is by no means comparable to the competences of an organisation like GATT in the field of trade.

labour, while Switzerland and France were the greatest demanders. Moreover, France received significant numbers of immigrants from North Africa.

From 1958 onwards, the *intra-EU free movement of labour* was gradually introduced among the six original member states. In the period between 1958 and 1973, the labour market was tight in all member states except Italy. That was one reason why the number of foreign workers originating from other EU member states remained, in general, limited. Only Italians migrated north but their numbers decreased rapidly during the period due to the catch up of Italy with the rest of the EU.

The EU member countries have extended their recruiting efforts *outside the EU* in order to provide the booming economies of the northern member states with the necessary labour. They set up recruitment bureaus in countries on the southern and eastern flanks of the Mediterranean, that often took upon themselves the organisation of transport, medical checks and housing. This means that the size and direction of the flows (see Table 7.1) was ultimately determined by policy.

Table 7.1   Estimate of the number of foreign workers in the member states, 1960–73, and their relative importance in the labour market of the host country

	Absolute figures (millions)			Percentage of labour force		
	1960[a]	1970[a]	1973[b]	1960[a]	1970[a]	1973[b]
EU6	2.0	3.8	4.8	3	5	7
EU9[c]	3.3	5.6	6.6	3	6	8
EU15[d]	n.a.	6.0	7.0	3	5	6

Notes: [a] *Labour force.* [b] *Dependent workers.* [c] *Given the free movement of labour existing between Denmark and Sweden, Norway and Finland, these figures have to be corrected upward.* [d] *Estimates for total: intra + extra EU12. Figures are rounded. Figures for Spain, Portugal and Greece are very low.*

Sources: *1960 and 1970: United Nations (1979, p. 324). For Italy, Denmark and Ireland: national statistics and estimates. 1973: EC, Beschäftigung ausländischer Arbeitnehmer, various years, Brussels.*

The ensuing migration flows were of considerable *size*, actually much larger than indicated by the figures of Table 7.1. Indeed most work licences were valid for a short period only. The holders of such licences, mostly unmarried, unskilled workers, used to arrive at workplaces in Western Europe, stay for a period of two years and then return to their home country. Around 1970, nearly one million migrants entered the EU, but about the same number returned home. Taking into account migration to other European countries, such as Sweden and Austria, and to a lesser extent the UK, we observe in Western Europe, in that period, a yearly gross migration of between two and three million people.[7] In the flows, cyclical patterns can be perceived.[8]

In the period 1960–73, *foreign labour was essential to the economies* of European receiving countries. In 1970, in five of the six member states (Italy being the exception) an average 7 per cent of total labour supply came from third countries, against some 3 per cent in 1960.

---

7   Böhning (1972). In interpreting these data, keep in mind that they should be corrected upwards because of the considerable clandestine migration going on. Some have estimated illegal migration at that time at certainly no less than 10 per cent. See also, for the long term developments, UN (1979).

8   Kayser (1972); Moulaert and Derykere (1982).

For certain sectors the dependency was actually much greater; in particular the metal industry, construction and some service sectors (catering) attracted much foreign labour in this period (Bhagwati *et al.*, 1984). Immigration enabled the EU to keep activities within its borders which otherwise would have had to relocate outside the EU (entailing outward direct investment flows).

THE FIRST ENLARGEMENT (1973–81)

In 1973, the UK, Ireland and Denmark became members and from that year onward the free mutual exchange of workers could be extended across the nine member states. Let us first see what the situation was at that moment with respect to the interpenetration of labour markets of the nine member states (see Table 7.2) and then see how migration has developed over the 1973–81 period.

The *intra-EU migration* consisted of three categories. The first refers to a hard core of workers stationed abroad by multinational companies and international organisations. The second type refers to emigrated Italians, already discussed in detail in the previous section (about one million). The third type refers to Irish emigrants (almost half a million of them), traditionally destined for the UK; that kind of emigration had already been regulated by bilateral agreement before 1973 (Böhning, 1972; Sexton, *et al.*, 1991). Together these groups amounted to some three million, so the degree of integration of the EU labour markets in 1973 was still quite modest (3 per cent).

The workers from *third countries* in the nine member states can be split according to their origin into three groups.

- *Greece, Spain and Portugal.* In 1973, 19 per cent of the labour force of Portugal, 9 per cent of the Greek and more than 4 per cent of the Spanish were employed in the EU9. Transfers of migrants to their home country equalled 24 per cent of imports for Greece, 9 per cent for Spain, and as much as 37 per cent for Portugal.[9]
- *Other Mediterranean countries.* Turkey and Yugoslavia were important emigration countries in 1973. Emigrants from North West Africa (Algeria, Morocco and Tunisia) were, however, forming the bulk of immigrants, most of them going to France and Benelux.
- *Other countries.* A small proportion of this group were citizens of third countries who work for multinational companies or international organisations (Americans, Japanese and other nationalities). Another limited part of this group was formed by foreign workers from Central and West African countries. The main body was formed by the approximately one million immigrants into the UK from Commonwealth countries.

Let us next look at the changes that occurred in the *1973–80 period* (Table 7.2). The first enlargement in 1973 coincided with the end of a long period of stable growth in Western Europe. The changed economic situation in the host countries led to a drop in GDP; many companies got into difficulties and the tension on the labour market rapidly diminished. Governments of immigration countries started to pursue restrictive admission policies *vis-*

---

9   See Salt (1976). Note that these national figures obscure even higher figures for certain regions: in some regions of Portugal, up to half the male labour force appeared to have emigrated to Northern Europe in 1973. In interpreting these data one should, moreover, keep in mind that all three countries are traditional emigration countries for other destinations than the EU: Iberians particularly to South America, Greeks to Australia and the USA (UN, 1980; Bernard, 1978).

à-vis citizens of non-EU countries and actively to stimulate return migration.[10] Moreover, schemes were developed to stimulate the assimilation or improve the integration of workers settled more permanently (that is, whose families were resident in the host country.[11] The developments and measures described above have led to a drop in the number of migrant workers in the EU. This decline varied in size for different groups of country of origin, depending on the degree of integration (Table 7.2).[12]

Table 7.2 Estimated total number of foreign workers (millions) in the EU, by country of origin and percentage share in total labour force, 1973–2000[a]

	Area	1973	1980	1990	2000
Intra-EU	Total EU15	3.3	2.6	2.4	2.9
Extra-EU	Mediterranean	2.2	2.1	2.3	n.a.
	Other	1.6	1.6	2.0	n.a.
	Total extra	3.8	3.7	4.3	5.2
Total	World	7.1	6.3	6.7	8.1
Share in total labour force (%)	Intra+Extra-EU15	6	5	5	5
	Extra-EU15	3	3	3	3

Note: [a] *In interpreting the magnitude and the evolution over time of the data presented one should keep in mind that their statistical basis is sometimes very weak and, moreover, very different over time.*

Sources: KEG, Beschäftigung ausländischer Arbeitnehmer, 1975 and 1982, Brussels; OECD (1992); see also Eurostat (1985, 1987, various sources); OECD Labour Force Statistics, various years.

- *EU partners*. The figures indicate an integration effect; that is to say, migration diminishes as free trade grows (see Box 7.1). For instance, on balance, 200 000 Italians working in other member states returned home in the 1970s once free trade among the EU countries had led to accelerated growth, more employment opportunities and better wages in their home country. The increasing number of British employed abroad in the 1970s may have been the initial effect of the UK workers' progressive integration in the common labour market, clearly helped along by economic (push factor) motives.
- *The three new member states*. The steep drop in the number of workers from Greece, Spain and Portugal employed in the rest of the present EU can be attributed to changes in admission policy in the receiving countries. Total return migration amounted to almost half a million (about 200 000 Spaniards, 100 000 Portuguese and 150 000 Greeks).
- *Other Mediterranean countries*. Here the restrictive policies have had less effect. Between 1973 and 1980, the number of Yugoslavians had decreased considerably, but those of North Africans and Turks had increased.
- *Third countries*. The doubtful measurement of the remaining group (UK) does not permit a clear-cut conclusion.

---

10 Böhning (1979); Hammar (1985). To stimulate return migration, measures of four types were introduced (Lebon and Falchi, 1980): (1) return premium to the person involved; (2) aid for setting up in business to person involved; (3) subsidies for professional training to the home country; (4) development aid for projects to home country.

11 See Council of Europe (1980, 1983); Castles and Kosack (1985); Edye (1987); EC (1985b).

12 Figures for later years are only marginally different from those for 2000.

SECOND AND THIRD ENLARGEMENT (1981–03)

Intra-EU migration has shown a slight decline in the 1980s (Table 7.2). There are several factors to explain this evolution (EC, 1991a). First, the enlargement of the EU with three Mediterranean countries coincided with a new impetus to European economic growth given by the internal market programme. The economic restructuring of the most advanced member countries that ensued diminished the pull factors for migration, as the demand for low-skilled jobs declined. Second, the access to the EU markets and the increased confidence of both domestic and foreign investors in the three new member countries (see next chapter) diminished the push factors: the large increase in investment and an accelerated growth of GDP increased domestic employment opportunities and wages.

BOX 7.1
COMPLEMENT OR SUBSTITUTION?

There is a debate on the question whether migration is a substitute for or complementary with goods and capital movements. The available evidence for the EU* suggests that:

Labour movements have to some extent been a substitute for goods movements (low-skilled immigrants maintaining certain productions in high-wage countries).

The movement of goods (after providing access to markets) and capital (due to direct investments in low-wage countries) has been a substitute for labour movement. This is reflected in the significant return migration after accession.

*   Very few authors have tried to test these hypotheses quantitatively, although the subject has been debated for a long time (see, for instance, Meyer and Willgerodt, 1956; Mihailovic, 1976). For evidence see, for example, OECD (1992) and data given in this section.

In the 1990s, migration within the EU picked up again. This has been the effect of larger numbers of employees of MNF and international organisations that are the result of a stronger interpenetration of the economies of the enlarged EU (see Chapters 14 and 18). However, the figures in Table 7.2 show very clearly that the freedom to move within the EU does not in itself bring about substantial migration; on the contrary, it seems that labour is rather immobile between EU member countries. The main reasons for the low level are to be found in the high friction cost within the EU (see Box 7.2).

However, even in the absence of such frictions migration is bound to be fairly small between the more developed countries of the EU as the experience of the Nordic countries shows. This may even be the case for the countries where larger differences exist.[13] In the period of transition even extreme shocks have not resulted in mass internal migration in the NMS. The introduction of the euro has not changed that situation; neither the pull nor the push factors seem to be significantly influenced by EMU.

The number of immigrant labourers from *third countries* into the whole EU increased in the 1980s and 1990s (Table 7.2). The causes of this increase differ within sub-groups:

- *Third countries of the Mediterranean basin*. These countries continued their sending of people and hence workers to the EU. Return migration, notwithstanding policy measures, remained

---

13   See, for instance, Fischer and Straubhaar (1996); Abraham and Konings (1999); Fidrmuc (2004).

BOX 7.2
CAUSES AND PATTERNS OF LABOUR MIGRATION

International labour migration depends on four factors:*

- push factors: low earnings and the lack of job opportunities in the sending country (LEC);
- pull factors: availability of jobs and better pay in the host countries (LIC);
- friction factors: cost of movement, dependent on distance and cultural and linguistic differences between LECs and LICs. Information networks between established and new migrants decrease such cost.** Friction is increased by lack of harmonisation of professional and vocational qualifications and of social security and tax regulations.
- legal limitations: immigration-restricting measures from receiving countries' policies.

Increasing values for the two first factors increase the size of migration flows; increasing values for the two last factors decrease these flows.

---

*   International migration studies have used a variety of approaches. Some were mostly theoretical (for example, Mueller, 1980). Others concentrated on the motives of individual migrants and employers (for instance, OECD, 1978). Yet others focused on phenomena well known from interregional migration analysis (for instance, Klaassen and Drewe, 1973; Heijke and Klaassen, 1979). The factors mentioned in the box were almost all found back in the analysis of Molle and van Mourik (1988, 1989a) explaining spatial patterns of international migration to and from Westen Europe.
**   Network effects have been found to be very important (Pederson et al., 2004).

---

low. On the contrary, again notwithstanding policy measures, immigration continued, mainly in the form of family reunion and illegal entrance. The main explanatory factor of this development is the push factor: low income and low employment possibilities due to a very dynamic population growth and a lagging economic growth in the home countries. Another important factor has been the civil war in former Yugoslavia.

- *Other third countries.* The developing countries of Latin America, Asia and sub-Saharan Africa have started to send people to the EU in significant numbers. Although often occurring officially on political grounds, this increasing migration appears in practice to be motivated by economic reasons, or a combination of both. Two cases in point are the migration from Argentina to Spain after the crisis in the former country; and the move of ethnic Germans from Central and Eastern Europe and Central Asia to Germany.

These migratory flows are very different from the ones that prevailed in the 1960s, for several reasons. First, they concern more sending countries over a much wider geographical area. Second, they concern more receiving countries: southern European countries that up to the mid-1980s had almost no immigration have become in the past decades the host countries of millions of third country immigrants. Third, recent migrants often go to the informal, sometimes even illegal, labour market (Pugliese, 1992). Fourth, the causes of migration tend to become more complex (intertwining of political, security and economic factors), leading to increased pressure. Finally, the conditions for integration in the receiving countries have deteriorated (lack of job opportunities and increasing cost of social integration). In view of all these factors we see that all countries of the EU15 have become immigration countries; however, as the wage differences between the southern and the north-western member states is still significant, it is logical that the percentage number of migrants is still significantly higher in the latter than in the former group.

As a consequence of the upsurge in migratory pressure on the EU, voices grew loud in the call to severely *limit immigration* into the EU.[14] In practice, the governments of all member countries have now resorted to a policy of restriction of immigration. Notwithstanding a clear convergence of national policies with respect to their targets and their instruments, it has not yet been possible to complete a common EU policy.[15]

FOURTH ENLARGEMENT: CENTRAL AND EASTERN EUROPE

The economies of the countries that have become members in 2004 have been going through a painful adjustment process, during which large numbers of workers, many of them highly skilled, have been made redundant. The job shortage and wage gap has pushed many to try to enter the EU15 to find a job. However, as the latter were almost all confronted with unemployment problems as well, they have not welcomed the idea of mass immigration. During the accession negotiations many of the EU15 member states have obtained a transition period, during which restrictions on migration from the NMS could be maintained. These permit EU15 countries to restrict for the period 2004–2011 inflows from the NMS to levels they consider acceptable and to take measures to prevent social security shopping.

Notwithstanding the big differences in job opportunities and wages between the new and the old member states, the migration flows between the two areas have been rather limited. On the eve of accession the number of CEEC nationals residing in the EU15 was less than one million. Most of them were in Germany, Austria and Italy. Several estimates have been made into the likely effect of the taking away of restriction to migration between the new and the old member states.[16] The results range around a long-run situation of about 100 000 labour migrants each year. Migrants for other reasons have to be added to this number. So we can estimate the number of residents from NMS in the OMS at about four million; a figure that corresponds to roughly 1 per cent of the EU15 population. The effects on wages and unemployment of this immigration into the EU15 depend very much on the rigidity of the national labour markets and the qualifications of the immigrants. However, the mainstream view is that they are limited but are likely to affect notably the lower skilled.[17]

These estimates suggest that the often heard concern that EU15 labour markets will be swamped by migrants from the NMS, seriously increasing unemployment, depressing wages and bleeding dry the social welfare system there are rather ill founded. However, the effects on regions (notably in Germany and Austria) bordering the NMS are far from negligible. So one can understand the putting into place of a set of temporary restrictive measures adjusting the immigration pressure to the speed of the restructuring processes in these regions.

---

14   See Eurobarometer of various years that report that a majority of EU citizens are in favour of a policy of severely restricting immigration. The economics of the policy are discussed in Böhning (1993); OECD (1993a); Siebert (1994).

15   The typical policy now is to stimulate integration into society for migrants already residing in the country and to restrict new immigration to persons who can fill in positions on the labour market that otherwise would not have been profitable. Active policies for stimulating return migration are difficult to implement. However, making clear from the outset to new immigrants whether their stay is permanent or temporary is welfare improving (see Dustmann, 1996). This policy should be complemented by a policy of aid to the labour sending countries, so as to restrict push factors (Molle et al., 1992; Molle, 1996).

16   For a review see EC (2001b); in particular Boeri and Bruecker (2000); and for an update Alvarez-Plata et al., (2003).

17   See Ochmann (2005) for a review of the relevant studies.

Wage structures

MOVEMENT AND MOVEMENT COST, PRICE CONVERGENCE

The effects of the integration of factor markets can be illustrated by comparing situations without and with migration of labour. That is done in Figure 7.1, where the upper part of the graph indicates the situation without, and the bottom part the situation with, migration. We have assumed that the world consists of two countries, A and B; the situation for A is depicted on the left-hand side, that for B on the right-hand side. For all practical purposes one may assume A to be the former EU15 and B the NMS. The situation on the labour market is given by the upward-sloping curves S_a and S_b representing labour supply, and the downward-sloping curves D_a and D_b representing demand for labour. Together they determine the price of labour (wages) and the number of workers employed.

In the non-integrated situation, in which the labour markets of countries A and B are separate, that is, without migration (upper part of Figure 7.1), the supply and demand conditions in country A lead to high wages and those in country B to low wages. Two national labour markets with such different wage levels can be kept separate only by dint of control measures, for instance 'permits' or restricted access to professions.

In the integrated situation such barriers are removed (bottom part of Figure 7.1). Now workers of country B will move to country A where they earn a higher income. As movement entails costs, both in economic and psychological terms, this will not lead to the complete equalisation of wages. We assume these costs to be equal to C. The inflow of migrant labour into country A pushes the wages down, which leads to a lower quantity supplied domestically (O_aM) and a higher quantity demanded domestically (O_aN). The difference (MN) indicates the number of migrants from country B in country A. In country B the opposite occurs: the higher wages lead to a lower quantity demanded (O_bP) and an increased quantity supplied (O_bQ); the difference (PQ) indicates the number of migrants from country B to country A. The number of out-migrants of country B (PQ) is of course just equal to the demand for foreign labour created in country A (MN). The new curves of domestic labour S_{a+m} and S_{b-m} demonstrate the consequences.

Now the problem in the EU is often with rigidities stemming from regulation. Suppose that in country A a system of minimum wages obtains. Suppose, moreover, that the minimum wage level is close to the average wage E in the left hand bottom part. It would mean that demand in country A stays around D. Supply would far exceed N (hypothetical intersection of Sa+m and horizontal line cutting through E). So the quantity OaN+ would transform itself in unemployment. If this unemployment hits the local workforce that is entitled to social security benefits, this implies a burden on the national budget (equal increase in volume times level of allowance).

AVERAGE WAGES: CONVERGENCE OR DIVERGENCE?

In the previous section we described a mechanism that was limited to the openness on the labour markets. The international integration of goods markets does change the rather simple situation described above. The classical way in which this has been analysed is with the theory of the equalisation of factor returns.[18] These models say that the change in demand

---

18   Generally called Heckscher/Ohlin/Samuelson models; see Chipman (1965–66) for a review.

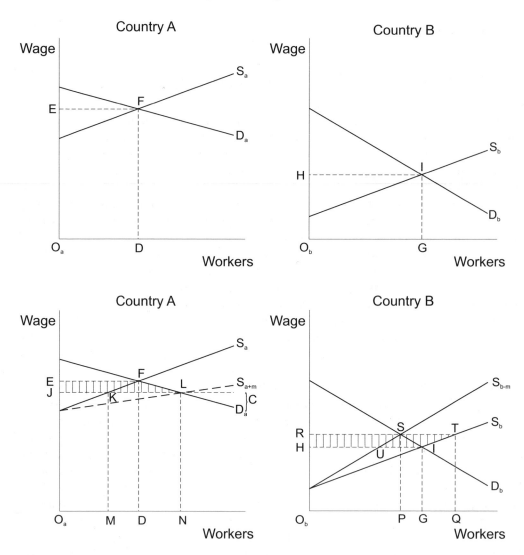

Figure 7.1   Integration of factor markets, price convergence

for production factors that follows international specialisation will lead to an equalisation of wages. This means that goods movements may actually be a substitute for factor movements (Mundell, 1957). However interesting from a theoretical point of view, this approach is not very helpful in practice, as the assumptions on which it is based are rarely realised (Markusen, 1983). So let us look at alternative approaches that bear more resemblance to reality. These show that *product market integration influences wages* through a number of channels, mostly trade in relation to capital mobility (Andersen *et al.*, 2000):

- Competitive pressures. The more integrated the economy is in international product markets, the more wages will converge to those of partner countries because of the need to stay competitive. Labour unions and governments will be pushed to accept structural reforms. Openness of product markets permits the entry of firms that have no allegiance to existing labour institutions. Depending on the initial situation this may lead to more divergence or more convergence.

- Foreign direct investment. The possibility of setting up plants in other countries and the reduction of distance cost may induce firms to split production vertically. Stages requiring lower qualified labour may then be located in low-income countries, with stages requiring highly skilled labour locating in high-wage countries. Depending on the relative changes of the demand and supply of labour in both types of country, the effects may be both convergence and divergence of wages.

The uncertainty in theoretical terms as to the outcome of the process of product and production factor integration has led to the development of two schools of thought.[19]

The *convergence school* is of rather neo-classical inspiration. It supposes that markets do work efficiently. Migration will bring equalisation of wages. Even in the absence of factor movements, the openness of product markets will induce the partners on the labour markets to align their wages to productivity. And productivity in low-wage countries will gradually increase due to catching up effects in which innovation plays an important role. Multinational firms will transfer technology and management practices to low-wage countries, thereby increasing the capacity to sustain higher wages. National governments of these countries will match this with investments in training of labour and infrastructure.

The *divergence school* maintains that the conditions for equalisation mostly do not obtain. Movement of labour tends to be restricted by factors like spatial and cultural distance and by institutional factors. Even in a customs union, trade can be impeded by collusive practices, transport costs, multinational firms monopolising new technology, and so on. The technological advance of certain countries implies that they will always select the new products with high value added as soon as they come on the market, abandoning products as soon as their value added drops and no longer sustains high wages. Thus the wage gap that accompanies the technology gap is not only perpetuated, but even accentuated. The liberalisation of European goods and factor markets was feared to have such an agglomeration effect.[20]

The answer to the question, which one of these two schools actually holds the truth depends on *empirical research*. This shows that convergence has prevailed in the period 1960–1990. This wage convergence was correlated with the increased integration of goods markets.[21]

There are still wide differences in average wages among the countries of the EU. On the whole they are highly similar to the international differences in GDP (see Table 16.2), with mostly high figures for the countries in Northern Europe, medium ones for the Mediterranean states and low ones in the NMS of Central Europe. There are several reasons that explain why the convergence of wage levels for the old member states is not complete. One is based on the limitations of *factor market integration,* as depicted in the previous section. The second reason has to do with *other aspects of integration*. The catch-up process of backward countries is indeed one of long duration. The restructuring of both the industrial base and the labour supply does take time as it implies many detailed decisions on the micro level. Lack of integration (for

---

19   For a more elaborate description of these schools, see Molle and van Mourik (1989b); compare also Chapter 16.

20   See, for example, Giersch (1949); Seers et al. (1979, 1980).

21   For an assessment of the differences in wages, see Saunders and Marsden (1981) and Molle and van Mourik (1989b). Rigorous testing of the alternative views on the development of wage differentials used to be very difficult because of deficient data (Tovias, 1982; Gremmen, 1985; van Mourik, 1987). However, for results of studies that have overcome these problems see respectively: Meyer and Willgerodt (1956); Fisher (1966); Butler (1967); van Mourik (1989, 1993); Andersen et al. (2000).

example, on service markets) may slow down the pace at which such decisions are actually taken.

Welfare effects

DISTRIBUTIONAL EFFECTS

The welfare effects of the migration caused by the joining of markets are also illustrated by Figure 7.1. They are fairly intricate and apply to both workers and employers in country A and country B (for a review, see Table 7.3).

Table 7.3 Welfare effects of integrated production factor markets

Category	Country	Gains	Losses
Workers	A	*	JEFK
	B	HRSU	*
	B to A	USTI	*
Employers	A	JEFL	*
	B	*	HRSI

*Note: * Not applicable.*

Workers from country A lose area *JEKF* because their wages are forced down. (For that reason, many trade unions in developed countries are against immigration.) On the other hand, workers remaining in country B gain from out-migration: there is less competition for jobs, which raises the wage rate from O_bH to O_bR. The gain is the producer surplus above the new supply curve (*HRSU*). The migrants also gain: they earn a higher income in A than they would have in B. However, account should be taken of cost factor *C*. So the gain is the area above the old supply curve S_b and below the new one S_{b-m} (*USTI*).

Employers in country A gain considerably: the area *JEFK* is redistributed to them from workers, while the area *KFL* is a net gain. In country B, on the contrary, employers are losers: they have to pay higher wages and hence lose profits. Of their consumer surplus (employers are demanders of labour!) they have to hand over area *HRSU* to workers remaining in the country, and area *USI* to migrants.

Countries A and B are clearly in different positions. The receiving country A has a net gain (*KFL*). The sending country B, on the contrary, has a net loss *USI* (difference between employers' loss and workers' gain). The migrants gain also: *USI* and *STI*. So the net gain to the world is *KFL* and *STI*; the distribution of welfare among countries depends on the allocation over countries of the gains to migrants.

The quantification of these effects in practice has not always been simple.[22] The effect of increased returns to capital for France was calculated at between 1.2 and 2.2 per cent of GNP in 1971. For Germany, employers' incomes have been estimated as being some 10 per cent above the level they would have had without immigration. The effects of immigrant labour on wages of local workers are rather contradictory.[23]

---

22   For early attempts, see, for example, Scott (1967).
23   See, for France, MacMillan (1982); for Germany: studies cited in Spencer (1994). Some find negative effects on wages of local workers (Haisken-De New, 1996), others find no effects (Pischken and Velling, 1994) and yet others

OTHER EFFECTS ON LABOUR-IMPORTING COUNTRIES

The most important welfare effects of migration have been enumerated in the first section of this chapter. The *static direct production effect* – in other words the increase in GNP as a result of the employment of immigrant workers – was limited.[24]

The *dynamic effects* of labour migration to LICs are less well known and there is much dispute over the question of whether the effects are positive on balance. Let us look at the different categories.

As to the *macro-economic effects*, some note a positive development because immigration, by taking away certain bottlenecks in the economy, has led to a permanently higher growth rate of GNP. Others note a negative effect: they argue that migration has prevented the economies of the LICs from adjusting structurally to the new global conditions in comparative advantages.[25] The effects of the latest EU enlargement on migration are not yet visible as many countries have taken protectionist measures during the transition period.

As to the effects on *public finance*, there is some confusion too. There is no evidence that active immigrants' demands on social (security) and public services (schools, hospitals and so on) exceed systematically their contributions. However, if one takes into account the cost of the second generation unemployed immigrants, the balance seems rather negative.[26]

On balance, labour-importing countries seem to have benefited somewhat from immigration;[27] this benefit is larger in periods of labour shortages and smaller in periods of considerable unemployment such as the 1990s. On the basis of these findings, many experts now plead in favour of a more selective or strategic immigration policy: letting in persons of working age with the required skills and keeping out all persons for whom the cost–benefit balance is likely to be negative.[28]

There is now a big debate about the question of whether immigration is the solution for the problem of the ageing population of Europe. The problem is as acute in the old as in the new member states, so internal migration is no solution. Without immigration from third countries the ratio of the numbers of inactive persons to active persons is likely to double over the coming decades. However, to compensate for the demographic effect, a yearly number of immigrants would be needed that seems to exceed by far the absorption capacity of the EU society. So the conclusion is that mass immigration can help but will not be the panacea for the problem (EC, 2003d).

EFFECTS ON LABOUR-EXPORTING COUNTRIES

The emigration of part of its labour force has both significant advantages and costs for a country. These differ according to category of migrant. Emigration of unskilled unemployed persons has little effect on total welfare. However, the outflow of skilled workers (Sexton *et*

---

even positive effects (Winter-Ebmer and Zweimueller, 1996). This confusion may be due to differences in the effect on branches: indeed for Germany it was found (Haisken-De New, 1996) that one needs to distinguish two cases. First is the case where one can presume that there is complementarity between foreign and native workers; here migration has had a positive effect on native workers. Second is the case where the foreigners seem to compete with natives; here the effect on native wages has been negative.

24   See MacMillan (1982); Askari (1974); Spencer (1994).
25   See Böhning and Maillat (1974); UN/ECE (1977); Zimmermann (1995); and the studies in the survey made by Leibfritz et al. (2003).
26   See Blitz (1977); Bourguignon et al. (1977); Löffelholz (1992); Spencer (1994).
27   This is also the experience of the USA, as noted in the studies of Simon (1989) and USDL (1989); later studies, such as Borjas (1995) and Friedberg and Hunt (1995), show more contradictory effects.
28   For example, Zimmermann (1995); see the final sub-section of this section.

al., 1991) is likely to have had a negative effect on LECs' welfare.[29] Temporary emigrants are supposed to have acquired *increased skills* while working abroad. However, once they have returned, the enhanced quality of human capital seems to have had little positive effect on the economies of LECs, for two reasons. On the one hand, the inability of LECs to offer sufficient employment opportunities to returning skilled workers has led to a net loss of human capital. On the other hand, returning migrants are generally disinclined to accept low-status jobs and frequently set up unprofitable service trades (Papadimetriou, 1978). Such factors have contributed to the rather negative welfare effects of policies that stimulated return migration (Dustmann 1996).

Migrants remittances count as a possible third positive effect of labour export. They amount to a considerable proportion of the LECs' GNP and in the short run constitute a very convenient means of financing deficits on the balance of trade. The long-run effects of remittances on the LECs' economy are limited, however, because on the whole they have been used for investment in houses and consumption purposes rather than for productive capital formation.[30] The increased consumption they have made possible has caused substantial price and wage increases and contributed to the misallocation of resources in LECs. And sometimes they have led to an overvalued currency. The transfer of savings, which also seemed promising, has proved rather disappointing in terms of investments in the emigration country, for too much money has been invested for purposes that are not directly productive.

Summary and conclusions

* Free migration of labour in the EU is a right of EU citizens. However, unlike the situation on goods markets, the further integration of labour markets is not meant to entail large migration flows. Politically the EU holds as a fundamental principle that nobody must be forced to submit to the socio-cultural and legal adjustments involved in international migration, and that ideally everyone should find sufficient work in his own country.
* The degree of interpenetration of EU labour markets (number of foreign workers divided by the total number of employed) has been stable over time at less than 2 per cent.
* Intra-EU migration is limited because of the taking away of barriers to goods, services and capital movement, the limited differences in wages compared to the cost of living, and the persistence of differences in culture and institutions such as social security systems.
* The fairly wide wage discrepancies prevailing among EU member states at the start of the integration period have decreased considerably since, which is in line with expectations fostered by the convergence school.
* Most migration comes from third countries. The welfare effects of these movements are not clear. The elaboration of a common EU policy in this matter is a complicated and difficult process as it touches sensitive areas such as internal security.

---

29   Interesting from a theoretical point of view, but difficult to implement, are proposals to compensate LECs for the negative effects of emigration by introducing an emigration tax (Bhagwati, 1987b) and to transfer financial means to LECs through an International Labour Compensatory Facility (for example, Kennedy Brenner, 1979).
30   Evidence in Keely and Tran (1989). See also, for the Maghreb countries, the contribution by Garson in OECD (1994a).

8 Capital

Introduction

Capital markets reveal many special characteristics that cause their integration to differ in practice profoundly from the way other markets are integrated, notwithstanding the basic theoretical similarity to, for example, labour market integration. To prepare this difficult ground we will start with a short description of the *basic concepts* of integration of capital markets, including of course the various barriers to movement, the advantages and so on. Next a brief sketch of the European *regulatory environment* for capital market integration will be given.

The central part of the chapter will be a description of the progress of integration measured by different types of private international capital market transactions. Many indicators come to mind. We have selected two: direct investment and long-term loans.[1]

The first subject we draw attention to is foreign direct investment (FDI). This phenomenon is of very high relevance for economic integration. We devote first a special section to the theoretical bases of FDI, explaining the logic of international production. Next we describe with some stylised facts how FDI has developed in the EU under conditions of integration; highlighting both sectoral and geographical patterns.

Next we go into the patterns of other *international movements of capital mainly in the form of long-term loans*. We will discuss in three sections the theoretical foundations and two important indicators of the degree of integration, namely, the volume of international transactions, and the equalisation of interest rates, that is, of the price of capital.

A short section on the *welfare effects* (both the theoretical analysis and the empirical measurement of the magnitudes) of capital market integration and a brief summary of the findings complete the chapter.

Some basic concepts

FORMS OF INTEGRATION

The movement of the production factor 'capital' can be considered free if entrepreneurs can satisfy their need for capital, and investors can offer their disposable capital, in the country where conditions are most favourable for them.

Once more a parallel can be drawn with free trade areas and customs unions. A free-capital movement area (FCMA) would then be a zone within which capital can move freely, each state

---

1   Other indicators often used to depict the progress of integration are the convergence of the prices of equity (notably those of listed stock), the percentage of foreign investments in the portfolio of pension funds or the percentage of the equity of major companies held by foreign investors. For evidence of the progress of integration on these scores, see, for instance, NIESR (1996).

making its own rules with respect to third countries. In a capital market union (CMU), on the contrary, there would be a common policy concerning the union's financial relations with third countries.

The integration of capital markets can be defined first of all as the removing of constraints on foreign exchange, of discriminatory tax measures and of other obstacles. This is the so-called 'negative integration'. Since capital is highly mobile and apt to go where the returns are highest, positive integration will also be needed; that is, the integration of capital markets by coordinating or harmonising the rules which govern their organisation and functioning, such as prudential regulations for bank credit, payments, and so on. Progress in capital market integration can be measured as progress on these various scores (Adams *et al.*, 2002). Given the interwovenness of the capital market with monetary policy, a certain integration of monetary policy, and coordination of the monetary relations with third countries, would be implied.

MOTIVES FOR IMPEDIMENTS

Integration of capital markets implies the removal of obstacles. This triggers the question why there exist so many obstacles. Arguments for restricting capital movements are based mostly on the disadvantages associated with long-term capital drain-offs.[2] The most frequently heard reasons for governments to impede the *exporting* of capital are the following:

- Bloodstream of the national economy. Capital drain-offs will reinforce the economies of other countries to the detriment of the country's own economy (for instance, there is less domestic investment, so the government receives less tax on the ensuing revenue).
- Loss of currency reserves. This jeopardises the ability to meet other international obligations; this is particularly relevant when the balance of payment is in disequilibrium and authorities are trying to prevent changes in the exchange rate.
- Internal equilibrium – an argument mainly associated with the price of capital. A large outflow of capital may compel a high rate of interest when a low rate would be recommendable for the development of the national economy.
- External equilibrium. Capital outflow may lead to currency devaluation even though the rate of exchange, as judged on other criteria such as the current account, is not unbalanced. In that way, the nation might be forced into imported inflation.
- Lack of confidence of international markets in policy measures of politically unstable countries. In order to maintain as much as possible the effectiveness of their fiscal and monetary policies, governments of these countries need the capital control instrument.

Rather paradoxically, arguments are also raised against the *importing* of capital, such as the following:

- Capital is power; therefore capital in foreign hands means loss of authority over one's own economy.
- Disturbance of the internal and external equilibrium: a large inflow of capital may entail a lower rate of interest than the monetary authorities think adequate for internal equilibrium.

Finally there are arguments pleading against *both the importing and the exporting* of capital:

---

2   See Cairncross (1973); Swoboda (1976); Mathieson and Rojas-Suarez (1994).

- Disturbance. Capital movements can be disturbing in cases where they are of a speculative nature, that is anticipating changes in the exchange rates of currency.
- Perversity. Free movement of long-term capital does not lead to optimum allocation, but to concentration in countries with a large market where capital is already in abundant supply, while states with smaller markets are deprived of capital.

The experience with controls both on inflows and on outflows has shown them in the long run to be ineffective instruments for preventing structural adjustments to the balance of payments. Modern technology and the development of 'offshore' international capital markets make it very difficult to make restrictive instruments effective even in the short run (Edwards, 1999). The arguments for fighting speculative capital movements, on the contrary, are on the whole economically sound (speculation often leads to overshooting); for that purpose other instruments may now be more effective (see Chapter 15, on monetary policy).

FORMS OF IMPEDIMENTS

A whole series of instruments can be used to restrict the importation and exportation of capital:[3] market-oriented instruments resemble tariffs in goods trade, as they influence the price of capital. They may take the form of lower (even negative) interests on foreign deposits, caused by taxes on interest or deposits, or otherwise.

- Administrative and legal instruments. These instruments are comparable to quantitative restrictions and non-tariff barriers. For instance, trade in securities may be impeded by reserving the right to hold domestic stocks and bonds to persons or institutions of the own nationality; or to restrict pension funds investments in foreign securities.
- Currency restrictions: authorities allotting only limited amounts of foreign currency for given capital transactions; split-currency markets, with a more (or less) favourable rate of exchange for current payments than for capital transactions.
- Tax: for example, heavier taxes on foreign profits than on domestic ones.
- Profits and interests transfers may be hindered by an obligation to reinvest in the host country all profits made with foreign capital, and by committing exporters to return as soon as possible (for instance, within five years) any capital drained off abroad.

ADVANTAGES OF INTEGRATION

Integration of capital markets is aspired to because it:

- diminishes the risk of disturbances such as tend to occur in small markets;
- increases the supply of capital, because better investing prospects mobilise additional savings, the investor being free to choose the combination most favourable to him in terms of return, solidity and liquidity;
- enables those who are in need of capital to raise larger amounts in forms better tailored to their specific needs;
- makes for equal production conditions and thus fewer disturbances of competition in the common market.

---

3   Whether or not speculative, compare Woolly (1974); Schulze (2000).

EU regime

RATIONALE AND PRINCIPLES

The liberty of capital movement as laid down in the Treaty of Rome was limited to *the extent necessary to ensure the proper functioning of the Common Market*. That restriction indicates that member states did not aspire to fully free movement of capital as an object in itself. The reason is that member states dared not give up the right to restrict external capital flows, because they needed the instruments for the effective control of internal macro-economic and monetary developments. Moreover full freedom of capital movement was hard to reconcile with the selectivity implicit in the measures of fiscal policy, investment stimuli and so on of many member states. As a consequence, the provisions of the EEC Treaty for freedom of capital were not directly applicable, unlike those for goods and labour. Indeed the Treaty did not enjoin upon the Community the creation of a veritable European capital market.

However, member states had committed themselves to go beyond the degree of liberalisation of capital movements prescribed by the Treaty, in so far as their economic situation, in particular the situation of their balance of payments, so permitted. Indeed efforts made towards the progressive liberalisation of capital movements have been made ever since the EU was founded, but up to 1987 they did not result in agreements reaching beyond the stipulations of the Treaty.

DIRECTIVES OF 1960–62

The Treaty is a framework agreement, setting out some general principles to be complemented later by further rules. For capital movements such rules were drawn up at an early date (1960–62) in the shape of two directives, which distinguish three groups of transactions by the degree of liberalisation:

- *Fully free*. The liberalisation of this group rested on the direct connection with the free movement of goods (short- and medium-term trade credits), of employees and self-employed (personal transactions) and the right to free establishment (direct investments and investments through participation in quoted capital stock).
- *Partly free*. This group comprised the issue and placing of shares listed on the stock market of a member state other than the one where the placing body resides; the acquisition of non-quoted shares by those not resident in the same country; shares in investment funds; and finally long-term trade credits.
- *No obligation to liberalise* existed with respect to such short-term transactions as the purchase of treasury bonds and other capital stocks and the opening of bank accounts by non-residents. The reason why these transactions were not liberalised is that they may be of a speculative nature and therefore a cause of disturbance.

So the EU was at its start rather an incomplete common market, the situation on the capital market resembling, in terms of goods market, rather a free trade area for selected products than an encompassing customs union. Between 1966 and 1986, many concrete proposals were made for further liberalisation and integration of markets[4] but in practice nothing was achieved. The

---

4   For example, Verrijn Stuart et al. (1965); Segré et al. (1966).

causes are involved but in the main associated with the conviction of many governments that restricting capital movement is an essential instrument for an effective monetary policy.

PROGRESS IN DEREGULATION AND LIBERALISATION

In the 1980s, the attitude towards international capital transactions shifted gradually but significantly (Lamfalussy, 1981) in favour of deregulation and liberalisation. What determinant factors brought this change about?

*   External position. The improvement of the balance-of-payments position of many European countries permitted them to abandon capital controls.
*   Poor efficiency of instruments. Governments had realised that restrictions on external capital movements often just delay structural adaptations that will be necessary anyway in the end and may become more costly if put off.[5]
*   General tendency to deregulate national financial markets. The progressive abolition of restrictions was stimulated by the experience in many countries with the negative effects of distortions created by such intervention of the public sector in the market.
*   Technological innovation. The telecommunication and automation revolution has greatly reduced the information and transaction costs of the financial sector. Information on financial markets anywhere in the world is now instantly available anywhere else.
*   Competition from largely unregulated 'offshore' markets. To avoid the problem of regulated home financial markets, a large unregulated international financial market had developed that proved increasingly efficient in coping with investors' and borrowers' needs.

Inspired by the worldwide trend to liberalise capital markets and by the will to complete the internal market (Chapter 14) also for capital, and comforted by the positive effects of unilateral liberalisation of countries such as the UK and the Netherlands, the EU decided to realise a free European capital market by 1992 (EC, 1986b). Capital movements between member countries have since been *fully liberalised*. At the same time the movement of capital between the EU and non-EU countries was gradually liberalised. The Maastricht Treaty has codified the free internal and external movement of capital in the following words: '*Within the framework of the provisions set out in this chapter, all restrictions on the movement of capital between member states and between member states and third countries shall be prohibited.*'

IMPROVING THE CONDITIONS FOR A PROPER FUNCTIONING OF EUROPEAN FINANCIAL MARKETS; HARMONISATION

To be effective, capital market integration cannot be limited to removing barriers; it also needs the creation of transparent markets and the harmonisation of the conditions enabling investors and creditors to be informed about the quality of foreign financial products (Seifert *et al.*, 2000). From the many measures taken by the EU in this respect we present three by way of illustration.

Taxes Differences in tax levels may distort the market as they may induce investors to locate in countries which offer the highest tax-adjusted profit rates (OECD, 1991). This applies notably to corporate taxes and to taxes on the revenues of capital (deposits, for example). We will come back to this point of harmonisation of taxes in Chapter 14.

---

5   For proof of the ineffectiveness of capital controls, see OECD (1980, 1982a) ; Gros and Thygesen (1998).

Company law Direct investors (for a takeover), investors in stock (for portfolio purposes) and subscribers to foreign companies' loans want to be able to judge the solvency and profitability of the company in question. A series of directives on company law have been adopted and more are in preparation. They concern the obligation to publish annual accounts according to certain specifications, minimum capital requirements, the qualifications of company auditors, national and international mergers, and the creation of a European company.[6]

Financial intermediaries A saver who places his deposit with a foreign bank wants to be reasonably sure that the bank is trustworthy. The directive of 1977 ('European Banking Law') lays down uniform criteria for admission to the banking trade and for the prudential control of banks in all member countries. Other directives determine the information banks have to give in their annual reports, the definition of the term 'own funds', and the application of common solvency and liquidity ratios, and even the specification of certain financial products (mortgages, for instance).[7]

EXTERNAL SITUATION

The external policy of the European Union with respect to capital movements has changed over time.[8] The Treaty of Rome does not set an objective for capital movements with third countries. Unlike the case for goods (where the Treaty established as a basic principle the greatest possible freedom with respect to traffic with third countries), the Treaty only urged member states to coordinate their capital movements with third countries (see Chapter 17).

The Maastricht Treaty has, however, installed a very clear principle for the common policy in matters of capital movement with third countries. Indeed the principle is that external movements need to be fully free, like internal movements. The reason is that many countries that had liberalised their capital transactions '*erga omnes*' (with respect to all other countries, partners and third countries alike) while a common European policy did not yet exist were not prepared to reintroduce restrictions towards third countries under a new common policy.

The policy of openness to third countries is not one of *laissez-faire*, though. Indeed according to the Treaty the EU may regulate the movement of capital to or from third countries involving direct investment (including investment in real estate establishment), the provision of financial services or the admission of securities to capital markets. The EU may even adopt restrictions on the freedom of capital movement with third countries if in exceptional circumstances movements of capital threaten to cause serious difficulties for the operation of the Economic and Monetary Union. Finally the EU promotes the adoption of liberal policies by third countries as well, so as to obtain symmetry in its external relations.

---

6   These directives guarantee that certain minimum rules are respected by all companies. The EU rules are stricter for companies listed on the stock exchange than for others. The directives establishing them concern the minimum requirements for listing, the information to be given with the application for listing (prospectus) and after admission (half-yearly reports). Other directives of interest concern the issue of prospectuses, insider trading and public takeover bids.

7   Harmonisation has not always been easy, owing to differences in the legal status of certain intermediaries, different traditions of prudential control and deep-rooted differences in culture (such as the opposition between the British view of finance as an independent industry and that of some continental countries of finance as an activity that should be placed at the service of the real economy). The Commission has put in place the Financial Services Action Plan to stimulate integration by regulatory convergence.

8   The attempts made by the European Commission to liberalise capital movements in Europe were in line with more general efforts in the same direction made by other international bodies, such as the International Monetary Fund (IMF) and the Organisation for Economic Cooperation and Development (OECD, 1968, 1982b, 1995a, 1995b).

Foreign direct investments; some theory

DIFFERENT FORMS OF CAPITAL MOVEMENT WITH FREE TRADE AND PROTECTION

The theory of international capital movements has developed a specific branch dealing with foreign direct investments. The *definition* of international direct investment (DI) is: the transfer of capital by a company in one country to another country to create or take over an establishment there which it wants to control. Typically DI involves the transfer by a firm not only of capital but also of other resources, such as technological know-how, management and marketing skills. Now it is the expected return on the total of the transferred resources rather than on the capital per se that is the rationale for firms to engage in foreign direct investment. A firm will engage in foreign direct investment if it:[9]

- possesses net *ownership (O) advantage vis-à-vis* firms of other nationalities. These are exclusive to the owner and can take the form of intangible assets (for example, a technological lead);
- considers it more beneficial to *internalise its advantages* through an extension of its own activities than to externalise them through licensing and similar contracts with foreign firms;
- utilises these advantages in conjunction with *locational (L) advantages*, consisting of at least some factor inputs (including natural resources) outside its home country; otherwise foreign markets would be served by exports and domestic markets by domestic production.

There are two main – and quite distinct – reasons why a firm goes multinational.

- To better serve a local market. This is often called 'horizontal' FDI, since it typically involves a duplication of the production process by establishing additional plants. This form of FDI usually substitutes for trade.
- To acquire low-cost inputs. This is often called 'vertical' FDI, since it involves relocation of specific activities of the value-added chain to low-cost locations. Unlike horizontal FDI, vertical FDI is usually trade creating.

Assume that capital movement for direct investment is free between two countries; the type of DI will vary according to whether or not trade in goods is free as well. We can distinguish two types of foreign direct investments dependent on the situation with respect to goods trade:

- *Protection.* If country A operates trade impediments, firms from B that want to export to A need a comparative advantage superior to the level of the tariff equivalent of country A's trade barrier. This advantage may be based on superior production technology, on the exclusive right to use a patent for the product, or, more generally, on better management or entrepreneurial skills. Exporting firms of country B who judge their advantage real but inferior to the tariff, and firms of B unwilling to have their profit margin taxed away by the tariff, will consider setting up production in country A to serve the markets of A. This

---

9   See notably Dunning (1979, 1980, 1988, 1993); further also de Jong (1981).

necessitates a direct investment of country B in country A. Such investments (often called 'tariff-jumping' investments) tend to be substitutes for trade.

- *Free trade*. Many firms following a strategy of growing through product specialisation opt for operation on several markets, wanting to export to foreign markets from their home base. However, this may not always prove the optimum solution, as production in other countries may be less costly. Within the market area, a location will be chosen for each plant that is optimal in view of the prevailing technology and market conditions (economies of scale) and locational determinants such as transport cost, taxes and so on. Some countries will specialise in one good, other countries in others. This type of direct investment, often called 'optimum location', is trade creating. The direction of FDI is contrary to that of trade; that is, the export of capital goes hand-in-hand with the importation of goods, and vice versa.

The abolition of tariffs is not a sufficient reason to stop the first type of direct investment. Indeed even in a customs union other equally important barriers may persist; these may include poor access to government contracts or the obligation to comply with national technical norms that compel firms to keep in close contact with national authorities (see Chapters 2 and 14).

CAPITAL MOVEMENTS UNDER CONDITIONS OF INTEGRATION

The creation of a common market implies the liberalisation of capital movement, including foreign direct investments. The pattern and magnitude of direct investment flows depend on the characteristics of a country. The more the firms in a country show entrepreneurial competitiveness (related to ownership advantages) the higher will be outward DI, as these firms will want to cash in on their advantages by investing abroad. The higher the locational attractiveness of a country, the higher the inward DI, as firms will have advantages in producing there rather than elsewhere (Sleuwaegen, 1987).

The DI flows will be affected by integration, as the different measures of goods and factor market integration affect firms in member and third countries in a different way (Yannopoulos, 1990) and hence will lead to different strategic responses of firms to their new production environment.

- *Intra-union*. The creation of a common market by the liberalisation of goods and factor movements leads to a restructuring of the economies of the partner countries and to an increase in trade. This increased specialisation entails a profound reorganisation and rationalisation of production and obliges firms to redefine their international investment strategies. The combined effect of the opening of goods markets and of capital markets will lead to an increase in DI of the optimal location type. The pattern of these increased DI flows will be determined by the combination of entrepreneurial and locational advantages of each country for each activity under new conditions of integrated markets.
- *Extra-union*. The trade diversion effect of the customs union formation will induce foreign producers that experience a loss in their export market to start production within the union (tariff jumping). Theory, moreover, predicts that other third country producers may want to exploit the dynamic growth effects caused by integration and decide to set up activities within the union (in other words, integration has enhanced the locational attractiveness of the union) (Motta and Norman, 1996). In both cases incoming DI increases, while goods imports decrease. Exports may increase too, as the union producers may have gained competitiveness on world markets. The effect on outgoing direct investment is not

certain. On the one hand, one may expect an increase, as the growth effects of integration may permit many union firms to obtain new ownership advantages that they will want to exploit in third countries. If the relative position of a location in a union country deteriorates relative to a third country, an increase in outgoing DI may follow. If, on the contrary, the union performs better than third countries, a decrease of outgoing union DI may be the result.

So it is not possible *a priori* to say whether trade and DI are substitutes or complements.

VERTICAL ORGANISATIONAL SPLIT; FDI STIMULATES TRADE

The modern multinational firm can be seen as a *functionally differentiated organisation* (NEI/ E&Y, 1992). It will internationally orient its investments by looking for optimal locations of its various functions. Headquarters will be located in central cities with good international communications. R&D facilities will be located in an environment that will stimulate innovation through contacts between researchers and the quality of the living environment. Distribution will be located at places from where relevant market areas can best be serviced. Production facilities again follow their own logic, to which we will devote more attention.

An interesting model permitting the combination of some of these elements in a simplified view of the determinants of the *location of production* is based on the product life-cycle theory.[10] This theory distinguishes four stages in the life of each product: (1) introduction, (2) expansion, (3) saturation, and (4) decline. At each stage in this cycle, the companies show differences in size, profitability and so on; the markets are differently structured and competition takes on different forms; and the division between capital, labour inputs and returns also displays wide variation.

The continuous process is set going by a technical change inspiring the development of a new product. At the first stage of its development this product will need close contact with existing customers, located in developed countries. At the second stage, it will still require special skills to produce and a strong market potential to sell; this means that the production will be located in developed areas where it generates a high value added and sustains high wages. At the maturity stage, margins will fall and, to cut costs, the production will be relocated to areas where wages are lower. The richer countries will change over to new products in the earlier stage of development.

Here again a common market is likely to influence the process. First the larger market will offer prospects to specialist producers who would not have been viable in smaller, nationally segmented markets. Next it presents a sufficient diversity in production environments, thereby offering better opportunities for the location of firms in the course of the expansion and saturation stages. Finally it makes it possible to find locations to accommodate within its territory the production of articles at the final stage of their life-cycle, and thus postpone the moment of delocation (outsourcing) of these activities to third (-world) countries.

The model described here tends to predict a strong flow from the rich capital-intensive countries to the less well-to-do countries that have much cheap labour. This FDI tends to create trade.

---

10   For further explanations of this theory (originating from Vernon, 1966, 1979) see, for instance, de Jong (1993b). Many elements of this framework are relevant to the process of integration. A common market may speed up innovation and enforce changes in industrial structure (see Chapter 10); it may sharpen competition (see Chapter 14) and thus lead to economies of scale, cost reductions, product improvement and a better export potential (see Chapter 5).

HORIZONTAL ORGANISATIONAL SPLIT; FDI LIMITS TRADE

In a situation where there are clear ownership and internalisation advantages of a firm (for example, an insurance firm that has a very good reputation, a strong brand name, skills in the management of risks and cheap access to international capital) and where that firm is confronted with high transaction costs, there will be no advantage in concentrating production in one office. Firms will then develop a network of offices and undertake more FDI the higher their transaction costs. Even in the presence of a single market, such FDI will be of the 'tariff-jumping' type, transactions cost related to distance having an equivalent effect to tariffs. Such FDI is not trade creating. It is of the horizontal type, whereby two-way relations may develop: firms from A investing in B and firms from B investing in A.

Some stylised facts on FDI

STRUCTURAL FEATURES

DI of some significance is a relatively recent phenomenon. Since the 1960s stocks of foreign direct investment around the world have grown four times faster than global GDP and three times faster than global trade. Most DI finds its origin in one of the three major economic areas of the world (USA, Japan, EU). The growth of FDI of the EU has been particularly vigorous (see Table 8.1).[11]

The *geographical pattern* of the flows of FDI from and to the EU reveals some interesting characteristics. Contrary to what one would expect from their relative levels of integration, the DI interactions between the EU and third countries have for a long time been larger than those among the member countries themselves. Despite the increased trade and policy integration within the EU (see Chapters 5, 14 and 17), DI flows with third countries grew much faster in the 1970s and 1980s than those among EU countries. The internal market programme has changed that situation; since then intra-EU DI outweighs extra-EU DI and in the most recent period it has become the dominant feature of EUDI activity.[12] Among the main partners of the EU both in outgoing and incoming investment we see the USA (due to strong links between multinationals that want to have a position on two sides of the Atlantic) and EFTA (strong links based on proximity).

The sectoral pattern of outward DI shows that manufacturing and services have about equal shares, the much smaller remaining share being taken up by energy. Inward DI shows a completely different pattern; here some two-thirds go to services and one-third to manufacturing, so that energy is hardly significant. Within both outward and inward DI the dominant branch is financial services. The structure of intra-EU DI strongly resembles the picture of incoming DI in the EU, with services again accounting for nearly two-thirds. This high share reflects two features of the service sector: first its dominance in all advanced economies; second the difficulty of trading its products. So DI is the only way to supply foreign markets.

---

11   More detailed figures for five-year periods show that the increase has been gradual and continuous. See also Spannent (1991).
12   See de Menil (1999); his model showed intra-EU FDI to be far higher than could be expected on the basis of the influence of the usual variables of a model of intra-OECD FDI.

Table 8.1 Direct foreign investment flows of EU by major partner (billion current euro), 1969–2003

	1969/78		1979/88		1989/98		1999/2003	
Origin or destination	I	E	I	E	I	E	I	E
EU	21	21	75	75	502	502	2069	2069
CEEC							8	77
Rest of World	34	41	74	174	331	515	670	1325
USA	16	11	23	114	179	252	316	558
Japan	—	—	5	2	23	6	42	17
EFTA	—	—	19	6	69	54	78	133
As a % of GFCF*								
EDIE		1		1		4		24
(FDIE+EDIF):2		1		2		4		6

Notes: Up to 1998: EU12. 1999/2003: EU15.
I = inflow into the EU.
E = outflow from the EU.

* five-year averages.

GFCF = Gross Fixed Capital Formation; EDIE = European Direct Investment in Europe; FDIE = Foreign Direct Investment in Europe; EDIF = European Direct Investment Abroad.

Source: Eurostat, Balance of Payments, several years; European Direct Investments 1984–93, EU Direct Investment Yearbook, several years; Quarterly National Accounts, several years.

The relative share of foreign direct investment in total investment (Gross Fixed Capital Formation: GFCF) used to be small. DI flows within the EU (EDIE) accounted for some 1 per cent in the 1970s, for 3 per cent since the 1980s and for some 5 per cent in the 1990s. Recently they have literally surged. This increase has been triggered by the increase in integration. Extra-EU DI (FDIE) flows have remained at some 2 per cent over the 1980s and early 1990s and have surged since.

EXTERNAL RELATIONS

The *role of the EU* in international DI has changed with time. From a net recipient in the 1950s and 1960s, the EU proceeded to a balanced situation around 1970 and since then has increasingly accentuated its role as a net direct investor, to become the largest direct investor in the world. It shows how the EU firms have gained over time O advantages; and that the L advantages of the production site EU have decreased over time. The high upsurge in recent years of European FDI in the world reflects a globalisation strategy on the part of many European firms; partly vertical and partly horizontal FDI. As Table 8.1 shows, other developed countries, such as the USA, count for about half the EDIF and FDIE; the other half of EDIF is mostly oriented towards the most vigorous emerging markets.

The structure of *inward* DI has for a long time been dominated by the USA; over time, Japan has become more important, while recently some other players (like Korea) have come on the scene.

- *USA*. Direct investment flows from the USA to the EU in the 1960s and 1970s sprang mostly from American companies, which capitalised on their ownership advantage in technology and management by conquering a portion of the growing European market. This direct investment was of the 'tariff-jumping' type. The export of capital was all the easier because during this period the USA had a strong currency and no balance-of-payment problems. The creation of the EU has had a clear impact on US direct investment in Europe (USDIE). In the 1950–58 period, the growth rate of US DI in the UK was almost equal to that of the countries on the continent. Between 1958 and 1973, the UK growth rate was half the EU6's; after 1973, when the UK joined, the two rates became equal again (Whichart, 1981). In the 1980s both the tariff jumping (the external tariff) and the global diversification strategy (market size) were important determinants of the pattern of USDIE.[13] Since 1987, there has been an upsurge in USDIE triggered by the single market. USDIE is now clearly of the market development type. The geographical orientation of USDIE within the EU is determined by differences in factor endowments and in taxation between EU countries.[14]
- *Japan*.[15] The reasons for the large DI by Japanese firms in the EU are rather diversified: we find the localisation strategy based on leads in the product and production technology, on economies of scope and on product differentiation. Other factors are financial strength, the 1992 programme and fears of a protectionist stand by the EU. This suggests that JFDIE has remained largely of the tariff-jumping type. The geographical orientation within the EU is very much a function of the type of activity; the high level of technology involved in the products make Japanese firms often choose central locations in the EU.
- *Other*. Some of the newly industrialising countries have begun following the same strategy as Japan. Hong Kong, Taiwan and Korea have become outward investors. Investing in the EU is not an easy task for companies from these countries, due to high transaction costs and competitive constraints. However, the attractions of a presence in the large and diversified EU market, aloof from anti-dumping threats, and of access to technological innovations are strong motives for overcoming these difficulties (Fujita *et al.*, 1997).

The structure of *outward* DI is quite different.

- *USA*. The USA has always been the main destination of European FDI (EDIUS). It springs on one hand from the wish of many European companies to profit from the possibilities offered by the American market for the development of a product at the 'growth stage'. On the other hand many European MNF believe they need a foothold in the three main economic centres of the world.[16]

---

13   The first econometric analyses (Scaperlanda, 1967; d'Arge, 1969; Scaperlanda and Mauer, 1969) showed considerable doubt about a possible effect of European external trade protection on the pattern of USDIE; they stressed the importance of access to the EU market. However, later analyses (for instance, Schmitz, 1970; Schmitz and Bieri, 1972; Lunn, 1980) showed that both were important.

14   See Aristotelous and Fountas (1996); Devereux and Griffith (1996); Morsink (1998); Clegg and Scott-Green (1999).

15   See Thomsen and Nicolaides (1991); Ozawa (1992); Buigues and Jacquemin (1994); Belderbos (1997); Barrell and Pain (1999); Clegg and Scott-Green (1999).

16   Sleuwaegen (1987); OECD (1987c); and Graham (1992).

- *Japan*. The importance of Japan as a destination for European DI is still very limited, owing to the (perceived) difficulties of successful competition with the local public–private interest coalitions.
- *Other*. This is a very diversified group, among which are many developing countries. In the 1990s the EFDI in this group increased rapidly as a consequence of the growing involvement of EU firms in the countries of Central and Eastern Europe on the one hand and the newly industrialising countries, and other emerging markets, such as developing Asia, on the other. In both cases EU firms have recognised the potential of the local markets and the possibilities of exporting to the EU from those locations (Fujita *et al.*, 1997).

INTRA-EUROPEAN RELATIONS

Internal direct investment flows have been completely free in the EU since the 1970s. On theoretical grounds we may expect that direct investments will increase as soon as companies become convinced of the advantages of selecting optimum locations within an enlarged market area (a 'free trade' type operation). In line with this, we see a rapid *growth over time* of intra-European direct investments. In the 1966–84 period, DI by companies from one member state in other member states than their home country (EDIE) showed double digit growth figures.[17] However, the real boom for EDIE came after 1985, when it doubled about every two years under the impetus of the 1992 programme (EC, 1996a). This is again in line with the optimum location hypothesis, as the taking away of the many remaining non-tariff barriers has a similar effect to the taking away of tariffs. Indeed the single market effect was highest in branches where NTBs used to be largest (such as insurance) (EC, 1996a). An analysis of the importance of DI in the total investment shows fairly low values (Table 8.1). This low percentage in terms of flows does obscure the fact that the accumulation of such DI over the years now makes for considerable percentages of production of each of the EU countries controlled by firms from other EU (or third) countries. Increasingly this no longer applies exclusively to large multinationals but also to small and medium-sized companies.

The *industry pattern* of EDIE is very stable over time. The service sector is increasingly dominant (accounting now for more than two-thirds); the manufacturing sector comes in second place (accounting for the remaining one-third); the EDIE of other sectors like agriculture, energy and construction is insignificant. Within the service sector, the branch of finance and insurance takes the lion's share (see the case study in Chapter 12 for more details). Much of this investment is made as part of the creation of a geographically diversified production and distribution network. The most active manufacturing firms are to be found in the branches of electronics and electrical equipment and chemical products. This DI is largely of an inter-industry type; for example, manufacturers of country A invest in country B, and vice versa (Cantwell and Randaccio, 1992). The recent liberalisation of markets and the privatisation of companies in branches such as energy, telecommunications and so on has led to a considerable international rationalisation of these industries and an explosive growth of FDI in these industries.

The *geographical pattern* of the flows of DI among EU countries (EDIE) (see Table 8.2) invites six remarks. First, the structure of the EDIE flows within the EU15 has been very stable over the whole period 1980–2000. In the most recent period a significant shift occurred. Second, EDIE is dominated by the relations between the countries in the core of the EU (mainly Germany,

---

17   Pelkmans (1983). Another indicator of this phenomenon is the number of subsidiary companies of multinationals in the EU that rose in the early integration period from 340 to 774 (Francko, 1976).

France, UK, Benelux and Italy); the underlying material shows that these are often made up of two-way flows of comparable size, indicating a considerable interpenetration. Third, there is an increasing flow of considerable importance from the core to the intermediate zone of the EU25 (mainly Spain, Portugal and Greece, which were considered as the periphery of the EU15). Fourth, the flow in the opposite direction is fairly modest. The net flow of capital towards the less developed EU countries (intermediate and periphery) confirms that private investment supports the convergence of wealth (see Chapter 16). Fifth, we see that the share of the flow from the core to the new periphery has quickly picked up during the period immediately preceding membership of these countries. Finally, we see that the flows between the intermediate and peripheral areas are very small or negligible.

Membership (or non membership) of the EU has a considerable influence on the magnitude of the flows of EDIE. We will illustrate this with three examples: the Mediterranean countries, EFTA, and (in the next section) the NMS.

The accession of Spain and Portugal to the EU has triggered important DI flows from the core countries.[18] Apparently the concentration effects which the divergence school had feared (Chapter 16) have not materialised. The patterns also suggest that there is a complementarity between goods and capital movements, whereas there is rather a substitution between capital and labour movements (in comparison with the results of Chapters 5 and 7).

The high growth of EFTA at the end of the 1980s and at the beginning of the 1990s (Table 8.1) can be attributed to the wish of industrial and service groups from the then still EFTA countries already to avail themselves of the opportunities of the completed internal market (Baldwin et al., 1996). Since 1996 the picture has changed considerably. Most EFTAns that joined the EU in the middle of the 1990s are non-typical peripheral countries (high income; strong MNF structures with ownership advantages). They have been very active in FDI both in the traditional core of the EU and in other EFTA countries. Hence a strong change in relative shares in the last column of the table. Since their accession the flows between the former EFTAns and the former EU12 have become more equilibrated.

An *explanation of the pattern* of these EDIE flows reveals several determinant factors. The financial strength of a country proves very important: the largest EDIE flows occur when the country of origin shows a net financial resource and the receiving country a high borrowing requirement. More specifically the strongest influence was found to come from the ownership advantage (high R&D leads to high outward DI, and vice versa); intermediate influence comes from factors like market size (+), transport cost (–), trade intensity (+) and exchange rate volatility (–). The trade intensity factor indicates that integration of goods markets stimulates that of capital markets, and highlights the point that EDIE is of the optimum-location rather than the tariff-jumping type. The exchange rate variable indicates that monetary integration, creating stable exchange rates, is likely to influence the EDIE flows positively. Finally some other factors did influence EDIE in a limited way: for example, differences in culture and taxation.[19] Other studies suggest that the level of real wages (unit labour cost) is a very significant variable: low wages tend to attract incoming FDI and high wages tend to stimulate outgoing FDI (Hatzius, 2000).

---

18   See Petrochilos (1989); Buckley and Artisien (1987); EC (1988a); Durán-Herrera (1992); Simões (1992).

19   The results on the various variables of the model by Morsink and Molle (1991), elaborated by Morsink (1998), are confirmed by those of Mortensen (1992) for the rate of return on capital, by Devereux and Freeman (1995) and Pain and Young (1996) for the real rate of interest and the tax wedge between the home and host country and by the studies summarised in EC (1996a) for the ownership advantage and the trade variable. The results for most variables are also confirmed by de Menil (1999) but for the influence of the exchange rate.

Table 8.2   Geographical distribution (%) of direct investment between groups of member countries of the EU, 1980–2003

	1980–84	1984–88	1988–92	1993–96	1997–2000	2001–03
Core to Core	77	80	71	79	76	56
Core to Intermediate	20	16	22	16	11	25
Intermediate to Core	3	4	5	3	4	8
Intermediate to Intermediate	—	—	2	2	5	5
Core to Periphery					3	5
Periphery to Core					0	0
Intermediate to Periphery					1	1
Periphery to Intermediate					0	0
Periphery to Periphery					0	0

Notes: *1980–96: EU12, 1997–2003: EU25.*
           Morsink has introduced some overlap to smoothen the data series.

Source: *Morsink (1998); based on Eurostat and OECD statistics and a number of unpublished sources, 1980–96 EU12, 1997–98 EU15: Eurostat: EU Direct Investment Yearbook. Eurostat, EU direct investment flows, breakdown by partner country and economic activity, 2005.*

THE CHANGED POSITION OF THE NEW MEMBER STATES

In the 1990s the CEEC have changed over to a market economy and the EU has gradually integrated them by offering access to its markets and pre-accession support. This has sparked off a strong movement of European FDI towards the accession countries (see Table 8.1). EU FDI in these countries accounted for about 80 per cent of their total incoming FDI. The motives for EU firms to invest in accession countries varied by type of activity. On one hand some firms (for example, in the food industry and in insurance) have moved in to capture local markets (horizontal FDI). On the other hand firms in branches such as textile, machinery or automobiles effectuated DI of a rather vertical, efficiencyseeking type (Djarova, 2004). Quite a considerable part of this FDI was in the form of the take-over of firms that the state wanted to privatise and where foreign ownership was deemed necessary to bring them quickly up to the necessary level of competitiveness. Next to that a considerable part of greenfield investment took place.

The pattern of these FDI from the original EU15 countries into the NMS reveals some interesting features. The *geographical orientation* within the NMS has been very uneven as is evidenced by Figure 8.1. There are several underlying factors to this pattern.[20] First it seems to coincide with proximity. Indeed FDI flows were found to follow the usual gravity model: the flow is mainly determined by the mass of the recipient and donor country and the distance between the two. Other determinant factors found were the quality of the infrastructure and of human resources and of institutions such as regulatory quality and absence of corruption. The question is often asked: has the EU15 FDI in the NMS been to the detriment of the FDI of the core to the now intermediate area of the EU25 (formerly, in the EU15, the periphery)? The various studies made come to controversial results.

---

20   See Bocconi (1997); Brenton et al. (1999); Martin and Turrion (2003); and Carstensen and Toubal (2004).

The *sectoral composition* of the FDI flows from the EU15 to the NMS has been dominated by the tertiary sector. Part of this preponderant position can be explained by the interest of EU15 firms in investment in utilities (water, telecommunications, electricity). Within the manufacturing sector there is at this stage no clear specialisation trend discernible. The only branch that stands out is the food sector.

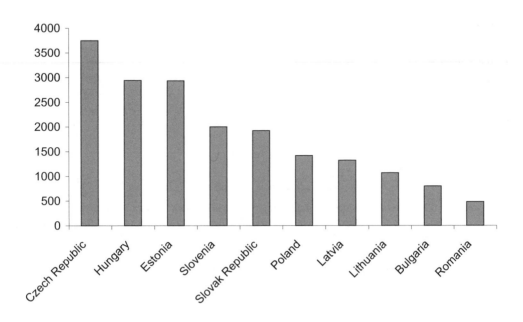

Figure 8.1   FDI (€) inflows per capita in the NMS, 1990–2003

Long- and short-term loans

LIBERALISATION OF MOVEMENT OF FACTORS; THEORETICAL POSSIBILITY OF FULL PRICE EQUALISATION

The integration of factor markets will lead to better allocation of capital. This can be illustrated by a neo-classical static two-country diagram (there is no influence from the rest of the world). In Figure 8.2, the horizontal axis gives the stock of capital. The sloping curves *AD* and *BE* indicate the level of production that can be obtained at each size of input of capital assuming a certain input of the complementary production factor. The curves of country B mirror those of country A, so that one picture describes the effects of integration on both countries.[21] The effects of integration of markets for production factors (on the assumption that goods markets are not integrated) can now be illustrated by comparing the situation in which there are barriers to movement with that of integration, in which these barriers have been removed.

We will first consider the situation in which the capital markets of countries A and B are completely separated (upper part of Figure 8.2); in other words, where capital is fully immobile

---

21   See Grubel (1981).

between nations. The vertical axis gives the price of capital; with perfect competition on the national markets, this price is equal to the marginal product of capital. The horizontal axis gives the supply of capital (O_aO_b, indicating the total stock of capital at the disposal of the two countries), demand of capital and supply of labour being given. Country A has a relatively abundant capital supply, hence a low interest rate; in country B capital is scarcer and hence the interest rate higher. The differential is ED. The downward-sloping curves for both country A and country B indicate that the marginal product of capital is lower as the capital stock is greater; with a given capital stock (K) in both countries (O_aC for A and O_bC for B) the price of capital is given for either: r_a for A and r_b for B. We assume there is no unemployment. From this picture the distribution of income can be derived. Total output is O_aADC for country A and O_bCEB for country B (the total production realised at all points on the horizontal axis; it consists of two components: capital income and labour income). Capital income (measured by the quantity of its input times the marginal product of capital at the point where the market is in equilibrium) corresponds to the rectangle O_ar_aDC in country A, and to the rectangle O_bCEr_b in country B. The triangles r_aAD and EBr_b represent labour income in countries A and B, respectively.

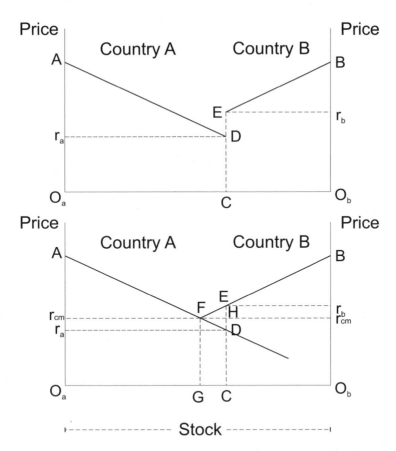

Figure 8.2   Integration of factor markets, price equalisation

What happens when the two countries integrate their national capital markets? The lower part of Figure 8.2 illustrates the effects. Owners of capital will now move their capital from the country where it earns a relatively low income (A) to the one where interest is higher (B). On the assumption of equal risks and uncertainty for foreign and domestic assets and of no other costs being involved (which implies the introduction of a common currency), this will lead to upward pressure on interests in A (smaller supply of capital) and downward pressure in B (greater supply of capital). In the end it will bring about the full equalisation of return on capital in both countries at level r_{cm} (representing the marginal productivity of capital in the common market). The capital stock of A declines while that of B increases by the amount GC, equal to A's net foreign asset. So country A will specialise in savings and country B in investment.

Even if there are no differences in factor prices between the two countries, the removal of controls is likely to favour a better allocation of resources. On capital markets, different liquidity preferences in the two countries will cause the importing of long-term capital and the exporting of short-term capital in A, and the reverse in B.

THE REMOVAL OF INTERNAL CONSTRAINTS

In the previous section we assumed full employment, at the national level, of the two production factors, labour and capital. However, that assumption is unlikely to be fulfilled in reality. In small segmented markets specialised labour will be hard put to find sufficient demand for its services, or the necessary capital with which to complement prevailing technological know-how. So in small segmented markets both the supply of and the demand for factors of production may be constrained, with negative effects on production and welfare. By taking away controls on the international movement of capital, both supply and demand can assert themselves, and an efficient allocation of all specialised factors of production will come about.

The 'trade' effects of removing the constraints on capital movement are illustrated in the upper part of Figure 8.3, which gives the supply and demand curves for capital for a given country A. The supply of capital comes from savers, its demand from investors. The country imposes controls on capital imports and exports that make its capital market inefficient. The financial products provided by the banking sector being inadequate, potential investors and savers refuse transactions, which implies that some capital remains idle; this is indicated in the figure by AB (given demand), investment and hence savings being limited to the amount OA. The price for the investor, or the borrowing rate, is OI, and the lending rate for savers is OG. The spread between the two, GI or FD, is the margin taken by banks for their intermediate role. Protection from foreign competition creates a monopoly rent of $GIDF$ (quantity OA times the margin GI). Assume now that controls on international capital movements are abolished. Fear of new entrants from abroad taking away profitable markets will induce banks in country A to propose new products, better adapted to the wishes of both savers and investors. This will bring additional supply and demand on the market. Let us, moreover, assume that all inefficiencies in the markets are removed for instance due to Union regulation and the introduction of a common currency. Let us further assume that the resulting rate of interest (OH) is just equal to the interest rate abroad. The rent will now disappear and savings and investment will expand to OB.

There is an important gain to society as a whole. First investors increase their 'consumer surplus' by the area $HIDC$. Next savers increase their 'producer rent' by the area $GHCF$. Of their monopoly rent $GIDF$, banks lose $HIDE$ to investors and $GHEF$ to savers. This leaves a net gain to society equal to the triangle FDC.

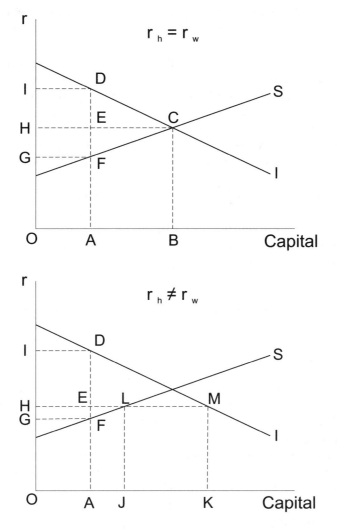

Figure 8.3   Welfare effect of capital market integration through deregulation

The effects of partial liberalisation are different. Under such conditions, the liberalisation of financial markets is unlikely just to balance out home supply and demand at the prevailing world market price. The lower part of Figure 8.3 represents the situation where the world interest rate *OH* is lower than the domestic equilibrium rate without international exchange. Now controls may affect only capital outflows, leaving inflows free, or alternatively, may affect only capital imports, leaving exports free. Let us analyse the effects of either case on the situation $r_w < r_h$.

In a situation of free outflow and controlled inflow, savers will take the opportunity of getting higher returns on the foreign market (*OH*) than on the domestic market (*OG*), and expand their supply to *OJ*. Under this pressure, domestic banks will have to diminish their margins from *GI* (= *FD*) to *HI* (or *ED*) to acquire the necessary capital (*OA*) for making the transaction with the domestic investors. The remaining supply *AJ* is invested abroad (either directly by savers or indirectly by banks). This will give rise to an inflow of interest payments equal to the area *AELJ*. The 'rent' of savers increases by the area *GHLF*, of which *GHEF* is gained at the expense (transfer) of the banking sector's monopoly rent, and *FEL* is the net welfare gain to society.

In the situation of free inflows and controlled outflows, the same reasoning applies. In the closed domestic market, investment was constrained by savings to *OA*. In the new situation, foreigners will acquire equity (portfolio investment) or companies (direct investment) and get higher returns than on the world market. That inflow will take total investment up to *OK* instead of *OA*, the quantity *AK* being imported, which entails payment of interest on foreign debt corresponding to the area *AEMK*. Investors find their 'surplus' increased by the area *HIDM*, of which *HIDE* is at the expense of monopoly 'rents' of financial intermediaries (that is, a transfer) and the triangle *EDM* is the net welfare gain.

A liberalised capital market has positive effects on economic growth (welfare effects) despite a possible initial deterioration of the balance of payments (from the equilibrium in the upper part of Figure 8.3 to the deficit of *JLMK* in the lower part of Figure 8.3). However, if the imported capital is used to create production units, the output of exportables may expand, compensating for the deficit in interest payments.

Some stylised facts on the international exchange of capital

QUANTITY EXCHANGED

The development of the integration of capital markets is indicated by the size of the transactions between savers and investors in different countries, much in the same way as the development of the goods market integration is measured by the trade in goods between different countries. Unfortunately there is no generally agreed common indicator based on a good statistical record of such transactions. So we have to work with a selection of indicators.[22]

The *share of foreign capital in total GDP* of the EU countries is an indicator often employed. Table 8.3 gives the development of both the total (average of foreign assets and liabilities) and of a special category (incoming and outgoing foreign portfolio investment; stocks).

We observe first that the ratios for total foreign capital are significantly higher than those for foreign portfolio: the difference is explained to a large extent by foreign direct investment (for details, see previous sections). Second we observe that for both indicators the figures for all countries increase significantly suggesting increased integration. Countries that have disposed of controls relatively early (like the UK and the Netherlands) show a higher degree of international integration than countries that did so later (like Germany or Italy). Some of the countries of the latter group seem, however, to be catching up, as the growth of their ratios over time is higher than for the former group. Fourth, the EU countries are on average much more open than major third countries, like the USA or Japan.

A special remark is in order on the integration of the NMS in international capital markets. Their liberalisation measures have borne fruit as is evidenced by a ratio of openness that is

---

22   An often employed indicator is based on the figures on international capital transactions (IMF or Eurostat) taken from the balance-of-payments statistics. These are rather deficient in quality, but their analysis permits us to highlight three features. First, there is considerable volatility over time of both portfolio and other categories of investment. Second, substitutability between these two categories is large because decreases of one often go hand-in-hand with equally large increases of the other. Third, an impressive magnitude that increases considerably over time; flows of the size of considerable percentages of GDP are increasingly common. Contrary to what we found for direct investment, the time and geographical pattern of these recorded flows does not show much relation to economic fundamentals.

Table 8.3   Foreign assets/liabilities and foreign portfolio investment, stocks (% of GDP[a])
EU, 1982–2003

	Total				Portfolio Investments			
	1982	1990	2000	2003	1982	1990	2000	2003
Germany	40	60	110	200	0	10	50	80
France	60	60	160	250	n.a	10	50	100
Italy	30	40	40	70	0	10	50	70
Netherlands	90	140	270	490	10	30	120	200
Belgium	130	200	260	490	10	30	80	130
Luxembourg	n.a.	n.a.	n.a.	n.a.	n.a.	n.a.	n.a.	50
UK	130	180	260	450	10	40	80	130
Denmark	n.a.	90	140	n.a.	n.a.	30	50	n.a.
Ireland	n.a.	n.a.	430	1090	n.a.	n.a.	360	600
Spain	30	30	100	180	0	0	40	70
Portugal	n.a.	n.a.	130	260	n.a.	n.a.	40	90
Greece	n.a.	n.a.	60	120	n.a.	n.a.	20	60
Austria	60	60	120	230	10	10	60	120
Finland	30	50	170	240	0	10	110	120
Sweden	50	70	140	160	0	10	60	60
Poland	n.a.	40	40	70	n.a.	0	10	10
Czech Rep.	n.a.	50	60	100	n.a.	0	10	20
Hungary	n.a.	n.a.	60	100	n.a.	n.a.	10	20
Slovakia	n.a.	n.a.	50	90	n.a.	n.a.	10	10
Slovenia	n.a.	50	40	60	n.a.	0	0	10
Lithuania	n.a.	n.a.	40	60	n.a.	n.a.	0	10
Cyprus	n.a.	n.a.	n.a.	280	n.a.	n.a.	10	50
Latvia	n.a.	70	60	100	n.a.	0	10	10
Estonia	n.a.	n.a.	60	130	n.a.	n.a.	10	30
Malta	n.a.	100	240	430	n.a.	20	30	100
US	30	40	70	110	10	10	30	40
Japan	20	60	40	80	10	20	20	40

Note: [a] *Rounded to the nearest ten.*

Sources: *NIESR (1996); OECD, Main Indicators, various years; IMF, International Financial Statistics, several years.*

similar to that of the southern member countries of the EU. At the same time, differences in the structure of the two groups remain. Portfolio flows are less important for the Central European countries than for Southern Europe today, but already have a higher share than in the latter countries prior to their accession (Buch, 1999).

Price convergence

INTEREST RATE PARITY

The *potentially determinant factors* of the evolution over time of the differences between countries in the price of capital were given at the beginning of this chapter as we discussed the reasons for capital controls. With integration we should see the fading away of most of these factors and subsequently a movement towards parity of interest rates for comparable financial products in different national markets. A distinction is thereby made between assets with a short- and with a long-term maturity. Differences in interest rates between countries stem mostly from two causes. First, there is the difference between supply and demand, a factor that should disappear with the taking away of barriers to international financial transactions in the framework of the integration of capital markets. Second, there is the inflation differential (related to the likely change in exchange rates: see Chapter 15), a factor that should disappear with monetary union. In addition, there is a set of factors such as the quality of the debtor, the differences in reserve requirements of financial intermediaries, fiscal regime, transaction costs in thick or thin markets, monetary unrest, and so on.

In the 1974–93 period (Lemmen and Eijffinger, 1996) the most relevant factor was inflation; out of line inflation puts pressure on a weak currency; governments wanting to avoid realignment and not willing to raise interest rates for domestic policy purposes (such as growth, debt burden) will then use capital controls to prevent capital from seeking higher returns abroad. The second factor was the instability of governments; indeed political instability limits the confidence of international investors in government policies, and capital controls are then needed to prevent capital movements that would make it even more difficult to pursue an effective policy.

The development of national interest rates[23] over the period 1960–2004 shows marked differences by sub-period, regime and maturity (Figure 8.4). Let us first analyse *sub-periods*. A certain tendency of convergence can be observed for the period up to 1973. The monetary unrest that was created by the first and the second oil crisis increased the divergence again. From the mid-1980s to 1993 convergence has again prevailed, notably due to the success of the stabilisation of exchange rates. Under the influence of the global monetary turmoil of 1993 a new upsurge of divergence occurred. However, in recent years convergence has prevailed again. The introduction of the euro has even led to equalisation of rates for the countries of the euro zone. Let us next turn our attention to *regimes*. We note that, since the early 1980s, the level of divergence was much lower for the five core countries of the Exchange Rate Mechanism (ERM) of the European Monetary System (EMS)[24] (see Chapter 15) than for the other EU countries. The figures for the most recent years of the evolution of the differences between the interest rate levels of the countries that form part of the EMU also show a very clear convergence (see also Chapter 15). If we finally turn to the aspect of *maturity* we note that for short-term rates the amplitude of the effects is very marked over time, while it is rather cushioned for long-term rates.

Actually we observe in Figure 8.4 an almost complete equalisation of prices. The remaining differences are due to a multitude of imperfections that we will not detail further.

---

23   In the past, several methods have been used (Frankel, 1989) for measuring the degree of capital market integration. Short-term interest rates figures for the 1970s show very little integration. In the 1980s, on the contrary, the markets of Germany, the UK, the Netherlands and Belgium became highly integrated, whereas the integration of the Italian and French markets remained poor. Real interest rate (RIR) parity among countries has not been found in empirical studies (Mishkin, 1984a, 1984b; Mark, 1985a, 1985b; Gaab et al., 1986; Caramazza, 1987).
24   The convergence measured seems to be on the low side; if trend behaviour is taken up correctly the movement towards convergence under EMS becomes very significant (Zhou, 2003).

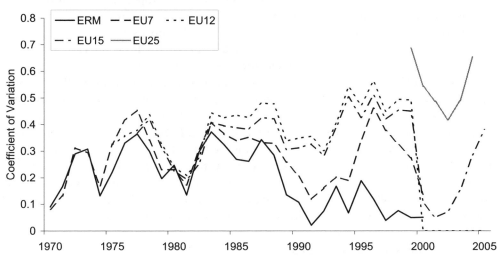

Short Term Interest Rate Variation

Figure 8.4   Divergence of interest rates between groups of member countries, 1970–2005

Note: *Divergence: unweighed coefficient of variation.*

Sources: 1960–85: Mortensen (1992); 1985–2000: own calculations, based on IMF, Financial Statistics; Euro-stat, Money and Finance, several years.

Welfare effects

SOME THEORY

The analysis of the *welfare effects* of capital restrictions (and of the removal of such restrictions) are rather complicated.[25] The welfare effects of integration can be described with the help of Figure 8.2. The first is an allocation effect; due to the lower cost of capital EU firms can produce more efficiently and thereby improve their competitiveness. The effects are different for different groups and hence lead to distributional disputes.

Let us look first at the *distribution over countries*. Total welfare will increase for both country A and B by the following process. The net domestic product of country A declines by *GFDC*, its net national product, composed of the domestic part $O_a AFG$ and the investment income earned abroad, *GFHC*, increases by *FHD*. The net domestic product of B increases by *GFEC*. As *GFHC* must be paid to A, the net gain for B is the triangle *FEH*. The total net gain arising from the better allocation of capital through integration corresponds for both countries to the triangle *FED* (*FHD* in A and *FEH* in B).

The distribution of income between the *main functional categories* (wage income versus capital income) changes when the factor markets are integrated. In country A the part of total income that accrues to labour is reduced in favour of the part that accrues to capital owners (by $r_a r_{cm} FD$), whereas in B the share of labour increases at the expense of owners of

---

25   See, among others, Grubel (1974) and Phylaktis and Wood (1984).

capital (by FEr_br_{cm}). This explains why trade unions tend to welcome incoming investment, but are opposed to domestic investment abroad, even if it leads to a higher aggregate income. Of course that effect will come about only if markets function properly; that is, if the wages are adjusted downward. If not, the result may be more unemployment, leading to reduced production, which the growth of capital income may fail to compensate in the short run.

The welfare effects of *foreign direct investment* are similar to those for capital flows as described in Figure 8.2. By shifting labour demand across countries, FDI raises the wage in the host country (B) and lowers the wage in the source country (A), thereby raising profits of source country firms at the expense of host country firms. The extent of cross-ownership of firms and the relative supply of skilled labour alter the impact of FDI on welfare (Glass and Saggi, 1999). However, there are also dynamic effects; these come notably from the improvement in the industrial and labour market structure that are induced by FDI.

Integration is bound to change government revenue springing from the taxation of international capital. If country B taxes foreign assets, a proportion of the area *GFHC* remains in B. If it exceeds the net gain of A (the triangle *FHD*), country A will suffer a net loss from opening up its capital market while country B had not done so completely.

EMPIRICAL ESTIMATES OF EFFECTS

The welfare effects of free internal flows of *European direct investment* occur in several ways (see Blomstrom and Kokko, 2001). Positive effects are dependent on the policies of the host country or host region. We analyse here two aspects: productivity and employment.[26]

FDI has been shown to stimulate *productivity growth*.[27] This relation is strongly substantiated for the NMS. However, FDI can only be effective in this respect in cases where other conditions are met as well. For instance, only if the quality of labour (skills of the workforce) is up to a required level does FDI bear positively on GDP growth. Much of the positive effects depend critically in the degree of transfer of technology that FDI brings. Apart from the direct effect, FDI also has an indirect effect in the sense that it stimulates productivity in indigenous firms through spill-overs. In this respect FDI has played a critical role in the process of the catch-up of the member states with below average income per head (see Chapter 16).

The *employment impact* of FDI seems to have been limited in both source and destination countries. The latter seem invariably to have benefited from DI. The effect on the former varies from negative, when exports from the home bases are replaced, to positive, when the penetration into a foreign market actually increases home employment. More generally, FDI will be low where unit labour costs are high compared to competing locations; this may lead to welfare losses due to high unemployment. The opposite will be the case for countries where wages are relatively low (given a certain productivity level).[28]

The impact on *wages* of FDI is not well documented.

Estimates of the welfare effects of the integration of *other capital markets* (made along the theoretical path indicated by Figures 8.2 and 8.3) resulted for the EU as a whole in a clear benefit (Price Waterhouse, 1988). Recently the benefits of a reduction in the cost of equity, bonds and bank loans have been estimated to amount to 1 per cent of EU GDP (LE/PWC 2002). The effects of the improvement of the quality of the financial services sector on growth have been estimated at only 0.2 per cent of GDP (Guiso *et al.*, 2004).

---

26   To our knowledge, no comprehensive studies have been carried out on the welfare effects of DI in the EU.
27   For instance for Italy studies referred to by Roberto (2004); for NMS: Borensztein et al. (1998); Campos and Kinoshita (2001); Goerg and Strobl (2002); Crespo and Velasquez (2003); Tondl and Vuksic (2003).
28   See Buckley and Artisien (1987); Hatzius (2000).

Summary and conclusions

- The objective of European capital market integration was initially fairly limited and for a long time remained practically restricted to direct investment; only lately has complete internal and external freedom of capital movements been installed.
- Direct investment in the EU has expanded considerably. The intra-EU pattern of DI shows a net flow from the 'core' (northern) towards the 'peripheral' (southern and eastern) member states, which has led to more convergence of wealth levels (see Chapter 16).
- Long-term and short-term loans were for a long time contracted on segmented markets. These markets have been progressively integrated both on the European and the global scale. As a consequence the percentage of foreign capital in each of the national markets in the EU countries has grown, while the price of capital in these countries has converged.
- The integration of European capital markets has produced very significant positive welfare effects, both for FDI and for long-term loans.

PART 3

Sectors of Activity

9 *Agriculture*

Introduction

The integration of the markets for goods generally refers implicitly only to manufactured goods. However, the advantages of integration do apply to the integration of agricultural produce markets too. Therefore the EU has decided right from the outset to also integrate agricultural markets.

In the first section below we will discuss in detail the principles of EU agricultural policy. The next section will give a summary description of the development of the agricultural sector under conditions of integration, detailing production levels, trade, production structure, concentration of firms and so on.

We will then give, with the help of three case studies, an idea of the workings of different EU regimes: two that are in the process of being phased out (guaranteed prices and quota) and the one that is now dominant (income support).

The regimes operated by the EU will next be evaluated from an economic point of view; in this last section we will concentrate on the welfare effects of the CAP on different segments of the economy.

To round off the chapter, a brief summary of the main findings will be given.

EU regime

RATIONALE AND PRINCIPLES

National governments have often regulated agriculture strongly. They tended to pursue four objectives: first, to protect farmers from the uncertainties of price developments; second, to make sure the country would be able to feed itself (security of food supply); third, to maintain the viability of small family businesses; and, fourth, to attain spatial planning objectives, such as maintaining a specific regional balance. To protect farmers from foreign competition and from large price fluctuations (see Box 9.1) many countries have established a policy of market control for agricultural products.

In many integration schemes agriculture has been excluded from the free traffic of goods (for example, EFTA), because the costs of adaptation were perceived to be higher than the advantages of integration. The EU has decided to integrate agriculture right from the outset. The economic motive was the strong association of the agricultural sector with the rest of the economy: differential prices for agricultural produce, affecting the cost of raw materials as well as labour cost (through food prices), lead to differential costs in other sectors and may thus disturb competition. The political motive was that, as a counterweight to the prospects the common market opened to German manufacturing industry, equivalent chances had to be created for French agriculture.

BOX 9.1
UNSTABLE MARKETS

Agricultural markets tend to be unstable – much more than, for instance, manufactured goods markets. The causes are as follows. On the demand side, agricultural products are vital necessities and so have a very low price elasticity. On the supply side, the vagaries of the weather may cause large fluctuations in production volume. Coupled with inelastic demand, this leads to large price fluctuations. The very many suppliers, by reacting simultaneously to price signals, may boost fluctuations even further. Indeed farmers are small producers compared to the size of the market. They tend to react to price changes without taking account of the underlying demand and supply changes.

An illustration of the inability of agricultural markets to achieve equilibrium is the so-called 'hog cycle', which owes its name to the German economist Hanau, who was the first to analyse the phenomenon with respect to the pig market. Figure 9.1 presents the relevant supply and demand curves. Suppose there is a sudden rise in demand (from D_1 to D_2); supply fails to adjust (it takes some time for pigs to be born and become fit for slaughter). As a consequence, the price rises to p_3 instead of p_2, which would be the new equilibrium price at which the equilibrium quantity OC would be sold. Producers considering the high price p_3 to be the long-term measure will extend the supply of pigs from OA to OB. However, demanders are not prepared to digest so much supply at that price, so that the price will drop to the p_1 level. Many producers now decide not to produce at this price; fewer pigs are raised, supply is after some time limited to OA, after which the cycle can start anew.*

---

* In its pure form the cyclical movement only occurs if the gradients of the demand and supply curves are equal. If the gradient of the demand curve is steeper than that of the supply curve, the system is explosive; that is to say, it progressively removes itself from the equilibrium; if the supply curve has a steeper gradient than the demand curve, the system converges (cobweb theorem).

The *objectives of the Common Agricultural Policy* (CAP) are:

* to increase agricultural productivity by promoting technical progress and the optimum use of production factors;
* to ensure a fair standard of living to the agricultural community by increasing their per capita income;
* to stabilise markets;
* to assure the availability of supplies;
* to ensure reasonable consumer prices.

The editors of the Treaty, realising that objectives were to some extent conflicting owing to the conflicting interests of consumers and producers, tried to give some indication of priority by the order of the points of this Article. From the position of points 1 and 2, to improve the income prospects of the producers is clearly the primary aim. We will see in subsequent sections that this has had very important consequences.

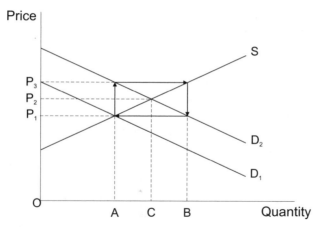

Figure 9.1   Disequilibria in agricultural markets: hog cycle

GRADUAL DEVELOPMENT OF COMMON POLICY[1]

During the 1960s and 1970s the EU agricultural policy was gradually elaborated. In line with the principles adopted, income support was the prime aim. Hence there has been a tendency under the market policy to set very high guaranteed prices. Moreover, generous support has been given to improving production structures. Together this has led to considerable overproduction (colloquially called milk lakes and food mountains). In turn, overproduction caused problems with taxpayers (in view of the very high budget outlays for stocking and subsidised sales) and with trade partners (due to the negative effects of EU-subsidised exports). So it became clear that the policy had to be reformed.

In the 1980s a number of changes were introduced that combined liberalisation and interventionist measures. The central element was the dissociation of market policy and income policy. The objective of the market order policy is to create stable and efficient markets; this implies the use of the *price instrument* for clearing the markets, maintaining some form of market regulation to stabilise prices.[2] At the end of the 1980s, the EU timidly set out on the road indicated by these proposals by introducing a system of so-called 'stabilisers' (for example, for cereals and oil seeds). They implied an automatic reduction in the intervention price in cases where the production exceeded a certain ceiling. The second element was to compensate the farmers for their loss of income by direct income support. This took away many of the welfare losses that the CAP had created for consumers (both final and intermediate) and for third countries, while limiting the losses for the taxpayer (see the final section of this chapter on welfare effects).

At the beginning of the 1990s a more fundamental change was made. The McSharry plan introduced considerable cuts in guaranteed prices (some 30 per cent for cereals), quotas for the production of milk, and a set of other measures to limit overproduction and budget outlays.[3] The reform introduced a system of direct payments to farmers in order to offset the impact of the cuts in guaranteed prices on producer incomes.

---

1   Over the years the policy has been elaborated in untold regulations, directives and decisions. For a detailed account of this policy, see Ingersent and Rayner (1999).
2   Proposals in this direction have been made by Koester and Tangermann (1976), Heidhues et al. (1978), van Riemsdijk (1972), Meester and Strijker (1985) and Tarditi (1984).
3   Much in the same way as the sugar regime, the milk system had been set up as provisional but proved to last a long time.

This was possible because in the 1990s the basis for support of the EU set-up eroded, while some new factors emerged that induced the EU to reform the CAP fundamentally (EC, 1995a).

- A need to *reduce budget outlays* and welfare losses. The Economic and Monetary Union obliges its members to observe strict criteria about their budget deficits (see Chapter 15). In view of this pressure on their national budgets political decision makers could no longer let the EU budget stay out of control due to unlimited guarantees.
- A change in the *external situation*. In the past there has been little achievement by international organisations in the regulation of world markets for agricultural products (production and trade).[4] However, in 1994, the GATT/WTO agreed on a programme for the worldwide liberalisation of trade in agricultural products. This implied the replacement of all non-tariff protection by tariffs,[5] the subsequent reduction of these tariffs by some 36 per cent, the reduction of subsidised exports by 36 per cent and, finally, the reduction of total support to the agricultural sector by 20 per cent (Tangermann, 1999).
- The enlargement of the EU by a number of Central and Eastern European countries. The agricultural sector in these countries is very important. (NMS' production is about one-third of the OMS' production.) Moreover, their prices are very low compared to the EU15 level. If the NMS were to bring their agricultural production capacity up to EU15 productivity levels, a considerable increase in production would ensue, exceeding by far the consumption levels of the enlarged EU.
- The increasing awareness of the size of the negative effects of the CAP on quality. First on the environment, notably due to pollution of the water as a consequence of the use of pesticides and chemical fertilisers (ECA, 2000). Second on animal welfare due to the confinement that industrialisation of production imposes. Third on the quality of the landscape; in areas of production it deteriorates as a consequence of the large scale and mono cultures; in areas where production is not economic by abandonment. Finally on health, mostly known due to the so called 'mad cow' and 'foot and mouth' diseases (EC, 1999a).

In the framework of the *Agenda 2000* a new reform has been agreed. This 1999 reform continued the one of 1992 (EC, 1998b) and comprised changes with respect to:

- Financial burden: the setting of a fixed ceiling for the budget outlays;
- Market support: reduction of prices[6] (ranging from 15 per cent for cereals to 20 per cent for beef); the maintenance of the quota system for milk up to 2006. As a consequence outlays for market support have decreased both in absolute terms and in relative terms (from about 90 per cent in 1991 to about 25 per cent in 2003);

---

4   Admittedly international agreements have been drawn up for certain products, aiming at some control of their world markets, so liable to great fluctuations through speculations and other causes. Such control schemes tend to be specialist in their orientation – to one product – and weak in their institutional structure. The Food and Agriculture Organisation of the UN is concerned in particular with worldwide aspects of food supply. The OECD's concern (for example, OECD, 1987d, 1996) has been of a coordinating nature (exchange of information and cautious adjustment of policy).

5   To give an indication of the external protection of the EU, 'tariffs' on wheat and beef were at some point some 150 per cent; on dairy and sugar some 300 per cent.

6   This is in line with earlier calculations about the size of the price cut to come to market equilibrium (EC, 1994a, 1995a; Tangermann, 1995).

- Income support: further increases in coverage. As a consequence expenditure on this category grew to reach some € 29 billion by 2003, or almost two thirds of total EU expenditure for agriculture;
- Multi-functionality: a role for farmers in the protection of the environment; the safety and quality of food; and the countryside.

In the course of the *2003 review* of the CAP the elements of the 1999 reform have been reconfirmed. Intervention in prices is further reduced so that market forces can play their role. Moreover, changes have been made in order to improve the delivery system for the remaining three aspects of the CAP. These implied first the introduction of a mechanism for financial discipline. Next the introduction of a system of single payments to most EU farmers; this was to be decoupled from production and related to compliance with a number of the objectives listed above under multi-functionality. Next the creation of the possibility for national governments to adapt the system to national, regional and local circumstances.

The adoption of the *CAP by the NMS* has been done on the basis of the reformed CAP. After much debate (EC, 2002a) it was agreed that the NMS would not benefit from price support, participate in the system of quotas for the relevant products and phase in the system of income support.

THE OLD SYSTEM: THE POLICY OF MARKET CONTROL

The common European policy of market control has been based on three *principles*,[7] important enough to be discussed in detail.

- *Unity of the market* implies, first, the free internal traffic of agricultural products (that is to say, no customs tariffs), second, the protection of the outer frontiers and third the harmonisation of national instructions with respect to health control and veterinary care.
- *Priority for EU's own products*. The needs of the market are in the first instance provided for by European production; only if that is insufficient will imports be resorted to.
- *Financial solidarity* among member states. A policy of market control yields (levies) as well as costs money (restitutions, storage costs and so on). All payments are made into and from the European Agricultural Guidance and Guarantee Fund, Guarantee Division (EAGGF). Because in general agricultural expenditure exceeds receipts, the European Agricultural Fund is fed additionally by the EU's other own financial means (see Chapter 4).

The common market regulation is not the same for all products. The three most important types of market control system operated by the CAP are the following:[8]

- *Outlet guarantee/intervention price*. This type of scheme guarantees a minimum price at which intervention agencies will buy up any domestic supply, the quantities involved

---

7   Another principle introduced by the Treaty is that agricultural production is largely exempted from the rules for competition that govern all other product and service markets (see Chapter 14).

8   Another interventionist strategy introduced by the EU is to regulate quantities in order to limit the use of the production factor, land. One option used is to pay the farmer for not using his land; crop-specific measures are a variation on the same theme. One such measure which has already been in operation for some time is that the area under viniculture is not allowed to expand.

being stored and sold when the market situation is favourable. It applied to by far the greater part of production – namely, cereals, sugar and dairy products.[9]

- *Quota.* In order to restrain production to levels that cover about internal consumption while nevertheless paying high support prices, an intervention in quantities is necessary. Right from the start of the CAP such production quota have been introduced for sugar; since the 1980s the system has also applied to milk.
- *Bonuses.* For some products, for instance those for which international agreements allow no protection at the border, a system of subsidies is applied. Such a system allows domestic production to be maintained at high producer costs, consumer prices being kept low nevertheless. It was applied, for instance, to oilseeds on the value of the produce. In other cases, subsidies by quantity produced, hectare cultivated or number of cattle are offered.

These different schemes have widely divergent welfare effects, depending on the domestic price level and the differences between the domestic guaranteed prices and the world market prices (see the three case studies hereafter).

THE COMPLEMENTARY SYSTEM: STRUCTURAL POLICY

If the EU policy of market control was worked out rather rapidly, things were different as far as structural policy was concerned. Given the pluriform production conditions and national regulations, until the early 1970s the Commission practically confined itself to some coordination of the member states' structural policies. The impulse towards a genuine European structural policy for agriculture was given by the so-called 'Mansholt Plan' (EC, 1968). Some relevant decisions were made around 1972, and from then on this policy has been gradually extended. The long-term aim of structural policy is to enhance the productivity of agricultural enterprise, an aim that derives directly from the first objective of agricultural policy. The main aspects of the structural policy as it has been pursued over the past decades are as follows:

Support to management means supporting investments aimed at technical progress, the improvement of education and training and of infrastructure, the realisation of re-allotment schemes and the building up of a network of consulting agencies.

Improving sales channels and processing of agricultural products involved dairy factories, slaughterhouses, packing establishments for fruit and vegetables, wine-bottling establishments, auction rooms, cold-storage warehouses and so on.

At the end of the 1990s the structural policy received a new impetus from the set-up of a European *rural development policy*. This puts the accent more on sustainability in environmental terms, on the diversity (non-food) and quality of the production, on animal welfare, on the preservation of genetic resources and on the social fabric of the rural areas (EC, 1998b, 1999a).[10]

The EU measures sketched above are not the only ones to be taken to improve the European agricultural structure. The main responsibility is still with the member states, as is apparent from the considerable expenditures on agriculture incurred by the national budgets.

9　There is a variant of this regime that uses only limited free price formation with the world market screened off. This type of scheme has been introduced for certain kinds of fruit and vegetables, flowers, eggs and poultry meat. These products do not count as basic foods and often have a short production cycle, which is why guarantee prices are not judged necessary and constraining the imports by levies and restrictions is thought sufficient. There were market schemes for pork, certain fruits and vegetables, and table wine, that put the emphasis on storage and processing support rather than on an automatic sales guarantee at fixed prices.

10　For an analysis of the economics of the new EU rural policy, see Mahe and Ortalo-Magne (1999).

The costs of the European structural policy are paid from the EAGGF, Guidance Division. In practice this often means that the EAGGF finances a certain proportion of a programme's total costs. That proportion is on average small in so-called 'strong' areas, but may be as high as 65 per cent in so-called 'weak' areas. The Guidance Division has considerable sums at its disposal, especially in comparison to the expenditures of the EU for other sectors of economic activity.

THE NEW SYSTEM: INCOME SUPPORT

The common European organisations of agricultural markets have many negative welfare effects (see subsequent sections). In order to do away with these negative effects the system of market support has been abandoned. Instead a new system of income support to farmers has been put in place. In the first instance these support levels were in different ways tied to production or capacity levels, and had the intention of compensating farmers for income losses due to the reduction of market support. The 2003 reform decouples income from production by introducing a single farm payment scheme. Farmers can decide what to produce according to market conditions. The income support is subjected to compliance with certain food safety and environmental standards. The NMS are to be gradually phased into these schemes; they have started with income allowances amounting to 25 per cent of the EU15 level; these will go up to 100 per cent in 2013. In order to limit the administrative burden and the risk of fraud, the NMS may start to apply simplified versions of the system.

Sketch of the sector

THE SECTOR AS A WHOLE

From the fact that agricultural policy is the EU's most elaborate policy area and has always been the focus of interest, one might presume that this sector is the most important in the EU economy. That was true in the distant past, but industry and, later, services have grown to a prominent position, reducing agriculture to a relatively modest position. Table 9.1 shows the steep drop in the relative significance of agriculture in the EU economy over the past half century.

Table 9.1 Percentage share of agriculture in total GDP and total employment of the EU, 1950–2003

Indicator	1950	1960	1970	1980	1990	2000	2003[a]	2003[b]
GDP	12	8	6	4	3	2	2	2
Employment	30	21	13	10	7	4	4	5

Notes: [a] *1950-2003: EU15* [b] *2003: EU25*

Sources: *GDP: Eurostat, OECD, National Accounts, various years; Molle et al. (1980). Employment: 1950–70 Molle et al. (1980); 1970–98 OECD, Labour Force Statistics, various years, some estimations.*

At the moment, about 2 per cent of total GDP is produced by the agricultural sector, with only 5 per cent of the total active population of the EU25 still employed in agriculture. In the 1950s these figures were six times as high. In those years the shares of agriculture differed widely among the countries of Europe (very high in Italy, France and other Mediterranean countries such as Spain, Portugal and Greece; modest in the UK). At the moment these differences are small within the EU15; they are fairly modest between the EU 15 and most NMS. Only Poland stands out with a share of some 12 per cent of the active population still in agriculture. This will change with the extension of the EU to 27 members; in 2000 Bulgaria and Romania had over 5 million people employed in agriculture, representing one third of their active population.

The main cause of the relative reduction of the agricultural share in the economy is the low income elasticity for food products. Indeed, as incomes rise, people tend to spend a smaller portion on food. Typical income elasticities in the EU are around 0.2 only, and for some products elasticity is even negative. Because the cost of food is increasingly made up of such industrial activities as processing, packaging and presentation, the share of agricultural products in the economy is even smaller than the elasticities seem to imply.

SUB-SECTORS

The broad sector of agriculture hitherto referred to falls into some important branches: (1) arable farming (cereals); (2) livestock farming (meat, milk, dairy products); (3) horticulture (vegetables, fruit, flowers and so on); (4) viniculture; (5) forestry (timber); and finally (6) fishing.[11] Each of them can be sub-divided into product groups. Table 9.2 shows the relative importance of each of these groups. It also indicates the stability of the shares of all the groups through time. Although there are many differences between agriculture in the EU15 and in the NMS, the broad structure of production in both is fairly similar (see the last two columns of Table 9.2).

Table 9.2   Percentage share of selected product groups in the total production value of EU agriculture, 1974–2002

Product		1974	1980	1990	2002a	2002b
1	Cereals (mainly wheat)	12	12	11	12	12
2.1	Dairy (mainly milk)	19	19	18	14	14
2.2	Meat (mainly beef and pork)	31	32	30	26	27
3	Vegetables, fruit, olives	13	14	15	23	22
4	Wine	4	5	6	5	5
5	Other	21	18	20	20	20

Source: CEC, *The Agricultural Situation in the EU*, Brussels, various years, 1974–80 EU9; 1990 EU12; 2002a EU15; 2002b EU25 .

SIZE OF FARMS

The structure of the agricultural market is characterised by almost perfect competition on the side of supply. Table 9.3 gives an indication of the evolution of the number of suppliers, in this case the number of farms. The picture excludes very small holdings, which are often run as side activities.

---

11   The fishery policy of the EU has some very distinctive characteristics. Interested readers are referred to Holden (1994) or EC (2003a).

Table 9.3   Development of the number and size of farms (agricultural establishments), EUª, 1960-2003

	EU10						EU15	
	1960	1970	1980	1990	2000	2003ᵇ	1990	2000
Number of holdings larger than								
1 ha (million)	8.1	6.6	5.5	4.7	-	-	-	-
2 ha (million)	-	-	-	3.6	3.4	3.1	4.9	4.2
Average size of holdings (in ha)								
Larger than 1 ha	11	14	16	17	-	-	-	-
Larger than 2 ha	-	-	-	18	21	22	18	24

Notes: ª *No comparable figures available for EU25.* ᵇ *Contains 2003 data for EU9 and 2000 data for Greece.*

Source: *Eurostat, Yearbook of Agricultural Statistics, various years; Statistical Yearbook, various years; some estimates.*

National and EU measures to improve the structure were among the causes of a rapid decline in the number of establishments in the past half century, by some 50 per cent. The figures on average size in Table 9.3 indicate that in particular the smaller farms have been closed down or taken over, or have had their land put to another use. As a consequence the average farm size doubled between 1960 and 2003. At present agricultural production in the EU15 is dominated by large farms. In 2000, holdings with more than 10 hectares represented 50 per cent of the number of farms and 90 per cent of the total agricultural land area. Holdings with more than 100 hectares represented 6 per cent of the number of farms but 43 per cent of the land.

There exist traditionally large differences between the EU member countries in average farm size. In countries such as Greece, Portugal and Italy the share of small holdings was one and a half times that of the EU15. Even larger differences exist now between the EU15 and the NMS.

Case study 1: guaranteed prices – cereals

REGULATORY FRAMEWORK

The common market organisation for cereals was created in 1962. It was based on intervention and external protection. Intervention consisted basically of the setting of an intervention price at which producers could sell unlimited quantities. External protection was based on variable levies and restitutions to compensate for the difference between world market prices and domestic prices. At the beginning of the 1960s wheat prices were highest in Germany and lowest in France. Because of the German position, the EU price finally resulting was well above the average of all other countries. Since among the objectives of the EU agricultural policy, farmers' income has pride of place, it is hardly surprising that intervention prices have been set as high as possible; and over time moved to levels well above world market level (p_3 in Figure 9.2).

The way in which this scheme of market control works and the effect it produces on various internal (national or EU) guaranteed and world market prices is shown in Figure 9.2. With the help of this figure we will depict the negative economic effects (lack of market equilibrium and increasing budget cost) of the political dynamics of the system. In Figure 9.2 S_{com} is the EU supply curve, which runs rather a level course, implying that a price increase causes a somewhat more than proportional production rise. D_{com} is the demand curve, drawn as rather precipitous, in concordance with the inelasticity of demand for most agricultural products.

We distinguish the following sequence of price setting:

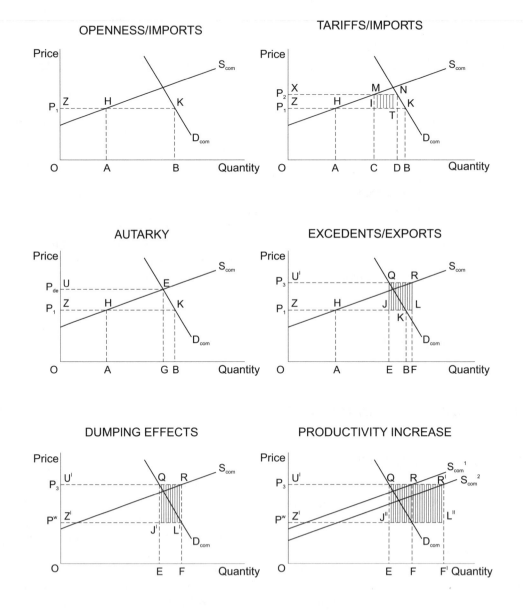

Figure 9.2   EU market regulation system for major agricultural products (guaranteed prices)

- The price on the world market is p_1, at which price any quantity wanted can be obtained (fully elastic supply). In an entirely open economy, domestic production will now become OA, domestic demand OB, and a quantity AB will be imported, everything at the price p_1. The domestic agricultural production is low in that case; so are consumer prices. Government subsidies do not apply, so the taxpayer is not asked for a contribution (left-hand upper part of Figure 9.2).

- At a guaranteed price p_2, domestic production will rise to OC and demand drop to OD. On the quantity imported, CD, an import levy of $p_2 - p_1$ will be imposed to make prices on the world and EU markets equal. That yields CD x $(p_2 - p_1)$ in tariff revenue (which can be translated into a relief for taxpayers in case total receipts are fixed), the shaded area IMNT in the right-hand upper part of Figure 9.2. The consumer is worse off: he consumes less at higher prices (consumer loss ZXNK, deadweight loss TNK). The farmer's gross return, achieved in one transaction, namely through selling to the intervention authority, will amount to OXMC. The area ZXMH represents an extra producer rent transferred to farmers from consumers (HMI deadweight loss).

- The price pde implies domestic equilibrium between supply and demand. This price level can be sustained without creating surpluses and without EU budget expenses to be borne finally by the taxpayer, albeit at a cost to consumers (left-hand middle part of Figure 9.2).

- At a price p_3, the situation changes profoundly, however. Demand will drop to OE, entailing an additional loss in consumer surplus. As supply rises to OF, market authorities have to buy up a quantity OF – OE at price p_3. That quantity has to be sold (in practice dumped) on the world market, which implies an export subsidy (or 'restitution' in EU jargon) of the difference between the guaranteed price (or intervention price) p_3 and the world market price p_1. The amount is JQRL, which is charged to the taxpayer. The gross return to the farmer, achieved in one transaction through the selling of production to the intervention authority, will amount to OU'RF (right-hand middle part of Figure 9.2).

- At price p_3 the extra supply that the EU dumps on world markets will decrease the world market price to pw. The internal market situation in the EU remains the same but the budget costs are considerable: the amount that has now to be paid to get rid of surpluses increases to the area J'QRL' (left-hand bottom part of Figure 9.2).

- At price p_3 the EU stops further price increases in order to limit further increases in budget cost. It does incur, however, the efficiency effects of its support to structural improvements. They lead to a downwards shift in the supply curve, that is represented by Scom' in the right-hand bottom part of Figure 9.2. As a consequence supply increases to OF'. Assuming demand and world prices stay the same, the cost to the budget doubles to J"QR'L".

The phasing out of the system has more or less been done according to a reverse of the sequence given. Prices decreased from p_3 to p_2 (assuming WTO rules permit a tariff of p_2-p_1). The demand curve has not changed much. However, the decrease in the supply curve is permanent and may in future even be accentuated.

BRANCH CHARACTERISTICS

On average EU prices have been almost double the world market ones over the years 1970–90. This does not mean, however, that European consumers have paid twice as much for their bread as they would have done without the CAP price system. As has been explained in the previous section, prices on the world market have been negatively influenced by the EU system. In the past decade prices in Europe have been lowered and hence European exports have dropped. As a consequence, prices on the world market have recovered.

Where domestic production is below the equilibrium levels of domestic supply and demand (upper part of Figure 9.2) the self-sufficiency ratio (SSR) is below 100. On the other hand, where domestic production exceeds domestic demand (middle and bottom parts of Figure 9.2) the SSR is above 100. For the period since 1960, Table 9.4 indicates the SSR for a set of important products, that are indicative for their categories.[12]

Table 9.4   Self-sufficiency ratio[a] of the EU for selected agricultural products, 1960–2000[b] (index)

Product	1960	1973	1974	1981	1990	2000	2000[a]
Wheat	90	111	103	117	127	116	113
Maize	64	67	58	66	77	97	100
Sugar	104	116	91	135	128	137	131
Wine	89	101	99	102	112	113	n.a.
Butter	101	118	101	120	121	n.a.	n.a.
Powdered milk	139	191	208	411	272	n.a.	n.a.
Beef	92	85	92	105	101	103	n.a.

Notes: [a] Bear in mind, in interpreting the SS-rates, that many of them are much too low, because the EU includes in demand the quantities which it has been forced to sell on the internal market to low-grade users and at special prices. [b] 1960–73: EU6; 1974–81: EU9; 1985: EU12; 1996, 2000 EU15, 2000a: EU25. n.a. = not available.

Sources: Eurostat, Basic Community Statistics; Yearbook of Agricultural Statistics; Statistical Yearbook Agriculture; Supply Balances; Animal Production and Crop Production; Quarterly Statistics; The Agricultural Situation in the EU, various issues.

The table shows the relevance of the sequence of Figure 9.2. Before the enlargement of 1973, the EU increased its self-sufficiency for many products to a considerable degree. The first enlargement entailed a drop in self-sufficiency for the EU9, due mostly to the UK's position as a large importer of many agricultural products. In the decade thereafter production of practically all commodities grew considerably; as a consequence the EU had by 1984 again become a net exporter of many of the products mentioned in the table. The extension of the EU to 12 countries first and to 15 next did not affect this situation very much. The latest years' figures for wheat show that the policy changes have gradually produced their intended effects as SSR have decreased. The latest figures also show that the accession of the NMS does not change the average picture very much.

---

12   For instance, the figures for wheat are very similar to those for rye and barley; the figures for butter similar to those for cheese, while the figures for beef are similar to those for pork and poultry.

Case study 2: production quotas – milk

REGULATORY FRAMEWORK

EU production of milk has for quite some time been regulated on the basis of price support. However, when in the early 1980s surpluses rose very quickly and several measures to curb production proved ineffective, a quota system was introduced. The system involves the fixing of maximum production levels for each country and, within each country, setting a maximum authorised production level for every farmer.[13] The advantage of quota schemes is principally to reduce budget cost. This is illustrated by Figure 9.3. At an intervention price of p_3, production will be at OF and demand at OE, the difference between the two being exported with a subsidy of $p_3 - p_1$ (intervention price minus world market price) at a cost of $JQRL$ to the budget. Introducing a quota system that limits total quantity to OW for the whole of the EU limits the budget cost to $JQTU$ (horizontally shaded in Figure 9.3). It also eases the strain on external relations because the quantity exported to (in practice dumped on) world markets is reduced by WF. However, under this quota system, the loss of consumer surplus remains at $ZSQK$ (the same as before in Figure 9.2), of which JQK is deadweight loss. The deadweight loss on the producer side diminishes by about $UYRL$; as some of the most inefficient producers will continue to produce their quota while some efficient producers have to cut down, the exact amount depends on the share each group has in the quota.

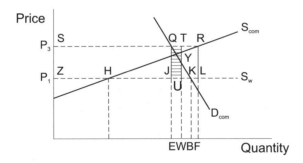

Figure 9.3   The effect of quotas

BRANCH CHARACTERISTICS

The milk market is specific in the sense that virtually all milk is sold from farms to a relatively small number of processing plants. This feature allows production to be controlled at the individual farm level. Had this market structure not prevailed in the milk sector, it would have been almost impossible to uphold a quota system. The device that is used to limit foreign producers' access to the EU market used to be the variable import duty and is now (since the GATT/WTO round) a tariff. Between 1995 and 2000 this tariff (p_3–p_1 or TU in Figure 9.3) has been reduced by 36 per cent.

---

13   For the origins, see Petit et al. (1987) and for more details EC (1997a).

Case study 3: income support

REGULATORY FRAMEWORK

The income support schemes introduced by the CAP reforms are not a novelty in a theoretical nor in a practical sense. A variant of the system used to be applied, among other countries, in the UK, where it was known as the scheme of *deficiency payments*.[14] However, EU income support schemes are a novelty in a systemic sense because no other socio-economic group receives direct income support from the EU. In an economic sense they are actually an oddity as the application of the subsidiarity principle or the rules of fiscal federalism would rather speak against the adoption of such a system. We will illustrate the workings of this system with the help of Figure 9.4.

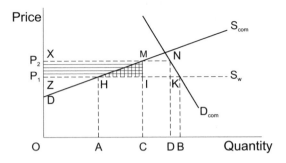

Figure 9.4   Income support schemes (deficiency payments)

- At a price p_1 (world market price or world market price plus tariff) demand will be OB and domestic production OA. The consumer enjoys high quantities OB at a low price and the government's (taxpayers') resources are not tapped. Farmer incomes come entirely from the sales of products. Only a few farmers are efficient, so incomes (triangle DZH) will be low.
- A country wanting to maintain production on marginal lands and or increase farmers' income will grant farmers a kind of subsidy. This can be made dependent on production. A subsidy of $p_2 - p_1$ will entail a domestic supply of OC and imports of CB. The price remains low for all consumers: p1. The taxpayer contributes ZXMI. The farmer's gross return consists of two parts: the market part OZIC and the subsidy part ZXMI. Even less costly is a system that is related not to the production volume but to the difference in cost and revenue. With such a system, based on information on production cost of groups of farms, producers in the OA range would not receive any subsidy, producers at point C the full subsidy $p_2 - p_1$, and producers in the AC range a subsidy that would be just sufficient to cover their cost. Costs to the government (taxpayer): the triangle HMI. Because with this system farmers' income support and price policies remain largely separate, a pressure strong enough to push up subsidies to orders of magnitude of $p_3 - p_1$ is not likely to build up easily. In the EU the total cost to the budget has been fixed. Assume that this limit

---

14   Such payments can be compared with production subsidies for industrial products, in cases where they serve a protectionist aim: to increase home production. For a detailed study of the effects of various schemes of income support to farmers, see OECD (1983b).

equals the area ZXMI. Any increase in the basis (OC) would then have to be compensated by a decrease in the subsidy per unit (XZ).

BRANCH CHARACTERISTICS

The EU policy differentiates according to size of farms, type of region, products and so on (for instance, tons per hectare for cereal producers, on livestock numbers for beef producers).

The production of oilseeds has increased tenfold over the period 1970–91, as a consequence of an expansion of the cultivated area and a very high increase in productivity. Expenditure to the budget increased in line with production. In order to limit budget problems (and thus production) the system has been made subject to maximum guaranteed amounts. Demand has also developed also and has been able to easily absorb this increased production. Even imports have grown in absolute terms. So the EU situation can best be represented by Figure 9.4 (with the exception of rape oil).

Welfare effects

LIMITED EFFECTS ON POLICY OBJECTIVES FOR THE AGRICULTURAL SECTOR

The common agricultural policy has a very controversial record.[15] On the positive side one remarks that it has realised its objectives on many points. In this respect we can mention that *productivity* has been increased, and that the sector has adapted to new technological possibilities. However, on the other objectives the scores are less positive.

A first objective of the CAP is to improve *farmers' incomes*. These have increased at about the same rate as those in the rest of the economy. On the negative side, however, one sees that the support to farm income has been extremely unequal. Indeed under the old regime 20 per cent of the European farms received 80 per cent of the EU money (EC, 1994a). This was a direct consequence of the EU system of market support. As CAP support was tied to production levels, most money goes to the largest farms. They represent only 20 per cent of the total. Yet from a perspective of income support these farms were least in need, as they produced generally at relatively low cost, so could create a good margin. For the other 80 per cent of farms things are quite different; they are small to very small holdings (less than 5 ha) that have to produce at high cost and hence create only a small margin. Small margin times small production level creates only a small total income. The new system of income support has not solved this problem. Recent figures (EC, 2002b; OECD, 2003) show that the distribution still confirms the 20-80 rule. So the switch in regime has not produced an improvement on this score. The explanation is that the income support system works out on the basis of criteria that are related to size. A final remark in this respect concerns the NMS. Support levels there are only gradually to be adapted to the EU15 levels which means that for some time to come the least support is given to the poorest brackets of farmers in the enlarged EU.

Another objective of the CAP is to *stabilise markets and safeguard supply*. Internal EU markets have indeed been stabilised in the sense that the play of supply and demand has been smoothened. Production has grown rapidly, ensuring a continuous supply. However, on another interpretation of the word 'stabilise' the record is negative. Large excess supplies

---

15   So the evaluation of the CAP, even on its own stated objectives, is that it has only in part been effective and in total extremely inefficient (Winters, 1990). For a more recent critical evaluation, see EC (2004j).

are a reflection of this failure. The regime changes have tried to solve these problems. The abolition of price guarantees has indeed worked out in this way. On the contrary, the record of the *quota system* to match supply with demand gives mixed feelings (Tangermann, 1984; EC, 1997a). In terms of the prime target set (which was to curb budget outlays) the system has performed satisfactorily. By the end of the 1990s outlays for the milk sector were less than 10 per cent of total agricultural market support compared to 30 per cent in 1980. However, on other scores the evaluation is less favourable. First, excess production continued (*QT* or *EW* in Figure 9.3), partly due to the rise in *productivity*, while demand is about stable. Second, there is the very heavy administrative burden (deadweight loss) of the system. Third, the existing market situations become fossilised and entry by newcomers blocked. Fourth, farms holding production authorisations claim rents that are not economically justified. Fifth, existing producers benefit from windfall gains provided by the sale, rent or lease of quota. As the higher values of quota have also had an upward effect on land prices, alternative uses of land have been frustrated. Finally, the system is particularly vulnerable to fraud; a famous case has been Italy which, due to administrative laxity, failed to comply with EU restrictions. It has been condemned by the European Court to pay a considerable fine. Unfortunately, these negative aspects will persist for some time as the system's complete abolition is foreseen for the year 2006.

CONSIDERABLE WELFARE LOSSES AND DISTRIBUTIONAL PROBLEMS FOR THE NON-AGRICULTURAL SECTOR

On the negative side one remarks that the attempt to keep up agricultural incomes by boosting price levels has led to a large overproduction: surpluses which could only be disposed of at very considerable cost. These have created enormous welfare losses. We can detail these as follows:

A first group of losers in the EU were *consumers,* because they have paid more for their products than necessary (see Figure 9.2 for the theoretical effect). The objective of the CAP is to set reasonable prices for consumers. The agricultural ministers who have been responsible for decisions on prices have apparently thought that high was still reasonable. However, they implied a very high cost to the EU consumer; estimated to amount to some € 250 per person per year (Kol and Kuypers, 1996; OECD, 1996). The reality is even worse than indicated by this average welfare loss. Indeed because food is a primary need for everybody, poor people spend a higher percentage of their total budget on food than rich people. It means that poor people also pay a higher percentage of their budget to support farmers than rich people. So the EU price support system has effectively worked out as a degressive income tax (Tarditi and Zanias, 2001).

A second group of losers in the EU were taxpayers. If consumers paid too much for products they needed, taxpayers paid for production nobody really wanted. The total cost of the CAP incurred by the European taxpayers can be estimated with the help of the analysis of the total expenditure for agriculture from the EU budget (Table 9.5). Since the end of the 1990s expenditure amounts to over € 40 billion; this implies a cost of some € 150 per head a year.[16] Note that the CAP regime changes that have been operated in order to take away many

---

16   See again Kol and Kuypers (1996) and OECD (1996). This is actually not the total cost as we need to add to the cost of the CAP the cost of national support schemes. The total of these outlays amounted in the mid-1980s to some 3 per cent of GDP; as a result of restrictive measures it is now some 1.5 per cent of GDP. If we compare this with the total contribution of agriculture to GDP (Table 9.1), one sees how large the distortions in allocation are. Indeed, on average some 50 per cent of agricultural production values stemmed from subsidies (47 per cent for wheat, 63 per cent for milk and 52 per cent for oilseeds). For some products this figure went up as high as 90 per cent (OECD, 1996).

of its negative effects are of little or no help to the taxpayer. They change the composition of the agri-budget but not the total outlays for agriculture; the burden to the taxpayer does not decrease significantly. A final remark concerns the distributional effects of the CAP for taxpayers. As poor countries tended to contribute more to the budget than they received in CAP support, the CAP had a perverse effect on distribution. However, this effect has in the meantime been largely annihilated.[17]

To wrap up, the CAP involves considerable welfare losses. The transfers of taxpayers and consumers (which amount to about € 100 billion a year) reach only to a very limited extent the target group (price support for 25 per cent, income support for 50 per cent), the rest is absorbed by all sorts of elements in the chain (input suppliers and landowners). The irrationality of the policy is illustrated by the fact that transfers make up 40 per cent of farmers' incomes and nearly 100 per cent of the total net value added produced by the sector. And the cost mentioned is not all; one needs to add the cost of national measures in favour of the sector and for the administration of many control and support programmes (EC, 2004l).

Table 9.5   Expenditure (in billion euro) on the European Agricultural Guidance and Guarantee Fund, 1970–2005

	1970	1980	1990[a]	2000[a]	2005[a]
1 Guarantee	2.0	11.2	29.2	36.6	37.6
2 Guidance	—	0.4	1.6	4.3	4.4
3 EAGGF	2.0	11.6	30.8	40.9	42.0
4 Total budget	2.4	16.8	49.1	92.0	106.3
3 as a percentage of 4	85	69	63	44	40

Note: [a] *Budget.*

Sources: EC, The Agricultural Situation in the Community, various years; Financial Forecast for the EU 2000– 2006. EC, General Budget of the European Union for the Financial Year 2005. EC, The Agricultural Situation in the European Union: 2002 Report.

Apart from the internal losses in the EU, the CAP creates losses to *third countries,*[18] many of them developing countries. In so far as they are net exporters, they have faced two problems: first, poorer prospects of exporting to the EU; and, second, lower revenues from their sales to world markets because of dumping by the EU. The predicament is serious, for it has brought the EU into conflict not only with developed countries like the USA (about cereals, for example) but also with developing countries which depend very much on the revenues of their exports (of sugar, for example) to pay their imports.[19] Thus the beneficial effects of EU development policy (see Chapter 17) have been partly undone by the detrimental external effects of the

---

[17]   The total cost to the taxpayer is not the only bone of contention; the distribution of the tax burden is another one. We recall that the burden of the budget is shared equally by the member states (see Chapter 4). The benefits of the CAP, however, tended to go to member states with a high national SSR (Strijker and de Veer, 1988). In some studies attempts have been made to measure these redistributive effects of the budget (Buckwell et al., 1982; Koester, 1977; Rollo and Warwick, 1979). The group of states with low national SSRs being relatively poor, large compensation amounts needed to be paid out to them.

[18]   See, among others, Tims (1987); Hine (1992); Zietz and Valdés (1986); and Valdés and Zietz (1995).

[19]   It has been estimated that the so-called 'Cairns group' of countries (composed of Argentina, Australia, Brazil, Canada, Chile, Colombia, Fiji, Philippines, Hungary, Indonesia, Malaysia, New Zealand, Thailand and Uruguay), who have a comparative advantage in agricultural production, have missed in this way some 50 per cent of their potential revenue from exports (Tyers, 1994).

CAP. On the other hand, the complete abolition of the EU protective system would favour the LDCs as a group only slightly. One reason is that the recovery of world market prices is to the detriment of the many LDCs who are themselves importers of food. Some doubts prevail about the stability of the recovery of world market prices and hence also about the net effects of the EU policy change on the LDCs as a group.

ADVERSE EFFECTS ON OTHER EU POLICY OBJECTIVES

The effects of the CAP also need to be seen in the framework of its effects on other EU policy areas. The effects of the CAP are in general not very positive. We will mention the following:

Allocation The CAP has led to a serious *misallocation of production factors and resources*. Agriculture and the industry producing inputs for it are using up resources that could have been better employed elsewhere. Biotechnological industries have had difficulties developing, among other reasons because their input prices were too high (sugar, for instance).[20] A considerable area of agricultural land, which could have been used for other products (wood, for instance, which is in very short supply in the EU) or for nature reserves, is tied up in useless production. In some countries, the high product prices have even led to the further extension of agricultural land at the expense of ecologically valuable areas. Moreover, the large claims agriculture makes on the budget frustrate the development of other EU programmes. Next, efficient allocation is seriously harmed, as the CAP has been found to be very susceptible to *fraud*.

Cohesion The objective of the EU is the balanced development of the different parts of its territory, in particular the peripheral areas with low incomes (see Chapter 16). In the beginning of the CAP, support levels were particularly high for so called northern products (for example, wheat). It implied a redistribution of income from the poorer regions that imported these products (such as Portugal) to the richer northern regions that produced them. With the shift of attention of market support to other products first and the shift from market support to income support next, this situation has changed. At the moment the implied redistribution of CAP spending benefits the lower income regions most; so it contributes to cohesion (Molle, forthcoming).

Environment Finally we have to account for the damage done to the environment, to health and to the scenery. To eradicate these negative effects, costly programmes have been necessary, for instance for the purification of polluted water. We do not know of welfare estimates of these effects but they add to an already very negative balance.

Summary and conclusions

- While under the EU regime a liberal spirit predominates, in the sense that market forces are to take care of the orientation of production and the price mechanism is to play its full role, the sector of agriculture has been set apart and is in fact intensely regulated.
- Heavy pressure has been brought to bear by the farmers – the directly interested – to create mechanisms for the transfer of money from both consumers and taxpayers to themselves. This has given rise to large welfare losses. The codification of rules in the Treaty of Rome

---

20   An example is Western Germany. For this country it was estimated that the liberalisation of the agricultural sector would entail some 3 per cent extra growth and a considerable increase in employment.

has made it politically extremely difficult to realise the structural reforms of the CAP that were imposed on economic grounds.[21]

- Since the mid 1980s the CAP has been fundamentally reformed. Market support (mainly in the form of guaranteed prices) has been reduced. A system of income support to farmers has been put in place. Finally, the structural policy has been transformed into a rural development policy.

- The objectives of the reforms were to do away with the negative welfare effects of the CAP. The record of reform is positive for three of them, viz. consumers, third countries and other policies (such as environment). No improvement can be seen on two scores. First, the level of the absolute budget cost remains the same, so no relief for taxpayers. Second, no improvement is observed in equality of the distribution of farm incomes.

---

21   See Pelkmans (1985) and Petit et al. (1987) for early assessments of the political economy reasons that have made it extremely difficult to reform the CAP.

10 *Manufacturing*

Introduction

The industrial sector is at the heart of most integration schemes as these tend to begin with the integration of the market for manufactured goods. However, this market integration is to be followed by policy integration. Indeed, given the importance of the industrial sector for the growth of the economy, most countries have pursued a national industrial policy. As these tended to lead to distortions in the common market, a European framework was needed.

The way in which the EU has regulated the integration of the manufacturing sector will be discussed in the next section.[1] After that, we will give a concise description of the structural development under conditions of international integration (highlighting such aspects as specialisation, concentration and firm structure). This will be followed by case studies of the dynamics of two branches (steel and motor cars). To complete this chapter we will devote a section to price convergence. In the final section we will recall briefly the most important features of the analysis.

EU regime

RATIONALE AND PRINCIPLES

The importance of the manufacturing industry for the welfare of a nation has induced many governments to pursue policies to foster industrial development.[2] The theoretical justification for such policies (which is also applicable to other sectors) are to be found both in the failure of markets and in the failure of government interventions in other areas (see Chapter 14). There existed several *national models* of industrial policies,[3] with varying levels of effectiveness.

*   The Rhineland model favoured public–private cooperation and networks of companies and public institutions to favour sustained growth.

---

1 Manufacturing is also subject to coordination efforts of other international organisations. The developed ('industrial') countries have formalised their international industrial cooperation in the OECD. Since its foundation, this organisation has carried out comparative studies, collected statistics of various sectors and compared national policies with respect to industry (and technology). The UNIDO (United Nations Industrial Development Organisation) stimulates industrial development in third-world countries by exchanging information and supporting projects.

2 Industrial policy is not well defined; some authors adopt a narrow definition, others a very broad definition, encompassing parts of macro policy, trade policy, competition policy and so on. We have chosen to define industrial policy as the set of government measures aimed directly at firms from the manufacturing sector with the objective of enhancing their development and their structural adjustment to new conditions of worldwide competition. To that end, young sectors are stimulated, the conditions of mature sectors guarded, and old sectors assisted in their restructuring.

3 These models are not only relevant for industrial policies, but have major components of social policy such as industrial relations (see Chapter 16).

- The Anglo-Saxon model was based on stimulating competitiveness by more general measures such as low tax levels and deregulation.
- The Mediterranean model relied very heavily on state intervention, public enterprise, support to national champions and so on.

The European integration process has taken away the instruments with which national governments furthered industrial development through state intervention. This applied notably to the Rhineland and Mediterranean models. The common commercial policy has taken away the instrument of external protection; the European competition policy has done the same with instruments such as state aids and government procurement, while the completion of the internal market policy took away the instruments for setting technical standards. The capacity for national industrial policies is further eroded by internationalisation and technical progress that leads to an increase in scale; indeed the scale of many new projects (as in aeronautics) is now such that it goes far beyond the capacity of one national state.

In order to cope with market failures there is a case for an EU industrial policy. In this way it is possible to recover at the European level the capacity to intervene that is lost at the national level. However, for quite some time it has been unclear how such a policy had to be shaped given the large differences between member countries with respect to the objectives and instruments. After some hesitation the EU agreed, in the 1990s, on the principles of an EU industrial policy dealing with structural improvements.

MARKET CONTROL POLICY: PRICES AND QUANTITIES

The EU market for industrial products is governed by the play of market forces. The EU does not regulate the prices and quantities. Although from time to time proposals have been made to give the Commission or the national states the authority to make such interventions, the practice has gone in a different direction. Price controls, where they still existed, were abandoned. There is of course some indirect influence of EU and national governments on markets. One example is competition policy: the Treaties give ample power to the EU to prevent companies taking action affecting trade negatively within the EU or abusing dominant positions (Chapter 14). Another is external trade: foreign producers have access to the EU market, subject to the rules of the Common Commercial Policy (see Chapter 17). However, such policies do not constitute market intervention in the proper sense.

There has been one exception to this rule. The ECSC Treaty permitted a far-reaching market regulation policy for the steel sector, allowing certain interventions in prices and quantities such as minimum prices, national production quotas, import restrictions and so on. In the past these powers have only been used in very particular instances (see the case study later in this chapter). As the ECSC Treaty expired in 2002, this instrument is no longer available.

STRUCTURAL POLICY

The *legal basis* of the EU industrial policy has developed only gradually. Nowhere does the EEC Treaty mention an industrial policy in the sense of setting the course for and stimulating structural development of the manufacturing sector (contrary to agriculture and transport). The designers were of the opinion that such a policy was not called for: healthy competition would keep prices low for the consumer, ensure the suppliers' efficient use of production factors and guarantee the continuous improvement of the quality of the product.

However, in due time, a mere competition policy was found insufficient to achieve certain desired changes, and a European structural policy for industry was contemplated. The uncertainties as to what would come under the heading of such a policy has caused quite some confusion.[4] In practice, however, the following *policy instruments* were gradually developed.

- *Sectoral policy*. In the 1970s, the pressure of the old industries (like steel and textiles) confronted by restructuring led to some involvement of the EU. Later attention shifted to stimulating key technology industries.[5]
- *R&D stimulation*. In the 1980s and 1990s growth industries obtained support for the stimulation of technological innovation via large multi-annual programmes financed by the EU. They applied to such fields as telecommunication equipment and information technology. To avoid problems with European competition policy, all schemes addressed the so-called 'pre-competitive' stage only. Each company is at liberty to exploit the results of these common R&D efforts to develop and market its own products.
- *Technical standards and norms*. The EU has steadily harmonised such national norms to facilitate low-cost production and has thereby enhanced competitiveness on EU and global markets. However regulation at the EU level has but rarely been used as an instrument to further innovation (as with car exhaust gas!) or to protect indigenous firms.
- *Government procurement* is frequently used to stimulate the development of certain products especially in sectors of advanced technology. The EU accepts the application of this instrument at the European level on the condition of non-discrimination between EU firms. Owing to the limited size of the EU budget and hence of EU public procurement, the instrument has little potential for EU industrial policy.
- *Trade policy*. So-called 'strategic trade policies' have attracted much attention from politicians and academics. Although the EU practice contained many elements of this (as a result of the action of lobby groups), no deliberate industrial development-oriented external trade policy has been developed.

After much experimentation with these industrial policy elements, the EU has decided that it would have a formal industrial policy. The Commission, in its memorandum 'European Industrial Policy for the 1990s' (EC, 1991b), put the accent on policies that aim to create good conditions for improving the competitiveness of EU industrial firms. The commitment of the EU to this type of industrial policy has next been codified by the inscription of its aims and principles in the Treaty.

The objectives of the EU policy are:

- speeding up the adjustment of industry to structural changes;

---

4   For a discussion of the origins, see EC (1970); Toulemon and Flory (1974); of the instruments: Hall (1986); Franzmeyer (1982); Buigues et al. (1995); and of the relations between the EU industrial policy and other EU policy fields: Buigues et al. (1995); see the same publication for the application of such policies to the steel and the motor industries, two of the case studies presented in this chapter.
5   Company regrouping is an instrument that has often been used by governments that have large stakes in the capital of manufacturing firms, or have other ways of putting pressure on private firms. In the early days the EU (EC, 1970) tried to help companies to acquire a sufficient size of operations by stimulating European mergers. Since the late 1980s, such ideas have been abandoned and the EU considers that the best tool to promote such a larger scale is the safeguarding of fair trade in an internal market under good competition conditions (Schwalbach, 1988; Helg and Ranci, 1988).

- encouraging an environment favourable to initiative and to the development of undertakings – particularly small and medium sized enterprises;
- stimulating cooperation between firms;
- fostering a better exploitation of the industrial potential of innovation, research and technological development policies.

The Commission may use the following *instruments to improve competitiveness* (see Chapter 14)

- Improving the regulatory and institutional environment of firms. Important in this respect is the concern for a consistent set of EU and national rules that are conducive to growth and limit the obligation of enterprises to what is strictly necessary.
- Exploiting synergies between the various EU policies. They comprise stimulating the early adoption of new technologies by user industries, support to R&D programmes for information and telecommunication in the framework of the development of a knowledge-based economy. Important in this respect is also the good functioning of the internal market and an efficient competition policy.[6]
- Promoting cross-border intra-EU cooperation between firms and member states and exchanging best practices.

Sketch of the sector

DEVELOPMENT OF BRANCHES

In the post-war period, the manufacturing sector became one of considerable importance to the economy of the EU countries, as Table 10.1 shows. Although its relative importance has declined since 1970 in favour of the service sector, the manufacturing sector still accounts for about one-fifth of total employment and wealth creation in the EU. The latest extension has changed that figure only marginally. This is due for one to the relatively limited weight of the NMS in the total of the EU25, and for another to the relative similarity of the sectoral structures.

Table 10.1 Percentage share of manufacturing in total GDP and total employment, 1950–2003

	1950[b]	1960[b]	1970[c]	1980[c]	1990[c]	2000[c]	2003[c]	2003[d]
GDP[a]	n.a.	40	36	33	27	21	19	20
Employment	29	32	33	27	24	19	18	19

Notes: *a Inclusive of mining, public utilities, energy (approximately 4 per cent). b 1950-1960: EU12. c 1970-2003: EU15. d 2003: EU25.*

Sources: GDP: OECD, Eurostat: National Account Statistics, various years; Employment: 1950–70 NEI FLEUR database; 1970–2000 OECD Labour Force Statistics, various years.

---

6   This is reflected by the studies of the Commission (for example, EC, 1982a, 1999c, 2004j) and of scholars who judge the horizontal policies of the EU (such as allocation, monetary, social and so on) in terms of their contribution to competitiveness (Lawton, 1999).

The development of this large sector is the result of diverging developments of its constituent branches. These again are dependent on the development of their major products.[7] The latter tend to follow a certain pattern that is called the 'product life-cycle'. It begins with an invention followed by an innovation. These processes give rise to whole new groups of products, which frequently coincide with branches of manufacturing industry. The economy is therefore often divided into new or growth industries and stagnating ones. The result of these dynamic processes is that the importance of branches within total industry tends to vary considerably over time.[8]

A picture of the long-term growth and decline of manufacturing branches in the EU economy is given in Table 10.2 (presenting employment figures, the only indicator for which long time-series could be made comparable in some detail). The metal industry (ranging from basic metals to transport equipment) is by far the largest sector. The table also indicates that employment in all sectors of manufacturing industry has declined in absolute terms since 1970. Much can be explained by improved productivity:[9] in terms of production (gross value added) many sectors have at least remained stable or have grown.

Table 10.2   Employment (millions) in manufacturing by branch (EU), 1950–2003

	EU15				EU25	
	1950	1970	1990	2003	2000	2003
Food, beverages and tobacco	3.3	4.0	3.6	3.1	4.9	4.6
Textile and leather products	7.4	6.2	3.8	2.4	3.4	3.1
Wood and wood products	2.0	2.2	1.9	2.2	1.2	1.2
Paper, publishing and printing	1.6	2.5	2.3	2.1	2.9	2.7
Petroleum, chemical products	1.7	3.1	3.6	3.0	4.0	3.8
Non-met. mineral products	1.4	1.9	1.4	1.2	1.8	1.8
Basic metals; machinery	7.8	12.9	11.8	10.0	12.9	12.6
Transport equipment	2.2	3.4	3.4	2.3	3.3	3.2
Others	1.1	1.7	0.5	0.1	2.1	2.1
Total	28.5	37.9	32.3	26.4	36.5	35.1

Note: *EU15 and EU25 data incomparable: figures based on different data definitions.*

Sources: *Ecorys: FLEUROPA data; Eurostat: various sources.*

In some industries the drop in employment due to technical progress and competition from Third World countries started early, especially in such traditional industries as textiles

---

7   These branches are distinguished by their different products and production processes. Most of them can be clearly delimited, as with foodstuffs, electronics and furniture. With some modern activities, however, the differences are steadily becoming vaguer. A case in point is informatics, a sector comprising classical industrial production (such as cables and equipment for telecommunication), less classical industrial activities like the graphic arts, as well as a large number of traditional service sectors such as libraries, telecommunication and so on.

8   For a general discussion of the relation between sectoral growth, life-cycles and industrial policy, see de Jong (1993a).

9   The quantitative side of employment change hides the technological progress of the last few decades, which has radically changed the production apparatus and the qualifications of the workforce. Large numbers of blue-collar factory workers have been replaced more and more by the grey and white collars of those concerned with management, research, control, checking, and sales, working in offices, showrooms and laboratories.

and clothing. Their share in total manufacturing employment fell in the 1950–2000 period by about two-thirds. By contrast, chemicals and metal were obvious growth industries in the period 1950–70: their shares increased considerably. The figures are totals only and hide important developments at the sub-branch level. For example, in recent years branches such as informatics and telecommunication equipment have shown considerable growth. The new member states are rather specialising in manufacturing; in these countries many manufacturing branches actually show dynamic growth.

SIZE OF EUROPEAN FIRMS

Size is mostly measured by turnover (sales), but employment is another much used indicator. Ranked[10] by employment, the largest European firms are shown in Table 10.3.

Table 10.3   The twelve largest manufacturing[a] firms based in the EU (private ownership, worldwide employment, thousands), 1970–2003

			1970	1980	1990	2000	2003
1	Siemens	Germany	300	350	370	447	417
2	DaimlerChrysler	Germany	150	190	370	417	362
3	Volkswagen	Germany	190	230	270	324	337
4	Unilever	UK / NL	340	320	300	261	234
5	Bosch	Germany	120	120	180	199	232
6	PSA Peugeot Citroen	France	80	250	160	172	200
7	Thyssenkrupp	Germany	178	237	211	193	190
8	Fiat	Italy	190	220	300	224	174
9	Saint-Gobain	France	115	164	105	171	173
10	Philips	NL	370	340	270	219	164
11	Renault	France	160	230	160	166	131
12	Bayer	Germany	100	180	170	122	115

Note: [a] Excluding financial trusts and energy

Source: Fortune, several issues.

The table shows three interesting features:

- *Branch*. The largest firms are concentrated in very few branches: transport equipment (5) and electric machinery and equipment (3).
- *Country*. Germany dominates the list, with six firms. The other six are all from core countries. So, most EU member countries do not show up on the list at all.
- *Rank*. During the 1970–2003 period the composition of the list of the largest firms in the EU did change very little. The same was true (albeit to a lesser extent) of the rank order of firms. However, in the second half of the period some significant changes occurred as the result of, among other things, mergers (Daimler-Benz), worldwide restructuring (Unilever) and competitiveness and strategic choices (Siemens vs Philips; Peugeot vs Fiat).

---

10   In the world rankings, most European firms fall outside the top 20; these rankings are dominated by US and Japanese firms.

SOME THEORY ON ECONOMIES OF SCALE

The EU has opened up the markets for industrial products that have previously been subject to considerable protectionism. This regime change has had important implications for industries that are subject to economies of scale. An establishment which can produce larger quantities more cheaply than smaller ones, and is constrained in its outlets by a market of limited size, does profit from the extension of the market offered by a customs union.[11] Figure 10.1 can help us to analyse the effect of 'economies of scale'. In this figure, D_a and D_b are the (identical) demand curves for countries A and B, and D_{cu} their common demand curve. S_w is the world supply curve; once more we assume a perfectly elastic supply. Contrary to the demand curves, the supply curves are not the same for countries A and B, country A producing, on average, at higher cost than country B. In both countries the cost decreases as the production increases in volume (definition of 'economy of scale').

We can analyse trade effects for situations of free trade, protection and integration.

- Free trade appears to be the most advantageous option: at price p_w, countries A (left-hand upper part of Figure 10.1) and B (right-hand upper part of Figure 10.1) both import their total demand (OQ for either) from the world market.
- Protection has drawbacks for welfare. If countries A and B both close their markets, in other words adopt a policy of autarky, country A consumes OL at price p_a, country B consumes OM at price p_b. Evidently, to prevent the national producer from making monopolist profits in this case, the tariffs must not be higher than $(p_a - p_w)$ for country A or higher than $(p_b - p_w)$ for country B.[12] The total demand in countries A and B would be $O_aL + O_bM$, appreciably less than the $O_aQ + O_bQ$ in the case of free trade.
- Integration, through the formation of a customs union between countries A and B, has different effects depending on the choice of the common external trade policy it wants to adopt. Suppose that this customs union decides to close its own market to competitors from the rest of the world. Evidently in that case, represented in the left-hand bottom part of Figure 10.1, demand in the union could be $O_{cu}R$ at a price of p_{cu} and a customs tariff of $p_{cu} - p_w$. The implication is that country B would take care of the entire production, production in country A being discontinued.[13] The effects of trade creation, diversion and expansion of this CU are in line with the definitions given earlier, albeit that account has to be taken of the slope of the supply curves.

What are the *welfare effects of the customs union of A and B* that protects itself against external competition by a tariff of $p_{cu} - p_w$ in comparison with a state of autarky of both country A and country B and with a state of free trade? (See Table 10.4 for an overview.) Compared to the case of autarky, consumption in country A becomes ON instead of OL, an advantage equal to $BDEG$. Part of it, namely $BDEI$, is the cost-cutting effect of the economies of scale, equalling trade creation O_aL; the other part, the triangle IEG, is trade expansion (LN). For country B, consumption becomes ON instead of OM; the advantage is $BCFG$, of which $BCFK$ represents the cost-cutting effect, which equals trade expansion (MN). This example shows once more that, to promote trade between partner countries, an external tariff has to be set which just

---

11   See, in this respect, Corden (1972a).
12   Assuming some extra transaction cost on long distance international transactions, we can assume that this tariff is just sufficient to prohibit world market producers from entering the markets of A and B.
13   Assuming low transport cost and a good functioning internal market.

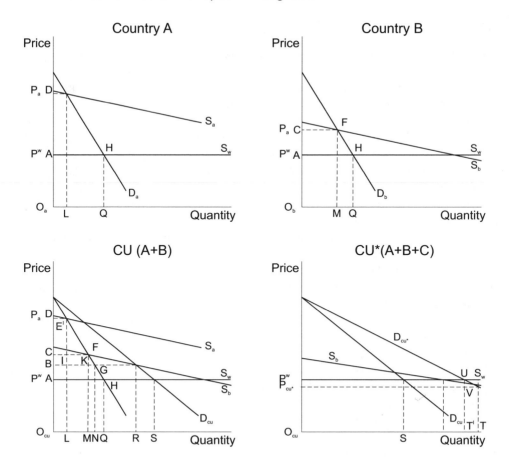

Figure 10.1   Economies of scale in production for individual countries A and B and for customs unions of A and B and of A, B and C

Table 10.4   Trade and production effects of a customs union under conditions of economies of scale, countries A and B

	Initial situation			
Effect	Free trade		Autarky	
	A	B	A	B
Creation	*	*	OaL	*
Expansion	−NQ	−NQ	LN	MN
Diversion	OcuN	OcuN	*	*

Note: * Not applicable.

protects the most efficient producer. Compared to free trade, the customs union produces for both countries A and B a negative trade contraction of NQ and a trade diversion of $O_{cu}N$.

For the customs union to be an advantageous alternative to overall free trade, the prices of the world producers must be equal to or higher than those of country B. That would be so if a third high-cost country C with a domestic market at least the size of ST' joined the customs union (the case depicted in the right-hand bottom part of Figure 10.1). The considerable advantage of such a large market achieved by the customs union is that it enhances the international competitiveness of the union. Indeed assuming no production in country C (or production at comparable costs to those in country A) this enlarged customs union enables the producer in country B to diminish his costs so as to deliver the good at price pcu*. At this price total demand of the customs union will increase to $O_{cu}T$. However, as this price is below pw, it is possible that the producer will also settle in his home market for the world market price which reduces total demand to $O_{cu}T'$. It will permit him to start to export his product to the world market and to earn a producer rent that on the domestic market is equal to the quantity sold times the margin between the price in the CU and the world market price. This will permit the customs union to abolish the tariff pcu – pw, which leads to a further trade expansion and creation in both countries A and B.

Do 'economies of scale', as described above, justify the creation of a customs union? That depends in the end on the net effects for the union as a whole, and the distribution of benefits and cost over partners. In our example, a customs union seems favourable on balance. However, the losing partner A is likely to demand compensation in terms of money transfers from country B, or to try and achieve a better starting-point than country B for other products, so that their manufacture can be concentrated in country A.[14]

SPECIALISATION, ECONOMIES OF SCALE AND LOCATION

The EU was conceived to bring about a better allocation of resources through specialisation and large-scale industrial production. Notably in manufacturing, economies of scale are very important[15] and, therefore, an analysis of the effects of the formation of the EU on production, direct investment and marketing is in order. We may refer in this respect again to Figure 10.1. Countries A and B can also be interpreted as plants of an MNF that are located in different countries. The management of the MNF will then base its decisions regarding location of production not only on cost and market considerations but also on the type of regime in place.

Strategy and internal organisation of multi-product, multinational companies also differ under different trade and direct investment regimes (see Table 10.5).

Philips is a good example of a firm that has experienced these changes in environment. Box 10.1 describes how its strategy has evolved over time (Muntendam, 1987; Teulings, 1984).

---

14   Imperfect competition may change the distribution of the effects over the customs union partner and third countries. If the supply curve of third country producers is not fully elastic, but also subject to increased returns, the decrease in third country exports to the CU due to the increase in the internal competitiveness of customs union producers depicted in Figure 10.1 will lead to an increase in the cost level of these producers and hence a further loss of their competitiveness on third markets (Venables, 1987).

15   See, among others, Pratten (1988).

Table 10.5   Production and trade patterns of multinational, multi-product companies under different trade regimes

Trade regime	Location of production units for each product	Dominant part of firm
Free trade	one plant (usually home base)	production and export
Protectionism	numerous plants (one in each major national market)	national companies
Integration	limited number of plants (at good locations)	matrix of national and product organisations
Free internal market	one plant (optimal location)	international product divisions

---

BOX 10.1
PHILIPS: EXPANSION AND ADAPTATION TO REGIME CHANGES

Taking advantage of the *liberalist trade environment* from the first decade of the 20th century, Philips rapidly increased its production of lightbulbs and other products, such as radio sets and domestic appliances. As early as 1910, Philips had established sales companies in 18 European and eight other countries of the industrialised world. Most were supplied by the home base, built for low-cost, large-scale production.

In the 1930s, the surge of *protectionist measures* (see Chapter 3) compelled the company to change its strategy thoroughly. It switched to the exploitation of ownership advantage. Its direct investments became of the tariff-jumping type (see Chapter 8). First, assembly lines for each of the major products were set up in every individual country in whose market Philips was well established. Next, national Philips companies were created, which became responsible for the production and local marketing of all Philips products. Quite naturally these national companies, having to gear their production to local taste, also acquired responsibility for product development. Conditions during and after the Second World War reinforced the system of geographically decentralised combined production and selling units.

In the 1960–90 period, characterised by the *opening of the EU markets,* all national companies were integrated in a centralised international system based on product division. This reflects a direct investment behaviour of the optimal location type (see Chapter 8). The major plants, which used to produce a whole array of products, were now made to specialise in only one or two products.

Recently this European strategy of specialisation and product division has been given a worldwide dimension under the impetus of global trade liberalisation.

CONCENTRATION

The creation of a large integrated market area like the EU has entailed an increase in firm size and a higher concentration in national and EU markets. In the 1962–1969 period the number of sectors in which the four largest firms (C4) had a share of over 50 per cent increased from

13 to 18 out of 46.[16] In the same period the situation in the UK (not a member) did not change. In the early 1980s, the concentration of manufacturing seems to have been more or less stable. The completion of the internal market (1992 process) has again induced further concentration; for the average industry the C4 index increased between 1987 and 1993 by two to three percentage points. As expected, the most significant increases have taken place in industries that used to be subject to regulation (related to public procurement and to food processing) or were subject to rapid market changes (technology-intensive industries) (EC, 1996a).

In the past many of the large European manufacturing firms performed poorly in comparison with their American and Japanese competitors in terms of outputs by employee and profitability. This was due to a significantly lower resilience of European industrial and market structures. It induced first the 1992 programme which did away with a large number of barriers to better performance and next the pursuit of an EU competitiveness policy (see Chapter 14).

PRICE EFFECTS OF INTEGRATION

The analysis of the evolution in the *differences in prices* made in Chapter 5 revealed that convergence has been observed over the 1975–99 period for the whole category of consumer goods. In the 1985–96 period this tendency towards convergence can be observed for all major sub-groups too (EC, 1996a; EC, 1999b). The decrease was highest for the groups for which initial dispersion was highest. This is in line with what one would have expected from integration theory. There is still quite some room for further price convergence as the average ratio of dispersion in the EU is significantly higher than the ratio for the US. Note that the remaining price dispersion is related to branch characteristics such as low import penetration and excise duties (beverages) or government regulation (pharmaceuticals). By contrast, mature markets, such as for clothing, show very low price divergence. In view of these factors it need not be a surprise that in recent years there is no clear tendency towards convergence any more, and that even the euro (see Chapter 15) has not yet fulfilled its promises of greater transparency and hence more similarity of prices (EC, 2004c).

Case study 1: steel

REGULATORY FRAMEWORK

The regime for the steel sector has differed from that of all other branches, as long as the ECSC Treaty (1952–2002) obtained. This Treaty bestowed special powers on the Commission to stabilise markets and restructure the industry. The Commission used this competence to overcome the 1975–80 crisis in this sector. Quantities were controlled by a system of production and supply quotas by country and by company for a large number of products. Prices were directly set through so-called 'price lists'. The practical implication was that the European

---

16   See EC (1974); Pryor (1972); Scherer (1974); Jacquemin and de Jong (1977); Locksey and Ward (1979); de Jong (1987). Other measures, such as the top eight, 30 and so on, convey the same message: their share in total output increased significantly in the 1960–75 period. After a hesitant start in the early 1960s, the 50 largest companies increased their shares in the output of the total manufacturing sector from 15 to 30 per cent between 1965 and 1980, accounting in 1980 for about one-fifth of the sector's total employment (Geroski and Jacquemin, 1984).

market broke down into national markets, largely fed by national production. To complement these measures the Commission has negotiated Voluntary Export Restraints with countries that were net exporters to the EU. The economic appraisal of this crisis management has been rather negative; adaptation has taken a very long time, welfare costs have been very high (Oberender and Rüter, 1993) and innovation has been retarded (Moore, 1998). For these reasons it was decided not to extend the duration of the ECSC Treaty when it expired in 2002, which implied that the steel sector is since under the EU rules that apply to all sectors of the economy.

SALIENT INDUSTRY CHARACTERISTICS

Technological change has determined the development of the European steel industry to a large extent. It has pushed the industry towards the use of large-scale integrated plants or of small-scale specialised plants (see Table 10.6). Between 1950 and 1980, one observes a tendency towards concentration of basic steel production in a limited number of integrated plants of (very) large scale. Since then the tendencies have changed. As a reaction to the crisis of the late 1970s, many of the smaller and some of the medium and largest integrated plants (those in sub-optimal locations) were closed. Other very large plants were scaled down to medium size. Next to these an increasing number of small scale specialised steelmaking plants were created in locations close to the market; a tendency that had already started in the 1960s in Northern Italy (Brescia).[17]

Table 10.6   Number of steel plants, by size category (Mt/y), in EU, 1960–2005

Capacity	1960	1970	1980	1990	2000	2005
0.5-1.0	35	24	15	13	n.a.	n.a.
1.0-2.0	29	46	24	18	23	14
2.0-5.0	7	18	29	25	16	16
> 5.0	-	1	8	4	5	5
Total	71	89	76	60	n.a.	n.a.

Source: Own estimates based on Iron and Steel Works of the World, Metal Bulletin Books, London/New York, several issues.

Continued technical progress in all parts of the industry leading to ever larger economies of scale increased the necessity for concentration of firms. In the period up to the Second World War, concentration had taken the form of vertical integration (coal, iron ore, iron and steelmaking, and metalworking). Since then, horizontal concentration has dominated the restructuring process (see Table 10.7).

The structural development of the EU steel industry has been very different in different sub-periods (see Table 10.8).

In the period between 1950 and 1974, capacity was expanded in line with the continuous growth in demand. EU firms were competitive on the world scale (reflected in net exports). The process of adjusting to the enlarged competition triggered by the new large ECSC market resulted in increased intra-industry specialisation among European firms (Adler, 1970) and intra-EU trade gradually expanding.

---

17   The data on these smaller plants do give a clear indication about the trend described. However, they do not permit quantitative comparisons over time. For that reason Table 10.6 does not give any figures for these smaller size plants.

Table 10.7   Output (Mt/y) of the largest EU steel-producing firms, 1980–2003

Present Company	Former Companies	Country	Mt/y EU output		
			1980	1990	2003
Arcelor	Usinor	FR	3		
	Sollac	FR	9	18	
	Sacilor	FR	3		
	Cockerill	B	4	4	37
	Sambre	B	3		
	Arbed	LUX	5	4	
	Sidmar	B	3	4	
Corus	British Steel	UK	8	14	19
	Hoogovens	NL	5	5	
ThyssenKrupp	Thyssen	GER	12	11	
	Krupp	GER	5	3	17
	Hoesch	GER	5	4	
Riva	Riva	ITA	14	12	16
Mittal	Various	NMS	n.a.	n.a.	12

Source: *International Iron and Steel Institute; websites of major producers.*

Table 10.8   Some characteristic data on the EU steel industry, 1950–2000

	1950	1960	1974	1980	1990	2000	2000[a]
Employment (1000)	787*	1 031	991	843	444	303	451
Capacity (effective (Mt/y))	n.a.	108	210	234	197	202	229
Crude-steel production (Mt/y)	51	105	181	152	149	163	186
Consumption (Mt/y)	44	92	158	123	120	144	149
Intra-EU trade as a percentage of consumption	n.a.	10	18	26	37	50	n.a.

Notes: ** Estimate based on preliminary data and extrapolation of figures for 1990–99. 1950–2000: EU15; 2000a: EU25*

Source: *OECD: The Iron and Steel Industry; The Steel Market and Outlook. Eurostat: Iron and Steel Yearbook, various years.*

In the period of economic crisis (1974–85) the total production of crude steel in what is now the EU15 dropped by 20 per cent. A considerable overcapacity (capacity-utilisation level in the 1980s approximately two-thirds) was the result, and the industry had to restructure in depth, closing down the older plants and laying off hundreds of thousands of employees. However, micro-economic as well as social factors spoke against the reduction. Given their very high fixed costs, firms were prepared to make drastic price cuts to stay in the market. When that strategy threatened to make some of them go bankrupt, governments moved in with subsidies to maintain employment. In the EU9, these amounted to a total of some € 50 billion for the 1979–86 period. They have led to the de facto nationalisation of large parts of the industry (in 1990, over 80 per cent in the UK, France and Denmark; over 60 per cent in Italy, Belgium and Luxembourg).

In the second half of the 1980s a normalisation of the situation occurred. Market integration was re-established gradually, one product group at a time, and was completed by the end of the decade. As a consequence of rationalisation and specialisation, employment was cut to less than half the 1980 level, capacity was reduced by some 20 per cent and integration of markets has increased (which means firms have become less oriented towards their home markets).

By the end of the 1980s a new crisis hit the industry as a result of the changes in Eastern Europe. The increased competition of Central and East European (CEEC) firms on both home and export markets of EU firms forced the latter into a new round of rationalisation and the laying off of substantial parts of the workforce (about 50 000 to 100 000 after 1990).

In recent years demand has picked up again (notably worldwide demand) and production has followed, and as capacity had roughly remained constant, the utilisation levels have improved considerably. Market integration has also increased considerably as witnessed by the indicator intra-EU trade as a percentage of consumption. This has, however, not resulted in a stabilisation of employment. On the contrary, the drive towards competitiveness and technological changes have led to a very large increase in productivity and hence a considerable drop in employment.

The accession of the NMS has changed the picture significantly. EU capacity and production levels grew significantly; EU consumption much less. Employment levels still remain high in the NMS; so there is ample room for further increases in productivity.

COMPANY STRUCTURE

We can distinguish five stages in the process of the restructuring of the industry in response to changing technological demands and economic integration. The key element in all these stages is further concentration. This is in line with the predictions of industrial economics with respect to mature industries (see de Jong, 1993b).

At the beginning of the 1950s, the situation of the European steel industry was marked by the existence of a large number of firms, tending to be linked (via financial groups) to other firms in the same sector, located in the same region. There was hardly any international integration. Some Belgian capital had penetrated into companies of the neighbouring French Lorraine district; the Dutch blast furnace company Hoogovens controlled the German firm of Hörder, and the Luxembourg and Saar industries were to some extent controlled by French and Belgian capital. International trade in iron and steel was limited.

In the 1960s, concentration followed a *regional pattern*. Evidently such technical factors as economies of scale, transport costs and labour force adaptations induced firms to join efforts with firms close by rather than with firms in other countries. First, concentration of firms occurred at a local level (Liège, Sambre and Dortmund, for example). Next the concentration movement was extended to operations on a regional scale.[18] The only international firm was Arbed which integrated steel firms in the Luxembourg/Saar/Lorraine/Flanders area. Later Estel merged the German Hoesch group with Dutch Hoogovens in another international regional grouping.

In the 1970s and 1980s a round of horizontal concentrations assumed a *national dimension*. The crisis of the mid-1970s induced many governments to step in with very substantial aid, given in exchange for a certain measure of control of the developments, which invariably led to nationalisation and concentration on the national level. Examples are the formation of British Steel, the merger between Usinor and Sacilor in France, the Thyssen/Krupp/Hoesch mergers in Germany, and the regrouping by RIVA of a number of smaller private companies

---

18   In France, the government stimulated the formation of regional groups: Usinor in the north and Sacilor in Lorraine; similar developments took place in the Ruhr area. Likewise, in Spain, Ensidesa regrouped firms in the Asturias, and Altos Hornos companies in the Viscaya district.

and the privatised parts of ILVA in Italy. The international Estel group fell victim to nationalist pressure (the German Hoesch group was forced to participate in a 'German' restructuring).

In the 1990s a further concentration with a *European dimension* occurred. Two major international mergers have been realised. The first is between Usinor (F), Arbed (L), Acelaria (SP) and Cockerill/Sambre (B) that formed Arcelor. The second one was the merger of British Steel with Hoogovens, creating Corus. In this way the number of large European steel companies has been reduced from 13 in 1980 to only four by the end of the 1990s. Each of these giants produces more than 13 million tons, more than double the capacity of the largest companies in 1995. Next to these giants there exist in the EU25 a limited number of medium-sized companies and a fairly large number of smaller producers. Among them one notes companies from the NMS such as Nowa Huta in Poland or Sidex from Romania.

Recently the *global dimension* of the steel industry has started to dominate the steel industry. There are two examples. The European group Arcelor has important production capacities in Brazil. The Mittal group (originally Indian) has acquired important positions in the EU, notably by taking over the major parts of the steel industries of the NMS (see Box 10.2).

BOX 10.2
THE EMERGENCE OF A NEW GLOBAL GIANT: MITTAL STEEL

The steel industry of the CEECs suffered from many problems, such as technological backwardness, inefficient logistics and poor marketing. Moreover, it caused problems to others as it was one of the worst polluters of the environment. The accession agreement with the EU involved a number of measures: privatisation of companies, closure of the most polluting production facilities, redundancy of most of the workers and considerable investment in new technology and facilities without capacity increases. Mittal Steel has acquired the steel companies of Poland, the Czech Republic and Romania (and Bosnia and Macedonia). It has thereby become by far the largest steel producer in the NMS and in the CEECs with a total capacity of some 14 million tons, of which half is in Poland (Nowa Huta). It has quickly turned the ailing operations into a profitable business, by bringing in technological and notably managerial know-how. It has thereby been able to capitalise on its unique experience with similar situations in India and Kazakhstan.

In 2005 Mittal Steel has become the largest steel maker in the world by acquiring the International Steel Group of the US. After that merger Mittal has production facilities in all major regions of the world and produces a total of some 70 million tons a year. Mittal is listed on the stock exchanges of Amsterdam and New York; a majority of the shares are, however, in the hands of its chairman Lakshmi Mittal, son of an Indian businessman (see: www.mittalsteel.com).

Notwithstanding the numerous horizontal mergers, the *concentration ratio* in the EU as a whole for quite some time did not rise very high. Between 1980 and 1995 the four largest companies accounted for about 30 per cent (C4) and the eight largest (C8) for about 45 per cent of total steel production of the EU15.[19] Since the recent upsurge of international mergers this situation has, however, dramatically changed. In 2000 the C4 stood at 52 per cent and the C8 at 69 per cent.

---

19   See Table 10.7; see also Oberender and Rüter (1993).

Case study 2: cars

REGULATORY FRAMEWORK

The regulations of the EU concerning the automotive sector apply to several areas, the most relevant of which are competition, taxation, external trade and technical standards.

The influence of *competition policy* on the car sector makes itself felt firstly in the system of distribution. Car makers want to control their outlets in order to protect brand images and technical quality. However, they thereby can also seal off national markets from competition. The EU allows exclusive dealership but also allows so called parallel imports. Competition policy also deals extensively with state aids. The car industry has benefited from considerable subsidies with considerable risks for distortion of fair trade. This is particularly relevant for the NMS that have attracted major investments in car making and are poised to attract more. The EU sees to it that this aid is transparent, below certain thresholds and only given for development of backward areas (see Chapters 14 and 16).

Harmonisation of *taxes* has not advanced very much. Major differences do indeed persist with respect to three types of taxation. Purchase taxes range from low levels in Germany to almost 200 per cent in Denmark. The annual circulation tax differs from € 100 to 1000 largely because of the choices made with respect to motor fuel taxes (see Chapter 14).

Another important part of the regulation of the automotive sector is *external trade*. Some member states have over a long period maintained protectionist measures against third country producers.[20] These barriers have been removed in the framework of the 1992 programme. At the same time, an EC-wide arrangement with Japanese exporters has been made, that ran to the end of the century. As from the year 2000, external protection with QR no longer exists.

A final important element of regulation is *technical harmonisation*. The myriad technical regulations that national states had established seriously hindered international trade. Technical standards have been harmonised with the 'EC Whole Vehicle Type Approval System'. EU regulations range from very important ones giving substance to other policies (for example, environmental policy leading to EU standards on exhaust emissions and noise levels), to very mundane ones, such as towing hooks. The Commission is pursuing its harmonisation efforts between EU and non-EU countries in order to facilitate global production strategies of firms.[21]

INDUSTRY CHARACTERISTICS

The car industry is a significant part of the EU economy. It provides some six million direct and indirect jobs, mostly medium and high skilled. The sector has shown that it is innovative and competitive on the global scale.

The industry is characterised by important *economies of scale*. To give an order of magnitude: if the production of 100 000 units cost € 10 000 per car, the production of 2 000 000 would bring this down to € 6 600. This also holds for intermediary products; producers can obtain large rebates from suppliers if they buy large quantities.

---

20   Italy, for one, restricted its imports of Japanese cars to 2300 a year, a quota dating from before the foundation of the EU. France has had, since 1977, a bilateral agreement with the Japanese government to restrict the Japanese share in the French market to 3 per cent. Finally, British and Japanese associations of car manufacturers have concluded VERs that restricted the Japanese share to 10 to 11 per cent (EC, 1983a; OECD, 1987e).

21   For a description of the policy process on automobile regulation, see McLaughlin and Maloney (1999).

The *overall trade position vis-à-vis the outside world* is characterised by both substantial exports and imports (see Table 10.9). The export performance of the EU has shown little growth since the 1970s, while producers from third countries have considerably increased their presence on EU markets. The European industry, while falling behind on export markets mostly in favour of the Japanese, has been able to retain much of its home market, initially thanks to important protectionist measures. However, against all kinds of impediment, the Japanese have managed to capture a very significant part of the market, from a negligible beginning in the years when the EU was established (both imports and local assembly).

Table 10.9 Production and consumption of, and external trade in, cars in the EU (millions), 1960–2002*

	1960[a]	1970[a]	1980[a]	1990[a]	2002[b]
Production	4.8	10.2	11.4	13.2	15.0
Imports	n.a.	0.2	n.a.	1.7	2.4
Japan	(—)	(0.1)	(0.9)	(1.2)	(1.0)
Exports	1.1	1.8	n.a.	2.7	3.1
Consumption	3.7	8.5	10.3	12.2	14.3

Notes: * Data on production, imports, etc. are not fully consistent. [a] 1960–90: EU12, [b] 2002: EU15

Sources: Owen (1983), Maillet (1977), Mueller (1981), additional estimates; JETRO, White Paper on International Trade. UK Department of Trade and Industry website. Eurostat, PRODCOM database. ACEA, the European Automobile Manufacturers Association, website.

The growing *interpenetration of markets in the EU* is indicated by a decrease in the share of the three largest producers in total sales on their four major national home markets (Table 10.10).[22]

Table 10.10 Shares (%) of the three largest national producers in home-market sales, 1960–2000

Country	Companies	1960	1970	1980	1990	2000
Germany	VW, GM, Ford	79	66	59	54	n.a.
France	Renault, Peugeot, Citroën	82	70	67	61	n.a.
Italy	Fiat, AR, Lancia	90	72	63	53	31
UK	BL, GM, Ford	79	76	57	55	31

Source: Tatsachen und Zahlen; Automotive News, various years. ACEA: Autodata; AID, 1996; for 2000 estimates based on additional information from the companies' homepages. The letters n.a. mean not applicable in this respect.

A second indicator is international trade.[23] In 1950 trade in cars was low, as it was hampered by high tariffs (20 to 40 per cent), by the intervention of governments in car production, the difficulty of creating dealer networks abroad, and so on. Scale economies are very important in the car industry, probably even more so for parts than for final goods, so there is ample impetus

---

22   In each of the four large countries given, a home producer was present. That was not always the case for smaller member states. Hence the relative share of imports in the smaller countries was much larger than for the four large countries (Hocking, 1980). We do not give figures for a later period, because the indicator is no longer adequate for two reasons. First, because mergers between companies have reduced the number of players. Second, because the relation between a producer and its home market has been loosened by the increased internationalisation of the production sites of the major producers (see also Table 10.11).

23   The trade structure of the finished product hides the international trade in parts (Hudson and Schamp, 1995). Already in the 1980s this was far advanced among the production facilities of each major car maker. Since then the exchange of parts, such as brakes, engines, and so on, has also been developed between all major companies. A highly developed European industry for components has been an asset to the EU car industry (Salvatori, 1991; Bongardt, 1993).

for scale-driven exports. Indeed large producers can use their savings on cost to penetrate foreign markets. To stop such inroads into their home markets, producers of other countries were forced to take up exporting as well. In the 1960s and 1970s, this determined the intra-EU pattern of trade (Owen, 1983). Since then the trade in cars between EU countries has surged; it was of the intra-industry type.

Table 10.11 Production (in thousands), by car manufacturer in the EU*, 1960–2002

Country	Company	1960	1986	1998	2002
Germany	VW/Audi	740	1 780	2 200	1 800
	GM (Opel)	330	900	1 050	870
	Ford	190	560	520	690
	Daimler-Benz	200	590	850	980
	BMW	60	430	640	750
France	Renault	430	1 300	1 190	1 160
	Citroën/Panhard	280			
	Peugeot/Talbot	190	1 470	1 370	1 600
	Simca[a]	220			
Italy	Fiat (AR/Lancia)	690	1 650	1 370	1 050
Belgium	Ford	n.a.	260	320	260
	VW (Seat)	n.a.	n.a	180	500
	GM (OPEL)	n.a.	n.a	300	330
Netherlands	Volvo (2000-: Ford)	n.a.	120	160	110
UK	BMC-Rover-BMW	450	400	470	160
	Ford[b]	340	350	340	280
	GM (Vauxhall)	130	160	280	140
	Rootes (Peugeot)[a]	120	80	70	200
	Nissan	—	—	290	290
	Honda	—	—	110	110
	Toyota	—	—	170	210
Spain	VW (Seat)	n.a.	320	740	670
	Renault	n.a.	230	460	460
	Ford	n.a.	260	300	370
	GM	n.a.	300	450	370
	Peugeot/Citroën	n.a.	170	250	360
Sweden	Volvo	n.a.	290	240	290
	GM (Saab)	n.a.	110	110	120
Poland	Fiat	n.a.	n.a.	n.a.	160
Czech Rep	VW (Skoda)	n.a.	n.a.	370	440
Slovakia	VW	n.a.	n.a.	130	230
Slovenia	Renault	n.a.	n.a.	n.a.	130

Notes: [a] Merged first with Chrysler, later with Peugeot. [b] Including Jaguar. * Not included are plants of less than 100 000 production, nor plants that only assemble, for example, in Belgium and Portugal.

Sources: L'Argus de l'automobile, various years; ACEA, Autodata; AID, Car Yearbook, Rhys (2004).

Table 10.11 gives an idea of the evolution of the *production of the most important car manufacturers by country of location*. The smaller producers, most of whom lost their independence in the past, have been left out. The table indicates five main features:

•   the steep increase in production up to 1986 and the more modest growth since;
•   the stagnation in production in the United Kingdom in the first period;

- the remarkable growth of Spain, where many firms have established production facilities (Hudson and Schamp, 1995);
- the rise in the assembly plants of Japanese firms located notably in the UK; and
- in the recent period, the stagnation of the EU15 and the vigorous growth in the NMS (to presently some 1.3 million units per year).

In the course of time international specialisation has increased further; in order to cut cost, parts of production were transferred to low-cost EU member countries, first to Spain and Portugal and next to even lower-cost NMS. The trend is likely to continue, as more investment is under way (notably from Japanese firms). This new investment favours in particular locations in the belt on the eastern border of the EU15 (for example, Bratislava, Poznan). This poses a formidable challenge to the present locations, some of which reveal fairly poor figures in terms of productivity (Rhys, 2004).

Appreciable differences between *car prices* have persisted for various reasons. First, car manufacturers, by their control over dealers, have been able to fix different prices on different national markets. Second, taxation differs; heavy tax pressure has led to low net prices in Denmark: companies selling there were forced to reduce pre-tax prices in a country with such a very heavy tax burden on cars. Third, national import restraints (VER, QR) matter: high penetration of foreign cars has led to low prices in Greece and Belgium. Fourth, alignment with prices of the major national producer and a market protected by driving on the left (few parallel imports) has led to high prices in the UK, where producers prefer greater benefits from limited sales volumes to higher market shares at lower prices. Finally, producers have set prices according to specific circumstances on national markets, taking into account stability of prices in local currency notwithstanding exchange rate movements.[24]

The Commission has tried to do away with this price discrimination between countries by favouring the possibility of parallel imports. Exclusive rights for sales networks are accepted, but consumers have the right to go and buy a vehicle in any other EU country. Some small firms specialise in this trade. Car manufacturers have to accept normal obligations of guarantee and so on for these cars. As a result of these measures, price differences have decreased markedly in the 1990s, notably for small and medium-sized cars, as here competition between manufacturers is fiercest (EC, 1999b; EC, 1999c). This tendency has continued in recent years. Its causes seem to lie more in changes in market structure than in increased transparency due to the euro (Goldberg and Verboven, 2004)

COMPANY STRUCTURE

In the *1950s and early 1960s*, the European volume producers were national champions in the sense that most of their production facilities were concentrated in one country, were controlled by capital from their home country and very often enjoyed government support. Standing up to international competition was often only possible with government assistance for restructuring of operations and development of new products. The European volume producers concentrated on family cars with idiosyncratic styles, oriented towards their national markets.

In the *1960s, 1970s and early 1980s*, under the pressure of US firms pursuing their concept of global industry, styles and technology converged into one rather homogeneous product,

---

24   For the various effects mentioned, see respectively: BEUC (1982); Murfin (1987); Gual (1993); Gil-Pareja (2003).

which could be sold both on national and foreign markets. Notably Ford and GM built up their German and British subsidiaries by rationalising their product ranges on a European level. More than before, attention was on minimising unit cost of development and production by large production series. In the face of increased competition, a tendency to concentrate along national lines prevailed, smaller firms being gradually absorbed by the larger ones (Fiat acquired Alfa Romeo and Lancia, Volkswagen acquired Auto Union, British Leyland resulted from a merger of UK companies, Citroën acquired Panhard). The only major attempt at an international take-over by a European firm (Citroën being acquired by Fiat) failed and, after considerable intervention by the French government, Citroën was finally merged with Peugeot.

By the *end of the 1980s* a new group of players came to the European market. Japanese car firms, which until then were satisfied with exporting to the EU, started to build production and assembly facilities in the EU. The total capacity of these plants amounted to some one million by the end of the decade.

In the 1990s a further wave of concentration occurred. This was mainly due to the 1992 programme on the completion of the internal market (Salvatori, 1991) that removed a number of obstacles in the field of taxes, technical standards and import restrictions. Other factors were the creation of the European Economic Area (see Chapter 17), the transition of Central and Eastern European economies and increased Japanese imports. Volkswagen (Germany) acquired Seat (Spain) and Skoda (Czechoslovakia); Renault has taken a large share in Revon (Dacia of Romania); Volvo (Sweden) was finally taken over by Ford; BMW acquired the Rover group;[25] and GM took over Saab.

The confidence that European car manufacturers have in their regained strength has led them to internationalise on a global scale. We can cite here first the recent merger of Daimler Benz with Chrysler and the large stake this new group has taken in Mitsubishi; second, the stake of Renault in Nissan and, third, the expansion of Volkswagen in China and Brazil.

In 2000, five of the eleven largest European manufacturing firms were in the automotive sector (see Table 10.3). This shows the importance of economies of scale in that industry. Consequently the concentration of firms in European car manufacturing is fairly high. From Table 10.11 we can calculate that the four largest producers accounted for about 50 per cent of total production in 1960 and somewhat less than 60 per cent in 2000. In the same period the C8 increased gradually from about 80 to about 90 per cent.

Summary and conclusions

- The EU industry has gone through a process of profound structural change. New sectors of activity have developed (electronics), older ones (shipbuilding) have faded out. This has caused the creation of many new jobs and new firms, on the one hand, and the loss of many jobs and firms, on the other. It has also meant the relocation of activities within and outside the EU.
- The creation of the EU has not affected all sectors in the same way; some have responded quickly (cars) and are now characterised by firms with European dimensions and much intra-industry trade; others have been subject to much protective regulation and have

---

25   The BMW Rover merger was very unsuccessful; BMW subsequently spun off again most of the Rover activities. This new group finally went out of business in 2005.

only fairly recently become subject to the Europeanisation and globalisation tendencies (steel).

- The new member states are quickly developing their manufacturing base. After their transition they have become the preferred location for many firms wishing to optimise their European production activities. This shift to the East is clearly illustrated by the car industry.

11 *Energy*

Introduction

The EU has from its very beginnings pursued the integration of energy markets. The regime it has created is described in the next section. It is a complicated one, because it needs to take account of the different ways in which all member states intervene in the energy markets and in the structure of the energy sector.

The third section sketches the changes, which in the past half century occurred in European energy markets (consumption, production and prices). The fourth and fifth sections treat the integration of certain markets in more depth; oil and electricity have been chosen as examples. In both case studies we will describe the EU regime, the development of the branch and the strategic responses of the major firms. A section with some conclusions will complete the chapter.

EU regime

RATIONALE AND PRINCIPLES

Energy is essential to economic development. Without the ample supply of energy the present levels of welfare would not be possible. The energy sector is dependent on very heavy infrastructure and its production, distribution and consumption have important external effects for instance on the environment (pollution) and social equity (connectivity and prices of essential goods). So, national governments have intervened in the sector to maintain a certain level of control over energy supplies and to check externalities of use by different forms of taxation and subsidies.

In an integration scheme, the equal access to energy is of great economic importance; as energy is a major input in many other productions, non-integrated energy markets coupled with integrated goods markets would lead to distortions. It is also of much political importance as the interdependency on strategic commodities may be the best guarantee for peace.

The objectives of the Common Energy Policy have been remarkably stable over time[1] as far as their essential characteristics are concerned. These are:

- *competitiveness* to ensure low-cost energy for producers and consumers; the most important instrument is to enhance the working of market forces;
- *security of supply* which aims to minimise risks and impacts of possible supply disruption on the EU economy and society;

---

[1]   See EC (1988b, 1992c, 1992d, 1995b, 1999d, 2002c and Art III 157 Draft Constitution).

- *environmental protection* which is integrated in both efficiency of energy production and energy use to safeguard sustainable development.

These objectives have been elaborated differently over time in view of the changing external conditions.

GRADUAL DEVELOPMENT OF POLICY

In the 1950s the EU energy policy started with development of a coal policy by the ECSC, followed by the set up of a common policy for the nuclear sector by the EAEC. Since then a coherent energy policy has gradually been developed on the basis of the three treaties.[2]

   In the 1960s, it was recognised that the situation in the energy field lacked balance. Since then, the Commission has submitted a series of proposals for a more coherent EC energy policy. The 1962 Memorandum on Energy Policy was followed in 1968 by a 'First Orientation to a Common Energy Policy'. It reflected the fundamental problems of the EU energy position and established the principles of EU policy, namely to ensure supply at the lowest possible price, with due regard to the specific structure of the energy sector. A common market for energy products and coordination of the member states' energy policy were to be the means. This led to the decision of the European Council in 1972 to develop a coordinated energy policy.

   The *1973–1985 period* is marked by the two energy crises, in 1973 and 1979, that showed that the EU was confronted by three major problems (EC, 1981a; d'Anarzit, 1982).

- Insecurity of supply. The EU was dependent for a large part of its energy on foreign oil. Some of the exporters used the cutting of supplies as a strategic weapon.
- Instability of prices. Fluctuations in the price of crude oil and the exchange rate to the dollar (see Figure 11.1) had caused huge disturbances of the European economy.
- Disequilibrium on the balance of payments. Between 1973 and 1981, the oil bill of the EU had multiplied by eight, despite a simultaneous decline of net imports by some 40 per cent.

The very divergent national responses to the 1973 crisis (virtually disintegrating the common energy market) made the EU painfully aware of the need for further action. This was reinforced by the second oil crisis of 1979. A central element of the EU policy is to render consistent the objectives and measures of energy policy as pursued by national governments. To coordinate the programmes of member states, the Commission organised periodical surveys

---

2   The EU energy policy was based on three different treaties, each containing rules for specific segments of the energy sector. The European Coal and Steel Community (ECSC) has pursued both a market regulation and a structural policy for the coalmining sector. Its first task concerned the adequate functioning of the market. In principle, free competition should govern the market process. However, in times of 'manifest crisis' or scarcity, the ECSC could intervene either directly in the prices or through production quotas and international trade. Its second task was to pursue a structural policy. To that end the ECSC has made indicative programmes, appraised individual investment programmes, supported investments and research, and finally supported restructuring.

   The European Atomic Energy Community (EAEC) had no powers as to the regulation of the demand side of the market. However, for the supply of ores, raw materials and fissionable material an EU monopoly was created. The EAEC's main tasks were: developing research, dispersing knowledge and making investments. Apart from supporting and coordinating, the EAEC could also participate directly in investments.

   The European Economic Community (EEC) Treaty contained no specific stipulations for the energy sector; therefore the functioning of the (crude) oil, (natural) gas and electricity markets was left to supply and demand forces regulated by the general stipulations of the Treaty, for example with respect to competition. Neither have provisions been made for structural policy measures for these sectors.

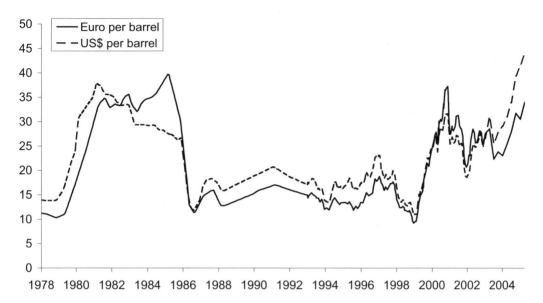

Figure 11.1   Import prices of energy: (crude oil)

Source: *EC (1986f, 1996b).*

of member states' energy policy schemes. The EU agreed on two common targets to improve the security of its supplies and the competitiveness of its energy sector. The first one was to diminish the ratio between the growth of energy consumption and the growth of GNP. The second one was to reduce the share of oil and stimulate the use of solid fuels and nuclear energy both in primary energy consumption and in electricity generation. The success of this policy, and the breaking up of the OPEC cartel, meant that, in the mid-1980s, the price of energy fell considerably, which changed fundamentally the market conditions and permitted the reorientation of the EU energy policy.[3]

In the period 1985–2000, major developments shaped a new framework for each of the three major objectives for EU energy policies.

- Competitiveness. Traditionally the markets for the different fuels were very heavily regulated on a national basis, and some of them (electricity, gas) were traditionally monopolies. As a consequence the European market was very segmented. The drive towards the completion of the internal market led to the creation of a competitive energy market with a pan-European regulatory framework, which implied a major restructuring and liberalisation of important segments of the sector.
- Security of supply. The EU will increasingly be dependent on imported energy, and the opening up of the Eastern European countries with their very important energy reserves has provided a new opportunity. A European Energy Charter has been signed between the EU and the CEEC to expand the infrastructure and subsequently the trade in energy

3   For the origins of the EU energy policy, see, for instance, Weyman-Jones (1986) or Jensen (1983); for coordination, Lucas (1977, 1985) and EC (1982b). Note that the EU was not alone; the OECD has also paid attention to the energy problem. A relatively advanced form of international cooperation, by OECD standards, was initiated after the first oil crisis by the creation of the International Energy Agency. This agency coordinates not only the national policies of the participating states, it can lay down uniform rules of behaviour which all member states are supposed to respect (OECD, 1987f).

between the two areas. This has fundamentally changed the external dimension of the EU energy policies (EC, 1992c, 1999d, 2002c).

- Concern with the environment. Indeed one of the major causes of air pollution is the burning of energy sources with a high carbon content, so the objectives of the policies became more oriented towards the limitation of consumption, and towards less polluting sources (EC, 1992d, 1995b). This objective has since been reinforced (EC, 1999d) as the EU has accepted higher targets in this field both internally (Treaty of Amsterdam) and externally (Kyoto conference).

MARKET REGULATION

An important impetus for EU regulation has come from the completion of the internal market for energy products, whereby the causes of distortions on the EU market for energy, such as differences in taxes on energy products, national monopolies, government interventions and protective national procurement, are taken away. The EU regulatory activity may be grouped under four headings.

- *Security*. To avoid the type of problem that occurred during the oil crises, member states are committed to maintain minimum stocks of oil and, in times of supply problems, to introduce a rationing scheme for these stocks.
- *Transparency*. Member states are committed to inform and consult the Commission on the development of prices and domestic and foreign supplies in the different sub-markets (oil, gas and so on). The market situation is quarterly reviewed.
- *Accessibility*. In the electricity and gas markets the monopoly power of the companies controlling the distribution networks has for a long time barred the access of efficient producers to potential clients. The EU now has common rules for market access (see section on electricity).
- *Externality*. The differences between member countries in taxation of energy cause distortions in the internal market and so some harmonisation is needed (see Chapter 14).

STRUCTURAL POLICY

The objectives of the common energy policy (CEP) cannot be realised without a certain restructuring of energy production, consumption and trade. The following measures of structural policy are in force in the framework of the CEP.

- *Stimulating EU production*. Support (financing and regulation) for alternative (permanent and renewable) sources: including research projects and demonstration programmes.
- *Saving energy*. One instrument is loans to manufacturing industries applying new technical procedures.
- *Supervising restructuring*. Support for and supervision of capacity adaptation by exchange of information, contacts and negotiations with industry representatives.
- *Supporting the improvement of Trans European Networks (TENs)* for the transportation of natural gas and the transmission of electricity. They concern notably the interconnection between isolated national grids and the access of peripheral regions to the grids. Particular attention is given to the connectivity of the NMS.

• *Checking external effects*. Energy is one of the main sources of greenhouse gases. The EU has agreed in the framework of the Kyoto protocol to reduce the emissions of such gases. To that end a system of tradable permits has been set up (for example, Endres and Ohl, 2005).

Sketch of the sector

EMPLOYMENT AND VALUE ADDED

Primary energy springs from a variety of sources. Historically human and animal muscle power, wood, wind and water (tides and rivers) were important. In more modern times fossil fuels have come to the fore (coal, oil, gas). Since the Second World War, nuclear energy has developed fast. Recently other forms of energy have regained interest, in particular the so-called 'renewable resources', like sun radiation, tidal waves, hydropower and biomass. Because primary energy sources are not always easy to use, they are converted into secondary ones, such as coke and gas from coal, petrol and liquefied petroleum gas (LPG) from crude oil. Some of these are converted a second time for the generation of electricity in coke- or oil-fired power stations.

The energy sector is composed of primary energy production (such as coal mining) and by secondary energy production and distribution (for example, electricity generation and oil refining). Each count for less than 1 per cent of total employment, which means that the entire energy sector represents about 2 per cent of total employment. In terms of gross value added, the percentage is about 3 per cent (because of the relatively high productivity and the large contribution the sector makes to government revenue). Although the sector does not represent a large part of total economic activity, we nevertheless devote a separate chapter to it because of its strategic importance.

TOTAL CONSUMPTION OF PRIMARY ENERGY

The 1950–73 period was characterised by high and stable economic growth (on average almost 5 per cent a year). Total energy consumption in the European Union increased very fast too (ratio between the increase of energy consumption and that of GNP was on average about one during the whole period).

The 1973–82 period started with some events which were to exert a strong effect on the entire consumption pattern. For one thing, the oil price, practically stable until then, rose almost fourfold. For another, the continuous supply of oil became uncertain as some oil exporters put an embargo on oil exports to certain consumer countries. An economic recession was the result, with, in 1975, the first decline of GNP and of energy consumption since the Second World War. The high price of oil induced its replacement by other sources of energy, as well as measures to diminish consumption by energy saving. In 1979 there followed the second oil shock, again multiplying the oil prices by almost four. It was the main cause of an actual drop in energy consumption. As the increase of GDP during that period was very low, the elasticity of demand was negative.

The 1983–2005 period started with economic growth accelerating and prices of energy decreasing drastically, and demand for energy picked up again too.

CONSUMPTION BY PRIMARY ENERGY SOURCE

Consumption has developed differently for the various primary energy sources,[4] as Table 11.1 illustrates. Certain trends can be discerned throughout the period 1930–2000, such as the fall in the share of coal (from a very dominant position), the rise and subsequent fall in the share of oil and the continuous rise of the shares of (natural) gas and primary electricity (mainly nuclear – (15 per cent, other renewables – 6 per cent). The table shows that there is some differentiation between sub-periods as far as the development of oil is concerned. In the period from 1950 to 1973, consumption switched fast from coal to oil. This trend reached a turning point in 1973: as a result of the considerable increase in oil prices and subsequent policy measures, the share of oil decreased from 1973 onward. In the second part of the 1980s there has been a steep fall in oil prices due to the breakdown of the OPEC cartel, which stimulated consumption and stabilised the share of oil. The effect of the recent steep rise in oil prices has not yet shown itself in the figures.

Table 11.1 Percentage shares of primary energy sources in total energy consumption (Mtoe), EU, 1930–2000[a]

	1930	1937	1950	1960	1973	1980	1990	2000[a]	2000[b]
Coal	95	90	83	63	23	23	22	15	18
Oil	4	8	14	31	61	51	44	41	39
Gas	—	—	—	2	11	15	17	23	23
Electricity	1	2	3	4	5	11	17	21	20
Total	100	100	100	100	100	100	100	100	100

Notes: *Figures for 2002 are highly similar to 2000 figures, so no more recent data included.* [a] *1930- 2000: EU15* [b] *2000: EU25.*

Source: *OECD, Energy Statistics, Energy Balances, Oil Statistics, various years; OECD (1966, 1973). European Commission, Energy and Transport Statistics, 2004.*

The determinant factors behind the substitution of one energy source for another are costs, consumer convenience and availability; of course, the latter two can also be translated into costs. The important switch from coal to oil in the post-war period is due to the divergence of their relative prices. While high labour costs of production and transport made coal more and more expensive, the consumption prices of oil could be reduced thanks to its capital-intensive production and the economies of scale achieved in conversion and transport.

The steady rise in the share of gas in total consumption has been due in particular to its convenient use in many installations and to the fact that it is more and more produced in the consumption areas. Finally the share of primary electricity has steadily been growing as a result of the high growth of demand for electricity and the stimulation of nuclear energy. Renewable primary energy sources, such as water, wind, sun and bio, are gaining in absolute and relative terms; but the high costs have been a delaying factor in their development.

The joining of the NMS has not altered the overall EU picture very much. Traditionally a number of the NMS depend rather heavily on (indigenous) sources, notably coal (for example, Poland). This is reflected in the figures for the last column of Table 11.1.

---

4   To be made comparable, the various energy sources (coal, oil and so on) have all been converted to the energy content of the dominant one: oil. The unit we have used is Mtoe, which stands for million tons of oil equivalent.

CONVERSION OF PRIMARY INTO SECONDARY ENERGY

Primary energy sources are not always convenient to users, which is why they are converted into secondary ones. *To convert energy costs energy.* On the one hand, oil refineries and coke ovens use energy to feed the production process. On the other, the return of thermal power stations is rather low: energy escapes through cooling into the water and through chimneys into the air. The cost of these conversion processes is justified by the higher efficiency in production, transport and consumption of the users of secondary energy. The primary sources differ widely in the extent to which they are converted into secondary energy. About one-half of all coal is converted, mostly in power stations. Brown coal is converted almost entirely into electricity. Crude oil is fully converted into oil products, of which a portion is processed further in electric power stations.

Table 11.2   Percentage shares of energy sources in the consumption of European power stations (calculated on the basis of a conversion in oil equivalent), 1960–2000

	1960	1970	1980	1990	2000a	2000b
Coal	56	45	42	37	27	32
Oil	9	24	20	9	6	6
Gas	2	5	7	7	18	16
Nuclear	0	4	13	34	34	32
Hydro	33	21	17	12	12	11
Other	0	1	1	1	3	3
Total	100	100	100	100	100	100

Note: *1960–2000a: EU15; 2000b: EU25*

Source: *OECD, Energy Balances of OECD Countries, Paris 2003.*

Apparently, then, many primary energy sources are ultimately converted into electricity. The relative volumes of the various primary energy sources utilised for the generation of electricity have changed over time (Table 11.2) under the influence of a combination of factors, such as the relative price (coal versus oil) and government policy (decrease of oil and increase of nuclear power for strategic reasons and increase in gas and renewable sources for environmental policy reasons). The figures for 2000 show that the NMS are still very much dependent on coal in matters of electricity generation.

PRODUCTION AND IMPORT

Along with the consumption pattern of energy in Western Europe, the pattern of production and import, and hence the *external dependence*, have greatly changed (EC, 1996b). The first change came when coal, a predominantly domestic energy source, was replaced by an imported one, oil. More and more coal was imported as well, because the West European mines could not compete with foreign ones. As a result, the dependence coefficient of the EU, defined as the share of net imports of energy in total energy consumption, rose rapidly (from just 1 per cent in 1930 to 7 per cent on the eve of the Second World War, to 15 per cent by 1950 and to 66 per cent in 1973: EU12 figures). The oil crisis of the early 1970s opened European eyes to the risk of such a development. Since then extensive schemes have been carried out to make Europe less dependent on foreign energy, notably oil: schemes to boost national production as well as reduce consumption. The policy has produced the desired effect: the external dependence coefficient of the EU15 was down to 42 per cent in 1985. Between 1985 and 2002 it has oscillated around 50 per cent. Let us look rather more closely at the individual energy sources.

Crude oil The EU's own production was practically negligible in 1950. In the 1985–95 period, the EU15 produced some 30 per cent of its total oil consumption (of which the UK had the lion's share).[5] By becoming increasingly self-supplying, Western Europe diminished its total dependence on foreign oil. Moreover, it reduced strategic risks by drawing oil from an increasing number of supplying (overseas) countries. In the 1980s, it was Norway and in the 1990s the Russian Federation that moved to first place as suppliers.

Solid fuels Traditionally Western Europe produced its own coal (main producers: UK, Germany, France, Spain and Belgium). In the 1950s and 1960s, less than 10 per cent of total demand for coal needed to be imported. By 1994, when the consumption of coal had picked up again, the EU15's dependence on imports had risen to some 35 per cent. Most imports came from the USA and Poland. For a long time, coal extracted in EU countries was able to hold its own against oil and imported coal only with the help of supporting measures. Now coal is of limited importance; only Germany is a producer of significant size. Notwithstanding substantial aid to the remaining coal industry, its present and future position is very weak (among other factors due to its contribution to pollution).

Natural gas The production in the EU has grown to become quite important (particularly in the Netherlands, and later on also in the North Sea (UK)). In Western Europe outside the EU, Norway is another large producer and recently (liquefied) natural gas has begun to be imported (LNG by tanker from North Africa, natural gas by pipe from the Russian Federation; the latter accounting for some 40 per cent of total EU imports).

Other Among the other sources of energy, nuclear is of particular importance. Because uranium can be stocked, the fiction is often maintained that nuclear energy is a domestic source of energy; that uranium has to be imported into Europe is overlooked. As for such alternative primary sources as hydro-power and wind, the EU is by definition independent of imports.

CONSUMPTION BY CATEGORY

To analyse the consumption pattern,[6] we distinguish three main sectors: industry, household/ commerce, and transport. The relative position of these consumer categories in total consumption was fairly stable throughout the 1950–2000 period (see Table 11.3). Up to 1990 industry invariably took first place, recently ceded to household/commerce. Transport invariably came in third position. In the course of time the share of industry has fallen, to the benefit of transport. The figures for the EU15 and the EU25 differ only marginally.

---

5   In addition, some 25 million tons of oil were produced by Norway.

6   The categories are not defined, as in Table 11.1, in terms of primary sources, but in terms of secondary sources (after conversion: 'liquid' comprises all oil products, 'solid' coal, coke and brown coal; 'gas' comprises natural gas as well as coke-oven and refinery gas and so on; and 'electricity' refers to power from nuclear as well as thermal power stations. Final domestic consumption is defined as total domestic production plus imports minus exports and minus the energy sector's own consumption. Contrary to the OECD definition, we count bunkers in final consumption; the OECD treats this category as exports.

Table 11.3   Final domestic consumption of energy (including for non-energy purposes) in the EU, by consumer category (%), 1950–2000

	1950	1960	1970	1980	1990	2000[a]	2000[b]
Industry (incl. non-energy)	41	47	47	41	37	34	34
Household/commerce	40	35	35	36	35	36	37
Transport (incl. bunkers)	19	18	18	23	28	30	29
Total	100	100	100	100	100	100	100

Notes: [a] *1950–2000: EU15.* [b] *2000: EU25.*

Sources: OECD (1987g); OECD, Basic Statistics of Energy, Energy Balances, various years. European Commission, Energy and Transport in Figures, 2004.

Industry   The iron and steel sector is the largest consumer. Coal (for blast furnaces) is in the lead, but other energy sources, especially electricity, are steadily gaining in importance. A second important sector is that of chemical products, in particular the petrochemical industry, which uses mainly oil products and gases.[7]

Household/commerce   Household consumption has accounted for half to two-thirds of the entire category's consumption over the whole period. The development of the various energy forms offers a striking picture: after a rise in the 1950s, coal was practically eliminated in the 1960s, obviously because it was inconvenient to the user. Electricity and gas, on the other hand, have grown fast, as did oil until the decline prompted by the oil crises.

Transport   Haulage (road) is by far the largest consumer group, accounting for more than half of the category's total consumption. Moreover, its share has steadily increased over time. The demand of the haulage sector is almost entirely for oil products, which is also by far the most important source of energy for air and water transport. Electricity is almost completely and exclusively used for rail transport; coal has lost most of its former important position in shipping and rail.

PRICES

Traditionally there are important differences in prices for energy products among the member countries of the EU. Disparity for certain fuels is much higher than for others. Determinant factors here are distances between major production and consumption sites (high for coal and natural gas, low for motor fuels) and degree of integration (low for electricity, high for motor fuels). These differences reflect, apart from differences in transport costs, and notably VAT and excise taxes (see Chapter 14), a lack of market integration. Under conditions of integration one generally expects a convergence of prices. For the period 1980–1993 (for which detailed figures exist) there is no such tendency for the major energy products (EC, 1996a). Unfortunately there are no comparable figures for the most recent period.

---

7   Note that the consumption of industry also comprises non-energetic consumption, for instance of naphtha as a raw material of the petrochemical industry.

Case study 1: oil refining

INDUSTRY CHARACTERISTICS

Economies of scale play an important role in the refining industry. Therefore production has been gradually concentrated in a relatively small number of large plants. This led to a continuous increase in the average size of refineries during the 1950–2000 period (see Table 11.4). The restructuring process of the European refining industry has followed a distinct pattern dependent on the different stages of the industry life-cycle (Molle, 1993).

Table 11.4   Number of refineries by size class and total capacity of refineries (Mt/y), EU15, 1950–2003

Class (Mt/y)	1950	1960	1970	1980	1990	2000	2003	2003[a]
0.1–1.0	60	53	31	17	6	4	4	6
1.1–5.0	11	45	81	55	28	33	34	37
5.1–10.0	—	5	30	57	40	28	27	30
10.1–15.0	—	1	7	16	14	24	23	25
15.1–20.0	—	—	5	6	5	3	2	2
Larger than 20.1	—	—	1	4	4	1	1	1
Total number	71	104	155	155	97	93	91	101
Distillation capacity	41	192	695	987	614	672	647	701
Average capacity	0.6	1.8	4.5	6.3	6.2	7.2	7.1	6.9

[a] *Last column refers to EU25*

Source: 1950-1990: *Molle and Wever (1983) and Molle (1993). 2002-2003 figures from Oil and Gas Journal, several issues.*

The *introductory stage* happened shortly after the Second World War, when a large number of relatively small plants were created.

The *expansion stage* lasted from the early 1950s up to the first oil crisis in the mid-1970s. During this period, the total capacity of the refinery sector in Europe increased rapidly, in line with the strongly increased demand. Part of that growth was achieved by the expansion of existing refineries, part by the creation of new ones. Notwithstanding a tremendous enlargement of the scale of plants (Table 11.4) there was no spatial concentration of production facilities. Throughout the period 1950–75, markets were indeed growing at an even higher rate than the optimal scale, which permitted refinery activities to orient themselves to national markets and to spread geographically (Molle and Wever, 1983). This orientation to national markets, based on location factors like transport cost, was consolidated by the strategy adopted by several governments to build up their own 'national' oil industries.

The *maturity stage* came suddenly in the mid-1970s. The causes were the dramatic increases in oil prices, which led to a slack in demand. New investment was halted but the extension of existing refineries and the coming on stream of new ones that had been planned before the events added to overcapacity. Only after 1980 was it realised that the fall in demand was of a structural nature and only then were measures taken: many plants were closed altogether, while most others were reduced in capacity. The pattern of these reductions was influenced less by considerations of competition between firms on integrated markets than by the need to adapt local capacity to local demand. This implied that most of the smaller refineries were closed; some others were scaled up to reach the minimum efficient size, while many of the largest ones have been scaled down considerably. Consequently there has not been much increase in international specialisation.

COMPANY RESPONSE

The European market for oil products is relatively competitive. The five *largest European companies* (see Table 11.5), together with some American companies, dominate the European market.[8]

Table 11.5   Rank order of EU oil companies by worldwide sales (billion euro)

Rank	Company	Country	1990	2003
1	BP	UK	57	190
2	Royal Dutch/Shell	NL/UK	81	164
3	Total	France	61	97
4	ENI	Italy	33	48
5	Repsol	Spain	13	34

Source: Fortune, 2004

Majors   To this group belonged, up to the mid-1970s, five American (Exxon, Texaco, Gulf Oil, Mobil Oil and Chevron) and two European companies (Shell and BP). In the turmoil of the oil crisis of the 1970s, two left the European scene: Gulf (operations taken over by KPC) and Chevron. The majors operate on a world scale and show a high degree of vertical integration. This means that they are active at all stages of the oil industry: in the exploration and exploitation of crude oil, the transport of crude and products, the refining and, finally, the marketing of the finished products. They are, moreover, active in such related activities as (petro)chemicals. The relative position of the original seven majors decreased quite a lot in the 1950–2000 period: while in 1950 they controlled 65 per cent of total EU15 refinery capacity, in 2000 they were down to about 30 per cent. Among these majors Shell (EU) and Exxon (USA) occupied the most important places. At the height of its influence, Shell possessed 23 refineries in ten European countries and controlled about 20 per cent of the total refinery capacity.

State-controlled European companies   In a deliberate policy to strengthen the national position in the refinery industry with respect to the majors, a number of countries have established state-owned or state-controlled refinery companies. Most of them confine their refinery activities within the national borders.[9] They usually held a very large share of the national refining sector. Among these companies were Total and Elf in France, ENI in Italy, Petrogal in Portugal. Other countries also had some national or semi-national companies, but their position in the EU refinery sector was relatively modest. In many countries the national oil companies were privatised during the 1990s. Some of them (for example, Total, Elf, Fina) merged and diversified their markets by expanding their operations into other countries, which makes them more like the traditional majors.

---

8   Apart from the majors and the state controlled companies there are three other categories that merit mentioning:
- Independent private companies: many have ceased production or were taken over by larger companies due to the weakness of their market position or their resource base.
- Chemical companies: some had taken a participation in or taken over oil-refining facilities. Most of these have now limited their activities to a joint venture or have pulled out altogether.
- National companies from producer countries have moved into Europe with production and distribution facilities; in particular KPC has gained a firm foothold.

9   Elf had a number of refineries abroad, in particular in Germany, which made it something of a multinational even before its merger with Fina and Total.

European integration has had some influence on the company structure, in that it has contributed to a certain *concentration*. But the main driving forces behind the company restructuring were worldwide changes in control over oil reserves and the privatisation of national companies. Up until recently the concentration was rather low: in 1995, the C3 index (indicating the share of the three largest EU companies in total sales) stood at 32 per cent. In 2000, however, the C3 (Shell, Total, BP) had risen to 80 per cent.

Case study 2: electricity

REGULATORY FRAMEWORK

Electricity used to be considered as a public utility that did not fall under the rules of the EU. It used to be heavily regulated by national governments. In the past the Commission has sometimes tried in vain to bring the sector under the usual EU regime (for example, under the 1992 programme). In the 1990s the Commission came under increased pressure from corporate consumers for a liberalisation of the electricity market. Indeed, large industrial users, considering they were paying too high prices, contested the monopoly power of the supplier by seeking access to the national grid in order to buy directly from other industrial producers in the same country or from a foreign electricity company. The Commission has adopted the view that electricity is not fundamentally different from other goods for which measures have been taken to complete the internal market. Notwithstanding very fierce opposition from many national governments, legislation has been adopted (Directive (96/92/EC) that establishes common rules for the organisation and functioning of the electricity sector and for access to the market. It combines (partial) liberalisation and framework regulation.

The EU regime obliges the electricity sector to maintain the *separation of production, transmission and distribution*. In principle production is free, and governments have to lay down rules under which they will authorise the construction of new electricity-generating capacity. Transmission of high voltage is entrusted to the transmission system operator. Producers supply this grid, and large industrial customers and distribution companies tap from it. Distribution system operators are entities that are responsible for the line to the final consumers. In principle these three functions are to be carried out by separate companies. However, if they are still operated by the same company, the EU obliges this company to take three basic measures: first, independent management for each function; second, full transparency of the accounts of the three parts (no cross-subsidies); and, third, appropriate mechanisms to avoid confidential information being passed by the transmission operator to other parts of the company.

The liberalisation of electricity supply means that production companies and customers are free to choose the partner they prefer. This freedom has been introduced in stages. The first stage started in 1999 with the largest clients, the next continued over the 2000–2003 period with clients in smaller-sized categories. These two stages liberalised about 33 per cent of the total market. The last stage was still in progress by 2005. Many member countries (such as the UK) have implemented their programme of liberalisation more rapidly than required by the directive; others (for example, France) have been slow to implement the necessary adaptations.

Given the monopoly of the transmission grid operator, the liberalisation of the electricity market hinges critically on the conditions under which third parties can gain access to this grid. The EU has provided for different systems, but the most common one is now the regulated third party access, in which the relevant authorities set the prices at which any user can transport electricity. This system has the advantage in the short run that it excludes discrimination against competitors and in the medium term that companies can plan future electricity deals with advance knowledge of transparent tariffs.

The regime put into place by the EU has a framework character. Much is worked out by national regulatory authorities for the electricity sector (independent from the electricity companies) in partnership with the usual national competition authorities and the Commission.

INDUSTRY CHARACTERISTICS

Electricity consumption has increased extremely fast in the last few decades. All the EU member states, in their efforts to be self-sufficient, have matched this increase in demand with a corresponding increase in the capacity of their generation plants and distribution lines. They have preferred to import primary energy rather than electric power.

Only a small percentage of total electricity production used to enter into international trade; intra-EU15 trade as a percentage of EU15 final consumption increased gradually from 2 per cent in 1960 to some 8 per cent in 1994, indicating the rather low degree of integration of the sector. Exchange with third countries during this period was limited to some imports. The explanation for these low figures is that the international exchange of electricity used to be limited to the volumes that were necessary to overcome specific shortages in the power provision of a country (for example, due to maintenance of major thermal power stations, temporarily low production of hydro plants or technical difficulties). This situation is at odds with the general philosophy of the EU, which is based on the notion that the rationale for the exchange of all goods and services is competitive advantage.[10] The liberalisation has not had a very high immediate impact on exchange, as adaptation of the infrastructure has taken some time.

The differences among EU countries in the price of electricity for typical household and industrial consumers used to be very substantial. We may give the following reasons for such differences.

- *Inefficiencies*. While markets are split and regulated to a very high degree, production is likely to be inefficient (as a result of bad allocation of resources and rent seeking). Some countries may have been better able to check such tendencies than others.
- *Policy*. In monopoly markets there is ample scope for setting different prices for different consumer categories. The public electricity companies have followed different strategies, based on the level of fixed costs of production and distribution and the possibilities of dividing these costs between different categories of users, taking account of market response and industrial, environmental and regional policy objectives.
- *Fuel mix*. In France, almost three-quarters of all electricity is generated in nuclear power stations, while Denmark's power plants are almost exclusively coal-fired. The more expensive producers were those that depended on oil or gas firing.

With the completion of the internal market for electricity, and the increase in trade in electricity that follows from this, a number of the above factors have lost importance and hence *price*

---

10   For theory, see Chapter 5; for clear examples, see Chapters 10 and 12.

differences have decreased. In the period 1996–99 the average decrease of prices in the EU amounted to some 6 per cent. In some countries, like Spain and Finland, the decrease was even three times as high. Since then further price decrease has been disappointing for a variety of reasons. In Italy, for example, the base price for the final consumer decreased by one third in the 1996–2003 period but the fuel charge neutralised this effect completely. Price convergence has also been disappointing because the cost bases of the various providers differ very much as they have made different technological choices as to the type of primary source used in their power plants. Moreover, government influence makes the position of many of the incumbents still very strong (for example, EDF in France) so the effects of further competition are weak. A final remark needs to be made on the most recent period: prices for crude oil have been sharply rising and as a consequence prices of electricity generated from oil have also risen. Further decreases in price differences can be expected as soon as the capacity for cross-border trading is sufficiently developed (see Faini *et al.*, 2004).

COMPANY STRUCTURE

The liberalisation of the EU electricity market has entailed a major upheaval in terms of company structure. All companies are now redefining their strategies. They have very different starting positions. Because the European market for electric power has long been fragmented along national lines, international integration of firms has been non-existent. In many countries economies of scale and scope have induced electricity firms to organise on the national level (for instance, France where EDF used to monopolise the generation, transmission and distribution of electricity). In the UK, following the liberalisation of the market in the early 1990s, various companies were created in the course of the privatisation process, each controlling parts of the generation and transmission and distribution process. Other member countries showed highly diversified patterns as to the organisation of the supply side, mainly depending on the institutional balance between different layers of government, and on the ideological balance between public services and private initiative.

The new EU regulatory framework has had two effects. First, it obliged companies to undo their vertical integration. That means that the network for distribution to the final customer and the transmission lines has to move into independent hands. Second, it has induced companies to concentrate on an international level in order to take advantage of the potential for cost cutting that goes hand-in-hand with scale. A few moves have already been made. Electricité de France (the largest company in the EU and one of the largest worldwide) has bought London Electricity, the UK capital's supplier. In addition, it also has stakes in a number of other EU countries, in some of the CEEC and in non-European countries. RWE Energie, one of the largest German producers (after having taken over power companies in the former East Germany) has acquired stakes in a Portuguese company and several companies in the CEEC. Two other major German producers, VEBA and VIAG, have merged their energy operations (VEBA had already acquired a majority stake in the Dutch EZH).

However, important national differences still remain as a function of the deeply rooted differences in the industry's internal institutions and their institutional environments (Glachant and Finon, 2000).

Summary and conclusions

- The involvement of the EU with energy was based on three different treaties: ECSC for coal, EAEC for nuclear energy and the EEC for all other energy products. Gradually a common energy policy has evolved.
- For a long time the dominant energy source was coal. From the mid-1960s, oil took over the lead. Electricity, generated from various primary sources, is becoming ever more important.
- Oil markets have gone through very turbulent times. Market partners, in particular the multinational oil companies, have responded by adapting and modernising the production, refining, transport and distribution systems, taking into account the integration of the European market and the linkages with world markets.
- Electricity, by contrast, is traditionally a highly regulated industry and until recently the market has remained fragmented along national lines. The liberalisation of the internal EU market has gradually been achieved.

12 *Services*

Introduction

While the European Union has always looked upon services as an essential part of the integration process, it has taken some time for the EU to devote much attention to them. In the present chapter we propose to look into the European service sector in some detail. The pattern of this chapter is the same as that of the previous ones.

First we will give a succinct description of the European policy regime. The mix of liberalisation and regulation of the EU had to take into account the fact that major segments of the service sector have been subject to considerable national government regulation. Convinced that a socially desirable organisation of quite large segments could not be left to private enterprise, governments have even assumed direct responsibility for production and distribution, especially for services associated with the welfare state (such as social security). Other branches (such as medical services) are a combination of public and private effort.

Next we will give a description of the service sector in Europe; we will focus in this chapter on the services that can in principle be traded by private agents, thus excluding the public sector from the discussion. Transport is also left out of the present chapter because of its special position in the European setting; it will be dealt with in a separate chapter.

We will then report the results of two case studies of integration. The first one is insurance, for which integration started some time ago. The second one is telecommunications, a branch that is expanding very quickly as a consequence of the development of the information society and is transforming itself very quickly as a result of recent privatisation and liberalisation.

A summary of the findings will complete the chapter.

EU regime

RATIONALE AND PRINCIPLES

The Treaty of Rome is fairly brief on services. Its general definition of services reads: 'all these activities normally provided for remuneration in so far as they are not governed by the provisions relating to freedom of movement for goods, capital and persons'. They include in particular activities of an industrial or commercial nature and those of craftsmen and professions. For all these activities the Treaty stipulates the freedom to:

- provide services: a company of member country A can provide services in member country B without having an office there; and
- set up an establishment: companies (or persons) wishing to set up an establishment (that is, a legal entity with, in general, premises, staff and so on) in another member country are

free to do so under the same conditions as are laid down for the nationals of the country of establishment.

The substantiation of the freedom to provide services has dragged on for a long time, for two main reasons. One was the difficulty in defining the equivalence of qualifications, another the access to certain markets that were organised by national governments or by private groups sanctioned to organise and protect them.

In the early 1970s, several rulings of the Court in principle liberalised all services connected with agriculture, manufacturing, craft and trade (commerce). However, until 1985 quite a few problems remained regarding the service branches. The programme to complete the internal market in services brought a solution by a combination of three elements (Chapter 6): (1) liberalisation – freedom for cross-border trade in services; (2) mutual recognition of the quality of the home country's control; and (3) harmonisation – minimum sets of European regulation.

The Commission has since made several attempts to complete the liberalisation of the internal service market. It has initially gone for a sector by sector approach. In this way separate regimes were agreed upon for financial services, telecommunication and transport.

MARKET REGULATION

Apart from its efforts to liberalise intra-Union trade in services, the EU does not pursue a *market regulation policy* for the service sector. The market for services is indeed organised in much the same way as that for most manufacturing and energy activities, for which EU institutions have neither responsibility nor power to intervene in prices and quantities. Service markets come under the general rules for competition (see Chapter 14), which are considered sufficient to have European markets function properly. Many service sectors are, however, heavily regulated at the national level, with governments influencing important aspects such as access to markets (for example, insurance, medical services) and prices (insurance and so on). Two principles govern the EU policy for the completion of the internal market of these sectors: first, to establish a minimum European framework of basic standards; second, to let companies working under different sets of rules compete freely, thereby obliging governments to compete with each other in optimal rule setting (see Chapter 14).

Until recently there was no European *policy vis-à-vis third countries* in matters of services, in stark contrast to the very elaborate schemes operative on goods markets (Chapter 17). Under the impetus of technological change (data transmission) and under pressure from third countries, questions about external trade in services were placed on the agenda of the Uruguay round of GATT/WTO.[1] This has finally resulted in an agreement to diminish the protection in trade in many service branches.

STRUCTURAL POLICY

Unlike agriculture, manufacturing and energy, the sectors discussed in the preceding chapters, the service sector is not subject to a European structural policy. There are no schemes to encourage innovation, support investments in infrastructure or production equipment, or

---

1   Indeed the growing importance of services in the economy did not immediately bring about a greater interest among international organisations. For a long time, services were considered an essentially domestic sector hardly in need of international attention. Since the 1970s, however, the awareness has grown that such lack of interest has bred many protectionist measures impeding the internationalisation of service activities (Griffiths, 1975, among others). Organisations like WTO now carry services as an important subject on their negotiating agenda.

improve human capital. This is in line with the situation we find back in the individual member countries: the private segment of the service sector is mostly left to fend for itself. There are two very important exceptions to this. The first relates to telecommunications. The structural policy of the EU for this sector of activity uses two instruments: (1) support for innovation via the large-scale technology programmes, and (2) support for infrastructure by the newly established possibility for support of trans-European networks.

The second relates to electronic commerce and the use of the Internet. The EU considers that the future competitiveness of its economy will be dependent on the speed with which it will be able to transform itself into a knowledge-based economy. It has set up an action programme for the stimulation of the so-called content industries (eContent). This umbrella term covers many traditional publishing products (books, periodicals and so on), radio and television, and the modern multimedia applications. This sector is estimated to account for some 5 per cent of GDP and is expected to grow at a rate of some 20 per cent a year. The action programme aims to take away the barriers to the development of a European market for these products. One of these barriers is the multilingual character of the products that the EU market needs. By providing solutions to this problem it is anticipated that the present handicap can be transformed into an asset, because it would permit the export of multilingual multimedia products to other parts of the world.

Sketch of the sector

EMPLOYMENT AND VALUE ADDED BY BRANCH

Since the Second World War, the service sector[2] has rapidly advanced to assume the leadership in the total economy of the EU. With increasing productivity and low income elasticities, the shares of the agricultural and manufacturing sectors first stagnated and then dropped, making room for the quickly expanding service sector. One reason why statistics show such a large expansion is that certain functions which had hitherto been carried out within other sectors (cleaning, auditing and so on) have become independent and are thus registered as such. This phenomenon results when technically progressive services break off from manufacturing for reasons such as the broadening of the scope of products, the improvement of the quality through specialisation, or the cutting of cost by using economies of scale.

When the service sector becomes dominant in an economy and many service activities concern the handling of information rather than trade in goods, the terms 'post-industrial' or 'information society' are often used. The EU has entered that stage. Indeed the total service sector that accounted for little over a third of total employment just after the Second World War now accounts for almost three-quarters of employment (Table 12.1). That spectacular growth has been accomplished by a few branches; while the relative position of the construction and transport branches stagnated, trade, and notably financial services and business and community services were very dynamic. The very fast growth of community services[3] has been closely related to the build-up of the welfare state and the ensuing increased involvement

---

2   Unlike the situation with other sectors of activity, a definition of the service sector is difficult to give. Services are often described as a 'rest sector' encompassing the activities other than primary and secondary. Another approach focuses on the intangible nature of the output, and thus excludes, among other things, construction. Statistical measurement is poor and hence also the possibility of quantitative analysis of the sector.

3   See Saunders and Klau (1985); Rose et al. (1985). The sector of community services consists of three branches of about equal size – public administration, education, medical – and a small group of other services.

of the public sector in society. The structural changes are difficult to measure for the NMS; however, the present situation in the NMS does not differ that much from the EU15; as witness Table 12.1.

Table 12.1   Percentage share of the service sectors in EU total employment, 1950–2003

Sub-sector	1950	1960	1970	1980	1990	2000[a]	2003[b]
5 Construction	7	8	8	8	8	8	8
6 Commerce	13	14	15	16	17	18	18
7 Transport	6	6	6	6	6	6	6
8 Finance and Business	3	4	5	6	7	11	11
9 Community and Social	9	12	19	24	27	28	27
Total services	38	44	53	60	65	71	70

Notes: [a] *1950–2000: EU15* [b] *2003: EU25*

Sources: NEI, Fleur data base; OECD, Labour Force Statistics, various years. Eurostat, Labour Market Statistics.

For GDP, the branch composition of these service sectors is comparable to that of employment.[4]

The growth of services has also been dependent on the specialisation of the other sectors of the economy that have spun off many services otherwise provided internally to specialised service firms. About one third of the gross output of the manufacturing sector consists of services. Network services (such as transport and telecommunication), financial services (such as banking), trade (such as wholesale) and other (such as consultancy) all play major roles (Faini et al., 2004). Consequently, changes in efficiency, quality and cost of the services impact heavily on the competitiveness of the overall economy.

EUROPEANISATION OR MULTINATIONALISATION OF FIRMS

The list of the largest service firms in the EU (excluding public enterprises and public and private transport companies) is dominated by firms from the telecommunications, retail and finance sectors. For each sub-sector of services, we have indicated in Table 12.2 the biggest firm (by employment), to give an indication of the intersectoral differences.[5]

Generally speaking, service firms have a considerably smaller average size than manufacturing firms. The size of firms in certain sub-branches, such as professional services or business services (marketing, legal and so on), are particularly low; concentration and multinationalisation have not yet advanced far in these branches (Rubalcaba-Bermejo, 1999).

Most firms have their home in one of the larger countries of North Western Europe (in particular Germany); this is true for all branches. Their large internal markets provide a good basis for initial expansion at home and subsequent expansion abroad. An example is Carrefour in France which is the result of a merger between two large French retail firms and has expanded in several European and third countries. Head offices of the major EU service firms. are mostly in London, Paris and Frankfurt. The Southern European countries and the NMS

---

4   Comparisons between the industry figures on GDP and employment need to be made with caution, as the differences between the two indicators may be due not only to productivity divergences but also to differences in sector delineation.

5   The service sector is a very mixed bag, and because firms from different service branches are difficult to compare (turnover for commerce, gross premium for insurance, assets for banks and so on) we have opted for employment figures as the best indicator of size.

Table 12.2   Service firms, largest by sub-sector, 2003

Name	Country	Branch	Employment (x 1000)
Carrefour	F	Retail trade	419
Deutsche Post	D	Mail, package, freight delivery	383
Deutsche Telekom	D	Telecommunications	249
HSBC Holdings	UK	Banking: commercial and savings	218

Source: Fortune, 2004.

are very poorly represented. This unbalanced situation has been reinforced by the completion of the internal market. In the past decades most mergers and acquisitions have indeed been initiated by companies from northern member states, often seeking to absorb companies from southern and eastern member states.

MARKET STRUCTURES

The markets for services of the EU member countries have long remained sheltered from competition, owing to lack of mobility of services across markets and firms within markets. This situation was due to three factors:

- *Natural determinants of the degree of concentration.* Among these factors we find economies of scale and of scope. For a service like telecommunications, for instance, the cost of a network determines the very high concentration; in other services large numbers of sellers appear on more diversified markets, as with hotels.
- *Barriers to entry.* Many service industries typically incur fixed costs in two types of assets: tangible (such as buildings) and intangible (such as reputation). Sunk costs in the tangible category occur, for example, in telecommunications (networks). Sunk costs in the intangible category consist, for example, in maintaining a good reputation for financial services (banks, insurance).
- *Government regulations.* These are usually divided into two categories: (1) those that affect the structure of the industry (for example, the entry of new firms) and (2) those that impinge upon the conduct of existing firms. Some branches have relatively little of both (construction, for instance), some have much of both (for example, insurance) and some are subjected to structural instruments only (for example, distribution).

Table 12.3   Market structure in services

Branch	Determinants			Degree of competition	
	Concentration	Sunk cost	Regulation	Before	After
Construction	low	low	medium	high	high
Distribution	low	low	medium	medium	high
Hotels	low	low	low	high	high
Telecom	high	high	high	low	medium
Banking/ insurance	medium	medium	high	low	medium
Business	low	medium	low	medium	medium

Source: EC (1993c, 1996a).

For a number of service branches we have indicated the scores on these three factors in Table 12.3 (first three columns). From this information we can assess the degree of competition in each branch (last two columns): first the situation that prevailed before the 1992 programme was implemented ('before' column) and second, the situation that prevailed around 1996 ('after' column).

Competition has in general increased (Table 12.3) as a consequence of the completion of the internal market; low competition has become medium and medium competition has become high. However, overall the increase in competition seems to be less strong in services than in manufacturing, reflecting the lack of implementation of the internal market programme in many domains of the service sector.[6]

The 1992 process has led to a better *allocation*; that is, to the provision of the European consumer with service products that are better adapted to his needs at lower cost. In some branches where competition has not increased much (such as banking) these effects were not very strong. In other branches, like mobile telecommunication and logistics/distribution, the scope of services has been substantially enlarged and their price substantially reduced. This in turn has increased the possibilities for EU-wide sourcing and improved the competitive position of the branches that use these services (EC, 1996a).

This process of restructuring has not led to big changes in the *location of production*, because of the high degree of proximity between consumers and producers that many services require. However, ownership of firms has been affected, as local service providers have increasingly become parts of multinational firms or networks. This may be as subsidiaries or via cooperation agreements (association, licensing, franchising). The latter are often used by branches such as accountancy, consultancy and distribution.

The impact of the 1992 programme on *concentration* has been very different for the various branches of the service sector. Sub-sectors with relatively light regulation, such as distribution, have shown increases in concentration both at the EU and the national level. Highly regulated services, such as retail banking, have shown only small increases in EU-wide concentration, while concentration at the national level tended to increase more (EC, 1996a). For sectors such as banking there is still a considerable potential for cross-border integration. However, for such services the cost benefit relation of such integration is less easily derived from arguments about economies of scale than in the manufacturing sector (Bos and Kolari, 2005).

There has been a general tendency towards *price convergence* in services over the 1985–96 period (EC, 1996a, 1999b). However, price dispersion in market services stays at levels much above those in manufacturing. The remaining price disparities are caused by a number of factors:

- *Wage levels*. Services for which international transaction costs tend to be prohibitive will be costed at the price of the local labour market inputs (real estate).
- *Regulation*. Important differences in government intervention still prevail in services like health, water distribution and so on.
- *Market structures*. Exclusive distribution systems (insurance) or licence for access to market regulations (telecommunications) hinder the arbitrage process.

---

6   An example of such slow growth of competition is the banking sector; see in this respect, for instance, Bikker (2004).

Case study 1: insurance

REGULATORY FRAMEWORK

Within the EU countries, the insurance industry has developed on a national basis, each national sub-market being regulated by a whole array of measures.[7] The only exception to this was the UK industry, which has always been of a highly international nature. The common market for services was scheduled by the EEC Treaty to be realised by 1970, but this has proved impossible. The Commission has tried to bring about a common European market for insurance services,[8] but for a long time has found it very difficult to convince national governments. In its *harmonisation* programme, the Commission has made a distinction between life and non-life. This principle of specialisation forbids life insurance companies to do other types of insurance, so as to protect the interests of life policyholders against considerable risks. In its *liberalisation* programme, the Commission has made a distinction between the freedom of establishment and the freedom to provide services abroad.

Freedom of establishment implies the possibility of creating a subsidiary in another member state; non-discrimination requires that such a subsidiary, a broker or an agent, be treated on a level with national companies. In the 1970s, several directives introduced this freedom of establishment (1973 for life, 1979 for non-life). The directives obliged every member state to subject all insurance business, of both local and foreign companies, on its territory to authorisation on the same conditions; as a result, all companies anywhere in the EU have come under supervision. The problem was, however, that this system tended to add to the cost for the insurer (for example, the French authorities, applying French standards, required minimum reserves that had to be franc-dominated and lodged in francs), which added to the costs of the foreign insurer. Subsequent directives have set minimum standards, to inspire mutual confidence in national regulations and to make sure that coverage would be similar (for example, in the motor insurance branch, so as to take away the need for border controls of insurance documents). In 1986, the European Court of Justice confirmed in a case of the Commission against four member states that national restrictions against foreign insurance companies were not acceptable; exceptions could be made, however, if the protection of the consumer so required.

Freedom to provide services abroad means that, for example, a French client can conclude an insurance contract directly with the London office of an English company and is not obliged to do so with a France-based firm. This situation used to be precluded by national regulations. In line with the general sense of Court ruling in other branches of activity, the Commission had proposed several schemes for liberalisation and harmonisation; however, up to the end of the 1980s, they had all failed to gain sufficient approval from the Council to reach realisation. The reasons for this are that national regulations were well entrenched, and opposition to further harmonisation and liberalisation was quite fierce (Finsinger *et al.*, 1985). Liberalisation was only half-heartedly supported by insurance companies. Indeed the latter were often well settled behind protecting regulations even in foreign markets. In that situation the German

---

7   The regulations have been made in the first instance to protect the consumer and to call for a certain prudence in the management of the resources that have been entrusted to the company. It goes without saying that these measures are easily used for protection against outside competitors. A classification of such protectionist measures can be made, along several lines. OECD (1983a); Ingo (1985); Carter and Dickinson (1992).

8   For a more elaborate description of the EU's initial involvement, see EC (1985c, ch. 2); for national systems of some member countries, see Finsinger and Pauly (1986); for the programme, see Pool (1990); and for the situation at the beginning of the 1990s, see EC (1992e).

broker Steicher went against the German regulations by arranging for insurance of his German clients directly with non-German insurers. The European Court of Justice, asked to consider the case, ruled in December 1986 in favour of Steicher, considering that corporate clients could very well be left free to choose between products of different companies at home or abroad. The far-reaching implications of that verdict were soon realised, which speeded up the discussions on the proposals for the common market for insurance in the framework of the 1992 programme. A number of directives have been agreed upon. Full freedom of insurance service provision both for the life and non-life markets was realised by the mid-1990s.

The European legislation covers such matters as the formation of an insurance company, the opening of branches and agencies and the subsequent supervision of technical reserves, assets, solvency margins and minimum guarantee funds. Harmonisation of these aspects is important to prevent companies from being pushed by competition into contracts that do not cover the cost of the risks involved. Theory[9] does not predict that a very tight regulation is the best option. So the EU regime is rather based on a rather limited set of rules. The Commission is counting on a tendency towards spontaneous harmonisation of national regulatory systems as increased international competition of firms implicitly entails competition of the national regulations under which they operate.

The supervision of insurance companies is carried out by national authorities. The coordination of this supervision is an important aspect of European legislation because it is the basis for a double target: (1) to permit a company to do business in several EU countries under a single licence supervised by the authorities of the country where it has its (European) head offices (home country control principle); (2) to afford persons seeking insurance access to the widest possible range of insurance products on offer in the EU.[10] In the 1990s this regulation proved to be in need of some clarification. This was due, on the one hand, to the development of new technological possibilities, such as remote contracting via electronic commerce, and, on the other, to the need to specify the possibility of limiting liberalisation for preserving the 'general good'. The Commission has clarified these issues in a recent communication (EC, 2000c).

In the past many governments have blocked the combination of insurance and banking in one company for reasons of consumer protection, quality of supervision and fair competition. Since the EU-wide deregulation, such barriers have been lifted. Now a number of banks and insurance companies see advantages in the combined marketing of products, the organisation of access to capital, and the spreading of risks. The strategy of combining the two into one corporate structure is called 'banc-assurance'.

INDUSTRY CHARACTERISTICS

The insurance business consists of two main branches, life and non-life (motor, fire and so on). The importance of both segments in the total market of the EU has varied over the past decades; in the 1990s each accounted for about half of total business. Insurance is a product for which demand is growing fast; as a result, the share of premiums in total GNP increased from 3 per cent in 1960 to 7 per cent in 1995. There is little national variation in the share of 'non-life' products in total expenditure. On the contrary, national differences in expenditure on 'life' products are fairly large, owing to differences in preferences, social security coverage and so on. There is some tendency towards convergence: in the countries with a low coverage,

---

9   For a concise overview of the theory behind the regulation see, for example, Rees and Kessner (1999).
10   See EC (1992e); Carter and Dickinson (1992); Pool (1990).

demand for life insurance has grown very fast in the past decades; growth has been less dynamic in mature markets.

Until recently integration had not developed far. The European insurance market used to be segmented into national markets. On each national market, concentration tended to be fairly high as a consequence of economies of scale and scope. The largest group typically held a 15 to 25 per cent share in the national market. In some countries (France, Ireland), a large portion of the business was covered by nationalised companies, but in most countries private firms dominated the market. In all countries, mutual-insurance companies also took a fair share of the market (EC, 1985c).

During the 1990s a general trend towards liberalisation took place, in which many state-owned companies were privatised. The very highly regulated German market was opened up, significantly reducing the high cost structure in that country. However, until now, two other effects that one would have expected did not happen: (1) the interpenetration of markets by cross-border trade; and (2) significant new entry into the German market. Apparently, the barriers to market access (no independent brokers, differences in legal stipulations) are still too problematic for a real internal market to develop (Rees and Kessner, 1999).

In the recent past, interpenetration of markets has been stimulated by the multinationalisation of firms. Firms have several motives to multinationalise by mergers and acquisitions:

- Need to spread risks. This can be done better by companies that have grown to a certain size and have diversified their geographical markets. Acquiring a large size[11] is not easy on small national markets, so companies have tried increasingly to get at their objective by internationalisation. As it is not easy to start branch operations in a new market from scratch, many companies have internationalised by acquisition and mergers.
- Demand from multinational firms. MNFs from other branches have increasingly centralised their buying of insurance services, asking for worldwide coverage of their operations by one insurance company. This factor does play its role notably in the non-life business.
- Completion of the internal market. This has entailed a process of restructuring of firms at the European level, and this has been facilitated by the large-scale privatisation of nationalised industries in a number of EU countries.

The *increase in multinationalisation* can be measured by several indicators. The share of foreign-owned firms in the total national premium income of the 15 member countries of the EU was only between 3 and 10 per cent in the mid-1980s. It increased in the first half of the 1990s by some 13 per cent on average. The ratio of foreign premium income in total domestic income from the various European insurance companies increased more than fourfold in the same period (Rietbergen, 1999). Recent figures are not available, but the process of mergers and acquisitions described must have led to considerable further increases in these two ratios.

In the past, segmentation of national markets led to large price differences among EU member countries. To illustrate their magnitude: in 1985, consumers in Portugal paid nine times as much for the same life insurance policy as consumers in the cheapest country, the UK (BEUC, 1988). Similar differences in prices were found for other categories of insurance (house, motor, fire and liability). Assuming that the average of the four countries with the lowest prices

---

11   Large size permits companies to achieve economies of scale in the marketing of their products. Large scale also permits one to improve one's bargaining position on financial markets. In order to reap these advantages even more fully, some companies have joined forces with banks in so-called 'total finance' companies. This has been made possible by the new deregulated environment.

would be a fair indication of the EU price after integration, the potential for price cuts was found to amount to more than 50 per cent for Italy, 30 per cent for Belgium, Luxembourg and Spain, 25 per cent for France and 10 per cent for Germany (Price Waterhouse, 1988). In the 1985–96 period the price dispersion decreased significantly (EC, 1999b). Moreover, productivity of the industry increased, implying efficiency gains to producers and consumers.

COMPANY STRUCTURE

The changes in the regulatory environment have led many companies to revise their strategies. The first is with respect to their legal form. As the founding principles of mutuals became difficult to uphold under the pressure of competition, a movement of de-mutualisation set in, leading to a significant rise in the market share of incorporated companies (based on shares). The second is with respect to markets. Many firms have recognised the necessity of becoming a multinational company, which has led to a frenzy of mergers and acquisitions. As a consequence, the number of companies in the EU fell by one-quarter between 1990 and 1997.

By way of example, we describe the *genesis and development of the five largest EU companies:*[12]

- AXA (F). The transformation of a small regional company into a multinational ranking first in the EU has been realised in the time span of a few decades through a series of take-overs and mergers. Initial take-overs concerned firms in the UK (Equity and Law) and the USA (Equitable). A major merger was concluded in 1996, when AXA joined forces with UAP.[13] The strategy of the AXA group is to stick to insurance as its core business.
- Allianz (G). This company has purchased RAS, the second largest Italian group, and a number of smaller companies in other countries. It has then strengthened its position on its home market by acquiring complete control over Vereinte and on the EU market by acquiring control over the major parts of the French group AGF. It also grew in the USA by taking over PIMCO. By acquiring Dresdner Bank it has gone into diversification.
- Generali (I). In the past this company has grown internationally by acquiring a series of companies. To strengthen its home base and to ward off the possibility of itself being taken over by one of the other large EU insurers, it acquired, in 2000, INA, the third largest insurer in Italy. It has expanded in the NMS and recently in China. Generali has insisted it does not want to become a banc-assurance group.
- ING (NL). This group is the result of a deliberate strategy of international banc-assurance. It has a strong position in both banking and insurance in Benelux, as well as important insurance activities in other EU countries and in the USA. Its objective is to become a major player in banc-assurance in all countries of Europe and the USA.
- Aviva (UK). This is the new identity of CGNU (the result of a merger between CGU and Norwich Union). The company owns, among others, Delta Lloyd (NL) Hibernia (IRL) and Commercial Union (PL).

---

12   The list excludes some very large reinsurance companies, such as Münchener Re. It equally excludes Lloyd's, the British firm that occupies a very special place in insurance brokerage. Apart from the companies based in a EU member state, some Swiss companies are also very active on the EU market.

13   UAP was itself already a multinational, having acquired (majority stakes in) companies like Royale Belge (B), GESA (SW), Sun Life (UK) and Groupe Victoire (F) (which included Colonia (G)).

During the past decades internationalisation by cross-border take-overs and mergers has been the result of the considerable advantages of rationalisation and scale (Dickinson, 1993; EC, 1996c). It is worth noting that companies that could start to exploit these advantages in a major home market had the best chances to get to top positions, as the list above shows.[14] This whole process of rationalisation has entailed three changes. First, the average size of the largest EU firms has greatly increased (some four times). Second, some European firms are now among the world leaders due to their global expansion. Third, the ranking of the largest EU insurance companies has been profoundly changed.

Case study 2: telecommunications

REGULATORY FRAMEWORK

Only a short time ago telecommunications was regarded as a clear case of a natural monopoly. More than one supplier would imply the duplication of a very costly network infrastructure and hence imply a welfare loss for society. In most EU countries public telephone operators were state-owned organisations which tended to cross-subsidise different services at the demand of government and privilege domestic equipment manufacturers. Technological developments have completely changed this situation. Networks for cable television or electricity distribution can be used for telecommunication services, while satellites offer even more versatility and have permitted the very rapid generalisation of the use of mobile phones with their associated services, such as pictures, music and so on. In view of these changed circumstances the national monopolies were no longer justifiable. Moreover, multinational corporate users of telecommunications services exerted increasing pressure to liberalise, as their competitiveness in world markets depended on good and cheap telecommunications. This became even more urgent with the opening up of a whole range of new services based on the Internet.

The EU has recognised that a change in the regulatory framework has become imperative. In the 1980s it decided that telecommunications were to be regarded as a market service, and hence formed part of the programme for the completion of the internal market. In addition, it has launched programmes to support European firms in the adoption of the new technologies. Examples of such programmes are RACE (Research in Advanced Communications in Europe) and ESPRIT (European Strategic Programme for Research and Development in Information Technologies). These have had a significant impact on the speed of innovation and industrial structure of the European telecommunications industry (Dumont and Meeusen, 1999). In 1993, after long hesitation, the EU committed itself to the liberalisation of the European telecommunications service sector. This went hand-in-hand with important reforms in member states[15]. Until 1998 the main concern of the regulatory policy focused on the liberalisation of

---

14   A large home market is not a necessary condition, however. This is indicated by ING. Another large firm that turned such a possible disadvantage into advantage is AEGON (NL), the result of a merger that was realised in the beginning of the 1980s between two Dutch companies, AGO and ENNIA, each the result of mergers between smaller companies. The constraints of a small home market stimulated the company to go international, which it has done via very large take-overs in the EU and the USA.
15   See Eliassen and Sjovaag (1999) and Hulsink (1999). A survey of the directive's decisions and recommendations has been given in the various reports of the Commission on the implementation of the telecommunications regulatory package (see, for example, EC, 1999e). The NMS have already begun to implement the regulatory package on telecommunications ahead of accession.

fixed line telephony. After that year attention moved to the mobile industry. These moves towards liberalised EU markets have been driven not only by technology but also by the global trend towards liberalisation of trade in services (see Chapter 17).

The first step towards the setting up of the new EU regime was to separate the regulatory functions from the operational functions. The next one was to make the operational functions subject to the usual competition policy and to replace discretionary powers of national regulators by rule based anti-trust control. The third step was to specify and organise the new regulatory functions.

The *EU system* consists of the following elements:

- National Regulatory Agencies (NRAs) have been created in all member countries. These authorities are in charge of the implementation of the EU regulation and need to be independent from both operators and government. Their main objectives are consumer protection and the establishment of an innovative, competitive and sustainable telecommunications industry.
- The specification of certain conditions for operators to obtain licences under which operators have to work. One example is interconnection, which means the linking of the facilities of different operators and providers. Interconnection is essential in safeguarding access of new providers to the existing network infrastructure.

A new set of directives was issued in 2002[16] that have as their prime objective to eliminate remaining restrictions to entry, to create a level playing field between incumbents and new entrants.

INDUSTRY CHARACTERISTICS

The range of products of the telecommunications sector has changed dramatically over the last decades. The major part of the market of telecommunications services is still with fixed telephony (and related services such as fax). These services have a very high penetration rate among households in the EU and growth rates are henceforth relatively modest, although still very substantially above GDP growth rate levels. Over the past decade two services, mobile telephony and the Internet, have developed at a spectacular speed.

In the past the sector was composed of national telecommunications companies that were monopolists. Although employment has been suppressed because the former monopolists have had to rationalise activities after having been submitted to international competition, this loss has been more than compensated by the employment creation of new entrants with new services.

Price dispersion has decreased under the influence of increased competition: the index went down by one third between 1993 and 1996 and by one fifth between 1995 and 2000 (EC, 1999b, 1999e, 2001a). This tendency has since been reinforced. In some countries, prices of international and national long distance calls (markets in which competition is fiercest) have been cut by 30 per cent or more. However, prices for local calls (a market still dominated by the former monopolists) have scarcely decreased at all. The decrease in prices of mobile phone services has been particularly significant in recent years. There is still quite some variation among the countries of the EU that can be explained by differences in regulation, notably on

---

16   See, for example, EC (2004b).

aspects that determine consumer switching cost such as number portability. Liberalisation of fixed lines also has a negative effect on mobile cost (Grzybowski, 2005).

So the sector provides an example where liberalisation has actually boosted total output, improved the product range, reduced prices and supported net job creation.

COMPANY RESPONSE

The company structure of the telecommunications industry changed very profoundly during the 1990s. Currently, the *major players* on the EU market are the incumbents (that is, the former national public telephone companies) of the major member countries. These are all very large even by world standards (they are all among the largest European companies on the *Fortune* list). Most of these are now fully or partly privatised. Since the liberalisation movement gained momentum, a significant number of alternative suppliers have entered the marketplace. At the beginning of the 21st century the number of those who had obtained licences for nationwide and international services exceeded 500. As a consequence the entire EU population now has the opportunity of choosing between at least two providers. The position of the incumbents remains, however, very strong; in most countries they still have a share in home market sales well above 50 per cent.

This situation is far from stable. On the contrary, a frenetic movement of regrouping consisting of building alliances, cooperating in joint venture projects and, notably, mergers and acquisitions, has been triggered by the new EU regime. This process is not limited to the EU. On the contrary, companies are increasingly struggling to acquire a sufficient scale of operations to become one of the major players on the world level. Incumbent companies from one country have often started by taking over one or two such alternative suppliers to start up business in other countries than their home market.[17] Mergers of incumbent companies from the bigger member countries have not yet taken place, but the merger movement between smaller ones has been quite important.[18] As technology in this field changes very rapidly and so do the services related to them, it is likely that this turbulence will continue for some time.

Summary and conclusions

- The EU had always considered services an essential part of the integration process, but paid little attention to it in practice. The growing importance of the sector in intra- and extra-EU trade has changed that situation, and now policies are being worked out for the liberalisation of the internal service market as well as for external trade in services.
- Many service firms have up till recently been sheltered from international competition by government regulations. For that reason, little multinationalisation of firms has occurred. The sector's low degree of integration is also apparent in the fairly high differences in prices among EU countries.
- The case studies of insurance and telecommunications, branches in which economies of scale are important, show that liberalisation (both the freedom to provide services in

---

17   For example, Deutsche Telekom took over One2one in the UK, SIRIS in France and acquired large stakeholdings in NMS companies (for example, Matav of Hungary). The British company, Vodafone, acquired the German company Mannesmann in a spectacular hostile bid.

18   For example, between Norway's Telenor and Sweden's Telia (which has stakeholdings in the Baltic countries).

another country and the freedom of establishment) has led to a growing interpenetration of markets and multinationalisation of firms.

13 *Transport*

Introduction

Economic integration implies that each member state specialises in the production of those goods for which it is best equipped in terms of economic, geographic or other conditions. Specialisation in turn implies the spatial separation of supply and demand, and hence increased international goods transport. The increased interaction that follows from the creation of an economic and monetary union (freedom to provide services, free movement of persons and so on) leads to increased international passenger transport. How profitable integration will be depends also on the cost of transport. In that respect, transport costs are not different from customs tariffs or other obstacles to the complete free trade of goods and movement of persons. Logically, therefore, the transport sector should not be overlooked as integration proceeds.

In the following sections of this chapter, the development of the transport sector in the course of the European integration process will be analysed in much the same way as the other economic sectors in previous chapters. First, we will describe the policy regime that the EU has created for the transport sector. Next some significant aspects of the development of the sector, such as production capacity, employment and firm size, will be discussed. Finally we will present two case studies. The first is on goods transport (notably by road), the second on passenger transport (notably by air). A summary of the major findings will complete the chapter.

EU regime[1]

RATIONALE AND PRINCIPLES

In the past, all national governments in Europe have become deeply involved in the regulation of transport markets. The *arguments for intervention* are manifold. Paramount among them is the lack of possibility of stocking up transport services. As capacity tends to be geared to peak demand and as a large proportion of the costs are fixed, inelastic supply in periods of low demand, combined with a low price-elasticity of demand, could lead to destructive price competition. Governments felt duty bound to prevent such a situation (which is by no means typical of transport alone). Another argument is that transport requires expensive, long-lasting infrastructure, which users are not willing to provide, so for which the government is mostly responsible. Because the construction costs of this infrastructure and their recovery differ widely among transport modes (compare the railways with inland shipping and road traffic), measures are needed to restore a balanced competition. Third, the specific characteristics of

---

1   For an overview of the various texts of the EU regulation, see EC (1999g).

railroads lead to a 'natural monopoly'; and the government needed to regulate this in order to safeguard the consumers' interest. Fourth, the general public is not able to judge the quality of the equipment of transport providers, so public standards are set for safety and access to the trade is restricted to firms able to comply with these. Finally, over the decades, the objectives of transport policy have increasingly become merged with other societal objectives such as cheap transport to backward regions, for certain social groups; moreover, many sectors of transport have so-called 'public service obligations'.

The *instruments* used for intervention are also quite varied, including the straightforward setting of prices, the licensing or nationalisation of operators, the restriction of access to markets for non-national operators, and so on.

In view of these circumstances, it is not surprising that the discussion on the *integration of the transport sector* has been a particularly difficult one. The package that came finally into the text of the treaties[2] was based on the following principles:

* an obligation to establish a Common Transport Policy (CTP);
* non-discrimination,[3] which puts an end to the practice of charging high prices on import destinations and low prices for export destinations;
* freedom of establishment – that is, the possibility of creating a company in another member state;
* no freedom of services – access to the market in other member states is dependent on the setting of common EU provisions;
* different regimes for different modes (see following sections).[4]

---

2   The three treaties give different stipulations for transport. The ECSC Treaty is concerned only with preventing the distortion of fair competition by tariffs for transport of coal and steel that discriminated by nationality origin/destination. For the rest, transport policy was explicitly reserved to the member states. The EAEC Treaty is not very important in transport matters. The EEC Treaty, on the contrary, provides (in its Article 3) for a common transport policy. The principles of such a policy are given in a separate title (V, Articles 70–80), a privilege shared only with agriculture. The modes of transport are treated differently. Remarkably the transport title as such applies only to the so-called 'inland traffic', namely transport by rail, road and inland waterway. With respect to navigation and aviation, the Treaty stipulates merely that appropriate provisions may be laid down (Article 80). Common rules for international inland transport must be laid down, as well as the conditions under which transport entrepreneurs are admitted to national transport in a member state in which they are not resident (Article 70). This shows that the right of establishment, contrary to the right to provide services, is directly applicable to transport.

3   Such tariffs were indeed practised by some countries. Just before the Coal and Steel Community was founded, coal produced in Germany was transported at tariffs up to a quarter below those for imported coal. An example of a low tariff for exports is that for French sodium salts, which paid up to two-fifths less for transport than salt destined for the domestic market.

4   The regimes for road and air transport are discussed in the next sections; some major features of the other modes of transport are as follows:

Rail: railways' heavy investment in infrastructure has led to state-owned monopoly enterprises, to a firm hold of governments on the tariff structure, and to railroad companies' obligation to provide transport. The EU has pursued two objectives: (1) a normal price-setting in commercial supply and demand situations; and (2) the abolition of subsidies. The harmonisation decision of 1965 committed member states either to reimburse the costs of charges and transport obligations foreign to the trade, or to abolish the obligations. Now governments have to conclude public service contracts with the railway companies. Railway companies are now obliged to be financially independent, and are encouraged to concentrate on the exploitation of the railways (leaving infrastructure to the public sector) and to regroup themselves internationally.

Maritime transport is of critical importance for the EU as well, as a very large share of external goods trade is made by ship. Moreover, maritime shipping regulation became particularly important when, with the joining of three new member states (two of them islands!) in 1972, some maritime shipping turned into intra-community transport. The Court has confirmed that sea navigation comes under the general rules of the Treaty. Market control in maritime shipping mostly takes the form of so-called 'shipping-line conferences': associations of ship-owners active in the same sailing area, which, in economic terms, are cartels. In the framework of UNCTAD negotiations, the EU was forced not only to accept the existence of such conferences, but also to concede a certain division of the market between developed and developing countries. Admittedly provisos have been made to the effect that the division of cargoes will not be applied to intra-EU

These conflicting principles sprang from considerable differences among member states in economic and geographical conditions and in conceptions of transport policy (Button, 1984; Erdmenger, 1981). Some countries (especially Germany and France) saw transport as a public service or as an integral part of the social structure, affecting the distribution of population and shaping the community's social life. They had regulated their transport sector in a very detailed way and considered that government intervention in both markets and structure was the only way to realise the social objectives of their transport policy. Others (the Netherlands and the UK) took a largely commercial view of transport; they considered that the application of market-economic principles was in the best interest of customers (shippers) and society.

All the national market-control schemes pushed up the costs for the users of transport services. If the objectives of the treaty were to be realised, national government interventions had to be partly harmonised and partly abolished. The experience in countries which decided to deregulate their transport markets was that service improved and prices dropped, without the market being disturbed (Auctores Varii, 1983). Economically, therefore, liberalisation of the European transport market was the most desirable solution and one in line with the EU regime for the rest of the economic sectors.

GRADUAL DEVELOPMENT OF A COMMON POLICY

1960–1982: the liberalisation–harmonisation deadlock The Commission started its activities in the early 1960s with the aim of establishing a common transport market for all inland transport modes, guided by the principles of market economics and inspired by the liberal attitude displayed in the Treaty of Rome with respect to the goods trade. It was hoped that a common transport policy, replacing the various national policies, would guarantee fair competition among and within branches of transport, as well as create conditions of equal competition for other sectors in the economy, such as agriculture, manufacturing industry and commerce. In that vein, the 1962 Memorandum of the Commission proposed three *objectives*:

- Removal of obstacles created by transport and impeding the common market for goods and persons (for example, abolition of tariff discrimination for reasons of nationality).
- Integration of the transport market. In addition to some intra-EU liberalisation of transport services, quite detailed regulations were to be made with respect to market control, namely for tariffs, market access and so on (comparable to the market regulations in agriculture).
- Establishment of a European transport system. This concerned, first, adjusting the infrastructure to the demands of increased international exchange (for example, frontier-crossing motorways) and next the harmonisation of technical (for example, axle load), fiscal (for example, motor vehicle tax), social (driving hours) and economic (professional requirements) stipulations.

---

sea traffic and that all EU ship-owners will have equal access to EU cargoes to third countries (Hart *et al.*, 1992). Recently a number of changes have been made (see Pallis, 2002).

    Inland shipping was practically free when the EU was created, thanks largely to the Mannheim Convention, which guarantees free traffic on the Rhine. The economic recession of 1973 inspired associations of ship-owners to enforce, through a blockade, a rotation scheme for the proportional allocation of freight on the canal systems of Holland, Belgium and France. The EU has opposed such a development, which is at cross-purposes with the Treaty. After lengthy negotiations a scheme has been adopted for the abolition of the limitation of free market access for all categories by the year 2000.

In practice these objectives and principles proved so difficult to realise that the common policy advanced at a snail's pace, and the integrated market for transport services hardly at all (see, for instance, EC, 1973a). For many years, harmonisation was the first concern, on the consideration that no fair competition would be possible or liberalisation admissible without it. In the second half of the 1970s, the progress of the CTP was slowed down even more by the economic recession, the increased concern for the environment, the higher energy costs and the extension of the EU.

1982–2000: liberalisation hand-in-hand with harmonisation Confronted with stagnation, the Commission then proposed new schemes, limiting its own involvement to laying down general principles and emphasising the harmonisation of national measures. The idea of working out a complete European regime for transport, following the pattern of agriculture, was abandoned. However, the new proposals, like the earlier ones, came to nothing because of the Council's indecisiveness. In that situation, in 1982, the European Parliament, always an active promoter of a European transport policy, summoned the Council of Ministers before the Court of Justice. That this unique procedure was resorted to characterised the regrettable situation that had evolved: 25 years after the founding of the EU, still no EU transport policy had been worked out.

In its verdict the Court stated that the Council:

- is committed to regulate within a reasonable period the liberalisation of frontier-crossing transport within the EU (including transit);
- shall establish the conditions under which entrepreneurs from one member state are permitted to take part in transport in another member state;
- may, but is not obliged to, take complementary measures (in practice social, technical, environmental and other harmonisation measures).

The Court left the question of timing open by using the term 'within a reasonable period'. The Commission and the Council specified the horizon, much in line with the other aspects of the internal market (Chapter 14), as the year 1992. In the following sections we will illustrate how this liberalisation and regulation have been given substance (see EC, 1999f).

MARKET ORDER

After much hesitation and negotiation the liberalisation part of the CTP has been worked out. The 1992 deadline was not met, but in the years after considerable progress has been made. This progress has been facilitated by the global tendency to liberalise the transport sector. As a consequence most of the markets for transport services are now operating under the same *liberal regime* that prevails for the other sectors of the economy. In order to let markets function properly, a set of detailed regulations specific for transport apply.

One of these applies to the *recovery of infrastructure cost*. Indeed, different systems can distort competition between transport modes as well as disturb international trade. Two conditions must be satisfied for the adequate recovery of costs: (1) correct computation of total costs and (2) correct attribution to users. Levies would have to satisfy two requirements: (1) to reflect marginal social costs and (2) to meet the demand of overall budget equality. The computation problem was solved in 1970, when the Council introduced a common system to establish the costs of road, railroad and waterway infrastructure. The attribution problem has not been solved yet. On the basis of the many studies made,[5] the Commission has submitted to the Council various proposals for directives. Notwithstanding considerable progress, the fair and efficient pricing (covering social and external cost) remains a major point of action (EC, 1999f).

The *external dimension* of the EU internal transport market is based to a very limited extent on common European rules; much is still dependent on bilateral deals of member states with third countries.[6] This is the case, for example, for road transport: the bilateral deals concluded by individual member states with third countries make it practically impossible for third-country hauliers to offer their services on the EU market. However, price competition from companies from Central and Eastern Europe is strong on the EU–CEEC links. The same problem did not occur with rail transport, because on the continent any international transport by rail required the cooperation of nationalised companies with monopoly power. In inland shipping, the Mannheim Act applies only to riverine states of the Rhine, which means in practice that third countries (apart from Switzerland) are banned from services on the Rhine. In civil aviation, national authorities regulate access to their territory for EU and third-country companies alike: a common external civil aviation policy has not yet got off the ground. The Commission considers the setting up of a common external policy in transport matters as a cornerstone of its policy. However, progress on this score has been slow.

STRUCTURAL POLICY

A coherent common policy for the development of the structure of the European transport sector has gradually been elaborated. The policy is concerned with both transport infrastructure (generally in the public domain) and production means (in principle in private hands, in practice also to a large extent in public hands).[7]

The first proposals made by the Commission for intensive coordination of national investments in *infrastructure* were refused by the Council as an intrusion of the EU in national autonomy; it accepted only a consultation procedure (Gwilliam et al., 1973). To that end, an Infrastructure Committee has been set up. Since the early 1980s the Commission has sought the competence to give financial support to projects[8] that remove bottlenecks in the networks for international transportation of goods, by road, railroad and inland waterways, and of information (telecommunication). Examples of such large-scale projects with evident European dimensions are the Channel Tunnel and the high speed trains network. Neither the planning nor the financing of such projects was a direct task for the Commission. However, as far as the latter aspect is concerned, the Commission may, since 1990, contribute its support.[9] With the Maastricht Treaty, the setting up of Trans-European Networks (TEN) in the areas of transport has become an EU task. The aim is to promote the interconnection and interoperability of

---

5   For the older proposals, see, among others, Allais et al. (1965); Malcor (1970); Oort (1975).

6   Some of the external aspects of the transport market are regulated by international organisations. Merchant shipping in particular has had the attention of such UN affiliates as ECE, UNCTAD and the International Maritime Organisation, and air transport that of the International Air Transport Association. European agencies concerned with transport problems are the European Conference of Transport Ministers, the OECD Transport Committee, the European Committee for Civil Aviation and the Central Rhine Shipping Committee.

7   Transport policy is also instrumental in pursuing some other objectives for which the EU has developed regulation. Examples are: the safeguard of sustainability (by the reduction of exhaust gases); the improvement of road safety (harmonisation of signs); the improvement of passenger rights (for example, compensation for delays).

8   See EC (1979b, 1982c, 1982d). This even extends to projects in third countries (Switzerland, CEEC) as far as is essential to intra-European traffic.

9   This support to infrastructure is based on considerations of transport policy; transport infrastructure in backward regions is supported, on regional–economic considerations, by the European Regional Development Fund (Chapter 16).

national networks as well as access to such networks. In the framework of this policy, support has been given to a number of individual projects for improvement of international transport links, to the amount of some € 300 million a year. The TEN programme has been extended to cover the NMS.

Infrastructure is not only roads, ports and so on. It also consists of systems. In the era of the knowledge economy these are becoming increasingly important for the competitiveness of transport and the economy as a whole. The EU has set its teeth in two problems.

- Air traffic control. In Europe, a multiplicity of national air traffic control centres (54) are active, working with different computer systems and programming languages. These complicated, time-consuming and costly procedures limit the capacity of the European skies. They lead to unnecessary costs to carriers (back-up aircraft and crew) and consumers (delays) (EC, 2000d). In view of the very high losses involved, European airlines and the Commission have been pressing for the setting up of a single system. (Compare the USA, which, over a much larger area, has 20 centres with one system!)
- Satellite systems. Modern transport is dependant on information. The EU contributes to the set-up of Galileo, a system that permits the improvement of a range of transport-related services. These concern, first, private services such as tracking of goods carried in different modes; next, semi-public services, such as the support to aircraft while landing and to ships while sailing into harbour; and finally public services, such as the control of transport of dangerous materials (for example, nuclear waste).

Policy concerned with the improvement of the production means varies among transport modes. EU measures to improve the production structure of road transport concern technical prescriptions as to axle load, brakes, permissible weight and so on. The Commission has taken some perfunctory steps towards a structural policy for inland shipping, more specifically with respect to the scrapping of obsolete ships. Regarding sea traffic, the structure-improving programmes concern measures like the setting-up of a European register of ships. In air and railroad transport no relevant EU measures have been taken.

Sketch of the sector

IMPORTANCE OF THE SECTOR

The transport sector is of strategic importance to the EU economy, though relatively modest in terms of wealth creation and employment, accounting throughout the 1950–90 period for a very stable 5 per cent of GDP and employment. By the beginning of the 2000s this share had gone down a little (to 4 per cent).

The branches of the sector have developed differently. Road transport, now accounting for almost half of employment, has taken the place that rail transport occupied in the 1950s (now some 25 per cent). The relative importance of water and air transport is less, but the latter is growing very fast.

PRODUCTION MEANS

The developments of production means reflect the structural changes in European transport. Table 13.1 neatly illustrates the fast rise of road and the decline of goods transport by railroad. The length of the railroad network dropped by 13 per cent between 1960 and 2000: the number of goods wagons fell by more than 60 per cent in the same period. By contrast, the number of lorries (commercial vehicles) increased fourfold. The relation between the data for units and for capacity (or production) reveals how much the scale of transport has grown. Such developments can be observed in most branches of inland transport: road haulage, pipeline transport and in inland shipping (taking into account the increase in capacity of self-propelled craft and barges).

Transport in the NMS is still more oriented towards rail than in the EU15. The last columns of the table show that, due to the accession, the quantity of goods transported by rail increased by 50 per cent, while the indicators of road transport all showed more modest increases.

Table 13.1   Characteristics of the inland transport system, EU, 1950–2002

	1950	1960	1970	1980	1990	2000[a]	2000[b]	2002
Road								
Motorways (1000 km)	2	4	16	31	39	52	55	n.a.
Cars owned (x 1 000 000)	7	22	63	103	146	179	199	208
Commercial vehicles								
(x 1 000 000)	3	5	8	11	16	21	27	n.a.
Railway								
Coaches (x 1000)	113	111	98	96	86	78	100	106
Passengers (x 1 billion pkm)	n.a.	n.a.	217	253	268	304	348	348
Goods wagons (x 100 000)	15	14	15	12	8	5	8	6
Goods (1 000 000 tkm)	n.a.	n.a.	283	287	256	250	374	354
Track total (1000 km)	163	175	171	165	160	152	202	199
Inland waterways[a,b]								
Self-propelled craft (x 1000)	n.a.	29	24	18	15	9	n.a.	n.a.
Dumb and pushed barges								
(x 1000)	n.a.	10	5	3	3	3	n.a.	n.a.
Pipe[b,c]								
Length in service (x 1000 km)	n.a.	6	13	18	20	23	28	n.a.

Notes: 1950: EU12. 1960-2000a: EU15. 2000b, 2002: EU25. [a] *Data indicated for 1960 apply to 1965; figures for 2000 and 2002 for B, D, F, NL, A.* [b] *Excluding Finland and Sweden.* [c] *Excluding DK, IR, PORT.n.a. = No comparable data available.*

Sources: UN/ECE, *Annual Bulletin of Transport Statistics for Europe, various years; Eurostat, Transport Annual Statistics, various years; some estimates based on various national statistics. CEC with Eurostat, Energy and Transport in Figures, 2004. CEC, Situation as Regards the Community Fleet per Country, various years.*

Case study 1: goods transport, haulage

REGULATORY FRAMEWORK

The *regulation* of the haulage industry is dominated by qualitative standards. These are derived from social (driving hours), safety (technical check-ups) and environmental (exhaust gases) considerations. In the past governments have also intervened by setting minimum prices and by regulating supply. National road transport used to be reserved for national companies susceptible to national market controls (licensing and permit systems, tariff setting, access restrictions based, for example, on expertise, finance and so on). In some countries, internal long-distance carriage was subject to licensing systems.

The *liberalisation* of the road haulage market in Europe started with international transport. To that end national trip permits (quotas) were replaced by an EU system of trip authorisation with national quotas. That system could never respond adequately to the needs of a market. Many vehicles were forced to return empty.[10] So further liberalisation was undertaken. The number of EU authorisations has been gradually stepped up to become large enough for the transition to a fully free common market for international road transport (finally reached by the end of 1998).

Integration has also been realised by *harmonisation*. Regulations have been introduced for the operating conditions of international road transport in the following fields:

- fiscal: exemption from customs duties for fuel in the tanks;
- social rules: mainly concerned with hours of driving and resting;
- admission to the profession: certificates and so on for firms, and a European driving licence;
- safety: periodic inspection of vehicles, speed limits;
- environment: energy consumption, emission of exhaust gases, dangerous materials.

INDUSTRY CHARACTERISTICS

Under conditions of integration, transport develops faster than total economic activity, as goods trade increases faster than industrial production. Intra-EU international transport has grown (in tons) faster than extra-EU international transport, which confirms the data derived from international trade statistics (Chapter 5).

The *modal split*, that is the relative importance of the various transport modes for goods transport in Europe, has undergone important changes over the past decades (Table 13.2). The major shift from railroad to road haulage is evident. Before 1960, road haulage played only a modest part in goods transport among EU member states, amounting to less than a fifth of railroad transport (Blonk, 1968). Now, some 40 years later, the roles are reversed: international road haulage accounts for the lion's share (three quarters) of inland transport. The NMS are still relatively more dependent on rail. However, there too the shift towards the road is very pervasive.

---

10   In the early 1980s, an estimated 40 per cent of international road haulage had no return cargo at all.

Table 13.2 Inland goods transport (in ton/km) by mode of transport (in percentages), EU, 1970–2002

Mode of transport	1970	1980	1990	2000a	2000b	2002
Road	48	56	68	74	70	72
Railroad	33	26	19	14	18	16
Inland waterway	12	10	8	7	6	6
Pipeline	8	8	6	5	6	6
Total	100*	100	100*	100	100	100

Note: 1970-2000a: EU15; last two columns (2000b, 2002): EU25. * Due to rounding, figures do not always add up to 100.

Source: European Commission, Transport in Figures, 1998, Energy and Transport in Figures, 2004.

What have been the *determinant factors* of this shift in the modal split of goods transport? The significance of the various factors such as price, speed and reliability varies with the nature of the product to be carried. For low-value bulk goods, rail and water transport are eminently suitable. Intermediary products and finished manufactures are generally carried in smaller quantities and to more dispersed destinations; here the lorry is most suitable. The latter type of product has an increasing share in the total, owing to the structural changes in the economy. Hence the rise in the share of road haulage. Regulation with regard to prices and quantities has affected the long-term change in the modal split only marginally (Voigt *et al.*, 1986). Recent liberalisation has, however, improved the position of the road haulage sector, the more so because the liberalisation of the rail freight sector has still not become effective. This is visible in the very high growth of the road sector (some 40 per cent in the ten years since 1990), which is poised to continue in the years up till 2010 (EC, 2003b).

COMPANY RESPONSE

International road haulage is dominated by small firms: 80 per cent of the firms have fewer than five vehicles, 10 per cent have five to 10 vehicles and another 10 per cent more than 10 vehicles. The average size does, however, grow over time and with it the degree of concentration.

The deregulation that the EU has carried through in the framework of the creation of the single market has had a number of effects (Sleuwaegen, 1993). Companies have lowered their prices for cross-border transport by an estimated 6 per cent. The greater efficiency has cut margins, as costs have grown in the same period (fuel, harmonisation: EC, 1996a). This reduction in transport cost has further stimulated demand for road transport.

There has been a substantial *restructuring* of the sector. First, there has been a shake-out of inefficient firms. Second, there has been a concentration both at the EU level and at the national level. Third, many small firms have entered the market. Differentiation has been accentuated. On the one hand, one sees the emergence of firms that are 'architects of transport and logistics': they have invested in international networks of firms with national client access, in telecommunication and in computerised handling and tracking. They try to realise greater efficiency and to reap the economies of scale and scope that are made possible by the larger market. On the other hand, one sees the emergence of smaller companies in the role of subcontractor or of jobber. Finally a number of specialists have developed (for example, for bulk chemicals). The middle group is often quasi-integrated into larger organisations. This is an efficient form, as it achieves economies of scale without being subject to moral hazard problems related to the use of vehicles (Fernandez *et al.*, 2000).

Since the accession of the NMS the EU road haulage sector is increasingly penetrated by companies from these countries that capitalise on their comparative advantage (low cost).

Case study 2: passenger transport by air

REGULATORY FRAMEWORK

The civil aviation industry is very heavily regulated. Everywhere in the world countries have pursued a national aviation policy that aims at protecting the market of the national flag-carrier(s). Governments maintain a firm grip on the air traffic market by holding controlling stakes in the stock of their national air transport company, by regulating their airspace control, by allocating landing rights and so on. Moreover, national airlines often used to enjoy a monopoly on internal routes in their country of origin, which allowed them to offset profit-making activities against loss-making activities connected with their public service role of providing services to outlying areas and on low-density routes. Internationally the situation was characterised by a veritable tangle of multilateral accords (Convention of Chicago) and bilateral agreements governing landing rights, capacity, frequency, routes, tariffs and market sharing.

Until recently the situation that prevailed worldwide also prevailed on the internal EU market.[11] As a result of this protection and of the segmentation of markets within the EU, prices were generally too high and services not optimal.[12] This situation involved many welfare losses. Consequently the Commission has tried several times to *liberalise the intra-EU air traffic market*. It has been helped by the Court which ruled in 1986 that the rules of EU competition apply also to air transport. Liberalisation has finally been made possible within the framework of the total programme for the completion of the internal market. Liberalisation has started with interregional air transport. Next, the market-sharing agreements were loosened and intervention in prices restricted. Since 1997 full freedom to provide airline services within the EU has existed for licensed companies from EU member states. Finally, strict rules on state aids were introduced. The situation with respect to *external liberalisation* is quite different. Here the whole panoply of protection based on bilateral agreements persists. Worldwide, the US government has been practically the only one to speak in support of liberalisation. The EU has not been able to make a stand on this. Whereas the UK and the Dutch governments are favourable to an 'open skies' policy, the governments of many other member states are rather afraid of the idea. The Commission has been trying to get a mandate for international negotiations, in line with the powers it has in matters of external trade relations. However, up to now the member states have not given up their prerogatives. Consequently, the Commission has decided to challenge these bilateral agreements in the Court of Justice and has won. It is now entitled to negotiate air service agreements with third countries. The international organisations that are in charge of international trade in services have for some time been studying the dossier of civil aviation, but the prospects for a successful negotiation of worldwide liberalisation still seem a long way off.

---

11   For a detailed description of the development of EU air transport policy, see Button et al. (1998).
12   For a price comparison of Europe and the USA, see, among others, EC (1979c); Gialloreto (1988) calculated that airline operating costs in Europe were 50 per cent above those in the USA.

INDUSTRY CHARACTERISTICS

Passenger transport has grown considerably since the Second World War. In 1960, the average EU15 inhabitant spent 8 per cent of his total net income on mobility. By 1990, the percentage had risen to approximately 14 per cent; air traffic comprised an important part of this increase. Since its partial liberalisation air transport has risen even faster. The tremendous growth of international passenger traffic by air is explained on the demand side by demographic growth, increasing incomes and leisure time and the integration of markets (which increased business contacts). Explanatory factors on the supply side have been the fast-decreasing cost due to increases in productivity and better services (as to time, destination and so on). The explosively growing demand could be satisfied thanks to the overall adequate extension of the infrastructure (notably airports). Air traffic has shown the most spectacular growth of all modes. Over the 1960–2000 period, the total number of passenger kilometres flown by the major European airlines increased more than twentyfold.

The *supply structure* has been heavily influenced by regulation. Over the period 1960–95 it changed very little. Such stability could only be sustained in the dynamic growth market of civil aviation because all major suppliers were nationalised companies that were heavily protected against competition. The following three indicators (based on the data in Table 13.3) clearly show the extent of segmentation of markets due to considerable protection.

* *The low overall concentration of supply of European air transport.* In 1995, calculated on total world operations, the C1 index (share of largest company in total operations) was 26 per cent; C4 (share of four largest companies) was 69 per cent.
* *The stability in participation of companies.* In the 1970–95 period, the list showed neither new entrants nor departures, and only a few mergers, regrouping companies of the same country. This seemed the best option for both internal political reasons (for example, Air France with UTA and with Air Inter) and external policy reasons (the whole international system is based on bilateral deals; multinational companies are at odds with this system).
* *The stability of the ranking of the eight major companies.* Between 1970 and 1995, four companies did not change places at all, while two pairs changed only one place.

COMPANY RESPONSE

The shift in the EU attitude towards civil aviation that occurred in the 1990s has brought about *increased competition*. The major airlines have entered into competition with other majors but also with new entrants. Between 1985 and 1994, this led to a shift in markets from full fare tickets for business purposes to discount fare tickets for a whole variety of purposes. It has pushed down the prices by some 15 per cent on the routes where competition was first introduced, which led to a decrease in the yield of airlines in real terms by almost 20 per cent (EC, 1999b, 1999c). Since then, due to further liberalisation measures the pressure on prices has continued; fares for economy and promotion tickets fell by up to 50 per cent between 1997 and 2000; the fall was largest for those connections where competition was fiercest (EC, 2000f). This change in conditions is bringing about great changes for all players.

All major carriers have had to *cut costs, raise productivity and improve service*. The main way of achieving this has been to reduce the labour force directly employed by the airline. Some airlines have been able to restructure successfully at an early stage (for example, BA, KLM, Lufthansa); others have been struggling for some time with the problem (for example, Air France, Iberia) and have been depending on heavy government support to recover.

Table 13.3 Total passenger kilometres (billion) on scheduled[a] services (international and domestic) of major international European airlines, 1960–2003

Rank	Company	Country	1960	1970	1980	1990	1995	2000	2003
1	British Airways	UK	6[b]	17	44	66	94	119	100
2	Air France	France	4	10	25	37	49[c]	92	99
3	Lufthansa	Germany	1	8	21	42	62	45	97
4	KLM	Netherlands	3	6	14	26	45	60	57
5	Iberia	Spain	1	6	14	22	24	25	42
6	Alitalia	Italy	1	8	13	23	32	26	28
7	Virgin Atlantic	UK	—	—	—	—	20	29	27
8	SAS	Scandinavia	2	5	11	17	19	23	23
9	Easyjet	UK	—	—	—	—	—	18	18
10	Ryanair	Ireland	—	—	—	0	—	5	18
11	Austrian	Austria	0	1	1	3	5	9	15
12	Hapag Lloyd	Germany	—	—	—	—	—	14	14
13	Air Berlin	Germany	—	—	—	—	—	1	13
14	TAP	Portugal	—	2	3	7	8	10	12
15	Aer Lingus	Ireland	0	2	2	4	5	10	10
16	Finnair	Finland	0	1	2	5	8	7	9
17	Bmi	UK	—	—	—	2	—	4	9
18	Spanair	Spain	—	—	—	10	—	9	9
19	Air Europa	Spain	—	—	—	n.a.	—	5	8
20	Olympic	Greece	0	2	5	8	8	9	6
21	LOT	Poland	n.a.	n.a.	n.a.	4	—	6	6
22	Czech Airlines	Czech Rep.	n.a.	n.a.	n.a.	2	—	4	5
23	Malev	Hungary	n.a.	n.a.	n.a.	2	—	3	4
24	Sabena	Belgium	1	2	5	8	9	19	—

Notes: [a] 2000–2003 is the sum of scheduled and non-scheduled flights. [b] BEA + BOAC. British Caledonian included for all years. [c] Including UTA.

Sources: IATA, *World Air Transport Statistics*, several years. CEC, *Energy and Transport Statistics*, 2004.

The market position of the major EU airlines[13] is given in Table 13.3. We see that the picture is dominated by carriers from the big countries in Western Europe. The air companies of the NMS are relatively small in size. The liberalisation of markets would normally entail a substantial *restructuring of the industry*, by the entry, mergers and exit of companies. Given the remaining constraints on the market such effects have only occurred recently (see last columns of Table 13.3).

- Many new *entrants* have indeed emerged and they have put much pressure on existing companies on many connections within the EU. Many of them are low cost carriers such as Easyjet or Ryanair. However, as the threshold for entry into the business of large-scale international air transport service is quite high, a major upheaval of the position of the major carriers from that type of competition has not occurred.
- *Exit* of companies that used to be national flag-carriers has occurred only recently. After the unsuccessful merger between Swissair (not on the list) and Sabena, both got into trouble and went bankrupt. Some of the companies that have been losing out have left the group of international carriers and have become more of a regional specialist (Olympic).
- *Mergers* between companies have changed in character. International mergers between EU companies have been tried. After the unsuccessful merger of Swissair and Sabena and the aborted attempt to merge KLM and Alitalia, Air France and KLM have concluded a successful merger.[14]

Given remaining constraints of international law and EU regulation, the response of many companies has been to form *alliances*.[15] These typically involve a major EU and a major US airline, plus a number of the former national companies of the samller EU member states and some companies from other parts of the world. One is the Star alliance, which groups Lufthansa (EU), United (US), Thai, SAS (EU), Varig (Brazil) and Spanair (EU). Another one is the One World alliance grouping British Airways (EU), American Airways (US) and, among others, Iberia, Finnair and Air Lingus (EU), and Cathay and Quantas. A third one is the Skyteam alliance of Air France/KLM (EU), Alitalia (EU), with NorthWest/Continental and Delta (US) and Aero Mexico. These alliances are very effective in increasing returns as they redirect traffic to the benefit of alliance members by means of code sharing and common frequent flyer bonuses, while permitting cost cuts by the exchange of slots and terminal facilities, the common use of agents and so on. However, experience has shown that they are not very stable and that switching of partners is a recurrent theme.

Summary and conclusions

- The European transport market has for a long time been very heavily regulated on a national basis and therefore much fragmented. Rulings of the Court have obliged the

---

13   There are many more companies that provide jet services (far more than 100 in 1990). Their number has grown quickly following the recent liberalisation of intra-EU traffic. Many of the larger charter companies are actually bigger than the smaller flag-carriers in terms of the total number of passenger kilometres flown. However, the overall picture is difficult to get hold of, as many flag-carriers have taken (sometimes majority) stakes in such (charter and feeder) companies operating mainly from their home country base.
14   The need to safeguard international positions within the present regulation meant that the two companies have kept much of their national identity even after the merger.
15   For the economics of international alliances in air transport, see Button et al. (1998) chs 5–6 and Hanlon (1999) for global airlines.

Council to work out a common transport policy along the same liberal lines that obtain for the rest of the economy. Liberalisation has been pursued in the framework of the completion of the internal market.

- Goods transport by road has increased much faster than industrial growth. However, this growth has not yet gone hand-in-hand with international integration of road haulage firms. A number of large European logistic firms have recently been created in a process of take-overs and mergers.
- Passenger transport by air has increased very rapidly, but the company structure has until recently remained practically unaltered, evidencing the lack of competition and international integration. In recent years, intra-EU liberalisation and worldwide competition have changed this situation profoundly, leading to the entry of new competitors, to some mergers of EU companies and to a strengthening of the linkages of major European companies with other major carriers in the world.

Conditions for Balanced Growth

14 *Allocation, Internal Market and Competitiveness Policies*

Introduction

The main objective of the European Union is to enhance the allocational efficiency of the economies of the member states by removing barriers to the movement of goods, services and production factors. Moreover, policies have been agreed upon to make the European market, once created, function properly. In the following sections we will describe in some detail a number of these policies.

Before we go into the specific policy areas, we will first specify some of the basic theoretical principles about government intervention in European markets. Next we will describe the EU regime in matters of allocation policies. To ensure the good functioning of the internal market, two types of policy are needed: competition and harmonisation.

Competition is the first specific policy area to which we will give attention. We will describe the economic rationale of the EU involvement with competition and the specific forms in which this policy has been elaborated over the past.

The *harmonisation* approach will be illustrated with two examples. The first concerns indirect influencing of markets through taxation. This applies both to goods and services markets (value-added and excise taxes) and production factors (corporate and income taxes).[1] The second applies to the regulating of market access by defining technical norms and standards for the quality of products. Such regulation used to be a major policy instrument for governments to protect their markets. The EU policy measures needed to remove such obstacles will be reviewed in a last policy section.

All distortions of efficient allocation take a heavy toll in welfare from the EU, and their removal has positive *welfare* effects. Some estimates of these effects will be presented, before a final section in which we present some conclusions and a summary.

Theoretical foundations

THEORY OF MARKET REGULATION (PRICES AND QUANTITIES)

The basic assumption of economics is that the workings of markets will bring the best outcome in terms of allocation efficiency and hence the best outcome in terms of wealth creation and growth. However, in some cases, market forces do not lead to optimal outcomes. In those cases government intervention may then correct non-optimal situations. One form of intervention uses *direct price and/or quantity controls*. These may be justified in the following cases:

---

1   The other side of the coin of indirect influences is subsidies. As these apply rather to production than to products, they are dealt with under competition policy.

- Acute scarcity may drive up the prices of products providing for basic needs (for example, food), which for social reasons must be kept low. To prevent excess demand in such cases, quantities need to be controlled as well. Such direct intervention is justified in exceptional circumstances such as those prevailing during and just after the Second World War.
- Natural monopolies (in electricity distribution, for instance) are inclined to charge too high prices and restrict production. Such potential abuse of market power calls for regulation to keep prices at the level that would prevail under competitive conditions.
- Unstable markets (like those for agricultural products) may cause grave social problems and a fragile production structure. Governments may use instruments such as guaranteed prices or selling and purchasing from public stocks to stabilise markets.
- Social considerations may lead to the setting of minimum wage levels, compulsory social security contributions and rules about equal pay for men and women in labour markets.
- External effects of the consumption of goods (health and environment, for instance) and the existence of public goods lead in some cases to the fixing of prices (for medical and pharmaceutical products and transport, among others).

Now, apart from its presumed beneficial effects, such intervention in markets also has some important negative effects.[2] So it need come as no surprise that in the past the use of the instrument has decreased considerably.

THEORY OF STRUCTURAL POLICIES

In Western-type market economies the prime task of economic development is left to private enterprise. Entrepreneurs have to compete with one another for markets and resources. Institutions safeguard the rules of the game under which this competition takes place. Governments set the rules so as to optimise the conditions for the competitiveness of firms. The question then becomes what intervention is best for the economy.

The theoretical foundation for the pursuit of an *'industrial'* or a *sectoral policy* is mainly found in market failures.[3] The reasons are monopolistic behaviour, the existence of public goods, economies of scale, external effects, the cost of gathering information and making adjustments, rigidities, entry barriers and so on. To correct such imperfections and to secure an optimum situation, the governments intervene in the market. A classical case in point is the infant industry argument: a firm should be protected (by subsidies, for instance) from its foreign competitors at the first stage of its development, because only in that way can it grow enough to profit from economies of scale and become competitive. The costs of protection in the first period are compensated by the benefits of production at a later stage (creation of private and tax revenue).

---

2   See the examples of agriculture (Chapter 9) and steel Chapter 10).

3   Governments intervene to smooth the continuous restructuring that marks modern economies, implying the balanced phasing out of old industries, the optimisation of the production environment of mature industries and support for the creation and development of new activities. At the first stage of new products, public intervention may be beneficial because the market is not well informed, the risks are considered too high for the participants, or the socio-economic cost/benefit ratio is greater than one while the private one is not, or not sufficiently (externalities). At the second stage of growing product volumes, disturbances may arise from uncoordinated private decision making (overcapacities); the cost of adjusting capacities to demand levels may be minimised by government intervention. Finally, at the recession stage, the public authorities can steer the sector through the rough waters of capacity reduction. (See, for instance, Jacquemin and de Jong, 1977; Urban, 1983; Odagiri, 1986; Wolf, 1987; Chang, 1996).

The quality of the arguments for intervention has been criticised[4] mainly on the grounds that the cost of intervention is often overlooked and that public authorities are generally no better equipped to evaluate future developments than are private decision makers (public sector failures).

The arguments for intervention for structural purposes apply not only to the manufacturing sector, but also to other sectors (agriculture and services) and factor markets. In the previous chapters we have described, for each sector, the way in which the EU involvement has developed.

Many of the instruments of structural policies tend to affect the allocative efficiency of the Union economy. An example in this field is state aids. For that reason, a common stance towards national measures of structural policy is an obvious necessity in a customs union. At later stages, common programmes for structural change may become a more efficient solution.

OTHER POLICIES

Governments intervene not only to stimulate economic activity, but also to safeguard a number of *social objectives*. A case in point is the protection of health. The instruments that are used to foster the realisation of these objectives are twofold: finance and regulation. The first relies on tax instruments such as excise duties to discourage the consumption of goods with negative external effects (for instance, tobacco and liquor) while subsidising goods with positive externalities (for instance, sports facilities). The second may lead to rules about the maximum hours that can be worked a week or on the quality of the paint in toys. There are other reasons for regulation; we just mention here those that have to do with market access (for instance permits to broadcast television or provide telecommunication services). Too much regulation tends to suffocate the economy.[5] This is particularly so in cases where countries have accumulated a technology gap (for example, with respect to ICT). So, governments should do away with unnecessary regulation. Deregulation in product markets should precede deregulation in the labour market (Blanchard and Giavazzi, 2003). There are several reasons for this. Excessive regulation in product markets tends to do more harm than in labour markets. Product market deregulation lowers the price of goods so it raises the real wages. It reduces barriers to entry which leads to a fall in unemployment. Moreover, it decreases total rents which reduces the incentives for workers to put efforts into the appropriation of a proportion of such rents. This in turn will facilitate labour market deregulation.[6]

Taxes and subsidies change the (relative) prices of goods. Differences in national practices of such indirect intervention can distort trade between partners. As compensatory import and export duties or quantitative restrictions are incompatible with the Customs Union, some EU harmonisation is called for (see the following section).

Differences in regulation between countries add to cost of business and so decreases the competitiveness of the EU. So EU harmonisation is called for to take such cost away.

---

4   For early discussions see, for example, Lindbeck (1981); Eliasson (1984); for later see Pelkmans (2001).
5   See, for example, Koedijk and Kremers (1996); Nicoletti and Scarpetta (2003).
6   As argued in Chapter 16, regulation on the labour market may actually enhance growth. Regulation brings confidence in the stability of conditions over time and thereby facilitates investment in human capital (and therefore improvement of production factors). Moreover, it facilitates consultation between social partners and the government and thereby limits industrial disputes. However, pushed too far it fossilises structures and inhibits the flexibility of firms and innovation that leads to fast growth – see, for instance, OECD (2004). Note that the intensity of labour market regulation is very highly correlated to the intensity of product market regulation.

EU regime

THE BASIC PRINCIPLE: A LIBERALISED MARKET

EU member countries entered the EU with very different traditions of state intervention in markets, be it control of prices and quantities, state responsibility for production and regulation of quality, or vigilance with respect to competition rules. Some countries – France for one – have a more interventionist tradition; others, like Germany, are more of the liberalist type (at least for markets of manufactured goods). However, no EU country defended a straightforward *laissez-faire* regime, nor had any country adopted a system of rigorous central planning. When the EU order had to be worked out, it was only logical that one would steer a course between the two extreme views.

The underlying *principle* of the order of the European Union is the *liberalist view*. Decisions as to production, consumption, investment, saving and so on are left to economic agents and the public authorities do not directly intervene in the markets. Within these general European rules set for the allocation process, there is room for a competition of national rules which is supposed to sort out the policy environment that is most conducive to growth. National governments are free to adopt a more interventionist or a more liberal approach; initially a number of governments were in favour of heavy regulation; recently, however, all member state governments have opted for a more liberal stand.

In certain cases EU *interventionist regimes* have been put in place. For instance the ECSC Treaty gave the EU institutions quite considerable powers to intervene in coal and steel markets. This instrument no longer exists (Chapter 10), however. The EEC Treaty accommodated two noticeable interventionist exceptions: agriculture (Chapter 9) and transport (Chapter 13). For the latter all, and for the former most of the direct influences on price and quantities have in the meantime been abolished.

A liberalised market needs certain conditions to function properly. Paramount among them is regulation. The EU has opted for a blend of regulatory policies that comprise both competition and the harmonisation of laws of national states.

MAIN OBJECTIVE: A SINGLE MARKET

The unity of the market is a basic principle of the EU. In defiance of this general principle, many impediments to the free movement of goods, services, capital and labour persisted up to the mid-1980s, some of which implied controls at internal borders.[7] Concern about the

---

7   National governments had three major reasons for such intervention:

- The need to comply with technical standards and norms adopted by some countries for environmental reasons or to protect consumers or workers. Related to this are the controls of movements of plants and animals to check whether they come up to national health standards.
- Different levels of indirect taxation. Goods need to be checked to establish the amount of VAT or excise duties to be levied in the country of destination.
- Public security measures, giving rise to personal checks at the internal borders (illegal immigrants, criminals, terrorists).

   However, the European Union itself has also contributed to the segmentation of the European Market in national markets:

- The Monetary Compensatory Amounts of the Common Agricultural Policy have for some time effectively let the unity of the market disintegrate.
- Multi-Fibre Agreement: the insufficiency of the Common External Policy has led to an elaborate system of

negative effect of these barriers to European growth increased, notably among industrialists who had to stand up to international competition on world markets. To arouse public interest, Philips' president, Dekker, in 1984 launched his Plan for Europe 1990. Following this impetus, the Commission (EC, 1985a) came up with a white paper containing the bold proposal for a consistent and comprehensive list of measures that would do away with all controls on goods, services, capital and persons at the internal borders of the EU by the end of 1992. This programme was endorsed by the Council and was made into a treaty obligation by the adoption of the Single European Act: 'The internal market shall comprise an area without internal frontiers in which the free movement of goods, persons, services and capital is ensured.'

The most important elements of this programme were successfully executed over the 1985–92 period, while other elements have taken more time. The *success factors* were fourfold:

- Complete comprehensiveness: it covered all measures needed to do away with internal frontiers; the continued presence of any one reason to maintain frontier controls could be enough to keep them intact.
- A clear timetable: the target set was the end of 1992. This recalls the approach of the Treaty of Rome to the abolition of all tariffs and quotas on internal trade by 1970.
- A simplified decision-making process: the new rule required only a qualified majority for decisions on most measures needed to accomplish the internal market, instead of unanimity.
- A balance between liberalisation and harmonisation: a sector-by-sector approach, that gradually liberalised increasing segments of each heavily regulated sector, while at the same time setting framework EU rules.[8]

There are two *reasons* why, more than a decade after the target date, *the internal market is not yet complete.*

- Difficulties of coming to agreement among member states about EU legislation: examples are the lack of full freedom for the movement of persons (owing to problems about safety checks, and absence of a common immigration policy), the complexity of certain issues in particular services (see Chapters 6 and 12) and the ailing harmonisation of taxation (see further sections in this chapter).
- Non-compliance of member states with EU legislation: the cases involve a range of single market directives including excise duties, public procurement and financial services.

In order to speed up work on the removal of the remaining problems, the Commission has introduced an annual cycle of setting of target actions and reporting on the progress of implementation (EC, 1999h). The latter consists of a so-called Scoreboard and reporting on, for instance, price convergence. The former encompasses initiatives and actions both at the EU and the national level with concrete deadlines for realisation.

---

national quotas for so-called 'sensitive' products.

8   This approach has removed in many instances the hesitations of national governments and of the sectoral interest groups (see, for example, Chapter 11 case study on electricity, Chapter 12 case studies on insurance and telecommunications and Chapter 13 case study on civil aviation).

Competition

THEORETICAL FOUNDATIONS FOR REGIME CHOICES

In Western industrialised countries, most decisions are left to private economic actors. Market forces are allowed to play their role and the price mechanism is largely relied upon to bring about an efficient allocation of resources. However, private actors may collude to avoid competition. Indeed Adam Smith wrote, more than 200 years ago, in his famous book, *Wealth of Nations*: 'People of the same trade seldom meet together, even for merriment and diversion, but the conversation ends in a conspiracy against the public or in some contrivance to raise forces.' In these cases, he argues, prosperity is less than with free competition; monopoly spells loss of welfare to consumers. To prevent it, public authorities must take it upon themselves to intervene with competition laws and policy.[9]

There are also advocates of limitations to competition – for instance, by cartels and monopolies. Cartels would permit enterprises to finance R&D, whereas competition would take away the margin that is necessary for making investments in innovation. Another argument often heard is that to beat foreign competition a sufficiently large margin has to be realised on home sales.

The balancing out of arguments pro and con has found its best expression in a school of thinking that advocates the '*workable competition*' concept. In this view an authority should be charged with the maintenance of such a workable competition in the various markets. This task used to be executed by national authorities. Their policies differed: some, like the Netherlands, used to be very lenient towards restrictions; others, like Germany, used to be fairly strict. A set of independent national competition policies is unlikely to be sufficient for establishing a good competition regime in integration areas.[10] Indeed, if two firms in different member states agree to refrain from competing on each other's home market, national competition policy probably cannot do anything against it. Yet such agreements obviously impede the trade between member states. Some form of union competition policy is indeed needed to ensure the fair play of common market forces.

THEORETICAL EFFECTS OF INCREASED COMPETITION DUE TO INTEGRATION

The principal *theoretical reason for governments to pursue competition policies* is indeed the need to avoid the misallocation resulting from:

- static inefficiency in resource allocation: a firm charging a price above the real (marginal) cost of production (because of monopolist power) keeps production and consumption below the optimum level (with excess profits to the firm and losses to the consumer);
- reduced technical efficiency: firms operate inefficiently (through overstaffing, higher wages, lack of response to new opportunities, poor management) in sheltered situations;
- dynamic inefficiency: this is an extension of technical inefficiency. To be dynamically efficient requires constant innovation in production and products.

---

9 See Demsetz (1982); Scherer (2000).
10 For an introduction to the theory and a review of the competition policies practised by the EU countries (and a comparison with those of the USA and Japan), see Shaw and Simpson (1987). For the origins of this variation in forms and their subsequent adaptation, see Martin (1999).

In this way the removal of barriers to competition has similar effects to the removal of barriers to trade.[11] The technical and dynamic efficiency effects are far more important than the static ones. This can be demonstrated with the help of Figures 14.1 and 14.2. The first step in the analysis of the effects on trade and welfare can be illustrated with Figure 14.1, which reproduces the market for good x in country A. Curves S_a and D_a represent supply and demand in country A itself (see Chapter 5 for the theoretical base). Supply from the world, fully elastic, is once more denoted by S_w. A change has occurred in the representation of the supply from country B; it is not indicated by a curve S_b here, but combined with supply S_a and incorporated in curve S_{cu}, which is valid for the entire customs union. The diagram has been drawn in such a way that the tariff t_2 is just sufficient to avoid any imports from the world market (S_{cu} cuts through N). Now suppose that, before the CU was established, country A operated a tariff of t_3. After creation of the customs union, the common external tariff will be set at t_2, and further lowering of this common outer tariff to t_1 is envisaged. Let us consider the static effects of this customs union; according to the model given in Figure 14.1, the lowering of the initial tariff from t_3 to t_2 would mean that total demand in A is now satisfied by supply from the customs union. This implies a trade-creation effect of KRL and a trade-expansion effect of MUN, against a trade-diversion effect of $HLMI$. As the area of the latter is about equal in size to the combined areas of KRL and MUN, this customs union would be about welfare-neutral. Reducing the tariff further to t_1, triggering off an import quantity $A'C$ from the partner country and CE' from the world market, would be highly welfare-creating, as the combined areas $K'RL'$ and $M'UN'$ clearly outweigh the area $XK'L''H'$ (AC being the trade diversion from W to B).

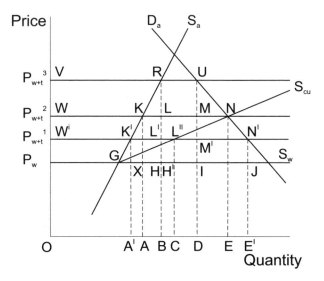

Figure 14.1 Effects of tariffs and improved technical efficiency, account being taken of the customs union supply curve, country A

---

11   See Geroski and Jacquemin (1985); Pelkmans (1984).

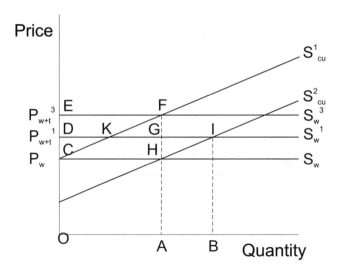

Figure 14.2   Advantages of improved (technical) efficiency

Now this is not the whole story. Manufacturers in A, finding themselves confronted by a great loss of sales markets (from OB with tariff t_3 to OA' with tariff t_1), rather than accept the loss will accomplish savings on production costs (Figure 14.2). As a result the supply curve of A will move down and the supply curve of the entire customs union will drop accordingly (from S^1_{cu} to S^2_{cu} in Figure 14.2). We have assumed that it dropped sufficiently to permit the customs union producers to satisfy total home demand in the CU under a tariff protection of t_1. The production and consumption effects of this drop in cost are indicated by the shift of the equilibrium point from F to I. To see the basic change in welfare effects, consider the change in cost of production of the initial quantity from OE to OD that producers have realised under the pressure of stronger competition. The cost reduction is equal to $DEFG$. This is a net positive effect and not, as in the earlier static examples, a redistribution effect of $DEFK$ and a new effect of KFG.

BASIC FEATURES OF THE EUROPEAN REGIME

The need for a Common European Competition Policy has been recognised right from the start; both the Treaty of Paris (ECSC) and that of Rome (EEC) contain a chapter on it. Over time a coherent EU competition policy has been worked out (Martin, 1999; Eekhoff, 2004). The basic features of this policy are as follows.

The *objective* of the European competition policy is to protect the competitive process, and hence the benefits of integration, by preventing distortions of the market process by either private (company) or public (national government) actions. To that end, different instruments can be used; these are given in Table 14.1. We will highlight in the following sections the three EU actions that are marked with an asterisk.

Table 14.1   Major components of the EU competition regime

Concerning	Private firms or groups	Member state or public enterprise
Instruments	Cartels* Dominant positions* Concentrations	Anti-discrimination Equivalent measures State monopolies Public enterprise State aids to firms*

Three *institutions* have in the course of the years developed and applied the fundamental European competition rules: the Council by its legislation, the Commission by its administrative practice and the Court by its jurisprudence.

- The Council's role is limited to the issue of regulations and directives on the general application of the rules laid down in the Treaty.
- The Commission has been given the central role.[12] It investigates violations of the rules on its own initiative or upon receiving complaints from member states, companies, private persons or institutions. When the Commission observes an infringement, it may order it to be rectified. In many cases such actions end with the company or member state's voluntarily changing its conduct. In other cases, where the Commission finds a complaint well founded and the company does not change its conduct, the Commission can order changes, and member states are obliged to help the Commission enforce such a ruling. All firms and public institutions are committed to allowing the officials of the Commission to make any investigations it thinks necessary to gather evidence. The Commission can impose fines, which may amount to tens of millions of euros.
- The Court deals with appeals from the allegedly infringing company. Since its creation, the European Court has treated a large number of cases, and 'case law' has greatly helped to define competition law and to make clear the interpretation of the rules.

The *field of application of EU competition rules* is very wide; they apply irrespective of:

- the company's location, so they also cover companies from third countries operating in the EU;[13]
- the legal or proprietary form, which means that government companies (with the exception of public utilities) are subject to EU competition rules too; to identify possible competition distortions, the financial structure of state-owned companies must be transparent;
- the sectors of private economic activity: notwithstanding the differences in market structure, all sectors are now subject to the EU competition policy.[14]

---

12   The role of the Commission has in the past been severely criticised, as it acts as investigator, prosecutor and judge. Due to the long time periods involved in Court dealings, the consequences of wrong Commission decisions often proved irrevocable in practice. In order to reduce the chances of erroneous decisions, the quality of the staffing and the internal procedures of the Commission have been improved. In order to minimise the uncertainties for firms, the Appeal procedures in the Court have been shortened.

13   The external dimension of EU competition policy has recently been enlarged to the European Economic Area (so including EFTA). The association agreements with Eastern European countries also contain a section on competition. Moreover, the Commission has made a cooperation agreement on competition with the US authorities.

14   In the past many branches of the telecommunication, transport, bank and insurance, and energy sectors were practically removed from competition policy. Deregulation, privatisation and the opening of markets in the framework of the 1992 programme have brought them into EU-wide competition and hence under the EU competition rules. Specific rules still exist for some of them.

The European competition policy is *complementary to national competition policy*; the former regards competition from the angle of inter-state trade, the latter from whatever angle is specific to it. However, as in all other fields, the European competition law prevails in cases where there is a conflict between EU and national laws. Such conflicts are less likely now than some time ago, as many national regimes have been profoundly recast and have adopted the EU principles (Laudati, 1998). The EU institutions share the responsibility for enforcing EU competition rules with national competition authorities and national courts. In order to promote consistent application, a European Competition Network regrouping the Commission and national competition authorities (such as the German *Kartellamt*) has been created.

The increasingly international character of many firms has made the EU have to take decisions that do influence very heavily firms from other countries. This applies in particular to the US. There is no international institution that assumes responsibility for such matters. The EU has made attempts to entrust competition to the WTO, but the ideas have been discarded by important players (Molle, 2003, chapter 11). So the EU has concluded bilateral cooperation agreements with, for example, the US. These limit, but do not exclude, conflicts as the famous cases of the Commission against Microsoft (abuse of dominant position) or General Electric/ Honeywell (blockage of merger) illustrate.

CARTELS (COMPANY AGREEMENTS)

The first basic rule for competition bans as 'incompatible with the Common Market all agreements between undertakings, decisions by associations of undertakings and concerted practices which may affect trade between Member States and which have as their object or effect the prevention, restriction or distortion of competition within the common market'. The objective of this article 81 is to prevent companies from re-establishing, by means of market-sharing agreements and export bans, less visible but equally effective barriers to trade to replace the customs frontiers that were abolished by the European Common Market for goods and services. Moreover, any agreement or decision prohibited by the treaty is automatically void.

The following groups of *activities are incompatible with the EU competition rules*:

- market-sharing agreements dividing the EU into national sub-markets;
- price-fixing agreements of groups of firms that control a large share of the European market;
- agreements to buy only from or sell only to specified manufacturers or buyers;
- exchange of company information on cost, production and sales;
- exclusive or selective distribution agreements that prevent parallel imports;[15]
- concerted practices whereby, without a formal agreement, partners align their policies.

Exemptions can be given for:

- capacity: in view of a reduction of structural overcapacity of a branch, agreements can be made on the phasing out of plants;
- research and development: cooperative research or agreements on specialisations may favour innovation and progress.

---

15   Selective distribution arrangements are sometimes permitted if they improve the quality of the service provided, but discrimination against retailers, especially for their pricing strategies, can be severely punished).

DOMINANT POSITIONS

The second basic competition rule reads: 'Any abuse by one or more undertakings of a dominant position within the common market or in a substantial part of it shall be prohibited as incompatible with the common market in so far as it may affect trade between Member States.' Abuse of a dominant position can damage either the consumer or the competitive process. Forms of abuse include unfair pricing, exclusion or limitation of supply and discrimination among trade partners (see Box 14.1).

BOX 14.1
FACTUAL ABUSE OF A DOMINANT POSITION

Hoffman-Laroche dominated the world market of vitamins in bulk (market shares of over 80 per cent). The company had passed 'fidelity' contracts with its customers, which would give it a permanent position of priority or even of exclusivity as supplier to these customers. The Commission fined Hoffman-Laroche, which thereupon appealed to the European Court. However, the Court confirmed the essentials of the Commission's decision, making it clear that the dominant firm may not limit a customer's supply possibilities, nor bar the entry of new suppliers which could put a downward pressure on prices.

Firms may be tempted to acquire dominant positions by merging. Mergers and acquisitions (M&A) have shown a very different dynamism during the various integration periods. In *the 1972–84 period*, merger activity stayed at a fairly low level. An analysis of the mergers among the thousand largest firms in this period (De Jong, 1993a) showed that the majority of mergers were of the horizontal type. The principal motive for such mergers was 'critical mass': to increase efficiency, obtain a better competitive position and spread R&D cost over longer series. Most mergers involved two firms based in the same country and were oriented towards the national market. Increased European integration during this period did not lead to more cross-border European mergers (Lemaitre and Goybet, 1984) because of differences in management strategies, cultural traditions, government intervention and legal practices.

Theory shows us that economic integration stimulates cross-border M&A (for example, Bjorvatn, 2004). Under the influence of the Single Market Programme (SMP) international intra-EU merger and take-over activity did indeed increase very spectacularly (EC, 1996c). The SMP incited many firms to try to acquire quickly the critical size for effective cost cutting. This has not only been accepted but actively promoted by the Commission because for many industries mergers offer real prospects of efficiency gains and access to world markets, while competition on the EU market of non-EU firms limits the disadvantages of the ensuing concentration (Directive on cross-border mergers). As a consequence the share of the largest enterprises in the total of a number of branches has risen substantially (EC, 1994b).

The composition of mergers changed very significantly over the past decades. As to branches, the picture became dominated by mergers between firms from service sectors (such as distribution, banking and insurance) that before were in sheltered markets (NTB). As to nationality, the merger activity between firms within the EU15 has decreased relative to two other types. First M&A activity has reoriented itself to the NMS. Second, it was increasingly aimed at obtaining strong positions on world markets. The latter fall again into two categories (see Figure 14.3). EU-based firms were initially very much oriented towards the US, but more recently increasingly in emerging markets.[16] The attractiveness of the single EU market for non-EU firms wanting to acquire a position there is reflected by the very high increase in the number of mergers and acquisition operations where a non-EU firm chose as its target an EU firm (EC, 2001e; 2004k).

To prevent firms acquiring dominant positions, the Commission has intensified its *monitoring of mergers*.[17] Since 1989 it also has the power to block a merger if it considers that it leads to a dominant position, or more generally that it will significantly impede effective competition (EC, 2004e). This concerns only mergers beyond a certain size. Smaller ones are dealt with by national authorities. In the past the vast majority of the notified cases obtained clearance in the first phase of examination, sometimes only after parties had offered to make changes to their original plans. Of some 2400 cases investigated over the period 1990–2004 only 18 were actually blocked (EC, 2004e) (see Box 14.2).

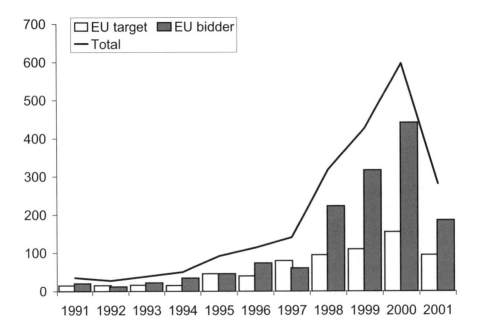

Figure 14.3　Number of international M&A in the EU, 1991–2001

The control of the EU Commission over M&A activity applies to the situation on the EU market not to EU-based firms. In 2001 the Commission blocked a merger between two US companies, General Electric and Honeywell, that together would have obtained a dominant position in large segments of the jet engine market. Coordination between the competition authorities of the EU and the US is set up to avoid the problems that may ensue in cases where they might take different positions, such as this one (see Chapter 17).

16　Compare in this respect the discussion on FDI in Chapter 8; acquisitions form a major component of FDI.
17　A good overview of the foundations of EU merger policy in terms of economic advantages and disadvantages of mergers is given by Jacquemin (1991) and Neven et al. (1993); for a broader treatment, see OECD (1984b).

BOX 14.2
MERGER BLOCKED BECAUSE OF RISK OF ABUSE OF DOMINANT POSITION

RTL, the Luxembourg broadcasting company, Veronica, the Dutch commercial television company, and Endemol, one of the largest producers of television programmes in the EU, had formed a joint venture (HMG) to which RTL's two Dutch television channels and Veronica's television channel were transferred. The case was submitted by the Dutch government to the EU. The Commission considered that HMG would have a dominant position in the Dutch market for television advertising and for television programmes and declared the merger incompatible with the common market.

STATE AID

Aid is given to correct market failures and to attain social objectives by influencing private economic decision making. Where subsidies are given for political reasons (for example, for the maintenance of employment in industries that have lost their competitiveness), resources are badly used. However, even where subsidies are given to industries for economic reasons, theory shows that this generally represents a distortion. These lead to losses in welfare for the domestic and international economy.[18] So, the prohibition of state aids actually increases welfare (Collie, 2000). For these reasons the EU in principle forbids state aid. State aid to firms is incompatible with the Common Market in so far as the unfair advantage it gives to certain firms distorts trade among member states or damages competing firms.

There has been a continuous debate on the implementation of this rule. As state aid is a major instrument for national governments to intervene in the economy to pursue certain important goals of socio-economic policy, some forms of state aid must be exempted from this general principle. Consequently the EU has defined the kinds of support that are permissible. As such it qualifies aid that aims at:

- Regional development. A maximum aid level has been established by the Commission for each problem area; the aid measures have to be public and transparent.
- Specific economic activity. This implies restructuring of old and stimulation of new industries. The former type of aid must be exceptional, limited in duration and geared directly to the objective of restoring long-term viability of firms or the reduction in capacity in declining industries like shipbuilding, steel and textiles. The latter type is often in the form of research and development, enabling companies to develop products and compete successfully on the world market (see Box 14.3).
- Important project of common EU interest. In this respect one might think of environmental improvement ensuring as much as possible the principle of 'polluter pays'; or the conservation and development of new indigenous resources of energy.
- Culture and heritage conservation; repair of damage done by natural disasters and exceptional circumstances.

---

18   See EC (1991c). In the past, state aid in the EU has amounted to some 2–3 per cent of total GDP. This is double the Japanese level and even four times the US level. Over the past decade, the amount of state aid as a percentage of EU GDP has gradually decreased.

To permit the Commission to implement this set of rules, plans for such aid must be submitted to the EU for prior approval. Controls have been tightened over time.

The constant drive of the Commission to reduce the distortion created by state aid has had a certain success. A very neat decrease has been registered since 1997. Particularly contentious cases involve aid to firms from sectors that until recently have been sheltered from competition (for example, airlines and defence industries). In recent years the EU has given new guidelines for state aid (EC, 2004f). They are set within the new policy environment of the EU (Enlargement; Lisbon strategy; Cohesion). Moreover, they specify the rules for activities that are in the (semi) public domain (such as urban transport) and the rules for improving the predictability and transparency of the process of decision making by the EU authorities.

BOX 14.3
AUTHORISED STATE AID

SGS Thomson had designed a programme of more than one billion euro to acquire the technology of key semiconductor products. The French government planned to subsidise this R&D programme with a capital grant of some € 300 million and submitted its case to the Commission. The Commission authorised the aid (IP/94/714), taking into account the objectives of its trade policy (limiting the considerable deficit for these products) and of its industrial policy (strengthening the position of EU firms in a sector dominated by US and Japanese firms).

Indirect influence on prices: taxes

SOME THEORY

In the course of time every country has set up an elaborate system of taxation for generating government revenue and for correcting undesirable effects of the working of markets. The structure, rates and exemptions of these systems reflect the history of a large number of choices about the functions of government in allocation, stabilisation and redistribution. Such systems affect the relative price of goods, services, labour and capital. In open economies these effects are transmitted to partner countries. This limits in practice the autonomy of nations in tax matters; actually, the more the economies are integrated, the more autonomy is lost.

What would be the best response by both national and EU authorities to the new situation created by further integration? In line with the principle of subsidiarity (see Chapter 2), nations should be left with maximum sovereignty and flexibility in arranging their own tax systems. That has induced some to favour full competition of rules (no coordination, at best some consultation), others to favour harmonisation or even unification of tax rules.[19] We will indicate the arguments in favour of and those against full competition.

Advantages The first argument for competition is that it promotes the efficiency of the public sector. Countries will be forced to examine critically the quality of the public goods they

---

19   See Dosser (1966), Brennan and Buchanan (1980), Gordon (1983), Puchala (1984), Cnossen (1987, 1990); and, for a survey of theories on competition, Wilson (1999).

provide and will try to provide the best service at the lowest cost to the taxpayer. The second argument is that it permits experimentation and quick adjustment. Different authorities, responsible for the operations of different systems, will react more quickly to new challenges of changes in external circumstances than large systems and will more easily try out novel approaches that may turn out to be more effective. The final argument is that it permits authorities to seek the lowest compliance cost by adapting the system to the exigencies and traditions of the local private sector.

Disadvantages The first argument against is that competition may yield a sub-optimal level of public goods because of lack of resources and the difficulty of matching taxes with the marginal benefits of public goods such as health. The second argument is that competition leads to solutions that frustrate equity. Inter-category equity is jeopardised because the high mobility of capital permits it to flee high-tax countries; to avoid this, countries will decrease their tax burden on capital. So competition will result in zero capital taxation in all countries. Consequently the full burden is put on the rather immobile factor, labour. Interjurisdictional equity is put in danger because residents from a low-tax, low-public service country may use the public goods of a high-tax, high-public service country.

The balancing out of advantages and disadvantages of competition leads to two *guidelines for the coordination of taxes* in an integration area:

1. Only those taxes need be harmonised that cause a real distortion in the process of integration.
2. Agreements on minimum levels of taxes should prevent the system evolving to sub-optimal low levels of taxation.

Which taxes should be subjected to harmonisation? The answer to this question differs with the stage of integration.

Trade (FTA and CU) National systems with different levels and structures of indirect taxation (VAT and excise duties) will lead to different prices for consumers in different national markets. That situation may encourage sales of goods from low-tax countries to residents of high-tax countries, at the cost of a loss of government revenue in the latter. To prevent this, national indirect taxation systems are usually complemented by trade controls and border adjustments of taxes. Liberalising trade entails the need for adjustment of indirect taxes.

Production factors (CM) Differences in levels of national direct taxes, such as the corporation tax and the wage (income) tax (including social security), will lead to differences in net income position of the different actors on the capital and labour markets. To prevent both supply (savers and workers) and demand (investors and employers) moving to countries where the net situation is most favourable, border controls are used. Liberalising movements of production factors means that another way has to be found to prevent distortions in allocation. This is most relevant for capital, as it is highly mobile (OECD, 1991, 1998b).

Policy (EMU) In moving towards higher forms of integration, more and more taxes (like the income tax) become Union competences. However, policy integration can proceed quite far without further harmonisation of taxes.

EU REGIME

The tax policy of the EU has followed the general principles indicated in the previous section. Indeed the EU tax policy has been designed and developed so as to serve the objectives of other policy fields, notably an efficient allocation (Neumark *et al.*, 1963). In line with the principle of subsidiarity, the EU tax policies have gradually developed; EU harmonisation has been applied only to those parts of the national taxation systems that caused significant distortions and inefficiencies at the EU level. The involvement of the EU with tax harmonisation has changed with the stage of integration.

Incomplete customs union   In the early 1950s, the workings of the ECSC made it apparent that the differences between member states in sales (turnover) taxes could lead to quite important distortions of the competitive positions of coal and steel producers located in different countries. The report by a study group set up to suggest solutions (Tinbergen, 1953) has actually given the basic principles on which harmonisation of this tax has been based.

Customs union   The Treaty of the EEC, basing itself on the ECSC experience, recognises the necessity of the 'harmonisation of turnover taxes, excise duties and other forms of indirect taxation to the extent that such harmonisation is necessary to ensure the establishment and the functioning of the common market'. It forbids the use of such taxes for discriminatory practices (such as high taxes on imported goods, low ones on home-produced goods). Although the major decisions on indirect taxes were made quite quickly, further progress proved slow.

Common market   Already in the early 1960s it was recognised that unharmonised direct taxes could distort the free movement of capital and workers, thus jeopardising the effectiveness of the European Common Market. The member states negotiated at an early stage the abolition of all double taxation of residents and firms. However, until the end of the 1980s the EU had not advanced very far towards a fully free market for capital and labour; the problems of direct taxation were not considered to be urgent and received little attention.

Internal market   The white paper on the completion of the internal market identified differences in national fiscal regimes as one of the main barriers to free internal movement; it made framework proposals to see them removed (EC, 1985a). Although much doubt was cast on the likelihood of success (fiscal matters needed to be decided with unanimity), the major decisions as to the harmonisation that was necessary to abolish border controls have all been taken. However, many problems remain, so that the internal market is still not perfect.

Economic and monetary union   The EU's adoption of an economic and monetary union has not so far necessitated a further integration of the tax systems of the participating member countries. The Commission has defined two challenges to the taxation policy in the EMU:[20]

- stabilisation of member states' tax revenues (tax competition between member states should not lead to a race to the bottom; see section on theory);
- promoting competitiveness and employment (for example, alleviating the tax burden on the immobile factor labour (see section on direct taxes hereafter).

---

20   Monti (1996); for the latest proposals of the EC, see their website (EC, 2005b) and for a good overview of the academic debate, see the special issue of the International Tax and Public Finance (2003) Vol. 10.6.

INDIRECT TAXES ON GOODS AND SERVICES: VALUE-ADDED TAX (VAT)

When the EU was created, member states were operating different systems of sales (turnover) tax. The need for a harmonised tax in the form of a value-added tax (which accounts for 12 to 20 per cent of total tax receipts and for 5 to 10 per cent of GDP in the member countries of the EU) has been quickly accepted by the member states. At each enlargement of the EU, VAT has been adopted by the new member states as part of the *'acquis communautaire'*. In the harmonisation process of this tax a series of directives have set up common principles, structures and modalities of application, leaving considerable variation as to rates and specific issues.[21]

Value-added   The different systems of EU countries, like the German turnover tax, the UK (wholesale) purchase tax or the French value-added tax, had certain common features. The French system of taxation had three distinct advantages. One is that it is neutral as to the degree of vertical integration of firms. The second is that it is a self-policing operation: the purchasing firm has an interest in having an invoice from its supplier certifying that the taxes on the inputs have been paid. The third is that it is a very stable and flexible source of government revenue. The essentials of the harmonised system were adopted in the 1970s and have since been elaborated.

Rate categories   The differences between the EU member countries are given in Table 14.2. All countries have a 'normal' or standard rate for most goods (and services) and a reduced rate for goods that are considered essentials, like food or clothing, or merit goods like cultural services. Some countries also applied an increased rate to goods labelled as luxury goods (video-recorders, for instance). The purpose of this differentiation is to achieve some redistribution (southern member states relied more on (differentiated) VAT, northern countries more on (progressive) income tax for redistribution). The EU has decided to do away with the increased rate and to define precisely which goods fall into each of the two other categories.

---

21   This harmonisation programme was prompted, not only by the need to remove distortions in the working of the customs union, but also by the wish to have a comparable base for the calculation of the contribution of member states to the budget (see Chapter 4).

Table 14.2   VAT rates* in member countries of the EU, 1970–2004

State	1970–74 Standard (Normal)	1970–74 Reduced (Essential)	1970–74 Increased (Luxury)	1985–1990 Standard (Normal)	1985–1990 Reduced (Essential)	1985–1990 Increased (Luxury)	2000–2004 Standard (Normal)	2000–2004 Reduced (Essential)
Germany	11	5.5	—	14	7	—	16	7
France	23	7.5	33	18.6	2/7	23	19.6/20.6	2.1/5.5
Italy	12	6	18	19	4/9	38	20	4/10
Netherlands	14	4	—	18.5	6	—	17.5/19	6
Belgium	18	6	25	19	1/6	25/33	21	6
Luxembourg	10	2/5	—	12	3/6	—	15	3/6
United Kingdom	10	—	—	15	0	—	17.5	5
Denmark	15	—	—	22	—	—	25	—
Ireland	16	1/5	30	23	0/10	—	21	4.4/13.5
Spain	n.a.	n.a.	n.a.	12	6	33	16	4/7
Portugal	n.a.	n.a.	n.a.	17	0/8	30	17/19	5/12
Greece	n.a.	n.a.	n.a.	16	3/6	36	18	4/8
Austria	16	8	—	20	10	—	20	10
Finland	n.a.	n.a.	n.a.	n.a.	n.a.	n.a.	22	8/17
Sweden	18	3/9	—	23.5	4/12.9	—	25	6/12
Poland							22	3/7
Czech Rep.							19/22	5
Hungary							25	5/15
Slovakia							19/23	
Slovenia							19/20	8.5
Lithuania							18	5/9
Cyprus							8/15	5
Latvia							18	5
Estonia							18	5
Malta							15/18	5
EU minimum	—	—	—	15	5	—	15	5

Note: * Rates are tax-exclusive – that is, based on selling prices before tax.

Source: EC, VAT Rates Applicable in the Member States, DOC/2008/2004 EN, 2004.

Rate levels   There used to be important differences between EU member states (Table 14.2). The EU has tried to arrive at a diminution of these differences. Initially governments were not very inclined to cooperate. High-rate countries (such as France) feared that they would not be able to raise equivalent income from other sources if they lowered their VAT rates. Low-rate countries (such as Germany) were loth to raise them as they were afraid of inflationary pressures. These attitudes changed with the imperative of the internal market. The experience in countries like the USA showed that small differences between the member states do not lead to significant distortions.[22] The option chosen by the EU has thus not been full unification, but the setting of minimum rates (of 5 per cent for reduced and 15 per cent for standard) with possible upward national variations. This has been considered preferable in the light of the subsidiarity principle, as it leaves member states free to operate their VAT systems in line with national social and economic policy objectives, albeit within the limits of EU regulation.[23] Convergence of rates has been minimal. Between 1985 and 2004 the spread decreased by only 1 percentage point. The NMS have all introduced VAT while preparing for membership; the spread of their standard rates was identical to that of the EU15 (see last column of Table 14.2).

The present system has a number of drawbacks.[24] The Commission has regularly made new proposals for directives with the double objective of rationalisation and simplification of the VAT regime and its adaptation to the situation created by modern technology (for example, sales on the Internet). However, progress on this score has been very slow. Decisions in the Council have to be taken by unanimity and a number of very thorny issues have to be solved.

INDIRECT TAXES ON GOODS: EXCISES

Excise taxes are less important than VAT to tax revenues of member states (6 to 12 per cent instead of 10 to 20 per cent). On the other hand, they apply to politically highly sensitive goods which, according to many, have serious negative external effects (alcohol and tobacco on health, energy on the environment). Excises, like sales taxes, need to be harmonised in a regime of open borders. The systems of excises of the member states had many elements in common, but differed markedly as to tax base and tax rates (see Table 14.3). So harmonisation measures of the EU have focused on these two aspects.

---

22   See Pelkmans and Vanheukelen (1988). For certain activities where this freedom could lead to distortions, as for companies selling directly to the client by mail, special rules have been made.

23   The need for such leeway had become clear in the 1970s and 1980s as many governments raised VAT to cope with the budget burden created by the economic crisis. In the years 1986–2000 national governments also made such moves for national political purposes. The standard rates were increased by Germany, confronted by the cost of reunification, and by Spain and other countries confronted with the need to fulfil the budget criteria of the EMU (see Chapter 15).

24   One thorny problem is the system of VAT applied to internal trade (destination principle) (see, for alternatives, Cnossen, 1987, Lockwood et al., 1995 and Hashhimzade et al., 2005). Other problems refer to the goods that fall under categories of zero rating and exemptions and so on (OECD, 1998a). Many proposals for improvement have been made by experts (for example, Keen and Smith, 1996).

Table 14.3   Examples of excise taxes (euro) in EU member states, 2004

Member state	Cigarettes[1] (per 100)	Beer[2] (per litre)	Wine (per litre)	Spirits at 40 % (per litre)	Unleaded petrol (per litre)
Germany	12.79	0.10	0	5.21	0.66
France	16.00	0.13	0.03	5.80	0.64
Italy	8.19	0.17	0	2.58	0.56
Netherlands	10.50	0.25	0.59	7.10	0.67
Belgium	10.26	0.21	0.47	6.64	0.57
Luxembourg	7.23	0.10	0	4.16	0.44
UK	22.12	0.89	2.32	11.10	0.70
Denmark	11.30	0.47	0.95	8.08	0.51
Ireland	19.06	0.99	2.73	15.70	0.49
Spain	6.07	0.10	0	2.96	0.41
Portugal	7.39	0.15	0	3.52	0.52
Greece	7.76	0.14	0	3.63	0.31
Austria	8.81	0.26	0	4.00	0.42
Sweden	10.57	0.81	2.43	22.08	0.46
Finland	11.51	0.97	2.12	11.3	0.60
Poland	3.30	0.19	0.30	3.85	0.38
Czech Rep.	3.12	0.09	0	3.32	0.37
Hungary	4.56	0.21	0.04	3.02	0.44
Slovakia	22.71	0.15	0	2.42	0.39
Slovenia	5.00	0.35	0	2.83	0.41
Lithuania	2.05	0.10	0.44	3.71	0.29
Cyprus	8.46	0.24	0	2.40	0.30
Latvia	1.35	0.09	0.46	3.27	0.29
Estonia	2.97	0.18	0.67	3.71	0.29
Malta	10.53	0.09	0	9.33	0.31
EU: minimum	57 %	0.09	0	2.20	0.36

Notes: [1] *These rates apply for filtered cigarettes; unfiltered cigarettes generally face lower excise burden.* [2] *At an alcohol percentage of 5%.*

Source: EC, Excise Duty Tables, 2004.

- *Base.* Adopting a European list of products subject to excise taxes has resulted in three categories – tobacco products, alcoholic beverages and energy products. This has been realised. Excises on other products (for instance on soft drinks) have been abolished.[25] For the three product categories common systems of taxation were defined.
- *Rates.* Limiting the variance of the rates applied for each product. The 1992 programme suggested a complete unification. This proved impossible to obtain, owing to political resistance on the part of several member countries. The Commission then put forward proposals for minimum rates, coupled for some products with a progressive convergence towards an EU standard. Decisions by the Council have been taken at the beginning of the 1990s.

The situation for each of the three main product categories is as follows. For *tobacco* products, some headway was made with harmonisation of the excises in the 1980s (Kay and Keene, 1987). In 1992 the EU set the minimum excise at 57 per cent of the retail price (excluding VAT) of the most common brands. For other tobacco products a minimum excise per kilo has been agreed

---

25   At the moment voices have become loud to reintroduce excises on soft drinks and products like candy to fight obesity.

upon. The system is due for revision in 2006 taking account of the Framework Convention on Tobacco Control recently adopted by the members of the World Health Organization. The NMS have not reached minimum levels of taxation at their date of accession and have been granted a transition period up to 2010.

With *alcoholic beverages*, member states tended to tax imported products more heavily than domestically produced ones, for instance wine versus beer in the UK, whisky versus cognac in France. The Commission in its harmonisation efforts took the view that excise taxes for different products should be based on the rationale of the excise, which is to compensate for negative health effects. Hence the rate should be proportional to the alcohol content. The Court has in many cases ruled against discrimination, considering that all these products were in competition with one another and therefore must be taxed on an equal footing. The option finally chosen is minimum rates for beer, wine and alcohol (for wine, the minimum rate is zero in view of the specific position of this product in southern member countries). The NMS have implemented these rules on accession (see columns 2, 3 and 4 of Table 14.3). In a recent report (EC, 2004g) the Commission concluded that more convergence is needed so as to reduce distortions and fraud. However, given the sensitivity of the matter proposals will only be made after a wide ranging public debate.

The harmonisation of taxes on *energy products* has proceeded very slowly. For instance for petrol member countries operate widely varying combinations of sales, cars, road and fuel taxes to raise money for the covering of the cost of traffic infrastructure and the removal of negative (environmental) effects. From Table 14.3, petrol excises appear to be fairly similar in the EU15. For all products (mineral oils, coal, gas and electricity) minimum rates are effective as of 2004 (EC, 1996d). Recently adopted new directives permit the NMS to apply temporary reductions in the levels of taxation (last column of Table 14.3).

DIRECT TAXES: LABOUR

The harmonisation of the taxes on the income of the production factor labour (wage tax for dependent workers, personal income taxes, encompassing also independent workers, and social security contributions) has not raised much interest in the EU up to now. This may surprise, given their quantitative importance (more than two-fifths of total tax receipts in the EU). For one thing, as we explained in Chapter 7, the free movement of labour has not created an interpenetration of the labour markets anything like that of the goods market. The creation of the EMU is not likely to change this. Hence tax differences on labour do not cause major distortions of international relations. Furthermore, as these taxes are not levied, controlled or balanced at the internal borders, the Commission does not consider their harmonisation a necessary condition for the completion of the internal market in general and the integration of labour markets in particular, and has not been intent on achieving this.

There are, nevertheless, two reasons for EU action. The first applies directly to the objective of safeguarding the internal labour market and concerns migrants and people who work in a country other than their country of residence. Problems such as the double taxation of the same income and the lack of coordination for individuals who pay taxes in one country and social contributions in another are not yet fully removed by the existing harmonisation (see Chapter 7). The second applies to the objective of employment growth (see Chapter 16). Between 1980 and 1993, the implicit tax rate on employed labour increased by about one-fifth, while the same indicator for other factors of production (mainly self-employed and capital) decreased by one-tenth (Monti, 1996). Since then the latter has further decreased (see next section). Decreasing labour cost by decreasing the tax burden on labour should have a positive effect on employment.

DIRECT TAXES: CAPITAL

The EU member countries operate systems of capital taxation that are quite different as to principles, rates, dividend withholding and so on. Some *harmonisation* of national tax provisions is needed, for two reasons: first, for a good functioning of the European capital market in a world of highly mobile capital; second, to avoid problems of unfair distribution of wealth due to erosion of the tax base of some member countries.[26] The history of the efforts towards harmonisation is one of many attempts and little success.

Paramount among capital taxes is the *corporate tax* (CT). The major differences between the national CT are the following.

- *Systems.* Most member states use systems that give shareholders credits on their personal income tax for the corporation tax imputed to the dividends due to them. In the others, widely divergent systems are in use. A gradual convergence of these systems can be observed.
- *Rates.* Traditionally the statutory rate varied very much among member states. Since 1985, the tariffs have converged, while the (unweighted) average has decreased to some 30 per cent. Before membership the rates of most applicant countries of Central Europe (not all shown in the table) were largely similar to the ones in the present EU. This is with the exception of Estonia which has refused to introduce a CT. However, over the past years they have been significantly reduced (see Table 14.4).

Although they are not very important in quantitative terms (EU average about 1 per cent of total tax receipts) corporate taxes may cause important distortions, as tax differences are an important determinant in the choice of the country of investment. Low corporate taxes are indeed used by member governments to attract investment. Distortion may stem from national differences in tax incentives, double taxation (by the countries of origin and destination of FDI), differential treatment of residents and non-residents and of corporate investments.[27] Tax incentives make the effective rate much lower than the posted rate. In the past there has been very fierce resistance by certain member states to any attempt to harmonise corporate taxes. This meant as a consequence that even a minimum rate and a common definition of the tax base could not be agreed upon. In 1999 member states all agreed to a politically binding Code of Conduct for Business Taxation. However, the practice up till now is rather in the direction of a fierce competition between member states and consequently a constant erosion of the tax rates and hence revenues. So further harmonisation is in order. In 2001/2002 the Commission made new proposals that aim at setting common rules for defining the tax base and for the apportionment of revenue of CT on MNF over member states. These have not yet borne fruit (McLure, 2005).

---

26   The external openness of the EU capital markets (Chapter 8) implies that not only EU but also worldwide harmonisation is called for (Giovannini, 1989; OECD, 1991, 1998b; and Devereux et al., 2002).
27   See EC (1966); Devereux and Pearson (1989); Ruding Committee (1992); Gardner (1992); Cnossen (1996). Some of the problems (for example, of double taxation) have been solved on a case by case basis by jurisprudence of the ECJ.

Table 14.4   Corporate taxes: systems and basic rates, 1977–2004[a]

Country[b]	1977	1985	1991	2000	2004
Germany	56	47/63	50	52/43	40
Italy	25	41	36	37	37
Greece	39	49	35	35	35
Netherlands	48	43	35	35	35
Spain	36	35	35	35	35
Austria	n.a.	n.a.	n.a.	34	34
Belgium	48	45	40	37	34
France	50	50	34	33	34
Denmark	37	40	34	32	30
Luxembourg	40	47	37	30	30
UK	52	52	33	30	30
Finland	n.a.	n.a.	n.a.	29	29
Portugal	36	40	36	34	28
Sweden	n.a.	n.a.	n.a.	28	28
Ireland	45	50	38	24 (10)	13
Poland				30	19
Czech Rep.				31	28
Hungary				18	16
Slovakia				40	19
Cyprus				24/29	10/15
Estonia				0	0

Notes: [a] *In many countries there is a surcharge, surtax or a local tax that makes the total rate of CT some 10 per cent higher than the rates shown here.* [b] *Some countries not listed due to data unavailability.*

Sources: *Cnossen (1987, 1996); Gardner (1992); KPMG, Corporate Tax Rate Survey, 2001 & 2004.*

Another important item in matters of capital taxes is *interest*. The EU-wide harmonisation of the taxation of interest on savings deposits held in another member country than the country of residence has only been realised in 2000. The agreement provides for the following rules:

- Member countries agree that they will inform each others' tax authorities about the capital income earned by non-residents.
- If they do not do this because of their national rules on bank secrecy, they will be charged a withholding tax of at least 20 per cent.

By 2015 this information system is bound to replace the withholding system for those member countries that have adopted it. New member countries will have to immediately adopt the information system.

Access to markets, technical barriers

SOME THEORY

Governments wish to limit market access for several reasons.

- Imperfect information makes it hard for consumers to judge the quality of goods and services, and may also spell material losses and risk to health and safety.
- Production and consumption may have external effects in the shape of costs or benefits to third parties. Environmental damage is a case in point.

To cope with such aspects, governments use various *instruments*.

- For goods, governments mostly rely on the specification of technical standards and norms with which goods must comply (for instance, safety windshields in cars).
- For services, governments tend to set minimum requirements which key persons in a profession must satisfy (for instance, pharmacists and lawyers). Continuous control of a company's financial soundness is another instrument; such prudential control is applied to financial institutions such as banks, pension funds and insurance companies, to whom the public entrusts large sums of money, sometimes on long-term contracts.
- Governments may reserve certain activities to themselves or to (state) monopolies, thus blocking the entry of other suppliers. Many social services belong to this category, along with, for instance, defence industries.

That a free market cannot be created by simply removing tariffs and quotas will now be clear. Indeed states can effectively use national standards like technical specifications to bar the importation of foreign goods, requirements for qualifications, diplomas and so on to curb the free movement of active persons and services, and prudential control of financial institutions to restrict the movement of capital. They have indeed done so in the past, with different countries having developed different requirements for quality and practices of testing the product's conformation to these requirements. If trade is not barred it is made more costly because of compliance with duplicative testing and certification procedures on imported goods. Specified requirements and the ensuing technical trade barriers have often been used to protect private interest groups rather than the general public. An example is the telecommunications industry, where the requirements which public companies set for the equipment they purchase were such that only domestic firms were likely to comply with them.

THE EUROPEAN UNION REGIME

Goods subjected to technical norms represent about 75 per cent of intra-EU trade. The segmentation of the EU market has for a long time compelled producers to adapt their products to a number of different sets of national norms and standards. As this situation is very costly in welfare terms, the EU has tried several approaches to do away with the differences.

Mutual recognition Technical specifications that are set up as measures of quantitative restriction are prohibited. In a number of rulings, the European Court has specified the application of this principle. The trendsetter was the 1979 ruling in the case of Cassis de Dijon, an alcoholic product not conforming to German liquor standards in that it contained only 18 instead of the prescribed 25 per cent of alcohol. Another famous case was that against the German *Rheinheitsgebot*, a prescription dating from the 16th century laying down that beer could only be made from certain ingredients. In these and similar cases the Court ruled that a good produced and marketed in one member country according to that country's national specifications should in principle gain free access to the markets of partner countries. Only in a case where a country can prove that 'mandatory requirements' of public interest justify higher national technical norms than those of the partner country can obstacles to free movement be imposed.

Harmonisation The approach here is the 'approximation of such provisions laid down by law, regulation or administrative action in member states as directly affect the functioning of the common market'. Since 1968, when the Commission proposed a general programme of harmonisation, experts of the Commission, national administrators and external institutions have exerted themselves to harmonise the technical standards for a large number of products, with meagre results, however (Pelkmans and Vollebergh, 1986). The poor record was notably due to the rule of unanimity in the Council, where agreement proved difficult to obtain as the experts tended to aim at excessive uniformity and the specification of many technical details. In the framework of the Single Market Programme a new approach was adopted. All matters are decided on in the Council by qualified majority. The EU switched thereby from the former monolithic conception in which national legislation and powers are replaced by European powers, to a pluralistic, pragmatic and federalistic conception in which national legislation is framed in a way that respects minimum European requirements (Padoa-Schioppa *et al.*, 1987). This takes somewhat different forms for goods and services.

For *goods*, the approach is based on mutual recognition of, and reference to, standards. The directives implementing the technical harmonisation henceforth define only the essential requirements with which products must comply to circulate freely all over the EU. They refer to European standards (technical specifications) defined by the competent normalisation organisations, such as CEN, CENELEC and CEPT. Each member state must give free access to any product manufactured according to the European standards; restrictions based on public interest may no longer be invoked.

For *services*, the approach is based on recognition of the quality of control in the home country. The segmentation of service markets is due to national regulations concerning products (insurance products, among others) but also to the prudential control exerted by national authorities on all establishments located in their territory. Of course this presupposes a minimum standard of surveillance.

Welfare effects

In the *early 1980s*, a few attempts[28] were made at quantifying the cost of the remaining non-tariff barriers and formalities at the internal borders of the EC and the other imperfections of the internal market. They could only provide a very limited and fragmentary view of the problem.

In the *late 1980s* the Commission tried to establish a more complete picture of the welfare gains to be obtained from the removal of the remaining obstacles.[29] In this ex-ante study a distinction was made between three types of effects:

---

28   For example, Albert and Ball (1983), Hartley (1987).
29   The results of a series of detailed sectoral studies have been put together in three volumes: (1) a scientific report (Emerson et al., 1988); (2) a volume containing the executive summaries of the detailed reports (EC, 1988c); and (3) a more popular book, which became known as the Cecchini et al. (1988) Report, after the chairman of the working group.

- *Border control removal.* In economic terms, the cost of administration of both importers and exporters, and the cost of delays for transporters are similar to tariffs that impede trade.
- *Market entry and competition effects.* The short-term effect is that prices will drop to the level of the most efficient producer in the EU. The long-term effect is the further reduction of cost through enhanced innovation and learning effects.
- *Economies of scale.* As competition leads industries to restructure, closing down inefficient plants, investing in new plants and expanding output, production will become more efficient.

The total welfare gains resulting from the completion of the internal market of the EU were rather optimistically estimated at some 6 per cent of GDP, provided the right macro-economic policies were carried out.

In the *mid-1990s*, the Commission made an ex-post evaluation of the effects of the completion of the internal market (EC, 1996a). It has thereby distinguished between two major effects:

- Allocation (this encompasses the three effects mentioned in the ex-ante study): the improvement of efficiency has been calculated for individual markets (for example, goods, capital) and industries (for example, manufacturing).
- Accumulation: the effect of the transformation on the improvement of the productivity of the production factors of the entire economy.

The effects on GDP were found to be considerably less than those calculated in the ex-ante study. Including the effects of the liberalisation of the so-called network activities (for example, telecommunications) the total effects were estimated to amount to some 1 to 2 per cent of GDP. The effect on employment was somewhat less, as a result of important productivity increases. However, as some of the medium-term (dynamic) effects may not have been fully captured, the growth bonus may be significantly higher. As a consequence the total employment effect is supposed to have been some 2.5 million jobs. The efficiency gains have anyway more than compensated for the initial losses due to restructuring.[30]

The latest developments concern the completion of *the internal market for services*. Services account for the lion's share of value added, employment and FDI in the EU. However, their share in intra-EU trade is very modest. The service markets are very fragmented (see Chapters 6 and 12). The completion of the internal market for services (conform the draft directive EC, 2004b) would lead to an increase of total intra-EU trade of 1 to 3 per cent and a growth impulse of some 1 per cent for GDP and 0.3 per cent for total employment (Kox *et al.*, 2004; Copenhagen Economics, 2005).

Summary and conclusions

- The main rationale for European economic integration is the enhancement of allocational efficiency; the main instrument to achieve it is the liberalisation of markets.
- In addition to liberalisation measures, the EU has introduced rules to create the conditions for the proper functioning of markets. The most important come under the heading of the

---

30   Allen et al. (1996, 1998); EC (2004c); for the effects of the functioning of product markets, see also Dierx, Ilkovitz and Sekkat (2004).

EU competition policy. Others concern the harmonisation of technical norms and of the segments of taxation that impact on the internal market, notably value-added tax.

- In the 1960s and 1970s, the internal market remained incomplete. In the 1980s and early 1990s, a new programme succeeded in bringing about the complete abolition of all controls at internal borders on goods, services, workers and capital. This programme had substantial positive welfare effects.

15 *Stablisation: Economic and Monetary Union*

Introduction

The progress along the road from free trade area to full union takes in the station of Economic and Monetary Union (EMU). We recall (Chapter 2) that such a union implies, on the monetary side, a single currency, and on the economic side, policies that sustain the internal market and the monetary union. One implication of this is the need for coherence of the budgetary policies of member states.

The policy integration needed for a monetary union has mostly to do with stabilisation. The purpose of stabilisation policies is to cushion the effects of internal and external shocks to the economy. An example is the intervention of monetary authorities in foreign exchange markets when speculations tend to put these out of alignment with fundamental economic factors. Budgetary policies to soften the effects of the business cycle on economic activity are another example. The latter, however, need to be dovetailed with anti-inflationary policies in order to retain consistency with monetary policy. As integration of markets erodes the possibility for independent national policies, stabilisation is an important European policy field. We will discuss this below in the following way.

First, we will go into the theoretical foundations. The main rationale for monetary integration is that it smooths trade and investment in the EU and hence contributes to the efficient allocation of resources. Now, for such relatively small open economies as most EU member states are, the independent pursuit of stability is very difficult. We will indicate the advantages and disadvantages of different degrees of integration.

Next, we will describe the way the EU has gradually developed its economic and monetary integration. We describe the evolution from its hesitant start on a narrow legal basis to the development of the precursor of the EMU, the European Monetary System.

In the section that follows we describe the set-up chosen for the European Monetary Union and the criteria for membership. Effective monetary integration imposes constraints on national macro-economic goals. We will discuss the forms these constraints on national policy take in terms of budgetary deficits, government indebtedness and so on. The EU has set a number of criteria that its member countries have to meet in order to participate in the EMU. We will indicate what the application of these criteria has given in terms of countries that participate in EMU and those that do not.

The next section will deal with the workings of the EMU. We will discuss in particular the independent monetary policy of the ECB and the coordination of fiscal policies of the member countries.

Finally, we will go into two important issues for the further development of the EU: the position of the UK (and the pound sterling) and the road of the new member states towards the euro.

As usual, we will end the chapter with an evaluation and some conclusions.

Theoretical foundations

THE PROBLEM: GROWING INTERDEPENDENCE NARROWS THE SCOPE FOR INDEPENDENT POLICIES

The creation of a customs union and a common market increases the specialisation of the constituent economies and the exchange of goods, services and production factors. As a result, the economies involved become increasingly interdependent, every country being dependent on its partner countries and affected by the developments there.[1] Interdependence has a strong bearing on the degree to which individual governments can influence the economy through budgetary (fiscal) and monetary (exchange rate) policies. For example, a budgetary policy intended to increase output by increased government spending may be ineffective if the additional purchasing power created is spent on imported rather than domestic goods. A monetary policy that restricts the money supply to keep inflation low may be frustrated by price increases of imported goods as a result of wage inflation in the partner (exporting) country. Interdependence of national economies means that developments on the national scale are apt to have spill-over effects in partner countries.

Increased integration implies a reduced ability to control the instruments of policy (such as the domestic money supply under a regime of fixed exchange rates) and to influence policy targets (such as the level of real output, the level of unemployment and the level of inflation). Now private decision makers in financial markets are very well aware of the reduced effectiveness of policies pursued independently, so public authorities have to make considerable efforts to remain credible. If they fail, private parties will go on responding to expectations of future exchange rates, irrespective of policy intervention, thus doing away completely with whatever room for manoeuvring there was left to the public authorities. This is particularly relevant under the now prevailing conditions of generalised free movements of capital using a technological infrastructure which makes it possible to move considerable sums from one country to another almost instantly. The enormous sums that private traders can now mobilise, compared to the limited means of monetary authorities, reinforce the need for partner countries to cooperate and in this way to regain collectively the control which they had lost individually.

THE SOLUTION: COORDINATION OR UNIFICATION THROUGH COMMON INSTITUTIONS

The central element of the solution to the problem of loss of autonomy is, then, policy coordination or unification. (This approach finds its theoretical underpinning in game theory). The important question arises as to why in the past cooperation has been the exception rather than the rule. The following reasons have been put forward:

---

1   Interdependence is more than openness. An open economy is dependent on the outside world, but small open economies do not necessarily have an impact on the economies of partners. Structural interdependence is notably not the only effect of integration with partner countries. To this needs to be added the effect of openness on the rest of the world. The vulnerability to shocks from outside the group (such as an oil shock) is changed under the influence of group integration, and an effective response will need coordinated action.

- *Uncertain relations between objectives and policy.* Players believe in different models of the real world (for instance monetarists versus Keynesians). Even if they agree on one basic model, the quantification of the parameters is very difficult, leaving large margins for error. Coordination can be introduced with success only if conceptual problems can largely be eliminated.
- *Absence of compensation mechanisms.* If, under coordination, country A is not worse off than before, while country B stands to reap large benefits, the scheme is unlikely to be considered a good deal by country A. Better deals may be concluded if side payments are made to countries that lose or gain but little from cooperation.
- *Rank and file.* Players (governments) are constrained not only by other players' strategies, but also by their national parliaments and pressure groups. The need to maintain a balance back home may preclude the choice of the optimum solution in Brussels.
- *High cost of coordination.* Negotiations can be long-winded, conditions may change while they are going on, welfare functions are hard to define, and the assessment of the advantages accruing to each group meets with conceptual as well as statistical obstacles. This leads to high transaction cost. Moreover, compromise objectives and policies (second best solutions) incur high welfare costs.
- *Complexity.* Even in a group with a limited number of members and confining its attention to only one or two objectives, the game is already complex. The complexity increases with the number of players (geographical extension) and the number of targets (extension of subjects to deal with). The difficulty increases further with the adding of objectives with different time horizons. So the feasibility of coordination depends critically on the limitation of the number of targets.

The conclusion from this analysis is that the setting up of institutions and the acceptance of common rules are important conditions for the durability and effectiveness of policy coordination.

GOALS: A HIERARCHY OF ULTIMATE AND DERIVED GOALS

Stabilisation is not a goal in itself. It is pursued because it brings economic benefits. For instance, limiting the effects of cyclical fluctuations by stabilising fiscal policies brings about a higher growth rate. This growth bonus occurs as short-term stability favours the process of building up human capital and learning by doing.[2] The principal goals for an EU stabilisation policy are at several levels.

Stability of exchange rates This second level goal is derived from the higher goal of creating the stable conditions for the efficient functioning of markets. The main instrument for arriving at this goal is contained in the very definition of the monetary union: the definitive fixing of the exchange rates with the currencies of all partner countries or the adoption of a single common currency. It is understood that there is full and irrevocable convertibility of MU currencies, which implies that unlimited foreign exchange is available for all international transactions among MU partners, be they related to trade, services, capital or remittances (essential for CU and CM).[3]

---

2   See, for empirical proof, Martin and Rogers (2000).
3   The goal of fully fixed exchange rates is not easy to attain, and therefore intermediate goals have been advocated. In one, the variability of exchange rates is limited to certain target zones around pivot rates. In another, a so-called

Alignment of inflation rates   This third level goal is derived from the goal of stable exchange rates; indeed in the long run the exchange rate has to be adapted to changes in the inflation rates between the two countries. So, to keep the former fixed, the latter have to be aligned. The instrument used to arrive at a target rate of inflation for the whole Union is the coordination or unification of monetary and budgetary policies. Obviously, in a complete EMU with only one currency, money supply and budgetary policies are agreed upon jointly by partners or decided by Union institutions.[4] On the way to an EMU, intermediate solutions are likely to be found, that gradually reduce the divergence of inflation rates through the coordinated use of policy instruments by member states.

Alignment of budgetary deficits   In order to comply with the previous goals and to make sure that budgetary policies can still play their role as stabilisers in the economy, national fiscal policies need to be coordinated. This results at the fourth level in the choosing of the budget deficit as a target variable. In order to keep national inflation rates low and the differences between countries small, budget deficits should be very limited. In order to keep some room for expansionary budgetary policies in a period of recession, without risking inflation, the budget needs to be close to balance in normal times. Coordination may take several forms. During the intermediate stage (preparing for EMU), governments retain some flexibility as to the degree of compliance with the goal, and as to the mix of instruments used. The stronger the commitment to an EMU the more closely will be the coordination of a whole series of policy elements, such as the composition of government spending and of tax and other receipts. The efficiency of the coordination process (consistent involvement of partners) and the effectiveness of its outcome (credibility in markets) depend critically on the gradual reinforcement of the regulatory and institutional set-up.

THE ROUTE: CONTROVERSIES BETWEEN 'ECONOMISTS' AND 'MONETARISTS'

Over the past years, reaching an agreement on the way in which these two objectives of the EMU could be realised has been made difficult by the deep-rooted differences of opinion among experts about the best way forward. Although everybody agreed that the benefits of monetary integration increase, and the costs of integration decrease, with increasing interdependence in terms of goods trade (see Figure 15.1), there were differences about the point where the two lines intersect. The main dividing line was between economists and monetarists. They have different conceptions about the balancing of the cost and benefits of the EMU, notably about the cost level of integration (see Figure 15.1).

The *economists* (found in particular among German and Dutch scholars) gave priority to the harmonisation of economic policies, and considered results on that score an essential condition for further monetary integration. Their argument was that divergent inflation rates (springing from different economic policies and the incapacity to overcome rigidities in the field of wages and immobility of labour) sooner or later lead to exchange rate adaptations. If that option is not open any more, some countries may be forced into a very costly deflation which for internal political reasons they would rather avoid. The ensuing tensions will almost certainly break up the fragile systems of exchange rate stabilisation agreed upon. The

'pseudo union' (Corden, 1972b) is established, in which exchange rates are fixed but monetary policies are not fully integrated; there is no Union monetary authority, and some doubt persists about the durability of the exchange rates.

4   Evidently the exchange rate with all third currencies as well as balance-of-payment questions with the rest of the world will then become matters of common policy, the Union Monetary Authority controlling the pool of exchange reserves.

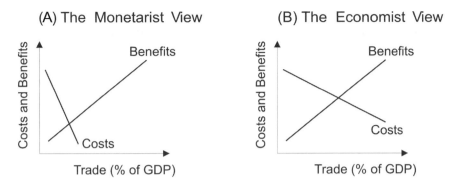

Figure 15.1   Two views of cost and benefits of a monetary union

Source: *de Grauwe (2000).*

economists held that the cost curve is far away from the origin (right-hand side of Figure 15.1) and hence that the full unification of economic policies must precede full monetary integration.

The *monetarists* (chiefly found among the Italians and in earlier years also among French and Belgians) defended the view that the use of exchange rates is in the long run ineffective to correct for imbalances. In this view (left-hand part of Figure 15.1) the cost curve is very close to the origin. Monetary integration (fixed exchange rates, controlled liquidity and so on) is the best way to commit national governments to take the necessary measures of economic policy to curb inflation. Their argument was that governments of high-inflation countries will not start adjusting their policies and curb the forces that tend to press inflation upwards, such as politicians (budget policy) and labour unions (wage-cost inflation), unless forced to do so by fixed exchange rates.[5]   The skirmishes between the two schools have flared up with every step taken towards further integration into an EMU. Both parties have finally agreed to the compromise that the two elements need to be gradually integrated in a balanced fashion.

PARTICIPATION: THE SEARCH FOR OPTIMALITY

Countries that participate in a customs union, and *a fortiori* in a common market, will come to realise that the costs of non-coordinated policies tend to increase. For one thing, the volumes of trade subject to exchange rate risks have become greater. For another, there are larger flows of capital, which tend to shy away from exchange rate risks in so far as they are of a structural nature, but tend to increase them inasmuch as they are of a speculative nature. These costs push CU partners and, even more, CM partners, to progress to an EMU eventually.

The question is then: who should take part in a scheme for monetary integration? In the literature the concept of the *Optimum Currency Area* (OCA) has been favoured (see also Chapter 2). To identify the group of countries likely to form an OCA, different indicators are used that refer to the stages of integration distinguished earlier (products, production factors and policy). The most popular indicator is openness of goods markets: pairs of countries with high import or export figures in respect of their domestic consumption are good candidates for a monetary union. Next follows the degree of openness to production factors (labour and capital). Indicators that relate to degree of diversification of the economic structures and

---

5   For example, Giavazzi and Pagano (1986).

the similarity in preferences and level of economic development have also been proposed. Finally comes the degree to which forms of integrated policy with respect to stabilisation and redistribution are realised. The higher the flexibility of the labour market (job mobility real wages adaptation) and the more effective the compensation mechanisms, the more likely it is that the group of countries can effectively cope with whatever asymmetric shocks occur. To some all the previous indicators are rather irrelevant as criteria for EMU membership; to them a monetary union cannot be sustained without full political unification.[6]

The search for optimality for defining membership of an EMU on the basis of such criteria as openness to trade, capital and so on has been severely criticised (by Ishiyama, 1975, among others). For one thing, the scores on these criteria are often difficult to measure. For another, which criterion would be best is hard to say; even a combination is of little avail, as we do not know what weights to attach to them. Finally, countries may value their independence so highly that the perceived cost of participation outweighs the advantages of integration. There is also a more institutional reason not to follow up the argument of the OCA. To be viable, an EMU must have a fairly strong institutional structure and real powers. Such a structure is unlikely to be created or sustained among countries that have not acquired some experience with the institutional set-up of less difficult forms of integration. This implies that countries already forming a CU or a CM will be the best candidates for participation in an EMU.

There is a much more fundamental reason why the OCA approach is not sufficient to decide on the participation of countries. This is *endogeneity*: the mere participation in an EMU actually helps countries to grasp the benefits of it while exclusion from it makes the meeting of accession criteria ever more problematic. One can compare this argument to the observation we made in Chapter 5 on the participation in the customs union of countries that did not seem to be first candidates for such membership. Yet their very participation did lead, after some time, to very high levels of goods market integration. The argument that the criteria are endogenous has also been developed for the monetary union;[7] participation in an EMU actually helps countries to fulfil the conditions for its sustainability. The business cycle correlation may rise with stronger trade ties that in turn are enhanced by the stability brought about by a common currency.

PARTICIPATION: THE BALANCE BETWEEN COST AND BENEFITS

The question of whether to create an EMU, then, becomes a much more pragmatic one: what conditions must be met for CM partners to realise monetary integration? That depends on the trade-off between the loss of autonomy in certain policy fields and the economic advantages which integration promises, to each member individually and to the union collectively. Governments will give up autonomy in sensitive policy areas only when they consider the

---

6   For an overview of the development of this theory, see Kawai (1992). The basis comes from the seminal article by Nobel prize winner Mundell (1961); the other indicators have been proposed by respectively McKinnon (1963); Kenen (1969); Ingram (1973); MacDougall et al. (1977); Allen (1983); Hamada (1985).

7   See, for example, Fatas (1997); Frankel and Rose (1998); de Grauwe (2000).

gains from integration will exceed cost.[8] So the identification and quantification of gains and losses becomes the essential point of analysis for the decision to move towards an EMU.[9]
The *gains* can be summarised under three headings.

- *Efficient goods, service, labour and capital markets.* The basic reason for monetary integration is to relieve traders and investors of transaction costs; that is, exchange losses on their international transactions. The second reason is that they take away the uncertainty as to future fluctuation of exchange rates and the fear of competitive devaluations. Indeed uncoordinated policies lead to 'overshooting' in a system of flexible exchange rates, and hence to largely unnecessary fluctuations in trade, production and investment. In general stability will increase the volume of international exchanges. This in turn is likely to improve the financial services needed for payments and hence reduce transaction costs even further. The third reason is that the single currency will eliminate significant information cost and price discrimination that is based on these imperfections.
- *Efficient monetary system.* An MU needs far smaller monetary reserves than the group of constituent countries operating individually. For one thing, no stocks need be kept of currencies of other MU members; for another, peak demands for the currencies of third countries are unlikely to occur in all member countries at the same time. Intervention in foreign exchange markets by MU authorities is more effective than individual actions because of the increased means and the unity of purpose. Moreover, the use of the common currency by third countries provides extra benefits to the common central bank; they can actually be seen as a lowering of domestic taxes. Finally, the easier management of the system will free part of the resources formerly tied up in it (both with the monetary authorities and with the banking system).
- *Faster economic growth.* The direct growth effects of the improved allocation and better coordinated budgetary and monetary policies will be complemented by some dynamic effects. These stem partly from more efficient markets (that have been discussed in Chapter 14), partly also from a better macro-economic situation (lower interest rates lead to lower budget deficits and to a lower burden on the economy).

The *cost* of monetary integration is to be measured in the loss of production and value added, employment and so on, and stems from three types of problems:

- *Changeover cost.* Both the public and private sector incur cost by the changeover from national currencies to a common currency. For both, these are in terms of adaptation of the hardware and software of administrative and financial systems. The problems are of course more acute for financial institutions than for the other segments of the economy.
- *Non-optimal policy mix.* Many governments assume that there is in the short run a certain relation between the level of inflation and the level of unemployment. Each country that used to 'choose' independently a combination of these two is now forced to accept a common inflation rate, and hence accept a different combination of inflation and

---

8   We have already seen that similar decisions had to be taken in earlier stages of integration. Countries participating in a customs union waive the right to use tariffs, quotas and other trade instruments vis-à-vis their partners, and the right to decide on their own to use such instruments towards third countries. Much in the same way, partners in a common market refrain from using instruments for the control of capital flows to pursue macro-economic objectives. All partners have given up part of their competences because they reckon that the benefits of cooperation outweigh the loss of room for manoeuvre.

9   See, for example, Thygesen (1990); Gros and Thygesen (1998); de Grauwe (2000); Eijffinger and de Haan (2000).

unemployment. The costs involved can be reduced if partners take long enough to realise convergence of national rates for these two variables so as to realign with the union targets that bring a definite strengthening of confidence in the long-run predictability and stability of the price level.

- *Rigidities*. Economies are regularly victims of external shocks. Some of these, that affect the whole union in the same way, and others, that are minor and country-specific, will be easily accommodated. However, an MU constrains domestic policy making in response to major country-specific shocks (as, for example, with a sudden fall in demand for a country's exports or a rise in import prices). Adjustment of the exchange rate is no longer feasible, so adjustment will have to occur in the real sector. The cost involved in that adjustment process (for example, the lay-off of production factors) will depend on the (lack of) institutional and social flexibility of the economy.

So the *basic cost–benefit assessment* of monetary union has to weigh a set of micro- and macroeconomic costs and benefits of very different sorts. The balance can come out differently for each participant country, depending on the structure of its economy, its past policies, its institutional arrangements (rigidities) and so on. One feature is prominent in all this, however: the more the cost of monetary integration in terms of the percentage of welfare (GDP) gets lower, and the benefits higher, the more open the national economy (in terms of trade and capital relations) and the more interrelated the economy in policy terms.

EU regime: from the start to the EMU

THE BEGINNINGS

The Treaty of Rome is not very explicit on the macro-economic and monetary integration of Europe. It provides for some embryonic integration on this score, designed to facilitate the proper functioning of the Common Market for goods, services and production factors. The main *objectives* of the EU in matters of economic and monetary policy at its start were to ensure a high level of employment and a stable level of prices. To attain these objectives, three *instruments* were to be used:

- coordination of national economic policies, particularly cyclical policies;
- stabilisation of rates of exchange;
- assistance (in terms of credits) in case of balance-of-payments problems.

The role of the European Union in matters of monetary policy is not foreseen by the EEC Treaty but not explicitly precluded by it either. That is, however, the case for one instrument of macro-economic policy: the EU cannot pursue a budgetary policy, as the EU outlays and receipts must be in balance every year. Should the resources of the EU fall short of needs, then member states have to put up the money; the EU can neither, like its member states, raise money by imposing taxes, nor finance spending by loaning on the capital market.[10]

Why was the Treaty so cautious in bestowing powers of monetary and economic policy on the EU? The answer to this question lies in the economic conditions of the period: the

---

10   But even if the EU had been authorised to pursue budgetary policies, their effect would have been doubtful with an EU budget amounting to no more than about 1 per cent of total GDP.

Bretton Woods system of fixed exchange rates was functioning smoothly, and the European economies were all at a stage of long-term economic growth, so that all attention could be given to short- and medium-term policies.

THE CREATION OF AN INTERMEDIATE STAGE (EMS)

While European integration was in progress it became apparent that the coordination system had some severe shortcomings. To cope with the problems more unification than coordination seemed necessary. Several proposals for the realisation of an economic and monetary union were made. At the Hague Summit of 1969 the heads of state and government agreed in principle to the creation of an Economic and Monetary Union.[11] However, due to the considerable monetary turmoil in the 1970s, these plans had to be shelved.

Theory had already shown that it is impossible to maintain all three of the following elements of the triangle: free movement of products and production factors (notably capital), fixed exchange rates, and national autonomy in the fiscal and monetary policies. As the first was an established fact by the progress in integration and the second was not accepted, the fixed exchange rate was sacrificed.

However, this choice had large negative effects. European governments (from both small and large countries) experienced repeatedly that their macro and monetary policies had lost effectiveness.[12] It convinced more and more academic, business and political circles that further progress towards the EMU was urgently needed.

In a period when economists were hopelessly divided over both the advantages of a system of free-floating exchange rates and the best road to monetary stability (see the previous section), a decision was taken by three statesmen (Giscard, Schmidt and Jenkins) to get out of the deadlock. They proposed an incomplete monetary union (see Chapter 2) as an intermediate stage to full monetary union. These ideas have been realised by setting-up the European Monetary System (EMS).[13]

The main aim of the EMS was to create short-term exchange rate stability in Europe. This has been put into practice by the creation of the European Currency Unit (ECU) and of an Exchange Rate Mechanism (ERM). The ECU was made up of parts of the currencies of all member states and so reflected the whole Union's financial identity. Each national currency contributed a certain part to the ECU. For the national currencies that participated in the ERM, reference parities (central or pivot rates) to the ECU were defined, which also defined all bilateral exchange rates between these currencies. Together they formed a grid of parities. The

---

11   A blueprint for such a union was the report called 'The Realisation by Stages of the Economic and Monetary Union in the Community', submitted in 1970 by a committee under the chairmanship of Werner. The Werner Report, adopted by the Council in 1971, proposed the realisation of the EMU in stages, and presented an ambitious calendar, foreseeing completion in 1980. The Werner plan soon proved an illusion. The monetary disorder of the mid-1970s made it very difficult to obtain adequate political support. While awaiting the single currency, a need has developed for a European monetary unit that does not have all the attributes of a currency. Indeed, accepting one of the member states' currencies (German mark) or a third currency (US dollar) as a vehicle for financial transactions in the EU is hard to defend politically. Therefore several forms of European units of account were developed in the past, all of which proved inadequate for the tasks ahead.

12   For problems and possible policy solutions, see, for example, Buiter and Marston (1985); Steinherr (1984, 1985).

13   Over the past decades, the EU has worked out several systems to reduce exchange rate uncertainty among its members (Steinherr, 1994). The first major attempt was the 'Snake' arrangement of April 1972. The widely varying policy responses of the European countries to the oil crisis reduced the arrangement to a small group of currencies around the DM. In 1979, the European Monetary System (EMS) started. For a description of the genesis of the EMS, see Ludlow (1982); for the basic text, see EC (1979d) and for an elaborate description of its genesis and evolution, see Gros and Thygesen (1998).

market value of the currencies changed continuously as a consequence of supply and demand conditions. Hence differences between the real rate and the central rate occurred.

Stability was realised by the intervention of monetary authorities on the exchange markets.[14] They let the market rate fluctuate only within certain margins. In the beginning these margins were small (for most countries 2.25 per cent above or below the central rate) but, in mid-1993, speculation forced many currencies out of these small margins, and some (like the UK pound) even out of the ERM. In order to make such speculative attacks much more costly for speculators and less costly for the authorities, the margins have been considerably widened, to some 15 per cent. In practice, however, the central banks of many countries kept much smaller margins.

Has the EMS delivered what is was meant to do? The answer is yes as far as the main EMS objective is concerned. On the whole, the system has worked very satisfactorily, producing a fair balance between flexibility (daily variations of exchange rates) and stability (central rates). The answer is also yes as far as a second objective is concerned: to stimulate the efficiency of markets. Intra-Union trade and capital movements[15] have indeed been stimulated by the decrease in exchange rate uncertainty (note that an increase in migration is not an objective – see Chapter 7). This result is not surprising; as a matter of fact, the decrease of exchange rate volatility and a fortiori the creation of a monetary union has been shown to lead to large increases in trade among the participant countries (Rose, 2000).

THE CREATION OF EMU

The EMS had some inherent weaknesses. Moreover, the advantages of the scheme fell short of those of a full monetary union. Under the impetus of the successful completion of the internal market, initiatives were taken to revitalise the plans for an EMU. A committee under the chairmanship of the president of the Commission set to work and drew up a new plan (Delors et al., 1989). The committee was composed of members of the Commission, of the governors of the national central banks and a number of independent experts. It was strongly supported by the business community, which had been made painfully aware of the disadvantages of the monetary disorder (AMUE, 1988). The proposal was the basis for the negotiations that finally resulted in the inclusion in the Treaty of the creation of the EMU.

In the debate that led to the adoption of EMU the evaluation of the costs and benefits of the operation in economic terms has played a relatively minor role. It proved very difficult to quantify the major components specified in the theoretical section. The benefits (notably from lower transaction costs) have been estimated at some 0.5 per cent of GDP (EC, 1990a). The positive effect of EMU on growth proved difficult to quantify. On the cost side a number

---

14   Uncertainty in exchange rates has an influence on both imports (sudden increases in production cost through intermediate goods) and exports (sudden fall in a country's competitiveness when its own currency appreciates) (de Lattre, 1985). Although financial markets have responded with different products (forward markets and hedging mechanisms) to cover the risk of floating, short-term exchange rate volatility still entails cost. Moreover, for many risks, coverage is difficult to obtain. This is notably the case for long-run misalignments (Steinherr, 1985). So, many firms remain exposed to such financial risk and prefer exchange rate certainty to floating. There is much controversy about the thesis that the exchange rate certainty of the EMS has contributed to intra-EU trade. Some empirical econometric research gives weak (Cushman, 1983; de Grauwe, 1987), other none (EC, 1995c), yet other very strong (Stokman, 1995) support for the thesis. Strong support also comes from inquiries among representatives of industry and commerce, which always indicate exchange rate turbulence as a major hindrance to trade (de Lattre, 1985; AMUE, 1988). It is mainly the long-run evidence that supports the case for a monetary union (Pugh et al., 1999).

15   Direct investment flows between EU countries have been negatively influenced by exchange rate uncertainty (Morsink and Molle, 1991; Morsink, 1998). The same applied to foreign transactions in loans and stock (NIESR, 1996).

of studies showed that the negative effects of a non-optimal policy mix[16] and of remaining rigidities were probably lower than initially foreseen.[17]

The EMU has been set up in several stages:

*   Stage 1 (start 1990). Removal of remaining barriers to capital movement.
*   Stage 2 (start 1994). Set-up of the forerunner of the European Central Bank that started monetary policy coordination.
*   Stage 3 (start 1999). Irrevocable fixing of the exchange rates of the participating currencies to the euro; introduction of the euro and transfer of monetary policy to the ECB.

EMU: BASIC FEATURES

The essential features of EMU are as follows.

*   A single currency, the euro, is issued by a European Central Bank.
*   Monetary policy is conducted by the independent ECB, largely along the lines of the Bundesbank. So the ECB inherits the credibility of the Bundesbank by having adopted the essentials of both its institutional set-up and its policy practice.
*   Economic policy is the responsibility of the member states that have, however, the obligation to coordinate their policies (see the following section).
*   Monetary relations within the EU between the members and the non-members of EMU that so wish are governed by an Exchange Rate Mechanism. This ERM2 has to provide exchange rate stability between the euro and the currencies of these non-EMU members. The euro has an anchor role in these relations. The central rates and the width of the band are set in mutual agreement between the ECB, the ministers of countries of the euro area, and the minister and governor of the central bank of the non-euro country. If appropriate, non-euro area member states can establish, on a bilateral basis, smaller fluctuation bands between their currencies and the euro. Supportive policy measures should be taken, including appropriate fiscal and monetary policies conducive to economic convergence.

The major outsider is the UK; the pound sterling has deliberately been kept out of the system. The other countries that have an opt-out are Sweden and Denmark. The NMS are in a different situation; they have all agreed to become members of the EMU as soon as they fulfil the convergence conditions. So, the ERM2 has considerable potential importance.

---

16   The limitation of the budget deficit was not regarded as a cost (Buiter et al., 1993; Allsopp and Vines, 1996), as it was due anyway for sound economic reasons. An overview of research (Perotti, 1996) indicated that the fall in public demand can under certain circumstances be (more than) offset by a rise in private demand (Alesina and Perotti, 1995). Moreover, it permits lowering of the high tax levels on labour, thus decreasing the barrier to enhanced employment (Masson, 1996).

17   There are several reasons why the loss of the exchange rate instrument was considered less costly in practice than in theory. First, a number of countries have already, over an extended period, refrained from using the instrument (for example, the Netherlands, which had a fixed exchange rate with Germany). Second, those countries that have used the instrument have found that it is not a very effective one in the long run. Third, the occurrence of asymmetric shocks in an EMU decreases (Rubin and Thygesen, 1996). Fourth, many shocks in Europe are region-specific rather than country-specific, which makes national exchange rate change an ill-adapted instrument (Decressin and Fatas, 1995). Fifth, some studies found that national monetary policies were already ineffective to cope with problems like unemployment (for instance, Erkel Rousse and Melitz, 1995). Finally, some authors observed that many shocks in the past had been more of a sectoral nature than of a country nature (for instance, Bayoumi and Prassad, 1995; Gros, 1996).

The implementation of the Economic and Monetary Union

CHALLENGES TO MONETARY AND FISCAL POLICY

The setting-up of the EMU is a unique experience and therefore the conditions that are essential for its success are not very well known. The theory of EMU is not sufficiently developed to help out. So the EU has distilled from various segments of economic thinking and of policy experience a set of rules about sound macro policies that have been imposed upon participating countries. These have been enshrined in the Treaty on European Union as the *criteria of convergence*[18] of national economic performance. They made joining EMU conditional on the member state's meeting the following criteria:

- inflation rate not higher than 1.5 per cent above the average of the three countries with the lowest inflation rates;
- budget deficits not in excess of 3 per cent of the GDP;
- government debt not in excess of 60 per cent of the GDP;
- long-term interest rate not more than 2 per cent above the rates of the three countries with the lowest inflation rates.

In the following sections we will go into more detail about these criteria, discussing the rationale of their introduction, the past performance of the EU member countries and the effect of their application on membership of the EMU.

INFLATION RATES

A monetary union cannot be sustained if inflation rates diverge too much. Indeed, as Figure 15.2 shows, in the long run higher than average inflation rates of EU countries inevitably lead to a corresponding depreciation of their currencies. The opposite is also true.[19] The conclusion is that countries need to bring their inflation rates in line (make them converge) with the inflation rates of their partner countries. However, this is not enough. Because inflation has a certain number of negative economic effects, low inflation is a desirable policy goal. So the double objective of a group of countries striving for an EMU must be to maintain low inflation rates that show only a small divergence from the EU average. Let us see how the EU countries have performed on these two scores.

First, inflation rates in the EU have shown wide differences *over time* (see Table 15.1, where the periods are given, marked by events that had a major influence on inflation). The economic crisis of 1973 brought about a tremendous increase in overall EU inflation. Since 1983, inflation has been cut back considerably following the adoption of anti-inflationary policies by many member countries. Average inflation in the EU15 has decreased even further in the 1993–2000 period, which was marked by the wish of many countries to participate in the EMU and hence to meet the convergence criteria. During this period most accession countries were feeling the pain of their transition and were struggling to keep inflation under control. As the table shows their efforts were crowned with success in the period since 2000.

---

18   This type of convergence is also called 'nominal convergence', in opposition to real convergence, which is the reduction of the differences in wealth levels between the member states. The latter is taken up in Chapter 16.
19   These relations remain the same if other OECD countries, including the larger ones, are also taken into account.

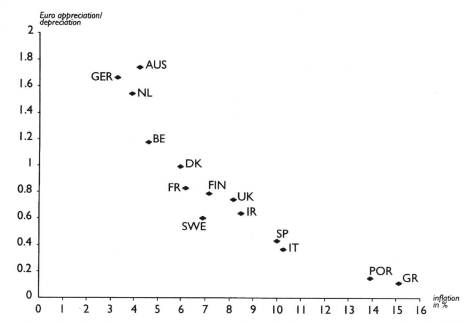

Figure 15.2   Inflation and currency depreciation or appreciation, 1973–1998

Since then all member countries (euro zone and others, including the NMS) have committed themselves to strive for a low inflation rate. It is the task of the European Central Bank to pursue a monetary policy that keeps inflation low; the ECB targets 2 per cent. Since 2000 not only the eurozone but also the EU25 as a whole meets this criterion. Some of the EMU member countries show relatively high inflation, notably those with relatively low GDP/P levels. This may spell problems for the development of their competitiveness.

Second, inflation rates have shown considerable *differences between EU15 countries* over the period 1973–92[20] and very small differences in the last decade. Since 2000 inflation rates in the NMS have decreased very significantly and the differences between the NMS have become within the brackets that prevailed for the EU15 in the 1993–1999 period.

What are the *causes* of the large differences between EU countries in inflation rates that existed in the past and of the recent convergence? Schematically the explanations can be grouped under the following headings.

Institutionalist: labour market   Increase in wages beyond the increase in productivity results in a cost-push. This has mostly occurred in countries with a fragmented labour market structure (like Italy). It has least occurred in countries with a neocorporatist structure (like the Netherlands). In the 1980s the strength of this factor has decreased as trade union power has decreased everywhere (Ferner and Hyman, 1992). In the 1990s the collective wage bargaining systems in most EMU countries have been adapted so as to take account of the exigencies of the EMU and the need for maintaining competitiveness in a rapidly globalising world (Kauppinen, 1998).

---

20   We can distinguish in this period three blocs of countries:

- below average rates, inflation-shy countries, mostly in northern Europe;
- about average rates (France, UK, Ireland);
- above average rates, 'inflation-prone' or 'inflation-permissive' countries, all lying in the Mediterranean basin.

Table 15.1   Average annual inflation rate (GDP price change) by country and period (%), 1960–2004

Country[a]	1960–72	1973–82	1983–92	1993–99	2000–2004
Austria	4.3	6.2	3.5	1.3	1.7
France	4.6	10.8	4.5	1.4	1.7
Germany	4.2	4.8	2.8	1.6	0.9
Netherlands	5.8	7.1	1.8	1.8	3.3
Denmark	6.3	10.1	4.4	1.8	2.1
Belgium	3.9	7.2	3.7	1.9	1.7
Sweden	4.8	10.0	6.8	1.9	1.6
Finland	6.3	12.0	5.4	2.0	1.6
UK	4.9	14.3	5.5	2.6	2.4
Luxembourg	3.7	7.8	3.8	3.1	2.3
Italy	4.9	17.0	7.7	3.5	2.7
Spain	6.7	16.1	7.9	3.5	4.0
Ireland	6.6	14.8	5.5	3.8	4.2
Portugal	3.6	17.8	15.8	4.5	3.5
Greece	3.3	17.5	16.9	8.3	3.6
Poland				18.6	3.1
Czech Rep.				7.8	2.9
Hungary				18.3	7.9
Slovakia				8.8	5.2
Slovenia				16.6	6.2
Lithuania				64.7	0.7
Cyprus				2.9	3.2
Latvia				21.1	4.0
Estonia				19.7	4.4
Malta				n.a.	2.2
Eurozone				1.7	2.0
EU15	4.9	11.5	5.6	2.1	2.0
NMS				14.2	6.8
EU25				2.6	2.1

Notes: [a] *Ranking by the 1993–99 performance.*

Source: Eurostat, several sources.

Institutionalist: monetary   The Central Bank's high degree of independence allows it to pursue effectively an anti-inflationary policy. Indeed, the independence of, for example, the German and Dutch central banks has been found to be one of the major reasons for the good performance of these countries in matters of controlling inflation.[21] EU countries, while striving for EMU membership, have all awarded independence to their Central Banks.

Monetarist   Price increases result from expansion of the money supply beyond the increase in the total product available. This results in general from governments spending more than their income, which is reflected in an increase in the public budget deficit. This largely explains

---

21   See, in this respect, Eijffinger and de Haan (1996); Berger, de Haan and Eijffinger (2001). Mind, however, that the independence is also challenged as a necessary condition for low inflation – see, for example, Aaron-Cureau and Kempf (forthcoming).

the high inflation that obtained in the past in the third group of countries (such as Italy and Greece). For some time most countries have pursued strict budgetary policies.

Structuralist Wage uniformity makes every branch and region follow the increase in the most productive part of the economy, notwithstanding differences in productivity between them; for example, manufacturing versus services or London versus a provincial town. Recently this factor has gained new attention in the framework of international catching up (see Chapter 16) as price level convergence (associated with convergence in wealth levels) has contributed to observed inflation differences in the euro area.[22]

GOVERNMENT DEFICIT, GOVERNMENT DEBT AND INTEREST RATES

In economic terms it might have been sufficient to specify only the inflation criterion for membership of the EMU and leave the type of measures that are needed to come up to that criterion to individual member states. However, in a world of free capital movements, an EMU is only sustainable if the markets are convinced of the *firm long-term commitment of the governments of the participating countries to sound principles of public finance*. Indicators of this commitment to disciplined behaviour are a small budgetary deficit and a sustainable size of the public debt of the member states.

In line therewith, the Treaty specifies two more criteria for joining the EMU: *no excessive budget deficits and no excessive government debt.* The concept of 'excessive' is not easy to translate into numerical values. On the one hand, one should allow governments sufficient flexibility to cope with problems of different nature; on the other, a limitation is necessary as governments will be tempted to use all the available leeway to avoid painful decisions. There is no way of scientifically determining the level at which these two criteria need to be set. So the practical solution chosen by the EU has been to set early 1990 EU average as criterion for the public debt (which should not exceed 60 per cent of GDP); consistent with this is a budget deficit of maximally 3 per cent.

The durability of the convergence achieved by the member states is reflected in the *long-term interest rate* levels. Indeed these rates are dependent, first, on the expectations of the financial markets as to the future rates of inflation in the country at hand and, next, on the solvency of its government. So a high long-term interest rate may signal a lack of policy discipline in the country in question (see Chapter 8). For that reason the EU has opted for the divergence of the long-term interest rate as an additional criterion for joining the EMU. In practice this criterion means that, observed over a period of one year before the examination, a member state has had a nominal long-term interest rate on its government bonds that does not exceed by more than two percentage points the rate of the three best performing member states in terms of price stability.

The development of these indicators for the EU15 between 1985 and 2004 is given in Table 15.2. We have added the same indicators for the NMS for the most recent years.[23]

---

22   See Maynard and van Ryckeghem (1976); Magnifico (1985); Rogers et al. (2001).
23   It should be recalled that government debt has increased considerably in the early 1980s.

Table 15.2 Nominal convergence towards EMU criteria, 1985–2004

	Deficit				Debt				LTIR			
	1985	1990	2000	2004	1985	1990	2000	2004	1985	1990	2000	2004
Germany	1	2	-1	4	43	44	60	66	7	9	5	4
France	3	2	1	4	46	47	57	66	11	10	5	4
Italy	13	12	1	3	82	98	111	106	14	14	6	4
Netherlands	5	5	-2	3	70	79	56	56	7	9	5	4
Belgium	9	7	0	0	120	128	109	96	11	10	6	4
Luxembourg	-6	-5	-6	1	14	7	6	8	10	9	6	3
UK	3	2	-4	3	59	40	42	42	11	12	5	5
Denmark	2	1	-2	-3	77	67	52	43	12	11	6	4
Ireland	11	3	1	-1	108	102	61	30	13	10	6	4
Spain	7	3	-4	0	45	45	38	49	13	15	6	4
Portugal	10	6	3	3	71	68	53	62	25	15	6	4
Greece	14	15	4	6	63	95	114	111	16	23	6	4
Austria	n.a.	2	2	1	51	58	67	65	8	9	6	4
Finland	n.a.	-5	-7	-2	17	15	45	45	13	13	5	4
Sweden	n.a.	-5	-5	-1	64	44	53	51	13	13	5	4
EU15	5	4	-1	-3	59	60	62	65	11	12	5	4
Poland			1	5			50	44			12	7
Czech Rep.			4	3			5	37			7	n.a.
Hungary			3	5			13	58			9	8
Slovakia			12	3			27	44			8	5
Slovenia			4	2			63	29			n.a.	n.a.
Lithuania			3	3			56	20			n.a.	4
Cyprus			2	4			18	72			8	6
Latvia			3	1			24	14			n.a.	5
Estonia			1	-2			55	5			n.a.	n.a.
Malta			6	5			37	75			6	5
NMS			3	-4			64	45			n.a.	n.a.
EU25			-1	-3			37	64			6	5

Sources: CEC, 'Annual Economic Report for 1993', European Economy, no. 54, March 1993; European Economy, Supplement A; Statistical Annex, 1996; European Economy, Annual Economic Review, 2000; Eurostat, Euroindicators, 2000. Eurostat, Economy and Finance, 2005.

WHICH COUNTRIES DO PARTICIPATE?

At the moment when the decision about participation had to be taken (in 1998) the EU member countries were divided into two groups. In the first we find 12 EU member countries that were striving for EMU membership. In the second group we find three countries that for political reasons had decided not to join (UK, Denmark and Sweden). The countries of the first group had all made considerable efforts to meet the convergence criteria specified at the beginning of the previous section (see Table 15.2). In the 1990s deficits decreased for all EU countries (EMU candidates and others alike). For debt the figures are somewhat less conclusive. But convergence of interest rates was very evident. During the 1998 examination of the performance of each member country it was clear that one country – namely Greece – did not qualify. All others did, albeit with some difficulty. So the EMU started on 1 January 1999 with 11 countries participating. Shortly after Greece was thought to have qualified for membership and joined the EMU too. Note that the recent performance of the NMS on the various criteria is in line with or better than the performance of the EU15 in the run-up to the EMU.

It is interesting to compare the practice with some of the theoretical notions we presented in earlier sections and in Chapter 2. The exercise of comparing the results of the application of the convergence criteria with those of the theory of *Optimum Currency Area* (OCA) proved rather complicated. Indeed, the empirical literature[24] did not give a straightforward answer to the question of which sub-group of EU15 member countries would constitute an OCA. Some agreement existed about a collection of 'core countries' (Germany, France, the Benelux countries, Austria and Denmark). For all other EU members the literature gave contradictory results. As there is no way to determine which of the criteria should predominate over the others, inclusion or exclusion tended to be rather a matter of personal judgement than the result of a scientific analysis. So one can conclude that the result of the application of the convergence criteria is not contradicted by the results of OCA analyses.

The application of the *domino theory* in matters of the EMU appeared less complicated. Indeed, many countries have gone through much trouble to be able to take part in the EMU because staying outside was a costly option for several reasons. First, non-EMU countries do not benefit as much from the internal market and the single currency as EMU countries (transaction cost argument). Moreover, non-EMU currencies may suffer from speculative attacks if financial markets do not believe that governments will keep their promises to avoid depreciations, cut public expenditures and keep interest rates low. This problem risked being perpetuated as weak countries outside the EMU risked being trapped in a sort of misery circle. Financial markets demand risk premiums on domestic interest rates, which increases interest payments on domestic debt stocks, which in turn increases budget deficits and makes compliance with the criteria more difficult. The lack of credibility means that higher than necessary unemployment would have to be accepted.[25]

THE EARLY EXPERIENCE

The euro was launched at the turn of the century and its introduction has been a clear success. Not only have the technical problems been overcome without difficulty, but acceptance has

---

24   See, for example, Bayoumi and Eichengreen (1993, 1997); Bofinger (1994); Jacquemin and Sapir (1995). After the decision was taken about participation in EMU the debate went further. Some favoured more restrictive criteria (for example Beine et al., 2000), others coming up with alternative assessments (Kim and Chow, 2003).
25   See Jacquemin and Sapir (1995) ; de Grauwe (1996).

been very great from the beginning. The euro has become the highly visible symbol of the European Union even if not all countries participate in it.

The endogeneity thesis of the EMU has proven very relevant; indeed most of the countries that were not obvious members of the OCA have proven to be able to meet the criteria for participating due to the dynamics of the EMU. Some (for example, Italy) have indeed been helped to put their public finances in order by the very quick convergence of their interest rates towards an EU level (see Chapter 8 and last columns of Table 15.2), that entailed a significant drop in the expenditure side of the national budget.

In the early years of the EMU many countries have made further progress towards meeting the criteria (for example, debt for Belgium and Italy). However, quite a few EMU member countries have had difficulty keeping to the deficit criterion. Among them are two major member countries (Germany and France) for which both deficit and debt went the wrong way. For interest rates, on the contrary, convergence has progressed very quickly and there is now almost complete price equality.

Has the adoption of the euro actually delivered the benefits that were expected? There is as yet not much evidence to answer yes to this question. The positive effects on trade have not yet shown up very clearly.[26] The reduced exchange rate volatility and the higher and less heterogeneous quality of the institutions seem to have had a weak effect on growth (Bagella *et al.*, 2004).

The institutional conditions for sustaining EMU

MONETARY POLICY: THE EUROPEAN CENTRAL BANK

The design and implementation of monetary policy in the euro area is the exclusive preserve of the European Central Bank (one money; one policy principle). The ECB is seconded in this task by the national central banks, together forming the European System of Central Banks. The ECB is primarily responsible for policy making, the national central banks for policy implementing.[27]

The *independence* of the ECB is safeguarded in several ways by provision in the EU Treaty. The first is by the long terms of tenure that obtain for the members of its Executive Board and for its governors. Next, there is the ban on national governments' attempts to influence the ECB's and national central banks' decisions. This very strong safeguard of the ECB's independence is justified by the empirically substantiated negative relationship between the rate of inflation and the degree of independence of central banks. Finally, there is the prohibition of any financing by the ECB of national governments or EU institutions. The ECB is accountable to the European Parliament for its policy. However, to many observers the accountability of the ECB is not well organised, given the exceptional degree of independence of the ECB.[28]

The prime *objective* of the ECB is price stability. Without prejudice to that objective the ECB shall also support the objectives of economic policy, such as sustainable growth, high employment and economic cohesion among member states. In pursuing its monetary policy

---

26   See in this respect the discussion in Economic Policy where Rose (2000) predicted very high results; these were challenged by Persson (2001) followed by Micco et al. (2003) who did as yet find little effect.
27   For an introduction to the principles and modalities of the ECB policy, see Issing et al. (2001). This is an insiders' view; all authors are eminent economists of the ECB.
28   See, for example, de Grauwe (2000), and further: http.//www.europarl.eu.int/comparl/econ/emu

the ECB will *target* both monetary aggregates and inflation. To that end it will monitor a variety of indicators such as the monetary base, price and wage changes, the exchange value of the euro and developments in assets markets.

FISCAL POLICY: THE STABILITY AND GROWTH PACT AND THE EXCESSIVE DEFICIT PROCEDURE

Member states cherish their fiscal autonomy. They consider this as an essential application of the principle of subsidiarity (Chapter 2). Indeed national budgets are the main instrument for delivering public goods according to national priorities. Among them we may cite coping with diverse shocks and stabilising of the economy by varying public expenditure levels (Oates, 1999). However, complete national fiscal autonomy is *inconsistent with the MU*. The EMU sets a Union target for inflation. One of the causal factors of inflation is budget deficits. So, in order to avoid inflation the total Union budget deficit needs to be limited. This can only be done by the setting of EU constraints on government spending in excess of income and by macro-economic policy coordination.[29]

The EU has chosen to preserve as much as possible national fiscal autonomy by putting in place only the constraints that are essential for safeguarding Union objectives (Gros *et al.*, 1999). The form chosen is that of the '*Stability and Growth Pact*' (SGP). The central element in this pact is the norm that forbids EMU member states from running a budget deficit of more than 3 per cent of GDP. Countries are invited to strive for a 'close to balance budget'. The margin between balance and a 3 per cent deficit is available for counter-cyclical policies in periods of economic downturn. This is thought to be sufficient to cope with most shocks, both normal cyclical ones and other more exceptional ones.[30] Besides, EMU member states need to observe the criteria of an inflation rate close to the EMU average and a public debt not exceeding 60 per cent of GDP.

In order to see whether national governments apply these rules of sound public finance, a *surveillance system* has been put in place. It is operated by the Commission and monitors the present and future position of each of the member states. The findings are regularly evaluated by the Council.[31]

Surveillance is not enough. One also needs measures to discipline those who do not observe the rules. To realise this the Pact has introduced the 'excessive deficit procedure'. This has two dimensions:

- Prevention. If a member state deviates significantly from the path (that is, it transgresses the limit on budget deficits) the Council will intervene in the form of a recommendation on the policy measures to be taken in order to bring the country back on track.
- Deterrence. If the Council decides that an excessive deficit exists, and that insufficient action has been taken, it can impose sanctions. In the first instance, this sanction takes the

---

29   Theory teaches us that national governments have an interest in adopting these EU rules in order to avoid other more difficult problems (Beetsma and Uhlig, 1999). However, the lessons from theoretical and empirical studies on the 'how' of macro-economic policy coordination were very poor (Mooslecher and Schuerz, 1999).

30   See Viñals (1994) and EC (1999i). Somewhat larger margins may be needed for coping with very heavy shocks such as an oil crisis or to cope with shocks while being simultaneously obliged to solve major structural problems, such as the decrease of a very large debt ratio or the cost of the 'greying' of the population.

31   Shortly after its introduction the surveillance system showed certain weaknesses. It appeared that some countries had not correctly reported their situation (for example, Greece due to the cost of the Olympic games). So the system was improved with the introduction of more precise definitions and more in-depth auditing. The monitoring of the indicators that represent the convergence criteria is part of a more complete monitoring of EU policies; we describe these in Chapter 18 (Broad Economic Policy Guidelines; see also EC, 1999j).

form of a non-interest bearing deposit. The amount is 0.2 per cent of GNP and, depending on the size of the excess deficit, may be as high as 0.5 per cent of GNP. If after two years the deficit has not been reduced, the deposit can be turned into a fine. The amount of the fine is then distributed among the EMU member states that respect the criteria as a compensation for the negative effects of the lack of rigour of the defaulting member state.

After the introduction of the euro it appeared that many member countries had difficulty in observing the rules about deficit, notably because expenditure was consistently higher than planned (EC, 2005c). The 3 per cent rule proved to be too constraining for three of the biggest member countries (Germany, France and Italy) and a number of smaller member countries (Portugal, Greece). The situation for Germany is particularly worth noting as this country had made the introduction of the euro conditional on the strict definition and application of the SGP. However, its budget deficits rose for several consecutive years above the 3 per cent norm due to the astronomical cost of German reunification and coping with structural change. Germany and France have asked for a new interpretation of the rules of the SGP. In early 2005 the Council decided that small and temporal deviations of the rules could be accepted. Moreover, countries can invoke exceptional cost (such as reunification in the case of Germany) to justify such deviations. In 2005 more countries have gone beyond the 3 per cent budget deficit ceiling and have agreed with the Commission on plans to come back to orthodoxy. Both political and academic circles have questioned the SGP for being too rigid and constraining growth. An interesting suggestion in this respect is to keep the Europe-wide margins (an optimal aggregate fiscal stance) and internal coherence, yet create more flexibility to individual countries by assigning national quotas for deficits and make them into tradable permits. Countries that temporarily need some leeway could then negotiate with other countries having negative deficits to use their permits.[32]

The position of the non-euro countries

THE UK AND THE POUND STERLING

On the EU side the position is that a change-over of the UK from the pound sterling to the euro would be welcomed as it is believed to lead to significant net welfare increases. These stem from the sheer size of the UK economy, the possibility of merging the international role of the pound sterling and the euro, and the strengthening of London as the major financial centre of the EU.

On the UK side there are many hesitations. Apart from the general reluctance that the UK has always had in matters of progress of integration (see Chapter 3) and that may weigh very heavily in public decisions, there are also serious questions about the balance of economic advantages and disadvantages for the UK. The government of the UK has adopted five conditions that must be met before it will agree to propose joining the EMU:[33]

---

32   See in this respect, among others, Casella (2001) and Collignon (2004).
33   These are strongly inspired by the OCA theory. Test 1 deals with the likeliness that asymmetric shocks occur; test 2 with the capacity to cope with them, in particular with respect to flexibility on labour markets; test 3 uses the criterion of capital mobility. See: www.hm-treasury.gov.uk

- *Convergence*: are business cycles and economic structures compatible so that the UK can live comfortably with euro interest rates on a permanent basis?
- *Flexibility*: if problems emerge, is there sufficient ability to respond to economic change quickly and efficiently and to ensure that shocks do not have long-lasting effects?
- *Investment*: would joining the EMU create better conditions for firms taking long-term decisions to invest in the UK?
- *Financial services*: will EMU have a positive impact on the competitiveness of the UK financial services industry, particularly the City of London's wholesale markets?
- *Growth, stability and employment*: would adopting the euro promote higher growth, stability and a lasting increase in jobs.

Until now the UK Treasury considers that the test on the first two criteria have not been met. Note that the criteria are fairly vague so that a decision that is largely politically inspired can be taken. In this respect it is important to consider that during the first half of the 2000s the UK economy has consistently outperformed the economy of the member countries of the EMU. Although according to economists there is no causal relation, public opinion in the UK tends to assume there is.

THE NEW MEMBER STATES

The new member states of the EU have all committed themselves by the accession treaties to adopt the euro as soon as they fulfil the convergence criteria of price stability, sustainable budget deficits and public debt and convergence in interest rates. To this list has been added exchange rate stability, which is to be realised by membership of the ERM2 for two years preceding adoption of the euro. Moreover, a number of institutional conditions need to be met, such as the independence of the national central bank and the quality of the prudential supervision of the financial system. The European Commission and the ECB monitor the performance of each of the NMS on these criteria. On the basis of their reports the Council will take a decision.

There has been no timetable fixed for the adoption of the euro; for each of the NMS a separate decision will be taken about the when and the how. The question is thus when will the NMS be ready? The 2004 ECB and Commission reports showed that all NMS still have a significant way to go, although each had very different positions with respect to the individual criteria (compare Table 15.2).

Now the willingness to strive for an early or late meeting of the convergence criteria and hence for the adoption of the euro[34] depends on the balance of the advantages and disadvantages.

There are several major *disadvantages* of early membership of EMU. First, inclusion of the NMS would reduce the capacity of the present EMU to cope with problems, as the chances of asymmetric shocks increase. Second, the early accession of the NMS to EMU will cause problems in the NMS due to the so-called Balassa Samuelson effect. High growth of productivity will lead to an increase in wages.[35] The wage increase will lead to price increases in the sheltered sector and inflation will tend to be much higher than the target rate of the ECB. This may lead to cost increases exceeding productivity increases and hence a loss of competitiveness.[36] Finally, the budget constraints of the SGP may limit the policy flexibility of the NMS and force them into

---

34   For example, de Grauwe and Aksov (1999).
35   This is good for real convergence (see Chapter 16) but bad for nominal convergence.
36   Compare in this respect the adoption of the DM by the new states of Germany.

an excessively restrictive budget policy with negative effects on growth and the speed of the restructuring process (for example, Orban and Szapary, 2004). This would mean that the cost of early adoption would be high for both the present EMU countries and the NMS.

There are also *advantages*, however. First, it produces for the NMS more stability, or in other words less macro-economic problems due to the disappearance of exchange rate volatility. This is particularly important as the NMS have been suffering in the early 2000s from an inflow of short-term capital that has pushed up their exchange rates against the euro, which is a negative point for their export chances.[37] Next access of NMS to foreign savings is improved while they may benefit from the stabilisation of the interest rate at a low level. Some observers (for example, Breuss *et al.*, 2004) point towards the reduction of administrative cost, stability due to serious commitment, and so on and suggest that these tend to outweigh or even reduce the remaining risks.

It need not be a surprise that the first NMS that want to join (target 2007–08) are the smallest ones as they are most vulnerable to outside influences and have least capacity to react. Moreover, some of them have already realised a considerable amount of convergence of their wealth levels with those of the EU average (see Table 16.2) and of their similarity in reactions to macro-economic disturbances with the old member states (Frenkel and Nickel, 2005). By mid-2005 three countries of this group had joined the ERM2 while others joining was imminent.

In theory there is an alternative way to the EMU and that is *unilateral euroisation*. It means that a country does away with its own currency and adopts the euro without the consent of the present EMU members. Such a strategy has not yet been followed with respect to the euro, but examples of this strategy exist for other major currencies. For instance in the 1990s some of the war-struck countries in former Yugoslavia had practically adopted the Deutschmark. Unilateral euroisation offers in the first instance the same advantages and disadvantages of formally joining the EMU; on the positive side stability and access to foreign capital, on the negative side loss of flexibility and competitiveness. However, it also presents additional disadvantages. The first one is that the country in question has no voice in EMU/ECB decisions. More important, however, is that a formal adherence to EMU at a later stage will become much more difficult. Existing EMU members will not forget that the country that has gone for unilateral euroisation has violated a fundamental EU principle that says that monetary policy is to be considered as a matter of common interest. In view of these implications it need come as no surprise that none of the NMS has opted for this strategy.

Summary and conclusions

- The EU has been slow to develop coordinated (let alone harmonised) stabilisation policies.
- Stable exchange rates were the main objective of European monetary cooperation in view of the welfare gains which they bring international traders and investors. The European Monetary System, with its centrepiece the ECU, has for quite some time been successful in bringing about such stability.

---

37   So the figures of the relation 'inflation-exchange rate' of the NMS do not correspond to the picture of Figure 15.2 but have been very erratic over the 1990–2005 period.

- With free capital movement and independent policy making of national governments, it is difficult to maintain the stability of the exchange rates. Therefore an EMU has been created. The euro was introduced at the start of the year 2000.
- Countries of the EU that want to participate in the setting up of the Monetary Union have to fulfil five criteria: low inflation, no excessive deficits on the public budget, not too heavy a debt burden, a long-term interest rate in line with the rates of the countries with low inflation, and no devaluation of their currency.
- Convergence towards the threshold values of these criteria did imply a significant policy effort for virtually all member countries. EMU has successfully started with 12 countries participating; the NMS will follow as soon as they meet the criteria.

16 *Redistribution: Cohesion Policies*

Introduction

Competitive markets (efficiency) may generate considerable inequality. Government intervention is then required to reduce this inequality by redistribution. The EU creates a need for such redistribution on the European scale. Indeed the EU's main objective is to step up efficiency and stimulate economic growth by integrating the markets of goods and production factors. The structural changes implied (relocation of economic activities, changing composition of sectoral activity) have negative consequences for certain sectors of society. The most vulnerable groups tend to be concentrated, on the one hand, in particular regions or even countries (regional dimension) and, on the other, in particular sectors of the labour force (social dimension).

The EU has taken it upon itself to redistribute funds so as to help these groups to adapt to the new situation. It considers that in this way the cohesion of its constituent parts will be improved.

Cohesion has no clear definition.[1] It is best understood as the degree to which disparities in social and economic welfare between different regions or groups within the Community are politically and socially tolerable. Whether cohesion is achieved is thus largely a political question.[2]

In the following sections we will go into the way the EU has devised its cohesion policies. The chapter is arranged as follows. In a first section we will examine the theoretical foundations. Next we give the essentials of the EU regime; which institutions are involved; how do they devise and implement the policies, and so on. We will deal with each of the major dimensions of cohesion (regional and social) policies in successive sections. For both we will follow the same approach, which consists, first, of the assessment of the major problems; second, of the presentation of the objectives of the policy; third, of its gradual development; fourth, of a critical examination of some of its major elements, in particular the funds; and finally, of an evaluation of its results. The chapter will be rounded off with a brief summary of the major findings.

---

1   There is some lack of precision in the use of the words 'cohesion', 'convergence', 'regional', 'redistribution' and 'structural'. Cohesion policy aims at decreasing the disparity between regions and social groups, in other words at making wealth levels converge to an EU mean. The main instrument for attaining this objective is redistribution of financial resources. The EU has created several funds to that end. They are called structural funds because they stimulate notably the improvement of the economic structure of problem regions and groups. In that respect one also speaks of structural policies. Decrease in disparities (for example, in wealth) is called convergence (of incomes). In the EU jargon this is also called 'real convergence' as opposed to 'nominal convergence'. The latter applies to macro-economic indicators like inflation and is relevant in the context of the criteria for joining the EMU (see Chapter 15).

2   However, the contribution of economics is in the study of the development of disparities and the possibilities of influencing the system in such a way as to decrease disparities (NIESR, 1991).

Theoretical foundations

DIVERGENCE OR CONVERGENCE IN DEVELOPMENT?

The distribution of welfare among the different partners in an integration scheme is an issue of overriding political importance. The objective is in general to stimulate poor countries to catch up with the richer ones. To that end the factors that determine the location of high income generating activities need to be influenced. Now the question whether integration contributes towards more or towards less disparity (catching up) is not easy to answer; there are theoretical arguments that plead for and others that plead against.[3]

*   *Convergence*. The neoclassical and Heckscher–Ohlin–Samuelson models lead to the conclusion that factor returns (that is, interests and wages) tend to converge when markets are opened up after the creation of a customs union and a common market (see Chapters 5 to 8). However, the outcome of such models depends on many assumptions, the most important probably being that markets function properly and that there are no impediments to movements. The model based on the life-cycle of the product may also lead to convergence between the levels of development of different areas in the common market. It comes about by the gradual absorption of skills and know-how in areas benefiting from direct investment to develop production at the middle stages of a product's life-cycle. This permits them to develop gradually their own research and innovation and to upgrade the quality of the production, at the same time increasing the capacity of their productive system to sustain high wages and high profits.
*   *Divergence* may occur as the effect of an initial imbalance being aggravated because investment tends to favour regions that have a technology lead, while labour tends to move to areas with the best career potential (in general already developed regions).[4] This may be illustrated with the help of Figure 16.1. If the environment in country A is better for growth, as the result, for example, of a higher input in technological innovation than in country B, the curve of country A may shift upwards while the curve of country B (B_1) remains where it is. The expectation of a continuation of this trend may lead to a situation where the expected returns on labour and capital are higher in A than in B and consequently where labour and capital may start to flow from B to A. This, in turn, may lead to further dynamic (cumulative) effects.

The debate between the proponents of the convergence and the divergence schools has acquired a new dimension with the new growth theory. Important factors in this theory are market access, human capital, technological change, international competitiveness, economies of scale, institutional efficiency and so on. Theory shows that some countries master good combinations and grow, others fail to do so and lag behind. This is irrespective of the initial situation. The effect is the synchronic occurrence of the convergence of some, and the divergence of other countries. The outcome of the process is not determined beforehand; depending on the details, the new theoretical models can produce both convergence and divergence. So, the effects of regional integration on cohesion may be both positive and

---

3   See Chapter 8 for the relationship of this phenomenon to wage convergence.
4   See Myrdal (1956, 1957); Vernon (1966); Krugman (1980).

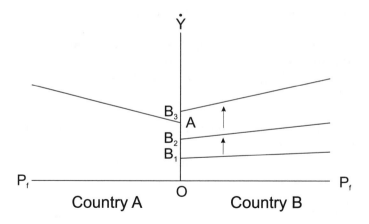

Figure 16.1   Policies for intra-Union balanced growth

negative. Much depends on the initial situation, the capacity of regions to adapt, the growth effects of integration and so on.[5]

WHY INTERVENTION?

Because the system appears on many occasions to be unable to achieve a socially desirable equilibrium, governments have devised policies to bring about a more equal distribution of wealth over persons, categories and regions. Traditionally two reasons for intervention are given.

Efficiency   This argument, of an economic nature, says that measures of regional and social policy help towards the efficient allocation of resources by taking away bottlenecks and barriers to development. Total welfare increases, as resources that are badly utilised or not utilised at all will participate (better) in production. Some examples may illustrate this.

- *Regional*. Where labour is rather immobile, unemployed human capital will not be put to work by private investors unless conditions for a profitable operation in that region (for example, in terms of infrastructure) are met. A government programme for such infrastructure removes the obstruction to development.
- *Social*. A programme for the retraining of workers for taking up jobs in a new industry after being made redundant in an industry that had lost its competitive position will adapt the human capital to new conditions. Private initiative would not have taken this up.

Equity   This argument, of a socio-political nature, says that large groups of the population feel that inequality is morally unacceptable. Total welfare would increase if the inequalities between groups and regions were removed. Again we may give some examples.

- Regional. Minimum standards of provision of public goods may be set for all regions (for example, number of hospital beds per inhabitant). The government's budget then

---

5   See, among others, Giersch (1949); Williamson (1976); Vanhove and Klaassen (1987, ch. 6); Molle (1990); Molle et al. (1993).

transfers the money to regions that do not have the capacity to generate sufficient revenues themselves.

- Social. Minimum personal income standards may be set. Transfer payments from the most to the least affluent can take the form of detailed schemes of social security: old age pensions, unemployment benefits, insurance against illness and so on – schemes generally associated with the welfare state.

The above arguments indicate why government intervention for cohesion purposes is needed. They do not say how much redistribution is needed to obtain the policy goals. To give an answer to that question one needs to make detailed economic calculations, on the one hand, and political trade-offs, on the other.[6]

WHY UNION POLICIES ?

Countries participate in integration schemes because they expect welfare gains from them. However, there are also costs involved in progressive integration that may be unevenly distributed. These are different for the various stages of integration.

Customs union   The internal liberalisation and the development of a common foreign trade policy deprives member states of the trade policy instruments by which they had supported activities of certain social groups or of regionally concentrated industries. In the process of specialisation, resources are set free that need to adapt to other occupations. This often entails the loss of expertise, costs of moving and so on. For some countries the benefits may take a long time to materialise, whereas the adjustment costs occur immediately. For others, gains may be quick to come about, while the costs are limited. In other words, costs and benefits may be very unequally distributed among countries.

Common market   The problems are aggravated when the free movement of production factors is introduced, and labour and capital begin to flow to the regions offering the best locations for investment. Now production factors may not always move in such a way as to bring about a better equilibrium. Capital in particular tends to move to those areas that have already secured the best position. Labour may move from low-wage to high-wage countries, but that may entail high social and personal cost. So these movements aggravate the risk of an unbalanced development.

Economic and monetary union   The setting up of an EMU further curtails the instruments available to national states. They are losing, for example, the possibility of influencing the equilibrium with partner countries by exchange rate and monetary policies. Furthermore, with the progress of harmonisation, especially on the industrial and social planes, national instruments lose much of their implicit power to control regional developments.

Countries that find incomes sinking below those of others may be inclined to opt out. Although solidarity with integration schemes is not marked solely by immediate economic gains, for some countries the absence of such gains may become a political factor important enough to inspire compensation schemes.

---

6   Okun (1975); Padoa-Schioppa et al. (1987); Breuss and Eller (2004).

Claims for redistribution are generally restricted to participants in schemes of social cooperation for mutual advantage. This has important consequences. Since such schemes coincide traditionally with nation states, claims can be made only by citizens of the specific state involved. Because for participants in economic integration schemes the boundaries of cooperation tend to extend beyond the national framework, it is logical to extend distributional justice to citizens of all member states of the union.[7]

WHAT FORM FOR INTERNATIONAL REDISTRIBUTION SCHEMES?

The need for redistribution changes as integration reaches higher stages.[8] Higher-stage integration in general means stronger institutions. It also means a stronger solidarity between the constituent parts of the integration area. These factors largely determine the type of instrument that can best be used for international or interregional redistribution schemes (see Table 16.1).

Table 16.1   Forms of redistribution at different levels of integration

Instruments/ Integration	Low PTA/FTA	Medium CU/CM	High EMU	Full FED
No action	0			
Expenditure:				
Compensation	*			
Specific purpose		*	*	*
General purpose			*	*
Receipts:				
Compensation	*			
Contribution		*	*	
Taxes			*	*
Social Security				*

During the *lowest stage of integration* (preferential trading agreements, free trade areas) redistribution is often absent from the policy toolkit, for three reasons: the embryonic character of the institutional set-up, the lack of solidarity among constituent parts and the lack of agreement about the way compensation has to be calculated. If these barriers can be overcome, the next step is a simple system of compensation; payments are made to member states that do not benefit from integration (for example, because trade diversion leads to higher cost to the consumer); contributions are made by member states that are net gainers.

The *highest forms of integration*, like federations, will use two types of instruments. The first is interpersonal transfers, such as progressive income tax and social security entitlements. Instruments dealing directly with the individual are most effective as federal powers over income taxes and social security are substantial and the federal budget represents a considerable portion of GDP. The second type is interregional. Poor regions may receive more from the central state to finance their programmes than their contribution to central government income.

---

7   The consequence of such limiting of claims to a well-delimited sub-set of the world, be it the nation or the union, is that international transfers to third countries (aid to development policies) become part of external policies (Chapter 17). The case of aid to potential member countries in Central and Eastern Europe is on the borderline between the two.

8   See, for the originals, MacDougall et al. (1977). For a more recent discussion, see Sapir et al. (2004).

During *the medium and higher forms of integration* (customs union, economic and monetary union) different combinations of income and expenditure instruments may be used. There is a preference for schemes using the expenditure instruments involving different layers of government because (1) expenditure can be tailored to specific needs (including compensation of negative integration effects) and (2) governments are generally reluctant to let unions decide on interpersonal redistribution matters.

There are two main ways to handle the redistribution of funds through the expenditure side of the union budget.

General-purpose grants take the form of block payments from the union to a member country. The underlying philosophy is one of needs. These have to be evaluated for each individual state against a standard for public-sector programmes and the capacity of the member state to finance them. The union has no control over the actual use of the funds thus transferred, which thus risk being used in a way not expedient to structural improvement.

Specific-purpose grants, not having the same drawback, are the most common. Here the union decides on the type of programme that should be set up and to which it is prepared to give financial aid. Such grants are considered to lead to optimum welfare in the long run, because they target investments in the improvement of production factors or of the production environment.

STRUCTURAL POLICIES

Redistribution schemes should thus be designed to support the creation of a viable base for future-oriented economic activities. Examples of this type are financial aid programmes for specific social groups, designed to retrain workers who have become redundant because of the structural changes of the economy due to integration. While such schemes are mostly short-term, others are of a structural nature. An example of the latter is a programme for the improvement of the infrastructure in regions that are far below the average level of development, aimed at creating the conditions required for self-sustained regional growth.

The rationale for and the equalisation effect of such structural policies are illustrated by Figure 16.1. Suppose income growth ($Y \cdot$) is determined completely by increases in production factor availability and productivity, together called P_f. Suppose further that country B is not only a slow-growth but also a low-level income country (OB_1), while country A is not only a fast-growth but also a high-level income country (OA). To make income levels in the union converge, the curve of country B has to move upwards, with the intercept moving from point OB_1 through OB_2 to OB_3, which is beyond point OA (the structural growth in country A).

EU regime[9]

INSTITUTIONS INVOLVED

There is a whole set of institutional interfaces that facilitate the design and delivery of EU cohesion policies. Some operate in a somewhat formal way (through participation in

---

9   EU involvement in matters of cohesion has developed gradually. In the 1950s and 1960s, a hesitant start was made. Real political commitment to a European regional and social policy was achieved at the 1972 Paris Conference

advisory committees of the EC), others in an informal way (by bilateral contacts). We cite the following:

- Committee of the Regions (CoR). The CoR has the right to give its advice on EU policy proposals. It is intended to smooth the coordination of more general issues between the EU and the regions. The CoR has not acted as a crystallising point of political change. Membership is extremely diverse and this makes it difficult to come to strong common positions.
- Economic and Social Committee (ESC). The ESC is composed of representatives of employees and employers, professionals and consumers. It advises the Commission and the Council on their policy plans. The role of the ESC is notably relevant in matters of social cohesion.
- Lobbies. Traditionally the employers' organisations were most important. They have been joined by trade unions and NGOs that take an interest in specific subjects. Many regions have also set up liaison offices in Brussels to handle their business with the EU; we find without exception all those who have a very strong constitutional position such as Scotland, the German Laender and the Spanish autonomous regions.

PARTNERSHIP

In matters of cohesion there are a range of actors involved. There is no hierarchical relation; the EU has adopted the principle of *partnership*. Partnership is a set of rules and procedures that prescribe that civil servants of the European Commission, national government and regional authorities, together with representatives of social actors (among them local business, labour unions and social action groups) collaborate closely and continuously together in the design, implementation and evaluation of EU-funded cohesion programmes.

This makes for a complicated set-up that is defined by some as a policy network.[10] The advantage of such structures resides in 'ownership'; it means that all parties involved are inclined to cooperate as they feel it is in their own interest. The disadvantage is the high cost involved in transactions due to unclear division of responsibilities and decision-taking power.

The principle of *partnership* is derived from the principle of subsidiarity. The latter prescribes that the lowest level of government that can efficiently deal with a subject has to be empowered to do so but in cooperation with the governments at other levels that deal with aspects they are best equipped for. In countries where internal subsidiarity had not been much of an issue and where many decisions were taken by central government, EU cohesion policy has been a factor of institutional change. Using the leverage of the structural funds the Commission has incited countries with very weak sub-national government structures (such as Italy) to empower the latter better.[11] So in all member states, old and new, specific forms

---

of the European Council. In the following 15 years the policies were given shape and substance. With the adoption of the Single European Act (Article 158), confirmed by subsequent treaties, cohesion by redistribution has become a constitutional obligation. It now has three dimensions: economic, social and territorial. For many practical purposes the economic and territorial dimensions are worked out in regional policy, while the social dimension has a more general scope. The rest of this chapter is based on this practice-oriented approach.

10   This form of multi-layer government is called cooperative federalism by Casella and Frey (1992); for networks, see, for example, Heinelt and Smith (1996).

11   See Lion et al. (2004). For the NMS the situation has been confused for some time. Initially the EU has put some pressure on the accession countries to come to formal regionalisation. This worked out well in countries that had already decided to go along this path (for example, Poland). After some time the EU has accepted for efficiency reasons more flexible solutions with a strong involvement of the central government (Hughes, Sasse and Gordon, 2004).

have been adopted that meet the needs of the EU cohesion policy and respect the national situation.

PROGRAMMING

Cohesion policy addresses major structural problems. So the actions need to be put in a long-term perspective. As a consequence the EU has adopted a multi-annual approach. Because the cohesion policy of the EU is complementary to that of its partners the EU has adopted a multi-partner approach. The two have come together in the adoption of the programming approach as major policy instrument. Programming involves all stages of the policy cycle: analysis of major problems; setting of priorities; choice of programmes and projects; allocation of funding; monitoring of operations and the evaluation and adjustment of objectives and instruments. Its purpose is first to provide predictability to all involved as to the financial envelopes that are available and the rules of the game to be played. The second purpose is to give substance to the principle of partnership by organising the involvement of all competent organisations at the regional, national and European level.

There are three stages in this programming:

- Preparation. In most cases a so-called 'Single Programming Document' is prepared. This co-production of a member state, a region and the Commission has three elements. First, it sets out the strategic choices of the regional and central authorities in the light of an analysis of the problems. Next, it identifies the areas for priority action, the financial resources and the forms of assistance (Community Support Framework). Finally, it details the concrete activities for each priority action in the various regions (operational programmes) and their likely impact on objectives (ex-ante evaluation).
- Implementation. The authorities of the member states and the regions ensure the implementation (one authority has to be designated to manage the whole programme). Monitoring committees in which the regions, member states and Commission are represented supervise the execution of the programmes and make a mid-term evaluation.
- Ex post evaluation. After the execution of the programme an evaluation has to be made; this has to indicate how far the results obtained correspond to the targets set.[12]

INSTRUMENTS

The main instruments to realise the objectives of the EU cohesion policy are in line with the general set-up discussed:

- Coordination of national policies (regulation). As cohesion is a matter of shared responsibilities between the Union and national authorities, such coordination is vital for effectiveness. The EU has used its regulatory powers to assure the correct spending of its finances and to set certain standards as to state aids and labour conditions. For many policies, notably the social policies, the EU uses a light form of coordination (OMC) where European objectives are served by national instruments.
- Structural funds (finances). The EU pursues a redistribution policy allocating funds to the disadvantaged regions for the improvement of their structure (economic) and accessibility (territorial) and to social groups to improve their employability and to avoid their social

---

12   For methods of monitoring and evaluation, see EC (1999k); for a critical comment on evaluation, see Bachtler and Michie (1995).

exclusion. The resources of the SF have been increased each time member states requested the compensation in budgetary terms for their consent to other measures (for example, enlargement, participation in the agricultural policy, and so on).

- Coordination of Union policies. The EU will take effects on cohesion into account while devising its other policies (some of which may be detrimental to cohesion).

Regional policy

ASSESSING THE PROBLEMS

There are considerable differences in wealth levels between the member countries of the EU (see Table 16.2). Immediately after the Second World War, some of the countries now making up the EU15 were rather poor (Portugal, Greece and Spain, to a lesser extent Italy, and initially also Germany) while others (Belgium, Denmark, the UK and France) were relatively well off. Differences in wealth in 2000 were much less marked than those in 1950. Indeed, much of this divergence had already disappeared by 1980; in the 1950–80 period disparity between countries decreased by half.[13] This was due on the one hand to higher than average growth rates for countries with an income level below the EU average. On the other hand, growth in the above average countries was below rather low.[14] A case to highlight is Ireland which has successfully fought its way into the league of above average countries over the past decades. However, a quite important deficit in wealth level still persists for the three Mediterranean countries that joined in the 1980s.

The recent enlargement with eight Central European countries has much increased the differences in wealth levels (Table 16.2). The new member states have much lower wealth levels than the EU on average. Only two of them fall in the middle group of the EU25. This situation differs very much from the one that occurred with the second wave of enlargement in the 1980s; the gap between the new and old member states then was about 30 per cent; this time it is about 60 per cent.

The disparity in national wealth levels determines to a large extent the disparities that exist between the regions of the EU.[15] The reason for this national dominance is that many of the underlying factors, such as resources, the level of schooling of the labour force, the access to markets and, in particular, the social and economic institutional infrastructure, are national rather than regional characteristics. So the improvement of national factors is an important condition for the catching up of the lagging countries and, subsequently, regional cohesion.

The EU shows considerable diversity in regional situations[16] (see Figure 16.2). The bars in the figure indicate the range of deviation of the various regions of a country with respect to the EU mean (100 line).

---

13   See Molle et al. (1980); Molle (1990); Molle and Boeckhout (1995).
14   For the reasons for the slow growth of the UK in this period, see Kaldor (1966); Boltho (1982); Murrell (1983).
15   Some 80 per cent; see Molle and Boeckhout (1995).
16   From the beginning, the Commission has reported on the regional situation and regional developments in the Community (EC, 1961, 1964, 1971, 1973b, 1981b, 1984c, 1987b, 1991d). Recently it has broadened its scope and now reports on cohesion (EC, 1996e; 2004c).

Table 16.2 Development of GDP/P (EU = 100), for the EU member countries, 1950–2004

Country	1950 euro	1990 euro	2000 euro	2004 euro	1990 PPP	2000 PPP	2004 PPP
Germany[a]	93	125	127	120	116	113	109
France	136	111	120	119	109	115	111
Italy	71	101	102	104	102	111	105
Netherlands	100	100	128	135	100	121	125
Belgium	166	104	122	122	105	116	119
Luxembourg	201	149	245	253	150	217	223
UK	140	89	135	129	99	114	119
Denmark	153	132	162	161	104	126	122
Ireland	81	71	139	164	74	127	141
Spain	35	69	79	88	77	93	99
Portugal	35	37	60	58	61	80	73
Greece	30	43	57	67	58	72	82
Austria	58	109	133	130	105	127	122
Sweden	170	142	148	139	108	119	116
Finland	114	143	128	128	102	114	115
EU15	100	100	115	114	100	110	109
Poland			24	23		46	47
Czech Rep.			30	38		65	70
Hungary			25	36		53	61
Slovakia			21	28		47	52
Slovenia			52	58		73	78
Lithuania			18	23		38	48
Cyprus			72	75		86	82
Latvia			18	22		35	43
Estonia			22	30		43	51
Malta			54	48		77	71
EU25			100	100		100	100

Notes: *PPP = purchasing power parities. [a] In 2000, inclusive of former DDR.*

Sources: OECD National Account Statistics, several years; Eurostat, National Accounts (ESA) Review, several years; Statistics in Focus 1996/5. National figures on GDP made comparable with exchange rate figures; EC, European Economy, No. 70, 2000, Tables 8 and 9.

Many regions do not give rise to particular concern at the European level. Others tend to show particularly difficult problems, resulting from deficiencies in the infrastructure, production sector, labour-force qualifications and so on. The considerable differences in

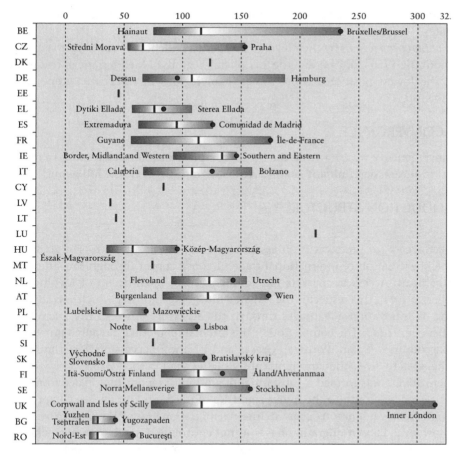

| Average of all areas of the country.

● Capital city area of the country.

Figure 16.2 Regional extremes in income per head* by EU member country (GDP/P based on PPP 2000)

Source: Eurostat. * *In the extreme right regions the GDP/P is overestimated due to very large incoming commuter flows.*

economic development between member countries, and between the regions constitute a threat to cohesion.

To approximate the development of cohesion over time we use the main indicator of disparity, the level of income per capita. In 2000 the ten most favoured regions in the EU15 were three times 'richer' than the ten 'poorest'.[17] The evolution over time of the disparity between all EU15 regions shows a significant decrease over the first part of the period of analysis. This tendency towards convergence also prevailed in all major EU countries.[18] However, from the end of the 1980s onwards, the tendency came to a halt. Recently disparities

---

17   Turbulence on exchange rate markets does influence disparity figures quite a bit. Another indicator of regional disparity is unemployment. As it appears to be highly concentrated in the same regions that also show a low GDP/P level we have not detailed unemployment here.

18   These results are confirmed by other studies such as Barro and Sala-I-Martin (1991); Molle and Boeckhout (1995); Sala-I-Martin (1996). For further details about the time and regional patterns of convergence in the EU, see the various contributions in Vickerman and Armstrong (1995).

between regions have even tended to increase; this applies both to the former EU15 and the new member states.[19]

The *ranking of European regions* by their level of prosperity evidences a remarkable stability. Indeed, throughout the 1950–2000 period, the 'peripheral' regions of Mediterranean countries were always in the lowest positions, while some urban regions in northern Europe were consistently at the top.

CAUSES FOR CONVERGENCE

The causes of convergence of wealth within the EU are complex. Integration has played a major part with respect to several determinant factors. We distinguish between the following.

MARKETS: PRODUCTION STRUCTURE[20]

- *Goods.* Market access for products is an essential prerequisite for growth. The dynamic effects of the liberalisation of international trade in goods appear through the structural adaptation of firms. Access to markets has resulted in the catching up of low-income countries. Illustrative in this respect is the Italian white goods industry which was capable of exploiting its innovation advantages through the access it gained to the markets of other member countries.[21] The completion of the internal market has favoured growth in the cohesion countries (Spain, Portugal, Greece and Ireland);[22] accession has stimulated growth in the NMS to levels that are significantly higher than in the EU15.[23]
- *Labour.* When the EU was formed a substantial migration of labour took place from the poorer countries in the south to the richer countries of northern Europe (see Chapter 7). After some time, return migration occurred. Internal migration in the EU has since been on a relatively low level. Labour migration has thus not contributed much to convergence.
- *Capital.* The most important category of capital movement in this respect is direct investment (DI). An analysis of the flows of DI in the EU does indeed show that these contributed to convergence: the 'poorer' member states are net importers of DI, while the 'richer' member states are net exporters (Chapter 8). This investment, triggered by market integration and accompanied by the transfer of technical and managerial skills, has helped the catching-up process.

POLICIES: PRODUCTION ENVIRONMENT

- *Infrastructure and labour qualification.* Large EU funds have gone and still go into the improvement of these two factors in backward regions. Recently infrastructure (transport,

---

19   Studies for individual EU15 countries show similar patterns. Convergence for the period up to the middle of the 1980s: Hofer and Woergoetter (1997); Suarez-Villa and Cuadrado Roura (1993); Cuadrado et al. (1999); Persson (1997); Kangasharju and Pekkala (2004). Divergence since: EC (2004c). Divergence is even prominent in the new member countries (Kozak, 2003; Tondl and Vuksic, 2003; Ehrlich and Szigetvari, 2003; Resmini, 2003; Roemisch, 2003).

20   An important role has been played by the gradual shift over a long period of high value-added economic activity towards low-income countries and regions (Klaassen and Molle, 1982; Bachtler and Clement, 1992; EC, 1996e). As a result, the branch structure of the regions and countries of the EU has become much more similar over time (Molle, 1997).

21   See, in this respect, Maillet (1977); Mueller (1981); Owen (1983); and Bianchi and Forlai (1993).

22   Note that access to the EU has had a very clear influence on the relatively high growth figures of France in the 1960–73 period (Hennart, 1983), and of Ireland, Spain and Portugal since their accession (EC, 1996e). The GDP of this latter group in 1993 was some 10 per cent higher than it would have been had the pre-1987 growth trends continued.

23   See, for example, Breuss (2002).

energy, telecommunications) has received more attention with the setting up of the Trans-European Networks (see Chapter 13).

- *Institutions and regulation.* By their collective action, special interest groups obtain regulation that shields them from competition and change. This reduces overall efficiency and hence aggregate income and growth. Integration makes collusion of firms under sanction of the government more difficult, it diminishes trade union power in sheltered industries, and so on.

REGIONAL POLICY: RATIONALE AND OBJECTIVES

The *arguments* for the EU regional policy follow the theoretical ones we have indicated before:

Efficiency   The economic argument for a European regional policy has been central in each of the stages of its development. An example from the crisis period of the late 1970s may be illustrative in this respect. The lack of alternative activities in 'steel regions', where substantial cutbacks in employment were necessary, induced certain member states to give heavy support to their steel industry, to which other member states responded by threatening to close their frontiers to these subsidised products. Now that would mean a direct violation of the founding principles of the EU (free market and international specialisation). The putting into place of an effective regional policy to help the steel regions develop new activities has avoided putting into jeopardy the very functioning of the EU.

Equity   The social argument for European regional policy has only gradually come to the fore. Until the mid-1980s, neither the social dimension nor the public support for a fiscal contribution to assist regional development in a different EU member country had developed much.[24] The EU now puts more emphasis on social and human aspects as necessary complements to purely economic ones.

The *main objectives* of European regional policy are:

- To improve the situation in existing problem regions. Many regional problems are very deep-rooted and hence require structural policy actions that are maintained over several decades.
- To prevent new regional disparities that could result from structural changes in the European and world economy. Some of these are due to integration, others are the result of the continuous changes that occur in technology, in environment, in social values and in world politics.

GRADUAL DEVELOPMENT OF POLICY

The European regional policy has developed gradually under the influence of progressive deepening and widening.[25] The major stages, that follow in practice the theoretical model of Table 16.1, can be described as follows:

---

24   See, for instance, EC (1980); Vandamme (1986).
25   See, for instance, EC (1979e, 1984d, 1985e; 1990a). For a comparison of the 2000 situation with the one prevailing in the previous period see EC (2004c). http//www.info.regio.cec.eu.int/wbdoc/docgener/guides/ compare/ info.en.pdf

- *1955–75.* The fathers of the EU were well aware of the regional problems; this is evident from the preamble of the Treaty of Rome, according to which the member states were 'anxious to reduce the differences existing between the various regions and the backwardness of the less favoured regions'. In spite of warnings by academics that European integration spelled problems for certain regions, the EEC Treaty made no provisions for a European regional policy in the proper sense.
- *1975–85.* The northern enlargement of the EU increased the regional imbalances. The UK, afraid of losing out to its continental competitors, on the one hand, and of an unfavourable distribution of receipts from and payments to the EU budget, on the other, had obtained in the negotiations of accession an assurance that a European regional policy would be set up. This was realised in the second half of the 1970s. Large sums of money were put into a distribution scheme using specific-purpose grants as the instrument.
- *1985–93.* Two factors caused a further stepping up of the regional policy efforts. The first was the drive towards more allocative efficiency through the completion of the internal market. The second was the enlargement with three less developed new member states. To improve the economic and social cohesion in a wider and deeper EU, the resources devoted to cohesion were doubled, the target groups restricted, the procedures improved and the instruments refocused.
- *1993–2000.* Similar factors played a role in the 1990s. Deepening concerned the setting up of the EMU and coping with international developments like the further decrease of external trade protection (Uruguay round). To deal with the EMU effect, a cohesion fund was set up. Widening concerned notably the integration of the new German *Bundesländer*. The extension with three EFTA countries did not constitute a major new challenge for EU regional policy, given their relative wealth. To deal with these new challenges, the resources devoted to structural adaptation were stepped up again.
- *2000–2006.* The enlargement of the EU with a number of CEECs has considerably increased the demands on the EU budget for cohesion. The 1999 regulation of the structural funds therefore limited the number of objectives and targets Moreover, the regulation improved the institutional set-up: each member state has to designate one managing authority that is responsible for supervising the implementation. Finally, the financial control system has been tightened.

Summarising these developments we may say that the EU set out without sufficient authority in regional matters, that it has gradually acquired the necessary instruments, and that now the regional element occupies a prominent place among the European policy areas.

THE ROLE OF THE EUROPEAN REGIONAL DEVELOPMENT FUND AND OTHER STRUCTURAL FUNDS

To offer effective help to regions in distress, the EU must have financial means. After several attempts the EU obtained in 1975 the necessary finance with the creation of the European Regional Development Fund (ERDF).[26] The tasks of the ERDF are to grant subsidies to stimulate investment and promote innovation in economic activities and develop the infrastructure in regions designated as European problem areas (see Figure 16.3). Eligible for investment support in these regions are those activities which are already receiving aid from the member

---

26   For a description of the proposals for the ERDF, see EC (1969); for the creation of the fund, see Talbot (1977); for the various recasts, see EC (1977, 1981c, 1990b); and for a review of its performance in the first ten years, see EC (1985e).

state in question or one of its agencies; the EU intervention is indeed meant to complement such aid.

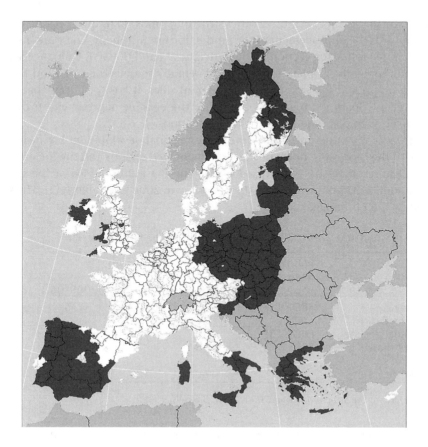

Figure 16.3   Regions qualifying for ERDF aid: (objective 1 convergence)

The problem regions tend to fall into two main types.

- *Lagging regions (objective 1)*. Many of these regions are traditionally backward, have failed to develop sufficient manufacturing or service industry and are still oriented to agriculture. Especially in southern member states, agriculture is often not very productive. This type of region is generally characterised by a peripheral situation, a deficient infrastructure, a meagre endowment with business services and a lack of skilled labour with a good industrial and service tradition. Below-average GDP per head is a main indicator of problems here; regions with a GDP less than 75 per cent of the EU average are eligible for aid.
- *Regions of industrial decline (objective 2)*. Many of these regions played a leading role at a certain stage of economic development, specialising in one or other sector. They have landed in difficulties as production conditions for these sectors changed. This type of region is generally marked by inadequate infrastructure and by serious problems in old industrial areas. They often have a highly specialised manpower whose skills are, however, at odds with modern requirements. High unemployment is the main indicator of distress here. Regions are eligible for aid if their unemployment rate is higher than the EU average,

their percentage share in agriculture or industrial employment is higher than the EU average, and there is a sudden drop in this employment.

The ERDF works together with three other structural funds, so termed because their efforts are oriented towards the improvement of the production environment. These are the European Social Fund (ESF, see following sections), the Agricultural Fund (EAGGF, Guidance Section; see Chapter 9) and the relatively small Fishery 'Fund'. Finally there is the Cohesion Fund that is of more recent origin and follows somewhat different rules. It has specifically been set up to compensate Ireland, Spain, Portugal and Greece for the possible negative effects of the EMU. The aim of the EU is to combine the efforts of these funds.

The total *size* of the structural funds devoted to regional development has been gradually stepped up with the increasing needs of the less advantaged regions and the increasing accent on cohesion. The resources have increased from some € 1 billion a year at the start, in the mid-1970s to some € 25 billion a year in the period up to 2006 (see Table 16.3). The structural funds are fed by the EU budget.

Table 16.3   Structural funds, distribution of aid by objective, 1989–2006

Objective		Funds involved	Billion euro		
Code	Name		1989–93	1994–99	2000–06
1	Backward (incl. ex GDR)	ERDF, ESF, EAGGF	43	102	136
2	Industrial decline	ERDF, ESF	9	22	23
3	Labour market	ESF	8	15	24
	Total		60	139	183

Source: *EC, Reform of the Structural Funds 2000–2006, Brussels, 1999.*

The *distribution over regions* of the structural funds favours in particular the main problem regions (see Table 16.3). Objective 1 (structural difficulties) regions received about 75 per cent of the resources available for some 25 per cent of the EU population. Objective 2 (industrial conversion) regions are rather dispersed geographically; here some 15 per cent of the resources were spent in regions representing some 18 per cent of the EU population.[27] The effect of this is that the financial means of the funds are attributed in such a way as to strongly favour low-income countries (two-thirds of the funds go to Spain, Portugal, Greece, Ireland and southern Italy).[28]

The *distribution over the type of project* of the funds has changed considerably. In the late 1970s and early 1980s, the bulk (80 per cent) of the resources was used to assist investment in basic economic infrastructure (transport, telecommunications, water, energy). Since then, resources devoted to productive investment in industry and services have increased significantly, and the same holds for projects that improve the business environment and develop human resources (EC, 1991a, 1996e). The accent on various categories differs from country to country.

---

27   Of particular importance are INTERREG, which emphasises the trans-border, trans-national and interregional dimension, and URBAN, which has as its objective the economic and social conversion of urban areas.
28   The efforts of Ireland have brought such welfare increases that the country no longer qualifies as an objective 1 region.

COORDINATION OF EU COHESION POLICIES WITH NATIONAL AND OTHER EU POLICIES

In the fight for more regional equity the EU and national governments are comrades in arms. However, there is also rivalry between the two. What from a national point of view may seem a grave problem justifying a substantial money outlay may seem trifling from the EU point of view. So the first task of the EU was to define the priority regions on the European level. The second task was to prevent governments from outbidding one another with subsidies, which would mean in practice that the richer member states would be able to match any package allowed to the less well-off ones. The EU has put a ceiling on aid levels in each type of problem region: that is, the bigger the problems, the higher the ceiling.

The different policies of the EU should reinforce each other, or at least should not be contradictory. So policies such as agriculture, trade and monetary should contribute to cohesion.[29] Although this seems self-evident in theory, it is not in actual practice. The reason is that EU policies have tended to be developed fairly much in isolation. This has indeed led to problems; at the end of the 1980s, the combined effects of the major EU policies tended to be positive for the non-assisted areas and negative for problem regions of long standing in southern Europe. So on balance they did not support the cohesion objective.

In the debate on cohesion effects of other policies, the following three receive particular attention.[30]

- Agriculture. The CAP (which consumed the lion's share of the EU budget and involved the largest redistribution of income among European citizens) mainly benefited the 'rich' regions. Since the 1992 reforms (see Chapter 9) most 'cohesion' countries seem to benefit increasingly from the CAP.
- Internal market. One of the main preoccupations of the EU has always been the competitiveness of its economy. The single market programme has been of outstanding importance in this respect. Although it is difficult to dissociate the effects of such programmes from those of simultaneous developments (like the accession of Spain and Portugal) the effects have been found to be rather positive.
- Economic and Monetary Union. EMU entails some new adaptation problems for the backward regions. In order to fight these a 'Cohesion Fund' was created (of € 3 billion a year) that finances infrastructure developments in the Mediterranean countries to support them in meeting the demands of the Stability and Growth Pact (see Chapter 15).

Some problems come up quite suddenly as the result of EU policy changes. Take the case of an agreement on the external trade in textiles. More openness for imports can spell problems for regions that have specialised in textiles. The EU has the possibility of reacting relatively quickly to such adverse regional developments, including regions other than those given in Figure 16.3.

---

29   Of course the opposite is also true. So, while carrying out regional policy (for example, with infrastructure projects), due account should be taken of other policy objectives, for example, environment. The Structural Funds Regulation does indeed make aid conditional on compliance with such other policy objectives.
30   See Molle (forthcoming) and the studies cited therein, notably Henry (1981); Franzmeyer et al. (1991); Molle and Cappellin (1988); Molle et al. (1993); EC (1996a, 1996e, 2001c).

EVALUATION

How effective is regional policy in realising certain objectives, such as growth of employment and decrease in disparity? The question has three aspects.

The choice of the EU as to the *system* seems to be a good one. Indeed the allotment of aid in the form of specific-purpose grants in the framework of Community Support Frameworks seems to be more efficient than a system that would operate with block grants. Moreover, the reform of 1989 concentrated aid to specific problem areas and improved the procedures and hence the workings of the system. Finally the system takes due account of aspects of allocational efficiency and policy consistency.

The *effectiveness of the operational efforts* is not easy to establish. Evaluation studies of individual projects and programmes suggest that the specific policy targets are generally met. The more general target is the decrease in disparity. So the real question to which research needs to give an answer is *whether the SF have contributed to a reduction of these disparities*. There exists a considerable controversy as to the effectiveness of the SF on this score.

Positive. On this side we find the Commission, which states: 'The Structural and Cohesion Funds do not only stimulate demand by increasing income in the regions assisted. By supporting investment in infrastructure and human capital they also increase their competitiveness and productivity and so help to expand income over the long term.' The same thesis is supported by many academics who have found empirical evidence for the positive effects of regional cohesion policy measures on the decrease in disparity.[31]

Negative. Other authors claim that the effect of the EU policy is at best neutral in the sense that the transfers from the rich to the poor do contribute only that amount to the wealth levels of the beneficiary regions. However, they doubt any long-term growth effects and suspect that the welfare effect is actually negative due to the ensuing distortions of taxation and bureaucracy and sub-optimal location of activities.[32]

Both camps base themselves on empirical results. The differences in results may be in part due to the complicated nature of the cause-effect relation and the difficulty to isolate the effects of cohesion policy from 'normal' development.[33]

The next question evaluation has to answer is about *efficiency*; in other words, whether the EU could have attained these positive effects using fewer resources; this is much more critical. The organisational and administrative costs of the present system are very high. The way to improvement may be to apply better the subsidiarity principle and leave more to the member states: this would involve a trimming of the flows to and from the richer member states (see the advantages of decentralisation proclaimed by the fiscal federalism school).

---

31   See, for example, EC (2001c, p. xxi) and EC (2004c) and, for academics, Martin and Saenz (2003); Beugelsdijk and Eijffinger (2003); Dall'erba and Le Gallo (2003). ERDF spending on public infrastructure and education in backward regions was found to have accelerated growth in these regions (for example, de la Fuente and Vives, 1995 for Spain and Bradley et al., 1995 for Ireland) by some percentage points. Other analyses of the supply-side effects of regional policy were less conclusive. Also macro-economic models that put the accent on the demand side of increased spending by the structural funds show significant effects (EC, 1996e).

32   For example, Boldrin and Canova (2001, 2003) state: 'current (EU) policies are ineffective, based on incorrect or at least unsubstantiated economic theory, badly designed, poorly carried out, a source of wrong incentives and in some cases of corruption'. The EU structural funds support has been at a cost to welfare because it tended to force R&D-intensive industries into regions not well endowed to make them competitive (Midelfart-Kvarnik and Overman, 2002).

33   The models used all have certain limitations. An early attempt at such modelling has been made by Molle (1983), relating sectoral growth of employment for the regions of the EU9 to a number of variables (location factors) among them regional policy. The effect of the latter variable could not be identified. Other models exist that explain well a significant part of the decrease in disparity by the usual growth factors, such as Crespo-Cuaresma et al. (2003) but do not include a policy variable. Other models that combine both the supply side and demand side have also been made. For a critical review of all three types of models, see Mairate and Hall (2001). An overview of demand side models is given in EC (1999k).

So the *conclusion* of this section is that there is much evidence to justify the EU regional policy; however, there remains some concern both for effectiveness and, notably, efficiency.

Social policy

ASSESSING THE PROBLEMS

The EU is confronted by many social problems. A prolonged situation of unemployment may lead to loss of job qualifications, lack of capacity to earn may inhibit people from investing in the acquisition of new skills. Adverse situations may lead to indebtedness. The factors that lead to this are mutually reinforcing and may lead to social exclusion. Despair may lead to crime.[34]

Unemployment overshadows all the other social problems in Europe. And within unemployment it is female unemployment that gives particular cause for concern (Table 16.4). Until the mid-1980s, it increased considerably as a consequence of the two crises in the 1970s. Unemployment declined in the second half of the 1980s under the impetus of the upswing related to the completion of the internal market. At the beginning of the 1990s it significantly increased again. This overall EU picture gets more contrast if we look at the differences between countries (Table 16.4). Unemployment has in the past been particularly problematic in many countries of the periphery of the EU (Spain, Italy, Greece, Finland) and in the new *Bundesländer*. At present it is also very high in more central countries such as France. The NMS show very large differences; very high rates for instance for Poland; very low for a country like Slovenia. The transition from command to a market economy has meant that in all of these countries certain groups of the labour force were ill adapted to the new demands. So unemployment has tended to increase everywhere. However, some countries have managed to overcome relatively quickly the problems; among them those that have made an early start with reforms, had a diversified economic structure, are located in proximity to the West and have flexible labour markets (for example, Hungary).

There is a set of *causes* for the high level of European unemployment.[35] First, there have been a number of adverse developments: in particular, movements in the terms of trade (for example, due to high import bills of energy) and the effects of counter-inflationary demand policies. Second, these shocks have had a large impact because of the low responsiveness of the European labour market. This poor functioning of the European labour market is thought to be due to rigidities coming from 'over'-regulation. Third, there are propagation mechanisms that lead temporary shocks to have persistent effects. And, last but not least, unemployment is due to the excessively rapid growth of the cost of labour. There is a chain of causes here. The increase in cost of labour is caused by the growth of the taxes on labour. These in turn are a consequence of the shift in the tax burden from capital and goods taxes to labour. This comes about because tax competition (see Chapter 14) shifts the burden to the most immobile factor. And the rise in labour cost has induced firms to substitute capital for labour.[36]

Differences in *the level of social protection* are perceived to lead to frictions within the EU. Over the years the richer countries of the EU have developed an elaborate system of

---

34 See, for example, Vleminckx and Berghman (2001).
35 See Bean (1994); Layard et al. (1991); Heylen and van Poeck (1995); OECD (1994b); Modigliani (1996); Blanchard and Wolfers (2000).
36 Daveri and Tabellini (2000).

Table 16.4   Indicators of social disparity in the EU, 1980–2004

	Unemployment (2004, %)			Expenditure on social protection per head (thousands of 1995 euros)		
	Total	Males	Females	1980	1990	2000
Germany	9.5	8.7	10.5	5.3	5.5	6.9
France	9.7	8.8	10.7	4.4	5.2	6.6
Italy	8	6.4	10.5	2.6	5.0	4.4
Netherlands	4.6	4.3	4.8	5.0	5.5	6.2
Belgium	7.8	7	8.8	4.4	4.6	6.0
Luxembourg	4.8	3.3	6.8	4.4	5.7	9.1
UK	4.7	5.1	4.2	3.0	3.8	6.4
Denmark	5.4	5.1	5.6	5.4	6.6	8.4
Ireland	4.5	4.9	3.9	2.0	2.2	3.3
Spain	10.9	8.1	14.9	1.4	2.7	2.7
Portugal	6.7	5.9	7.6	0.6	1.3	2.2
Greece	10.5	6.6	16.2	0.7	2.9	2.4
Austria	4.8	4.4	5.4	n.a.	5.2	6.9
Sweden	6.3	6.5	6.1	n.a.	8.9	8.5
Finland	8.8	8.7	8.9	n.a.	6.3	5.8
EU15	8.1	7.1	9.3	3.4	4.3	5.4
Poland	18.8	18	19.7	n.a.	n.a.	0.5
Czech Rep.	8.3	7.1	9.9	n.a.	n.a.	0.8
Hungary	5.9	5.8	6	n.a.	n.a.	0.5
Slovakia	18	17	19.3	n.a.	n.a.	0.6
Slovenia	6	5.6	6.5	n.a.	n.a.	1.8
Lithuania	10.8	10.3	11.3	n.a.	n.a.	0.4
Cyprus	5	4	6.3	n.a.	n.a.	n.a.
Latvia	9.8	9.2	10.3	n.a.	n.a.	0.4
Estonia	9.2	10.3	8.1	n.a.	n.a.	0.4
Malta	7.3	6.9	8.3	n.a.	n.a.	1.5
EU25	9	8.1	10.2	n.a.	n.a.	4.6

Source: Eurostat.

protecting their citizens in general and their workers in particular against loss of income due to unemployment, sickness, accidents and so on. Moreover, legislation protects workers against hazards at their workplaces. The levels of protection are lower in the less well-off member countries of the EU15 and even much lower in the NMS (Table 16.4) In the member states that have high social standards, labour cost will be higher than in states with low standards. This has given rise to the accusation of *social dumping*: employment will be lost in the former and won in the latter because firms faced with losses in market shares will relocate to low-cost, low-protection locations. Those demanding protection against this social dumping can neither use the instruments that apply to goods and service markets (free movement), nor those of a macro-economic nature (a devaluation is precluded by the monetary union). So, they advocate countering a downward pressure upon social conditions by setting for all member states minimum wage levels, social provisions and health and safety standards.

GRADUAL DEVELOPMENT OF POLICY

European social policy is a complement to national social policies. Social policy is closely associated with, and may even encompass, labour market policy, which addresses issues like unemployment but also education, training and working conditions. Many other social problems are aggravated by the unemployment problem, so it is only logical that the EU has placed the fight against unemployment at the centre of its policy actions. The promotion of social cohesion requires the reduction in disparities, which arise from unequal access to employment opportunities.

The main *instruments* for putting in place the policy are financial support through the European Social Fund and regulation (for example, minimum standards).

European Social policy has to be seen in the light of the fundamentals of the *European Social Model*, defined by the European Council of Barcelona in 2002 as good economic performance, a high level of social protection and education and social dialogue. In all national systems of EU member countries one finds this consistency between economic efficiency and social progress.

The *objectives and actions* of the European Social (cohesion) Policy have changed as the EU has moved into higher stages of integration.[37]

1952–74 The experience of the ECSC was used when the social policy paragraphs of the EEC Treaty were devised. However, that treaty shows a dichotomy between aims and means. Indeed the aims set are broad and ambitious (promote improved working conditions and an improved standard of living for workers). However, the instruments provided are not very specific; the improvement is largely to be achieved through the beneficial effects of the Common Market. To enhance the allocational efficiency of the EU labour market, in other words, occupational mobility, the ESF supported schemes for vocational training or retraining.

1974–85 As a reaction to the deterioration of the economic situation, the Council agreed in 1974 to an action programme for social policy. Objectives were the improvement of living and work conditions, codetermination of workers and full employment. It proved very difficult to move forward. At the end of this period some bits and pieces of social legislation had been passed, but the overall progress was very limited. EU involvement consisted first of support to employment via the Social Fund, of which the resources were increased from some € 250 million to € 1.5 billion. In this period the redistribution objective of the ESF overtook the allocation objective. Indeed half the fund's money went to the less developed regions. The second segment of EU social policy was the coordination of social security systems to secure freedom of movement for workers.[38]

1986–92 The discussion assumed a different perspective when the plans for the single market were set up. There was much concern that the increase in economic efficiency would entail considerable social problems, for two reasons. First, the adaptation to new circumstances would lead to unemployment. Second, the competition from low-wage countries that also have low social protection would lead to an erosion of the high social protection in the richer countries. The Social Charter was adopted, that covers aspects such as working conditions, freedom of movement, social protection, collective bargaining, worker participation, health and safety, and so on. In 1986 the ESF's volume was increased to € 2.5 billion. In allocation of

---

37   Collins (1983); EC (1993d, 2004n); Hantrais (1995); Degimbe (1999); and Ferrera (forthcoming).
38   Workers who migrate from one national system of social security to another need protection to safeguard their rights, but that does not necessarily mean that the systems themselves need to be changed.

the fund's resources, emphasis was placed on the redistribution towards the most distressed regions.

1993–2006   The Social Chapter has considerably broadened the scope of the regulatory action of the EU in the social field (minimum hours of work per day, social security, health and safety requirements and so on). The concern for subsidiarity has meant that it expressly excludes certain areas from EU involvement (wages, strikes and so on). The Treaty of Amsterdam introduced a European policy to promote employment through EU guidelines for national policies. The main objective set for the ESF was developing high quality employment (objective 3 in Table 16.3), in particular by promoting the reinsertion of the unemployed in jobs and the development of human resources (also in innovation, technology and so on).

The extension of the EU with ten new members that have very different traditions from the ones in the former EU15 poses a formidable challenge to EU social policy. The NMS have accepted to take over the *acquis* in terms of institutions such as the social and civil dialogue. However, in order to circumvent the occurrence of problems, such as the ones that have occurred in the Mezzogiorno of Italy and in East Germany, the NMS will need to keep quite some flexibility as to their social policy infrastructure (for example, Belke and Hebler, 2002).

EMPLOYMENT POLICY

The European Council has on several occasions confirmed that the fight against unemployment is the *number one priority* of the EU. The European Employment Strategy specifies three *strategic objectives*: 1) full employment; 2) productivity and quality of work; and 3) social cohesion and inclusive labour markets.

The *implementation* has to be executed by the EU and the member states.

*   Member states assume the primary responsibility for taking policy actions. They set up National Action Plans specifying targets and implementation measures. These actions, that come under the heading of so-called Active Labour Market Policies, aim at improving the functioning of the labour market by enabling persons to take on new job opportunities, by developing skills of employees, the promotion of equal opportunities and by keeping the potentially unemployed in contact with the labour market.
*   The EU sets frameworks and gives policy guidelines. Some of these contain quite detailed quantitative targets, for example, with respect to participation rates of men and women, and increases of productivity. Others deal with the decrease of social exclusion and poverty. The Commission monitors progress annually . The EU, moreover, gives financial support from the ESF. Finally the EU works on the improvement of conditions (for example, improvement of the working of the internal market, investment in human capital, consistent monetary and macro policies).

The *employment policy* is intricately connected to other EU policies. Very important in this respect is the so-called Lisbon strategy that aims at stronger competitiveness of the EU economy (see Chapter 18). The actions under the various strategies have in common that they address structural impediments that national governments need to tackle in order to unblock their development potential and increase the competitiveness of their economies. They relate to reforms of the tax system and of labour market regulation, to the reduction of government deficits, to the enhancement of the effectiveness of R&D spending, to the removing of the obstacles to entrepreneurship, and so on. Until now such reforms have proved to be very difficult to implement as each regulation is defended by very strong interest groups that have the capacity to stop politicians from taking the necessary action.

The European Social Fund (ESF) is the *main instrument* to combat unemployment. The fund is administered by the Commission, assisted by a committee of representatives of governments, trade unions and employers. An example of *ESF action* is the EMPLOYMENT programme in operation during the late 1990s. It consisted of four interrelated sub-programmes to promote the labour market chances of women (NOW), of the disabled (HORIZON), of people under 20, especially those without basic qualifications (YOUTHSTART), and those threatened by social exclusion (INTEGRA). Another initiative targeted groups not yet integrated into the information society (ADAPT). About a million people received training or other support to improve their job prospects in an increasingly competitive EU labour market (EC, 1996e). For the 2000–2006 period the set-up has been recast. A new initiative called EQUAL promotes new means of combating all forms of discrimination and inequalities in connection with the labour market.

SOCIAL PROTECTION POLICY

One of the values that are shared by all EU countries is *solidarity*. It has given rise to the European Social Model, that is characterised by high levels of public support for insurance against income loss (unemployment benefits) and particular risks (for example, health). Important differences existed between member states in the level of social protection. To many this was thought to be incompatible with market integration. The question thus came up how the preservation of the benefits of these national systems could be brought in line with the pursuit of market integration. In this debate, broadly two views can be distinguished: the 'economic or liberalist' and the 'social progress or regulators' view.[39]

In the *economic view*, the social security systems need only be harmonised as far as necessary for the proper functioning of the Common Market. Long-term productivity growth has to be based on increased competitiveness on world markets; such growth in turn is a necessary condition for the further improvement of social protection. The EU should favour a competition between rules and refrain from any major policy action. The argument of the 'competition school' is that standards restrict the functioning of markets. This has two aspects. First, standards increase the cost level of the below-average-income member states, which restricts their chances of competing successfully on product markets, which in turn increases the possibility of their becoming dependent on transfer payments.[40] Second, EU standards increase the rigidity on labour markets, which is one of the major causes of unemployment (see previous section).

In the *social progress view*, the EU is more than a common market, and has the clear task of enhancing welfare. Factors like a highly developed social security system and the stability of labour market institutions are considered to strengthen investments in human capital and to lead to a motivated labour force. High EU standards prevent the negative effects of a downward spiral in social protection occurring. Such negative effects are of two types: first, serious social problems may lower productivity; second, labour market institutions may become less efficient as the positive external effects of regulation are forgone. This view has led to proposals to eliminate at least the gravest shortcomings of the systems in certain member states.

---

39   See, for example, Holloway (1981); Dearden (1995); Brown et al. (1996).
40   See in this respect, for example, OECD (1994c); de Molina and Perea (1992). The example of the new German Laender is in this respect a warning for the EU not to move too far in harmonisation. It could work out negatively for, notably, the NMS.

The outcome of the debate between economists and social progressionists has changed over time. Initially the economists won. The Commission, which had associated itself with the social progress approach, was forced, in 1966, to adopt the economic line advocated by all member states. This line was followed during the period 1965–90. In the 1990s, things changed. The European Social Charter established that any citizen of the EU is entitled to adequate social protection, including social security; the determination of the level and form is, however, to be arranged by each member state. The 1994 white paper of the Commission on European Social Policy presented competitiveness and social progress as complements. This is now the mainstream view;[41] case-by-case solutions will have to be found so that social protection and competitiveness can be improved in step.

EVALUATION

Up to the end of the 1980s, European social policy consisted mainly of (1) a set of rules defining the rights of migrant workers to social security benefits, (2) a loose cooperation in the form of exchange of information on other aspects of social policy, and (3) a means of redistributing European funds among member countries for the retraining of workers in the poorer regions. The various elements of this stage of European social policy have drawn mostly unfavourable critiques.[42]

In the 1990s, the social policy of the EU has been extended. The EU has engaged considerable resources in its fight against *unemployment,* its first policy priority. The problem is that there is a whole range of ESF support, which means that the effectiveness of the policy cannot easily be evaluated in general terms. However, many of the instruments used come under the heading of Active Labour Market Policies whose effectiveness was found to be rather ambiguous.[43]

There are various ways to attack the problem. The EU makes evaluations of all expenditure on programmes of the SF. These studies use very different methodologies and data. The main aim was, however, to answer three questions. Are the strategies appropriate for the objectives? Has the programme reached the target groups? What improvements in the delivery system can be made to increase effectiveness? The general conclusion drawn from this wide range of results is positive (EC, 2000g, 2004m). Another approach to evaluation is measurement of the combined effect of the SF in total, that is of both economic and social policies on the main target variable. This type of study shows that the SF have contributed to decrease unemployment.[44]

Summary and conclusions

- Cohesion policy is pursued in partnership between EU Commission and national and local governments. All actions are set in a multi-annual programming framework. EU cohesion policies involve redistribution. They absorb a very large part of the EU financial resources.

---

41   Bean et al. (1990); Addison and Siebert (1994); Brown et al. (1996).
42   For example, Laffan (1983); Steinle (1988) who argue that, at best, the ESF has served the redistribution of European money (equity), but failed to attain any specific Community objectives on efficiency.
43   Layard et al. (1991); Martin (1998). The effect of regional policy measures on employment is very hard to measure by econometric models (Molle, 1983; EC, 1996e).
44   For example, Bradley, Morgenroth and Untiedt (2004).

- The most important parts of EU cohesion policies are regional and social policies. The instruments used for both reflect the wish of the EU to make these policies conducive to more allocational efficiency as well.
- The regional policy's objective is a decrease in disparity. Notwithstanding a gradual decrease over the past decades, considerable differences in wealth remain. European integration has helped to diminish the disparity in national wealth, and that is a major determinant of regional disparity.
- The social policy has ambitious objectives: in practice the essential features of the policy are (1) a redistribution of resources through the European structural funds for the fight against unemployment and (2) the harmonisation of a large variety of labour market regulations.
- Evaluations of the effectiveness of both policies are fairly critical; the contribution to growth of employment and wealth convergence appears to be unsatisfactory.

17 *External Relations*

Introduction

Integration schemes need to define rules not only for their internal functioning, but also for their external relations. Owing to the high degree of worldwide economic interdependence, each member country has developed a whole panoply of relations with third countries. The higher the stage of economic integration, the smaller the scope for independent action by member countries. Indeed a matter which has been regulated internally by the Union cannot be treated in external international relations without the participation and consent of the Union. In the next sections we will first go into these fundamental principles and next describe the EU regime in its international institutional setting.

As the EU is based on a customs union, trade policy will receive ample attention below. Two sections will be devoted to the common external trade policy, one to the objectives and instruments and the other to the specific relations with different groups of trading partners. The EU has developed from a customs union via a common market into an economic and monetary union and is on the move towards a political union. This means that other matters than trade are the object of gradual integration and are thus becoming the concern of the common external policy. The subsequent sections of this chapter therefore review other economic policies (such as labour and capital movements, international economic and monetary coordination) and development aid, and will finally touch upon external policies less associated with economic issues, such as foreign and defence policy. Some general conclusions will round off the chapter.

Theoretical foundations

DYNAMICS OF INTEGRATION

The setting up of common policies is more efficient than the pursuit of independent policies by member states if the common policy produces better results with less effort than independent ones. This will often be the case in international matters, where the power relations between the various partners determine in part the outcome of negotiation processes. The scope of the common external policies is determined by the stage of the integration process.

A *customs union* lays the basis for a common external policy by setting up a common commercial policy. It generally covers both a common external tariff and rules on the common use of non-tariff barriers to prevent member countries using such instruments to obtain supplementary competition advantages for their industry. As international trade in goods and services is welfare-improving, customs unions have an interest in pursuing a policy of openness towards third countries (trade leads to a better allocation of resources and the competition of imports has a disciplining effect on domestic supplies). However, strategic considerations may nevertheless induce trade blocks to use impediments (for example, accepting provisionally some protection for some industries to get sufficient political support for the liberalisation of most other industries' trade).

A *common market* will entail common policies in the fields of labour and capital. For labour, the abolition of internal border controls for workers, and *a fortiori* for all persons, will induce a common policy for immigration from third countries. It will likewise create a need for the harmonisation of other policies (such as crime prevention and social security). For capital, a similar reasoning applies: the liberalisation of movements between members will imply capital flowing into the whole of the common market through the country that gives the easiest access to capitalists of third countries; a common stance is therefore necessary.

An *economic and monetary union* also brings a need for an extension of the scope of external policy. Let us take just a few examples for illustration. In terms of allocation policies, foreign firms need to know whether they have to comply with the rules on competition and whether they qualify for financial support of technological innovation from one of the EU programmes. The setting up of a monetary union requires a common exchange rate policy, whereas a common external redistribution (aid) policy may be required to enhance the effectiveness of the various efforts.

A *full union* will have an essential responsibility for matters such as security and defence and many cultural aspects. These will thus become part and parcel of Union external policies.

EU regime

OBJECTIVES AND INSTRUMENTS

The competence of the EU as to external relations has been gradually expanded over time. The original Treaty bestowed on the EC only the competence to deal with external trade matters. The expansion of the EU competence to *other economic policy areas* implied that it also acquired external competences in these fields. In practical terms this means that the European external policy has been extended by new subjects as integration progressed through the stages we distinguished in Chapter 2.[1] The increased weight of the EU implies that it will have to take increasingly into account the effects of internal policies on third countries. In the course of time the Commission has taken action in such economic matters as civil aviation, distortion of competition and monetary stabilisation.

The EU has increasingly assumed responsibility for non-economic external matters. It has elaborated a common foreign, security and defence policy. The objective of this set of policies is to contribute to the dissemination of the principles that lie at the basis of the Union, such as democracy, rule of law, human rights and compliance with international law.

The increased role of the EU in economic and in foreign and security matters has led to a new type of external relations of the EU. It specifies for each area in the world packages of trade advantages, financial aid to development (infrastructure, education, and so on) and agreements on other matters such as migration controls, compliance with EU internal market regulations, the fight against terrorism and drugs trafficking and the promotion of values such as democracy. Important in this respect is the new neighbourhood policy that defines

---

1   See Molle and van Mourik (1987); Ward (1986).

relations between the EU and countries on its eastern (former Soviet Union) and southern borders (Mediterranean countries).

The choice of *instruments* of external policy integration for the EU will depend on the advance of internal policy integration. With external policies that are a complement to a clearly defined internal union competence, unification of instruments may be the answer (for instance, a common external customs tariff for a customs union). In areas where powers are not yet clearly vested in the 'union', the definition of the stance towards third countries will be carried out by consultation or coordination among member countries. The instruments that are used for the reaching of agreement with third countries will depend on the international institutional framework – negotiations in the WTO for trade, but consultation and information in the G8 for macro policy. In cases where such international fora do not exist the EU uses very diversified instruments. It sets up platforms for consultation on matters of common interest and where possible concludes cooperation agreements covering such diverse aspects as FDI, aid, regional integration and social cohesion. Examples are the Transatlantic Economic Partnership (with the US) and the Mediterranean Partnership (with southern neighbours).

FINANCIAL FLOWS

The importance of the categories of an economic union's external relations can be derived from its balance of payments, which is the financial record of its transactions with the rest of the world. These transactions include current ones concerning merchandise, services and so on, as well as long- and short-term capital transactions. We have rearranged the headings in the statistics of the current account of the European Union to fit the four parts of the common market; the results are given in Table 17.1.

Table 17.1   Percentage share of categories in total external payments of the EU;[a] average of assets and liabilities on the current account,[b] 1970–2003

	1970	1980	1990	2000	2003	2003[c]
Merchandise	67	64	64	60	61	60
Services (commercial)	20	19	18	20	21	22
Labour (inc.)	1	1	1	1	1	1
Capital (inc.)	12	16	17	19	17	17
Current account (CA)	100	100	100	100	100	100

Notes: [a] *1970–80: EU12; 1990–2003: EU15. 2003[c]: EU25.* [b] *Figures of assets being very much like the liability figures for all headings, we have preferred this presentation to the more common one of net figures (assets minus liabilities).*

Source: *Eurostat, Balance of Payments, Geographical Breakdown, various years; IMF, Balance of Payments, Washington, various years.*

A few brief comments on the results are in order. The first is that the structure of the external transactions has been fairly stable through time, irrespective of the composition of the EU. The prominence of merchandise exports is striking; they accounted for almost two-thirds of total current transactions. This justifies the considerable attention we will devote in the next sections to the external trade in goods of the EU. Services occupy a modest place in comparison. Among the payments associated with production factors, the returns on capital invested abroad are growing in importance; the payments made by and to the EU for labour (earnings from work and remittances by emigrant workers and so on) are very small in comparison. Next to these current account transactions there are those of the capital account, whose total volume, as a matter of fact, is by far the greater. This justifies an ample discussion of the involvement of the EU in world policies on stabilisation and development.

INTERNATIONAL INSTITUTIONAL SETTING

The process of European integration takes shape in the framework of a rapid globalisation of economic activities. As a consequence there is an increasing need for international institutions to set the policies to accompany these developments. However, these have developed to very different degrees according to the subject. Most is done for trade, very little for other elements such as allocation policies and macro-economic and monetary policies (see Chapter 20 and Molle, 2003).

Trade relations (manufactured goods) have for a long time (1950–95) been regulated by GATT, the General Agreement on Tariffs and Trade. In 1995, the WTO, the World Trade Organization, took over the responsibilities of GATT. It has, moreover, been given responsibility for trade in services, agricultural products and ideas (intellectual property) and for trade-related investment measures. All member countries of the EU were contracting parties to the GATT and are now members of its successor, the WTO. The *essential functions* of the WTO are as follows.

- Administering and implementing the multilateral and plurilateral trade agreements. Central to this set of rules of conduct for international trade has been the so-called 'most-favoured-nation clause'. It means that any advantage affecting tariffs or other trade regulation instruments which is granted to one of the members must immediately be granted to all other members as well. Exempt from this rule of non-discrimination are arrangements with the objective of creating a free trade area.
- Providing a forum for multilateral trade negotiation. Members have agreed that changes in trade policy, such as the imposition or raising of tariffs, the setting of quotas and so on, cannot be decided unilaterally by one national government, but must be subjected to international negotiation. That rules out unilateral increases in protection which might lead to retaliation and tariff wars, and at the same time provides countries prepared to make concessions in the direction of free trade with a lever to obtain similar concessions from other nations (reciprocity).

The WTO conducts regular reviews of members' trade policies and practices. Unresolved disputes between signatories are brought before a panel of independent experts for conciliation and adjudication.

Production factors are much less well covered by international institutions. Some consultation on capital transactions (including FDI) is done by the OECD, and was in earlier days in the framework of the IMF. For labour markets, the ILO has done relevant work on labour standards, while both the OECD and the ILO have worked on migration issues.

Economic policy coordination, again, has been done in the OECD. This organisation has covered the whole range of subjects discussed in this book, from policy coordination for economic sectors to stabilisation. Regular work on worldwide monetary coordination has been done by the IMF, which has the task of monitoring and promoting the stability of the international financial system. Relevant in terms of macro-economic and monetary policy coordination has been the G8, the yearly summit meetings of the heads of government of the largest economic powers in the world. Finally, redistribution is the realm of the World

Bank, but this organisation is directly responsible for aid and does relatively little in terms of coordination of national aid.

Trade policy: a fan of instruments

PRINCIPLES AND OBJECTIVES

The EU *trade regime* is based on a number of theoretical principles. Indeed, the literature on external trade relations indicates that a regime of openness is most conducive to growth. The possibility of imports and the rivalry of foreign firms that have made direct investments put the local producers under constant pressure, leading to more dynamism than would occur in a country with a closed economy. The EU practice is meant to be in line with these theoretical recipes.

The Treaty of Rome (in its Article 18) says that the EU wishes to contribute, in the common interest, to the harmonious development of world trade, the progressive abolition of restrictions on international trade and the lowering of customs tariffs. The Rome Treaty (in its Article 29) gives the following *motives* for a common commercial policy (CCP):

* the need to promote trade among member states and third countries;
* the possible improvement of the competitive capacity of undertakings;
* the avoidance of competitive distortions in finished-goods markets, related to supplies of raw materials and semi-finished goods;
* the avoidance of serious disturbances in the member states' economies, while ensuring the growth of production and consumption within the EU.

At present the treaty objectives of the CCP are limited to contributing to the harmonious development of world trade and the gradual abolition of all impediments to international trade.

The common commercial policy covers not only tariffs but other trade instruments as well. So all powers regarding changes in tariff rates, conclusion of trade agreements, export policy, the achievement of uniform liberalisation, and anti-dumping or countervailing duties are within the competence of the EU institutions. Nevertheless, the mixed nature of their economies caused member states to use independently all sorts of instruments on the borderline of trade policy, which has given rise to lengthy competence battles between the Commission and member state governments. Over the years a trade policy practice has been worked out that uses fairly complicated procedures and a very elaborate panoply of instruments (EC, 1993b).

COMMON EXTERNAL TARIFF

The Common External Tariff (CET) of the EU was established for each category as the arithmetic average of the tariffs applied by the member states. Thus the first CET reflected the whole history of the trade relations of all member countries. The EU has effectively worked towards global free trade. Major reductions in the CET for manufactured products have regularly been made in the framework of GATT negotiations. The so-called 'Dillon round' of 1960–62 and the subsequent 'Kennedy round' of the mid-1960s cut the tariffs by about half. A further tariff cut of some 30 per cent of the 1978 level was agreed upon during the so-called 'Tokyo round' of the mid-1970s. The 'Uruguay round' has resulted in yet further cuts. Consequently the general level of tariff protection of the EU is now very low, only a few per cent. For many the EU tariff actually applied is nil or negligible. Moreover, the dispersion has become very narrow. The recent discussions in the WTO framework apply now also to the segments of economic activity that were until recently excluded, such as agriculture and services. This has incited the EU to dismantle its protective system for agricultural products (see Chapter 9).

NON-TARIFF BARRIERS

Less visible than tariffs but no less effective as instruments of trade policy are the so-called 'non-tariff barriers' (NTBs). In line with its policy objectives the EU has tried over the years to *free its external trade from NTBs*. Let us analyse the progress for three forms of NTB.

- Many *quotas* applied to imports from non-EU members date from pre-EU times. Although the Treaty of Rome had allowed member states to retain such quotas, the Commission has been pushing to dispose of them. Other quotas have been introduced over the past decades with the objective of protecting so-called 'sensitive sectors'.[2] The completion of the internal market made national quotas impractical as border controls were no longer permitted. As a result, all national ones have now been removed; the few remaining are EU-wide quotas.
- *Voluntary export restraints* (VERs) (by one exporting country) and *orderly marketing arrangements* (OMAs) (multilateral voluntary restraint agreements) existed outside the GATT framework, and were therefore, from a political point of view, more expedient than quotas. They have been widely used. In the WTO Agreement on Safeguards, the EU has done away with these 'grey area' measures.
- *Technical regulations*. The internal EU rules on mutual recognition have had an external liberalisation effect as well (see Chapter 14). Indeed, a product imported from a non-EU country that is legally marketed in one of the member states, because it comes up to the technical specifications of that country, has free access to the other member states as well.

The main attention of the EU has now shifted towards trade in services, where NTBs are of a more regulatory nature (see Chapters 6, 12, 14).

ANTI-DUMPING PROTECTION AGAINST UNFAIR TRADE PRACTICES

In their attempts to conquer a new export market, firms sometimes adopt the strategy of first selling at a loss in foreign markets to force local producers out of business, and afterwards raising their prices to very profitable levels. The practice is known as *dumping*. GATT/WTO rules allow the importing country to take protective measures against such practices, in particular to impose anti-dumping duties which level off the difference between the selling prices the dumping firm charges in its home and export markets. GATT/WTO rules permit such measures

---

2   Sensitive sectors are composed of low-technology manufacturers, using relatively standardised, labour-intensive production technologies, the very sectors in which LDCs have been gaining increasing comparative advantage. Paramount among them is the textile and clothing sector. Under the Multi-Fibre Arrangement (MFA), negotiated between the EU and the principal textile-exporting developing countries, the latter have agreed to a voluntary restriction of their textile exports to the EU. In practice, the MFA had deteriorated into a scheme by which the individual EU member countries had fixed the quantities of textile products they will import from each separate exporting country. The abolition of the MFA has taken a lot of time but is now a fact. This policy change has brought considerable welfare increases (Koekkoek and Mennes, 1988).

to be taken only if it can be shown that (1) imports have increased substantially, (2) there is a substantial price difference between home and export prices of the exporter, and (3) the imports cause material injury to the home producers.

These GATT/WTO rules have inspired the EU anti-dumping regulation.[3] The EU *procedure* is as follows:

* a complaint is lodged by (groups of) firms directly concerned; the regulation indicates in detail what information the Commission requires;
* verification by the Commission of the information given by the complaining party;
* if a dumping margin is found to exist and if injury has been done, the Commission may either accept the exporters' offer to adjust prices and/or subsidies, or, if the adjustment is insufficient, impose a duty.

Anti-dumping investigations have grown over the 1980–2000 period. By the end of the century, some 183 EU anti-dumping measures were in force. The geographical pattern of anti-dumping measures has changed also. Those against the former communist countries have fallen, while those against the newly industrialising countries (NICs) have increased. The cases where anti-dumping duties have been applied represented only a small percentage of total EU imports.[4]

LIBERALISATION VERSUS PROTECTIONISM

There are sound economic arguments for the abolition of all protective measures. Theoretical analyses and empirical analyses (Chapter 5) have, indeed, shown that trading partners obtain net welfare gains from getting rid of protective measures. In the case of the EU, the total cost of its trade protection measures could amount to as much as 7 per cent of its GDP (Messerlin, 1999a). Large welfare benefits have also been found in studies on the effects of the various GATT/WTO rounds of trade liberalisation (see, for an overview, François *et al.*, 1996). Now, if economic considerations plead so convincingly against the use of protective instruments, why have they been so widely used? The reasons are of a political economy nature.

* The negative effects of liberalisation on welfare in terms of jobs lost is not easy to determine, yet in many people's eyes the unemployment in certain sectors is directly attributable to trade.[5] Claims for protection were found to be higher as (1) the industry is more concentrated corporately or regionally, (2) the historical levels of protection are higher, (3) the industry is better organised, and (4) the macro-economic performance (including the balance of payments) is weaker.
* The positive effects of liberalisation are more general and diffuse and hence less visible. Export industries and consumers have no interest in protection. However, in contrast to the sectors demanding protection, they tend to be poorly organised and have little influence.

Adjustment costs are only a small element in the balance of cost and benefits. Nevertheless the former tend to carry more weight than the latter. Politicians anxious to be re-elected,

---

3   The EU does not have any anti-dumping rules on intra-EU trade; here the competition rules should safeguard the fair play of competitors.
4   See Tharakan (1988); Messerlin (1988); EC (1993b); WTO (2000).
5   In the EU it was found that other factors are much more important in explaining unemployment (see Dewatripont et al., 1999).

whatever their ideology, tend to listen more to the slogans of well organised pro-protection pressure groups than to the pleas of anti-protectionists.[6] The state will only override the pro-protection interest groups if considerations of international relations carry enough weight. This is the case under international agreements that liberalise trade across the board: a country that gives special protection to a specific group risks the revocation of the agreement, which puts in jeopardy the advantages of free trade for all other groups. So under such schemes it is unlikely that the political pressure of special interest groups will be strong enough to override the general interest.

Trade policy differentiation by area

A HIERARCHY OF TRADE RELATIONS

EU external trade relations are governed by GATT/WTO rules, notably the most-favoured-nation (MFN) rule. However, there have been strong pressures on the EU to use the loopholes in the GATT system and discriminate in practice between (groups of) countries. This has resulted in special advantages being given to specific groups of countries with which the EU wanted to retain special relations. Table 17.2 gives a summary idea of the highly differentiated system that has evolved. It gives at the top of the hierarchy, or pyramid[7] the arrangements for which relations are closest, while it gives at the bottom the relations for which most protection persists.

Table 17.2 The hierarchy of EU trade relations (2004)

Countries concerned	Form of relationship	Share[a] in EU external trade (%)	Population (millions)
EFTA	Free trade area; incomplete common market	12	10
Central and Eastern Europe	Association	3	60
Mediterranean	Mixed[b]	8	240
ACP[c]	Special one-way preference[d]	4	600
Other Third World	Generalised preference[d]	32	4500
US, Japan, CIS, etc.	Most-favoured nation	41	900

Notes: [a] See Table 5.4; 2004 imports and exports divided by two. [b] Customs unions, free trade areas, reciprocal and non-reciprocal (one-way) tariff preferences. [c] African, Caribbean and Pacific countries. [d] One-way (non-reciprocal) preferences: the EU reduces/eliminates its tariffs on imports from the partner country but obtains no reciprocal (reverse) concessions on its exports; generalised preferences apply to all developing countries, special preferences to a selected group.

---

6   See Baldwin (1984) and Weiss (1987). For a survey of categories of cost and benefits, see Matusz and Tarr (1999).

7   See Mishalani et al. (1981); Hine (1985); Pomfret (1986).

We will detail this overall picture for each group in the following sections. Mind that there are certain situations that give rise to overlap. Moreover, the EU has embarked upon agreements with other preferential trade agreements in the world such as Mercosur.

We will thereby analyse how far this discrimination has had the effects that were expected of it. From the vehemence of the political debate on changing the clauses of discriminatory arrangements, the advantages accruing to their beneficiaries do seem to be well worthwhile. However, in practice, the discrimination is seen to be hardly effective, owing to the low level of tariffs, on the one hand, and the high level of uncertainty as to prices and exchange rates, on the other.

EFTA (OTHER WESTERN EUROPE)

The relations between the EU and the EFTA have been very deeply influenced by the fact that, at regular intervals, groups of EFTAns joined the EU.

At the end of the 1960s, the UK and three other EFTA member countries decided to leave EFTA and apply for EU membership. A major problem arose: trade among former free trade partners risked being greatly disturbed by the trade barriers still remaining between the EU and EFTA.[8] The solution chosen was that of a large European free trade area, of which the EU is the core. In this way, full free trade in manufactured goods in Western Europe took effect in 1977; as in EFTA, agricultural goods were excluded from the arrangements. As a consequence, trade relations between the EU and EFTA intensified throughout the 1960–85 period (Table 5.4).

In the mid-1980s, a similar problem arose. Once again the EU was joined by some EFTAns. The completion of the internal EU market tended to have a negative effect on the remaining EFTA countries. The solution found has been to associate the EFTA to internal market regulations; this has increased EFTA–EU trade relations (see Table 5.4) and improved welfare in the EFTA group (Norman, 1989, 1991).

In the early 1990s, a third group of EFTAns joined the EU. Although the economic weight of the remaining EFTA is now very small (Norway, Iceland, Switzerland, Liechtenstein) the trade relation is important for both partners.

CENTRAL AND EASTERN EUROPE

The trade relations of the EU with the countries of Central and Eastern Europe have seen revolutionary changes, due to two factors: first, the change of economic system that these countries have implemented since the turn of the decade; second, the acceptance of a group of CEECs as new members by the EU. As a consequence the CEECs have moved from the bottom to the top of the EU trade hierarchy. Let us briefly look at both the old and the new situation.

Up to the end of the 1980s, the CEE countries had centrally planned economies. Most of them were not contracting parties to the GATT (Lopandic, 1986). They were grouped in the Council of Mutual Economic Assistance (CMEA or Comecon). As trade was a matter of the state in CMEA countries, most East–West trade was based on bilateral agreements. Consultation between the EU and the CMEA was difficult: so the EU found itself compelled to set the

---

8   The remaining EFTA countries were unable to join the EU for reasons of foreign policy (neutrality, lack of democracy). A customs union was out of the question: the EU clearly stated that it was not prepared to share its responsibility for trade matters in the framework of the CCP with countries that were not full members. The formula chosen for this FTA was that of bilateral agreements between the EU and individual EFTA countries.

conditions for imports from each Comecon country unilaterally. It is not surprising that, under such conditions, trade relations did not develop much (see Table 5.4).

Since 1989/90, the EU has assumed a new responsibility for the CEECs.[9] It has concluded with each of them bilateral association agreements (so called Europe agreements) that have an important trade component. Over the past decade the EU has abolished tariffs and quantitative restrictions on its imports from the CEECs of almost all industrial products. The CEECs from their side have gradually liberalised their imports from the EU. Trade in agricultural goods was subject to reciprocal preferential treatment. For a while a tangle of bilateral agreements existed between the EU and the CEECs and among the CEECs. An attempt to come to a multilateral agreement among the CEECs (CEFTA, the Central European Free Trade Area) never got off the ground.

In the lead-up to accession this inefficient discriminatory system has gradually been abolished. Since 2004 eight CEECs have become members of the EU. With the remaining countries, bilateral agreements exist. Trade relations between the EU15 and the CEECs have expanded very quickly. The welfare effects of this change in trade relations are as positive as those of earlier enlargements.[10]

MEDITERRANEAN COUNTRIES (NORTH AFRICA AND MIDDLE EAST)

In the period 1960–85, the EU trade relations with Mediterranean countries were of a special nature. Some North African countries used to have colonial ties with one of the EU member countries and wanted to maintain the special trade relations that had been established. Yet others wanted to obtain advantages on the EU market similar to those their neighbours had obtained. The EU gave way to the strong political pressures for preferential treatment, the form chosen depending on political aspirations, on the one hand, and GATT limitations, on the other. For some time the EU has made efforts to put the agreements on a more uniform basis.[11]

For the period 1985–95, the following categories of bilateral agreements existed:

- *Cooperation agreements* with the Maghreb (Morocco, Algeria and Tunisia) and Mashreq (Egypt, Lebanon, Jordan and Syria) countries. The parts concerned with trade were in the form of a one-way preference scheme, which means that these countries had tariff-free access to the EU market for industrial goods and preferential access for agricultural commodities. The EU has settled for an MFN treatment of EU goods on the home markets of these countries. For some sensitive goods the imports into the EU were limited by quotas.
- *Association agreements*, possibly leading to full EU membership. Under these agreements, these countries have obtained tariff-free access to the EU for manufactured goods. These agreements aspired to accession (which has recently been realised for Malta and Cyprus) and to a full-fledged customs union (which has been realised between the EU and Turkey).
- *A free trade agreement*, on the principle of full reciprocity, with Israel.

---

9   We distinguish between three groups of countries. The first consists of the countries west of the former Soviet Union, plus the Baltic countries and Slovenia; they are dealt with in the remaining part of this section. The second group consists of the successor states of the Soviet Union; they now come under the MFN category. The third consists of countries for which the relations still have to be defined (Albania) or are suspended for political reasons (former Yugoslavia). We disregard the latter group here.

10   The relations with non-EU Mediterranean countries on the European shores come under the CEEC heading.

11   See Shlaim and Yannopoulos (1976); Pomfret (1986); Hoekman and Djankov (1996).

The Mediterranean countries appear to have been able to increase their share in EU imports considerably, while their share in EU exports has stagnated, which is an indication of their improved position *vis-à-vis* the EU and other countries exporting to the EU (see Table 5.4). The preferential access to the EU market has brought substantial gains for these countries (Pomfret, 1986). For the EU itself, the economic effect of its Mediterranean policy seems to be small. Generalised system of preference (GSP) countries seem to have suffered from the policy's trade-diversion effects.

Recently the EU has recast the relations with the countries of North Africa and the Middle East in the form of so-called 'Euro-Med-Partnerships'; together these bilateral association agreements will result in a vast free trade area for most manufactured goods and a zone of preferential and reciprocal access for agricultural products. The beneficial effects of these agreements for the Mediterranean countries stem partly from the locking in of the effects of structural reform (Hoekman and Djankov, 1996) but mostly from their increased exports to the EU, estimated at some 20-27 per cent since the entering into force (Peridy, 2005).

THE LOMÉ CONVENTION (AFRICA, CARIBBEAN, PACIFIC)

Right from the start, the EU has taken over the responsibility for easy access of producers of the former French colonies in sub-Saharan Africa to the EU market. After the UK joined the EU, the schemes were extended to the former British colonies, whose economic structure resembled that of the associated states. The present scheme applies to some 70 so-called ACP countries, including practically all countries in sub-Saharan Africa and some few, very small countries scattered across the Caribbean and Pacific areas.[12] The main provisions of the scheme are the following.

- *Tariff preferences*; almost the entire ACP exports have access to the EU market free of any tariff or quota.[13] In that sense the ACP countries have a better deal than the other developing countries (see below), which are subject to formal and informal quantitative restrictions.
- *MFN.* The EU tariff preferences are non-reciprocal; the agreement stipulates only that the ACP countries grant imports from the EU the same favourable treatment that is allowed to the most-favoured developed country.
- *Agriculture.* ACP exports to the EU of products coming under the CAP receive, within some quantitative limits, a reduction of the EU levies on many agricultural imports (Chapter 9).

The *effects* of these agreements have been disappointing for ACP countries. The early association agreement has, as its main effect, produced slight windfall gains (due to higher export prices) to exporters in ACP countries (Young, 1972). The first Lomé convention produced small trade-creation effects for its participating countries. The ACP countries have not benefited from the extension of the EU; their losses on EU6 markets were hardly offset by their gains on the UK market (Moss, 1982). The experience of the 1980s and 1990s is not any better; notwithstanding some success stories of export growth and diversification, the ACP share in total EU imports

---

12   The ACPs are neither a political group nor an economic entity: ACPs as a group exist only in the framework of relations with the EU. So it seems as if the group might better be split up into three sub-groups, the countries of each sub-group joining strong regional integration schemes in their own geographical area.

13   Access is granted for goods which can be shown to originate for more than 50 per cent of the value added in the country itself, in other ACP countries, or in an EU country.

has halved over the period. The main reasons for this poor performance are armed conflicts, lack of initial endowments and absence of stable institutions and sound policies (realistic and stable exchange rates, good governance, reduced trade protection) (EC, 1996f).

The value of the ACP preferences stands to decline further as a consequence of multilateral liberalisation and other EU-centred preferential trade agreements (for example, the Mediterranean).

GENERALISED SYSTEM OF PREFERENCES (GSP) (LATIN AMERICA AND ASIA)

The group of developing countries is confronted with considerable problems in accessing world markets. The EU has tried to alleviate certain of these problems[14] by establishing preferential trade relations with this group of countries. The UNCTAD adage 'trade instead of aid' has been important in this context. The European Generalised System of Preference (GSP) was set in place in 1971 and follows ten-year cycles; the last one covered the period 1995–2005. It has the following distinctive features:[15]

- Status. The EU version of GSP is not an agreement concluded between two or more parties after negotiations. It is autonomously granted by the EU to a number of beneficiary countries. The EU can unilaterally decide to change it or even withdraw it completely.
- Instrument. The scheme offers a tariff preference: in general, goods coming under the GSP are imported into the EU tariff-free, whereas non-GSP countries face the full CET. There is no reciprocity; EU exports to GSP countries receive MFN treatment.
- Product coverage. The GSP is confined to semi-manufactured and manufactured goods and excludes agriculture.[16] For a list of sensitive goods,[17] it used to be limited to sometimes fairly restricted quotas. The 1995 GSP abolished tariff quotas and ceilings. A critical look at the product structure reveals that the products that are of most interest to GSP countries have received the least benefits.
- Countries selected. The GSP is in principle available to all developing countries, but the EU has specified those to which it agrees to give GSP status. In 2004 it applied to 178 countries. Some countries (such as ACP and Mediterranean) prefer other, more advantageous schemes; that leaves Latin American and Asian countries as the most important beneficiaries.
- 'Graduation'. Although the GSP was initially a non-discriminatory scheme, in practice it has developed into a highly complicated and selective arrangement. Indeed the trade advantages are differentiated according to the level of development of the country

---

14   See Stevens (1981). The major problems facing developing countries participating in world trade are:
- Agriculture. In the developed countries, demand is growing only slowly owing to the low income elasticity of food, while production is increasing owing to support schemes and increased productivity. World markets are distorted by dumping and export subsidies to agricultural production in the developed world. Prices tend to fluctuate very heavily around a downward trend.
- Manufacture. Developing countries face protective tendencies on the part of developed countries, because their competitiveness threatens the viability of the older sectors in developed countries.
15   See Hine (1985); Langhammer and Sapir (1987); EC (2004i).
16   The CAP has repulsed external suppliers from the EU market and it has thrown its huge agricultural surpluses on the world market with almost unlimited subsidies. This has driven developing countries out of their traditional home and export markets, and caused a steep drop in world market prices, and hence in the export earnings of developing countries (see, for instance, Matthews, 1985; IBRD, 1985).
17   For a list of so-called 'sensitive products' (goods whose increased imports would cause serious damage to certain European producers) quotas were set on a national basis, both on the EU (importer) side and on that of the exporters. Davenport (1986) reported that the EU GSP involved some 40 000 different EU-wide and bilateral quotas and ceilings. Moreover, some products, such as textiles, which were ruled by the Multi-Fibre Arrangement (MFA), were completely excluded from the application of the GSP.

involved (low for relatively highly developed) and the type of goods traded (for example, low for relatively high tech).[18]

The *evaluation* of the effect of the GSP on EU–LDC trade starts from an analysis of the penetration of LDCs into the EU market. For quite a few branches of manufactured products (such as textiles and clothing) the picture is positive. For others (food), market shares have stagnated.[19]

The welfare gains of the GSP differed by area. In the first decades of its existence the scheme produced gains to the beneficiary GSP countries that amounted to some 2 per cent of GDP. The EU registered a loss of about 0.5 per cent. Third countries had lost no welfare as far as the manufacturing sectors were concerned, but about 1 per cent in agriculture (Davenport, 1986; Langhammer and Sapir, 1987). In the late 1980s and 1990s, the effect of the tariff preference was very small as a consequence of two factors: first, the multitude of controls for sensitive products, and second, the decrease of the preference margin as a result of the decrease in MFN tariffs. This latter factor increases in importance, as the EU concludes free trade agreements with a whole spectrum of countries at the same or at a lower level in the EU trade pyramid. Cases in point are the successor states of the Soviet bloc and the members of integration schemes like Mercosur (South America) and NAFTA (Mexico).

A particularly interesting case among countries with GSP status is China. Exports from China to the EU have been developing at a very high pace. As EU exports have lagged behind, a considerable trade deficit of the EU has developed. China has overtaken both the ACP and the Mediterranean countries groupings as a trade partner of the EU and is poised to grow even further.

MOST-FAVOURED-NATION (MFN) (USA, JAPAN AND OTHERS)

There is a group of countries with which the EU has established trade relations on the basis of the most-favoured-nation treatment. To this group belong all non-European industrialised countries. Among these, the USA and Japan take pride of place, while others, like Australia, are less important to the EU. We have already indicated that trade among GATT/WTO partners has been considerably liberalised in successive rounds of tariff reductions.

The trade relations with the *USA* reveal a special importance. The EU and the USA are the two most important trading partners in the world, each accounting for some 20 per cent of total trade in goods and services. Moreover, the EU and the USA are each others' most important trading partner (see Table 5.4). We recall that a similar situation applies to FDI (see Table 8.1). With such intensity of contacts it need come as no surprise that there is also much room for conflict. The trade relations between the USA and the EU have for a long time been strained over the CAP. Other disputes concern competition matters (the conflict over state subsidies to Airbus and Boeing). In the latest GATT/WTO negotiations the EU and the USA have agreed to a fair amount of liberalisation of trade in agricultural products. In the same way substantial progress has been made in the liberalisation of the trade in services. They have,

---

18   The most generous preferences have been given to the 49 least developed countries; under the 'everything but arms' initiative virtually all imports of these countries can enter the EU duty free. EU support is given to GSP countries on programmes to combat drugs production and trafficking, compliance with environmental protection agreements or the implementation of labour standards.
19   See Kol (1987). More recent data are based on OECD Foreign Trade and Industrial statistics. Note that the impact has been different for different sub-periods. By the mid-1970s GSP had led to a trade expansion of some 15 per cent of all eligible exports; trade diversion was slight (about 2 per cent) (Baldwin and Murray, 1977).

moreover, agreed to regular bilateral talks on trade and related matters in the framework of Transatlantic Economic Partnership.

The trade relations of the EU with *Japan* have been strained for one major reason, namely the considerable deficit on the commercial balance between the two. While in 1970 the trade balance was still practically in equilibrium, in the early 1990s EU exports to Japan covered only 30 per cent of its imports from that country. In recent years the situation has become more balanced again. The EU has made an agreement on mutual recognition, limiting the number of disputes over regulatory differences that hinder trade.

Other economic policies

COMMON MARKET, PRODUCTION FACTORS

For the external relations engendered by the Common Market there is nothing comparable to the regime for trade. The competence of the EU with respect to the external dimension of production factors (already touched upon in Chapters 7 and 8) are limited and different for labour and capital.

For *labour* the EU has for most of the past period resembled a free trade area. There is full freedom of internal movement for EU nationals. External relations with respect to the movement of both workers and non-active persons from third countries were governed by unilateral policy measures of individual member states and by bilateral agreements that each of the individual member countries had concluded with third countries. Member states have worked out administrative rules for controlling immigration of non-EU citizens. As these controls cannot be perfect, countries are confronted with illegal immigration. The EU has recently committed itself to work out a common policy towards immigration (permanent stay) and a common visa policy (temporary stay), which would bring the EU in line with the definition of Common Market in this area. Unlike the situation for trade, there is no institution on the world level that is empowered to deal with migration matters, so the EU is likely to proceed by unilateral rules or bilateral agreements with the most concerned third countries. The rules that apply now are as follows:

- *European Economic Area.* The EEA Treaty stipulates that the present internal EU rules on freedom of movement will be applicable over the whole EEA area for nationals of all EU and EFTA countries; additional rules for third country nationals.
- *Central and Eastern Europe.* The association agreements between the EU and the CEEC liberalise the movement of workers to the extent that this is conditional for the transformation of the CEEC economies (for example, specialists and managers). For the rest it is regulated by bilateral agreements.
- *Other.* There is some coordination of member states' immigration policies (both for workers and others); however, this has not yet resulted in a common policy.[20]

Restrictive measures do not take away the 'root' causes of migration, which means that the pressure on the EU will continue. To step up the effectiveness of the restrictive immigration policy, two types of complementary measures are taken. The first, with a short-run objective,

---

20   On many detailed points, such as visas, passports, asylum seekers and so on, some form of coordination has existed for some time on the basis of concerted practices of the national administrations.

concerns the introduction of a clause in the cooperation agreements which the EU concludes with the countries on the southern and eastern borders of the EU: (1) to take back their citizens who are expelled from the EU because they have no permit to stay; and (2) to take responsibility for sending back to their home countries those citizens of third countries having passed illegally into the EU through the territory of the country in question. The second, with a long-term objective, is the improvement of the conditions in the sending countries: hence the importance of aid programmes like Phare and Tacis for the CEECs and like MEDA for North Africa (see next sections and Molle, 1996).

For capital, external free movement has practically been realised by the mid-1990s; some EU countries maintain specific types of capital controls in view of specific internal policy objectives. Much of the integration in capital markets was not achieved by EU countries among themselves (see Chapter 8), but by individual EU countries with the offshore capital markets. The efficiency of these markets required that the full liberalisation of the EU capital market be accompanied by a policy of external openness of EU countries 'erga omnes'; that is, free movement towards partner and third countries alike. Indeed the capital-diversion effects of any EU-wide control would have been too costly to be acceptable for countries that had already opened up to the rest of the world. The Maastricht Treaty installed such an EU policy of complete openness towards third countries for capital transactions; it permits, however, some restrictions in the form of safeguard measures. The EU policy of external openness is based on a unilateral decision; there is no GATT/WTO type of international agreement concluded for capital transactions. The agreements that the EU has concluded with its partners hardly mention capital movements, and in cases where they do (for example, the EU–Med programme) the relevant clauses do not seem to have much effect in practice.

ECONOMIC UNION: MARKET POLICIES

In the past little progress has been made with the external dimensions of the *various policies* that define an economic union.

Allocation policies are hardly coordinated with third countries. The noteworthy exception is competition policy. There are two origins of distortions which determine that this policy should be coordinated. The first are national governments; state aids do distort trade and the WTO has set rules against it.[21] The second are giant multinational firms that may inhibit competition by their inter-firm agreements. Cases in point are the control of mergers that can impede fair competition on both the EU and the US markets. There is in the meantime an understanding between the EU and US competition authorities to coordinate their actions in cases that involve companies from either partner. Attempts to come to a multilateral approach (through the WTO) have been aborted as many developing countries were very opposed to the idea (see also Chapter 18).

A special form of unification of internal market policies applies to the EFTA, the CEECs and Turkey that adapt their legislation in such a way that it becomes compatible with the EU rules on the internal market. Farthest advanced along this road are the *EFTA* countries. The EU has concluded an arrangement with EFTA countries that implies the implementation of the *acquis communautaire* by EFTA, with flanking policies in the fields of social affairs, transport, R&D and environmental protection. The European Court of Justice has been made competent to settle any disputes according to common rules. The *CEEC* have in the past embarked on similar programmes to adopt the *acquis* in the framework of their accession to the EU. For ten

---

21   See Box 20.1.

of them this has been superseded by their membership of the Union; for the remaining CEECs and for Turkey progress is as yet very uneven (see the next section and Chapter 18).

MONETARY UNION; MONETARY AND FISCAL POLICIES

Stabilisation policies, if coordinated internationally, have the same type of advantages as was pointed out for internal EU coordination (Chapter 15). Such global coordination is progressing only slowly, however. The EU involvement in the work of the groups charged with coordinating the macro and monetary policies (the Group of Seven largest developed countries) is increasing. The need for coordination and stabilisation of exchange rates on the world scale is most acute for the stabilisation of the key currency, the US dollar. The variations in the dollar/euro exchange rate (see Figure 17.1) were particularly wide in the 1970s and 1980s. Since the introduction of the euro the exchange rate of the US dollar has again shown significant variability. The determinants of these changes are ill-understood, and few models have been able to heed the past, let alone predict the future.[22] However, differences between countries in government spending and productivity levels (growth) are important next to monetary variables and the swap of holdings of international currencies by Central Banks of third countries. Taken in a historical perspective the recent euro/dollar exchange rate volatility does not seem to be exceptional.

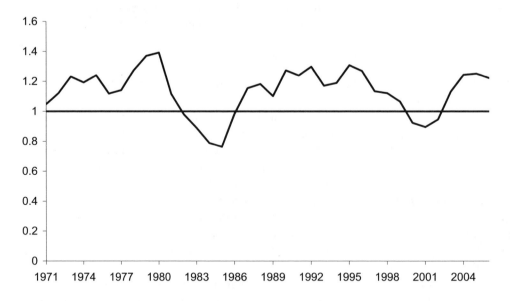

Dollar/euro exchange rate over time, 1971-2006

Figure 17.1   Dollar/euro exchange rate over time: (€/$)

The creation of the euro changes the relations of the EU to the outside world because the euro has a certain potential to become an international currency. Indeed the euro covers a quarter of world GDP and two fifths of world trade. At present, however, the US dollar fulfils the role of international currency practically alone. The various functions that are implied are given in Table 17.3.

---

22   See, for example, Helleman and Hens (1999); Rogoff (1999).

Table 17.3 Private and public functions of an international currency

Money function	Private sector use	Public sector use
Means of payments or medium of exchange	*Vehicle currency* used to settle international trade and to discharge international financial obligations	*Intervention currency* used in foreign exchange markets and currency used for balance of payments financing
Unit of account (numeraire)	*Quotation currency* used to denominate international financial instruments and to invoice foreign trade transactions	*Pegging currency* used in expressing exchange rate relationships and as an anchor for other currencies
Store of value	*Investment currency* used to denominate deposits, loans and bonds	*Reserve currency* used as international reserves by monetary authorities

Source: Hartmann (1998).

Having a dominant international currency offers the country concerned on one hand political and economic benefits. But there are, on the other hand, significant costs (Eijffinger and de Haan, 2000). In the past, the balance between the two was such that Germany was not willing to let the deutschmark take on the functions of an international currency. As long as the British pound and the NMS currencies have not become part of the euro, the potential for the euro to take on the various functions described in Table 17.3 outside the realm of the relations of the euro zone with third parties seem to be rather limited.

External Aid

AID TO DEVELOPMENT

The EU and its member states have both a moral obligation and good economic reasons to cooperate to achieve a better distribution of wealth at the world level. A large share of the population of the world has not participated in the considerable increase in wealth that the world has witnessed over the past decades and still lives in conditions of (sometimes extreme) poverty. Right from its beginnings the EU has committed itself to contribute to a better distribution of global wealth and notably to poverty alleviation. As development depends to a large extent on trade conditions, and trade policy is a common EU policy, there were good reasons for a common EU development policy too. So the Treaty of Rome provided for a common EU aid policy by setting up a European Development Fund (EDF). The EU gives aid in the form of grants and loans. It is complementary to that given on a bilateral basis by the individual EU member states, and to the aid given on a multilateral basis by other donors (for example, the World Bank).[23]

The distribution of EU aid by countries has changed over time as a function of changing geopolitical circumstances.[24] Initially, aid has been concentrated on the ACP countries but, recently, more attention has been given to other countries, for example, the Mediterranean countries (including Palestine) and South Africa.

The total amount of *aid to ACP countries* is some € 2 billion a year, financed from the European Development Fund (EDF). Most of the aid is given in two basic forms:[25]

- *Investment.* The EDF provides loans and grants to facilitate investment in infrastructure, both of an economic type (roads, ports, water) and of a social type (hospitals, schools, information and trade-promotion institutions) and to productive investments in agriculture, mining, industry and energy. Investment is also promoted by loans from the European Investment Bank (EIB).[26]
- *Stabilisation of export earnings.* If the value of an ACP country's exports to the EU drops by more than a certain minimum percentage, the EU compensates for the initial loss with a transfer of money. The STABEX (agricultural) and SYSMIN (mineral products) systems apply only to products contributing substantially to the country's total export earnings.

The *evaluation* of the EU development policy *vis-à-vis* the Lomé countries produces a mixed picture. In general, EU aid does not seem to have been less effective than other aid schemes. Financial and technical cooperation matches in general both the objectives of the donor and the needs of the recipient countries. Effectiveness is found to be relatively high, notably as regards infrastructure and social projects. However, the poor state of the institutions and ill-devised economic policies have, in many of the recipient countries, been major constraints in raising living standards and the level of development.

EU development policy towards the *Mediterranean countries* has gradually got off the ground. Many Mediterranean countries receive aid in various forms from the EU. The MEDA programme, which is destined for the eastern and southern Mediterranean region, is the principal one. It makes about € 1 billion a year available. Approximately half this amount is spent on aid to structural adjustment, development of private enterprise and the improvement of production factors. The other half is available for projects in technical and social infrastructure.

During the 1990s the EU diversified its aid in terms of recipient countries. There is some € 1 billion a year available for aid to countries in *Asia, Latin America and South Africa*. The reason for this greater attention is largely of a political nature. The EU supports projects in countries that are in line with EU objectives. Examples are the support to the set-up and functioning of regional integration schemes (see Chapter 19) and to countries that are willing to cooperate with the EU in international fora to come to solutions for worldwide problems

---

23   Redistribution policies towards third countries are hardly the subject of coordination on the world level. This adds to the difficulties of many recipient countries in devising consistent programmes of development. In order to help developing countries with their structural reform, equilibration of the balance of payments and the establishment of sound public finance, the EU provides macro financial assistance in the form of loans.

24   For a more thorough treatment, see Cox and Chapman (1999).

25   There are two more forms worth mentioning:
- *Structural adaptation.* See note 23
- *Food aid.* The provision of food to people in areas struck by acute famine is taken from the EU stocks (or surpluses from the farm policy; see Chapter 9). Recently an evaluation study of independent experts concluded that the 'impacts of EU programme food aid have been, on balance, marginally positive, but its provision has involved very high transaction cost suggesting the need for radical changes to improve effectiveness and efficiency' (Clay *et al.*, 1996).

26   The EIB can only help to finance profitable projects.

(such as global warming). Finally, EU aid is given for purely humanitarian purposes (famine, relief for countries that recover from war, the fight against HIV).

AID TO TRANSITION AND ACCESSION

The European Union has supported the CEECs in their transition from a centrally planned economy to a market economy. The major programme is Phare (originally an acronym for Poland and Hungary Action for the Restructuring of the Economy; subsequently applicable to all CEECs that are candidate members of the EU). Similar programmes exist for the NIS (newly independent states or the successor states of the former Soviet Union and Mongolia). The major programme is Tacis (originally an acronym for Technical Assistance to the Commonwealth of Independent States).

Most CEECs have rapidly opted to become members of the EU. They saw large advantages in the adoption of the EU model for setting up their market economy institutions, as this would provide stability and predictability for all those involved in transition and modernisation. The EU has replied by defining the criteria for membership. These choices have entailed a change in the basic objective of the *Phare programme*; it has been mainly oriented towards the objective to prepare the beneficiary countries for EU membership. The basic features of Phare are:

- Funds are offered as non-reimbursable grants and not in the form of loans.
- Projects eligible for support must enhance (1) the process of reform (for example, privatisation), (2) the build-up of technical infrastructure (transport, telecommunications) and social infrastructure (institutions, public administration, social services and health), (3) the development of private enterprise (agriculture, energy), (4) the improvement of human capital (training), and (5) conditions for sustained growth (environmental protection).
- Recipient countries need to propose the relevant programmes for EU support; the EU, however, often provides technical assistance, studies and so on, to set them up.

Two other funds were created:

- ISPA (Instrument for Structural Policies Pre Accession) has been set up, which is mostly oriented towards projects in environment and transport infrastructure.
- SAPARD (Special Action Programme for Agriculture and Regional Development) provides support for the structure of agriculture.

The three different programmes mentioned have their own rules as to eligibility of projects, administrative operations, and so on. These have been adapted to resemble more the mechanism of the structural funds (see Chapter 16). This helped the candidate countries to become familiarised with the EU way of providing financial support to development.

The size of the budget for implementing the pre-accession strategy (Phare, ISPA and SAPARD) is very considerable (more than € 3 billion a year after 2000). The Tacis programme is smaller in size, accounting for some € 1 billion a year. Additional financial support comes from the European Investment Bank and from the European Bank for Reconstruction and Development.[27] In order to step up the *effectiveness* of aid to the CEECs, the EU has assumed the role of coordinator of the support of both EU and third countries' aid to them.

---

27   For more details on aid to CEECs and NIS, see Cox and Chapman (1999).

Non-economic external policies

FOREIGN POLICY

External *policies for non-economic areas* have gradually become an EU matter for two reasons. Third countries increasingly tended to look upon the Union as one political entity and expect a common EU stand on a large variety of diplomatic issues (such as human rights in China, or peacekeeping in former Yugoslavia). Moreover, the member states have increasingly become aware of the fact that coordinated foreign policies tend to increase the effectiveness of individual member states' actions (for instance, in the fight against terrorism). In the 1960s a timid start was made with regular meetings of the Ministers of Foreign Affairs of EU countries regarding diplomatic questions. In the 1970s, the European Political Cooperation (EPC) was created as an intergovernmental 'institution', not linked to the EU framework. The centrepiece of the EPC was the commitment to consultation with partners before adopting final positions or launching national initiatives on all important questions of foreign policy common to EU member countries, and to the joint implementation of actions. Over the years the cooperation has steadily intensified and its scope has continually broadened. The dissociation of the EPC from the normal EU institutions was increasingly felt to be a problem. This led, first, to the regular participation of the president of the Commission and the Commissioner for External Relations in the EPC conferences. Next the EPC was formally hooked onto the EU institutional framework by the Single European Act, without much alteration to its objectives or its intergovernmental features. The Treaty on European Union has brought the Common Foreign Policy (CFP) under the EU umbrella. As external economic and diplomatic issues are closely intertwined, the Presidency (Council) and the Commission have to ensure the consistency of the two policies.[28]

The EU common foreign policy is closely intertwined with the external economic policy. On one hand the EU uses economic instruments (carrots and sticks) to foster non-economic objectives. The carrots are generally increased aid to countries that comply with agreements on, for instance, the combating of global warming (Kyoto Protocol), cooperation in the fight against terrorism or peace processes (Palestine). Sticks are less in use, although the EU has used sanctions (for instance, against South Africa), or imposed export restrictions on strategically important goods (for instance arms to China).[29]

SECURITY (DEFENCE) POLICY

A particularly important matter in the context of a European external policy is defence. The history of this starts right from the birth of the EEC. One of the major objectives envisaged with the creation of the EU was to contribute to a durable peace; however, its pursuit was to be made by economic means, not by military ones. We may bring to mind that, after the failure of the European Defence Community in the 1950s, European defence matters were

---

28   To improve the effectiveness of common foreign policy making and implementation, the draft Constitution introduced a European Minister of Foreign Affairs (Art III 197), who combines the roles of the Commissioner for External Relations and the acting president of the Council of Ministers of Foreign Affairs.
29   For the limited effectiveness of economic sanctions, see Hufbauer and Scott (1985), van Bergeijk (1987) and Kaempfer and Loewenberg (1992). Mind that the EU can also be the target of such instruments. An example was the selective oil embargo of Arab states against some EU countries in the 1970s. Such a situation is unlikely to occur again as the EU CFP mechanism is designed to prevent such selectivity from occuring, while the high level of internal integration makes its implementation practically unfeasible.

treated in international bodies such as NATO (North Atlantic Treaty Organisation) and the WEU (Western European Union). Most of the EU member states (the exceptions being Ireland, Sweden, Finland and Austria) were members of both NATO and the WEU. The WEU was created by the Treaty of Brussels in 1954 to strengthen peace and security. In the past attempts have been made to merge its institutional structure with that of the EU. That has been realised by the Treaty on European Union; the WEU has since been indeed considered an integral part of the development of the European Union, since most of the WEU's role and resources for intervention have been transferred to the EU. Like foreign policy, defence policy is carried out in an intergovernmental way (under the responsibility of the Council of Ministers deciding with unanimity).

In the 1990s the EU assumed a role in the solution of the civil war in Yugoslavia. The record of this intervention is generally considered poor. In other matters of global importance (crisis in Afghanistan, Iraq war) the EU has been completely overshadowed by the US. The evident importance of effective defence for the security of the EU has incited the EU leaders to set up a common European Security and Defence Policy (ESDP). This has to be carried out in line with the obligations which the EU countries have in the frameworks of NATO and the UN (Security Council). The ESDP consists mainly of political and military coordination and decision structures and the capacity to react quickly and independently with the use of military force, with the objectives of preventing crises, keeping peace and containing conflicts.

Summary and conclusions

- The EU is based on a customs union; in practice its external relations are mostly trade relations. However, its progress towards economic and monetary union has drawn other areas, such as immigration, international capital and monetary matters, into the domain of EU external policy. Moreover, the EU has recently integrated a number of non-economic elements in a full-dress EU external policy.
- A complicated system of trade advantages, differentiated according to specific groups of countries, has been drawn up for mainly political reasons. The system has not produced the economic effects hoped for. Under pressure from GATT/WTO, the EU system has been considerably simplified.
- The common commercial policy has used a spread of instruments to regulate trade and protect EU industry. However, the EU has consistently moved towards greater liberalisation of world trade and, apart from agricultural matters, is fairly open to third country suppliers.
- The external relations implied in the establishment of the Common Market (labour, capital) and the Economic and Monetary Union (for example, competition and currency policy) have only very timidly developed. Part of this is due to the absence of global institutions that could provide the platform for negotiations and the framework for agreements.
- The EU has concluded cooperation agreements and partnerships with a kaleidoscope of individual countries and groupings of counties covering a large diversity of issues. These are the results of efforts to reach EU policy objectives such as wealth creation, democracy, sustainability by a coordinated use of instruments of external economic policies and the common foreign and security policy.

5 *Conclusions and Lessons*

18 *Evaluation*

Introduction

The objective of this book has been to present an economic analysis of the process of European integration. To that end we described in the first part the conceptual basis, the historical roots and the institutional framework of integration. In the second part we discussed the theoretical foundations and empirical dynamics of the customs union and common market, with at their centre the freedom of movement of goods, services, labour and capital. The changes in the organisation of economic activity in the various sectors of the economy under the influence of economic integration occupied the central place in this book. As freedoms cannot flourish nor economic sectors develop unless government creates the proper conditions, a discussion of the policies pursued with these goals in mind complemented the book.

At the end of this analysis of separate segments, a more general view of the dynamics of the whole process of European economic integration seems in order. To measure the progress of integration we will make a distinction between indicators of a more economic nature, such as the share of trade in total GDP, and the more policy-oriented indicators, such as the limitation of power of nation states in different segments of economic policy. As economic integration is to be instrumental to the attainment of higher goals, we will evaluate its contribution to the growth and the distribution of welfare and to a number of non-economic objectives of integration.

The economic integration of Europe is a process of long duration that is far from being completed. In the future, integration will further progress along the axes of deepening (new fields of competence) and widening (the geographical extension of the EU). We will sketch the likely developments on these issues in a somewhat speculative approach that is quite different from the rigour with which we have presented the theoretical and empirical results in all previous parts of the book. As usual a short summary completes the chapter.

Progress of integration; economic indicators

QUANTITIES

A usual way to measure the progress of integration is by looking at the evolution of the quantities traded or exchanged. For goods and services this is done in practice by measuring the extent to which the production of one country is consumed in another. In much the same way, the advance of integration on the markets for production factors can be assessed by the change in the extent to which the labour and capital of one country are put to work in another. Both indicators have been employed in the detailed analysis of the preceding chapters. Table 18.1 combines the dispersed results.

Table 18.1 Growth of market integration in the EU (goods, services, labour and capital) (%), 1960–2003

		1960[a]	1970[a]	1980[a]	1990[a]	2000[a]	2003[b]
Customs Unions							
Goods[c]	Intra	6	10	13	15	16	19
	Extra	9	8	10	9	10	9
Services[c] Intra		1	2	3	3	4	5
	Extra	1	1	1	2	4	3
Common Market							
Labour[d] Intra		2	2	2	2	2	n.a.
	Extra	1	3	3	3	3	n.a.
Capital DI[e]	Intra	n.a.	1	1	3	26	n.a.
	Extra	n.a.	1	2	2	13	n.a.
Capital income[f] Intra		n.a.	—	1	2	5	4
	Extra	n.a.	1	2	3	3	4

Notes: [a] *EU15* [b] *EU25* [c] *Average of imports and exports as a percentage share of GDP; EU15; 1960 estimates.* [d] *Non-nationals as a percentage of total labour force.* [e] *Direct investment; four-year averages. Average of inflows and outflows as a percentage share of Gross Fixed Capital Formation; 1960–90: EU12.* [f] *Income from investments abroad as a percentage of GDP; 1970–80: EU12.*

Sources: Goods: Chapter 5; services: Chapter 6 plus some estimates based on balance-of-payments data; labour: Chapter 7; capital: Chapter 8, plus some estimates based on balance-of-payments data.

For goods and services, the figures leave little room for doubt. By 2003, EU countries had become far more integrated with their partners than in 1960. The integration of the EU in the world economy has not suffered from this dynamism; the ratio of extra-EU imports and exports to GDP for goods and services remained more or less stable during the study period. Looking specifically at the goods trade, we observe that the orientation of trade has changed under the influence of integration. In 1960, trade in goods was more oriented towards third countries than to (potential) partner countries, whereas in 2003 intra-EU relations largely outweighed the extra-EU ones. For services, intra-EU trade has always been of the same order of magnitude as extra-EU trade. The increase in internationalisation is visible for both intra- and extra-EU trade; the latter, of course, reflects the growing importance of the world economy (for example, transport, insurance) for EU producers and consumers.

For *labour*, the figures indicate that only a small percentage of labour in EU countries is of foreign origin, and that this percentage has been very stable over the last decades. The average percentage share of labour from other EU member countries in the total labour force of the member countries of the EU15 oscillated within a narrow band around 2 per cent between 1960 and 2000. For workers from outside the EU15, the level is rather low, too. A steep increase in the 1960s was followed by a levelling off in the 1970s and 1980s. (Another increase in recent years is not visible in the figures due to rounding.) In interpreting this indication of limited integration, one should remember that massive migration flows were never an objective of the EU. On the contrary, the movement of capital to, and the differential growth of, the economies of poor member countries were intended to keep intra-EU migration in check (see Chapter 7), while national admittance laws regulated immigration from third countries.

For *capital*, the quantities exchanged can only be studied for direct investment, figures for other forms of capital movement not being available. Within the EU, foreign direct investment has been fully liberalised since the 1970s. Although its volume increased considerably in the past decades, its share in total Gross Fixed Capital Formation (GFCF) remained modest. EU countries used to be less oriented to their partners than to third countries; this was due as much to heavy EU investment activity abroad as to foreign (third country) investment in EU countries. However, in recent years the interrelations among EU countries have been developing very rapidly (even faster than those with third countries) and now outweigh extra-EU relations. The recent figures reflect the effect of the single market and of the general upsurge of FDI in recent years.

Another indicator of the integration of capital markets is the income received from investment abroad (both DI and portfolio). The figures available show a very fast increase for both external and internal EU relations. The increasingly global character of capital markets is reflected in the relative importance of the extra-EU relations with respect to the relations among EU countries themselves.

PRICES

The progress of integration can also be measured by the convergence of prices for the same goods and services and production factors in the various countries of the EU. However, the international comparison of prices is beset with difficulties, both of a methodological and a statistical nature. The few figures available are reviewed hereafter (Table 18.2).

Table 18.2   Price convergence for goods, services and production factors, 1975–2000

Indicator	1975	1980	1985	1990	1995	2000
Customs Union[a]						
Consumer goods						
(tax-inclusive)	21	20	19	20	18	12
(tax-exclusive)	16	19	18	19	17	14
Equipment goods						
(tax-inclusive)	14	13	13	12	13	n.a.
(tax-exclusive)	14	13	13	n.a.	n.a.	n.a.
Common Market[b]						
Capital[c]						
LT interest rate	20	23	23	14	24	n.a.

Notes: [a] *Index of dispersion (see Chapter 5); the lower the indices the higher the integration. EU12, 1995=93, 2000=1999, EU15.* [b] *Data on wages not available (see Chapter 7).* [c] *Divergence indicator (see Chapter 8) of the long-term interest rates; the lower the indicator the higher the integration. EU7. Value of the indicator in the 1960–70 decade: 15. No data for 2000, given the differences between EMU and non-EMU countries.*

Goods   There was significant convergence of the prices of consumer goods and almost no convergence in prices for equipment goods. More detailed material shows that this is the result of two opposing trends: in branches open to competition, prices tended to converge, while they diverged for branches with many NTBs. The internal market programme has led to stronger competition for an increasing number of branches; in the figures for the most recent period, the effect is visible in the decreasing value of the disparity indicator (Chapter 5).

Services   The few data available for the period up to the end of the 1980s show considerable price differences and no tendency towards convergence, which is in keeping with the limited integration of this sector. As a result of the liberalisation programme, prices have converged somewhat in recent years (Chapters 6 and 12).

Wages   The price of labour appears to have shown a gradual convergence. However, the measuring of this trend is not very easy, while it is even less easy to identify the integration effect (Chapters 7 and 16).

Capital   Prices on the markets for short-term and long-term loans have shown about the same tendencies over the past integration period; the amplitude of the changes has been higher for the short term than for the long term. There was some convergence up to 1973. The turbulence of the first oil shock brought a clear divergence. From the mid-1980s to 1993, capital prices converged again, under the influence of the stabilisation of exchange rates in the European Monetary System and the measures of liberalisation of capital movements by many countries. Under the influence of the monetary turmoil of 1993, divergence occurred again. Recently, owing to the creation of the EMU, very strong convergence has been observed among EMU member countries and some between EMU and non-EMU countries (Chapters 8 and 15).

Progress of integration; policy indicators

INSTITUTIONS; GROWTH OF OPERATIONS

Looking at the European Union as an organisation, we can measure the progress of integration in several ways. The most obvious indicator is the increase in the *number of members*. Indeed widening has been a distinct feature of the dynamics of the EU. Membership has increased at almost regular intervals, from six to 25.

    A second indicator of integration that visualises growth, even to the casual observer, is the *number of people and organisations* involved in EU policy making (input). We give evidence for three groups (Table 18.3).

    EU civil servants employed by the Commission and other EU institutions form the core. Their number has rapidly increased; for example, with the Commission, from 1000 to 24 000 between 1960 and 2000 (in the same period, the total number of civil servants in the member countries of the EU rose from 4 million to about 9 million).

Table 18.3   Growth of activity of those involved in EU operations, 1960–2005[a]

Indicator	1960	1970	1980	1990	2000	2005
Permanent civil servants (x 1000) of EU Commission[b]	1	5	11	17	24	n.a.
Committees[c]	n.a.	70	150	300	1 000	2 700
Number of lobby organisations[d]	167	309	410	3 000	n.a.	n.a.

Notes: [a] *Estimate based on extrapolation of figures for 1990–99.* [b] *Sources: EC General Reports; Official Journal (several years); Eurostat; own estimates.* [c] *Estimates based on, for example, van Schendelen (1998); for 2005 the estimate consists of some 1700 advisory committees and some 1000 plus management committees (list of all committees by DG published in February 2005 at http:europa.eu.int/comm/secretariat_general/) .* [d] *In 1990 transnational producer and professional groups were estimated at some 700; new lobby groups at some 2300; the 3000 groups totalling some 10 000 lobbyists (Anderson and Eliassen, 1991).*

    National civil servants and experts can be found in the first ring around this core. Their increased involvement is reflected by the figures on the growth of the number of committees; their number exploded during the last decades as a consequence of the Commission's increased involvement in many detailed issues of a large number of policy areas. This growth is the more marked as the number of meetings of each committee has also increased. (By the way, the same holds for the meetings of the Council of Ministers, of its working parties and of other institutions such as the European Parliament).

Interest groups form the outer ring of this system. In the 1960–85 period, new lobbyist groups were regularly established, and older ones increased their efforts to influence European policy and decision making by extending their membership and consolidating their presence in the centre of EU decision making. The first to be set up were transnational interest groups in the industrial, commercial and professional spheres. From 1985 to 1990, an upsurge in the growth of lobby groups occurred under the impetus of the single market. Alongside the growth of the traditional ones, many new lobby groups have since appeared on the scene, notably due to the extension of the competences of the EU into areas such as security and home affairs (local authorities, extra-EU interest, and so on).

A third set of indicators concerns the *yearly production of the EU institutions* (output). One can read the rise of the output for instance by the growth in the number of pages of the Official Journal (from 2000 in 1960 to 55 000 in 2000). This growth is parallel with the growth of the number of documents that are made during the preparatory stages preceding the actual publication of policy measures, such as expert studies, committee reports, white papers, communications and so on) with which even the casual observer is in the meantime familiar. We give a more detailed view of the output growth for four other indicators in Table 18.4.

Table 18.4   Growth of production of the EU institutions, 1970-2000

	1970/75	1976/80	1981/85	1986/90	1991/95	1996/2001
Legal acts x 1000						
Regulations, Directives	2.6	6.4	9.0	12.9	12.6	11.4
Recommendations, Opinions	0.1	0.1	0.1	0.1	1.2	1.5
Court Decisions	0.7	1.2	1.8	2.1	2.0	2.5
International Agreements	0.5	0.5	0.5	0.5	0.9	1.2
EU expenditure:						
% EU GDP	0.4	0.7	0.8	0.9	1.0	1.1
% National Budgets	1.0	1.5	1.6	1.8	2.0	2.4

Source: Alesina et al. (2005).

The growth in the number of European *legal acts* (Regulations, Directives, and so on) has been very high particularly at the end of the 1980s and beginning of the 1990s. This reflects a particular effort on two scores. First, the completion of the internal market, entailing a long list of detailed regulation on product qualifications, and abolition of existing national measures. Second, the effort to give substance to the EU environmental policy; with regulation about noise levels, water quality, and so on. We see that the number of Court decisions has grown more or less in step with the other indicators. Particularly interesting, finally, is the growth of the number of international agreements, which shows that the EU has confirmed its identity both *vis-à-vis* third countries and in international fora such as the WTO.

A final indicator may be the *financial resources* deployed in the EU policies. The data for this indicator are given in the bottom part of Table 18.4. One sees that the percentage of GDP that goes via the EU budget has increased from less than half a percentage point to somewhat over one percent. This does indeed reflect a small Europeanisation of the budgets as the EU budget has increased in the same period from 1 to 2.4 per cent of the total of the national budgets.

SUBJECT MATTERS; THE MOVEMENT TO HIGHER STAGES

There are sound economic as well as political reasons to start economic integration with goods markets (customs union), continue with production factors (common market) and conclude with intensified policy integration (economic and monetary union). In that view, the progress of economic integration in Europe can be measured by the stage it has reached at different points in time. Remember, however, that the stages are not strictly successive in the sense that the lower ones have to be fully realised before the higher ones can be tried for. Rather, as remarked earlier (Chapter 2), progress in the higher stages is a condition for the full realisation of the lower ones.

The *Customs Union* was to be realised before the end of the 1960s. The evidence from internal and external trade in goods (Chapters 5, 10 and 17) shows that for large parts of the economy (manufactured goods) that objective has indeed been realised quickly. However, services and some other sectors have remained protected for a long time (Chapters 6, 12 and 17). For these sectors the CU has also been implemented in the framework of the 1992 programme (see Chapter 14). Apart from relics (such as rail transport) and border issues (such as the private provision of services that are generally considered public) this programme is now completed and hence the CU can for all practical purposes be considered as fully realised.

The *Common Market*, implying the abolition of obstacles to the free movement of capital and workers, is an old target. Progress on it has been fairly rapid for large parts of both the labour and capital markets (see Chapters 7 and 8). However, until recently, large sections of both remained excluded. The 1992 programme has almost completely abolished the remaining barriers. Some exceptions persist, such as the lack of freedom to move between the old and new member countries and the lack of a common external regime of the labour market.

Economic and Monetary Union became an objective of the EU in the 1970s. Before that time, a number of common policies had been adopted and the coordination of monetary policy had been prepared. Notably the creation and successful operation of the EMS has paved the way for the creation and implementation of the EMU.

With regard to *full economic union*, in the past, work started on a number of subjects engaging the EU in an even closer integration than that implied by the CM and the EMU. The EU has penetrated fields such as environmental, foreign and defence and science policy.

The growth of the EU through these stages can actually be decomposed in smaller events such as the realisation of the CAP, the adoption of the common external tariff, the start of the European Exchange Rate Mechanism and so on. To each of these events scores can be given in such a way that an index emerges running from 0 (no integration) to 100 (full integration) (Dorrucci et al., 2003). The results are given in Figure 18.1. The growth indicated is for the original members; members that have joined at different moments in time show steeper growth. Some members have caught up with the line in the graph (for example, Austria), some non-euro countries stay somewhat below the line (for example, the UK).

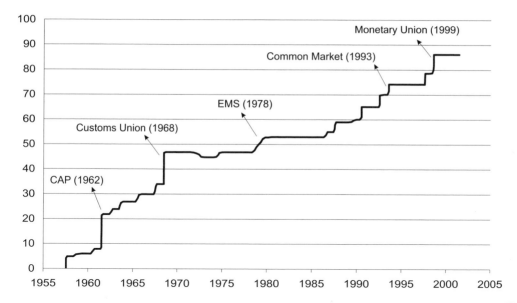

Figure 18.1   Index of integration

Source: Dorrucci et al. (2003) page 177.

INSTRUMENTS: THE SHIFT OF COMPETENCE FROM NATIONAL TO EUROPEAN INSTITUTIONS

All progress of integration tends to curb the freedom of action of the member states' policy makers. The more use is made of higher instruments from the hierarchy (ranging from information via consultation and harmonisation to uniformity; Chapter 2), the more the autonomy of the member states will be limited and the further integration has apparently progressed. The progress in policy integration made since the EU came into existence is indicated in Table 18.5.[1] We limit ourselves here to the period 1960–2000; although on many scores cooperation has intensified and harmonisation become more encompassing, we think that the scores for the year 2000 are still quite adequate for the situation in the first half of the decade.

Before we go into policy issues, let us recall that the situation for the *four freedoms* – of goods, services, labour and capital – is very clear: from the outset their regimes were fully uniform. In principle the member states ceded from the start all relevant authority to the EU. Important limitations have for some time existed for services, capital and labour. Indeed large segments of the service sector were practically unaffected by European integration until the 1992 programme. Until 1990 capital movements were only liberalised as far as was necessary for the functioning of the Common Market. Labour movements have, in transition periods, been restricted.[2]

---

1   The progress on the intensity with which the EU pursues certain policies has been measured in a somewhat different manner by Schmitter (1996) followed by Longo (2003). They define an indicator of the level of authority of the EU and apply it to different policy fields at different years in the period 1950–2000. The scores range from 1 (low) to 5 (high). A comparison of the results of the Schmitter/Longo approach with our approach shows a very high correlation.
2   Although the freedoms were not immediately implemented, we have considered a U to be the best for 1960; a U also for 1990, notwithstanding some rudiments of national discretion.

Table 18.5 Synoptic view of the development through time (1960–2000)[a] of the degree[b] of policy integration,[c] by activity area[d]

Field of action	1960	1970	1980	1990	2000
Allocation					
competition	U*	U*	U*	U*	U*
fiscal	C*	H*	H*	H*	H*
technical	C*	H*	H	H	H
structural	C*	C	C	H	H
Stabilisation					
monetary	C	C	H*	H*	U
macro + budgetary	C	C	C	C	H*
growth policy	I	I	C	C	H*
Cohesion					
regional	I	C	H*	U*	U*
social	H*	H*	H*	H*	H*
External					
trade: goods	U	U	U	U	U
trade: services	I	C	H	U*	U*
prod. factors: labour	O	I*	C	C	C
prod. factors: capital	I*	C	H	U	U
development aid	U*	U*	U*	U*	U*

Notes: [a] *The first column presents the situation at the moment of birth of the EU; the last column describes the recent situation; the middle columns describe the situation just before the first and second extensions.* [b] *O means that there was no EC involvement; I = Information; C = Consultation; H = Harmonisation and U = Unification.* [c] *Evidently, each situation is liable to be characterised differently by different observers; we think, however, that the table gives a fair overall picture.* [d] *The asterisk indicates that only part of the policy field is affected by the indicator given; for that part the highest form is indicated.*

Allocation covers policies that aim at the proper functioning of the common (internal) market, including those that try to improve the structure of productive activity. Right from the start, competition policy was harmonised, some would say even partly unified. Although the scope of the European competition policy has since been broadened and the intensity with which it is pursued stepped up, the situation of the division of competences has remained virtually unchanged. For fiscal, technical and related internal market policies, a timid start with consultation was soon followed by partial harmonisation efforts (for example, for value added in fiscal matters). The EU accepted very early responsibility for a limited part of structural sectoral policy (agriculture, and coal and steel) but, for most sectors, integrating efforts of industrial policy have not passed beyond the stage of consultation. In the 1980s, some large-scale European supply-side programmes were implemented (Esprit, Monitor and so on), for which harmonisation seems to be an apt description.

For *stabilisation* policies – mostly monetary and macro-economic – consultation was foreseen right from the start.[3] In the 1970s and 1980s, consultation was broadened to cover also growth policy. The EMS, created to stabilise exchange rates, can be regarded as a form of harmonisation. EMU brings with it a uniform monetary policy and the harmonisation of macro and growth policies.

---

3   The EEC treaty refers to coodination, but the standard term, 'consultation', describes more adequately the situation that prevailed during this period. Note that the U for 2000 is only partial as not all EU member countries are participating in EMU.

In *cohesion*, we have distinguished between regional, social and territorial policies. The EU started in 1958 without a clear idea about regional policies.[4] By 1973, a consultation procedure had been put into practice. With the creation of the European Regional Development Fund (ERDF), national regional policies were subjected to European harmonisation; with the extension of the scope of the ERDF, partial unification seems the more adequate characterisation. For social policies, the situation is different; the European Social Fund (ESF) was created right at the start of the EU, and there has been considerable development since. Notwithstanding this extension, we indicate partial harmonisation even for 2000, as some very important fields, such as social security, remain largely unaffected by the integration process.

External policies cover a whole array of policies, from trade to defence. The common trade policy (implying uniformity) has been quickly realised for goods, but for services it has only recently got off the ground. External policies for production factors were absent in the 1960s; some coordination began in the 1970s. Recently a common policy for capital was decided on (full external freedom). A part of development aid has been uniform right from the beginning, but the better part of it remained in national (uncoordinated) hands.

Other policies (not discussed in this book) have, in the course of the years, become the object of EU consultation and harmonisation, cases in point being, respectively, environment and home and justice affairs. In the 1980s, some consultation on diplomatic and defence matters started (EPC); this policy has since received new foundations. For many more policies (for example, education) the stage of information has started recently.

Summarising, we find that the use of higher instruments clearly increased over time. Between 1960 and 2000, the number of H scores rose from 1 to 7, the number of U from 3 to 5, while the number of uncoordinated areas diminished (0 scores going down from 5 to 0), I scores from 4 to 0.

Objectives and results

ECONOMIC GROWTH AND EQUAL DISTRIBUTION

Economic integration is not an end in itself but is pursued to realise faster economic growth, that is, wealth improvement. The income effects of market and policy integration of the EU have been substantial. We can summarise the various empirical studies, reported on in the previous chapters, as follows.

For *product markets* the effects have been calculated mostly for manufactured goods, leaving agriculture, energy and services largely out of account. The combined effects of better market entry, increased competition, more innovation, quicker learning and economies of scale amounted to several per cent of GDP.

For *labour markets* the welfare effects spring in particular from the immigration of people from third countries, as migration among EU countries has on the whole been on a low level. The effects of the employment of immigrant workers are not well quantified. Some believe that immigration, by removing certain bottlenecks from the economy, has led to a permanently higher growth of GNP; others point out that immigration has prevented the economies of the EU from adjusting structurally to the new world conditions in comparative advantages.

---

4   Although the EEC Treaty set regional equilibrium as a common objective (as there was a few of the negative side-effects of EU allocation policies), the practice of the formative years of the EC was one of information (see Chapter 6).

For *capital markets* the empirical evidence on the welfare effects of integration is very thin, and differs from one sub-market to another. For direct-investment flows, attention has been limited to employment effects. These seem invariably positive for the host country, but for the home countries vary from negative (when exports from the home bases are replaced) to positive (when the DI facilitates penetration of a foreign market, thus enhancing activity at home as well).

For *common policies* the situation as regards the welfare effect is rather unclear. Although the study of individual policies shows in general positive net effects, the quantification of the growth and welfare effects of the integration of policies (like macro and monetary policies in the framework of the EMU) is still not satisfactory.

A major objective of the EU is to achieve a balanced distribution of this wealth. In other words, the EU strives for a harmonious development of the European economy by reducing the differences in wealth among the various countries and regions. It implies the pursuit of policies leading to higher than average growth rates for low-income countries and regions. The EU has managed to come closer to this objective. Indeed a comparison of the growth figures of the individual member countries with the EU average shows two things: first, that many of the countries that had below average incomes in 1950 have grown at a more than average rate; and, second, that countries that were rich at the outset grew at a below average speed. So in 2000 there was more equality than in 1950. The access to the EU is believed to have had a marked influence on the high growth figures of Italy in the 1960s and of Spain and Portugal in the late 1980s and the early 1990s. For the latter countries this market integration went hand-in-hand with the transfer of considerable amounts of money from the structural funds.

BEYOND ECONOMICS

Economic integration is first and foremost a device to enhance balanced economic growth. However, it is also a method for attaining some non-economic objectives. In recent European history (see Chapter 3) two such objectives have been paramount:

- *Peace.* Countries that are very dependent on one another will not enter easily into an armed conflict.
- *Democracy and human rights.* Attempts to overthrow this order will have little chance of success in an integrated framework that makes membership conditional on respect of these values.

The three objectives – growth, peace and democracy – have had different weights in the setting up and extension of the institutions that in the past have given form to European integration. The Benelux Economic Union only pursued economic objectives, the EU strove for both growth and peace, while EFTA's objective was only growth. The first extension of the EU only had an economic target, whereas for the second both the growth and the democracy argument were used. The enlargement of the EU with three EFTA countries only pursued an economic objective. However, for the extension with the CEEC all three arguments were again very relevant.

PATTERN OF DEVELOPMENT

The objectives of the EU in matters of deepening can be detailed in terms of stages of integration. They have been pursued while at the same time working on the objective of widening. The gradual stepping up of ambitions on both scores and their realisation over time has been summarised in Table 18.6.

Table 18.6   The process of deepening and widening of European integration

Deepening	Widening					
	1944 Benelux	1958 EU6	1972 EU9	1986 EU12	1993 EU15	2004 EU25
ICM		*	*			
CM				*	*	*
EU	*			*	*	*
MU					*	*
PU						*

Looking at the overall process of deepening and widening, we may conclude that the EU has needed in the past about 14 years to forge strong links between the members of a group, working towards the attainment of a well-defined objective. This turned out to be the basis on which a new extended group could start work on a higher objective (for example, EU12 working towards the realisation of the internal market). However, if we analyse the process in rather more depth, we see that there are intermediate steps, too (1952 for the ECSC; 1967 for the first, unsuccessful, negotiations with the UK; 1981 for the accession of Greece; 1993 for the accession of three EFTAns). Extending this dynamism with the same periodicity from the past to the future, we predicted in previous editions of this book that both deepening and widening would proceed in parallel. In line with our predictions, deepening has led to the creation of the EMU by the year 2000 while widening has resulted in a (new round of) accession in 2004.[5]

SUCCESS FACTORS

From the various strands of literature we have distilled the following general factors that have conditioned, in the past, the success of progressive integration.

Unity of purpose   The EU started with a limited number of members around the strong axis of France and Germany. The risk of dilution was limited as extensions were few, occurred only after considerable periods of internal strengthening, and new members were only admitted on the condition that they accepted the '*acquis communautaire*' of the past and the new objectives for the future.

Limited diversity   Differences in levels of development between the members are not very large by world 'standards'. All EU countries belong, indeed, to the category of (highly) developed countries. As a consequence, one could start without intra-EU financial transfers, always a bone of contention, and continue with a redistribution scheme that kept transfers at a relatively low level. This set-up has made it possible to continue to work on programmes for improving allocational efficiency (for instance, the completion of the internal market) and macro-economic stability (for instance, EMU) without the discussion being distorted by distributional issues.

---

5   This implies a period of 18 years, breaking the neat periodicity of the past.

Safety mechanism against reverse developments   The integration of markets, once achieved, cannot be rejected by a member state. Safeguards are the whole EU legal system and the heavy cost that a breakaway would inflict on business that has organised itself on the assumption of durable and reliable access to markets, complemented by common policies.

Institutional strength The powers of the EU to make laws on the basis of qualified majority voting that are, moreover, directly applicable in all member states have permitted this supranational organisation to function relatively effectively and efficiently. The institutional set-up of the EU has reduced very significantly the cost of bargaining, that is of reaching cooperative solutions to political problems in areas where national policies have lost effectiveness.

Operational flexibility   The EU has a diversity of regulatory forms. In many cases the directive is used. This permits much flexibility as to the way in which national authorities actually implement EU regulation in their legislation. If needed, the EU has temporarily permitted exceptions to general rules – for example, with longer transition periods for Mediterranean countries to comply with the rules of the internal market or environmental policy. In some cases it has even permitted the opting out of certain members for whole sections of its activity (as with the UK for the Social Chapter).[6]

CONDITIONS FOR MAJOR PROGRESS

Specific accelerations of the integration process have occurred when a set of conditions was fulfilled. We make here a distinction between deepening and widening.

Success with *deepening* depended on the following conditions:

- clear-cut objectives that can be easily understood by large sections of society (for example, removal of all barriers for the completion of the internal market; one market, one money for EMU);
- tangible gains; felt directly by influential interest groups like big business and supported by independent assessments or by academics (as with the studies on the cost of non-Europe for the benefits of the 1992 programme);
- coherent action for realisation, with a timetable and a clear distribution of roles for the various actors (Commission, industry associations and so on).[7]

The process of *widening* has deliberately started from a narrow base. Extension came on three conditions:

- excess of economic advantages over cost (an acceleration of the growth of GDP offsetting short-term restructuring cost);
- taking away of political barriers (for example, lack of democracy and human rights in Mediterranean and Central and East European countries) and institutional barriers (functioning market economy in CEECs);
- limited strain on the functioning of the EU (no renegotiation of the *'acquis communautaire'*; limited budget outlays; institutional continuity).

---

6   This practice, which has developed over the past, has been enshrined as a constitutional right by the Treaty of Amsterdam. It permits groups of member states to use the EU institutions framework for forms of closer cooperation.
7   See, for instance for the internal market programme, the white paper (EC, 1985a) and subsequent work programme for '1992'.

FAILURES

The EU has not only had successes. On the contrary, its past performance also shows some important failures. These are of two types. The first applies to things that the EU has done and should not have done. The two principal examples, reported in earlier parts of this book, are both related to allocation:

- For a long time the EU has tended to *over-regulate* the economy. It has changed its approach only with the advent of the internal market programme, focusing now on subsidiarity and proportionality.
- The regimes for *agriculture* (and for some time, to a lesser extent, those for steel, energy and transport) have occasioned considerable distortion in markets, leading to inefficient redistribution, to persistent large losses of welfare and to international tensions.

The second type of failures applies to things the EU has not done and should have done. This is a much more difficult nut to crack, as it implies the identification of a number of integration measures that would have led to large welfare increases yet have not been realised or have not been realised in due time. Many things come to mind in this category, such as: the incomplete tax harmonisation leading to tax evasion and fraud; the non-existence of a European corporate statute, which prevents firms from organising themselves efficiently; the late integration of the service sectors and so on. However, the evidence for these examples is less clear than for the previous category, and furthermore the losses incurred by not acting seem to be less important than the losses related to the EU acting wrongly.

The major *reasons* for failures (doing things wrongly) were as follows:

- The EU started out as an experiment that could neither use historical examples, nor a solid theoretical base to guide its actions.
- The special constitutional standing of a number of regimes for specific sectors, coupled with a sector-specific bureaucracy, made them resistant to change even after conditions had changed radically.

Future deepening

FOUNDATIONS

The theoretical foundations for the explanation of the EU's past dynamism, as reflected in the growth of intra-EU trade and investment and the considerable increase in its scope of competences, have been given in Chapter 2. The most encompassing concept in this respect is the idea of spill-over. This concept starts from the benefits that can be had from trade integration by using to the full the advantages of economies of scale, dictated by technology. Once markets have been opened, integration spills over into other areas, as one economic function is related to others. For example, common policies are needed as they enhance the effectiveness of market integration. This economic interpretation of the progress in integration needs to be complemented by factors from political science in order to formulate a full explanation of the specific forms that integration has adopted.

In the past a projection into the future of the subjects that integration would cover could be based on this notion of movement through principal stages, and this approach has indeed permitted us to correctly forecast three major developments: first, the completion of the internal market by 1992 (Molle, 1985); second, the successful set-up of the economic and monetary union by the end of the last century; and, finally, the increased weight that redistribution policies have taken in total EU activity during the 1990s (Molle, 1989). With hindsight this appears to be the single logical outcome of a long-term course of events. However, at the time of writing these issues were highly controversial.

As the EU has arrived at the highest stage of integration short of the full economic union, the approach of the movement through stages can no longer be used to predict how integration will move on. We can, however, predict two rather general features of this process:

- European regulation will cover an increasing number of detailed subjects from a very wide array of economic policies. The form that this integration will take depends on the specific configuration of the political forces of the principal players involved in the field at hand; no grand design is likely to emerge from this.
- For the regulation of these subjects the less committing instruments will be selected. Indeed, the EU has understood the advantages of subsidiarity/proportionality and has set on a course of increasingly using the open method of coordination rather than unification.

From the standpoint of the *public authorities*, in charge of creating the conditions for a good functioning of the EU, this implies a shift in attention. In the past it concentrated on the elaboration of a common legal framework. Now it concentrates on the systematic support for the structural reform of the (national) markets and policies by the benchmarking of each others' performances, the selection of the best practices and the exertion of peer pressure to implement the necessary changes.

THE AMBITION; THE LISBON STRATEGY (LS)

The European Union and its member countries pursue many goals. However, they have seen in the past that for their realisation a basic condition needed to be fulfilled, and that is the increased capacity of the economy to sustain these efforts. The Lisbon European Council of 2000 (strengthened by the subsequent Councils) has recognised this and has established the goal for the European Union to *become the most competitive and dynamic knowledge-based economy in the world, capable of achieving a sustainable economic growth with more and better jobs and a greater social cohesion.*

The key word in this respect is competitiveness. Unfortunately competitiveness (see, for example, CE/ECORYS, forthcoming) is an elusive concept. It is influenced by a whole series of factors. One is thus well advised to take these as policy indicators and not the final outcome. We name here by category:

- Industrial structure: specialisation in high value added; degree of internationalisation; entrepreneurial talent; clusters of activities; risk taking culture.
- Innovation: R&D levels research institutes and universities; linkages between companies and R&D; linkages in international networks.
- Human resources: knowledge-intensive skills; educational facilities; demographic trends; training and teaching institutes.

- Infrastructure: transport but certainly telecommunication; quality of place (cultural amenities and so on).

So in order to realise the LS ambition one needs to attack all these elements, which implies policies for the information society, R&D and innovation, the completion of the internal market, notably for services, and the reform of the labour market and the welfare state.

Several attempts have been made to translate this ambition into objectives[8] and the objectives into *concrete targets and measurable outputs*. However, the problem is that the Lisbon Strategy covers very many fields and thereby lacks focus. So it is difficult to monitor progress. Different policy fields already have specific monitors for the measurement of progress in realisation and performance. We mention as an example the European Innovation Scoreboard that contains data on such aspects as innovative behaviour in firms, science and engineering base and so on. Moreover, the Commission draws up an annual synthesis report on the basis of the structural indicators. These provide an instrument for the objective assessment of the progress made towards the objectives (Eurostat, 2003).

The *means* that are applied are very diverse. The LS covers strategies, guidelines, communications, action plans, task forces and councils on a whole range of EU policies. Moreover, much of the implementation has to be done through national policies. Indeed, many of the instruments are in the hands of the member states. So EU objectives need to be realised by the application of the open method of coordination, which means the exchange of knowledge and good practices among member countries. Now there are problems with the operationalisation of the LS on each policy level:

- EU. The various DGs responsible for parts of the LS have not all made an equally satisfactory systematic policy set-up. Moreover, the overall set up seems to lack coherence. This was notably the case in so far as the dovetailing between the SF and the LS is concerned.
- Member state. National priorities tend to overshadow the EU ones. This is so on the level of ambition, but notably so on the level of specification of targets and focus of resources.
- Region. Uncertainty as to the degree to which regions are actively involved in the process. This is not the least important point as most of the financial means for the LS have to come from the SF.

A point that complicates even further progress on the LS is the constant flux of the policy environment. We need but mention: the need for a major revision of the budget (and notably the CAP and the structural funds), the limits of the European Social Model, the terms for the accession countries (including Turkey) and the legal framework of the draft constitution.

COORDINATION OF VARIOUS POLICIES

Recently, the EU has enlarged the scope of policy coordination. It now covers three principal objectives:

---

8   As an illustration of the relevant literature we cite here (by subject): for innovation, Bloom et al. (2002), Furman et al. (2002) and EC (2003c); for industrial policies, Lawton (1999); for active labour market policies, Martin (1998); and for product market regulation in combination with technology, Nicoletti and Scarpetta (2003); for labour market regulation, Teulings and Hartog (1998) and Broadway and Cuff (2001); for the influence of governance structures, Kaufmann et al. (2002); for the role of the state in general, OECD (1997).

- macro-economic and budgetary stability (Stability and Growth Pact)
- improving competitiveness;
- improving the employment situation (Employment Pact)

In order to improve the effectiveness of the policies that are pursued to attain these objectives, the EU has started a new coordination procedure. Major instruments in this framework are the so-called Broad Economic Guidelines which make an inventory of the structural problems and suggest policy actions, both at EU and individual member state level (see EC, 1999j). Although these guidelines are not legally binding obligations, they can nevertheless lead to effective coordination, as they use three types of tool: first, the setting of benchmarks and the identification of best practices; second, the monitoring of the progress of policy implementation and the attainment of targets; and, third, the use of peer pressure on member states that do not comply with the common stances. The package of policy measures differs between different parts of the EU.

1. *East.* On the basis of economic theory and past experience with the effectiveness of cohesion policies, we may expect that the type of catch-up growth that is foreseen in the NMS and in the present candidate countries will in large part be supportive of the realisation of the goals of the Lisbon Strategy. It will for a large part be oriented towards manufacturing industry. For this sector a long tradition exists of support to R&D, to innovation and so on. Here the structural funds will play a big role and will do so largely in line with the governance structures that have themselves proven to be effective in the past.
2. West. Western Europe's economy will be largely service based. Growth is relatively low and needs to be enhanced for several reasons: 1) to accommodate the constant restructuring following from the dynamics of the global economy; 2) to spur growth in NMS, the other CEECs (and by extension in the LDCs) and 3) to provide the basis for safeguarding of the European Social Model (EC 2004z).

Future widening

ECONOMIC FOUNDATIONS

The *theoretical foundations* for the explanation of the widening of an existing framework of regional economic integration have been given in Chapter 2. We distinguished there between a number of approaches.

The theoretical concept that has received most attention is the *optimum integration area* (OIA). It suggests that countries that have reached among themselves a certain degree of exchange, and show a certain degree of convergence of policy, can participate, whereas countries that do not fulfil such criteria should be excluded from participation. In practice, however, it proved rather difficult to implement this theory, for a number of reasons already given in Chapter 2.

The solution has been to translate the discussion on the criteria into a discussion *about cost and benefits*. For countries that are part of the OIA the benefits will in general outweigh the cost; the opposite is the case for countries that are not part of the OIA. Incidentally this economic balancing does not fully determine the outcome: many political arguments may come into play and may even overshadow the economic ones in the final decision. In the past the decisions about the enlargement of the EU have been taken in a manner that is in line with these theoretical foundations (see previous chapters). Indeed, economic studies have produced evidence of the advantages of enlargement for both the EU and the accession countries. In those cases where political arguments have tipped the balance in favour of the decision, the very functioning of the EU (market and policy integration, including the participation of old and new member countries in EU redistribution schemes) has made it possible for countries to come up to the requirements. This finally tipped the balance of advantages and disadvantages, not only in political but also in economic terms. These advantages have been influenced by such factors as the increase in the efficiency of firms of the new member countries in having direct access to the European internal market. Staying out proved to be costly, which induced firms in non-EU countries to lobby for accession. This phenomenon described by the domino theory of widening, proved to give a quite adequate view of the process.[9]

The mostly influential view has probably been the *theory of clubs* (see Chapter 2). As a matter of fact the EU, as the dominant organisation, is capable of setting the rules and the criteria for membership. It then negotiates with the candidate countries the modalities of their access to the EU. For each individual country the decision is taken on the basis of the net effect of the economic and political benefits. The domino theory also comes to mind again. Indeed, for the CEECs the alternatives to membership of the EU were (and are) not very attractive; this applies both to a stand-alone situation and to participation in an alternative club.[10]

THE CRITERIA FOR MEMBERSHIP

The EU is open for membership of other democratic countries in Europe, which respect the rule of law and human rights. Before such a country can become a member it also needs to fulfil some economic criteria. The first of these is that it needs to have a functioning market economy. Whether this is achieved is judged on the answer to a number of questions; the most important of which are:

- Are market forces allowed to play their role? In other words, is there freedom of economic actors to set prices and to trade freely?
- Have obstacles to the entry of new firms and to the exit of existing firms (bankruptcy) been lifted?
- Is there an effective legal system that sets rules for the fair play of market forces, such as property rights, and is there an effective system to enforce compliance?
- Has macro-economic stability – that is, low inflation, a low budget deficit and a sustainable position of the balance of payments – been achieved?
- Is there a sufficient consensus about the main orientations and principles of the major policies?
- Is there a developed financial sector that permits savings to be channelled effectively into productive investment?

---

9   A preliminary empirical test of the domino theory has been done by Sapir (1997) with the help of a gravity model estimated for the period 1960–92. His results clearly show that EFTA members have been urged to join the EU due to loss of competitiveness.

10   Only Russia and its associated states may hope to be able to present a credible alternative to the EU. The participation of the CEECs in agreements with the EU gave them the perspective of joining the club, offering CEEC governments a commitment which helped them to implement reforms that otherwise would not have come through, due to time inconsistencies. This applies both to economic reforms such as the liberalisation of the trade regime and political reforms such as democratisation (Fernandez, 1997).

The second criterion is about *competitiveness*. A country is thought to be competitive if it has a positive score on the following sub-criteria:

- *Trade integration into the EU*. If the country exports to the EU this can be taken as a proof of competitiveness. Of course, the sectoral composition needs to be taken into account – that is, exports should come from the manufacturing and service sectors and not only from the natural resource sectors.
- *Balanced composition of firms in the economy*. The past dominance of state firms should have been brought to an end by successful privatisation. Moreover, small and medium-sized enterprises must have developed.
- *Good health of the private sector*. Indicators of health that can be used are the growth of output, the rate of investment, the degree of innovation and the profitability of operations.

A number of additional criteria that are *conditions for competitiveness* are also used. They are of a more qualitative nature. The most important ones are:

- *Production structure*. Are those types of intermediate product that are essential for many activities – such as energy, capital, telecommunications and so on – available?
- *Production environment*. Is there an adequate provision of infrastructure, of education, of R&D and of environmental services?
- *Institutions*. Are matters of competition, corporate governance, investment and so on well-regulated and are there organisations that can effectively implement them? Cases in point are, for instance, the markets for securities and a competition authority. In general, however, the efficiency of the whole public administration should be judged.

CANDIDATE COUNTRIES ON THE ROAD TO MEMBERSHIP

At the moment of writing (2005) there are four official candidate countries. First Bulgaria and Romania; the negotiations with them are at a very advanced stage. Next Croatia, which fulfils in the meantime the political criteria for accession; negotiations have started in 2005. Finally Turkey, which is a special case for several reasons; its long-term relations with the EU dating back to the 1960s; its mere size (in terms of population it would become the biggest member country by 2020); its economic problems (macro-economic weaknesses, very low GDP/P); its geography (largely outside the European subcontinent); its internal disparities (very considerable between west and east) and finally, its culture (predominantly Muslim).

A number of countries on the western Balkan peninsula are potential candidates. The EU has said that it considers as such Albania, Bosnia-Herzegovina, Serbia, Montenegro and Macedonia. The situation in these countries is characterised by their GDP/P position that is (often considerably) below the EU average and a political instability due to ethnic tensions. The EU is fostering the economic growth of these countries by its external development policy and their stability by its security policy. Bringing these countries into the EU zone of prosperity, democracy and security is a very important task ahead.

The Commission analyses on a regular basis the performance of all candidate countries in meeting the criteria for membership.[11] What would be a *realistic timetable*? This depends, on

---

11   Reports on the progress of reform and on the implementation of the 'acquis' are regularly given by the Commission (see, for instance, EC, 2000e). Up-to-date information on the enlargement process can be obtained from the

the one hand, on the internal restructuring of the EU itself (institutions, agriculture and so on) and, on the other, on the speed with which the applicants will be able to meet the criteria. Bulgaria and Romania already have indications about the date of their potential accession and this will be between 2007 and 2010. The process is so far advanced that for future purposes we may count them under the group of the members. If we take the time that has elapsed between the start of the negotiations and the accession of the CEECs as an indication, the accession of the other candidates (Croatia and Turkey) will take at least ten years. For the potential candidates (the countries on the western Balkan peninsula) it is very unlikely that they will speed up the process, so their accession will not come in the coming ten years, either.

THE EU AND CANDIDATES MAKE COMMON EFFORTS FOR PREPARATION OF MEMBERSHIP

The EU gives pre-accession aid to the western Balkan peninsula countries and Turkey, which will help these countries to adopt the *'acquis communautaire'*, to speed up their economic restructuring and to catch up with the EU average. To fulfil the criteria the candidates will have to make considerable progress with respect to liberalisation of the movement of goods and factors, and with economic, legal and institutional reform.[12] The pre-accession strategy of the EU consists of the following elements:

- Accession partnerships. They set out the key short- and medium-term priorities to be met in order to prepare for membership. They also indicate the financial assistance available from the EU in support of these priorities and the conditionality attached to that assistance.
- Europe Agreements institutions. At regular intervals a systematic examination is made of each candidate country's progress. To that end committees and sub-committees have been set up.
- National programmes. These specify the resources and the timetable foreseen for the adoption of the *'acquis'*. In addition to the agreed partnership priorities, most applicant countries have defined their own priorities for accession.
- Participation in Community programmes. This allows the accession countries to become familiar with Community policies and working methods. (These concern fields such as vocational training, energy and environment.)
- Financial and expert assistance. Traditionally this assistance has been given through the Phare programme, which focused on investment in infrastructure, on institution building and on the adoption of the *'acquis'*. From 2000 onwards the Phare programme has been joined by two new instruments (see also Chapter 17, 'External Relations').

Summary and conclusions

- Integration has made considerable progress in Europe in the post-war years. That is evidenced by many indicators: economic ones, such as the interpenetration of markets and the convergence of prices; and policy ones, such as the fields covered, and the strength of instruments used by EU institutions.

---

web site of the Commission: http://europa.eu.int.comm. enlargement/index.htm
12   Critical in this respect is the freedom of movement of persons. The EU wants to preclude large migration flows from notably Turkey to the present EU. In an internal market that would only be possible where the differences between the richest and the poorest participant do not exceed the ones that exist in the present EU.

- Integration has reached its objectives: peace and democracy have been safeguarded, and wealth has increased while the distribution of wealth has improved.
- New objectives have been set for future economic integration. In terms of deepening, the most important goals are: (1) the completion of the Economic and Monetary Union and (2) the making of a competitive Europe in the electronic age, characterised by new economic sectors (such as e-commerce) and new infrastructure (such as the Internet). In terms of widening, the most important goal is the integration of the countries of Central and Eastern Europe.

19 *What Lessons for Regional Integration Schemes?*

Introduction

Many countries all over the world are facing problems of development and ask themselves the question whether regional integration or cooperation can give a boost to their development efforts. They try to get together with their neighbours to see what objectives they have in common and what institutional solutions should best be adopted for their ventures. They see the success of the EU and ask themselves the question of how far this European experience contains lessons for them. The objective of the present chapter is to analyse how far that is the case.[1]

To tackle this problem effectively we will proceed as follows. First we will describe the way in which regional integration in the world has progressed and the salient features of the most important regional integration schemes (RIAs). Next we will use the set-up given in Chapters 1and 2 to compare these RIAs with the EU and draw lessons from the experience of the latter for the development of the former. We will do so for the rationale and ideology that lie at the basis of the schemes (compare Chapter 1); for the public goods these schemes should provide (corresponding to the stages of integration of Chapter 2) and finally for the instruments and governance systems used to make them deliver (also Chapter 2). As usual the chapter will be concluded with a short overview of the most important findings.

The dynamics of regional integration in the world

A FIRST UNSUCCESSFUL WAVE OF REGIONALISM

Many countries have realised for quite some time already that their domestic market was too small to grasp the combined benefits from economies of scale and competition. So they have tried to join forces with others through regional cooperation. After the Second World War many countries implemented policies of import substitution as the main avenue for growth and industrialisation. Regional cooperation between such countries logically adopted the same model. This included in general:

- trade liberalisation among partners;
- considerable protection towards third countries;
- regional industrial planning;
- concessionary measures for the weakest members.

---

1   In drawing lessons we have been inspired by, for example, Winters (1997), Jones and Plummer (2004) and Artesis and de Paula (2003).

This model or policy package has not been very effective. It failed to boost welfare as it was in general trade diverting instead of trade creating. Many of the groupings were just too small to create the economies of scale that would have led to competitiveness. Fear of concentration of activities in one member state led to devising schemes for political and bureaucratic distribution of industry and resources. Lack of progress in such distributional negotiations often led to a stop in the negotiations on trade concessions as well. Debt crises and monetary unrest led to currency misalignments and political problems. So it need come as no surprise that evaluations of the regional ventures of this period in terms of trade and growth creation were in general quite negative.

THE CONTROVERSY: BUILDING BLOCK – STUMBLING BLOCK

Partly on the basis of the experience with regional groupings based on the policy choices depicted in the previous section, regionalism was thought by many to be the wrong option. Others maintained that, provided the right policies were chosen, regional groupings could be beneficial.[2] Let us detail the arguments of both schools.

Opposition to regional integration ventures came from the dominant power (the USA) and under their influence also from the major international organisations (WTO, IBRD, IMF). They were supported by many academics who considered on the basis of their theoretical and empirical studies that regionalism was poised to lead to an inefficient system globally and to loss of wealth regionally (due to trade diversion effects). These forces were joined by countries that thought that their interests were better served by enhanced integration in the world economy than by a cumbersome regional integration (see Langhammer, 1992). This applied both to highly developed countries such as Japan and developing countries such as Chile. Other arguments against regional integration were that RIAs tended to absorb too much of the scarce negotiation capacity notably of small and poor countries and that they created idiosyncratic frameworks for regulation and dispute settlement that may have risked becoming incompatible with the emerging multilateral system. In this view RIAs are 'stumbling blocks' to global integration.

Supporters of regional integration (main proponent, the EU) use as their main argument that RIAs can lead to positive results provided the right conditions are created. Paramount among them is the increased openness of the grouping towards the outside world and a market-oriented domestic economy. Supporters of this view of open regionalism accept that the first best solution would be globalism, but as this is very difficult to realise one should adopt the next best solution, which is regionalism. Progress in trade liberalisation and associated domestic policy reform is then faster, albeit on a more limited regional scale. Regional integration breaks down the level of protection for many industries so that the resistance to multilateral changes is weakened. So it can help to transform the economic structure into one that is more competitive, which would teach producers to take advantage of global markets. So in this view regional integration schemes are actually 'building blocks' for global integration.

CHANGING ATTITUDES LEAD TO A CHANGE IN SUPPORT FOR REGIONAL VENTURES

In the course of the past decades the positions towards regionalism have changed. This is partly induced by economic factors, partly by political factors.

---

2   See, for this discussion, Bhagwati (1991) and de Melo and Panagariya (1993).

The *economic* background is formed by insights from theoretical and empirical work showing that under certain conditions RIAs do have positive effects. Indeed economic and geographical characteristics (distance) can predict the formation of FTAs (Baier and Bergstrand, 2004).

The *political* background is formed by the conviction of an increasing number of governments that globalisation has very deep effects and that part of the implied loss of sovereignty might be gained back by sharing it with regional partners. The coming to agreement among few participants (region) is much easier than among multiple partners (global). At the regional level policy makers feel more in control of the outcomes and can more flexibly adjust the agenda to their own preferences. As many governments made the same assessment of the future, many countries feared they could be confronted with strong blocks from others and saw in the cooperation with partners to create their own block a good answer to the perceived threat (for example, Gibb and Michalak, 1994; Ghosh, 2002).

These two factors have changed the attitudes of the major players in the following way (Memedovic *et al.*, 1999):

- *Developing Countries.* Since the mid 1980s many countries, including LDCs, have changed the ideology and principles that are at the roots of their policies. In the face of the disappointing results of the protectionist approach they have opted for more market-oriented policies. They now put the accent more on competitiveness of their export industries. In line therewith many RIAs have been revitalised on a new basis; they have abandoned the idea of high tariff walls and embraced the approach of 'open regionalism'. They have largely abandoned industrial planning and put the accent on the creation of advantageous FDI regimes. In many countries the support for RIAs has also come from the political advantages of locking in domestic reforms and creating a controlled learning process for liberalisation. Support for RIAs has been enhanced by the fear of a world dominated by hegemonic blocks (US/EU).
- *USA.* The USA has switched its position and has gradually accepted regional integration as a convenient middle station on the road to worldwide integration. This was due to a particular political constellation. By the end of the 1980s the US became afraid that the Uruguay round might actually fail and that new protectionism would ensue. It decided to take an active part in the setting up of its own RIA (NAFTA) and to give support to the conclusion of RIAs by others.
- *EU.* The European Union has always been convinced of the merits of regional integration, within and outside Europe It has supported the creation of regional integration arrangements in several parts of the world by giving technical advice on the set-up and by giving financial support to the integrating countries for the ensuing restructuring of their economies and for the necessary capacity building of national and RIA officials (for example, EC, 1995d). Moreover, it has concluded a large number of bilateral agreements with individual countries and with blocks to stimulate mutual trade relations and development. This has given rise to a complex pattern of preferentialism.[3] The EU has, moreover, concluded a number of parallel (mutually reinforcing) agreements with regions concerning political and economic cooperation and external assistance. They take the form of Regional Strategy

---

3   The effects of such preferential agreements are not easy to establish. However, they tend to have a positive effect on development in cases where certain national conditions with respect to governance structures are fulfilled (see, for instance, Hinkle and Schiff, 2004). We may assume that due to increased pressure from the WTO, such preferentialism will gradually decrease.

Papers (RSP), containing inter alia the EC policy objectives and strategies for the region, and cumulating in a multi-annual Regional Indicative Programme.

A NEW WAVE OF REGIONALISM ON A DIFFERENT FOOTING

During the last decades these changes in conditions have led to an upsurge in new regional integration schemes and the revitalisation of exiting ones. Some have called this the result of a *'race to regionalise'* (Thomas and Tetreault, 1999). Many of the present day RIAs deal with trade. Now in order to be acceptable to the international community such agreements need to be notified at the WTO. The number of such notifications has more than doubled over the 1990s. This is only part of the picture, however. Numerous new projects are under study at the moment, of which some have passed the proposal stage and of which only a few are actually in the negotiation stage. Although the speed of implementation of the agreements already concluded has sometimes been disappointing, the trend towards increased regionalism is clear. We can see that in three dimensions:

*   *Larger geographical coverage (widening).* The enlargement tendency concerns first many of the existing regional ventures. An important case in point is ASEAN; an agreement has been signed between China and ASEAN to let the former become a member of the latter and talks are going on between Japan and ASEAN to make Japan an associated member to this grouping. It concerns next the merging of existing groupings. In Asia proposals have been made to merge ASEAN with CER (Australia and New Zealand). In Africa SADC and COMESA are trying to join forces. In Latin America an agreement (of Cuzco) has been signed to merge Mercosur and Andean plus the remaining countries (such as Chile) in the South American Community of Nations, which has as its main objective the fostering of political, economic and infrastructure integration. It concerns finally the extension from regional to interregional and thereby the association of countries at different levels of development. Examples are the projects for a Free Trade Area of the Americas (FTAA, comprising virtually the whole of North and Latin America) and for APEC, encompassing both Russia, North America, ASEAN and countries in Latin America and the Pacific.
*   *Higher ambitions (deepening).* Most RIAs deal with trade and trade-related matters only. However, the revitalisation of many of the RIAs creates a dynamic to go beyond that stage. These new ambitions are logically mostly in the stages completing the FTA (for example, to include services) and those immediately following the FTA (for example, to include trade facilitation such as common customs rules). They concern first the creation of common markets (investment and labour); next the adoption of some common policies. Indeed the conviction has grown that successful trade integration cannot be realised without the coordination of a set of policies, such as allocation policies (competition, standards, anti-dumping, investment), external policies (NTBs, beyond the border measures), common resource policies (water, energy) and other policies such as transport and environment. Proposals are also recurrent to set up cooperation schemes for financial and monetary cooperation; some have even proposed forms of economic and monetary union, but concrete steps have not as yet been set.
*   *Stronger institutions (structuring).* Most RIAs have very weak institutions. This has proven a barrier to the delivery of the expected results. Improvements relate to both the system of negotiation of agreements, the implementation of those agreements and finally the settlement of disputes.

Salient features of the main regional integration schemes

AN OVERVIEW OF THE MAIN RIAS

Over time a panoply of regional integration areas have developed. They are too numerous to present here. We have selected the most salient ones in each continent outside Europe. We give their membership,[4] their objective and size in Table 19.1.

The list of RIAs that exist at this moment in the world is a long one. There is a considerable diversity as to the economic weight and practical relevance of these RIAs. It is, in the framework of this chapter, unfeasible to be exhaustive.[5] The list of RIAs given in Table 19.1 is thus incomplete.[6]

CHARACTERISTICS OF THE MOST IMPORTANT RIAS

Table 19.2 gives an overview of the main features (in the rows) of the major regional economic organisation in each continent (columns). In the top rows we refer to such basic notions as the definition of the common interest that countries have in order to get together. This is made more concrete in terms of the stages of integration. Next we detail some governance aspects, in particular the institutional set-up and the most important instruments that are used to get results and to make members comply.

AMBITIONS

Tables 19.1 and 19.2 indicate that the *ambition* of most of the RIAs is limited. All integration schemes cover trade of manufactured goods (this covers both liberalisation and the accompanying measures such as customs facilities, standards, and so on). Some have also realised the free movement of other goods (agricultural goods are often a bone of contention) and services. The latter part is almost invariably realised through the freedom of establishment. For investment, most RIAs assume free FDI; and some have worked to establish rules that

---

4   The composition of the RIAs suggests that countries belong to one RIA only. However, in practice there is a complex situation of overlapping regionalism and bilateralism. Indeed, many countries (notably in Africa but also in Asia) belong to several agreements. Some of them are of the South-South type, others of the North-South type.

5   A more comprehensive overview of regional integration ventures of the past and of their effects is given in de la Torre and Kelly (1992). For up-to-date information the reader is best referred to the WTO website: www.wto. org/regionalisms. Another interesting source is IRBD, 2005. Note that we use a more restrictive definition of regional agreements than the WTO. We exclude reciprocal bilateral agreements (for example, EU agreements with individual countries). For clarity it needs to be said that unilateral systems (for example, the EU initiative 'Everything but Arms') are also excluded from our definition.

6   It does not contain:

•   Ventures of the past that have proven unsuccessful. There are many of them, notably in Africa. Others that have been revived are taken up under their present form.

•   RIAs between countries that carry less economic weight than those in the table. In the Americas we mention CACM, the Central American Common Market and CARICOM, an FTA in the Carribean area. Another case worth mentioning is CER, a cooperation agreement between Australia and New Zealand that is the nucleus of a wider area: SPARTECA, the South Pacific Regional Trade and Economic Cooperation Agreement, which also encompasses a whole series of smaller South Pacific countries (islands). Finally we mention the Gulf Cooperation Council in the Middle East.

•   Many bilateral and biregional arrangements. Many of these are of the so-called South-South type, arrangements between developing countries. We find in this category, for instance, the overlapping COMESA (founded 1994) and SADC (South Africa has only been in it since 1994). Others are of the so-called North-South type, arrangements between a Northern country (for example, USA) or trade block (for example, EU) and one Southern country (for example, Chile) or a block of developing countries (for example, the ACP or Mercosur). The EU in particular has been keen to enter into such North-South agreements.

Table 19.1 Objectives, membership and size of major regional integration agreements, 2005

Acronym	Full name	Objective	Member countries	Size of population (millions)
Americas				
NAFTA	North American Free Trade Agreement	FTA	USA, Canada, Mexico	435
Mercosur	Mercado Comun del Sur	CM	Brazil, Argentina, Paraguay and Uruguay	591
CAN	Andean Community	CM	Bolivia, Colombia, Ecuador, Peru, Venezuela	118
Asia				
ASEAN (AFTA)	Association of South East Asian Nations (Asian Free Trade Area)	FTA	Brunei, Darussalam, Cambodia, Indonesia, Laos, Malaysia, Myanmar, Philippines, Singapore, Thailand, Vietnam	570
SAARC/ SAPTA	South Asian Association for Regional Cooperation/ South Asian Preferential Trade Arrangement	FTA	Bangladesh, Bhutan, India, Maldives, Nepal, Pakistan, Sri Lanka	1437
Africa				
COMESA	Common Market for Eastern and Southern Africa	CM	Angola, Burundi, Comoros, Congo, Djibouti, Egypt, Ethiopia, Eritrea, Kenya, Madagascar, Malawi, Mauritius, Namibia, Rwanda, Seychelles, Sudan, Swaziland, Uganda, Zambia, Zimbabwe	402
SADC[1]	Southern African Development Community	CU	Angola, *Botswana*, Congo, *Lesotho*, Malawi, Mauritius, Mozambique, *Namibia, Seychelles, South Africa, Swaziland*, Tanzania, Zambia, Zimbabwe	216
ECOWAS[2]	Economic Community of West African States	FTA EMU	*Benin, Burkina Faso*, Cape Verde, *Cote d'Ivoire*, Gambia, *Ghana*, Guinea, Guinea Bissao, Liberia, *Mali, Niger, Nigeria, Senegal*, Sierra Leone, Togo	252

1 The countries mentioned in italics form SACU: the Southern African Customs Union; it is now the nucleus of the SADC. SADC is the successor of the SADCC established in 1980 by the frontline states to reduce their dependence on the apartheid regime in South Africa. After the abolishment of apartheid, SADC was formed including South Africa.

2 The countries in italics are members of WAEMU, or the West Africa Economic and Monetary Union (Franc CFA).

Notes: The countries mentioned in italics form SACU: the Southern African Customs Union; it is now the nucleus of the SADC. SADC is the successor of the SADCC established in 1980 by the frontline states to reduce their dependence on the apartheid regime in South Africa. After the abolishment of apartheid, SADC was formed including South Africa. [2] The countries in italics are members of WAEMU, or the West Africa Economic and Monetary Union (Franc CFA).

Source: CIA, The World Factbook.

Table 19.2   Salient features of selected regional integration schemes

		North America	South America	Asia	Africa
Main organisation		NAFTA	Mercosur	ASEAN (AFTA)	SADC
Stages of integration	Trade liberalisation and facilitation	Manufactures Services Agricultural	Manufactures Services	Manufactures Services	Manufactures (Services in practice not integrated)
	Investment liberalisation	Yes	Yes	Restricted	In practice not integrated
	Labour	No provisions for permanent[3] labour mobility; temporary market access for certain groups; labour standards	Existing labour mobility provisions not implemented; restricted movement of persons as service suppliers	Only promotion of free flow of skilled labour related to investment	None
Instruments for realisation and compliance	Fora for negotiations	No central coordinating body; free trade commission; secretariat; meetings of heads of state	Council of common market; secretariat; trade commission	No supra-national institutions; central secretariat; meetings of competent ministers and heads of government	Meetings of competent ministers
	Rules for dispute settlement	Role of secretariat (relative robust procedure)	Bilateral negotiations; common market group; council of common market	Bilateral negotiations; senior economic officials; final arbiters: economic ministers	Dispute resolution tribunal

facilitate the cross-border operations of its firms (for example, Andean Community). Freedom of other capital flows depends on the policy the member countries follow in this matter. Labour market integration (the element that would complete the common market) is in all cases very rudimentary. So we can conclude that only a few RIAs go timidly a bit beyond trade integration.

Some go a little bit further. For instance the agreement of Cartagena creating the Andean Community does contain explicit provisions for the harmonisation of exchange rates, monetary, financial and fiscal policies. The same is true for Mercosur; its member countries have recently created a high-level civil servants group on the coordination of macro policies and environmental policies, and they have worked on the definition of common standards for goods. COMESA goes into allocation policies; its treaty forbids cartels and one of its aims is (like Mercosur) to come to a regional competition policy. The NAFTA treaty contains provisions that govern domestic labour standards and other regulatory issues, such as the environment. Many schemes refer to democracy, security and peace as motives for regional integration; they provide fora for debate and negotiation that should prevent tensions from deteriorating into armed conflicts.

N.B. In comparison to the EU all this integration is still at a very low scale. While the index of integration for the EU has recently approached 90, the index for Mercosur stood at only 25 (Dorrucci et al. 2003). We can deduce from the table that the values of the integration index for the other RIAs mentioned were even lower, with the exception of NAFTA.

RIAs: what have they delivered?

EFFECTIVENESS; POOR RECORD FOR THE FIRST WAVE

Comparing the results with the objectives of the first round of regionalism, one can only be disappointed. Little was achieved, and what was achieved often came with considerable delays. The causes of such lack of success are manifold. We cite here:

- Lack of clear advantages (limited potential for realising economies of scale) and distributional disputes.
- Inefficient national administrations. Governments have to implement nationally what they have agreed on internationally. Often the quality and capacity of the national administrations is so low that instruments do not work.
- Disturbances. Macro-economic, monetary and financial crises have in the past induced governments to resort to reinstalling barriers to trade and investment.
- Insecurity. Armed conflicts either within countries or between countries of the same RIA have been a major barrier to trade (and economic) integration and development. In this respect it is of utmost importance to take away that constraint. In this light one can welcome recent initiatives such as NEPAD, New Partnership for Africa's Development. It is a continent-wide approach to the major problems with which Africa is confronted: marginalisation in the global economy, high debt, poor food security, enormous health problems (HIV), and so on.

EFFECTIVENESS; THE SECOND WAVE IS ON TRACK BUT NOT ON TIME

The recent wave *of regionalism* has achieved considerable trade and investment liberalisation in the framework of open regionalism. To give one example: ASEAN is to abolish all tariffs among ten of its members by 2007; the other (poorer) members will follow later and realise this target by 2012. Mercosur has liberalised internal trade for almost all products and plans to realise the customs union by 2006. Although the African RIAs are all still far from completion of even an FTA, they have moved already into a number of common policies such as investment. AFTA has liberalised internal trade ahead of schedule and is now deepening integration on a number of points.

The measurement of the *effects of regional integration* is a function of the degree of integration. We give here the results for the two most current indicators of integration.

- *Goods trade.* For all RIAs the share of intra-regional imports in total imports increased.[7] A common criticism of RIAs is that they are trade diverting. However, recent empirical studies give a differentiated picture. They find, over the past decades, for many RIAs, increased trade with both regional partners and third countries.[8] Only in the case of some RIAs among developing countries (for example, the Andean Community and Mercosur) do they find stagnating or reduced trade with non-members.
- *Capital movements.* Unfortunately there is very little evidence on this score for the regional integration schemes selected. But the available information does not suggest large effects. The recent FDI boom in Mercosur has been mainly national market-oriented and only to a limited extent oriented towards the regional market. The ensuing productivity gains have not been sufficient to start exporting to the rest of the world (compare Figure 10.1) (Chudnovsky and Lopez, 2004).

The main point to analyse is how far integration has actually led to a growth of GDP/P. In a study for the period 1970–1990 on growth determinants the usual variables showed up (investment, HR, and so on) but no effect was found for the existence of RIAs (apart from the EU) (Vamvakidis, 1998). Other studies do not come up with clear-cut conclusions on positive integration effects either (IBRD, 2005). One cannot exclude that this is due to limits of statistical analyses, but it may also be that structural factors prevent integration benefits from being reaped (many RIAs are too small to grasp economies of scale). One can also think of institutional aspects: many factors may actually inhibit internally the realisation of the potential growth effects of integration.

EU SUPPORT TO RIAS

The EU supports all main RIAs in the world (apart from the NAFTA for obvious reasons). This support covers a wide range of subjects. Some of them have to do with the taking away of the physical barriers to exchange of goods, aiming mainly at the construction of transport infrastructure. Others concern regulatory issues, such as single vehicle licence systems, and so on. Yet others aim at capacity building by improving the functioning of government services (training of staff of customs offices, and so on). Moreover, some other measures move further into areas that improve the structure of the economy (such as support for major regulatory reform and industrial development) or enhance factor productivity (such as education and regulation). Finally support goes to environmental disaster prevention, drugs combating and mechanisms of conflict prevention and resolution.

An example of such aid is SADCC/SADC. Since the early 1980s the EU has donated through the European Development Fund a total amount of almost € 300 million. The broad division over the sectors is as follows: infrastructure (mainly transport corridors) 54 per cent; food

---

7   It is interesting to note that in many instances intra-regional trade already actually started to grow ahead of the putting in place of the regional integration schemes. In ASEAN for instance, they seem to have accelerated an autonomous trend, based on the need to procure close by parts of the manufacturing exports to the developed world.
8   See, for example, Clarette et al. (2003); IBRD (2005). Some think that this may be explained by the removal of invisible trade barriers as a result of trade facilitation measures (Cernat, 2001).

and agriculture 17 per cent; trade and finance 6 per cent. The Regional Indicative Programme for the South East Africa region for the period 2002–07 allocates some € 100 million; again infrastructure and related services take up the lion's share. However, about a third of the resources are now devoted to measures related to regional economic integration.

Lessons on systemic choices

RIAS

Many regions in the world have a history of military conflicts and political instability. This is notably the case for Asia and Africa. Economic integration is a method of diminishing such conflicts. However, we know from the experiences of the past and from the theory of international institutions that the emergence and development of international regimes, as of RIAs, is rather triggered by a clear economic rationale, in practice the *economic benefits* that members expect from them. To many countries the adherence to an RIA is also a means to secure these benefits: they lock in the results of internal structural reforms that under other conditions might be reversed. A very clear example of this is Mexico which adhered to NAFTA.[9]

However, the economic rewards of integration vary significantly (see Chapter 2) between the low forms (PTA or FTA), the medium forms (CU, CM) and the highest forms of economic integration (EMU).

- The FTA is only about the reduction of tariffs between members. In principle this does not imply any coordination of policies. Hence it can be realised between countries that have very different views about their economic systems and the way in which they pursue their objectives and can be set up without common institutions.
- The customs union and common market are fundamentally different. They require a common stand towards third countries (in practice not only for trade policy but, related to this, other policies). Moreover, there is common revenue that can be devoted to common objectives. Finally the customs union is not sustainable without a minimum of coordination of fiscal policies.
- For EMU even higher demands need to be met, such as deep integration and strong common institutions.

So all projects of integration that target a stage beyond the FTA have to be part of a project that has wider objectives than just trade gains. The consequence is that it also requires that the conditions for such cooperation are fulfilled. These are to be found in convergence of values and ideology and in the principles that guide institutional development.

Now, there are large differences in tradition, ideology and hence political choices between countries in the same region. Moreover many countries are small and poor which means that they have fragile economic structures and weak institutions. In this perspective it need come as no surprise that most of the RIAs that have been tried out initially were limited to the stage of FTA. However, the very dynamics of such integration pushes many to go beyond that stage (see Chapter 2 for causes).

---

9   See Chapter 2 and de Melo and Panagariya (1993).

EU ASPECTS

Let us now see what the situation of the EU is on this score. The EU has developed in a sense as a by-product of the political will to create a zone of political stability and peace in Europe. To that end it has committed itself to a deep integration. This is a fundamental choice; it was in opposition to the choices other countries in Europe had made, notably EFTA.[10] However, the EU has never made any blueprint of the final situation it aspired to. As integration progressed it has gradually set new concrete objectives for which cost and benefits could clearly be mapped out. Examples are the completion of the customs union by 1970, the internal market by 1992 and the EMU by 2000. In each of these steps the EU has chosen to move over a large front (covering all related issues) so as to distribute widely the cost and benefits and so avoid stalemates on individual cases. We must thereby take into account that the EU is a grouping of mostly highly developed countries that had in general rather resilient economic structures and strong government institutions to cope with the policy demands of such deep integration.

The EU has, moreover, given much attention to the interests of third countries. To give an example: the creation of the customs union went hand in hand with a decrease in its external tariff.

LESSONS

Comparison of the experience of the various RIAs with that of the EU suggests that the former should take account of the following lessons while making their choices as to the design of their system:

- Do not look upon the EU as an institutional blueprint for integration. Institutions and rules have to evolve according to contextual specificity, which means according to the cooperating countries' philosophical basis, political structures, public attitudes.
- Make the fundamental choice for a level of integration, set clear and shared objectives in function thereof and translate these into realisable deliverables.
- Analyse whether conditions for further integration are fulfilled. Mind that it is better to develop well an FTA rather than performing poorly on a higher (unrealistic) objective.
- Be realistic in the benefits which integration can achieve and about the cost to pay for reaching goals.
- Make sure that the RIA is a building block and not a stumbling block for multilateral (global) integration.

Lessons for the lower stages of integration: trade plus

RIAS

The objective of all RIAs is to provide certain public goods that neither the market nor the national governments can provide as efficiently as the RIA. Paramount among these is trade liberalisation. As has been said in a previous section most countries now see the benefit of opening up their economies to stronger possibilities of economies of scale and subject in their

---

10   The EU model has proved to be the strongest one and so others have rallied to it. However, one still sees that the fundamental choice of some of those countries which might have preferred only market integration is visible in their reluctance to adhere to the euro.

industries to the discipline of the markets. However, protectionist measures are often deeply entrenched and defended by strong interest groups. So liberalisation tends to take time and exceptions for specific products are often needed to come to an agreement on across the board tariff cuts.

There is a pressure to come to some form of common policies even in the lower stages of integration. This stems from the need to make sure that the liberalisation of markets is not distorted by so-called behind the border measures. A company that has a strong position back home may realise in this way the financial buffers it needs to compensate for the losses it incurs while dumping its products on the markets of its neighbours; hence the need for an anti-dumping or even better a full dressed competition policy. The same is true for social protection. Low levels of protection mean low production cost, which gives rise to claims of social dumping by competitors faced with the high cost of high levels of social protection. A possible solution may be to refrain from common policies and to refer to global standards; for instance ILO standards on labour protection (see next chapter).

The recent past has shown that RIAs can come under very heavy strain due to changes in the balance-of-payments position of one or more of its members. There is thus a real coherence problem to be solved. Some form of stabilisation of exchange rates is necessary; the more so in cases where internal liberalisation stretches beyond manufacturing trade and also covers capital movements and financial services. This entails, moreover, a need for maintaining coherence of other macro policies.

A subject that has bedevilled many RIAs is *divergence/convergence*. Many RIAs show considerable differences in wealth levels among participating countries. The ratio between the richest and the poorest member country is 4 for the Andean Community, 5 for Mercosur, 7 for NAFTA and about 100 for ASEAN (Singapore and Laos). All countries want to gain from the RIA, but in general one would like to see that the least developed countries gain most. Fortunately we have seen that in many cases the spontaneous development goes in that direction and that concentration tendencies of integration are limited. So real convergence can be expected to result from the process of integration.

EU ASPECTS

The EU has set out to define first its strategy towards liberalisation of markets and next to hammer out its flanking policies. In doing the first it has opted for a gradual approach; it has liberalised its markets in batches. It started with manufactured goods for which it used a comprehensive approach, that is across the board decrease of barriers. In the framework of the 1992 programme it liberalised the more sensitive areas; again in a comprehensive way as it was the result of the taking away of physical borders. This internal liberalisation went hand in hand with important regulation of the EU market.

The common policies of the EU have been developed in step with the integration of markets, giving priority to policies that were supportive of market integration. Policies that sustain what has been called the EU model (social and environmental objectives are pursued in step with the pursuit of competitiveness through market-oriented policies) have only come to development after evidence of convergence in political terms among the quasi-totality of its members.

Differences in wealth levels between the member countries of the EU (see Chapter 16) were relatively low (ratio about 3). So the EU has been able to develop over the first 25 of its 50 years of existence with a very simple system for promoting cohesion. The combination of (privileged) access to EU market and cost advantages has permitted integration to produce real convergence. As the convergence was thought to be too slow, cohesion has become a political objective in the second half of the life of the EU. Cohesion is now the major segment of the EU budget (notably if one also considers the transfers of the agricultural policy as redistribution). However, it is still limited if compared to national levels of redistribution.

LESSONS

The following lessons can be drawn from the development of low stage integration schemes:

- Reduce trade barriers only across the board; accept only very few exceptions.
- Couple integration with domestic liberalisation, but do not count too much on economies of scale.
- Do not rush to liberalisation of services and factor markets; but for FDI.
- Check possibilities for common policies that foster integration as they help to reap supplementary benefits.
- Organise first market access policies and policies that facilitate trade and investment, such as product standards and transport facilities.
- Formulate common competition policies in the first instance only with respect to extreme cases (monopolies; state aids) and probe carefully further into this area.
- Coordinate macro and monetary policies only as far as necessary to create conditions for market integration; provide for a mechanism to deal with shocks.
- Provide for simple mechanisms to cope with distributional issues only for cases where these become a hindrance to integration of markets.

Lessons from higher stages of integration: EMU

RIAS

The previous sections have made clear that most RIAs struggle in one way or another with the creation of stable conditions. They have experienced, sometimes at very high cost, that macro-economic and monetary disturbances can have very negative effects on trade. So countries are thinking of diminishing such disturbances and one option that is often considered is to radically do away with monetary and macro-economic stability issues and pave the way to monetary union.[11] The chances of such schemes succeeding are dependent on a multitude of factors. Most of them are found back in the Optimum Currency Area approach (see Chapter 2). We give the scores of the major RIAs on the most common criteria of the OCA in the next table. They range as usual from the openness to trade and production factors to the macro-economic conditions for EMU.

---

11   For a number of such ideas in Latin America, see the different contributions to Haegen and Vinals (2003) and to Artesis and de Paula (2003), and for similar ideas in Asia, several contributions in the 5th issue of Vol 15 (2004) and the first issue of Vol 16 (2005) of the Journal of Asian Economics.

Table 19.3 Optimum currency area indicators for major RIAs (2000)

Indicator	Statistics	NAFTA	Mercosur	ASEAN	SADC
Trade openness	% of GDP	25	15	52	n.a.
Trade interdependence	% share of total trade	65	36	n.a.	25
Labour mobility	several	very low	very low	very low	very low
Overall financial openness	IMF restriction Indicator	very high	high	very different for different member countries	very different for different member countries
Intra-regional financial integration	% share of partners in total capital inflow	high	low	low	low
Macro-economic convergence	Fiscal deficit; Publ.debt/ GDP; Inflation	high	low; average	very low	low
Credibility problems of monetary institutions	Past performance	small	serious	serious (recall Asian crisis)	serious

Source: Arroyo (2003) for NAFTA and Mercosur; own calculations and estimations for ASEAN and SADC.

There is only one conclusion possible from this table; all of the RIAs analysed are still far away from fulfilling even the economic conditions for the launching of a successful EMU. Trade integration is relatively low; internal capital market integration is low. The convergence achieved is far from significant. None of the regions has an anchor currency that may give credibility to other members such as the Deutschmark (Bundesbank) in the EU. In the case of NAFTA the dollar exists but the other member countries are not ready to surrender their policies to the domestic preferences of the USA in matters of currency. In none do we see a fiscal transfer mechanism to check possible divergence tendencies or an operational system to stimulate macro-economic convergence. Both are often considered as necessary conditions for monetary integration.

EU ASPECTS

It took the EU some 50 years of progressive integration to realise an EMU for the majority of its members. It was indeed the pinnacle of the integration process; and accepted only at a moment when the political conditions happened to be united (trade-off between German reunification and monetary union). In the meantime some intermediate solutions of monetary cooperation have been tried out (such as the ERM – see Chapter 15). Although they have helped the EU on the path to further convergence, they have also sometimes implied expensive lessons. The strength of the global capital markets exceeds by far that of the monetary authorities of RIA members working in isolation, and even of those of an RIA working in combination.

Although many economists have warned the EU not to move to EMU because it did not yet meet the criteria of an OCA, the EU has nevertheless moved ahead as a core group of member countries had achieved a very high degree of convergence for all criteria. The EU has set up an original combination of institutions to govern the EMU. It has created a centralised monetary authority in the independent European Central Bank that oversees the financial sector in cooperation with the national central banks. It has maintained a decentralised system of national fiscal authority that is coordinated by the Stability and Growth Pact. Internal labour movement in the EU is very low; nevertheless the EMU functions satisfactorily without this adaptation mechanism.

The perceived cost of staying out has induced many countries that were initially not considered to form part of the OCA to fulfil the criteria for membership. Endogeneity has worked in the sense that many of these countries now perform well on the conditions of the Stability and Growth Pact, whereas some of the countries that were considered to form the stable core of the OCA are struggling to keep to the rules (see Chapter 15).

LESSONS

The following lessons should be taken into account by countries considering the creation of an EMU:

- Do not move to monetary union until the basic conditions, including the political commitment, is there.
- Refrain from half-way solutions such as pegging systems. Having opted for open capital relations with the rest of the world, such intermediate forms will collapse under the attacks of the international markets. Moreover, the complications of managing such a system may actually delay instead of foster convergence.
- Reinforce institutions in order to prepare for EMU. The integration of financial markets needs to go hand in hand with institutional reinforcement of the system of macro-economic steering of the economy. Central Bank independence is a point to consider. Finally binding rules for fiscal coordination may help to create the conditions for a stable development of the CM.
- Avoid unnecessary social instability; labour mobility is not a prerequisite for EMU as long as other mechanisms work.

Lessons on institutions and governance

RIAS

In matters of governance one has to see three important aspects. These are the quality of the legal framework, the way in which decisions are made and the way in which they are implemented. Effectiveness on these scores speeds up the integration process and hence the grasping of the benefits of integration. However, this supposes willingness to surrender part of sovereignty to an international body. Many countries are afraid of doing so for two reasons: first, they value their independence very highly; second, they are afraid of the international organisation becoming subjected to special interest or to parasite behaviour of its governors and civil servants.

Institutional identity is weak. Most RIAs are based on an international treaty, some only on agreements. The lack of international legal personality means that RIAs such as the NAFTA, notwithstanding their clear economic importance, do not speak with a single voice in international organisations that serve as negotiation fora, such as the WTO. Some try to palliate this by setting up a common negotiating machinery for the period of negotiations.

Decision making in all RIAs is by consent. They are all based on the intergovernmental method, where all parties negotiate until they agree with the outcome. Results in this system can often only be had in cases where there is some sort of side-payment to the partners that gain least from the agreement or in some cases could, on specific points, even lose out. However, the RIAs analysed have no provision for such a system. It means that progress can only be achieved where the benefits exceed the cost for all partners.

Implementation methods are weak. The lack of compliance mechanisms mean that there is no way of making things that have been agreed happen in practice. Theory shows that in order to solve a problem, a group will opt for the lightest form of governance structures for getting compliance. Much in line herewith we find that the institutional and governance structure of the various RIAs is very rudimentary. In many cases disputes have to be resolved by negotiations among the partners that are party to the dispute. The recognition of the fact that such features prevent the organisation from reaching its goals sometimes leads the RIA to reluctantly resort to slightly stronger forms of governance (a case in point is ASEAN, see Box 19.1). Another case in point is the dispute settlement procedure of NAFTA. It involves a clear departure from the unilateralism that the US is often prone to use, as the US is obliged (notwithstanding its hegemonic power) to use the dispute settlement procedure.

BOX 19.1
THE ASEAN WAY

ASEAN countries have created the organisation as a 'low cost-high reward' one. All member countries are very keen on keeping their sovereignty and have a particular aversion to centralisation. They have chosen to transfer as little power as possible to the new organisation. This has had a series of consequences.

Legal matters. ASEAN has no formal treaty or charter. It is based on a series of agreements. Moreover, there are very few legal acts. So the organisation is not based on formal regulation but rather on trust and personal relationships (the Asian way).

Decision making. Partners talk until they reach agreement (consensus). Originally ASEAN had only a loose coordination structure between ministers of foreign affairs. After some time it became clear that this was not efficient and the structure has been strengthened. Meetings of the ministers of economic affairs and the heads of government have been installed for deciding on operational matters, while meetings of the heads of government are held to decide on the more strategic matters.

Dispute settlement. ASEAN does not rely on formal standard procedures. On the recognition of a problem (no solution to a dispute found), parties have to renegotiate; if this does not work out, further negotiations under the auspices of a mediator can be realised.

The weaknesses of this structure incite, from time to time, claims for a strengthening (for example, Charativat *et al.* 1999).

The lack of *strong institutions* does, however, also have some advantages. These show up notably in situations where external conditions have changed and ask for a new approach. Institutions based on strong regulation and strong governance will have to adapt a whole set of things which may be very difficult given the vested interest. Moreover, a strong system when misused can lead to substantial welfare losses. If no such formal agreements exist, the practices can be simply changed overnight.

EU ASPECTS

The EU has been formed by member states that all had long traditions of codification of rules, of efficient bureaucracies and of impartial judiciary. In this light it is understandable that it has opted for the *set-up of a strong supranational institution* to give form to its ambition of integration. This is to be detailed at several levels.

Constitution. Most countries of the EU have written constitutions that lay down the principles on which the state is based (for example, democracy) and the way it is organised, notably the division of powers and the checks and balances. The EU has for a long time worked on the basis of treaties that have an increasingly constitutional character. They define the institutional framework for coming to decisions and for implementing those decisions.

Decision. In many matters the EU arrives at decisions with qualified majority. This avoids many a stalemate. A member country that knows it can be overruled will, during the negotiations, orient itself towards alternatives, possibly by making package deals, where it benefits on one part of the deal while losing out on another.

Laws. EU law is directly applicable in all its aspects in member states. This means that compliance can be realised by any citizen invoking the EU rules in national courts. Disputes between member states are settled by the European Court of Justice.

Compliance. The European Commission is the Guardian of the Treaty and the trustee of the Community interest. It can use strong instruments to have the rules respected (like fines in cases where competition rules are violated). It has been bestowed with powers to negotiate with third parties on all matters where the EU has internal competences.

The advantages of this strong institutional set-up have been coupled with the advantages of a *flexible approach* towards the reaching of targets. In order to reach higher targets, a small group can actually move forward; it is not necessary for the whole fleet of countries to go at the speed of the slowest ship. The EU tries to accommodate the member countries that had unfavourable starting positions and opted to stay slow in reaching targets in two ways. First, by accepting (sometimes long) transition periods. Second, by giving financial support through its structural funds. A very good case in point were the funds (for example, Phare) that financed projects in accession countries in Central and Eastern Europe to help them in their transition from a planned economy towards a market economy.

The specific set-up of the institutions of the EU has, however, caused a major problem. The closed circuit of the agricultural interests and the political and managerial decision makers has created a very wasteful system of support that has successfully resisted many a tentative attempt at reform. The blame for this is mostly due to the special status that was given to this sector by the Treaty.

LESSONS

The experience of the EU in matters of governance suggests the following lessons for RIAs that want to improve their performance:

- Limit unanimity and introduce as quickly as possible qualified majority voting rules for all regular decisions.
- Resist the urge to write regulation centrally; limit this to the essentials only and give as much leeway under some form of subsidiarity to the constituent parts.
- Set up an independent guardian of the integration process (such as a Commission); this is essential in periods of crisis to prevent recursive effects.
- Avoid political and bureaucratic dealing with disputes; adopt procedures involving a Court of Justice or an independent Appellate Body.
- Lodge responsibility for external trade matters in one clear institution; an executive subject to broad periodic guidance and review from elected legislatures.
- Account for flexibility, for instance by accepting long transition periods. They essentially decouple the institutional commitment from the stresses of adjustment, postponing the latter until the former looks more or less indisputable.
- Do not give special constitutional status and/or a distinct bureaucracy to one or other segment of the economy.

Summary and conclusions

- The major RIAs of the world reveal very important differences in internal homogeneity, population size and institutional structures.
- Most RIAs have faced considerable problems in realising even relatively modest ambitions; however, in recent years real progress has been made and integration has moved beyond incomplete FTAs with positive effects on growth.
- The EU experience does contain a number of lessons for other regional integration schemes. However, the experience of the EU cannot be applied one to one in another context. One needs to see in all cases the specificity of each regional situation.

20 *What Lessons from the EU for the Design of Global Integration?*

Introduction

The present era is one of *globalisation*. As a consequence, for a large number of subjects, the optimal area for regulation is no longer the EU or the national state. Optimal regulation areas will increasingly correspond to the whole world. Globalisation puts a number of challenges to the Global Institutional System. So solutions have to be found to problems stemming from the inadequacies of the present situation. In the past the EU has been able to find solutions for similar problems by regaining collectively the power that its member countries had lost individually. So the objective of the present chapter is to analyse what lessons could be drawn from the EU experience[1] for improving global institutions.

The chapter is structured as follows. In the first section we give an overview of the basic features of the global regimes that make up the global economic institutional system. In the subsequent sections we detail each of the major features of this system. We define in this way the rationale of different regimes, the provision of public goods, the organisational form and finally the instruments that are used for realising the objectives. In each of the sections of this part we will discuss the global and the EU models and the lessons that the EU can provide to the world. In the final section we will analyse the consistency of proposals for enhanced integration on the regional level for different parts of the world (see previous chapter) with the enhancement of global integration (this chapter). As usual the chapter will be rounded off with a summary and some conclusions.

Background to the analysis

FACTORS THAT STIMULATE THE EMERGENCE OF GLOBAL INSTITUTIONS

The international economy has seen profound changes over the past half a century. Fundamental changes in matters of technology (for example, a decrease in the cost of transport), the structure of the economy (for example, from agriculture to information) and politics (for example, the demise of communism) have produced a substantial intensification of global interchange and integration. These changes in the world economy have had important effects on the roles of the major actors, such as private firms, public authorities and representatives of civil society. Large multinationals now control much of international trade and direct investment. Public authorities have seen that some of the policy instruments they used to intervene in the economy are no longer effective. NGOs have internationalised and, helped by modern technology (Internet, mobile phones), give voice to the needs of the civil society.

---

1   This chapter draws heavily on the last chapter of Molle (2003).

The increased global interchange has certainly contributed to the growth of economic welfare. However, it has also engendered some quite *negative effects*. Many feel that they are threatened in their existence by international competition. Moreover, there are real problems of lack of equity, labour protection and environmental sustainability.[2] As individual national governments can no longer deal effectively with many of these problems, there is a clear need for collective action at the global level and for the strengthening of the system of world government. Such collective action is not simple.

After the Second World War a bold and imaginative initiative created a set of specialist international organisations. In line with theoretical propositions (see Chapter 2 and Molle, 2003) they have developed as answers to a sectoral problem and hence are specialised on a functional basis. So, each of them is responsible for dealing with one problem of global governance, or in other words providing a specific *public good* that neither the market nor national governments can provide adequately. Also in line with theory is that these organisations have all adopted the lightest forms of governance structures for getting *compliance*.

PRESENT AND FUTURE CHALLENGES

The 'system' that has thus emerged has functioned reasonably well during the past half century. Its scope has been gradually widened while the structure of several specialists' regimes has also been strengthened.

In the *recent past* external conditions have changed profoundly and significant limitations have become visible. First, increased openness has created a greater interdependence and hence greater instability and vulnerability (notably in finance). Second, old needs do not yet have a solution (for example, poverty) while new needs have become apparent (for example, security) that ask for action. The present global institutional set-up is inadequate to deal effectively with these concerns. Moreover, there are considerable misgivings among developing countries about the ideological fundamentalism of the West and about the lack of voice that many (developing) countries have in major parts of the present system. So there is a great need for adaptation.[3]

In future it is likely that even more demands will be put on the system. On one hand technology and business will continue to press for more interaction and openness. On the other hand the forces that claim a stronger role for global institutions in a variety of matters are also likely to increase. So it is becoming an urgent matter to bring the global system up to the needs of the global community. Now realising such change is not an easy matter. The past shows that once regimes exist and show a certain level of effectiveness, it is difficult to adapt them. It also shows how difficult it is to set up new regimes. But change is possible provided one fulfils the right set of conditions (Kapur, 2002).

SALIENT FEATURES OF THE PRESENT SYSTEM

Table 20.1 gives, for each of the major global economic regimes and their associated organisations (columns), an overview of their main features (rows). The columns have been

---

2   However, theoretical and empirical investigations (Molle, 2002a) show that these do not justify sweeping statements such as: 'Globalisation is grinding the poor'; or: 'Globalisation hurts workers worldwide'; or: 'Globalisation destroys the environment'. Our analyses show that relations between variables reveal great complexity and the effects of globalisation show great diversity.

3   This has been expressed very clearly as follows: 'We have a system that can be called global governance without global government, one in which a few institutions…and a few players… dominate the scene, but in which many of those affected by their decisions are left almost voiceless… It's time to change some of the rules governing the international economic order, to think once again about how decisions get made at the international level' (Stiglitz, 2002: 21).

ordered more or less according to the stages of integration; starting with allocation (trade and some investment, so common market) followed by several aspects that make us move to some rudimentary sort of economic union (respectively stabilisation, sustainability, social matters and redistribution or equity). In the rows we follow a hierarchy of features. In the top rows we refer to such basic notions as the definition of the common interest that countries have in order to get together; in other words the motive (rationale) for their collective action. This is made more concrete in terms of specific public goods that need to be provided to the international community. In the middle rows we indicate the organisations that deal with the problems of public good provision. Next we detail some governance aspects, in particular the most important instruments that are used to get results.

Table 20.1   Salient features of the global order

	Trade	Finance	Environment	Labour	Aid
Rationale	Enhancing growth by better allocation	Enhancing growth by improving stability	Safeguarding sustainable development	Enhancing social equity	Enhancing spatial equity
Public good provision	Enhancing free trade in goods and services	-Stable financial relations -Avoiding crisis and contagion	-Stabilisation of climate -Prevention of ozone layer depletion -Maintaining bio-diversity	-Improve labour conditions -Prevent race to bottom	-Overcome barriers to growth - Improve global cohesion
Main organisation	WTO	IMF	UNEP	ILO	WB
Instruments for realisation and compliance	-Dispute settlement -Sanctions -Retaliation	-Standards -Surveillance -Financial assistance -Incentives/ Aid	-Standards -Pollution rights -Tradable permits -Bans on products -Reputation	-Standards -Reputation -Aid -Tri-partite negotiation (labour unions, employers, government) - Complaint ICJ	-Financial development aid -Technical assistance

Source: Adapted from Molle (2003).

One sees that there is no unified institutional framework but a rather disparate set of organisations and agreements (see Molle, 2003). Many of the global regimes seem to be rather embryonic and inadequate for the increased demands that will be put on it.

Rationale

GLOBAL ASPECTS

Globalisation has eroded the capacity of national governments to deal independently with problems and it has thereby increased the need for international cooperation in the framework of international organisations. The efforts of these institutions need to be oriented towards a set of basic goals. Among them *economic growth* takes pride of place, in particular in those countries that have a considerable poverty problem. But other societal concerns also call for action; traditional ones such as the respect of human values in labour relations and more recent ones such as a sustainable environment. Individual regimes that deal with these concerns have developed without much concern for a balanced and consistent global government system.

The second aspect of global regimes is the economic order they represent. All have been conceived as a function of the basic norms and traditions (ideologies) of the Western countries. After the demise of the centrally planned economies and the transition of these countries to a market economy, most major countries have now accepted the idea of a market economy along the lines of the West. The same is true for the group of developing countries that after decolonisation tried in their own way to come to grips with the challenges they were confronted with. Their more interventionist attitudes have led to the creation of UNCTAD. Both transition countries (including Russia and China) and less developed countries (including the proponents of UNCTAD) have now become members of the global economic organisations such as the WTO.

However, this has not done away with another major problem on the global level. Indeed, many of the protests of the past can be interpreted as opposition to the further development of the liberal market and of its hallmark organisations, the WTO and the IMF, without due attention being given to societal concerns. There is indeed a very serious imbalance between the degrees of development of the major functions. The allocation (market) regime is relatively far developed with a relatively strong organisation (WTO). The regimes for the other functions are ill developed and some are dependent on weak organisations (for example, ILO and UNEP).

EU ASPECTS

The fundamental design criteria that characterise the socio-economic institutional set-up of Western countries are twofold.

The first is based on a *division and hierarchisation of functions*. This notion has also shaped the set-up of the European Union.[4] The construction of the EU consists indeed of three layers.

- The foundation of the EU consists of the internal market. The basic principle in this area is the free internal movement of goods, services, labour and capital. In this way the allocation function is optimised, which is conducive to growth.
- The second layer consists of enabling policies. In order to create the conditions for a good allocation and hence for growth, a number of common policies are pursued, such as competition, macro-economic stability, monetary, and so on.

---

4   This basic set-up is not unchallenged. Time and again pleas are made to introduce social considerations at the level of the definition of market policies by setting constraints that are supposed to foster such social objectives. In some cases such actions have led to regime changes, but these do not affect the fundamentals just described.

- The third layer is composed of policies that relate to the social function. Indeed, the outcome of the processes in the two previous layers may not always be in line with social preferences. As such we may think of the equality of income distribution over social groups and geographical areas, the access to jobs for men and women, and so on. To improve the situation in these domains policies are needed such as regional policy, on which the EU spends a considerable part of its budget. Another component we may cite are environmental policies. All these third layer policies tend to respect the autonomy of the first layer policies (in environmental matters for instance by applying the polluter pays principle).

The second one relates to the *blend of market and intervention*. The EU has gradually made its choices as to the best economic order. On one hand it has put the accent on the liberalisation of markets. On the other hand there is a strong accent on coordination and harmonisation. The EU model is often characterised as socio-liberal. It is composed of elements, such as social-market economy (with the combined strive for competitiveness, social progress and environmental sustainability), democracy, security and respect for human rights. Each of these elements precluded the adhesion of some EU states at some point in time. The most obvious cases were Central and Eastern Europe (no market economy), or the Mediterranean countries (no democracy) or some Nordic countries (neutrality). When these factors changed they became candidates for membership. Within the broad framework the EU permits, however, considerable national diversity. These show themselves in the degree in which the state intervened in economic life, in tax structures and so on.[5]

LESSONS

The comparison of the global and the EU situation in matters of rationale and system suggest that one should:

- Focus the present regimes more precisely on the improvement of one of the three functions (allocation, stabilisation, redistribution).
- Avoid aggravation of the serious imbalance between organisations caring for liberal markets and those caring for other concerns (redistribution).
- Develop gradually pragmatic solutions to practical problems. See how far differences in values and ideology can be sublimated in new principles and common approaches.

Public goods

GLOBAL ASPECTS

The next interesting point we turn to is the sequence in which the need for global public goods arises and the reaction of the authorities in providing such public goods. Given constraints on collective action, regimes only come about in cases where there are very good reasons (see Chapter 2). Factors such as 'awareness' and 'knowledge' are important but the factor that

---

5 In Chapter 10 we distinguished between three types of national models, of which two (Rhineland model and Mediterranean model) are more oriented towards stability and state intervention, while the Anglo-Saxon model is more market-oriented and oriented towards flexibility.

carries most weight is actually 'interest'. So the development of the various regimes can be related to the balance between economic advantages and political cost.

Theoretical insight indicates that the first level of integration should apply to the integration of goods markets, since clear advantages can be had here, while government power in essential domains is not lost. The early development of the WTO and its predecessor GATT (which concentrate on trade issues and aspects that are immediately related to trade) is thus in line with these insights. The experience of regional integration schemes such as the EU shows that the good functioning of the liberalised markets need some common allocation policies.[6]

The second early development has been in finance. This is in line with the insight that trade and investment relations are facilitated by stable monetary conditions. The problems of the interwar period were still very vivid after the war and increased the awareness of the problem and the need to do something about it. The main public good has, however, gradually shifted from stability on foreign exchange markets towards the stability of the international financial system. This seems to be a logical step in the sequence of regime building. Indeed, the 'interest' argument applies here in full as actions for the improvement of exchanges in matters of trade (and investment) can only bear their full fruits in cases where stable financial conditions prevail.[7]

It is a well-known fact that concern for environmental problems is taken seriously only after a society has been able to safeguard the provision of its basic needs. The emergence of global environmental action and its subsequent development in the 1970s would then fit in the total picture of 'interest', as wealthy societies develop interest in more long-term aspects and in immaterial goods.

The development of a regime for social aspects, notably of labour standards, would have been stimulated by the almost universal interest in the improvement of such standards. Although it made an early start, its further development ran into formidable obstacles.

Finally, equity. Concerns about unequal distribution give rise to the set-up of policies only in two cases. First, if the situation threatens the security of a society or the stability of its economic base. Second, if solidarity between participants has grown enough to induce people to have part of their resources redistributed to those who are (temporarily) in a less favourable position. Both factors play a role at the global level, but only to a limited extent. Moreover, there exist serious doubts about the effectiveness of the present forms of redistribution to bring about less inequality. As a consequence the development of redistribution mechanisms has not gone very far on the global level.

EU ASPECTS

The development of the EU in terms of subjects covered is in general explained with a different set of theories. Most of it is associated with the functional spill-overs and the distinction in stages of integration. In each stage a specific (set of) public good(s) is added to the previous ones. There are sound economic as well as political reasons to start integration with goods markets (free trade area and customs union) and to continue with the markets for production factors (common market). The EU has indeed started with these subjects much like most

---

6   The good functioning of markets is enhanced by rules about competition policy. The case for the setting up of such an international (multilateral) competition policy is strong (Meiklejohn, 1999) and merits the overcoming of the obstacles to its realisation, among which the inadequacy of the existing institutional framework (WTO) is not the least. A compelling case can also be made for the setting up of an investment regime (such as the OECD project on multilateral agreement on investment) even if the political circumstances have aborted its set-up.

7   However, this sequence on the world level is only partly in step with the development on the regional level; here financial integration has not come to the fore at an early stage.

other regional integration areas in the world. However, it took half a century to arrive at near completion of these stages and to gradually integrate all economic sectors.

During the progressive development of the EU it became clear that the completion of one stage changed the cost-benefit relations for the next stage and showed that some more public goods could no longer effectively be provided on the national level. The EU included from the start a fair bit of competition policy and an embryonic social and macro-economic policy. Later it integrated environmental policies and a series of others, notably cohesion policies, with the objective of coming to a more equitable income distribution. In the course of time these policies were intensified, in other words they covered more aspects of the general public good. With increased integration, monetary instability became more and more of a problem and after some experimentation with intermediate forms of monetary integration, the EU moved towards a full monetary union at the turn of the century. With the realisation of the Economic and Monetary Union, it has set the pinnacle of economic integration.

Recently the EU has also integrated aspects of foreign and security policy and justice and home affairs, thereby entering the stage of a political union.

LESSONS

The EU experience suggests the following rules of conduct for those in charge of the improvement of the global provision of public goods:

- Do not try to transpose the EU model of functional spill-overs to the global level. Rather count on interest translated into cost and benefits. Bear in mind that the lack of coherent institutions makes collective action difficult. Bear also in mind that the problems and solutions need to respond to the basics of very different national systems.
- Move only to the second stage of integration (*free movement of production factors*) in cases where the benefits exceed the cost for all participants. This condition is far from being fulfilled for capital let alone for labour and population.
- Do not attempt to force the way for far-reaching global *stabilisation policies*. The need for a strengthening of the present system can be done by gradually expanding and refining the toolkit of the present organisations.
- Improve the effectiveness of the present global redistribution system but do not go for systems that necessitate a strong solidarity among the members of an organisation. On the global level this is not likely to develop in the foreseeable future.

Organisations

GLOBAL ASPECTS

Overlooking the past development we see that the main international organisations that are responsible for governing the world economy were founded in the aftermath of the Second World War. This applies notably to the UN responsible for security, to GATT/WTO responsible for trade and to the Bretton-Woods institutions responsible for finance and redistribution. Some of the organisations are even older, such as the ILO, dealing with social and labour issues. Others have come to the fore under the pressure of new needs, such as UNEP dealing with the environment.

The total set up of organisations seems to suffer from *several systemic problems*. First, responsibilities of the various organisations tend to overlap each other, giving rise to unnecessary high cost. Second, there are gaps in the responsibilities leaving room for defaults of the system. Third, the regulatory forms used by the various organisations are all very idiosyncratic, giving rise to high transaction cost to economic actors that need to come to grips with the system. Finally, each of these global regimes risks being captured by specific interest groups.[8] A particularly problematic point is voting power. Whereas the US, and to a lesser extent the EU, dominate organisations such as the IMF and World Bank (one dollar one vote), the LDCs dominate the UN (one country one vote) even in organisations that require unanimity to come to conclusions (such as the WTO).

Many national governments consider that most international organisations are not very good at delivering the products and services they promise (lack of effectiveness) and what is worse that they have developed large and costly bureaucracies (lack of efficiency). These concerns are confirmed by public choice theory that shows that bureaucrats in general tend to pursue their own objectives which are different from those of the organisation, and that bureaucrats of international organisations have particularly strong incentives to do so. Unfortunately, objective ways of performance measurement of international organisations are still lacking.

Many proposals have been made for improvement of this global 'system' of organisations. A first approach is based on specialisation. This approach suggests that the IMF should deal better with the problem of volatility of financial markets, the UNEP with the problems of environmental deterioration[9] and the ILO with the enhancement of labour standards. This strategy is clearly advocated on the global level by organisations such as the WTO that considers, for example, that all international labour issues need to be dealt with by the ILO and not by the WTO. A second approach tries to bring constraints on the basic rules of the major economic organisations. It advocates the use of instruments to influence the actions of present organisations in such a way as to foster side objectives (for example, equity in trade matters). A case in point has been the past acceptance by the WTO of generalised systems of preferences for LDCs (violating the principle of non-discrimination). Included in all such proposals is a better distribution of power over the various members.

More far-reaching proposals have been made. For instance for a world government that can take a consistent view of all the major problems. Or for the adoption of a common world currency that would do away with uncertainty for international business, with some of the causes of instability in the financial system. In view of the difficulties of collective action on the international level and the limited interest of major partners, these are rather unrealistic and we will not deal with them further.

EU ASPECTS

In Europe the need for integration of an increasing number of functional areas resulted in the creation of a whole series of organisations. In matters of trade the first was the European Coal and Steel Community (ECSC) followed by the European Economic Community (EEC) and the competing European Free Trade Association (EFTA). In matters of finance we cite the European Payments Union. For security the Western European Union (WEU) was created, while the

---

8   A case in point is the IMF which is very much dominated by treasury ministries that tend to be sympathetic to interests in financial markets (Stiglitz, 2002: pages 19, 20).
9   A fairly far-reaching proposal in this respect is the creation of the World Environmental Organisation (WEO) that should oversee all regimes in the environmental field (Tussie and Whalley, 2002 and Whalley and Zissimos, 2002).

Council of Europe (CoE) took responsibility for cultural affairs. The Organisation for European Economic Cooperation (OEEC)[10] did deal with many diverse matters of economic policy such as industry, productivity, tourism and so on.

In the fourth quarter of the 20th century the EEC emerged as the dominant organisation. While the EEC developed into the European Union, it took over the tasks of quite a few other organisations that have subsequently been phased out (ECSC, EFTA, WEU). The determinant element in this evolution may have been the strong interest (economic growth) on one hand and the strong governance structure (qualified majority voting, unified legal instruments) on the other hand.

The EU thus encompasses a wide variety of different regimes. Many of these have developed in a fairly autonomous sense, however, taking into account a certain basic structure. They have shown a considerable capacity for adaptation in the course of time. The evaluation of their performance is in general positive. However, in the previous chapters we have found one case of an unfortunate regime that moreover showed itself very resistant to change, viz. *agriculture*. It is a very clear example of an institution having been captured by a special interest. The Fathers of the European Union, while drafting the Treaty of Rome, have given a special constitutional status to agricultural policy. Budget outlays for agriculture fall in the so-called compulsory category to which special decision-making rules apply. Such decisions have been entrusted by the EU to the Council of Ministers on which sit the national ministers of agriculture who have proven to be strong defendants of their sector's interest at the cost of the interest of many others (see Chapter 9).

Much uncertainty existed at the creation and during the growth of the EU about the detailed features of its institutional structure. So there has been much experimenting. With hindsight it seems that the result of these innovations (that is the strong EU institutions) are rather adequate. Its three essential features are:

- A system of main institutional actors (Commission, Council, Parliament, Court, European Central Bank, and so on) that deal with all issues falling under the competences of the EU.
- A set of decision-making rules; its system of qualified majority voting (that is weighted votes per country) has shown that one can effectively deal with the problem of the differences in size of member countries.
- A system of governance, with legal and financial instruments for implementing its policies.

The system has shown itself to be capable of integrating over time more functions and more countries; accepting where needed some variable geometry. It has for instance accommodated the development of an embryonic monetary unit such as the ECU (comparable to the SDR of the IMF) and later a single currency.

---

10   The OEEC as an organisation did not amalgamate with the EU; it enlarged its membership to become OECD. However, its tasks for the Western European countries have been taken over by the EU. The work of the Council of Europe has only partly been taken over by the EU but cultural matters have mostly stayed with the national member states under the application of the subsidiarity principle.

LESSONS

To improve the total architecture of global organisations and regimes one might work along the following list of actions:

- Work towards a unitary structure for accommodating the development of the functional regimes, in the knowledge that the chances of it being put into practice in the short term look rather bleak.
- Work in the meantime in a piecemeal way on the improvement of the various international regimes taken individually. In this way the coherence and the efficiency of the system can be gradually improved.
- Do not put hopes on the natural selection of a nucleus organisation that gradually brings under its wings the other specialist organisations. The WTO seems to qualify most as such as it is the strongest in terms of economic interest and governance, but it lacks the capacity to encompass other aspects, while the UN cannot be bypassed.
- Do not let special interest groups capture regimes at the cost of other important groups; to prevent this from happening avoid giving constitutional status to such special groups.
- Do not be afraid of trying out new original forms, make use of room for experimenting and innovation, taking into account lessons from other experiments.
- Take time. It may take a long time before change becomes feasible. On the relatively small scale of Europe the development took half a century. So on the global level much more time may be needed as interests are more diverse and solutions more difficult to reach.

Instruments (governance)

GLOBAL ASPECTS

International regimes differ in the way they take decisions and in the way they make sure that members comply with these decisions.

With respect to *the taking of decisions* the global organisations are almost without exception organisations where voting is either by unanimity, or, if majority rules have been accepted, by the method of one country one vote. This may be judged as a problem where interests are very different and sizes are very different. The exceptions to this are the Bretton Woods institutions where the size of the contribution to the capital is very important. To some this boils down to one dollar one vote.

In matters of *compliance* international organisations are in general weak. They rely very much on national governments to implement. To make such a layered situation work, countries must observe the rule of transparency. Only under that condition is a system of monitoring and surveillance possible at relatively low cost. The monitoring does not need to be done by the international organisation in question. Some regimes rely on monitoring that is done by interested parties (trade). In other cases (for example, the environment) NGOs play an important role. Whatever the situation, the regime always has an interest in using instruments that optimise the situation with respect to transparency. The WTO has, for instance, consistently been pushing in this direction by the abolishment of opaque measures such as non-tariff barriers and their replacement by transparent measures such as tariffs. Once a good monitoring system is in place, reputation should then do most of the job to make countries comply with regimes.

Some global regimes are stronger in matters of compliance than others. We may list the compliance mechanisms (compare also Chapter 2) as follows:

- Reputation. All partners know that the quality of the deals they get in future will depend on their reputation. So this will not be easily foregone. NGOs target both companies and countries on the aspect of reputation to enhance compliance.[11]
- Coercion. In order to create the conditions for financial stability the IMF gives conditional loans. If the country in question does not agree to this, the IMF can withdraw support for national plans and, as alternatives will be hard to find, a country will in general comply.
- Sanctions. The WTO admits retaliation in cases where a country does not live up to the result of a dispute settlement procedure.
- Incentives. The World Bank can give debt relief to countries complying with environmental programmes.

Although all these instruments have their merits, many of the ones in use are actually sub-optimal. Better instruments are available but are not used because they are difficult to implement on the global level. In this respect one can see the proposals that have been made to improve financial stability by limiting the volatility of capital flows.[12] Such proposals have not materialised for a list of reasons.

Next, one would save substantially on transaction cost by adopting a common set of legal instruments and rules of governance (within which some diversity could be accepted to accommodate the details of the various regimes).

EU ASPECTS

The EU has over time developed a whole series of *decision-making procedures* (see Chapter 4), all applicable in particular circumstances. However, the one that is most representative of the EU practice is the so-called Community method that applies a system of qualified majority voting.

In matters of *compliance* the EU has fairly strong instruments at its disposal. First of all it needs to be underlined that EU legislation (regulation) is directly applicable in member states. So it can be invoked in national courts. The EU falls short of national states in matters of ultimate means of coercion, such as the use of military or police forces. However, it can use sanctions; the Commission can impose fines on countries or companies that breach competition rules. In general the EU has had a better hand than some of the global organisations in the choice of its compliance instruments. One can see this with the example of the constraints on state subsidies. The WTO instruments are clearly sub-optimal compared to those of the EU (see Box 20.1).

---

11   Compliance to standards, for instance, signals to the international community that you are part of a respectable set, which leads to lower cost of capital or higher inward investment.
12   One option is the so-called Tobin Tax. There is an abundant literature on this subject. We limit ourselves here to a reference to Haq, Kaul and Grunberg (1996) and Artesis and Sawyer (1997).

BOX 20.1
EU AND WTO INSTRUMENTS COMPARED

State aids (subsidies) can have important negative effects. So both the WTO and the EU have policies that regulate the use of state aids. There are, however, important differences between the two on many scores.

The objective of the WTO regime is to prevent subsidies from nullifying the abolishment of protectionist measures such as tariffs. For the EU the objective is the protection of fair competition on the internal market.

The procedure of the WTO is the lodging of a complaint, and the set-up of a panel that checks whether there has been injury to the complaining partner. The EU gets a complaint and that leads to the Commission investigating the case; findings of the Commission can be challenged before the European Court of Justice.

Compliance in the WTO has to be done by negotiation first and retaliation next. In the EU the Commission can oblige the member state to stop the aid and oblige the beneficiary of a non-permissible subsidy to pay it back.

The EU system is more economically sound as it takes away the origin of the problem, whereas the WTO system permits retaliation, which creates another distortion. Moreover, the institutions of the EU are more likely to come to economically sound conclusions. The EU does indeed rely on permanent staff in the specialist Directorate General of the Commission, whereas the WTO relies on trade diplomats who take alternate roles in the Subsidy Committee.

Source: Messerlin (1999b), 167–74.

LESSONS

The global system might benefit from observing the following EU lessons in matters of compliance:

*   Enhance the effectiveness of *decision making* in international organisations by introducing some form of qualified majority rule. Redistribute power by assigning weights (number of votes) for example, on the basis of population figures.
*   Enhance the quality of *implementation and compliance* by opting for first best solutions, wherever possible.

Consistency between global and regional integration

GENERAL ASPECTS

In the previous chapter we have discussed the question of whether the experience of the EU can provide lessons to other integration schemes. The idea was based on the observation that regional integration is positive because it can help to improve world welfare. In the present chapter we have seen that there are also lessons for the world institutional system as a whole. This idea assumes that improvement of the global system is necessary to enhance global welfare. From theory we know that action by small groups forming clubs (regions) is much easier than action by large groups (world). This observation has inspired the EU to stimulate and support regional cooperation in the interest of better world governance.[13]

Combining the two lines of thought (increased regionalism with increased globalism) creates a three-layer hierarchical structure (global, regional, national), in which the middle part deals with regional matters for the nations and represents the national part on the global level.[14]

The *advantages* of the option are seen to be fourfold:

- limiting the demands on the provision of global public goods by providing more on the regional level;
- limiting the cost of collective action and transaction by simplifying coordination and decision making;
- improving the voice of (groups of) LDCs and thereby limiting the distributional issue;
- bringing the decisions to a lower level where in principle a better trade-off between various aspects can be made than at the higher level (subsidiarity).

WHAT PUBLIC GOODS?

On the regional level economic integration tends to apply first to trade matters. Some regional organisations have developed into more encompassing ones in terms of public goods and have added some aspects of labour, finance, environment, and so on. The EU has gone furthest along this path. NAFTA has also made quite some headway. But going along that path for regional integration ventures outside the developed world is not simple. As said in the previous chapter, the conditions that the EU venture could fulfil and that made the EU capable of moving each time into higher stages of integration are not easy to replicate in other regions of the world. As a consequence there is a lack of match between the global and the regional regimes for all public good provision except for trade and investment.

- *Trade.* The WTO is the farthest developed international organisation with clear objectives and a relatively strong institutional set-up; notably its dispute settlement procedure stands out in this respect. On the regional level most ventures have been set up to deal with trade and related matters. The regional ventures are by definition in agreement with the WTO rules as that is the condition *sine qua non* for member states to participate in FTAs and CUs. For a multi-level set–up, however, there is a problem in terms of geographical coverage, as not all countries participate in regional schemes.
- *Finance.* The IMF as a global organisation uses a direct line in its contact with member countries. At this moment there are no equivalent structures dealing with monetary and macro-economic matters on the regional level apart from the EU. This is unlikely

---

13   This model has been proposed as an option by a working group that has prepared the EU white paper on governance. See Madelin et al. (2001).
14   The improvement of the global layer of international organisations (IO) is a problem, due to the diffuse power structures and the lack of incentives for major actors. To circumvent this problem proposals have been made to create IOs as clubs of clubs, instead of as platforms for intergovernmental cooperation (see, for example, Fratianni and Pattison, 2001).

to change in the near future; regional organisations such as ASEAN have very limited capacity to reform themselves quickly enough so as to be able to cope effectively with financial crises (Park and Wang, 2000; Teunissen, 2002).

- *Environment.* The UNEP deals in a somewhat disparate manner with a list of global environmental problems, which has resulted in a series of individual international agreements. Next to it are a host of regional agreements. These are all specific legal constructs and regimes, showing a great diversity as to geographic coverage, forms, instruments and so on. The EU is also the exception here, in the sense that as a regional organisation it has extensive powers in matters of the environment. The value added of newly created regional institutions for the environment that assume responsibility for harmonising regional matters consistent with global regimes is far from self-evident.
- *Aid.* The WB deals directly with all countries involved, both recipients and donors. Next to it exist a number of regional development banks. The set-up of a confederate structure of these institutions would imply that regional banks would be the main operational arms, while the WB would limit itself to a role in worldwide redistribution and the exchange of information. The coordination problem between donors would be lessened, the more so in cases where regional banks would also assume this role for bilateral donors.
- *Labour.* No match between world and regional level as virtually no regional integration schemes exist that have the competence to deal with the issue.

HOW TO REALISE OVERALL CONSISTENCY?

At present there is a lack of consistency between the various global regimes. All international organisations have different objectives, rules, audiences, and so on. Their dispersed actions are geared to effectiveness in a segment of the global 'system', not bringing about consistency between regimes.

For some time there has been some effort to achieve better coordination. In matters of trade and finance efforts have been made to achieve a greater consistency between the main multilateral agencies dealing with trade, development and finance. Notably trade-related assistance and market access for developing countries is a case in point. Cooperating organisations comprise the WTO, WB, IMF, UNDP, UNCTAD and ITC. More specifically there has been a link (observer status on the level of the Board members and cooperation on the level of staff members) between the IMF and WTO. Although these increased efforts at coordination help, they do not produce conformity in governance and consistency in results.

So the major challenge facing the system is to organise consistency between the global level and the regional level. The difficulties on this score are indeed immense. In the previous sections we have already seen the lack of coverage in public goods of most regional integration schemes; which means that they cannot serve as relay points for many global institutions such as the World Bank or the UNEP. But other problems exist too. For instance the value added of an additional organisational layer would have to be proved and the risk of creating another level of bureaucracy put aside. Finally a sort of unifying structure for the various regional and global regimes would have to be worked out. This would imply resolving difficult questions regarding the mandate of the regions in the global institutions, the governance of the new set-up (including weighted votes, and so on). So the option of the three-layered system, including enhanced regionalisation, is not very likely to be implemented.

Summary and conclusions

- The global institutional 'system' is very fragmented. It is actually more a patchwork than a system. The patchwork consists of a large variety of international regimes and organisations, each of which has been created to cope with a specific (set of) global problem(s).
- This 'system' has come under heavy criticism as many find that it has proved to be inadequate to cope with the problems of global public good provision; in other words to provide good global government.
- The EU experience does contain a number of lessons for world integration and institutional development. However, few of the experiences of the EU can be applied one to one in the global context. One needs to see in all cases the specificity of the problem at hand.
- The setting up of a consistent global system does not start from scratch. The (sometimes embryonic) individual regimes can be fitted into that new system. With respect to the function of government, the specialised agencies of the UN and various separate organisations could be seen as the global ministries of trade (WTO), finance (IMF), environment (UNEP), and so on.[15]

---

15   The General Assembly of the UN could act as a parliament. The International Court of Justice could be seen as the Court.

Bibliography

Aaron-Cureau, C. and Kempf, H. (forthcoming), 'Bargaining over monetary policy in a monetary union and the case of appointing an independent central banker', *Oxford Economic Papers*.

Abraham, F. and Konings, J. (1999), 'Does the opening of Central and Eastern Europe threaten employment in the West?' *The World Economy*, vol.22.4, pp.585–602.

Adams, K., Japelli, T., Menichini, A., Padula, M. and Pagano, M. (2002), *Analyse, compare and apply alternative indicators and monitoring methodologies to measure the evolution of capital market integration in the European Union*, EC Internal Affairs, http://europa.eu.int/comm/economy_finance/publications/economic_papers/2002/ecp/179en.pdf.

Addison, J.T. and Siebert, W.S. (1994), 'Recent developments in social policy in the new European Union', *Industrial and Labour Relations Review*, vol.48, no.1, pp.5–27.

Adler, M. (1970), 'Specialisation in the European Coal and Steel Community', *Journal of Common Market Studies*, vol.8, pp.175–91.

Agresano, J. (2004), 'European Union integration lessons for ASEAN +3: the importance of contextual specificity', *Journal of Asian Economics*, vol.14, pp.909–26.

Aitken, N.D. (1973), 'The Effect of the EEC and EFTA on European Trade; a Temporal Cross-Section Analysis', *American Economic Review*, vol.63, pp.881–91.

Albert, M. and Ball, R. (1983), *Towards European Economic Recovery in the 1980s*, European Parliament Working Documents 1983/84, Luxemburg.

Alesina, A., Angeloni, I. and Schuhknecht, L. (2005), 'What does the European Union do?', *Public Choice*, vol.123, pp.275–319.

Alesina, A. and Perotti, R. (1995), 'Fiscal expansions and fiscal adjustments in OECD countries', *Economic Policy*, vol.10, pp.205–48.

Alesina, A. and Spolaore, E. (1997), 'On the number and size of nations', *Quarterly Journal of Economics*, pp.1027–56.

Allais, M., Duquesne de la Vinelle, L., Oort, V.J., Seidenfus, H.S. and del Viscoro, M. (1965), 'Options in Transport Policy', *The EEC Studies*, Transport Series no.4, Brussels.

Allen, C.B., Gasiorek, M. and Smith, A. (1996), *Competitiveness, impact, and the quantification of trade creation and trade diversion due to the MSP* (background study to EC, 1996b), Brussels.

Allen, C., Gasiorek, M. and Smith, A. (1998), 'The competition effects of the Single Market in Europe', *Economic Policy; a European Forum*, pp.441–86.

Allen, P.R. (1983), 'Policies to Correct Cyclical Imbalance within a Monetary Union', *Journal of Common Market Studies*, vol.21.3, pp.313–27.

Allington, N.F.B., Kattman, P. and Waldmann, F.A. (2004), 'One market, one money, one price? Price dispersion in the European Union', *Working paper Judge Institute of Management*, Cambridge.

Allsopp, C. and Vines, D. (1996), 'Fiscal policy and EMU', *National Institute Economic Review*, pp.91–107.

Alvarez-Plata, P., Bruecker, H. and Siliverstovs, B. (2003), *Potential migration from Central and Eastern Europe into the EU 15 – an update*, DIW Report for the European Commission, DG Employment and Social Affairs, http://europa.eu.int/comm/employment_social.

AMUE (Association for the Monetary Union of Europe) (1988), *European Business and the ECU*; results of a survey carried out by FAITS et OPINIONS among 1036 business leaders in the European Community with the help of the ECU Banking Association and the European Commission, Paris.

Anarzit, P. d' (1982), *Essai d'une Politique Pétrolière Européenne*, Editions Techniques et Economiques, Paris.

Andersen, T., Haldrup, N. and Soerensen, J.R. (2000), 'Labour market implications of EU product market integration', *Economic Policy, a European Forum*, vol.30.2, pp.107–33.

Anderson S. and Eliassen, K. (1991), 'European Community Lobbying', *European Journal of Political Research*, vol.20, pp.173–87.

Arge, R. d' (1969), 'Note on Customs Union and Direct Foreign Investment', *Economic Journal*, vol.79, pp.324–33.

Aristotelous, K. and Fountas, S. (1996), 'An empirical analysis of inward foreign direct investment flows in the EU with emphasis on the market enlargement hypothesis', *Journal of Common Market Studies*, vol.34, no.4, pp.571–83.

Arroyo, H.T. (2003), 'Latin America's integration processes in the light of the EU's experience with EMU', in P. van der Haegen and J. Vinals (eds), *Regional integration in Europe and Latin America, Monetary and financial aspects*, Ashgate, Aldershot, pp.65–130.

Artesis, Ph. and de Paula, L.F. (eds) (2003), *Monetary Union in South America; lessons from EMU*, Edward Elgar, Cheltenham.

Artesis, P. and Sawyer, M. (1997), 'How many cheers for the Tobin tax?' *Cambridge Journal of Economics*, vol.21, pp.753–68.

Askari, H. (1974), 'The Contribution of Migration to Economic Growth in the EEC', *Economica Internazionale*, vol.27, no.2, pp.341–5.

Auctores Varii (1983), 'Issues and Experience of Transport Regulation Reform', *International Journal of Transport Economics*, vol.10, no.1–2.

Bachtler, J. and Clement, K. (eds) (1992), '1992 and regional development', special issue of *Regional Studies*, vol.26, no.4, pp.305–419.

Bachtler, J. and Michie, R. (1995), 'A new era in EU regional policy evaluation: The appraisal of the Structural Funds', *Regional Studies*, vol.29, no.8, pp.745–52.

Badinger, H. and Breuss, F. (2004), 'What has determined the rapid growth of intra EU trade?' *Review of World Economics*, vol.140.1, pp.31–51.

Baele, A., Ferrando, A., Hoerdahl, P., Krylova, E. and Monnet, C. (2004), 'Measuring European Financial integration', *Oxford Review of Economic Policy*, vol.20.4, pp.509–30.

Baer, W., Cavalcanti, T. and Silva, P. (2002), 'Economic integration without policy coordination; the case of Mercosur', *Emerging Markets Review*, vol.3, pp.269–91.

Bagella, M., Becchetti, L. and Hasan, I. (2004), 'The anticipated and concurring effects of the EMU: exchange rate volatility, institutions and growth', *Journal of International Money and Finance*, vol.23.7/8, pp.1053–83.

Baier, S.L. and Bergstrand, J. H. (2004), 'Economic determinants of free trade agreements', *Journal of International Economics*, vol.64.1, pp.29–63.

Bairoch, P. (1976), *Commerce Extérieur et Développement Economique de l'Europe au XIXe Siècle*, Mouton, Paris.

Balassa, B. (1961), *The Theory of Economic Integration*, Irwin, Homewood, Illinois.

Balassa, B. (1966), 'Tariff Reductions and Trade in Manufactures among Industrial Countries', *American Economic Review*, vol.56, pp.466–73.

Balassa, B. (ed.) (1975), *European Economic Integration*, North-Holland/American Elsevier, Amsterdam.

Balassa, B. (1976), 'Types of Economic Integration', in F. Machlup (ed.), *Economic Integration, Worldwide, Regional, Sectoral*, Macmillan, London, pp.17–31.

Balassa, B. (1977), 'Revealed Comparative Advantage Revisited: an Analysis of Relative Export Shares of the Industrial Countries 1953–1971', *The Manchester School*, pp.327–44.

Balassa, B. (1986), 'Intra-Industry Trade among Exporters of Manufactured Goods', in D. Greenaway and P.K.M. Tharakan (eds), *Imperfect Competition and International Trade*, Wheatsheaf, Brighton, pp.108–28.

Balassa, B. and Bauwens, L. (1988), 'The Determinants of Intra-European Trade in Manufactured Goods', *European Economic Review*, vol.32, no.7, pp.1421–39.

Baldwin, R. and Murray, T. (1977), 'MFN Tariff Reductions and Developing Country Trade Benefits under GSP', *Economic Journal*, vol.87, pp.30–46.

Baldwin, R.E. (1984), 'Trade Policies in Developed Countries', in R.W. Jones and P.B. Kenen (eds), *Handbook of International Economics*, vol.I, North-Holland, Amsterdam, pp.571–621.

Baldwin, R.E. (1994), 'Towards an integrated Europe', CEPR, London.

Baldwin, R.E. (1997), 'The causes of regionalism', *CEPR discussion paper*, no 1599 London.

Baldwin, R.E., Forslid, R. and Haaland, J.I. (1996), 'Investment creation and diversion in Europe', *The World Economy*, vol.19, no.6, pp.635–59.

Baldwin, R.E., Francois, J.F. and Portes, R. (1997), 'The cost and benefits of eastern enlargement; the impact on the EU and central Europe', *Economic Policy; a European Forum*, vol.24, pp.127–76.

Barrell, R. and Pain, N. (1999), 'Trade restraints on Japanese direct investment flows', *European Economic Review*, vol.43, pp.29–45.

Barro, R.J. and Sala-I-Martin, X. (1991), 'Convergence across states and regions', *Brookings papers on Economic Activity*, 1991.1, pp.107–82.

Bartel, R. (1974), 'International Monetary Unions, the 19th Century Experience', *Journal of European Economic History*, vol.3, no.3, pp.689–723.

Bayoumi, T. and Eichengreen, B. (1993), 'Shocking aspects of European Monetary Integration', in Francisco Torres and Francesco Giavazzi (eds), *Adjustment and Growth in the European Monetary Union*, Cambridge University Press, Cambridge, pp.193–229.

Bayoumi, T. and Eichengreen, B. (1997), 'Ever closer to heaven? An optimum currency area index for European countries', *European Economic Review*, vol.41, pp.761-70.

Bayoumi, T. and Prassad, E. (1995), 'Currency Unions, economic fluctuations and adjustment: some empirical evidence', *CEPR discussion paper*, no. 1172.

Bean, Ch. (1994), 'European Unemployment: A Survey', *The Journal of Economic Literature*, vol.32.2, pp.573–619.

Bean, Ch., Bernholz, P., Danthine, J.P. and Malinvaud, E. (1990), *European labour markets: a long-run view*, CEPR Macroeconomic Policy Group, Centre for European Policy Studies, Brussels.

Beetsma, R. and Uhlig, H. (1999), 'An analysis of the Stability and Growth Pact', *The Economic Journal*, vol.109, pp.546–71.

Begg, D., Cremer, J., Danthine, J-P., Edwards, J., Grilli, V., Neven, D., Seabright, P., Sinn, H-W., Venables, A. and Wyplosz, Ch. (1993), 'Making sense of Subsidiarity; how much centralization for Europe?', *Monitoring EU Integration,* no 4, CEPR, London.

Beine, M., Candelon, B. and Hecq, A. (2000), 'Assessing a perfect European Optimum Currency Area; a common cycles approach', *Empirica*, vol.27.2, pp.115–32.

Belderbos, R.A. (1997), 'Antidumping and tariff-jumping: Japanese firms' DFI in the European Union and the United States', *Weltwirtschaftliches Archiv*, vol.133.3, pp.419–57.

Belke, A. and Hebler, M. (2002), 'Towards a European Social Union, Impacts on labour markets in the acceding countries', *Constitutional Political Economy*, vol.13, pp.313–35.

Bergeijk, P.A.G., van (1987), *The Determinants of Success and Failure of Economic Sanctions, Some Empirical Results*, Development and Security, Groningen.

Berger, H., de Haan, J. and Eijffinger, S. (2001), 'Central Bank independence, an update of theory and evidence', *Journal of Economic Surveys*, vol.15.1, pp.3–40.

Bergstrand, J.H. (1983), 'Measurement and Determinants on Intra-Industry International Trade', in P.K.M. Tharakan (ed.), *Intra-Industry Trade: Empirical and Methodological Aspects*, North-Holland, Amsterdam, pp.201–55.

Bernard, P.J. (ed.) (1978), *Les Travailleurs Etrangers en Europe*, Mouton, The Hague.

Berthold, N., Fehn, R. and Thode, E. (1999), 'Real wage rigidities. Accomodative demand policies and the functioning of EMU', *Weltwirtschaftliches Archiv*, vol. 135.4, pp. 545–72.

BEUC (1982), *Report on Car Prices and Private Imports of Cars in the EC Countries*, BEUC 105892, Brussels.

BEUC (1988), *Term Insurance in Europe* (Report nr. 51/88), Brussels.

Beugelsdijk, M. and Eijffinger, S. (2003), *The effectiveness of structural policy in the European Union; an empirical analysis for the EU 15 during the period 1995-2001*, Mimeo, CentER, Tilburg.

Bhagwati, J.N. (1987a), 'Trade in Services and the Multilateral Trade Negotiations', *The World Bank Economics Review*, vol.1, no.4, pp.549–69.

Bhagwati, J.N. (1987b), 'International Factor Mobility', in R.C. Feenstra (ed.), *Essays in International Economic Theory*, vol.2, MIT Press, Cambridge, Massachusetts.

Bhagwati, J. (1991), *The world trading system at risk*; Princeton University Press, Princeton.

Bhagwati, J. and Panagariya, A. (1996), 'The theory of preferential trade agreements: historical evolution and current trends', *AEA papers and proceedings*, vol.86.2, pp.82–7.

Bhagwati, J.N., Schatz, K.W. and Wong, K. (1984), 'The West German Gastarbeiter System of Immigration', *European Economic Review*, vol.26, pp.227–94.

Bianchi, P. and Forlai, L. (1993), 'The domestic appliance industry; 1945–1991', in H.W. de Jong (ed.), *The Structure of European Industry*, 3rd edn, Kluwer, Dordrecht, pp.171–202.

Bikker, J.A. (2004), *Competition and efficiency in a unified European banking market*, Cheltenham; Edward Elgar.

Bjorvatn, K. (2004), 'Economic integration and the profitability of cross border mergers and acquisitions', *European Economic Review*, vol.48, pp.1211–26.

Blanchard, O. and Giavazzi, F. (2003), 'Macroeconomic effects of regulation and deregulation in goods and labor markets', *Quarterly Journal of Economics*, vol.118.3, pp.879–908.

Blanchard, O. and Wolfers, J. (2000), 'The role of shocks and institutions in the rise of European unemployment; the aggregate evidence', *Economic Journal*, vol.110, pp.1–33.

Blitz, R.C. (1977), 'A Benefit–Cost Analysis of Foreign Workers in West Germany 1957–1973', *Kyklos*, vol.30, pp.479–502.

Blomstrom, M. and Kokko, A. (2001), 'Foreign direct investment and spill-overs of technology', *International Journal of Technology Management,* vol.22.5/6, pp.435–54.

Blonk, W.A.G. (1968), *Enige Aspecten en Problemen van het Goederenvervoer tussen de Lidstaten van de Europese Economische Gemeenschap, met Name ten Aanzien van de Kwantitatieve Beperkingen en Kwalitatieve Belemmeringen*, Born, Assen.

Bloom, N. Griffith, R. and Van Reenen, J. (2002), 'Do R&D tax credits work? Evidence for a panel of countries, 1979-1997', *Journal of Public Economics*, vol.85, pp.1–31.

Bocconi (university of) (1997), 'EU foreign direct investments in Central and Eastern Europe', mimeo, Milan.

Boeri, T and Bruecker, H. (2000), 'The impact of Eastern enlargement on employment and labour markets in EU member states', *Report for the EC/DG Employment*, http://europa. eu.int/comm/employment_social.

Bofinger, P. (1994), 'Is Europe an optimum currency area?', *CEPR discussion paper series*, no.915, Centre for Economic Policy Research, London.

Böhning, W.R. (1972), *The Migration of Workers in the UK and the EC*, Oxford University Press, London.

Böhning, W.R. (1979), 'International Migration in Western Europe, Reflections on the Last Five Years', *International Labour Review*, vol.118, no.4, pp.401–15.

Böhning, W.R. (1993), *International Aid as a Means to Reduce the Need for Emigration*, ILO/UNHR, Geneva.

Böhning, W.R. and Maillat, D. (1974), *The Effects of the Employment of Foreign Workers*, OECD, Paris.

Boldrin, M. and Canova, F. (2001), 'Europe's regions: income disparities and regional policies', *Economic Policy*, vol.32, pp.207–53.

Boldrin,M. and Canova, F. (2003), 'Regional policies and EU enlargement', *CEPR discussion paper series*, No. 3744.

Boltho, A. (ed.) (1982), *The European Economy; Growth and Crisis*, Oxford University Press, Oxford.

Bongardt, A. (1993), 'The Automotive Industry; Supply Relations in Context', in H.W. de Jong, (ed.), *The Structure of European Industry*, 3rd edn, Kluwer, Dordrecht, pp.147–70.

Borensztein, E. *et al.* (1998), 'How does foreign direct investment affect economic growth?' *Journal of International Economics*, vol.45, pp.115–35.

Borjas, G.J. (1995), 'The economic benefits of immigration', *Journal of Economic Perspectives*, vol.9, no.2, pp.3–22.

Bos, J. and Kolari, J. (2005), 'Large bank efficiency in Europe and the United States; are there economic motivations for geographic expansion in financial services?' *Journal of Business*, vol.78.5, pp.1-38.

Bourguignon, F., Gallast-Hamond, G. and Fernet, B. (1977), *Choix Economiques liés aux Migrations Internationales de Main d'oeuvre; le Cas Européen*, OECD, Paris.

Brabant, J.M. van (1989), *Economic integration in Eastern Europe; a handbook*, Harvester Wheatsheaf, New York.

Bradley, J., Morgenroth, E. and Untiedt, G. (2004), *Macro regional evaluation of the Structural Funds using the HERMIN modelling framework*, paper for the Slovenia conference.

Bradley, J., O'Donell, N., Sheridan, N. and Whelan, K. (1995), *Regional Aid and Convergence, Evaluating the Impact of the Structural Funds on the European Periphery*, Avebury, Aldershot.

Brennan, G. and Buchanan, J.M. (1980), *The Power to Tax, Analytical Foundations of a Fiscal Constitution*, Cambridge University Press, Cambridge.

Brenton, P., di Mauro, F. and Luecke, M. (1999), 'Economic integration and FDI, an empirical analysis of foreign direct investment in the EU and in Central and Eastern Europe', *Empirica*, vol.26.2, pp.95–121.

Breuss, F. (2002), 'Benefits and dangers of EU enlargement', *Empirica,* vol.29.3, pp.245–74.

Breuss, F. and Eller, M. (2004), 'The optimal decentralisation of government activity; normative recommendations for the European Constitution', *Constitutional Political Economy*, vol.15, pp.27–76.

Breuss, F. Fink, G. and Haiss, P. (2004), 'How well prepared are the New Member States for the European Monetary Union?' *Journal of Policy Modeling*, vol.26.7, pp.769–91.

Broadway, R. and Cuff, K. (2001), 'A minimum wage can be welfare improving and employment enhancing', *European Economic Review*, vol.45.3, pp.553–76.

Bröcker, J. (1984), *Interregionaler Handel und ökonomische Integration*, Florentz, Munich.

Brown, S., Button, K. and Sessions, J. (1996), 'Implications of Liberalised European Labour Markets', *Contemporary Economic Policy*, vol.14, no.1, pp.58–69.

Bruecker, H. (2002), 'Can international migration solve the problems of European labour markets?' *UN/ECE Economic Survey of Europe*, no.2, pp.109–41.

Brugmans, H. (1970), *L'idée Européenne 1920–1970*, De Tempel, Brugge.

Buch, C. (1999), 'Capital mobility and EU enlargement', *Weltwirtschaftliches Archiv*, vol.135, no.4, pp.629–56.

Buchanan, J. (1965), 'An Economic Theory of Clubs', *Economica*, vol.32, pp.1-14.

Buchanan, J. (1987), 'Constitutional Economics', *The New Palgrave*, Macmillan, London.

Buchanan, J. (1998), 'Constitutional Economics', *The New Palgrave Dictionary of Economics and Law*, London Macmillan, pp.585–88.

Buckley, P.J. and Artisien, P. (1987), 'Policy issues of intra-EC direct investment; British, French and German multinationals in Greece, Portugal and Spain, with special reference to employment effects', *Journal of Common Market Studies*, vol.26, no.2, pp.207–30.

Buckwell, A.E., Harvey, D.R., Thomson, K.T. and Parton, K.A. (1982), *The Cost of the Common Agricultural Policy*, Croom Helm, London.

Buigues, P. and Jacquemin, A. (1994), 'Foreign direct investments and exports to the European Community', in M. Mason and D. Encarnation (eds), *Does Ownership Matter? Japanese Multinationals in Europe*, Clarendon Press, Oxford.

Buigues, P., Jacquemin, A. and Sapir, A. (1995), *European Policies on Competition, Trade and Industry*, Edward Elgar, Aldershot.

Buiter, W., Corsetti, G. and Roubini, N. (1993), 'Excessive deficits: sense and nonsense in the Treaty of Maastricht', *Economic Policy*, April, pp.57–100.

Buiter, W.H. and Marston, R. (eds) (1985), *International Economic Policy Coordination*, Cambridge University Press, Cambridge.

Butler, A.D. (1967), 'Labour Cost in the Common Market', *Industrial Economics*, vol.6, no.2, pp.166–83.

Button, K.J. (1984), *Road Haulage Licensing and EC Transport Policy*, Gower, Aldershot.

Button, K., Haynes, K. and Stough, R. (1998), 'Flying into the future; Air transport policy in the European Union', Edward Elgar, Cheltenham.

Buzan, B. (1984), 'Economic Structure and International Security; the limits of the liberal case', *International Organization*, vol.38, pp.597–624.

Cairncross, A. (1973), *Control of Long-Term International Capital Movements*, Brookings Institution, Washington.

Campos, N. and Kinoshita, Y. (2001), 'FDI as effective technology transferred', *paper Dep. of Economics*, University of Newcastle upon Tyne, Newcastle.

Canny, N. (ed.) (1994), *Europeans on the Move; studies in European migration 1500–1800*, Clarendon Press, Oxford.

Cantwell, J. and Randaccio, F.S. (1992), 'Intra-Industry Direct Investment in the EC, Oligopolistic Rivalry and Technological Competition', in J. Cantwell (ed.), *Multinational Investment in Modern Europe*, Edward Elgar, Aldershot, pp.71–106.

Cappellen, A., Castellacci, F., Fagerberg, J. and Verspagen, B. (2003), 'The impact of EU regional support on growth and convergence in the European Union', *Journal of Common Market Studies*, vol.41.4, pp.621–44.

Caramazza, F. (1987), 'International Real Interest Rate Linkages in the 1970s and 1980s', in R. Tremblay (ed.), *Issues in North American Trade and Finance*, North American Economic and Finance Association, vol.4, no.1, pp.123–50.

Carstensen, K. and Toubal, F. (2004), 'Foreign Direct Investment in Central and Eastern European countries, a dynamic panel analysis', *Journal of Comparative Economics*, vol.32.1, pp.3–22.

Carter, R.L. and Dickinson, G.M. (1992), 'Obstacles to the Liberalisation of Trade in Insurance', *TPRC*, Harvester Wheatsheaf, London/New York.

Casella, A. (1994), 'Trade as an engine of political change, a parable', *Economica*, vol.61, pp.267–84.

Casella, A. (2001), 'Tradable deficit permits', in A. Brumilla, M. Buti and D. Francko (eds), *The Stability and Growth Pact; the architecture of fiscal policy in EMU*, Palgrave, Basingstoke, pp.394–413.

Casella, A. and Frey, B. (1992), 'Federalism and clubs; towards a theory of overlapping political jurisdictions', *European Economic Review*, vol.36, no.2/3, pp.639–46.

Cassis, Y. (ed.) (1991), *Finance and Financiers in European History 1880–1960*, Cambridge University Press, Cambridge.

Castles, S. and Kosack, G. (1985), *Immigrant Workers and Class Structure in Western Europe*, Oxford University Press, London.

Caves, R. (1982), *Multinational Enterprise and Economic Analysis*, Cambridge University Press, Cambridge.

Caves, R. and Jones, R. (1984), *World Trade and Payments*, 3rd edn, Little, Brown, Boston, Massachusetts.

Cecchini, P. *et al.* (1988), *The European Challenge 1992*, Gower, Aldershot.

CE/ECORYS (forthcoming), 'Factors for regional competitiveness', study commissioned by the EC DG Region and carried out by Cambridge Econometrics and ECORYS in cooperation with Prof. R. Martin, WIFO, CEET and IPD.

CEPII (1996), *Intra- versus inter-industry trade flows inside the EU due to the internal market programme* (background study for CE, 1996b), Brussels.

CEPR (1992), 'Is Bigger Better? The Economics of EC Enlargement', *CEPR/MEI* Series 3, London.

CEPR (1993), 'Making Sense of Subsidiarity; How much Centralization for Europe?', *CEPR/MEI* series 4, London.

CEPR (2002), 'Financial market integration, corporate financing and economic growth', London.

Cernat, L. (2001), 'Assessing regional trade arrangements; are South–South RTAs more trade diverting?', in *Policy issues in international trade and commodities study series*, no 16, UNCTAD, New York.

Chang, H.J. (1996), 'The political economy of industrial policy', Macmillan, London.

Charativat, S., Pachusanond, C. and Wongboonsin, P. (1999), 'ASEAN prospects for regional integration and the implications for the ASEAN legislative and institutional framework', *ASEAN Economic Bulletin*, vol.16.1, pp.28–50.

Chen, N. (2004), 'The behaviour of relative prices in the European Union; a sectoral analysis', *European Economic Review*, vol.28, pp.1257–86.

Chenery, H. (1960), 'Patterns of Industrial Growth', *American Economic Review*, vol.50, pp.624–54.

Cherif, M. and Ginsburgh, V. (1976), 'Economic Interdependence Among the EEC Countries', *European Economic Review*, vol.8, pp.71–86.

Chipman, J.S. (1965/6), 'A Survey of the Theory of International Trade', *Econometrica*, part I, vol.33, no.3, pp.477–519; part II, vol.33, no.4, pp.685–761; part III, vol.34, no.1, pp.18–76.

Chryssochoou, D.N. (1997), 'New challenges to the study of European integration; implications for theory building', *Journal of Common Market Studies*, vol.35.4, pp.521–42.

Chudnovsky, D. and Lopez, A. (2004), 'Transnational corporation strategies and foreign trade patterns in Mercosur countries in the 1990s', *Cambridge Journal of Economics*, vol.28.5, pp.635–52.

Clarette, R., Edmonds, C. and Seddon Wallack, J. (2003), 'Asian regionalism and its effects on trade in the 1980s and 1990s', *Journal of Asian Economics*, vol.14, pp.91–129.

Clark, C. (1957), *Conditions of Economic Progress*, Macmillan, London.

Clay, E., Dhiri, S. and Benson, Ch. (1996), *Joint evaluation of European Union programme food aid, Synthesis report*, ODI, London.

Clegg, J. and Scott-Green, S. (1999), 'The determinants of new FDI capital flows into the EC; a statistical comparison of the USA and Japan', *Journal of Common Market Studies*, vol.37.4, pp.597–616.

Cnossen, S. (ed.) (1987), *Tax Coordination in the European Community*, Kluwer, Deventer.

Cnossen, S. (1990), 'The Case for Tax Diversity in the European Community', *European Economic Review*, vol.34, pp.471–9.

Cnossen, S. (1996), *Reform and harmonisation of company tax systems in the European Union*, OCFEB RM9604, Rotterdam.

Coase, R. H. (1937/1988), 'The nature of the firm', *Economica*, vol.4, pp.386–405; reprinted as chapter 2 in R. H. Coase (1988), *The firm, the market and the law*, University of Chicago Press, Chicago

Collie, D.R. (2000), 'State aid in the European Union; the prohibition of subsidies in an integrated market', *International Journal of Industrial Organisation*, vol.18, pp.867–84.

Collignon, S. (2004), 'Fiscal Policy and Democracy', *Oesterreichische National Bank (OeNB) Discussion papers*, no 4, Vienna.

Collins, D. (1983), *The Operations of the European Social Fund*, Croom Helm, London.

Cooke, T.E. (1988), *International Mergers and Acquisitions*, Basil Blackwell, Oxford.

Copenhagen Economics (2005), 'Economic assessment of the barriers to the internal market for services', Appendix A, Study for the EC.

Corden, W.M. (1971), *Theory of Protection*, Clarendon, Oxford.

Corden, W.M. (1972a), 'Economies of Scale and Customs Union Theory', *Journal of Political Economy*, vol.80, no.1, pp.465–75.

Corden, W.M. (1972b), 'Monetary Integration', *Essays in International Finance*, no.93, Princeton University, Princeton, NJ.

Corden, W.M. (1974), *Trade Policy and Economic Welfare*, Clarendon, Oxford.

Council of Europe (1980), *European Migration in the 1980s, Trends and Policies*, Strasbourg.

Council of Europe (1983), *The Situation of Migrant Workers and their Families; Achievements, Problems and Possible Solutions*, Strasbourg.

Cox, A. and Chapman, J. (1999), 'The European Community External Cooperation Programmes; policies, management and distribution', Overseas Development Institute, London.

Craigh, L.E. and Fisher, D. (1996), *The Integration of the European Economy*, Macmillan, Basingstoke, St. Martin's Press, New York.

Crespo, J. and Velasquez, F.J. (2003), 'Multinationals and the diffusion of technology between developed countries', *Working paper no 26-2003,* FSEC/UCM, Madrid.

Crespo-Cuaresma, J., Dimitz, M.A. and Ritzberger-Gruenwald, D. (2003), 'The impact of European integration on growth; what can we learn for EU accession?', in G. Tumpell-Gugerell and P. Mooslechner (eds), *Economic convergence and divergence in Europe; growth and regional development in an enlarged Europe*, Edward Elgar, Cheltenham. pp.55–71.

Cuadrado-Roura, J-R., Garcia-Greciano, B. and Raymond, J-L. (1999), 'Regional convergence in productivity and productive structure; the Spanish case', *International Regional Science Review*, vol.22. 1, pp.350–53.

Cushman, D.O. (1983), 'The Effects of Real-Exchange-Rate Risk on International Trade', *Journal of International Economics*, vol.15, pp.45–63.

Dall'erba, S. and Le Gallo, J. (2003), *Regional convergence and the impact of European Structural Funds over 1989-1999 ; a spatial econometric analysis*, Paper for the ERSA conference, Jyvaskyla.

Dangerfield, M. (2000), *Subregional Economic Cooperation in Central and Eastern Europe; the political economy of CEFTA*, Edward Elgar, Cheltenham.

Davenport, M. (1986), *Trade Policy, Protectionism and the Third World*, Croom Helm, Beckenham.

Daveri, F. and Tabellini, G. (2000), 'Unemployment and taxes; Do taxes affect the rate of unemployment?' *Economic Policy; a European Forum*, vol. 30, pp.47–104.

Dearden, S.J.H. (1995), 'European Social Policy and Flexible Production', *International Journal of Manpower*, vol.16, no.10, pp.3–13.

Deardorff, A. and Stern, R. (1981), 'A disaggregated model of world production and trade; an estimate of the impact of the Tokyo Round', *Journal of Policy Modeling*, vol.3, no.2, pp.127–52.

Decressin, J. and Fatas, A. (1995), 'Regional labour market dynamics in Europe', *European Economic Review*, vol.39, pp.1627–55.

Degimbe, J. (1999), *La politique sociale Europeenne*, Institut Syndical Europeen, Bruxelles.

Delors J. *et al.* (1989), *Report on the Economic and Monetary Union in the European Community*, CEC, Brussels.

Demsetz, H. (1982), *Economic, Legal and Political Dimensions of Competition*, North-Holland, Amsterdam.

Devereux, M.P. and Freeman, H. (1995), 'The impact of tax on foreign direct investment; empirical evidence and the implications for tax integration schemes', *International tax and public finance*, vol.2, pp.85–106.

Devereux, M.P. and Griffith, R. (1996), 'Taxes and the location of production; evidence from a panel of US multinationals', *IFS working paper*, 14–96, London.

Devereux, M., Griffith, R. and Lemma, A. (2002), 'Corporate income tax reforms and international tax competition', *Economic Policy*, vol.17, pp.450–95.

Devereux, M. and Pearson, M. (1989), 'Corporate Tax Harmonisation and Economic Efficiency',

Report Series, no.35, Institute of Fiscal Studies, London.

Dewatripont, M., Sapir, A. and Sekkat, K. (eds) (1999), 'Trade and jobs in Europe; much ado about nothing', Oxford University Press, Oxford.

Dickinson, G. (1993), 'Insurance', *European Economy/Social Europe*, no.3, pp.183–210.

Dierx, A., Ilkovitz, F. and Sekkat, K. (eds) (2004), *European integration and the functioning of product markets*, Elgar, Cheltenham.

Djarova, J. (2004), *Cross border investing; the case of Central and Eastern Europe*, Kluwer, Boston, NY, Dordrecht.

Dorrucci, E., Firpo, S., Fratzscher, M. and Mongelli, F.P. (2003), 'What Lessons for Latin America from European Institutional and Economic Integration?' in P. van der Haegen and J. Vinals (eds), *Regional Integration in Europe and Latin America; monetary and financial aspects*, Ashgate, Aldershot, pp.171–218.

Dosser, D. (1966), 'Economic Analysis of Fiscal Harmonisation', in C.S. Shoup (ed.), *Fiscal Harmonisation in Common Markets*, Columbia University Press, New York.

Drabeck, Z. and Greenaway, D. (1984), 'Economic Integration and Inter-Industry Trade, the CMEA and EEC compared', *Kyklos*, vol.37, pp.444–69.

Dumont, M. and Meeusen, W. (1999), 'The impact of the RTD policy of the EU on technological collaboration; a case study of the European telecommunications industry', in W. Meeusen (ed), *Economic Policy in the European Union, Current Perspectives*, Edgar Elgar, Cheltenham, pp.135-156.

Dunning, J.H. (1979), 'Explaining Changing Patterns of International Production: in Defence of an Eclectic Theory', *Oxford Bulletin of Economics and Statistics*, vol.41, pp.269–95.

Dunning, J.H. (1980), 'A Note on Intra-Industry Foreign Direct Investment', *Banca Nazionale del Lavoro Quarterly Review*, vol.34, December.

Dunning, J.H. (1988), 'The eclectic paradigm of international production; a restatement and some possible extensions', *Journal of International Business Studies*, vol.19, no.1, pp.6–12.

Dunning, J.H. (1993), *The Globalisation of Business; the challenge of the 1990s*, Routledge, London.

Dur, R. and Roelfsema, H. (2005), 'Why does centralisation fail to internalise policy externalities?', *Public Choice*, vol.122, pp.395–416.

Durán-Herrera, J.J. (1992), 'Cross Direct Investment and Technological Capability of Spanish Domestic Firms', in J. Cantwell (ed.), *Multinational Investment in Modern Europe*, Edward Elgar, Aldershot, pp.214–55.

Dustmann, C. (1996), 'Return Migration: the European experience', *Economic Policy*, vol.2, pp.215–50.

EC (1961), *Document de la Conférence sur les Economies Régionales*, vol.II, Brussels.

EC (1964), *Reports by Groups of Experts on Regional Policy in the European Economic Community*, Brussels.

EC (1966), *The Development of a European Capital Market*, Segré Report, Brussels.

EC (1967), *Critère à la Base de la Fixation des Salaires et Problèmes qui y sont liés pour une Politique des Salaires et des Revenus*, Brussels.

EC (1968), *Mémorandum sur la Réforme de l'Agriculture dans la Communauté Economique Européenne*, Agriculture 1980, COM 68/100e, Luxemburg.

EC (1969), *A Regional Policy for the Community*, Brussels.

EC (1970), *De Industriepolitiek van de Gemeenschap*, memorandum van de Commissie aan de Raad, Brussels.

EC (1971), *Regional Development in the Community: Analytical Survey*, Brussels.

EC (1973a), *Communication from the Commission to the Council on the Development of the Common Transport Policy*, COM (73), Brussels.

EC (1973b), *Report on the Regional Problems in the Enlarged Community* (Thomson Report), COM 73/550, Brussels.

EC (1974), *Third Report on Competition Policy*, Brussels.

EC (1977), 'The Regional Policy of the Community, New Guidelines', *Supplement 2/77 to Bulletin of the European Communities*, Luxemburg.

EC (1979a), *Etude Comparative des Conditions et Procédures d'Introduction et d'Accès à l'Emploi des Travailleurs de Pays tiers dans les Etats Membres de la Communauté*, Brussels.

EC (1979b), 'A Transport Network for Europe, Outline of a Policy', *Supplement 8/79 to Bulletin of the European Communities*, Luxemburg.

EC (1979c), 'Air Transport, A Community Approach', *Supplement 5/79 to Bulletin of the European Communities*, Luxemburg.

EC (1979d), *The European Monetary System: Commentary Document*, European Economy no.3, Brussels.

EC (1979e), 'The Regional Development Programmes', *Regional Policy Series*, no. 17, Brussels.

EC (1980), *The Europeans and their Regions*, internal EC document DG XXVI no. 9, Brussels.

EC (1981a), *Energy Strategy to be Adopted by the Community*, Brussels.

EC (1981b), *The Regions of Europe: First Periodic Report*, Brussels.

EC (1981c), *Proposal for a Council Regulation Amending the Regulation (EEC), no. 724/75, establishing a European Regional Development Fund*, Brussels.

EC (1982a), *The Competitiveness of the Community Industry*, Brussels.

EC (1982b), *Review of Member States' Energy Policy Programmes and Progress towards 1990 Objectives*, Brussels.

EC (1982c), 'Experimenteel Programma betreffende de Vervoersinfrastructuur', COM 82/828 def., Brussels.

EC (1982d), 'European Transport, Crucial Problems and Research Needs, a Long Term Analysis', *Series FAST*, no.3, Brussels.

EC (1983a), *Commission Activities and EC Rules for the Automobile Industry 1981–1983*, COM 83/633 final, Brussels.

EC (1984c), *The Regions of Europe; Second Periodic Report on the Situation and Socioeconomic Evolution of the Regions of the Community*, Brussels.

EC (1984d), *Les Programmes de Développement Régional de la Deuxième Génération pour la Période 1981–1985*, Collection Documents, Brussels.

EC (1985a), *Completing the Internal Market*, Cockfield White Paper, Brussels/Luxemburg.

EC (1985b), *Migrants in the European Community*, European File 13.85, Brussels.

EC (1985c), *The Insurance Industry in the Countries of the EEC, Structure, Conduct and Performance* (S. Aaronovitch and P. Samson), Documents, Brussels.

EC (1985d), *Main Texts Governing the Regional Policy of the EC*, Collection Documents, Brussels.

EC (1985e), *The European Community and its Regions; 10 Years of Community Regional Policy and the ERDF*, Luxemburg.

EC (1986a), *Programme for the Liberalisation of Capital Movements in the Community*, Brussels.

EC (1986b), *Directory of European Community Trade and Professional Associations*, 3rd edn, Brussels.

EC (1986f), *Bulletin of Energy Prices*, Luxemburg.

EC (1987a), *Treaties Establishing the European Communities*, abridged edition, Luxemburg.

EC (1987b), *Regional Disparities and the Tasks of Regional Policy in the Enlarged Community* (Third Periodic Report), Brussels.

EC (1988a), 'The Catching-up Process in Spain and Portugal', *European Economy*, Supplement A, no.10, Brussels/Luxemburg.

EC (1988b), *Major Results of the Survey of Member States' Energy Policies*, COM 88/174 fin, Brussels.

EC (1988c), 'Research on the "Cost of Non Europe" – Basic Findings', vol.1, *Basic Studies; Executive Seminaries*, Brussels.

EC (1988d), *La Dimension Sociale du Marché Intérieur*, Rapport d'Etape du groupe interservices présidé par M.J. Degimbe, Brussels.

EC (1990a), '"One Market, One Money", an Evaluation of the Potential Benefits and Cost of Forming an Economic and Monetary Union', *European Economy*, no.44, Brussels/Luxemburg.

EC (1990b), *Guide to the Reform of the Community's Structural Funds*, OOPEC, Luxemburg.

EC (1991a), 'Immigration of Citizens from Third Countries into the Southern Member States of the European Community', *Social Europe*, Supplement 1/91, Brussels/Luxemburg.

EC (1991b), 'European Industrial Policy for the 1990s', *Supplement 3/91 to Bulletin of the European Communities*, Luxemburg.

EC (1991c), 'Fair Competition in the Internal Market; Community State Aid Policy', *European Economy*, no.48, pp.13–114, Brussels/Luxemburg.

EC (1991d), *The Regions in the 1990's; Fourth periodic report on the social and economic situation and development of the regions of the Community*, OOPEC, Luxemburg.

EC (1992a), 'Social Security for Persons Moving within the Community', *Social Europe*, OOPEC, Luxemburg.

EC (1992b), *Social Europe*, 2/92, Luxemburg.

EC (1992c), 'Energy policies and trends in the EC; focus on the East', *Energy in Europe 19*, OOPEC, Luxemburg.

EC (1992d), 'Energy policies and trends in the European Community', *Energy in Europe 20*, OOPEC, Luxemburg.

EC (1992e), 'A Common Market for Services', vol.I, *Services Completing the Internal Market*, Brussels.

EC (1993a), 'The economics of Community public finance', *European Economy*, Reports and Studies, no.5, Luxemburg.

EC (1993b), 'The European Community as a World Trade Partner', *European Economy*, no.52, Luxemburg.

EC (1993c), 'Market Services in the Community Economy', *European Economy*, Supplement A, no.5, pp.1–11, Luxemburg.

EC (1993d), *European Social Policy; options for the Union* (green paper), OOPEC, Luxemburg.

EC (1994a), 'EC agricultural policy for the 21st century'; *European Economy*, no.4.

EC (1994b), 'Mergers and acquisitions', *European Economy*, Supplement A, February, Brussels.

EC (1995a), *Agricultural situation and prospects in the Central and Eastern European Countries*, working document, Brussels.

EC (1995b), *An energy policy for the EU* (white paper), Brussels.

EC (1995c), 'The impact of exchange rate movements on trade within the single market', *European Economy*, no.4.

EC (1995d) (European Council) *Support for regional integration efforts by developing countries*,

Document 7711/95 Annex III Brussels.

EC (1996a), 'Economic evaluation of the internal market', *European Economy*, Reports and Studies, Luxemburg.

EC (1996b), 'Energy in Europe', *1996 Annual Energy Review*, special issue, Luxemburg.

EC (1996c), 'Mergers and acquisitions', *European Economy*, Supplement A, no.7, Brussels.

EC (1996d), 'Council directive for restructuring the Community framework for the taxation of energy products and electricity', (COM03/96) Brussels.

EC (1996e), *First cohesion report*, COM (96)542 final, Luxemburg.

EC (1996f), 'Green paper on relations between the European Union and the ACP countries on the eve of the 21st century; challenges and options for a new partnership', COM 96, 570, Brussels.

EC (1997a), 'Commission action plan on the free movement of workers', COM 586, Brussels.

EC (1997b), 'CAP 2000 working document; Situation and outlook, Dairy sector', http://europa. eu.int/comm/dg06/publi/cap2000/dairy-en/dairyen.pdf.

EC (1998a), 'Financing the European Union, commission report of the operation of the own resources system', Brussels (DG 19).

EC (1998b), 'The CAP reform; a policy for the future', COM 98.158 final/.

EC (1999a), *Agriculture, environment, rural development: Facts and figures - A challenge for agriculture*, DG Agri Brussels.

EC (1999b), 'Market integration and differences in price levels between EU member states; study 4 in EU economy 1999 review', http://europa.eu.int.comm.dg02/document/ ggreview/ctent.pdf.

EC (1999c), 'The competitiveness of European industry', COM1999.465, Luxemburg.

EC (1999d), 'The shared analysis project; economic foundations for energy policy', http:// www.shared –analysis.fgh.de/pub-fr.htm.

EC (1999e), 'Fifth report on the implementation of the telecommunications regulatory package', http://europa.int/comm/dg13/5threp99-eng.pdf.

EC(1999f), 'Guide to the transport acquis', http.//europa.eu.int/en/comm/dg07/enlargement/ guide2acquis/en.polf).

EC (1999g), 'The common transport policy; sustainable mobility, perspectives for the future', http://europa.eu.int/en/comm/dg7/ctp-action-prog/documents/en.pdf.

EC (1999h), *The strategy for Europe's internal market*, COM(1999)624 final/2, Brussels.

EC (1999i), 'Budgetary surveillance in EMU; the new stability and convergence programmes', *European Economy*, Supplement A no.3.

EC (1999j), 'Broad Economic Policy Guidelines 1999', *European Economy*, no.68.

EC (1999k), *Better management through evaluation; mid term review of Structural Fund programmes; Objectives 1 and 6 (1994-1999)*, Brussels.

EC (2000a), *The Community Budget; the facts and figures*, Brussels.

EC (2000b), 'Single market, two proposals to facilitate the cross border provision of services', http:/europa.eu.int./comm/internal-market/en/services/services/53.htm.

EC (2000c), 'Insurance, Commission clarifies concepts of freedom to provide services and general good', http//europa.eu.int/comm/internal-market/en/finances/insur/genralgood.htm.

EC (2000d), 'Air transport', http://europa.eu.int/comm/transport/themes/air/english/at2en. html.

EC (2000e), *European Economy*, Supplement C: Economic Reform Monitor, Brussels (see also http://europa.eu.int/comm/economy-finance/document/eesuppc/eecidxen.htm).

EC (2000f), *Internal market, EU consumers continue to benefit, but reforms must be accelerated*,

COM (2000) 881.

EC (2000g), 'Conclusions of the ESF final evaluations', Master 2/08/00, available from website europa.eu.int/comm/employment_social/evaluation/eval_concl_en.pdf.

EC (2001a), 'Price levels and price dispersion in the EU', *European Economy*, Supplement A, no.7, pp.2-20.

EC (2001b), *The free movement of workers in the context of enlargement*, Information note, Brussels.

EC (2001c), 'Unity, solidarity, diversity for Europe, its people and its territory', *Second report on Economic and Social cohesion*, Vol.1, Brussels.

EC (2001d), *European Governance*, a white paper, COM (2001) 428 final, 25 July 2001.

EC (2001e), 'Mergers and Acquisitions', *European Economy*, Supplement A, No.12, pp.2-19.

EC (2002a), *Enlargement and agriculture; successfully integrating the new member stats into the CAP*, Issues paper, SEC 2002.95.

EC (2002b), *Agriculture in the EU – Statistics and economic information*, Brussels.

EC (2002c), *Final report on the green paper "Towards a European Union strategy for the security of energy supply"*, COM 2002/321, Brussels.

EC (2003a), *The new common fisheries policy*, see website http://europa.eu.int/comm/fisheries.

EC (2003b), *European Transport policy for 2010, time to decide*, www.europa.eu.int/comm/dgs/energy_transport.

EC (2003c), *Innovation policy; updating the Union's approach in the context of the Lisbon strategy*, COM (2003) 112, available via web site: http://europa.eu.int/comm/enterprise/innovation/communication/doc/innovation_comm_en.pdf

EC (2003d), *Communication ...on immigration integration and employment*, COM 2003/336, Brussels.

EC (2004a), *Building our common future; Policy challenges and budgetary means of the enlarged Union 2007-2013*, COM 2004/101, Brussels.

EC (2004b), 'Proposal for a directive of the European Parliament and the Council on services in the internal market, (Bolkestein directive)', COM 2004 2 def, Brussels.

EC (2004c), 'A new partnership for cohesion; convergence, competitiveness, cooperation', *Third report on economic and social cohesion*, Brussels.

EC (2004d), *Preliminary analysis of price data*, DG Internal Market (EEB3), Brussels.

EC (2004e), *A pro-active competition policy for a competitive Europe*, COM (2004)293 final, Brussels.

EC (2004f), *33rd Report competition policy, 2003*, SEC 2004 658final, Brussels.

EC (2004g), Report from the Commission to the Council, the European Parliament and the European Economic and Social Committee on the rates of excise duty applied on alcohol and alcoholic beverages (presented pursuant to Article 8 of Council Directive 92/84/EEC on the approximation of excise duty on alcohol and alcoholic beverages), available from the EU web site.

EC (2004h), *The macro-economic effects of the Single Market Programme after 10 years*, http://europa.eu.int/comm./internal_market/10years/background_en.htm.

EC (2004i), *The EU's Generalised System of Preferences – GSP*, http//.europa.eu.int./comm/trade.

EC (2004j), 'Fostering structural change: an industrial policy for an enlarged Europe', COM 274 final, Brussels (Communication from the Commission).

EC (2004k), 'Mergers and Acquisitions', *DG ECFIN Notes*, no.1, pp.2-14.

EC (2004l), 'Economics of the Common Agricultural Policy' (by R. Wichern), *European Economy/Economic Papers*, no.211 (available from http://europa.eu.int/comm/economy_finance.

EC (2004m), 'The ex post evaluation 1994-1999 of ESF operations under objectives 1, 3 and 4 and the Community Initiatives Employment and Adapt', (EU synthesis report; executive summary), Brussels.

EC (2004n), 'Report of the High Level Group on the future of social policy in an enlarged European Union', DG Employment and Social Affairs, Brussels.

EC (2005a), 'Strategic Objectives 2005–2009; Europe 2010: A Partnership for European Renewal; Prosperity, Solidarity and Security', *Communication from the President in agreement with Vice-President Wallström, 26.1.2005*, COM (2005) 12 final, Brussels.

EC (2005b), see http://europa.eu.int/comm/taxation_customs/whatsnew.htm.

EC (2005c), 'Public Finances in EMU', *European Economy*, 3, 2005, SEC (2005) 723, (Full Report).

ECA (European Court of Auditors) (2000), 'Greening the CAP', *Special report no 14*, Brussels.

Edwards, S. (1999), 'How effective are capital controls?', *Journal of Economic Perspectives*, vol.13.4, pp.65–84.

Edye, D. (1987), *Immigrant Labour and Government Policy*, Gower, Aldershot.

Eekhoff, J. (ed.) (2004), *Competition policy in Europe*, Springer, Berlin.

Ehrlich, E. and Szigetvari, T. (2003), 'Transformation and Hungarian regional development; facts, trends, dilemmas and objectives', *Working papers, no.137*, Institute for World Economics, Budapest.

Eijffinger, S. and Haan, J. de (1996), 'The political economy of central bank independence', *Special papers in international economics*, no.19, Princeton University, Princeton, NJ.

Eijffinger, S. W. and Haan, J. de (2000), 'European monetary and fiscal policy', Oxford University Press, Oxford.

El-Agraa, A.M. and Jones, A.J. (1981), *Theory of Customs Unions*, Philip Allan, Oxford.

Eliassen, K. A. and Sjovaag, M. (eds) (1999), 'European telecommunications liberalisation', Routledge, London.

Eliasson, G. (1984), 'The Micro Foundations of Industrial Policy', in A. Jacquemin (ed.), *European Industry: Public Policy and Corporate Strategy*, CEPS, Clarendon, Oxford, pp.295–326.

Emerson, M. (1977), 'The finances of the European Community; a case study in embryonic fiscal federalism', in W. Oates (ed.), *The political economy of fiscal federalism*, Lexington, Mass, pp.129–72.

Emerson, M., Aujean, M., Catinat, M., Goybet, P. and Jacquemin, A. (1988), 'The Economics of 1992; an Assessment of the Potential Economic Effects of Completing the Internal Market of the European Community', *European Economy*, no.35/3, pp.5–222.

Engel, Ch. and Rogers, J.H. (2004), 'European product market integration after the euro', *Economic Policy*, vol.39, pp.347–84.

Endres, A. and Ohl, C. (2005), 'Kyoto, Europe? – An economic evaluation of the European emission trading directive', *European Journal of Law and Economics*, vol.19.1, pp.17–39 .

Erdmenger, J. (1981), *The European Community Transport Policy*, Gower, Aldershot.

Erkel Rousse, H. and Melitz, J. (1995), 'New empirical evidence on the costs of monetary union', *CEPR discussion paper*, no.1169.

Eurostat (1974), *Statistics of Energy*, Special Nr 4, Luxemburg.

Eurostat (1983), *Monthly Bulletin of Foreign Trade*, special issue 1958–1982, Luxemburg.

Eurostat (1985), *Foreign Population and Foreign Employees in the Community*, Luxemburg.

Eurostat (1987), *Employment and Unemployment*, Theme 3, Series C, Luxemburg.

Eurostat (1992), *International Trade in Services, 1979–1988*, Series 6D, Luxemburg.

Eurostat (1995), *Labour Force Survey*, Luxemburg.

Eurostat (2003) 'Structural indicators' (europa.eu.int/comm./eurostat/Public/datashop/print-product/EN?catalogue).

Eurostat (several years), *Electricity Prices*, Luxemburg.

Faber, R.J. and Stokman, A.C.J. (2004), *Price convergence in Europe from a macro perspective: Trends and determinants (1960-2003)*, DNB Working Paper no. 12.

Faber, R.J. and Stokman, A.C.J. (2005), *Price convergence in Europe from a macro perspective: Product categories and reliability*, DNB Working Paper no. 34.

Faini, R., Haskel, J., Barba Navetti, G., Scarpa, C. and Wey, C. (2004), *Contrasting Europe's decline; do product market reforms help?* Available from www.frdb.org.

Fatas, A. (1997), 'EMU; countries or regions? Lessons from the EMS experience', *CEPR Discussion Papers*, 1558, London.

Fernandez, A., Arrunada, B. and Gonzalez, M. (2000), 'Quasi integration in less than truckload trucking', in C. Menard (ed.), *Institutions, contracts, organisations (perspectives from new institutional economics)*, Edward Elgar, Cheltenham, pp.293-312.

Fernandez, R. (1997), 'Returns to regionalism; an evaluation of non-traditional gains from RTAs', *CEPR discussion papers*, no.1634, CEPR, London.

Ferner, A. and Hyman, R. (eds) (1992), *Industrial Relations in the New Europe*, Blackwell, Oxford.

Ferrera, M. (forthcoming), *The boundaries of welfare; European integration and the new spatial politics of social protection*, Oxford University Press, Oxford.

Fidrmuc, J. (2004), 'Migration and regional adjustment to asymmetric shocks in transition economies', *Journal of Comparative Economics,* vol.32.2, pp.230–47.

Finsinger, J., Hammond, E. and Tapp, J. (1985), *Insurance: Competition on Regulation, a Comparative Study*, The Institute for Fiscal Studies, London.

Finsinger, J. and Pauly, M.V. (eds) (1986), *The Economics of Insurance Regulation*, Macmillan, Basingstoke.

Fischer, P. and Straubhaar, T. (1996), *Migration and economic integration in the Nordic common labour market*, Nord (Nordic Council of Ministers), Copenhagen.

Fisher, M.R. (1966), *Wage Determination in an Integrating Europe*, Sythoff, Leiden.

Forte, F. (1977), 'Principles for the Assignment of Public Economic Functions in a Setting of Multi-Layer Government, EC', *Report of the (McDougall) Study Group on the Role of Public Finance in European Integration*, vol.II, Collection of Studies of Economics and Finances, Series no.B 13, Brussels.

Francko, L.G. (1976), *The European Multinationals; a Renewed Challenge to American and British Business*, Harper and Row, London.

François, J.F., McDonald, B. and Nordstrom, H. (1996), 'A user's guide to the Uruguay round assessments', *Working Paper*, no.ERAD 96.003 WTO.

Frankel, J.A. (1989), 'Quantifying International Capital Mobility in the 1980's', *NBER Working Paper*, 2856, NBER, Cambridge, Massachusetts.

Frankel, J.A. and Rose, A.K. (1998), 'The endogeneity of the optimum currency area criteria', *The Economic Journal*, vol.108, pp.1009–25.

Franzmeyer, F. (1982), *Approaches to Industrial Policy within the EC and its Impact on European Integration*, Gower, Aldershot.

Franzmeyer, F., Hrubesch, P., Seidel, B. and Weise, Ch. (1991), *The Regional Impact of Community Policies*, EP, Luxemburg.

Fratianni, M. and Pattison, J. (2001), 'International organisations in a world of regional trade agreements; lessons from club theory, *The World Economy*, vol.24.3, pp.333–58.

Frenkel, M. and Nickel, C. (2005), 'New European Union members on their way to adopting the euro; an analysis of macroeconomic disturbances', *Global Finance Journal*, vol.15, pp.303–20.

Frey, B. (1985), 'The Political Economy of Protection', in D. Greenaway (ed.), *Current Issues in International Trade*, Macmillan, London, pp.139–57.

Frey, B. S. and Eichenberger, R. (1997), 'FOCJ: creating a single European market for governments', in D. Schmidtchen and R. Cooter (eds), *Constitutional law and economics of the European Union*, Edward Elgar, Cheltenham, pp.195–216.

Friedberg, R.M. and Hunt, J. (1995), 'The impact of immigrants on host country wages, employment and growth', *Journal of Economic Perspectives*, vol.9, no.2, pp.23–44.

Fuente, A. de la and Vives, X. (1995), 'Infrastructure and education as instruments of regional policy; evidence from Spain', *Economic Policy*, vol.20, pp.13–51.

Fujita, M., Mallampally, P. and Sauvant, K.P. (1997), 'European Union direct investment in developing Asia and developing Asia direct investment in the European Union', *Transnational corporations*, vol.6.1, pp.83—100.

Furman, J., Porter, M.E. and Stern, S. (2002), 'The determinants of national innovative capacity', *Research Policy*, vol.31, pp.899–933.

Gaab, W., Granziol, M.J. and Horner, M. (1986), 'On Some International Parity Conditions: an Empirical Investigation', *European Economic Review*, vol.30, no.3, pp.683–713.

Gardner, E.H. (1992), 'Taxes on capital income; a survey', in G. Kopits (ed.), *Tax Harmonization in the European Community: policy issues and analysis*, IMF occasional paper 94, Washington, pp.52–71.

Gartzke, E., Li, Q. and Boehmer, Ch. (2001), 'Investing in peace, economic interdependence and international conflict', *International Organization*, vol.55.2, pp.391–438.

Gasiorek, M., Smith, A. and Venables, A. J. (2002), 'The accession of the UK to the EC; a welfare analysis', *Journal of Common Market Studies*, vol.40.3, pp.425–47.

Gaspar, V. (1995), 'Cohesion and Convergence: the economic effects of EC structural transfers', *Working paper no 257*, Universidade Nova de Lisboa.

Gavin, B. (2001), *The European Union and Globalisation; towards global democratic government*, Edward Elgar, Cheltenham.

Geroski, P. and Jacquemin, A. (1984), 'Large Firms in the European Corporate Economy and Industrial Policy in the 1980s', in A. Jacquemin (ed.), *European Industry: Public Policy and Corporate Strategy*, CEPS, Clarendon, Oxford, pp.343–67.

Geroski, P. and Jacquemin, A. (1985), 'Industrial Change, Barriers to Mobility and European Industrial Policy', *Economic Policy*, vol.1, no.1, pp.170–218.

Ghosh, M. (2002), 'The revival of regional trade arrangements; a GE evaluation of the impact on small countries', *Journal of Policy Modeling*, vol.24, pp. 83–101.

Gialloreto, L. (1988), *Strategic Airline Management*, Pitman, London.

Gianetti, M., Giuso, L., Japelli, T., Padula, M. and Pagano, M. (2002), 'Financial market integration, corporate financing and economic growth', *European Economy*, vol.179, pp.1–81.

Giavazzi, F. and Pagano, M. (1986), 'The Advantages of Tying one's Hands; EMS Discipline and Central Bank Credibility', *European Economic Review*, vol.28, pp.1055–82.

Gibb, R. and Michalak, W. (eds) (1994), *Continental trading blocks; the growth of regionalism in the world economy*, Wiley, Chichester.

Giersch, H. (1949), 'Economic Union between Nations and the Location of Industries', *Review of Economic Studies*, vol.17, pp.87–97.

Gil-Pareja, S. (2003), 'Pricing to market behaviour in European car markets', *European Economic Review*, vol.47, pp.945–62.

Giovannini, A. (1989), 'National Tax Systems versus the European Capital Market', *Economic Policy*, pp.346–86.

Glachant, J-M. and Finon, D. (2000), 'Why do European Union's electricity industries continue to differ; a new institutional analysis', in C. Menard (ed.), *Institutions, contracts, organisations (perspectives from new institutional economics)*, Edward Elgar, Cheltenham, pp.313–34.

Glass, A. J. and Saggi, K. (1999), 'FDI policies under shared factor markets', *Journal of International Economics,* vol.49, pp.309–32.

Glejser, H. (1972), 'Empirical Evidence on Comparative Cost Theory from the European Common Market Experience', *European Economic Review*, vol.163, pp.247–59.

Goerg, H. and Strobl, E. (2002), 'Multinational companies and indigenous development; an empirical analysis', *European Economic Review*, vol.46, pp.1305–22.

Goldberg, P.K. and Verboven, F. (2004), 'Cross country price dispersion in the euro area; a case study of the European car market', *Economic Policy*, vol.40, pp.483–522.

Gomes, L. (1987), *Foreign Trade and the National Economy; Mercantilist and Classical Perspectives*, Macmillan, London.

Gordon, R.H. (1983), 'An Optimal Taxation Approach to Fiscal Federalism', *Quarterly Journal of Economics*, vol.48, no.4, pp.567–86.

Graham, E.M. (1992), 'Direct Investments between the US and the EC, Post 1986 and Pre 1992', in J. Cantwell (ed.), *Multinational Investment in Modern Europe*, Edward Elgar, Aldershot, pp.46–70.

Grauwe, P. de (1987), 'International Trade and Economic Growth in the European Monetary System', *European Economic Review*, vol.31, pp.389–98.

Grauwe, P. de, (1996), 'Monetary union and convergence economics', *European Economic Review*, vol.40, pp.1091–1101.

Grauwe, P. de (2000), *Economics of Monetary Union*, 4th edn, Oxford University Press, Oxford.

Grauwe, P. de and Aksov, Y. (1999), 'Are Central European Countries part of the European Optimum Currency Area?' in P. de Grauwe and V. Lavra (eds), *Inclusion of Central European Countries in the European Monetary Union*, Kluwer, Dordrecht, pp.13–36.

Greenaway, D. (1983), *International Trade Policy, from Tariffs to the New Protectionism*, Macmillan, London.

Greenaway, D. (1987), 'Intra-Industry Trade, Intra-Firm Trade and European Integration; Evidence, Gains and Policy Aspects', *Journal of Common Market Studies*, vol.26, no.2, pp.153–72.

Greenaway, D. and Milner, C. (1986), *The Economics of Intra-Industry Trade*, Basil Blackwell, Oxford.

Gremmen, H. (1985), 'Testing Factor Price Equalisation in the EC: An Alternative Approach', *Journal of Common Market Studies*, vol.23, no.3, pp.277–86.

Griffiths, B. (1975), *Invisible Barriers to Invisible Trade*, Macmillan, London.

Grinols, E.J. (1984), 'A Thorn in the Lion's Paw; Has Britain Paid Too Much for Common Market Membership?', *Journal of International Economics*, vol.16, pp.271–93.

Gros, D. (1989), 'Paradigms for the Monetary Union of Europe', *Journal of Common Market Studies*, vol.27, no.3, pp.219–30.

Gros, D. (1996), 'A Reconsideration of the Optimum Currency Area Approach: The Role of External Shocks and Labour Mobility', *National Institute Economic Review*, October, pp.108–17.

Gros, D., Blanchard, O., Emerson, M., Mayer, T., St Paul, G., Sinn, H. and Tabellini, G. (1999), *Macro economic policy in the first year of euroland*, CEPS, Brussels.

Gros, D. and Thygesen, N. (1998), *European Monetary Integration*, 2nd edn, Longman, London.

Grubel, H.G. (1974), 'Taxation and the Rates of Return from some US Assets Holdings Abroad', *Journal of Political Economy*, vol.82, pp.469–87.

Grubel, H.G. (1981), *International Economics*, Irwin, Homewood, Illinois.

Grubel, H.G. and Lloyd, P. (1975), *Intra-Industry Trade: the Theory and Measurement of International Trade in Differentiated Products*, Macmillan, London.

Grzybowski, L. (2005), 'Regulation of mobile telephony across the European Union, an empirical analysis', *Journal of Regulatory Economics*, vol.28.1, pp.47–67.

Gual, J. (1993), 'An Econometric Analysis of Price Differentials in the EEC Automobile Market', *Applied Economics*, vol.25, pp.599–607.

Guiso, L., Japelli, T., Padula, M. and Pagano, M. (2004), 'Financial market integration and economic growth in the EU', *Economic Policy*, vol.40, pp.525–77.

Gwilliam, K.M., Petriccione, S., Voigt, F. and Zighera, J.A. (1973), 'Criteria for the Coordination of Investments in Transport Infrastructure', *The EEC Studies, Transport Series Nr 3*, Brussels.

Haaland, J. (1990), 'Assessing the Effects of EC Integration on EFTA Countries; the Position of Norway and Sweden', *Journal of Common Market Studies*, vol.28, no.4, pp.379–400.

Haaland, J. and Norman, V. (1992), *Global Production Effects of European Integration*, paper for the CEPR Conference Paris.

Haas, E.B. (1958), *The Uniting of Europe; Political, Social and Economic Forces 1950–1957*, Stevens, London.

Haegen, P. van der and Vinals, J. (2004), *Regional Integration in Europe and Latin America; monetary and financial aspects*, Ashgate, Aldershot.

Haisken-De New, J.P. (1996), *Migration and the inter-industry wage structure in Germany*, Springer, Berlin.

Hall, G. (ed.) (1986), *European Industrial Policy*, Croom Helm, London.

Hamada, K. (1985), *The Political Economy of International Monetary Interdependence*, Cambridge University Press, Cambridge.

Hammar, T. (1985), *European Immigration Policy*, Cambridge University Press, Cambridge.

Hanlon, P. (1999), *Global Airlines, competition in a transnational industry*, 2nd edn, Butterworth/Heinemann, Oxford.

Hantrais, L. (1995), *Social Policy in the European Union*, Macmillan, Basingstoke.

Haq, M.U., Kaul, I. and Grunberg, I. (eds) (1996), *The Tobin tax; coping with financial volatility*, Oxford University Press, Oxford.

Hart, P., Ledger, G., Roe, M. and Smith, B. (1992), *Shipping Policy in the European Community*, Avebury, Aldershot.

Hartley, K. (1987), 'Public Procurement and Competitiveness: a Community Market for Military Hardware and Technology?', *Journal of Common Market Studies*, vol.25, no.3, pp.237–47.

Hashhimzade, N., Khodavaisi, H. and Myles, G.D. (2005), 'Tax principles, product differentiation and the nature of competition', *International Tax and Public Finance* (forthcoming).

Hatzius, J. (2000), 'Foreign direct investment and factor demand elasticities', *European Economic*

Review, vol.44, pp.117–43.

Heidhues, T., Josling, T., Ritson, C. *et al.* (1978), 'Common Prices and Europe's Farm Policy', *Thames Essays*, no.13, Trade Policy Research Centre, London.

Heijke, J.A.M. and Klaassen, L.H. (1979), 'Human Reactions to Spatial Diversity, Mobility in Regional Labour Markets', in H. Folmer and J. Oosterhaven (eds), *Spatial Inequalities and Regional Development*, Nijhoff, The Hague, pp.117–30.

Heinelt, H. and Smith, R. (eds) (1996), *Policy networks and European Structural Funds*, Avebury, Aldershot.

Helg, R. and Ranci, P. (1988), 'Economies of Scale and the Integration of the EC, the Case of Italy', in *Research into the Cost of Non-Europe, Basic Findings*, vol.2, CEC, Luxemburg, pp.205–85.

Helleman, S. and Hens, L. (1999), 'Towards a monetary model for the euro-USD exchange rate', in W. Meeusen (ed), *Economic Policy in the European Union, Current Perspectives*, Edward Elgar, Cheltenham, pp.103–20.

Hennart, J.F. (1983), 'The Political Economy of Comparative Growth Rates; the Case of France', in D. Mueller (ed.), *The Political Economy of Growth*, Yale University Press, New Haven, pp.176–203.

Henrekson, M., Torstenson, J. and Torstenson, R. (1997), 'Growth effects of European integration', *European Economic Review*, vol.41, pp.1537–57.

Henry, P. (1981), *Study of the Regional Impact of the Common Agricultural Policy*, EC, Luxemburg.

Heylen, F. and Poeck, A. van (1995), 'National Labour Market Institutions and the European Economic and Monetary Integration Process', *Journal of Common Market Studies*, vol.33, no.4, pp.573–95.

Hine, R.C. (1985), *The Political Economy of European Trade*, Wheatsheaf, Brighton.

Hine, R.C. (1992), *The Political Economy of Agricultural Trade*, Edward Elgar, Aldershot.

Hinkle, L.E. and Schiff, M. (2004), 'Economic partnership agreements between Sub-Saharan Africa and the EU; a development perspective', *The World Economy*, vol.27.9, pp.1321–34.

Hirsch, S. (1981), 'Peace Making and Economic Interdependence', *The World Economy*, vol.4, pp.407–17.

Hirschmann, A.O. (1981), 'Three Uses of Political Economy in Analysing European Integration', in *Essays in Trespassing; Economics to Politics and Beyond*, Cambridge University Press, Cambridge, pp.266–84.

Hocking, R. (1980), 'Trade in Motorcars between the Major European Producers', *Economic Journal*, vol.90, pp.504–19.

Hodgson, G.M. (1988), 'Economics and Institutions', Polity Press, Cambridge.

Hodgson, G.M., Samuels, W.J. and Tool, M.C. (eds) (1994), 'The Elgar companion to institutional and evolutionary economics', Edward Elgar, Aldershot.

Hoekman, B. and Djankov, S. (1996), 'The European Union's Mediterranean Free Trade initiative', *The World Economy*, vol.19, no.4, pp.387–406.

Hoekman, B.M. and Kostecki, M. (1996), *The Political Economy of the World Trading System; from GATT to WTO*, Oxford University Press, Oxford.

Hoeller, P. and Louppe, M.O. (1994), 'The EC's internal market; implementation and economic effects', *OECD Economic Studies*, no.23, Paris.

Hofer, H. and Woergoetter, A. (1997), 'Regional per capita income convergence in Austria', *Regional Studies*, vol.31.1, pp.1–12.

Holden, M. (1994), *The Common Fisheries Policy; origin, evaluation and future*, Blackwell, Oxford.

Holloway, J. (1981), *Social Policy Harmonisation in the European Community*, Gower, Aldershot.

Holtfrerich, C.-L. (1989), 'The Monetary Unification Process in Nineteenth-Century Germany', in M. de Cecco and A. Giovannini (eds), *A European Central Bank?*, Cambridge University Press, Cambridge, pp.216–41.

Hudson, R. and Schamp, E.W. (eds) (1995), *Towards a new map of automobile manufacturing in Europe; new production concepts and spatial restructuring*, Springer, Heidelberg.

Hufbauer, G.C. (1990), 'An Overview', in G.C. Hufbauer (ed.), *Europe 1992; An American Perspective*, Brookings Institution, Washington.

Hufbauer, G.C. and Scott, J.J. (1985), *Economic Sanctions Reconsidered; History and Current Policy*, Institute for International Economics, Washington.

Hughes, J., Sasse, G. and Gordon, C. (2004), 'Conditionality and Compliance in the EU's Eastward Enlargement', *Journal of Common Market Studies*, vol.42.3, pp.523–52.

Hulsink, W. (1999), 'Privatisation and liberalisation in European telecommunications: comparing Britain, the Netherlands and France', Routledge, London.

Hymer, S. (1966), 'The international operations of national firms, a study of direct foreign investment', (later 1976) published by MIT Press, Cambridge, Mass.

IBRD (1985), *World Development Report*, Oxford University Press, New York.

IBRD (World Bank) (2005), *Global Economic Prospects; Trade, Regionalism and Development*, Washington.

IMF (1984), *Exchange Rate Volatility and World Trade*, IMF occasional paper, no.28.

Ingersent, K.A. and Rayner, A.J. (1999), *Agricultural Policy in Western Europe and the United States*, Edward Elgar, Cheltenham.

Ingo, W. (1985), 'Barriers to Trade in Banking and Financial Services', *Thames Essays*, no.41, Trade Policy Research Centre, London.

Ingram, J.C. (1973), 'The Case for European Monetary Integration', *Essays in International Finance*, no.98, Princeton University, Princeton, NJ.

Ishiyama, Y. (1975), 'The Theory of Optimum Currency Areas, a Survey', *IMF Staff Papers*, vol.22, pp.344–83.

Issing, O., Gaspar, V., Angeloni, I. and Tristani, O. (2001), *Monetary policy in the euro area; Strategy and decision making at the European Central Bank*, Cambridge University Press, Cambridge.

Jacquemin, A. (1991), *Merger and Competition Policy in the European Community*, Blackwell, Oxford.

Jacquemin, A. and de Jong, H.W. (1977), *European Industrial Organisation*, Macmillan, London.

Jacquemin, A. and Sapir, A. (1988), 'European Integration or World Integration?', *Weltwirtschaftliches Archiv*, vol.124, pp.127–39.

Jacquemin, A. and Sapir, A. (1995), 'Is a European hard core credible? A statistical analysis', *CEPR discussion paper series*, no.1242, Centre for Economic Policy Research, London.

Jensen, W.G. (1983), *Energy in Europe 1945–1980*, Fouls, London.

Johnson, H.G. (1958), 'The Gains from Freer Trade in Europe, an Estimate', *Manchester School*, vol.26, no.3, pp.247–55.

Jones, E. and Plummer, G. (2004), 'EU–Asia; links and lessons', *Journal of Asian Economics*, vol.14, pp.829–42.

Jones, K. (1984), 'The Political Economy of Voluntary Export Restraint Agreements', *Kyklos*, vol.37, pp.82–101.

Jong, H.W. de (1981), *Dynamische Markttheorie*, Stenfert Kroese, Leiden.

Jong, H.W. de (1987), 'Market Structures in the European Economic Community', in M. Macmillen, D.G. Mayes and P. van Veen (eds), *European Integration and Industry*, Tilburg University Press, Tilburg, pp.40–89.

Jong, H.W. de (1993a), 'Market Structures in the EEC', in H.W. de Jong (ed.), *The Structure of European Industry*, 3rd edn, Kluwer, Dordrecht, pp.1–42.

Jong, H.W. de (ed.) (1993b), *The Structure of European Industry*, 3rd edn, Kluwer, Dordrecht.

Kaempfer, W.H. and Loewenberg, A.D. (1992), *International Economic Sanctions; a Public Choice Approach*, Westview Press, Boulder, Colorado.

Kahler, M. (1995), 'International institutions and the political economy of integration', Brookings, Washington.

Kaldor, N. (1966), *The Causes of the Slow Growth of the United Kingdom*, Cambridge University Press, Cambridge.

Kangasharju, A. and Pekkala, S. (2004), 'Increasing regional disparities in the 1990's; the Finnish experience', *Regional Studies*, vol.38.3, pp.255–67.

Kapur, D. (2002), 'Processes of change in international organizations', in D. Nayyar (ed.), *Governing globalization, issues and institutions*, UNU/WIDER Oxford University Press, Oxford, pp.334–55.

Karsenty, G. (1999), *Just how big are the stakes?; an assessment of trade in services by mode of supply*, World Trade Organization, Geneva.

Kaufmann, D., Kraay, A. and Zoido-Lobaton, P. (2002), 'Governance matters II; Updated indicators for 2000-2001', *Policy Research Department Working Paper no 2772*, Washington, IBRD (World Bank).

Kauppinen, T. (ed.) (1998), *The impact of EMU on industrial relations in European Union*, Finnish Labour relations Association, Publication no.9. Helsinki.

Kawai, M. (1992), 'Optimum currency areas', in P. Newman, M. Milgate and J. Eatwell (eds), *The new Palgrave dictionary of money and finance*, Macmillan, London.

Kay, J. and Keene, M. (1987), 'Alcohol and Tobacco Taxes, Criteria for Harmonisation', in S. Cnossen (ed.), *Tax Coordination in the European Community*, Kluwer, Deventer, pp.85–112.

Kayser, B. (1972), *Cyclically Determined Homeward Flows of Migrant Workers*, OECD, Paris.

Keely, C.B. and Tran, B.N. (1989), 'Remittances from Labour Migration: Evaluations, Performance and Implications', *International Migration Review*, vol.23, no.3, pp.500–25.

Keen, M. and Smith, S. (1996), 'The future of value added in the European Union', *Economic Policy; a European Forum*, vol.23, pp.373–420.

Kenen, P. (1969), 'The theory of optimum currency areas', in R. Mundell and A. Swoboda (eds), *Monetary problems of the international economy*, Chicago University Press, Chicago.

Kennedy Brenner, C. (1979), *Foreign Workers and Immigration Policy*, OECD/DC, Paris.

Kennedy, P. (1988), *The rise and fall of the great powers*, Fontana Press, London.

Kenwood, A.G. and Lougheed, A.L. (1999), *The Growth of the International Economy 1820–2000, an introductory text*, (4th edn) Routledge, London.

Keohane, R.O. and Hoffmann, S. (1991), 'Institutional Change in Europe in the 1980's', in R.O. Keohane and S. Hoffmann (eds), *The New European Community, Decision Making and Institutional Change*, Westview Press, Boulder, Colorado, pp.1–39.

Keynes, J.M. (1936), *The General Theory of Employment, Interest and Money*, Harcourt, Brace & Co., New York.

Kim, Y. and Chow, H.K. (2003), 'Optimum currency area in Europe; an alternative assessment', *Economic Letters*, vol.81.3, pp.297–304.

Kirchner, C. (1997), 'Competence catalogues and the principle of subsidiarity in a European Constitution', *Constitutional Political Economy*, vol.8, pp.71–87.

Klaassen, L.H. and Drewe, P. (1973), *Migration Policy in Europe*, Saxon House, Farnborough.

Klaassen, L.H. and Molle, W.T.M. (eds) (1982), *Industrial Migration and Mobility in the European Community*, Gower, Aldershot.

Kock, K. (1969), *International Trade Policy and the GATT, 1947–1967*, Almquist and Wicksell, Stockholm.

Koedijk, K. and Kremers, J. (1996), 'Market opening, regulation and growth in Europe', *Economic Policy; a European Forum*, vol.23, pp.443–67.

Koekkoek, A., Kuyvenhoven, A. and Molle, W. (1990), 'Europe 1992 and the Developing Countries, an Overview', *Journal of Common Market Studies*, vol.29, no.2, pp.111–31.

Koekkoek, K.A. and Mennes, L.B.M. (1988), 'Some Potential Effects of Liberalising the Multi-Fibre Arrangement', in L.B.M. Mennes and J. Kol (eds), *European Trade Policies and the Developing World*, Croom Helm, Beckenham, pp.187–213.

Koester, U. (1977), 'The Redistributional Effects of the Common Agricultural Financial System', *European Review of Agricultural Economics*, vol.4, no.4, pp.321–45.

Koester, U. and Tangermann, S. (1976), *Alternative der Agrarpolitik*, Hiltrup, Münster.

Kohler, W. (2004, 'Eastern enlargement of the EU; a comprehensive welfare assessment', *Journal of Policy Modeling*, vol.26.7, pp.865–88.

Kol, J. (1987), 'Exports from Developing Countries; Some Facts and Scope', *European Economic Review*, vol.31, pp.466–74.

Kol, J. (1988), *The Measurement of Intra-Industry Trade*, Erasmus University Press, Rotterdam.

Kol, J. and Kuypers, B. (1996), *The cost for consumers and taxpayers of the Common Agricultural Policy of the European Union; the case of the Netherlands*, Erasmus University Press, Rotterdam.

Kool, C. and Olie, R. (1997), 'De EMU als fusieproces (the EMU as a merger process)', *ESB*, vol.82, no.4111, pp.495–98.

Kox, H., Lejour, A. and Montizaan, R. (2004), 'The free movement of services within the EU', *Document no 69*, CPB, The Hague.

Kozak, M.W. (2003), 'The consequences for Polish regions of integration with the EU', in Auctores Variie, *Cost and benefits of Poland's membership in the European Union*, Natolin European Centre, Warshaw.

Kozma, F. (1982), *Economic Integration and Economic Strategy*, Nijhoff, The Hague.

Krauss, H.B. (1979), *The New Protectionism, the Welfare State and International Trade*, Basil Blackwell, Oxford.

Krauss, L.B. (1968), *European Integration and the US*, Brookings Institution, Washington.

Kreinin, M.E. (1973), 'The Static Effects of EEC Enlargement on Trade Flows', *Southern Economic Journal*, vol.39, pp.559–68.

Krugman, P. (1980), Scale economies; product differentiation and the pattern of trade', *American Economic Review*, vol.70.5, pp.950–59.

Kuznets, S. (1966), *Modern Economic Growth; Rates, Structure and Spread*, Yale University Press, New Haven.

Laffan, B. (1983), 'Policy Implementation in the European Community: The European Social Fund as a Case Study', *Journal of Common Market Studies*, vol.21, no.4, pp.389–408.

Lamfalussy, A. (1981), 'Changing Attitudes towards Capital Movements', in F. Cairncross (ed.),

Changing Perceptions of Economic Policy, Methuen, London, pp.194–217.

Landesmann, M.A. and Petit, P. (1995), 'International trade in producer services', *The Service Industries Journal*, vol.15.2, pp.123–61.

Langhammer, K.J. and Sapir, A. (1987), *Economic Impact of Generalised Tariff Preferences*, TPRC, Gower, Aldershot.

Langhammer, R. (1992), 'The developing countries and regionalism', *Journal of Common Market Studies*, vol.30.2, pp.211–31.

Lannes, X. (1956), 'International Mobility of Manpower in Western Europe (I + II)', *International Labour Review*, vol.73, pp.1–24 and 135–51.

Lattre, A. de (1985), 'Floating, Uncertainty and the Real Sector', in L. Tsoukalis (ed.), *The Political Economy of International Money: In Search of a New Order*, Sage, London, pp.71–103.

Laudati, L.L. (1998), 'Impact of community competition law on member state competition law', in S. Martin (ed.), *Competition policies in Europe*, North Holland, Amsterdam, pp. 381–408.

Lawton, T.C. (ed.) (1999), *European Industrial Policy and Competitiveness*, Macmillan, Houndsmill/Basingstoke.

Layard, R., Nickell, S.J. and Jackman, R. (1991), *Unemployment*, Oxford University Press, Oxford.

Lebon, A. and Falchi, G. (1980), 'New Developments in Intra-European Migration Since 1974', *International Migration Review*, vol.14, no.4, pp.539–73.

Leibfritz, W., O'Brien, P. and Dumont, J.C. (2003), 'Effects of immigration on labour markets and government budgets; an overview', *CESifo Working paper*, no.874, Munich.

Lejour, A., Mooy, R. de and Nahuis, R. (2001), 'EU enlargement; economic implications for countries and industries', *CPB documents*, no.011, The Hague.

Lemaitre, P. and Goybet, C. (1984), *Multinational Companies in the EEC* (IRM Multinational Report no.1), John Wiley, Chichester.

Lemmen, J.J.G. and Eijffinger, S.C.W. (1996), 'The fundamental determinants of financial integration in the European Union', *Weltwirtschaftliches Archiv*, vol.132, no.3, pp.432–456.

LE/PWC (2002), *Quantification of the macroeconomic impact of integration of EU financial markets*, London Economics, London (http://europa.eu.int/comm/internal_market/en/finances/mobil/overview.htm).

Lindbeck, A. (1981), 'Industrial Policy as an Issue of the Economic Environment', *The World Economy*, vol.4, no.4.

Linder, S.B. (1961), *An Essay on Trade and Transformation*, Almquist and Wicksell, Uppsala.

Linnemann, H. (1966), *An Econometric Study of International Trade Flows*, North-Holland, Amsterdam.

Lion, C., Martini, P. and Volpi, S. (2004), 'Evaluation of European Social Fund Programmes in a new framework of multinational governance; the Italian experience', *Regional Studies*, vol.38.2, pp.207–12.

Locksey, G. and Ward, T. (1979), 'Concentration in Manufacturing in the EC', *Cambridge Journal of Economics*, vol.3, no.1, pp.91–7.

Lockwood, B., Meza, D. de and Myles, G.D. (1995), 'On the European Union VAT proposals; the superiority of the origin over destination taxation', *Fiscal Studies*, vol.16, pp.1–16.

Löffelholz, H.D. von (1992), *Der Beitrag der Ausländer zum wirtschaftlichem Wohlstand in der BRD*, mimeo, RWI, Essen.

Longo, M. (2003), 'European integration; between micro-regionalism and globalism', *Journal of Common Market Studies*, pp.475–94.

Lopandic, D. (1986), 'The European Community and Comecon', *Review of International Affairs*, vol.876, no.3, pp.12–14.

Lorz, O. and Willmann, G. (2005), 'On the endogenous allocation of decision powers in federal structures', *Journal of Urban Economics*, vol.57, pp.242–57.

Lucas, N. (1977), *Energy and the European Communities*, Europa Publications, London.

Lucas, N. (1985), *Western European Energy Policies, a Comparative Study*, Oxford University Press, Oxford.

Ludlow, P. (1982), *The Making of the European Monetary System*, Butterworth, London.

Lundberg, L. (1992), 'European Economic Integration and the Nordic Countries' Trade', *Journal of Common Market Studies*, vol.30, no.2, pp.157–73.

Lunn, J. (1980), 'Determinants of US investment in the EEC; Further Evidence', *European Economic Review*, vol.24, pp.93–101.

MacDougall, G.D.A. *et al.* (1977), *Report of the Study Group on the Role of Public Finance in European Integration*, CEC, Economy and Finance Series, vol.1, General Report, Brussels.

Machlup, F. (1977), *A History of Thought on Economic Integration*, Macmillan, London.

MacMillan, M.J. (1982), 'The Economic Effects of International Migration; a Survey', *Journal of Common Market Studies*, vol.20, no.3, pp.245–67.

MacNamus, J. (1972), 'The theory of the international firm', in G. Paquet (ed.), *The multinational firm and the nation state*, Collier, Macmillan.

Madelin, R., Ratchford, R.W. and Juul Jorgensen, D. (2001), 'Strengthening Europe's contribution to world governance', *Report of working group* no 5, Brussels.

Magnifico, G. (1985), *Regional Imbalances and National Economic Performance*, Office of Official Publications of the EC, Luxemburg, pp.85–95.

Mahe, L.P. and Ortalo-Magne, F. (1999), 'Five proposals for a European model of the countryside', *Economic Policy; a European Forum*, vol.28, pp.89–134.

Maillet, P. (1977), *The Construction of a European Community*, Praeger, New York.

Mairate, A. and Hall, R. (2001), 'Structural policies', in R. Hall, A. Smith and L. Tsoukalis (eds), *Competitiveness and cohesion in EU policies*, OUP, Oxford, pp.316–48.

Majone, G. (1996), *Regulating Europe*, Routledge, London.

Majone, G. (2002), 'What price safety; the precautionary principle and its policy implications', *Journal of Common Market Studies*, vol.40.1, pp.89–110.

Malcor, R. (1970), 'Problèmes Posés par l'Application Pratique d'une Tarification pour l'Usage des Infrastructures Routières', *The EEC Studies*, Transport Series no. 2, Brussels.

Maloney, J. and Macmillen, M. (1999), 'Do currency unions grow too large for their own good?', *The Economic Journal*, vol.109, pp.572–87.

Mark, N.C. (1985a), 'Some Evidence on the International Inequality of Real Interest Rates', *Journal of International Money and Finance*, vol.4, no.2, pp.189–208.

Mark, N.C. (1985b), 'A Note on International Real Interest Differentials', *Review of Economics and Statistics*, vol.67, no.4, pp.681–84.

Markusen, J.R. (1983), 'Factor Movements and Commodity Trade as Complements', *Journal of International Economics*, vol.14, pp.341–56.

Marks, F., Scharpf, F.W., Schmitter, P.C. and Streeck, W. (1996), *Governance in the European Union*, Sage, London.

Marks, G. (1996), *Governance in the European Union*, Sage, London.

Marques-Mendes, A.J. (1986a), 'The Contribution of the European Community to Economic Growth', *Journal of Common Market Studies*, vol.24, no.4, pp.261–77.

Marques-Mendes, A.J. (1986b), *Economic Integration and Growth in Europe*, Croom Helm, London.

Martin, C. and Saenz, I. (2003), 'Real convergence and European integration; The experience of the less developed EU members', *Empirica*, vol.30.3, pp.205–36.

Martin, C. and Turrion, J. (2003), 'Eastern enlargement of the European Union and Foreign Direct Investment adjustments', *Working paper no 24.2003*, FSEE/UCM, Madrid.

Martin, J.P. (1998), 'What works among active labour market policies; evidence from OECD countries' experiences', *OECD, Occasional papers*, no 35, Paris.

Martin, P. (1996), 'A sequential approach to regional integration; The European Union and Central and Eastern Europe', *European Journal of Political Economy*, vol.12, pp.581–98.

Martin, P.H. and Rogers, C.A. (2000), 'Long-term growth and short-term economic instability', *European Economic Review*, vol.44, pp.359–81.

Martin, S. (ed.) (1999), *Competition policies in Europe*, North Holland, Amsterdam.

Masson, P. (1996), 'Fiscal dimensions of EMU', *The Economic Journal*, vol.106, no. 437, pp.996–1004.

Mathias, P. and Davis, J.A. (1991), *Innovation and Technology in Europe; from the Eighteenth Century to the Present Day*, Basil Blackwell, Oxford.

Mathieson, D.J. and Rojas-Suarez, L. (1994), 'Capital controls and capital account liberalisation in industrial countries', in L. Leiderman and A. Razin (eds), *Capital Mobility; The impact on consumption, investment and growth*, Cambridge University Press, Cambridge.

Matthews, A. (1985), *The Common Agricultural Policy and the Less Developed Countries*, Gill and Macmillan, Dublin.

Matusz, S.J. and Tarr, D.G. (1999), *Adjusting to trade policy reform*, Policy research working paper no.2142, World Bank.

Mayes, D. (1978), 'The Effects of Economic Integration on Trade', *Journal of Common Market Studies*, vol.17, no.1, pp.1–25.

Maynard, G. and Ryckeghem, W. van (1976), 'Why Inflation Rates Differ, a Critical Examination of the Structural Hypothesis', in H. Frisch (ed.), *Inflation in Small Countries*, Springer, Berlin, pp.47–72.

McKinnon, R. (1963), 'Optimum Currency Areas', *American Economic Review*, vol.53, pp.717–25.

McLaughlin, A.M. and Maloney, W.A. (1999), *The European automobile industry; multilevel governance, policy and politics*, Routledge, London.

McLure, C.E. (2005), 'The European Commission's proposals for corporate tax harmonisation', *CESifo Forum*, vol.6.1, pp.32–41.

Meade, J.E. (1955), *The Theory of Customs Unions*, North-Holland, Amsterdam.

Meerhaeghe, M.A.G. van (1998), *International Economic Institutions*, 7th edn, Kluwer, Dordrecht.

Meester, G. and Strijker, D. (1985), *Het Europees Landbouwbeleid voorbij de Scheidslijn van Zelfvoorziening* (WRR, V46), State Publishing Office, The Hague.

Meiklejohn, R. (1999), 'An international competition policy, do we need it? Is it feasible?', *The World Economy*, vol.22, pp.1233–49.

Melo, J. de and Panagariya, A. (1993), *New dimensions in regional integration*, Cambridge University Press, Cambridge.

Memedovic, O., Kuyvenhoven, A. and Molle, W. (1999), 'Economics and politics of different routes towards global free trade', in Memedovic, O., Kuyvenhoven, A. and Molle, W. (eds), *Multilateralism and regionalism in the post-Uruguay round*, Kluwer, Boston,

Dordrecht, pp.3–28.

Memedovic, O., Kuyvenhoven, A. and Molle, W. (eds) (1999), *Multilateralism and regionalism in the post-Uruguay Round era; what role for the EU?*, NEI/Kluwer, Dordrecht.

Menil de, G. (1999), 'Real capital market integration in the EU; how far has it gone? What will the effect of the euro be?', *Economic Policy, a European Forum*, vol.28, pp.167–204.

Messerlin, P.A. (1988), *The EC Anti-Dumping Regulations; a First Economic Appraisal 1980–1985*, paper presented to the First International Seminar on International Economics, Oxford, August 1988.

Messerlin, P.A. (1992), 'Trade Policies in France', in D. Salvatore (ed.), *National Trade Policies, Handbook of Comparative Economic Policies*, vol.2, Greenwood Press, New York.

Messerlin, P.A. (1993), 'Services in EEC; the European Community as a World Trade Partner', *European Economy*, no.52, pp.129–56.

Messerlin, P.A. (1999a), *Measuring the cost of protection in Europe*, Institute for International Economics, Washington.

Messerlin, P. (1999b) 'External aspects of state aids, state aid and the single market', *European Economy, Reports and Studies* 3, pp.161–95.

Meyer, F.W. and Willgerodt, H. (1956), 'Der Wirtschaftspolitische Aussagewert Internationaler Lohnvergleiche', in *Internationale Lohngefaelle, Wirtschaftspolitische Folgerungen, und Statistische Problematik*, Bundesministerium für Wirtschaftspolitische Zusammenarbeit, Deutscher Bundesverlag, Bonn.

Meyer, G. (1973), *Problems of Trade Policy*, Oxford University Press, London.

Micco, A., Stein, E. and Ordonez, G. (2003), 'The currency Union effect on trade; early evidence from the EMU', *European Policy*, vol.37, pp.315–65.

Midelfart-Kvarnik, K.H. and Overman, H.G. (2002), 'Delocation and European Integration; is structural spending justified?' *Economic Policy*, vol.35, pp.322–61.

Mihailovic, K. (1976), 'Migration and the Integration of Labour Markets', in F. Machlup (ed.), *Economic Integration, Worldwide, Regional, Sectoral*, Macmillan, London, pp.163–86.

Miller, M.H. and Spencer, J.E. (1977), 'The Static Economic Effects of the UK joining the EEC, a General Equilibrium Approach', *Review of Economic Studies*, vol.44, pp.71–93.

Mishalani, P. *et al.* (1981), 'The Pyramid of Privilege', in C. Stevens (ed.), *The EEC and the Third World, a Survey I*, Hodder and Stoughton and ODI/IDS, London, pp.60–82.

Mishan, E.J. (1982), *Introduction to Political Economy*, Hutchinson, London.

Mishkin, F.S. (1984a), 'The Real Interest Rate; a Multicountry Empirical Study', *Canadian Journal of Economics*, vol.17, no.2, pp.283–311.

Mishkin, F.S. (1984b), 'Are Real Interest Rates Equal Across Countries? An Empirical Investigation of International Parity Conditions', *Journal of Finance*, vol.39, no.5, pp.1345–57.

Mishkin, F.S. (1999) 'Global financial instability; framework, events, issues', *Journal of Economic Perspectives*, vol.13.4, pp.3–20.

Mitchell, B. (1981), *European Historical Statistics 1750–1975*, 2nd edn, Sythoff/Noordhoff, Alphen a/d Rijn.

Mitrany, D. (1966), *A Working Peace System*, Quadrangle Books, Chicago (reprint from earlier book of 1940s).

Modigliani, F. (1996), 'The shameful rate of unemployment in the EMS: causes and cures', *De Economist*, vol.144, no.3, pp.363–96.

Molina, J.L.M. de and García Perea, P. (1992), 'European Economic Integration from the Standpoint of Spanish Labour Market Problems', in David W. Marsden (ed.), *Pay and Employment in the New Europe*, Billing and Sons, Worcester, pp.99–122.

Molle, W.T.M. (1983), *Industrial Location and Regional Development in the European Community, the FLEUR Model*, Gower, Aldershot.

Molle, W.T.M. (1985), '"1992", De Europese interne markt voltoooid?' ("1992" Will the European Single Market be completed?), *Economische Statistische Berichten*, vol.70, p.837.

Molle, W.T.M. (1989), 'De Europese Gemeenschap in 2000', (The European Community in 2000), *Economisch Statistische Berichten*, vol.74, pp.1271–1273.

Molle, W.T.M. (1990), 'Will the Completion of the Internal Market Lead to Regional Divergence?', in H. Siebert (ed.), *The Completion of the Internal Market*, Institut für Weltwirtschaft, Kiel.

Molle, W.T.M. (1993), 'Oil Refining and Petrochemical Industry', in H.W. de Jong (ed.), *The Structure of European Industry*, 3rd edn, Kluwer, Dordrecht, pp.43–63.

Molle, W. (1996), 'The contribution of international aid to the long term solution of the European migration problem', in D. Corry (ed.), *Economics and European Migration Policy*, IPPR, London, pp.50–75.

Molle, W.T.M. (1997), 'The Regional Economic Structure of the European Union: an Analysis of Long-Term Developments', in K. Peschel (ed.), *Regional Growth and Regional Policy within the Framework of European Integration*, Physica-Verlag, Heidelberg, pp.66–86.

Molle, W. (2002a), 'Globalization, regionalism and labour markets', *Regional Studies*, vol.36.2, pp.161–72.

Molle, W. (2002b), 'The role of small states in the European Union; coping with the Calim-Eco effect', *Actes de la VIIe Chaire Glaverbel*, P.I.E. Peter Lang, Bruxelles, pp.135–58.

Molle, W. (2003), *Global Economic Institutions*, Routledge, London.

Molle, W. (forthcoming), 'Are EU policies good or bad for cohesion?', chapter 9 in *European cohesion policies; economic, social, territorial*, Ashgate, Aldershot.

Molle, W.T.M. and Boeckhout, I.J. (1995), 'Economic disparity under conditions of integration; a long term view of the European case', *Papers in Regional Science, the Journal of the RSA*, vol.74, no.2, pp.105–123.

Molle, W.T.M. and Cappellin, R. (eds) (1988), *Regional Impact of Community Policies in Europe*, Avebury, Aldershot.

Molle, W.T.M., de Koning, J. and Zandvliet, Ch. (1992), 'Can Foreign Aid Reduce East–West Migration in Europe; with Special Reference to Poland?', *ILO Working Paper 67*, Geneva.

Molle, W., Sleijpen, O. and Van Heukelen, M. (1993), 'The Impact of an Economic and Monetary Union on Social and Economic Cohesion; Analysis and Ensuing Policy Implications', in K. Gretschmann (ed.), *Economic and Monetary Union; Implications for National Policy Makers*, EIPA, Maastricht, pp.217–43.

Molle, W.T.M., with the assistance of Van Holst, B. and Smit, H. (1980), *Regional Disparity and Economic Development in the European Community*, Saxon House, Farnborough.

Molle, W.T.M. and van Mourik, A. (1987), 'Economic Means of a Common European Foreign Policy', in J.K. de Vree, P. Coffey and R.H. Lauwaars (eds), *Towards a European Foreign Policy*, Nijhoff, Dordrecht, pp.165–92.

Molle, W.T.M. and van Mourik, A. (1988), 'International Movements of Labour under Conditions of Economic Integration; the Case of Western Europe', *Journal of Common Market Studies*, vol.26, no.3, pp.317–42.

Molle, W.T.M. and van Mourik, A. (1989a), 'A Static Explanatory Model of International Labour Migration to and in Western Europe', in I. Gordon and A. Thirlwall (eds), *European*

Factor Mobility, Trends and Convergences, Macmillan, London, pp.30–52.

Molle, W.T.M. and van Mourik, A. (eds) (1989b), *Wage Structures in the European Community, Convergence or Divergence?*, Gower, Aldershot.

Molle, W.T.M. and Wever, E. (1983), *Oil Refineries and Petrochemical Industries in Western Europe*, Gower, Aldershot.

Monnet, J. (1976), *Mémoires*, Fayard, Paris.

Monti, M. (1996), '"Monti memorandum" on fiscality', *Europe Documents*, no.1981, Luxemburg.

Moore, M.O. (1998), 'European steel policies in the 1980s; hindering technological innovation and market structure change', *Weltwirtschaftliches Archiv*, vol.134.1, pp.42–68.

Mooslecher, P. and Schuerz, M. (1999), 'International macroeconomic policy coordination; any lessons for EMU? A selective survey of the literature', *Empirica*, vol.26.3, pp.171–99.

Moravcsik, A. (1993), 'Preferences and Power in the European Community: A Liberal Intergovernmentalist Approach', *Journal of Common Market Studies*, vol.31, no.4, pp.473–524.

Morsink, R.L.A. (1998), 'Foreign direct investment and corporate networking; a framework for spatial analysis of investment conditions', Elgar, Cheltenham.

Morsink, R. and Molle, W.T.M. (1991), *Direct Investment and Monetary Integration, European Economy*, special edition, no.1, pp.36–55.

Mortensen, J. (1992), 'The Allocation of Savings in a Liberalised European Capital Market', in A. Steinherr (ed.), *The New European Financial Market Place*, Longman, London, pp.208–20.

Moss, J. (1982), *The Lomé Conventions and their Implications for the US*, Westview Press, Boulder, Colorado.

Motta, M. and Norman, G. (1996), 'Does economic integration cause foreign direct investment?', *International Economic Review*, vol.37.4, pp.757–83.

Moulaert, F. and Derykere, Ph. (1982), 'The Employment of Migrant Workers in West Germany and Belgium', *International Migration Quarterly*, vol.2, pp.178–97.

Mourik, A. van (1987), 'Testing Factor Price Equalisation in the EC: An Alternative Approach: A Comment', *Journal of Common Market Studies*, vol.26, no.1, pp.79–86.

Mourik, A. van (1989), 'Countries, a Neo-Classical Model of International Wage Differentials', in W.T.M. Molle and A. van Mourik (eds), *Wage Differentials in the European Community, Convergence or Divergence?*, Gower, Aldershot, pp.83–103.

Mourik, A. van (1993), *Wages and European Integration*, PhD, RL, Maastricht.

Mueller, C.F. (1980), *The Economics of Labor Migration, a Behavioral Analysis*, Academic Press, New York.

Mueller, D. (1981), 'Competitive Performance and Trade within the EEC, Generalisations from Several Case Studies with Specific Reference to the West German Economy', *Zeitschrift für die Gesamte Staatswissenschaften*, vol.137, no.3, pp.638–63.

Mueller, D.C. (1989), *Public Choice II*, Cambridge University Press, Cambridge.

Mundell, R.A. (1957), 'International Trade and Factor Mobility', *American Economic Review*, vol.47, no.3, pp.321–35.

Mundell, R.A. (1961), 'A Theory of Optimum Currency Areas', *American Economic Review*, vol.53, pp.657–64.

Muntendam, J. (1987), 'Philips in the World, a View of a Multinational on Resource Allocation', in B. van der Knaap and E. Wever (eds), *New Technology and Regional Development*, Croom Helm, London, pp.136–44.

Murfin, A. (1987), 'Price Discrimination and Tax Differences in the European Motor Industry', in S. Cnossen (ed.), *Tax Coordination in the European Community*, Kluwer, Deventer, pp.171–95.

Murrell, P. (1983), 'The Comparative Structure of Growth in West Germany and British Manufacturing Industries', in D. Mueller (ed.), *The Political Economy of Growth*, Yale University Press, New Haven, pp.109–32.

Musgrave, R.A. and Musgrave, P. (1989), *Public Finance in Theory and Practice*, McGraw-Hill, New York.

Myrdal, G. (1956), *An International Economy, Problem and Prospects*, Harper and Bros, New York.

Myrdal, G. (1957), *Economic Theory and Underdeveloped Regions*, Duckworth and Co., London.

Nayyar, D. (2002), 'The existing system and the missing institutions', in D. Nayyar (ed.), *Governing globalization, issues and institutions*, UNU/WIDER, Oxford University Press, Oxford, pp.356–84.

NEI/E&Y (1992), 'New location factors for mobile investment in Europe', *CEC Regional Development Studies*, no.6, Brussels.

Neumark, F. *et al.* (1963), 'Report of the Fiscal and Financial Committee', *The EEC Reports on Tax Harmonisation*, International Bureau of Fiscal Documentation, Amsterdam.

Neven, D., Nuttall, R. and Seabright, P. (1993), *Merger in Daylight; the Economics and Politics of European Merger Control*, CEPR, London.

Nicoletti, G. and Scarpetta, S. (2003), 'Regulation, productivity and growth; OECD evidence', *Economic Policy*, vol.36, pp.11–72.

NIESR (1991), *A New Strategy for Economic and Social Cohesion after 1992*, London.

NIESR (1996), *Capital Market Liberalization in Europe*, London.

Norman, V. (1989), 'EFTA and the Internal European Market, *Economic Policy*, vol.2, pp.424–65.

Norman, V. (1991), '1992 and EFTA', in L.A. Winters and A. Venables (eds), *European Integration, Trade and Industry*, Cambridge University Press, Cambridge, pp.120–41.

Oates, W. (1972), *Fiscal Federalism*, Harcourt, New York.

Oates, W. (1999), 'An essay in fiscal federalism', *Journal of Economic Literature*, vol.37.3, pp.1120–49.

Oberender, P. and Rüter, G. (1993), 'The Steel Industry, a Crisis of Adaptation', in H.W. de Jong (ed.), *The Structure of European Industry*, 3rd edn, Kluwer, Dordrecht, pp.65–89.

Ochmann, R.O. (2005), 'Potential migration after the first round of EU eastern enlargement. Impacts on Germany's labour market and welfare system', *IWE, Working Papers*, no.156, Budapest.

Odagiri, H. (1986), 'Industrial Policy in Theory and Reality', in H.W. de Jong and W.G. Shepherd (eds), *Mainstreams in Industrial Organisation*, Book II, pp.387–412.

OECD (1964), *Industrial Statistics 1900–1962*, Paris.

OECD (1965), *Wages and Labour Mobility*, Paris.

OECD (1966), *Energy Policy*, Paris.

OECD (1968), *Capital Market Study*, five volumes, Paris.

OECD (1973), *Oil, the Present Situation and Future Prospects*, Paris.

OECD (1978), *The Migratory Chain*, Paris.

OECD (1979), *International Direct Investment; Policies, Procedures and Practices*, Paris.

OECD (1980), *Controls on International Capital Movements; the Experience with Controls on International Portfolio Operations in Shares and Bonds*, Paris.

OECD (1981b), *Regulations Affecting International Banking Operations*, two volumes, Paris.

OECD (1982a), *Controls on International Capital Movements, the Experience with Controls on International Financial Credits, Loans and Deposits*, Paris.

OECD (1982b), *Code of Liberalisation of Capital Movements*, Paris.

OECD (1982c), *Controls and Impediments Affectinq Inward Direct Investment in OECD Member Countries*, Paris.

OECD (1983a), *International Trade in Services; Insurance: Identification and Analysis of Obstacles*, Paris.

OECD (1983b), *The Implications of Different Means of Agricultural Income Support*, Paris.

OECD (1984a), *International Trade in Services; Banking: Identification and Analysis of Obstacles*, Paris.

OECD (1984b), *Merger Policies and Recent Trends in Mergers*, Paris.

OECD (1985b), *Tourism Policy and International Tourism*, Paris.

OECD (1985c), *Cost and Benefits of Protection*, Paris.

OECD (1986a), *International Trade in Services; Audiovisual Works*, Paris.

OECD (1986b), *SOPEMI; Continuous Reporting System on Migration*, Paris (also 1973–86).

OECD (1987a), 'Science and Technology', *Newsletter* no.10, Paris.

OECD (1987c), *Recent Trends in International Direct Investment*, Paris.

OECD (1987d), *National Policies and Agricultural Trade*, Paris.

OECD (1987e), *The Cost of Restricting Imports; the Automobile Industry*, Paris.

OECD (1987f), *Energy Policies and Programmes of IEA Countries*, 1986 Review, Paris.

OECD (1987g), *Energy Balances of OECD countries 1970–1985*, Paris.

OECD (1991), *Taxing Profits in a Global Economy: Domestic and International Issues*, Paris.

OECD (1992), *Trends in International Migration*, SOPEMI, Paris.

OECD (1993a), *The Changing Course of International Migration*, Paris.

OECD (1993b), *Employment Outlook*, July, Paris.

OECD (1994a), *Migration and Development, new partnerships for cooperation*, Paris.

OECD (1994b), *The OECD Jobs Study, Evidence and Explanations*, Part II: The Adjustment Potential of the Labour Market, Paris.

OECD (1994c), 'Labour standards and economic integration', *Employment Outlook*, July, Paris, pp.137–66.

OECD (1995a), *Code of Liberalization of Capital Movements*, Paris.

OECD (1995b), *Introduction to the Codes of Liberalization*, Paris.

OECD (1995c), *Code of Liberalization of Current Invisible Operations*, Paris.

OECD (1995d), *The OECD Jobs Study: Investment, Productivity and Employment*, Paris.

OECD (1995e), *Economic Outlook*, no.58, Paris.

OECD (1996), *Agricultural Policies, Markets and Trade in OECD Countries; Monitoring and Evaluation*, Paris.

OECD (1997) *Industrial competitiveness in the knowledge-based economy; the role of governments*, OECD, Paris

OECD (1998a), *Value added taxes in Central and Eastern European countries; a comparative survey and evaluation*, Paris.

OECD (1998b) *Harmful tax competition; an emerging global issue*, Paris.

OECD (1998c), 'Public financial management and fiscal goals', *Working paper*, ECO/CPE/WP/1 (98)10.

OECD (1999), *EMU; Facts, challenges and policies*, Paris.

OECD (2003), *Farm household income; issues and policy responses*, Paris.

OECD (2004), 'Employment protection regulation and labour market performance', *OECD Employment Outlook*, Chapter 2 , Paris.

Okun, A. (1975), *Equality and Efficiency; the Big Trade Off*, Brookings Institution, Washington.

Olie, R.L. (1996), *European transnational mergers*, Universiteit Maastricht, Maastricht.

Olofsdotter, K. and Torstensson, J. (1998), 'Economic integration, market size and the welfare effects of trade liberalisation', *Weltwirtschaftliches Archiv*, vol.134.2, pp.302–19.

Olson, M. (1965), *The Logic of Collective Action*, Harvard University Press, Cambridge, Mass.

Oort, C.J. (1975), *Study of the Possible Solutions for Allocating the Deficit which may Occur in a System of Charging for the Use of Infrastructures Aiming at Budgetary Equilibrium*, CEC, Brussels.

Orban, G. and Szapary, G. (2004), 'The Stability and Growth Pact from the perspective of the New Member States', *Journal of Policy Modeling*, vol.26.7, pp.839–64.

Owen, N. (1983), *Economies of Scale, Competitiveness and Trade Patterns within the European Community*, Clarendon, Oxford.

Ozawa, T. (1992), 'Cross Investments between Japan and the EC. Income Similarity, Technological Congruity and Economics of Scope', in J. Cantwell (ed.), *Multinational Investment in Modern Europe*, Edward Elgar, Aldershot, pp.13–45.

Padoa-Schioppa, T. *et al.* (1987), *Europe in the 1990's; Efficiency, Stability and Equity; a Strategy for the Evolution of the Economic System of the European Community*, Oxford University Press, Oxford.

Page, S. (1981), 'The Revival of Protectionism and its Consequences for Europe', *Journal of Common Market Studies*, vol.20, no.1, pp.17–40.

Pain, N. and Young, G. (1996), *Tax competition and the pattern of European direct investment*, paper of the Institute of Fiscal Studies Conference on Public Policy and the Location of Economic Activity, London.

Pallis, A.A. (2002), *The common EU Maritime Transport Policy; policy europeanisation in the 1990s*, Ashgate, Aldershot.

Palmer, M., Lambert, J. *et al.* (1968), *European Unity; a Survey of the European Organisations*, PEP, Unwin University Books, London.

Panagariya, A. and Findlay, R. (1996), 'A political economy analysis of free trade areas and customs unions', in R. Feenstra, G. Grossman and D. Irwin (eds), *The Political Economy of Trade Policy*, London, MIT Press, pp.265–87.

Papadimetriou, D.G. (1978), 'European Labour Migration (Consequences for the Countries of Workers' Origin)', *International Studies Quarterly*, vol.22, no.3, pp.377–408.

Park, Y.C. and Wang, Y. (2000), 'Reforming the international financial system, prospects for regional financial cooperation in Asia', in J. Teunissen (ed.), *Reforming the international financial system, crisis prevention and response*, Fondad, The Hague, pp.21–42.

Pederson, P.J., Pytlikova, M. and Smith, N. (2004), 'Selection or network effects? Migration flows into 27 OECD countries 1990-2000', *IZA Discussion paper, 1104*.

Pedler, R.H. and Schaefer, G.F. (eds) (1996), *Shaping European Law and Policy; the role of the committees and comitology in the political process*, EIPA, Maastricht.

Pedler, R.H. and van Schendelen, M.P.C.M. (eds) (1994), *Lobbying the European Union; Companies, Trade Associations and Issue Groups*, Dartmouth, Aldershot.

Peeters, T., Praet, P. and Reding, P. (eds) (1985), *International Trade and Exchange Rates in the Late Eighties*, North-Holland, Amsterdam.

Pejovich, S. (1998), *Economic analysis of institutions and systems*, rev. 2nd edn, Kluwer, Dordrecht.

Pelkmans, J. (1980), 'Economic Theories of Integration Revisited', *Journal of Common Market Studies*, vol.18, no.4, pp.333–54.

Pelkmans, J. (1982), 'The Assignment of Public Functions in Economic Integration', *Journal of Common Market Studies*, vol.21, no.1, pp.97–121.

Pelkmans, J. (1983), 'European Direct Investments in the European Community', *Journal of European Integration*, vol.7, no.1, pp.41–70.

Pelkmans, J. (1984), *Market Integration in the European Community*, Nijhoff, The Hague.

Pelkmans, J. (ed.) (1985), *Can the CAP be Reformed?*, EIPA, Maastricht.

Pelkmans, J. (1986), *Completing the Internal Market for Industrial Products*, CEC, Brussels.

Pelkmans, J. (1991), 'Towards Economic Union', in P. Ludlow (ed.), *Setting EC Priorities 1991–92*, CEPS/Brasseys, London.

Pelkmans, J. (2001), *European Integration; Methods and Economic Analysis*, Longman, Harlow, New York 2nd edn.

Pelkmans, J. and Vanheukelen, M. (1988), 'The Internal Markets of North America. Fragmentation and Integration in the US and Canada', *Research on the "Cost of Non-Europe", Basic Findings*, CEC, vol.16, Luxemburg.

Pelkmans, J. and Vollebergh, A. (1986), 'The Traditional Approach to Technical Harmonisation: Accomplishments and Deficiencies', in J. Pelkmans and M. Vanheukelen (eds), *Coming to Grips with the Internal Market*, EIPA, Maastricht, pp.9–30.

Peridy, N. (2005), 'The trade effects of the Euro-Mediterranean partnerships; what are the lessons for ASEAN countries?', *Journal of Asian Economics*, vol.16.1, pp.125–39.

Perotti, R. (1996), 'Fiscal Consolidation in Europe: Composition Matters', *The American Economic Review*, vol.86, no.2, pp.105–10.

Perroni, C. and Whalley, J. (2000), 'The new regionalism, trade liberalisation or insurance?, *Canadian Journal of Economics*, vol.3 pp.1–24.

Persson, J. (1997), 'Convergence across the Swedish counties 1911-1993', *European Economic Review,* vol.41, pp.1835–52.

Persson, T. (2001), 'Currency unions and trade; how large is the treatment effect?', *European Policy*, vol.31, pp.433–59.

Persson, T. and Tabellini, G. (2003), *The economic effects of constitutions*, CES, MIT, Cambridge, Mass.

Pertek, J. (1992), *General Recognition of Diplomas and Free Movement of Professionals*, EIPA, Maastricht.

Peschel, K. (1985), 'Spatial Structures in International Trade; an Analysis of Long-Term Developments', *Papers of the Regional Science Association*, vol.58, pp.97–111.

Peschel, K. (1999), *The development of integration areas in Europe*, mimeo, IRF Christian Albrecht Universitaet, Kiel.

Petit, M. *et al.* (1987), *The Agricultural Policy Formation in the European Community; The Birth of Milk Quotas and the CAP Reform*, Elsevier, Amsterdam.

Petith, H.C. (1977), 'European Integration and the Terms of Trade', *Economic Journal*, vol.87, pp.262–72.

Petrochilos, G.A. (1989), *Foreign Direct Investment and the Development Process*, Avebury, Aldershot.

Phylaktis, K. and Wood, G.E. (1984), 'An Analytical and Taxonomic Framework for the Study of Exchange Controls', in J. Black and G.S. Dorrance (eds), *Problems of International Finance*, St Martin's Press, New York, pp.149–66.

Pinder, J. (1986), 'The Political Economy of Integration in Europe, Policies and Institutions in

East and West', *Journal of Common Market Studies*, vol.24, no.1, September, pp.1–14.

Pischken, J.-S. and Velling, J. (1994), 'Wage and employment effects of immigration to Germany', *CEPR discussion paper 935*, London.

Polachek, S.W. (1980), 'Conflict and Trade', *Journal of Conflict Resolution*, vol.24, pp.55–78.

Pollard, S. (1981a), *Peaceful Conquest, the Industrialisation of Europe 1760–1970*, Oxford University Press, Oxford.

Pollard, S. (1981b), *The Integration of the European Economy since 1815*, George Allen and Unwin, London.

Pomfret, R. (1986), *Mediterranean Policy of the European Community; a Study of Discrimination in Trade*, Macmillan, London.

Pool, B. (1990), *The Creation of the Internal Market in Insurance*, EC, Luxemburg.

Poon, J. and Pandit, K. (1996), 'The geographic structure of cross-national trade flows and region states', *Regional Studies*, vol.303, pp.273–85.

Pratten, C. (1988), 'A Survey of the Economies of Scale', *Research into the Cost of Non-Europe; Basic Findings*, vol.2, pp.11–165, Luxemburg.

Prebisch, R. (1950), *The economic development of Latin America and its principal problems*, United Nations Economic Commission for Latin America, New York.

Price Waterhouse (1988), 'The Cost of non-Europe in Financial Services', *Research into the Cost of Non-Europe; Basic Findings*, vol.9, CEC, Brussels.

Pryor, F. (1972), 'An International Comparison of Concentration Ratios', *Review of Economics and Statistics*, vol.54, no.2, pp.130–40.

Puchala, D.J. (1984), *Fiscal Harmonisation in the European Communities, National Policies and International Cooperation*, Pinter, London.

Pugh , G., Tyrall, D. and Tarnawa, L. (1999), 'Exchange rate variability, international trade and the single currency debate; a survey', in W. Meeusen (ed.), *Economic policy in the European Union, current perspectives*, Edgar Elgar, Cheltenham.

Pugliese, E. (1992), 'The New International Migration and Changes in the Labour Market', *Labour*, vol.6, no.1, pp.165–79.

Quaglia, L. (2003), 'European Monetary Integration and the "constitutionalisation" of macro economic policy making', *Constitutional Political Economy*, vol.14, pp.235–51.

Rees, R. and Kessner, E. (1999), 'Regulation and efficiency in European insurance markets', *Economic Policy, a European Forum*, vol.29, pp.365–400.

Resmini, L. (2003), 'Economic integration, industry location and frontier economies in transition countries', *Economic Systems*, vol.27, pp.205–21.

Resnick, S. and Truman, E. (1975), 'An Empirical Examination of Bilateral Trade in Europe', in B. Balassa (ed.), *European Economic Integration*, North-Holland, Amsterdam, pp.41–78.

Rhys, D.G. (2004), 'The motor industry in an enlarged EU', *The World Economy*, vol.27.6, pp.877–900.

Riemsdijk, J.F. van (1972), 'A System of Direct Compensation Payments to Farmers as a Means of Reconciling Short Run to Long Run Interests', *European Review of Agricultural Economics*, vol.1, no.2, pp.161–89.

Rietbergen, T. van (1999), *The internationalization of European Insurance Groups*, KNAW/FRWUU, Utrecht.

Rijksbaron, A., Roobol, W.H. and Weisglas, M. (eds) (1987), *Europe from a Cultural Perspective. Historiography and Perceptions*, Nijgh and Van Ditmar, The Hague.

Roberto, B. (2004), 'Acquisition versus greenfield investment; the location of foreign manufacturers in Italy', *Regional Science and Urban Economics*, vol.34.1, pp.3–25.

Robson, P. (1971), 'Current problems of economic integration; fiscal compensation and the distribution of benefits in economic groupings of developing countries', *UNCTAD* no. TD/B/322/Rev1, United Nations, New York.

Roemisch, R. (2003), 'Regional disparities within accession countries', in G. Tumpell-Gugerell and P. Mooslechner (eds), *Economic convergence and divergence in Europe; growth and regional development in an enlarged Europe*, Edward Elgar, Cheltenham, pp. 183–208.

Rogers, J.H., Hufbauer, G.C. and Wada, E. (2001), 'Price level convergence and inflation in Europe', *Working paper 01.1*, Institute for International Economics, Washington.

Rogoff, K. (1999), 'Monetary models of dollar/yen/euro nominal exchange rates; dead or undead?', *The Economic Journal*, vol.109, pp.655–9.

Rollo, J.M.C. and Warwick K.S. (1979), 'The CAP and Resource Flows among EEC Member States', *Working Paper* no.27, Government Economic Service, London.

Rosamond, B. (2000), *Theories of European Integration*, Palgrave, Houndmills, Basingstoke.

Rose, A. K. (2000), 'One market, one money; the effect of common currencies on trade', *Economic Policy; a European Forum*, vol.30, pp.7–47.

Rose, R. *et al.* (1985), *Public Employment in Western Nations*, Cambridge University Press, Cambridge.

Rubalcaba-Bermejo, L. (1999), *Business services in European Industry; growth employment and competitiveness*, EC, Luxemburg.

Rubin, J. and Thygesen, N. (1996), 'Monetary union and the outsiders: a cointegration– codependence analysis of business cycles in Europe', *Economie Appliquée*, vol.XLIX, no.3, pp.123–71.

Ruding, O. *et al.* (1992), *Conclusions and Recommendations of the Committee of Independent Experts on Company Taxation*, OOPEC, Luxemburg.

Ruigrok, W. and Tulder, R. van (1995), *The logic of international restructuring*, Routledge, London.

Sala-I-Martin, X. (1996), 'Regional cohesion; evidence and theories of regional growth and convergence', *European Economic Review*, vol.40, pp.1325–52.

Salt, J. (1976), 'International Labour Migration, the Geographical Pattern of Demand', in J. Salt and H. Clout (eds), *Migration in Post-War Europe, Geographical Essays*, Oxford University Press, Oxford, pp.126–67.

Salvatori, D. (1991), 'The Automobile Industry', in D. Mayes (ed.), *The European Challenge, Industry's Response to the 1992 Programme*, Harvester Wheatsheaf, London, pp.28–90.

Sampson, A. (1977), *The Seven Sisters*, Corgi, London.

Sannucci, V. (1989), 'The establishment of a Central Bank; Italy in the nineteenth century', in M. de Cecco and A. Giovannini (eds), *A European Central Bank?*, Cambridge University Press, Cambridge, pp.244–74.

Sapir, A. (1997), 'Domino effects in West European trade 1960-1992', *Discussion Paper* No.1576, CEPR, London.

Sapir, A. (2000), 'Trade regionalism in Europe; towards an integrated approach', *Journal of Common Market Studies*, vol.38.1, pp.151–62.

Sapir, A., Aghion, Ph., Bertola, G., Hellwig, M. Pisani Ferry, J., Rosati, D., Vinals, J. and Wallace, H. (2004), *An agenda for a growing Europe*, Oxford University Press, Oxford.

Saunders, C. and Marsden, D. (1981), *Pay Inequalities in the European Communities*, Butterworths, London.

Saunders, P. and Klau, F. (1985), 'The Role of the Public Sector, Causes and Consequences of the Growth of Government', *OECD Economic Studies*, no.4, pp.1–239.

Scaperlanda, A.E. (1967), 'The EEC and US Foreign Investment; Some Empirical Evidence', *Economic Journal*, vol.77, pp.22–6.

Scaperlanda, A.E. and Mauer, L.J. (1969), 'The Determinants of US Direct Investment in the

Scharpf, F.P. (1999), *Governing in Europe; effective and democratic?*, OUP, Oxford.

Scharpf, F. (2002), 'The European Social Model, coping with the challenges of diversity', *Journal of Common Market Studies*, vol.40.4, pp.645–70.

Schendelen, M.P.C.M. van (1993), *National Public and Private EC Lobbying*, Dartmouth, Aldershot.

Schendelen, M.P.C.M. van (1998), *EU committees as influential policy makers*, Ashgate, Aldershot.

Scherer, F. (1974), 'The Determinants of Multi-Plants Operations in Six Nations and Twelve Industries', *Kyklos*, vol.27, no.1, pp.124–39.

Scherer, F.M. (2000), *Competition policy, domestic and international*, Elgar, Cheltenham.

Schmidtchen, D. and Cooter, R. (1997), *Constitutional Law and Economics of the European Union*, Elgar, Cheltenham.

Schmitter, P.C. (1996), 'Imagining the future of the Euro polity with the help of new concepts', in G. Marks, F.W. Scharpf, P.C. Schmitter and W. Streeck (eds), *Governance in the European Union*, Sage, London, pp.121–51.

Schmitz, A. (1970), 'The Impact of Trade Blocks on Foreign Direct Investments', *Economic Journal*, vol.80, pp.724–31.

Schmitz, A. and Bieri, J. (1972), 'EEC-Tariff and US Direct Investment', *European Economic Review*, vol.3, pp.259–70.

Schulze, G.G. (2000), *The political economy of capital controls*, Cambridge University Press, Cambridge.

Schwalbach, J. (1988), 'Economies of Scale and Intra-Community Trade', in *Research into the Cost of Non-Europe, Basic Findings*, vol.2, CEC, Brussels, pp.167–204.

Scitovsky, T. (1958), *Economic Theory and Western European Integration*, Allen and Unwin, London.

Scott, N. (1967), *Towards a Framework for Analysing the Cost and Benefits of Labour Migration*, Institute for International Labour Studies, Bulletin, Geneva, February.

Seers, D., Schaffer, B. and Kiljunen, M.L. (1979), *Underdeveloped Europe: Studies in Core-Periphery Relations*, Harvester Press, Hassocks, Sussex.

Seers, D., Vaitsos, C. and Kiljunen, M.L. (1980), *Integration and Unequal Development, The Experience of the EC*, St Martin's Press, New York.

Segré, C. et al. (1966), *The Development of a European Capital Market*, EC, Brussels.

Seidel, B. (1983), *Wage Policy and European Integration*, Gower, Aldershot.

Seifert, W.G., Achleiter, A.K., Mattern, F., Streit, C.C. and Voth, H.J. (2000), *European capital markets*, Macmillan Business, London.

Sellekaerts, W. (1973), 'How Meaningful are Empirical Studies on Trade Creation and Trade Diversion?', *Weltwirtschaftliches Archiv*, vol.109, no.4, pp.519–51.

Sexton, J.J., Walsh, B.M., Hannan, D.F. and McMahon, D. (1991), *The Economic and Social Implications of Emigration*, NESC, Dublin.

Shapiro, C. and Varian, H.R. (1999), *Information rules; a strategic guide to the network economy*, Harvard BS Press, Boston.

Shaw, R.W. and Simpson, P. (1987), *Competition Policy; Theory and Practice in Western Economies*, Wheatsheaf, Brighton.

Shlaim, A. and Yannopoulos, G.N. (1976), *The EC and the Mediterranean Countries*, Cambridge

University Press, Cambridge.

Siebert, H. (ed.) (1994), *Migration; a Challenge for Europe*, Mohr, Tübingen.

Simões, V.C. (1992), 'European Integration and the Pattern of FDI Flows in Portugal', in J. Cantwell (ed.), *Multinational Investment in Modern Europe*, Edward Elgar, Aldershot, pp.256–97.

Simon, J.L. (1989), *The Economic Consequences of Immigration*, Basil Blackwell, Oxford.

Sleuwaegen, L. (1987), 'Multinationals, the European Community and Belgium; Recent Developments', *Journal of Common Market Studies*, vol.26, no.2, pp.255–72.

Sleuwaegen, L. (1993), 'Road Haulage', *European Economy/Social Europe*, no.3, pp.211–50.

Soete, L. (1987), 'The Impact of Technological Innovation on International Trade Patterns: the Evidence Reconsidered', *Research Policy*, pp.101–30.

Sosvilla-Rivero, S. and Gil-Pareja, S. (2004), 'Price convergence in the European Union', *Applied Economic Letters*, vol.11, pp.39–47.

Spaak, P.H. *et al.* (1956), *Rapport des Chefs de Délégation aux Ministres des Affaires Etrangères*, Brussels.

Spannent, A. (1991), *Direct Investment of the European Community*, Eurostat, Luxemburg.

Spencer, S. (ed.) (1994), *Immigration as an Economic Asset; the German Experience*, IPPR, London.

Steinherr, A. (1984), 'Convergence and Coordination of Macro-Economic Policies: Some Basic Issues', *European Economy*, no.20, pp.71–110.

Steinherr, A. (1985), 'Competitiveness and Exchange Rates; some Policy Issues for Europe?', in T. Peeters, P. Praet and P. Reding (eds), *International Trade and Exchange Rates in the Late Eighties*, North-Holland, Amsterdam, pp.163–90.

Steinherr, A. (1994), *30 years of European Monetary Integration; from the Werner Plan to the EMS*, Longman, London.

Steinle, W. (1988), 'Social Policy', in W. Molle and R. Cappellin (eds), *Regional Impact of Community Policies in Europe*, Avebury, Aldershot, pp.108–23.

Stevens, C. (ed.) (1981), *EEC and the Third World; a Survey*, Hodder and Stoughton, London.

Stiglitz, J.E. (2002), *Globalization and its discontents*, Norton and Co, New York and London.

Stokman, A.C.J. (1995), 'Effects of exchange rate risk on intra-EC trade', *De Economist*, vol.143, no.1, pp.41–54.

Streit, M. E. and Voigt, S. (1997), 'Towards ever closer union – or ever larger? or both?; Entry to the European Union from the perspective of constitutional economics', in D. Schmidtchen and R. Cooter (eds), *Constitutional law and economics of the European Union*, Edward Elgar, Cheltenham, pp.223–48.

Strijker, D. and de Veer, J. (1988), 'Agriculture', in W. Molle and R. Cappellin (eds), *Regional Impact of Community Policies in Europe*, Avebury, Aldershot, pp.23–44.

Suarez-Villa, L. and Cuadrado-Roura, J.L. (1993), 'Regional economic integration and the evolution of disparities', *Papers in Regional Science*, vol.72.4, pp.369–87.

Swoboda, A. (ed.) (1976), 'Capital Movements and their Control', in *IUHEI,CEI*, no.3, Sythoff, Leiden.

Tabellini, G. (2003), 'Principles of policy making in the European Union, an economic perspective', *CECifo Economic Studies*, vol.49.1, pp.75–102.

Talbot, R.B. (1977), 'The European Community's Regional Fund', *Progress in Planning*, vol.8, no.3, pp.183–281.

Tangermann, S. (1984), 'Guarantee Thresholds, a Device for Solving the CAP Surplus Problem?', *European Review of Agricultural Economics*, vol.11, no.2, pp.159–68.

Tangermann, S. (1995), 'Eastward enlargement of the EU; will agricultural policy be an obstacle?', *Intereconomics*, vol.30(b), pp.277–84.

Tangermann, S. (1999), 'Europe's agricultural policies and the Millenium Round', *The World Economy*, vol.22.9, pp.1155–79.

Tarditi, S. (1984), 'La Crise de la PAC: un Point de Vue Italien', *Economie Rurale*, vol.163, pp.28–33.

Tarditi, S. and Zanias, G. (2001), 'Common Agricultural Policy', in R. Hall, A. Smith and L. Tsoukalis (eds), *Competitiveness and cohesion in EU policies*, Oxford University Press, Oxford, pp.179–216.

Teulings, A.W.M. (1984), 'The Internationalisation Squeeze: Double Capital Movement and Job Transfer within Philips Worldwide', *Environment and Planning*, A, vol.16, pp.597–614.

Teulings, C. and Hartog, J. (1998), *Corporatism or competition, labour contracts, institutions and wage structures in international comparison*, Cambridge University Press, Cambridge.

Teunissen, J.J. (ed.) (2000), *Reforming the international financial system, crisis prevention and response*, Fondad, The Hague.

Teunissen, J.J. (ed.) (2002), *A regional approach to financial crisis prevention; lessons from Europe and initiatives in Asia, Latin America and Africa*, Fondad, The Hague.

Tharakan, P.K.M. (ed.) (1983), *Intra-Industry Trade; Empirical and Methodological Aspects*, North-Holland, Amsterdam.

Tharakan, P.K.M. (1988), 'The Sector/Country Incidence of Anti-Dumping and Countervailing Duty Cases in the EC', in L.B.M. Mennes and J. Kol (eds), *European Trade Policies and the Developing World*, Croom Helm, Beckenham, pp.94–135.

Thomas, K.P. and Tetreault, M.-A. (eds) (1999), *Racing to regionalize*, Lyne Riener, London.

Thomsen, S. and Nicolaides, Ph. (1991), *The Evolution of Japanese Direct Investments in Europe*, Harvester Wheatsheaf, Brighton.

Thygesen, N. (1990), 'The Benefits and Costs of Currency Unification', in H. Siebert (ed.), *The Completion of the Internal Market*, IWW/Mohr, Tübingen, pp.347–75.

Tichy, G. (1992), 'The European Neutrals', in S. Borner and H. Grubel (eds), *The European Community after 1992. Perspectives from the Outsiders*, Macmillan, London, pp.165–91.

Tims, W. (1987), 'EC Agricultural Policies and the Developing Countries', in L.B.M. Mennes and J. Kol (eds), *European Trade Policies and the Developing World*, Croom Helm, Beckenham, pp.135–87.

Tinbergen, J. (1953), *Report on Problems Raised by the Different Turnover Tax Systems Applied within the Common Market*, ECSC, Luxemburg.

Tinbergen, J. (1954), *International Economic Integration*, Elsevier, Amsterdam.

Tinbergen, J. (1959), 'Customs Unions, Influence of their Size on their Effect', *Selected Papers*, North-Holland, Amsterdam, pp.152–64.

Tinbergen, J. (1965), *International Economic Integration*, 2nd edn, Elsevier, Amsterdam.

Tinbergen, J. (1991), 'The Velocity of Integration', *De Economist*, vol.139, no.1, pp.1–11.

Tinbergen, J. and Fischer, D. (1987), *Warfare and Welfare, Integrating Security Policy into Socio-Economic Policy*, Wheatsheaf, Brighton.

Tondl, G. and Vuksic, G. (2003), 'What makes regions in Eastern Europe catching up? The role of foreign investment, human resources and geography', *Working paper B12*, ZEI, Bonn.

Torre, A. de la and Kelly, M.R. (1992), 'Regional Trade Arrangements', *Occasional Papers* No.93, IMF, Washington.

Toulemon, R. and Flory, J. (1974), *Une Politique Industrielle pour l'Europe*, PUF, Paris.

Tovias, A. (1982), 'Testing Factor Price Equalisation in the EEC', *Journal of Common Market Studies*, vol.20, pp.165–81.

Tovias, A. (1991), 'A Survey of the Theory of Economic Integration', *Journal of European Integration*, vol.XV, no.1, pp.5–23.

Tucker, K. and Sundberg, M. (1988), *International Trade in Services*, Routledge, London.

Tulder, R. van and Ruigrok, W. (1997), 'The nature of institutional change: managing rival dependencies', in A. Amin and J. Hausner (eds), *Beyond markets and hierarchy; interactive governance and social complexity*, Edward Elgar, Cheltenham, pp. 129–58.

Tussie, D. and Whalley, J. (2002), 'The functioning of a commitment based WEO: lessons from experience with the WTO', *The World Economy*, vol.25.5, pp.685–95.

Tyers, R. (1994), 'The Cairns Group perspective', in K.A. Ingersent, A.J. Rayner and R.C. Hine (eds), *Agriculture in the Uruguay Round*, London, Macmillan, pp.88–110.

UN (1979), *Labour Supply and Migration in Europe; Demographic Dimensions 1950–1975 and Prospects*, UN/ECE, Geneva.

UN (1980), *Tendencies and Characteristics of International Migration since 1950*, Geneva.

UN/ECE (1977), *Intra-European Temporary Migration of Labour, its Consequences for Trade, Investment and Industrial Co-operation*, TRADER 341, Geneva.

Urban, G. (1983), 'Theoretical Justification for Industrial Policy', in F.G. Adams and C.R. Klein (eds), *Industrial Policies for Growth and Competitiveness: an Economic Perspective*, Heath, Lexington, MA, pp.21–40.

USDL (1989), 'The Effects of Immigration on the US Economy and Labor Market', *Migration, Policy and Research*, report 1, Bureau of International Labor Affairs, Washington.

Valdés, A. and Zietz, J. (1995), 'Distortions in world food markets in the wake of GATT; evidence and policy implications', *World Development*, vol.23, no.6, pp.913–26.

Vamvakidis, A. (1998), 'Regional Integration and Economic Growth', *World Bank Economic Review*, vol.12,2; pp.251–70.

Vandamme, J. (ed.) (1986), *New Dimensions in European Social Policy*, TEPSA, Croom Helm, London.

Vanhove, N. and Klaassen, L.H. (1987), *Regional Policy, a European Approach*, 2nd edn, Gower, Aldershot.

Vaubel, R. (1986), 'A public choice approach to international organisation', *Public Choice*, vol.51, pp.39–57.

Vaubel, R. (1994), 'The Public Choice analysis of European integration; a survey', *European Journal of Political Economy*, vol.10, pp.227–49.

Vaubel, R. (1996), 'Constitutional safeguards against centralisation in federal states; an international cross section analysis', *Constitutional Political Economy*, vol.7, pp.79–102.

Venables, A. (1987), 'Customs Union and Tariff Reform under Imperfect Competition', *European Economic Review*, vol.31, pp.103–10.

Venables, A.J. (2003), 'Winners and Losers from Regional Integration Agreements', *The Economic Journal*, vol.113, pp.747–61.

Verdoorn, P.J. (1952), 'Welke zijn de Achtergronden en Vooruitzichten van de Economische Integratie in Europa en welke Gevolgen zou deze Integratie hebben, met name voor de Welvaart in Nederland?', *Overdruk no. 22*, Centraal Planbureau, The Hague.

Verdoorn, P.J. and Schwartz, A.N.R. (1972), 'Two Alternative Estimates of the Effects of EEC and EFTA on the Pattern of Trade', *European Economic Review*, vol.3, no.3, pp.291–335.

Vernon, R. (1966), 'International Investment and International Trade in the Product Cycle', *Quarterly Journal of Economics*, vol.80, pp.190–207.

Vernon, R. (1979), 'The product cycle hypothesis in a new international environment', *Oxford Bulletin of Economics and Statistics*, vol.41, no.4, pp.255–67.

Verrijn Stuart, G.M. *et al.* (1965), 'Europees Kapitaalverkeer en Europese Kapitaalmarkt', *European Monographs*, no.5, Kluwer, Deventer.

Viaene, J.M. (1982), 'A Customs Union between Spain and the EEC', *European Economic Review*, vol.18, pp.345–68.

Vickerman, R. and Armstrong, H.W. (eds) (1995), *Convergence and divergence among European Regions*, Pion, London.

Viñals, J. (1994), 'Building a monetary union in Europe: is it worthwhile, where do we stand, and where are we going?', *CEPR Occasional Paper*, no.15, Centre for Economic Policy Research, London.

Viner, J. (1950), *The Customs Union Issue*, Stevens and Sons, London.

Vleminckx, K. and Berghman, J. (2001), 'Social exclusion and the welfare state; an overview of conceptual issues and policy implications', in D.G. Mayes, J. Berghman and R. Slais (eds), *Social exclusion and European policy*, Edward Elgar, Cheltenham, pp.27–46.

Voigt, F., Zachcial, M. and Rath, A. (1986), *Regulation and Modal Split in the International Freight Transport of the EC*, mimeo, University of Bonn, CEC, Brussels.

Vromen, J.J. (1995), *Economic evolution; an enquiry into the foundations of new institutional economics*, Routledge, London.

Waelbroeck, J. (1976), 'Measuring the Degree of Progress of Economic Integration', in F. Machlup (ed.), *Economic Integration, Worldwide, Regional, Sectoral*, Macmillan, London, pp.89–99.

Ward, E. (1986), 'A European Foreign Policy', *International Affairs*, no.4, pp.573–82.

Weiss, F.D. (1987), 'A Political Economy of European Community Trade Policy against the LDCs', *European Economic Review*, vol.31, pp.457–65.

Werner, P. *et al.* (1970), 'Report to the Council, Commission on the Realisation by Stages of the Economic and Monetary Union in the Community', *Bulletin of the EC II*, Supplement.

Wessels, W. (1997), 'An ever closer fusion? A dynamic macropolitical view on integration processes', *Journal of Common Market Studies*, vol.35, no.2, pp.267–99.

Weyman-Jones, T.G. (1986), *Energy in Europe; Issues and Policies*, Methuen, London.

Whalley, J. (1985), *Trade Liberalisation among Major World Trading Areas*, MIT Press, Cambridge, Massachusetts.

Whalley, J. and Zissimos, B. (2002), 'An internationalisation-based World Environmental Organisation', *The World Economy*, vol.25.5, pp.619–42.

Whichart, O.G. (1981), 'Trends in the US Direct Investment Position Abroad, 1950–1979', US Department of Commerce, *Survey of Current Business*, vol.61, no.2, pp.39–56.

Williamson, J. (1976), 'The Implication of European Monetary Integration for the Peripheral Areas', in J. Vaizey (ed.), *Economic Sovereignty and Regional Policy*, Gill and Macmillan, Dublin, pp.105–21.

Williamson, J. and Bottrill, A. (1971), 'The Impact of Customs Unions on Trade in Manufactures', *Oxford Economic Papers*, vol.23, pp.323–51, reprinted in M. Kraus (ed.) (1973), *The Economics of Integration*, Allen and Unwin, London, pp.118–51.

Williamson, O.E. (1985), *The economic institutions of capitalism*, The Free Press, New York.

Wilson, J.D. (1999), 'Theories of tax competition', *National Tax Journal*, vol.52, pp.269–304.

Wilson, K. and Dussen, J. van der (eds) (1995), *The History of the Idea of Europe*, Routledge, London.

Winsemius, A. (1939), *Economische Aspecten der Internationale Migratie*, Bohn, Haarlem.

Winter-Ebmer, R. and Zweimueller, J. (1996), 'Immigration and the earnings of young native workers', *Oxford Economic Papers*, vol.48, pp.473–91.

Winters, L.A. (1985), 'Separability and the Modelling of International Economic Integration', *European Economic Review*, vol.27, pp.335–53.

Winters, L.A. (1987), 'Britain in Europe: a Survey of Quantitative Trade Studies', *Journal of Common Market Studies*, vol.25.

Winters, L.A. (1990), 'The so-called "non-economic" objectives of agricultural support', in *OECD Economic studies no. 3*, pp.237–66.

Winters, L.A. (1997), 'What can European experience teach developing countries about integration?', *The World Economy*, vol.20.7, pp.889–911.

Wolf, Ch. (1987), 'Market and Non-Market Failures; Comparison and Assessment', *Journal of Public Policy*, vol.7, no.1, pp.43–70.

Woolly, P. (1974), 'Integration of Capital Markets', in G. Denton (ed.), *Economic and Monetary Union in Europe*, Croom Helm, London, pp.23–55.

World Bank (2001), *Global economic prospects and the developing countries*, Washington.

WTO (2000), *Annual Report*, World Trade Organization, Geneva.

Yannopoulos, G.N. (1990), 'Foreign Direct Investment and European Integration; the evidence from the formative years of the European Community', *Journal of Common Market Studies*, vol.28, no.4, pp.235–57.

Young, C. (1972), 'Association with the EEC; Economic Aspects of the Trade Relationship', *Journal of Common Market Studies*, vol.11, no.2, pp.120–35.

Zhou, S. (2003), 'Interest rate linkages within the European Monetary System; new evidence incorporating long run trends', *Journal of International Money and Finance*, vol.22, pp.571–90.

Zietz, J. and Valdés, A. (1986), 'The potential benefits to LDCs of trade liberalization in beef and sugar by industrialized countries', in *Weltwirtschaftliches Archiv*, vol.122, pp.93–112.

Zimmermann, K.F. (1995), 'Tackling the European migration problem', *Journal of Economic Perspectives*, vol.9, no.2, pp.45–62.

Websites for further research:

http://www.euro.ecb.int/en.html

http://www.hm-treasury.gov.uk/documents/the_euro/euro_index_index.cfm

Index